SECURITY SUPERVISION:
THEORY AND PRACTICE OF ASSET PROTECTION

SECOND EDITION

International Foundation for Protection Officers

edited by

Sandi J. Davies
Ronald R. Minion

An Imprint of Elsevier Science
AMSTERDAM BOSTON LONDON NEW YORK OXFORD PARIS
SAN DIEGO SAN FRANCISCO SINGAPORE SYDNEY TOKYO

Butterworth Heinemann is an imprint of Elsevier.

 This book is printed on acid-free paper.

Library of Congress Cataloging-in-Publication Data
Security supervision: theory and practice of asset protection/
 authors, International Foundation for Protection Officers; co-
editor, Sandi J. Davies, Ronald R. Minion.—2nd ed.
   p.   cm.
 Previously published under the title: Security supervisor training
manual, c1995.
   Includes bibliographical references.
   ISBN 0-7506-7199-8 (pbk.: alk. paper)
   1.   Police, Private-Training of Handbooks, manuals, etc.
   2.   Private security services Handbooks, manuals, etc. I. Davies,
Sandi J. II. Minion, Ronald R. III. International Foundation for
Protection Officers. IV. Security supervisor training manual.
   HV8290.S39   1999
   363.28'9'0683—dc21   99-30933
                           CIP
British Library Cataloguing-in-Publication Data
A catalogue record for this book is available from the British Library.

The publisher offers special discounts on bulk orders of this book.
For information, please contact:
Manager of Special Sales
Elsevier Science
200 Wheeler Road
Burlington, MA 01803
Tel: 781-313-4700
Fax: 781-313-4802

For information on all security publications available, contact our World Wide
Web homepage at http://www.bhusa.com/security

10 9 8 7 6 5 4
Printed in the United States of America.

DEDICATION

To all the professionals within our industry who strive for the "Knowledge to Protect!"

To all who contributed to provide this knowledge embodied in this new and exciting book.

To Christopher A. Hertig, CPP, who coined the expression "The Forgotten Soldiers of an Invisible Empire."

We dedicate this book to all the professionals within our profession who have risen to the challenge: the challenge to protect life and property throughout the private and public security industry. We know this publication will provide help and guidance to those who strive for excellence in the sustainment of organizational life safety/asset protection.

Good Luck

TABLE OF CONTENTS

FOREWORD
by Louis A. Tyska, CPP and Lawrence J. Fennelly, CPO

This is, in our opinion, a one of a kind text which has been specifically written and offered to you – the Supervisor or Manager. There is no substitute for experience but this goes a long way in preparing for your journey on the management career path. When we were both supervisors, there was no text and very little additional training provided for supervisors. We salute all of the many contributors who assisted in putting the text together and sharing their expertise to make the path easier to attain supervisory skills and abilities.

WHAT IS A SUPERVISOR?

- The person who represents higher authority.
- The person who assesses situations and conditions, to make on the spot judgments without favor, prejudice or fear.
- The person who is a responder to any and all situations.
- A person who must galvanize the efforts of many to attain stated goals.
- A person who must assign tasks and ensure compliance and constant quality performance.
- A person who is accountable and, therefore, first in line to shoulder reaction, both good and bad.
- Finally, the person who must make a decision for management based on his or her professional development.

What does it mean to be a Supervisor/Manager? First, you may be called upon to handle numerous conflicts. Second, you will be required to meet management's or your client's expectations in the daily routine of operational activities.

PROFESSIONAL DEVELOPMENT

Professional development is a critical key word. It is the pathway for supervisors to become managers. By professional development we are referring to:
- Your leadership and networking skills.
- Your communicative ability, which includes oral, written and computer skills.
- Your reasoning and logical thinking ability.
- Your receiving formal training, accreditation or certification for your professional growth and personal satisfaction.
- Your developing a personal and professional code of ethics and high standards by which to guide yourself.

NEW MANAGERS/SUPERVISORS

We feel it is important to advise new managers that as a new manager, you have to learn how to develop and exercise (not abuse), your newly acquired authority, power and influence effectively. This can be done by your establishment of credibility—the earning of your subordinate's commitment and support.

Management is an art, not a science and new managers are at the crossroads, looking to make the right turns. Your leadership will guide them.
- A new manager is the person in charge. His/her elevation to the status of manager through promotion has given them the authority.
- A new manager is a person with a level of power and is a decision-maker.
- A new manager is knowledgeable in his/her field.
- A new manager uses his developed skills, ideas, education and experience.
- A new manager supervises their subordinates and passes information down the line as well as up the chain of command.
- A new manager has the responsibility to call the shots. He/she is paid to make decisions.
- A new manager has the responsibility to be aware of corporate policy as well as the client's requirements.

- As you develop your on-the-job experience as a new manager and you start to understand and accept your new responsibilities as well as what it means to a manager, consider this:
  - Learn how to supervise.
  - Develop your Leadership Skills.
  - Develop your Interpersonal Skills.
  - Develop knowledge of who you are. Know yourself.
  - Learn how to cope and deal with stress and emotion associated with management concerns.

By becoming a manager/supervisor you bring with you all of the above skills which you develop along your career path and these learning points become part of your new self.

CONCLUSION

You will be called upon to make decisions every day: some will be easy; others will be difficult decisions that could not have been made properly without a foundation of experience and education, and supported by "street smarts." Those abilities cannot be learned in a classroom or from a book, but only acquired through experience. Being on the front line and being prepared and willing to make the tough decisions is what being an effective supervisor or manager is all about.

ACKNOWLEDGMENTS

To compile a book of this nature is something that requires a tremendous amount of team work. The "team" that worked on this project without a doubt, put their hearts, heads and souls behind their efforts. The result of this "team project" is something that we should all be very proud of. With this book comes a tool that will provide the knowledge that will only enhance our industry. The "team" that so unselfishly contributed to this project should not go unrecognized.

A very special thanks to all of the professionals who contributed by way of submitting chapter(s) in their area of expertise. The time, effort and commitment of each and every contributor is greatly appreciated. These contributions and "team members" have become the framework of a significant undertaking that will focus positive recognition upon the private/public security sector. It will help those who implement and manage security to find the tools to work with; it will help those who need protection better understand the horrendous challenges involved in making the organization and the people in it feel and be secure.

Special thanks to Christopher A. Hertig, CPP, for without his energy, direction, dedication to the team goals . . . we could not have developed this purposeful reference text which will serve so many.

The technical support of Ann Hyndman and her professional direction, not to mention her patience and understanding, has been of enormous assistance in the successful completion of this project.

Other members of the team included Chuck Thibodeau, CPP, CSS; Larry Fennelly, CPO; Brendan Kirby, CPO, CSS; in addition to many students of York College of Pennsylvania.

Space precludes us from individually recognizing all contributing authors; hence, we respectfully draw your attention to the outstanding credentials of each of the 30 plus writers.

And finally, a salute to the International Foundation for Protection Officers (IFPO). The unselfish commitment to professionalism by this organization is evident through this notable contribution.

INTRODUCTION
by Sandi J. Davies and Ronald R. Minion, M.S., CPP, CPO

Sandi J. Davies, co-editor

Sandi began her career in contract security in 1980 with a primary focus on personnel administration. She became deeply involved in training and was instrumental in developing Security Officer training programs for a major national guard company. Her interest in security training grew and in 1988 she joined the newly founded International Foundation for Protection Officers (IFPO) as an administrative assistant. In 1991 she was named executive director of the IFPO and has been a driving force in Foundation program development and administration. Sandi is a longtime member of the American Society for Industrial Security (ASIS), having served in executive positions at the chapter level.

Ron R. Minion, M.S., CPP, CPO, co-editor

Ron began his career as a police officer at age 18 and after eight years of law enforcement service, he founded and owned a large, well known contract security company. He played a key role in developing the International Foundation for Protection Officers (IFPO) and the Certified Protection Officer (CPO) program. He was one of the first examined Certified Protection Professionals (CPP). He is a graduate of Mount Royal College and earned his master's degree through Columbia Pacific University. He is a former Chapter Chairman and a longtime supporter of the American Society for Industrial Security (ASIS). In 1988 he was named international vice president for his outstanding contributions to ASIS.

SECURITY SUPERVISOR TRAINING MANUAL

Demand for the Security Supervisor program, which was developed in 1990 by the International Foundation for Protection Officers (IFPO), has continued to grow. As new components were added to the program, a more current, relevant course text had to be developed.

The IFPO embarked upon the task of completing a new program manual and engaged security professionals to contribute to this effort. The result was the forging of an alliance between the IFPO/Butterworth–Heinemann and some of the industry's leading security supervisors, authors, educators and consultants, who collectively contributed to the production of this text.

The book for security leaders is here, it will serve participants in the Security Supervisor Program and it will be a valued reference for all protection practitioners.

SECURITY SUPERVISOR PROGRAM/CERTIFICATION

Objective:

To facilitate Security Professionals who aspire to enhance their leadership skills. To deliver a functional supervisory training program developed to heighten each candidate's ability to master the techniques of security personnel superintendency. To provide a meaningful accreditation which will lend professional recognition to those candidates who exhibit the knowledge and skills required to be a Certified Security Supervisor (CSS).

HISTORY OF THE PROGRAM

The International Foundation for Protection Officers (IFPO) was founded in 1988. A dedicated group of well known senior members of the international security community set out to develop a non-profit organization that would address the professional training and certification needs of line and senior Security Officers.

Through the commitment and vision of these industry leaders, who became members of the Board of Directors, the IFPO was formed. The Foundation's first and foremost undertaking was to develop the Certified Protection Officer (CPO) Program. Since the inception of the program, thousands of Officers have earned their CPO accreditation, now the recognized designation for Professional Officers employed by proprietary and contract security guard forces throughout North America and abroad.

As the IFPO grew, so did the need for Foundation leadership in addressing the professional development requirements of members of the security industry. Security Officers earned seniority and often assumed leadership roles within their respective security organizations. The IFPO recognized that there had to be a learning progression, a better defined professional development/career path. To address this condition, Board of Directors and Foundation Administrators developed the Security Supervisor's program/certification.

SECURITY SUPERVISOR PROGRAM LOGISTICS

To facilitate each reader's learning opportunities, at the conclusion of each chapter, the author has included a selection of fill-in-the-word, true/false and multiple choice questions. To complete the Security Supervisor program, each candidate must successfully achieve a score of no less than 70% on both an interim and final examination. Once the applicant has successfully completed the Security Supervisor program and has been awarded their completion certificate, they may then apply for the Certified Security Supervisor (CSS) designation.

The (CSS) program candidates are required to select and analyze a series of workplace scenarios that describe on-the-job conditions which are frequently encountered by the working Security Supervisor. Each situation demands immediate leadership remedial action. Candidates must describe in detail, the appropriate actions recommended to bring the matter to successful conclusion. The corrective measures employed by the supervisor must be supported from the contents of the course text.

Candidates seeking the (CSS) accreditation must submit an affidavit in the prescribed form, declaring that the written portion of the program is authored entirely by the applicant seeking accreditation.

The (CSS) certification committee will review the scenarios, application along with the candidate's complete file, to determine eligibility for the certification

CONCLUSION

IFPO has developed an important professional relationship with Butterworth–Heinemann (B/H), who have responded positively to the need to recognize the security professional who works the line, those who physically occupy the site and protect people and assets. Without B/H it would be difficult for the IFPO to exercise its mandate; to bring professional development opportunities to the entire security service community.

WRITERS' GALLERY

Michael J. Apgar, CPO

Mike is currently a student at York College of Pennsylvania majoring in Criminal Justice. He has been a patrol officer for York College's Security Department since September, 1997. He is also employed as a hospital security officer for York Hospital. He is a Certified Protection Officer (CPO) and a Certified Security Supervisor (CSS).

Daniel R. Baker, Ph.D

Dan is currently a teacher educator in the College of Education, School of Occupational and Adult Education, Oklahoma State University. He is a graduate of the School of Public Administration at the University of Southern California and holds an advanced graduate certificate in Police Administration. With 25 years of protection experience, he holds instructor certifications in security and law enforcement from Oklahoma Council on Law Enforcement Education and Training.

Daniel J. Benny, M.A., CPP, CPO, CSS

Dan is a private investigator and security consultant in Harrisburg, Pennsylvania. He is the author of over 300 articles which have been published nationally and internationally, and the IFPO book *The Private Investigator's Professional Desk Reference*. He is an adjunct instructor for Harrisburg Area Community College for its Security Administration and Criminal Justice Study Abroad in London programs. He served ten years as an officer in the U.S. Naval Intelligence Reserve and holds a Master of Arts degree from Vermont College of Norwich University and is a graduate of the U.S. Naval War College.

John T. Brobst, Jr., CPO, CSS

John is a Security Officer at Pottsville Hospital, Pottsville, Pennsylvania. He also serves as the Director of Crisis Intervention at Pottsville Hospital. He is employed as an associate director of the Paladin Security Group, a Pennsylvania consulting service. John has extensive experience in healthcare security and instructs in Nonviolent Crisis Intervention. He holds the titles of Certified Protection Officer (CPO), Certified Security Supervisor (CSS) and Certified Healthcare Security Officer.

Tom M. Conley, M.A., B.Sc., B.A., CPP, CFE, CPO

Tom M. Conley is the President & C.E.O. of Conley Security Agency / PSG which is headquartered in Des Moines, Iowa.

Mr. Conley has earned and been designated a Certified Protection Professional (CPP), by the American Society for Industrial Security, has earned and been designated a Certified Fraud Examiner (CFE) by the Association of Certified Fraud Examiners, and has earned and been designated a Certified Protection Officer (CPO) by the International Foundation for Protection Officers. He is a former police captain and is a commissioned officer in the United States Naval Reserve, where he possesses a secret security clearance.

Mr. Conley has earned a Master of Arts degree in Business Leadership with an emphasis in Quality Management from Upper Iowa University, where he graduated with a 4.0 GPA. He earned two undergraduate degrees from Upper Iowa University, a Bachelor of Science degree in Business Management and a Bachelor of Arts degree in Psychology from Upper Iowa University. He graduated with honors from both degree programs. He is also a graduate of Executive Security International, a highly regarded executive protection academy, where he became certified as a Protective Agent. He is a Certified Emergency Medical Technician, has earned a bona fide black belt in karate, and is a certified expert with the handgun and rifle.

Darren S. Estes, CPO, CSS

Darren is the Security Manager/Consultant, Imperial Marketing, Inc., Las Vegas, Nevada. He has served as a Security Officer with Flamingo Hilton in Las Vegas and was a Correctional and Field Training Officer with Idaho Department of Corrections, Boise, Idaho. Formerly, he was a Personnel Management Specialist, United States Army, and Honorary Regional Officer, British American Security Executive Consultants. He is a Certified Protection Officer (CPO) and Certified Security Supervisor (CSS).

Mary Lynn Garcia, M.S., CPP

Mary Lynn Garcia received a BA in Biology from the State University of New York at Oswego. She also holds an MS in Biomedical Sciences from the University of New Mexico and a Certificate in Electronics Technology from the Albuquerque Technical-Vocational Institute in New Mexico. Her previous employment has been with the University of New Mexico, Sperry Flight Systems (now Honeywell Defense Avionics Systems), and Intel Corporation. Ms. Garcia has worked for the past 13 years at Sandia National Laboratories in international safeguards and physical security. Her past projects include development of an automated video review station, video and lighting design for a demonstration physical security system at a major U.S. airport, and project management of an integrated alarm communication and display system. She is currently teaching a series of courses at three U.S. universities to initiate new programs in security engineering. Ms. Garcia has been a Certified Protection Professional since November 1, 1997.

Ms. Garcia has given presentations at many professional conferences including the Institute for Nuclear Materials Management, the American Defense Preparedness Association, and the American Society for Industrial Security. She has also taught several classes in security system design and evaluation within the DOE complex, to government agencies and corrections personnel, and to foreign students participating in the International Training Course jointly sponsored by the Department of Energy, department of State, and the International Atomic Energy Agency.

Eric L. Garwood, CPO, CSS

Eric is a Security Advisor, Corporate Security, DuPont, Wilmington, Delaware. He is responsible for security at two DuPont facilities. He has served with DuPont for seven years and has been deeply involved in a major installation of card access and CCTV systems at DuPont Experimental Stations. Prior to his career in security, Eric served with the Delaware State Prison System for five years. He is a Certified Protection Officer (CPO) and a Certified Security Supervisor (CSS).

Brion P. Gilbride, CSS, CPO

Brion is a graduate of York College of Pennsylvania. During his college career he worked for several years as a Security Supervisor for the York College Security Department. He has also been employed as a seasonal Police Officer for the town of Dewey Beach, DE. Brion was a station manager for Spartan Oil Company in Dover, NJ, in 1995. He is both a Certified Protection Officer (CPO) and a Certified Security Supervisor (CSS).

Dr. Martin Gill

Dr. Martin Gill is deputy director of the Scarman Centre at Leicester University and a senior lecturer in crime and security management, and course director of the MSc in the Study of Security Management, and the MSc in Security and Crime Risk Management, distance learning courses that include students from around the world. Dr. Gill is a member of the ASIS Standing Committee on Academic Programs and a member of the ASIS Taskforce to develop a body of knowledge for the security world. He has published articles on crime, security and policing in a wide range of refered journals and professional magazines.

His books include *A Special Constable* (Avebury); *Volunteers in the Criminal Justice System: A Comparative Study of Probation Police and Victim Support* (Open University Press); *Crime Victims: Needs Services and the Voluntary Sector* (Tavistock), all with Professor Rob Mawby. In order to draw attention to the problems facing businesses, he initiated the Crime at Work series; volume 1 was entitled *Crime at Work: Studies in Security and Crime Prevention* published in 1994, and volume 2 is entitled *Crime at Work: Increasing the Risk for Offenders* published in 1998 (both by Perpetuity Press).

He is co-editor of the *SecurityJournal* and co-editor of *Risk Management: an International Journal* which feature articles on a range of security and risk related topics.

Mark Gleckman, M.S., CPO

Mark is the owner of Security Management Services, Acton, California. He is a Crime Prevention Consultant and serves in that capacity for the San Fernando Police Department. He is a Technical Reserve Crime Prevention Specialist for the Los Angeles Police Department. Mark holds a Master of Science degree in Security Administration. He has completed the Department of Defense

Security Institute's curriculum in Industrial Security Management. He is a Certified Protection Officer (CPO).

Michael A. Hamilton, CSS, CPO, CFSO, BCFE

Mike is the Director of Corporate Security for SRA Technologies, Inc., a government contractor, located in Falls Church, Virginia. He is responsible for the development, implementation and management of all security policies, practices and procedures. Mike is a graduate of the USMC Command and Staff College, the USA Ordnance Officer basic course and the DOD Security Management program. He is a Certified Protection Officer (CPO) and a Certified Security Supervisor (CSS).

Alexander M. Hay, CPO, CSS

Alex has a broad and diverse background in security service, teaching and management. He began his career in teaching telecommunications for the British government, Department of Civil Aviation. He also held an administrative position with a university in Scotland prior to immigrating to Canada. In Canada he has served in educational institution and industrial security for more than 25 years. Alex is a Certified Protection Officer (CPO) and a Certified Security Supervisor (CSS).

Martin Hershkowitz, M.S.

Martin is the Principal Consultant of Hershkowitz Associates and a Senior Associate of Pedrick and Associates. He has been a senior operations research manager and analyst in Polaris submarine vulnerability, anti-ballistic missile systems and submarine logistics. He holds a Master of Science degree in Mathematics and Numerical Analysis. His works have been published extensively. He has chaired numerous conferences, symposia and presented many study papers.

Christopher A. Hertig, CPP, CPO

Chris Hertig is on the faculty of York College of Pennsylvania where he teaches courses in security management and criminal justice. He has also taught several physical education courses. Prior to coming to York, Mr. Hertig was a training administrator in the nuclear industry where he developed and taught various classes for both line officers and supervisory personnel. He was a security supervisor for several years and has completed graduate courses in Adult Education at Penn State University. The author of *Avoiding Pitfalls in the Training Process* (International Foundation for Protection Officers) as well as numerous other publications; he is active in both writing and consulting. Hertig is a member of the American Society of Law Enforcement Trainers, the Academic Program Committee of the American Society for Industrial Security and the International Association of Campus Law Enforcement Administrators. He serves as the Director of Accreditation for the International Foundation for Protection Officers. He is a Certified Protection Professional (CPP), a Certified Protection Officer (CPO) and a Master Level Instructor in Non-Violent Crisis Intervention.

David W. Hill, CPO, EMCA

Dave is presently employed at Williams Operating Corporation, Marathon, Ontario. He is the training officer within the Security Department and is responsible for on-site training in both Security and E.M.S. Dave is involved in the Occupational Health Department in which he instructs first-aid and C.P.R. programs to company employees. He has worked air and land ambulance in the Ottawa Valley and city ambulance in Sault Ste. Marie. Dave is a Certified Protection Officer (CPO).

Christopher Innace, CPO

Christopher is a graduate of York College of Pennsylvania with a degree in Criminal Justice with a concentration in Asset Protection/Security. He has worked as a protection officer for a contract service firm in providing special event coverage and currently works as a Loss Prevention Agent for Frank R. Booth Associates in Pottstown, Pa.

Stevan P. Layne, CPP

Stevan P. Layne, CPP is principal consultant and CEO of Layne Consultants International (LCI). He is a former police chief, criminal investigator, and public safety director. Steve serves as guest lecturer and faculty member for several colleges and universities, is a regular presenter at ASIS Annual Seminars and the Smithsonian Institution's Annual Cultural Property Protection Conference.

He is a graduate of the FBI's Police Management Program, and an instructor for the National Crime Prevention Institute.

Steve's publications include "Business Security Guidelines," "The Official Library Security Manual" and, due out this spring, "You Don't HAVE to be a VICTIM!".

Gary Lyons, B.A., CPO, CSS, CPP

Gary M. Lyons is the Des Moines, Iowa, District Operations Manager of Conley Security Agency / PSG which is headquartered in Des Moines, Iowa. Conley Security Agency / PSG has been in the security business for more than 20 years and specializes in providing highly qualified uniformed and plainclothes security services, security patrol services and covert investigative services to their clients.

Mr. Lyons earned his Bachelor of Fine Arts from Iowa State University. He earned and has been designated a Certified Protection Officer (CPO) and a Certified Security Supervisor (CSS) by the International Foundation for Protection Officers. He is now pursuing the designation of Certified Protection Professional (CPP) by the American Society of Industrial Security.

Before joining the Conley Security Agency / PSG team, Mr. Lyons spent ten years in training and management at two major international companies. His career in the United States military provided him with extensive experience in law enforcement and investigations. His military experience includes the Drug Enforcement Academy (DEA); FBI School of Auto, Off-Road Vehicle and Aircraft Larceny; Family Violence School; and Military Police and Investigator, Drill Sergeant, Paratrooper/ Pathfinder and Military Intelligence Analyst Academies. Mr. Lyons served as Chief Military Police Investigator at Ft. Riley, Kansas, and is a certified Military Police Instructor. In 1997, he obtained a Top Secret Clearance.

Johnny R. May, B.S., M.S., CPP, CPO

Johnny is currently employed by Henry Ford Community College (Dearborn, Michigan), where he serves as a security supervisor/crime prevention specialist with the college's campus safety department, and as the Program Coordinator for HFCC's Security and Private Investigations Program. He is also a licensed private investigator and adjunct professor at the University of Detroit-Mercy, where he teaches graduate level Security Administration courses. Johnny has had articles published in various security publications. He is a graduate of the University of Detroit-Mercy, where he earned his B.S. in Criminal Justice, and his M.S. in Security Administration.

Robert Metscher, B.S., CPO, CSS, PPS

Robert is a District Assets Protection Manager with a nationwide retailer and has been a retail investigator for over five years with various nationwide retailers. He is a graduate of York College of Pennsylvania's Security Curriculum and is currently working towards his Master's degree in Business Administration. Robert's other publications include articles on crowd management and supervisory ethics. Robert is a Certified Protection Officer, Certified Security Supervisor and Personal Protection Specialist.

Timothy D. Michener, M.S., CPP, CSS, CPO

Tim is Director of Public Safety and Security, Philadelphia College of Pharmacy & Science, Philadelphia, Pennsylvania.

He has been involved with campus security since 1987 when he retired as a municipal police officer. He has a Master's degree in Criminal Justice, is a Certified Protection Professional (CPP), a Certified Security Supervisor (CSS), and a Certified Protection Officer (CPO). He is actively involved in the International Association of Campus Law Enforcement Administrators.

Cole Morris, MPA, CSS

Cole Morris serves as the administrative security officer of MicroAge, Inc., a Fortune 500 technology integrator and distributor. A widely published author, his security-related work has appeared in such publications as *Security Management, Law Enforcement Technology, Law & Order, Security Management Bulletin, Police,* and *Police and Security News.* Morris' primary professional interest is the prevention of high-technology theft and he believes it should be a top concern for all private security practitioners.

Morris holds degrees in criminal justice and public administration. He has completed numerous courses in security, law enforcement, intelligence, aviation and military topics. When not protecting his company's profits, Morris works as a freelance writer for various general interest magazines. He also hosts *The Online Security Academy* which serves as an excellent resource for security officers, managers and executives. It can be found on the Internet at http://www.goodnet .com/~ej59217/index.html

Joan Mulder, M.A.

Joan is the coordinator of Program Development at Alberta Vocational College (AVC), Calgary, Alberta. She is responsible for the development of an entry level Security Officer Training program, which has been positively endorsed by the local security community. Prior to assuming her present responsibilities, Joan coordinated the establishment of AVC's Learning Assistance Center. She is a graduate of the University of Calgary, specializing in adult reading and writing skills.

David H. Naisby, Jr., CPO

David H. Naisby, Jr. is a Parole Officer in York County, Pennsylvania, where he supervises adult offenders. In addition to this role, David co-facilitates a "Life-Skills Program" that increases the skills of offenders as they are reintegrated into the community. David is also pursuing a Master's degree in Criminal Justice Administration at Villanova University.

David is a recent graduate of York College of Pennsylvania where he obtained a Bachelor's degree with two concentrations in Criminal Justice, and minors in Sociology and Criminal Investigation. David was the President of Alpha Phi Sigma, The National Criminal Justice Honor Society, and was a member of Phi Sigma Pi, National Honor Fraternity. David is an Eagle Scout and a member of "Who's Who among Students in American Universities." David has completed the Security Supervisor Program.

Lowell A. Nelson, B.A., CPP, CPO, CSS

Lowell is the Manager of Security, Storage Tek, Louisville, Colorado. He earned his Bachelor's degree from Columbia College, in Business Management. He is presently working towards his Master's degree in business. He was previously employed as a Colorado State Trooper and was the Assistant Director of Security at the Denver Art Museum. Lowell has earned his Certified Protection Professional (CPP), Certified Security Supervisor (CSS) and Certified Protection Officer (CPO) accreditations.

Brion K. O'Dell, CPP, CSS

Brion began his career as a contract security officer in 1981 in the greater Chicago area. As he gained experience and seniority, he had the opportunity to develop emergency preparedness procedures. He was instrumental in designing Security Officer drills, which focused on real work-place emergencies. In 1984 Brion joined the Waukegan Port District, Waukegan Harbor, Illinois, as Chief of Security, creating the District's first security police operation, the Waukegan Harbor Patrol. In 1994 he was appointed to the position of Chief of Security, Hotel Asheville in North Carolina.

Patricia A. O'Donoghue, CPO, CSS

Tricia is the Training Consultant for the Corporate Security Department at John Hancock Mutual Life Insurance Company in Boston, Massachusetts. She is responsible for the coordination and implementation of training activities for all of the members of the company's protective services. She is co-editor of the Security Department's monthly newsletter, the *Security Post*. Tricia is a Certified Protection Officer (CPO) and has completed the Security Supervisor Program/CSS.

Ivan E. Pollock, CPO, CSS

Ivan is a Security Supervisor, Avenor Forest Products, Dryden, Ontario. He began his career in security with Avenor in 1981 and supervises members of the company's in-house guard force. He has completed specialized training in Non-Violent Crisis Intervention. Ivan is a Certified First Aid and CPR Instructor/Trainer. He is responsible to train members of the company guard force in life safety. He is a Certified Protection Officer (CPO) and a Certified Security Supervisor (CSS).

Ramdayal K. Ramdeen, CPO, CSS

    Kelvin is a senior security training officer for the National Maintenance Training Company Limited, Trinidad, W.I., where he has served as a field supervisor and training officer for 17 years. In his current position, he is responsible for the coordination of classroom and OJT courses for a 1,300-Officer Security Force. Kelvin is an active reserve police officer with Trinidad and Tobago Police Service. He is a Certified Protection Officer (CPO) and a Certified Security Supervisor (CSS).

Benn H. Ramnarine, M.A., CPO, CSS

    Benn is the security training officer with the National Maintenance Training Security Company Limited, Mount Hope, Trinidad, W.I. He is responsible for the coordination, design, development and implementation of security training programs on a national basis. Benn is a graduate of Norwich University (Military College of Vermont). He is a member of IFPO, ASLET, IALEFI, FSTMA and MESA.

David L. Ray, B.A., LL.B

    Dave is a Private Corporate Security Consultant, Calgary, Alberta. He spent 10 years as Manager Corporate Security for Shell Canada Limited. Prior to that he held the position of Director, Corporate Security with MacMillan Bloedel Limited. Before his work in the public sector, Dave spent 14 years in the Royal Canadian Mounted Police. He instructs Security Administration and Security Law at the university level. Dave holds a Bachelor of Arts from York University and Bachelor of Law from Osgoode Hall Law School.

Randy J. Rice, CSS, CPO

    Randy J. Rice, CSS, CPO currently works as the Mail Services Coordinator for York College of Pennsylvania and is a Supervisor/Training Officer for a local mall. Rice has experience in Retail Security, Mall Security, Hospital Security, Hotel Security and VIP Protection. He has a B.S. from York College of Pennsylvania in Criminal Justice with a major in Law Enforcement and a minor in Security. Randy is active in several regional mail associations across the United States and frequently writes and speaks on mail security issues. He is also an associate member of the Fraternal Order of Police and The Law Enforcement Alliance Association.

Guy A. Rossi

    Guy A. Rossi is a retired Sergeant with the Rochester, New York Police Department. Sgt. Rossi's last assignment was in charge of the Recruit and Field Training Unit. He has over 21 year's experience as a street cop and trainer. His certifications include many descriptions of defense tactic and firearms training as an instructor-trainer. He is one of the founding members of the American Society of Law Enforcement Trainers (ASLET).

Randy W. Rowett, CPO, CSS

    Randy is an Assistant Security Manager with Captain Development Ltd., Toronto, Ontario. He was previously employed with the Metropolitan Toronto Police as a Special Constable, Court Detail. He has worked in hotel and harbor security and served as a private investigator and consultant. He conducts seminars to law and security students at two Ontario business colleges. He is a Certified Protection Officer (CPO) and a Certified Security Supervisor (CSS).

Henry C. Ruiz, CPO

    Henry is a security specialist for a major biotechnology company and a Program Associate for the International Foundation for Protection Officers. He is involved in various areas of security and related areas including training management, crime prevention research and high-technology aspects of security operations. In addition to being a member of the IFPO, Henry is a longtime member of ASIS and the Association of Certified Fraud Examiners. He holds the CPO, CPP and Certified Fraud Examiner (CFE) professional accreditations.

Steven R. Ruley, CPP, CFE, CPO

    Steve is a technical services supervisor with the Walla Walla Police Service, Walla Walla, Washington. His primary role with the department includes major crime scene investigations and forensic services. Prior to assuming his position in law enforcement, Steve has worked as a security consultant. He holds his Bachelor of Science degree in Paralegal Studies. He is a Certified Protection Professional (CPP), a Certified Fraud Examiner (CFE) and has completed the Security Supervisor Program.

Sidney Sappington, M.B.A., JD

Sidney S. Sappington, MBA, JD is a Business Law professor at York College of Pennsylvania where he teaches courses in law, business and management. He has 18 years of experience as a specialist in commercial and contract law with a property management and land development corporation. Professor Sappington holds both a Master in Business Administration degree from Mt. St. Mary's College and a Juris Doctorate from the University of Baltimore School of Law.

S. Robert Sherwood, M.S., CPO, CSS

Bob is the Emergency Medical Services Director and Security Officer for Bowater Incorporated, Southern Division in Calhoun, Tennessee, the largest newsprint mill in North America. He has 20 years of law enforcement industrial and institutional security experience. His educational background includes an Associate Degree in Law Enforcement and Bachelor's and Master's degrees in Criminal Justice. Bob is a nationally Registered Emergency Medical Technician.

Charles T. Thibodeau, M.Ed., CPP, CSS

Chuck is a prominent Minnesota Consultant and College Instructor. He is the owner and senior consultant of Q/A Systems and Consultants in Minneapolis, Minnesota. He is currently the lead instructor and coordinator of the Security Management program at Pine Technical College. Chuck has a Bachelor of Arts degree in Psychology. He has also served in a number of chapter executive positions with the American Society for Industrial Security. He is a Certified Protection Professional (CPP).

Neal E. Trautman, M.S.

Neal is the founder and director of the non-profit National Institute of Ethics, where he is responsible for all aspects of ethics related services. He is the founder of the Law Enforcement Television Network (LETN), the nation's largest provider of law enforcement training, serving more than 120,000 officers. During Neal's 16 years as a sworn officer, he has received many prestigious awards including two decorations for heroism. He has authored 8 textbooks and is the founder of the nationally recognized Florida Criminal Justice Trainer's Association.

Christopher L. Vail, M.S.

Chris is President of Law Enforcement Development, a firm specializing in training security and law enforcement personnel in such topics as First Line Supervision, Testifying in Court, and Investigative Techniques. Mr. Vail began his career as a Military Policeman with the United States Marine Corp. His security experience includes being in charge of security for a high profile Congressional Committee. He has also served as Director of Security on a college campus. Mr. Vail has served as President of the Georgia Criminal Justice Educator's Association. Chris is also presently the executive director of the Police Supervisors Group.

Ernest G. Vendrell, Ph.D.

Ernest G. Vendrell has over 20 years of law enforcement experience with the Miami-Dade Police Department in Dade County, Florida. He is a Sergeant currently assigned to his Department's Training Bureau as a Training Coordinator. In addition to membership in IFPO, he is a member of the International Association of Emergency Managers as well as the American Society for Industrial Security where he serves on the Standing Committee on Disaster Management. He earned a Ph.D. in Public Administration and Policy and Masters degrees in Management and Criminal Justice. He is also a Certified Protection Professional (CPP), a Certified Protection Officer (CPO), and a Certified Emergency Manager (CEM).

Mavis Vet, CPO, CSS

Mavis has been employed by Llewellyn Security Group since 1986 as a security supervisor. She has completed the private investigator's program through the International School of Investigations and Protective Services. She has also achieved special protective service training in narcotic and explosive detection techniques and leadership training in behavior symptom analysis. She is a Certified Protection Officer (CPO) and a Certified Security Supervisor (CSS).

R. Gene Watson, CSS, CPO

Gene is Protection/Investigation Chief for Bank IV Oklahoma, Tulsa, Oklahoma. He is a retired police officer and Town Marshall. He is considered an expert in financial security and emergency security management. Gene is a certified instructor in private security and private investigations in Oklahoma. His professional training includes completion of the FBI specialized protection training courses. His security policy manuals have been published by several financial institutions.

PROTECTION OFFICER CODE OF ETHICS

The Protection Officer Shall

1.   Respond to employer's professional needs.
2.   Exhibit exemplary conduct.
3.   Protect confidential information.
4.   Maintain a safe and secure workplace.
5.   Dress to create professionalism.
6.   Enforce all lawful rules and regulations.
7.   Encourage liaison with public officers.
8.   Develop good rapport within the profession.
9.   Strive to attain professional competence.
10.   Encourage high standards of officer ethics.

Today business and the public expect a great deal from the uniformed security officer. In the past there has been far too little attention paid to the ethical aspects of the profession. There must be solid guide lines that each officer knows and understands. More importantly, it is essential that each manager and supervisor perform his or her duties in a manner that will reflect honesty, integrity and professionalism.

Every training program should address the need for professional conduct on and off duty. Line officers must exhibit a willingness to gain professional competency and adhere to a strict code of ethics that must include:

LOYALTY

To the employer, the client and the public. The officer must have a complete and thorough understanding of all of the regulations and procedures that are necessary to protect people and assets on or in relation to the facility assigned to protect.

EXEMPLARY CONDUCT

The officer is under constant scrutiny by everyone in work and public places. Hence it is essential that he/she exhibit exemplary conduct at all times. Maturity and professionalism are the key words to guide all officers.

CONFIDENTIALITY

Each officer is charged with the responsibility of working in the interests of his/her employer. Providing protection means that the officer will encounter confidential information which must be carefully guarded and never compromised.

SAFETY & SECURITY

The foremost responsibility of all officers is to ensure that the facility that must be protected is safe and secure for all persons with lawful access. The officer must fully understand all necessary procedures to eliminate or control security and safety risks.

DEPORTMENT

Each officer must dress in an immaculate manner. Crisp, sharp, clean and polished are the indicators that point to a professional officer who will execute his/her protection obligations in a proficient manner and will be a credit to the profession.

LAW ENFORCEMENT LIAISON

It is the responsibility of each officer to make every effort to encourage and enhance positive relations with members of public law enforcement. Seek assistance when a genuine need exists and offer assistance whenever possible.

STRIVE TO LEARN

To become professionally competent, each officer must constantly strive to be knowledgeable about all his/her chosen career. How to protect people, assets and information must always be a learning priority for every officer.

DEVELOP RAPPORT

It is necessary to be constantly aware of the image that our profession projects. All officers can enhance the image of the industry, their employer and themselves. Recognize and respect peers and security leaders throughout the industry.

HONESTY

By virtue of the duties and responsibilities of all officers, honest behavior is absolutely essential at all times. Each officer occupies a position of trust that must not be violated. Dishonesty can never be tolerated by the security profession.

PREJUDICE

The job of protecting means that the officer must impose restrictions upon people who frequent the security workplace. All human beings must be treated equally, with dignity and respect, regardless of color, race, religion or political beliefs.

SELF-DISCIPLINE

With the position of trust comes the responsibility to diligently protect life and property. These duties can only be discharged effectively when the officer understands the gravity of his/her position. Self-discipline means trying harder and caring more.

CONCLUSION

The job of protecting life and property focuses much attention on the individual security officer. Hence, it is essential to be aware of the need for professional conduct at all times. By strictly adhering to each section in this Code of Ethics, it may be expected that we as individuals and the industry as a whole will enjoy a good reputation and gain even more acceptance from the public as well as private and government corporations. You as the individual officer must be a principal in this process.

LEARNING SKILLS—STUDY HABITS
by Joan Mulder, M.A.

To everything there is a season.
And a time for every purpose under heaven:
A time to be born, and a time to die;
A time to plant and a time to reap ...

Ecclesiastes 3:1-8

The idea expressed in these lines has endured for centuries. The words originated in the Book of Ecclesiastes, were popularized in the 1960s by Pete Seeger's folk song "Turn! Turn! Turn!", and have been read at funerals and weddings and used as titles of books on various subjects.

The thoughts and feelings of "to everything there is a season" are also appropriate when applied to the experience you are embarking upon as an adult learner—it is again a "time to learn," but at a different level of intensity and purpose than when you were in high school or college.

As you know, learning does not simply occur by magic nor by spending time with textbooks. Learning requires your specific organized effort and your investment of time and energy.

The purpose of this chapter is to provide you with strategies in the "art" of learning. Three specific areas are targeted:

1.   How to be effective as an independent learner;
2.   How to read efficiently and effectively study this manual;
3.   And how to score higher on the objective tests required for your certification.

While this chapter will not provide you with the "perfect" way to study and learn, because no two people are exactly the same in their learning styles, it will give you many study and learning skills, suggestions and techniques. Try them out, modify and adapt them to your personal way of learning and your individual situation.

A bibliography is included as reference for a more in-depth look at the areas presented, and for other academic skills not elaborated in this chapter (such as writing essay exams, writing reports and research papers, taking notes from the lecturer ...).

First, though, do you know how you compare with other adult learners? To begin your "time to learn," try this short quiz to find out how you rank in the range of efficient, effective adult students.

STUDY SKILLS QUIZ

Answer the following questions by placing a check mark in the box that best describes when you do the stated activities. The choices in the boxes are:

4: Almost always   3: More than half the time   2: About half the time
1: Less than half the time   0: Almost never

Being an Independent Learner:						
1	Do you have a study schedule in which you set aside time each day for studying?	4	3	2	1	0
2	Do you estimate how long it will take you to read an assignment and plan your study time in accordance with this?	4	3	2	1	0
3	Do you reward yourself when you complete a set amount of studying?	4	3	2	1	0

	Being an Efficient, Effective Reader and Learner:					
4	Before studying a chapter in detail, do you make use of any of the clues in the book such as headings, illustrations and chapter summaries?	4	3	2	1	0
5	Do you spend at least 50% of your study time reciting (testing yourself)?	4	3	2	1	0
6	Do you read with a pencil in hand in order to underline or make notes?	4	3	2	1	0
7	Do you know your best time of day for studying?	4	3	2	1	0
8	Do you vary your reading speed according to the type of material that you're reading?	4	3	2	1	0
9	Do you read without daydreaming?	4	3	2	1	0
	Being a Smart Test Taker					
10	At the start of an examination, do you make plans for suitably distributing your time among the questions?	4	3	2	1	0
11	Can you write an exam without feeling overly nervous or anxious?	4	3	2	1	0
12	Do you plan to answer all easy questions first, leaving the more difficult ones until the end?	4	3	2	1	0

How did you score?

- If you got 40 or above, you are using many of the right techniques in your learning already.
- If you scored between 30 and 40, you need to apply some specific strategies in order to be an efficient student
- Below 30 means that you are probably spending too much time on your studying, probably with negligible results.

What strategies and techniques can you apply? Over the years, adults returning to school have discussed their concerns and their study methods. I've made note of the most interesting comments and the most common concerns that these people have expressed.

Following are the eight most often heard comments (along with one comment about memory that I've only heard once!). The discussion following each is based, for the most part, on research in human learning. Practical ideas for applying this research to your daily study habits are suggested.

You will note that there is an overlap among some of the concerns and suggestions. I urge you to integrate, modify, personalize, and transfer the suggestions to various areas of your learning. By doing so, you will be more efficient and effective in your "time to learn".

Comment 1: How many times have I heard this one!?

"I'm 40 years old—I can't remember as well as I could when I was younger. Because I'm older, it is more difficult for me to learn."

As an adult, you bring to any learning situation many years of experience. Research has shown that your ability to learn *does not* decrease with age. Apps, in his book *Study Skills for Those Adults Returning to School* states that " ... the accumulated experiences of learning are a considerable asset to you as an adult learner. As you face new experiences, you can often relate parts or all of the new experiences to something you have experienced previously." (Apps, page 10)

In fact, studies have shown that older students in colleges and universities consistently earn higher grades than their younger classmates. A number of years ago, a group of 50-year-olds were given the same intelligence test that they had taken when they were 19. They consistently made higher scores on all but one section of the test.

Tony Buzan, in his book *Use Your Head*, talks about age and human mental performance. He concludes that older people who have remained "active and explorative" have the ability to understand and learn new areas of knowledge far surpassing that of "equally enthusiastic but younger and less experienced minds." (Buzan, page 63)

Comment 2:   This is the concern expressed by 90% of adult students who enroll in non-traditional programs or courses.

"With independent study courses, I find it difficult to get started. There is no instructor telling me to read Chapter 2 for next week, and there are no set dates for exams—it is all up to me! I tend to procrastinate for the first month, and then I have to hustle to finish the course. I could have done a lot better if I had started the first day I got the book."

Procrastination is a basic trait that we all possess. Some of us are worse than others, only doing our work when the deadline is the next day. A proven technique to break the procrastination habit involves time management. Use these weekly and monthly schedules to keep track of where you are and where you are going. The forms are presented as examples. Remember to try out the various formats and use the system and forms that will work for your unique situation.

TIPS FOR SCHEDULE PLANNING

1. The first day you begin your program, sit down with a schedule sheet (see examples) and a list of the required readings. Plan when you will complete each section. Treat the self-quiz at the end of each chapter as a real test. Keep track of your scores.

2. On all schedules, it is often easy to get started by writing in all the things that you cannot change, e.g. appointments, work times, community responsibilities, children's activities, and things that involve other people in your life. Now you can see when your free time is and how much free time you have. Remember to schedule some recreation time for yourself.

3. Many study-skills experts recommend that you do not open a book for one day of the week - maybe a Saturday, a Sunday or a Friday night. Their idea is that you will be "fresher" that way and will be able to concentrate more effectively during the five or six "study days." See if that works for you.

4. Plan as far ahead as possible—note your final test date and work toward that. At the beginning of each month or week, fill in details (times, pages and rewards). Be as specific as possible —set hours, number of pages, type of reward.

Comment 3:

"I sit and read this chapter from beginning to end, over and over. I guess I can't concentrate. Last night I sat for two hours reading Chapter 5, but halfway through I caught myself daydreaming about that great party we had last weekend."

You should have a basic time planning schedule(s) in place. Look at your use of time within the schedules. You need to get off the "procrastination trip" and on with some high-speed learning.

1.   First, decide when your "best" time of day is in terms of being energetic, productive, active and ready to learn. If you don't know, try out some times. Wake up at 5:30 a.m. and after a quick shower, get a coffee and study for an hour when the house is quiet. Maybe you didn't know that you were a "morning person." One student I know works best during the hours of 10 p.m. to 2 a.m. He knows his best body time - his peak time for productivity - and he capitalizes on it.

2.   How long can you expect yourself to sit in one place and be productive in your studying? Research has shown that the average student needs a break after 40 to 60 minutes of reading or studying.

3.   I recently heard a speaker state that after 40 minutes of listening, people tend to shuffle in their seats and look through the program to see what is coming next. After 45 minutes, people begin to think about their financial problems. After 60 minutes, they tend to have wild sexual fantasies.

With that in mind, you should plan your 2-hour study session in terms of:

- 40 minutes of study and 10 minutes break;

- 40 minutes study and 10 minutes break; then

- 20 minutes review.

Other combinations may work better for you:

- 60 minutes study and 20 minutes break;

- 40 minutes study with 10 minutes review.

Be sure to experiment with various time frames. At your peak times or when you are reading about a particular subject, you may be able to concentrate longer.

Comment 4:

"When I get a new textbook, I sit down and begin reading at page one."

Never treat a textbook like a mystery novel. Authors of textbooks, or manuals such as this, use many aids to help you prepare to read, to help you organize as you read and to help you review.

First, let's look at the total book. Plan to spend about 45 minutes at previewing or surveying the total book. Think of previewing as you're planning for a car trip to visit Aunt Hilda in New York City. In the initial planning stages, you get an AMA road map of North America and plan the best route—"best" in terms of shortness, scenery and good highways. You plan an estimated day and time of departure and arrival, what you will see there, as well as along the way.

The analogy holds for your study "trip" as well—you do some organizational work (study schedules), but you also plan your way through the book by doing the following:

1.   Look at both front and back covers (book jacket flaps as well). Read the preface and/or the introduction. From all of this, you will get important background on why the author or editor wrote or compiled the book, for whom the book is intended, and the credentials of the author(s). Note where the book was printed and in what year. (It may have U.S. examples; it may not be up-to-date.)

2.   Go through the table of contents and, if it has one, the index in the back. This gives you an overview of the book's contents.

3.   Leaf through, noting the visual aids (research substantiates the fact that "a picture is worth a thousand words"). We tend to remember better when visual aids such as pictures, graphs, charts and cartoons are used. More on that later.

4.   Check to see if other "goodies" are provided; reading lists, a glossary of specialized words with their meanings. (The glossary can save you many trips to your dictionary.)

5.   Spend time reading over the summaries. This gives you a good idea of what the book covers and gives you a sense of direction—"map" of the total book.

Comment 5:

"I try to be really neat when I take notes. By this I mean I keep the textbook spotless—no writing in the margins or underlining. In my notebook, I write in complete sentences, but I often have about one page of notes for every page of textbook."

Notes should *never* be particularly neat. They should *never* be in complete sentences. You spend valuable time writing when you really should be "reciting" or asking yourself questions. Your notes should have lots of diagrams or little charts—remember the old Chinese proverb that a picture is worth 1,000 words.

What is the most efficient and effective way of taking notes? Following are proven "tips."

1.   Survey

The 10 minutes that you spend at surveying the chapter is perhaps the most valuable time (along with the 10 or 15 minutes you spend reviewing at the end).

- Read the chapter *title* for a general idea of what the author is discussing. With colored pen or highlighter in hand, go through the chapter, checking for the *organization*, using the headings and subheadings.

- Note the typeset. The important items are set in bold type and in capitals.
  Glance through any *pictures* and *diagrams*—read the captions. If you know anything about the subject from past experiences (you've worked in The Bay and know their alarm system), these key words and diagrams or charts will trigger what you have stored in your memory about these past experiences, and bring them up from your subconscious mind.

- Read through the *summary*, noting the specific areas. When you go back to read the chapter, you will know what the author thinks is important and thus you can pay more attention to those areas.

2.   Now for the actual *note-taking*. Many methods are detailed in the books listed in the Bibliography. Following is one way that has worked for the majority of my adult students.

- Take one sheet of paper, *only one,* and outline the chapter in order to get the big picture or the total map of the chapter. You know that you must get *all* the notes for the chapter on *one* page. This system discourages too much writing. You save your valuable time for "reciting" or learning the material, not writing it down.

- Develop your own shorthand system. For example, use H_2O for "water," "exting" for "extinguisher," etc. Give yourself credit for being able mentally to fill in words in your notes. The example on the review cards makes use of only "key" words.

- As you come to the 40 minute mark of your study session, you need to take four or five minutes to test yourself on the review cards. You need to set aside the ones that you need more practice on, for a second review.

- Your "learning schedule" could be outlined as:

1)	survey chapter and do "map" sheet	10 min.
2)	read each section, make notes	40 min.
3)	review	5 min.
4)	before sleep; review	5 min.
5)	next day (lunchtime), review	5 min.
6)	end of week - review	5 min.
7)	end of month - review	5 min.

Remember, by the week- and month-end, you will have a number of chapters to review.

Comment 6:

"Usually I try to do my studying in the evenings at the kitchen table. The kids sometimes bother me, I get a few phone calls, and the T.V. is noisy, even though the door is closed."

1.   The *physical environment* for studying effectively is extremely important. Research indicates that instrumental music—particularly with headsets—provides a "cover" for distracting noises. The ideal situation is to have a room set aside as your study (preferably off the traffic pattern for the rest of the family). Equip it with a desk, good lighting, a firm chair, a clock, a dictionary, pencils, pens—everything you need (and lock the door so your 10-year-old doesn't take off with the ruler, pencils and your walkman!).

2.   Make it a habit to begin studying as soon as your bottom hits the chair in that room. Psychologists have long told us that certain behaviors are "habits" in certain places. For example, when people go to a football stadium, yelling and cheering behavior is automatic. Likewise, certain behaviors are habitual in church. Never let yourself sit and daydream or read the newspaper in your study—it is too easy to fall into an avoidance-behavior pattern.

3.   Remember to inform your family of your schedule and then stick to it. *Post a schedule* on the study door indicating that you are not to be disturbed from 8:00–8:45; you will then have a 15-minute break when you can deal with any phone calls, concerns, etc.; go back in from 9:00–9:45. It is amazing how people will cooperate when they know the rules and know that you are adamant about enforcing them. (A woman I know has cautioned her children that unless one of them is gushing blood or smoke is rising, they are not to disturb her until the posted time. She plugs in her special study music, and after 45 minutes, comes out for some "quality" time with her children.)

Comment 7:

"My memory is like the muscles in my body and I'm working at expanding my brain power. When I jog, I do mental exercises. I memorize the number of houses on my route, the names of all the streets I cross, and the number of poplar trees that I pass. The more I exercise my 'memory muscle,' the stronger it will be, just as the more I work out on my weight machine, the stronger my body muscles will be."

MEMORY PRE-TEST

Before you read the response to the above comment, try this little pre-test:

1.   Copy the following words on a sheet of paper.

2.   Have someone time you exactly one minute as you study the list.

3.   After one minute, turn your study sheet over, and in the correct sequence, write all ten words from memory.

4.   Score one point for every word in the correct sequence.

| man | table | pop | counter | brush |
| tree | swing | flower | dress | tap |

We have tried this little test with adult learners and found that the average score is 7. The average score on a similar test by University of Minnesota students was 6.5 (Ragor, p.130).

What is the best way to memorize? Is it "strengthening your memory muscle"? A study done by Professor Woodrow at Michigan State was designed to answer this. He pre-tested a group of students and randomly divided them into two groups. The memory muscle group spent three hours memorizing poetry and nonsense syllables—drilling themselves over and over. The other group learned techniques for remembering and did limited practice. The results from the post-test? The memory muscle group made a 4.5 percent improvement; the technique group a 36.0 percent improvement. (Ragor, p. 132-133).

What are some of the techniques that Woodrow taught his students?

1.   First, *select* what you want to remember. This is probably the most difficult part of the whole process. You can get a good idea from the summary and the practice tests. By reading, underlining and making notes (on review cards) on each chapter, you focus yourself on what is to be remembered.

2.   *Visualize* - Build a mental picture (remember, a picture is worth a thousand words!) Dream up a vivid, even outrageous picture of a pot-bellied *man*, standing on a little wooden *table*, balancing a can of pop as he tries to reach across to the kitchen *counter* to get a *brush*.

3.   *Group* - It's easier to remember two groups of five things than ten separate things. Build some type of organizational "tree." This also makes use of the "picture" idea; for example:

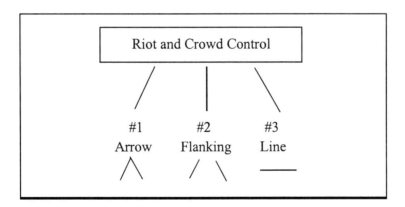

4.   *Number* - If you know that you must remember ten items at Safeway or have three methods of crowd control, your mind will tend to work toward remembering that number.

5.   *Use Color* - Another wonderful property of the brain is that it tends to remember best when a color is involved. Somehow when you're sitting in the test room, you visualize the seven types of communication systems circled with red ink.

6.   *Use Memory Formulas or Association* - You may want to use mnemonic (pronounced "nee-mon-ic") devices to help you recall such things as items on a list, steps to a procedure, or the nine types of alarm systems. Remember how to spell "arithmetic": *a red Indian thought he might eat turnips in church.*

Remember that nothing engages the senses as well as the real thing. As you walk by a fire extinguisher, check it out. If it says "soda acid," you would immediately recall "Type A fires, and small type 'B', has a little bottle of sulfuric acid in the neck which, when inverted, mixes with the soda and water to form CO_2 which forces water out." You may even pull the review card out of your pocket to confirm your knowledge.

The human brain seems to have an almost infinite capacity for memory. Some scientists have speculated that an average brain:

- can store up to 199 billion different bits of information;

- has 10 billion individual neurons or nerve cells; and

- could have about a million different chemical reactions taking place every minute.

The human brain is indeed complex. Dr. Houston states: "We are just beginning to discover the virtually limitless capacities of the mind ..." (*Super Learning*, p.3)

Super Learning and *Use Your Head* discuss, among other things, the concept of discovering the enomous potential of the human brain. Both books suggest excellent systems and techniques in "learning how to learn".

However, very simplistically, the brain may be said to have three areas of memory:

> Short Term
>
> Middle Term
>
> Long Term

- *Short term* - all kinds of information hits here and bounces right back out again unless you *select* that information as worth remembering and then do something in order to force the information into the:

- *Middle term* area where a lot of it stays for a few weeks or months before fading.

- *Long term* memory is reserved for such details as your name, the ages of your children and your telephone number.

Now that you know some techniques, try a post-test; same format as the pre-test:

1. Copy the words.
2. Memorize for one minute.
3. Turn your page over and write from memory, scoring one point for each word in the correct sequence.

beer	dog	grass	book	jar
flour	sky	stove	lady	deer

In our study skills workshops, 90 percent of the students score 100 percent on the post-test.

IT'S NOW UP TO YOU!

By knowing the principles and the "best" techniques for learning, you need to develop your personal study and learning system.

Don't be hesitant in experimenting—in growing by challenging yourself. This is your time to achieve excellence in your personal and academic life—"your time to learn."

And, remember to keep it all in perspective.

If you have comments, queries or would like to share a favorite "learning to learn" tactic, write to Joan Mulder at Alberta Vocational Center, 332 - 6 Ave. S.E., Calgary, Alberta T2G 4S6.

BIBLIOGRAPHY

Adams, W. Royce. *"Reading Skills: A Guide for Better Reading."* Toronto: John Wiley & Sons, 1974. A programmed format with lots of exercises to provide practice in all kinds of reading activities such as skimming, scanning, vocabulary development, study reading procedures.

Alberta Manpower, Career Services Branch. *"The Adult Back-to-School Book,"* 1985. (Free copy from Career Services Branch, Alberta Manpower, 201 Sun Building, 10363 - 108 St., Edmonton, Alberta   T5J 1L8).

Apps, Jerold W. *"Study Skills for those Adults Returning to School."* New York: McGraw Hill, 1978.

Buzan, Tony. *"Use Your Head,"* London: British Broadcasting Corporation, 1982. A terrific little pocketbook that talks about how to use your mind to the best advantage in reading, studying, memorizing. Includes practice exercises.

Carman, R.A. & W. Royce Adams. *"Study Skills, A Student's Guide for Survival,"* Toronto: John Wiley & Sons, 1972. (If I could buy one book, it would be this one! It is organized in a programmed format and written in a humourous style with lots of diagrams and exercises. Probably not to be used in its entirety; it contains excellent ideas for you to become a more effective, efficient adult learner (and it's fun to read!)

Gilbert, Sara. *"How to Take Tests."* New York: William Morrow & Co., 1983.

Grassick, Patrick. *"Making the Grade."* Toronto: MacMillan of Canada, 1983. Grassick has tested out his ideas with University of Calgary students who have participated in his Exam Skills Workshops. Good sections on the Global Map approach to note-taking, and on a step-by-step approach for reducing test anxiety.

Kasselman-Turkel, Judi & Franklyn Peterson. *"Study Smarts: How to Learn More in Less Time."* Chicago: Contemporary Books, Inc., 1981.

Ostrander, Sheila and Lynn Schroeder, *"Super Learning."* New York: Dell Publishing, 1979. Based on Dr. Lazanov's research on learning systems, this pocket book talks about a relaxed method of accelerated learning.

Raygor, Alton L. and David M. Wark. *"Systems for Study."* Toronto: McGraw-Hill, 1970. Designed for the college student; contains interesting implications of what has been learned from research for students' study behaviors.

And last, a good little booklet designed to help you improve your child's study and homework behavior (with a few tips for you as well):

Zifferblatt, Steven. *"Improving Study and Homework Behaviors."* Champaign, Illinois: Research Press, 1970.

Music Cassettes available from the Lind Institute, P.O. Box 14487, San Francisco, California 94114 USA.

UNIT ONE
THE SECURITY INDUSTRY

The Evolving Discipline of Security
The Future of Private Security

THE EVOLVING DISCIPLINE OF SECURITY
by Dr Martin Gill[1]

Despite the large amount of criminological work on a variety of different types of victims, there is still very little research on offences within, by and against businesses.[2] There are numerous very good studies on crime, crime prevention, management and risk but few attempts have been made to integrate the knowledge and experience being gained. And there has been very little attempt to learn from the experience of both practitioners and academics. Each has worked in relative isolation and thus there has been a lack of thinking on the links between theory and practice: academics are suspicious of solutions to problems whose impact have not been precisely measured, while practitioners on the other hand dislike the delay inherent in the academic process, claiming that the commercial realities demand a swift reaction. Moreover, practitioners are sometimes confused by the mode of presentation which is weighted with jargon.[3]

But it would be a mistake to see the divisions as being merely between academics and practitioners. Academics do not offer an accepted universal explanation for the causes of crime, and the background of criminologists is generally confined to two main disciplines: sociology and law.[4] Perhaps as a consequence the contribution that other disciplines (for example, economics, genetics, psychology, political science and in particular management and risk management) can make has yet to be fully exploited.

Similarly, the approach of practitioners is fragmented. This is evidenced by the range of security associations and institutes that exist often with conflicting aims and there is no single voice that can speak for what is a diverse range of activities. If one was starting from scratch the structures of the security world would look very different to the way they do now. It is no wonder that those working within the security world should argue that there is a need to take steps to ensure that they are regarded as a profession, while those outside point to the lack of formalized training, and in many countries the absence of statutory regulation (or the poor status of it) as evidence that it has a long way to go. In reality both camps are right. The security world is full of dedicated and very highly skilled individuals but the world in which they work has yet to find the right structures to ensure that minimum standards are maintained for all those practicing its skills. This remains a challenge for the future. In the meantime works goes on, security practitioners continue to offer excellent service to their clients, associations continue to push for recognition of their members' work and form the basis on which a recognition as a profession can one day be built. Associations have been instrumental in the development of a range of very good training courses which have their own impact on raising standards.

However, in this paper I want to look at the role of universities, or more specifically at some of the research which has evolved in recent years which is making its own contribution to practice. The good news for the security world is that a range of universities now offer postgraduate courses. In particular the Scarman Centre at Leicester University here in England has something like 200 students studying for Masters degrees. These are mostly professional people who are keen to obtain the academic credibility to accompany the skills they have acquired over many years. I am often intrigued by the types of comments that our students make on the successful completion of the program, such as "how come I have been a security practitioner for years and never have taken a course in crime prevention?" And I have to say "I don't know." Universities are able to develop theories, provide frameworks and generate new ideas to guide practice. This is where universities have made a difference to the lives of security professionals and to the development of the security world on its road to a profession.

An academic discipline, and the study of security aspires to be just this, is dependent on knowledge. And universities are beginning to publish research to develop that knowledge. Certainly here in Leicester all staff are required to be actively engaged in research. A range of research studies are being developed and reported, which greatly impact on the contribution to the body of knowledge, and there does need to be a recognized body of knowledge. In this paper I would like to highlight just three areas where this is the case, where research is already appearing. They are the workplace as a locale for crime, on policing and on the role of management in responding to crime.

THE WORKPLACE AS A LOCALE FOR CRIME

It has long been recognized that businesses are offenders and that this impacts upon the community.[5] Rather less has been said about the extent to which crimes committed against businesses and against workers impact upon society. Workplaces are commonly victims. A recent study of the retail sector in Britain found that while some types of outlet suffered from criminal attack more frequently than others, overall retailers were well over four times more likely than households to be burgled.[6] I came up with similar findings.[7,8] The 1988 British Crime Survey, which surveyed individuals rather than businesses, also found that those in some types of job were more likely to become victims of crime. It concluded that workers blamed their occupation as the cause of about a quarter of violent incidents and personal thefts and of over a third of threats.[9]

Research conducted in other countries has tended to replicate these findings. For example, a study of 966 businesses in Australia found that crime was more common in certain types of business (particularly retail and tourism/recreation), that the majority of those who suffered from burglary did so more than once, and that repeat victimization was common where workers had suffered from violence.[10] Similarly, in the USA survey findings indicate that 8% of rapes, 7% of robberies and 16% of all assaults occur while victims are working.[11]

It needs to be stressed that crime at the workplace has a direct impact on people: organizations include employees, employers, contractors and customers[12] and it is right to be concerned when they are victimized, all the more so given the legal requirement on employers under health and safety legislation to provide a safe working environment. Moreover, crime is expensive.[13] At least some of the resulting costs are passed on to consumers in increased prices; and it is the poorer sections of the community who can least afford this burden.

A good illustration of the impact of workplace crime is provided by a study of small businesses in New York.[14] It found that over a quarter of respondents (and half of wholesalers) experienced difficulties in recruiting workers because of crime, while about a seventh claimed that workers had resigned because of local crime levels (a figure that is put in perspective by the fact that over a fifth reported that a member of staff had been robbed while on duty or when traveling to or from work). As a result, firms experienced reduced sales, operated for fewer hours and canceled expansion plans.[15] New York may be atypical but without comparable data there is no basis for allaying fears that other businesses in other cities might experience similar problems. In any event the Institute of Directors[16] is among those who have drawn attention to these problems in the United Kingdom:

> *Crime is one of the enemies of the enterprise culture. It impedes the regeneration of our inner cities by deterring employers establishing businesses. It exacerbates skill shortages where potential employees refuse to work in areas with a high crime rate. In certain sectors this has a serious demoralizing effect on employers who themselves become victims of crime within the workplace.*

Much of the current work on crime prevention is addressing broader issues of community safety.[17] These include the prevention of substance abuse, interpersonal violence, racial attacks and harassment. More generally, there is concern to promote antisocial behavior strategies such as noise abatement. These issues affect people and also the workplace and we can no longer treat the two as separate areas of study and interest.

The workplace is an area where crime control has been practiced as a specialism for many years. It is usually referred to as security management but, as will be seen, evaluations of policing or discussions of crime prevention have generally avoided this area. But even without drawing on the techniques of security management there is much, potentially, that businesses can do to improve crime control in the community. As Shapland and Vagg[18] observe:

> *Businesses could be said to be sinks of opportunity for crime for the (predominantly local and youthful) offenders in the area. Their crime prevention practices and attitudes substantially affected people's views of the amount of crime in the area, since incidents of disorder on public property and against business premises were the mostly widely known.*

These authors also discuss the contribution businesses make by watching and guarding the street immediately in front of their premises: here they serve an important crime prevention and policing function which some "watch" schemes have been able to tap into. It is incredible that those researching security and those researching crime prevention have paid so little attention to each other because on many occasions they have been doing much the same thing.

The commercial sector has not been sold the merits of community crime prevention. A frequent lament I hear at meetings of business people is that they are often approached for finance on the assumption that the feel-good factor or the publicity given to the fact that they are helping will be sufficient return for them. But businesses have a stake in the community. Precisely because they are made up of people, and because they are part of community life, they are in a position to influence both perceptions (and hence the fear of crime) and policies. The lessons of a declining neighborhood where "no-one cares" have often been noted[19] and initiatives that tackle the causes of crime offer an opportunity for businesses to reduce the risk that they themselves or their workers will be victims of crime.

POLICING

There is a considerable amount of research on "the police" but only a few studies focus on private policing (and contract and in-house security). Private security is often viewed negatively, but one study[20] found that both public and management hold very favorable views on the role of private security in shopping centers. However, Speed et al[21] found that retailers "were not overwhelmingly favorable to the police." One explanation is that the types of crime that occur in organizations are mostly not a priority for the police. Willis and Beck[22] studied the police charter of 42 police forces in England, Wales and Scotland and found that only two included comments on tackling crime in the commercial sector. In short, the police response to crime in business is judged to have achieved mixed results.

But what is to be done when the organization is the offender? Clarkson[23] has drawn attention to this issue. Prompted, in part, by the finding that the last decade has seen 5,774 people killed at work—"the result of people being crushed, electrocuted, asphyxiated or burnt"—he has highlighted the need to rethink the official response in Britain.[24]   Indeed, there have been a number of disasters resulting in deaths that have led to legal proceedings, not all of which have been successful. This is an area where risk assessment and improved perception and communication may be able to contribute to the understanding of incidents that may be criminal or threaten security. It is surprising that this issue has not been given greater prominence and it is one which the journal seeks to address.

MANAGEMENT

Evaluations of responses to crime, whether within an organization or in a community setting, need to take account of both technological and management factors, and not just the former. As Hayes[25] has summarized:

> *Swiftly changing technologies will greatly enhance loss control efforts, but good, sound leadership and management provide the ultimate resolution to loss control problems.*

It is interesting to note that the literature on security management (which consists more of guides and manuals than of studies) includes relatively few evaluations of management approaches.[26] Indeed, the security world has often found solutions before defining the problems and there is a need here for more and better evaluations. In healthcare it is accepted that an aspirin will help cure a headache and a bandage will help to heal a cut finger. But in the field of crime prevention all too often a bandage is being used to cure a headache and it is assumed that an aspirin will stop a cut finger from bleeding. There are countless examples of such inappropriate treatments, some involving the management of technology. For example, there has been a massive investment in closed circuit television (CCTV) but evidence as to its effectiveness is sometimes conflicting. Part of the problem is that frequently CCTV is installed without a clear definition of objectives. Moreover, where there have been evaluations they have seldom been undertaken by independent and skilled evaluators. Indeed, one review has concluded that most such evaluations are "wholly unreliable";[27] often the most positive comments have come from those who have much to lose by negative findings.[28] The point is not that CCTV is not useful or of central importance; it is. But it may be more effective in some circumstances than in others, or against certain types of crime than others. Where, however, are the independent evaluations which provide the answers?

Of course one of the realities of crime prevention (and of management), and one of the difficulties too, is that it is sometimes more important to be seen to be doing something, anything, than to be doing the right thing. Purchasing a CCTV system is a more visible sign that safety and security are being taken seriously (especially when rivals are doing so) than minor changes in policy, such as altering operating procedures for cashiers or security staff or by focused training of staff. Yet these may be more appropriate and cheaper. It is unlikely there will be uniform solutions even to common problems. There are too many variables which need to be taken account of, including personnel, culture, language, laws, products, markets, competitors and finance. But there may be simpler responses that are also better.

There is a desperate need for more research. In terms of workplaces and workers more data are needed on the scale of victimization (including repeat incidents) and the relationships between a host of variables. These include: the nature of the offences; the characteristics of the victims and offenders; the type, location and size of the organization and its type of business; the type of security policy and procedures being followed and their sophistication; staff awareness of security; and company culture to name but a few. Much of the data on crime in organizations is limited to a few types of offences; data on the scale of sexual harassment, extortion and bribery remains elusive. There needs to be a closer scrutiny, via qualitative research, of community issues and examples of good practices need to be identified and then tested in different environments.

TOWARDS A BODY OF KNOWLEDGE

So the signs are good, more research is being produced which greatly enhances the development of security into a recognized field of study, but there is a need to bring this work together to create a recognized body of knowledge, a set of theories and frameworks that can be readily identified with the security world. They already exist, at least in parts. The world of risk management, for example, has identified distinct approaches, and there are a range of areas where security can benefit from work that has been developed, for other purposes over many years, different areas of the study of management, including disaster management, organizational studies, the sociology of work, and of course crime prevention to name but a few. Indeed, within the world of crime prevention a considerable amount of effort has been devoted to understanding how offenders make decisions at the scene, the sorts of things that make them think about the desirability of carrying out an offence in what is called rational choice theory. And that in turn has led to a set of techniques to reduce opportunities for offenders, known as situational crime prevention. This entails changing the situation or location of a shop, office, workshop, home, to make the crime less likely. In effect this is much of what security or crime risk management is about, and yet the links are rarely made.

Recently I have tried to enhance these links via the development of what I have called the crime risk management process. There is not the space here, nor is this the right place to discuss all the thinking that has gone behind the process, but it is an example of a framework, about managing crime and security issues that has evolved from the world of criminology. It has been designed as a guide to those responsible for managing a response.

The process begins with an *assessment*, and it is important that this is accurate for a good *decision* to be made, to *accept* the risk, to *transfer* it or by developing a more *specific strategy,* to tackle the problem.[29] The response can have at least three different *foci*; these identify the various levels at which *actions* can be taken, which in turn will dictate the variety of *techniques* available at the level of the *organization, situation* or *society. Management techniques* can be used to tackle some (situational) problems and they will certainly influence the effective management and work ability of different situational approaches. *Situational techniques* are based on the work of Clarke. Some *social/political/economic techniques* are used to tackle situational problems.

The process indicates the main stages one may go through when planning to tackle crime, and indeed a range of other problems. It may be possible in time to widen the scope of the model to look at safety issues and others too. Crime risk management (and indeed security management) in organizations involves making situations less conducive to crime. Environments need to be manipulated to make potential offenders think that their chances of success are quite low, indeed, too low to make the perpetration of a crime worthwhile. The process and the diagram are ways of simplifying what can be done—indeed there is a danger that they are an oversimplification. However, based on a theory of rational choice, itself derived from the behavioral patterns of offenders and built on the thinking of situational crime prevention, the process offers a guide to practitioners. I would welcome comments from any of you who could help me develop the model; even small ideas would be very welcome.

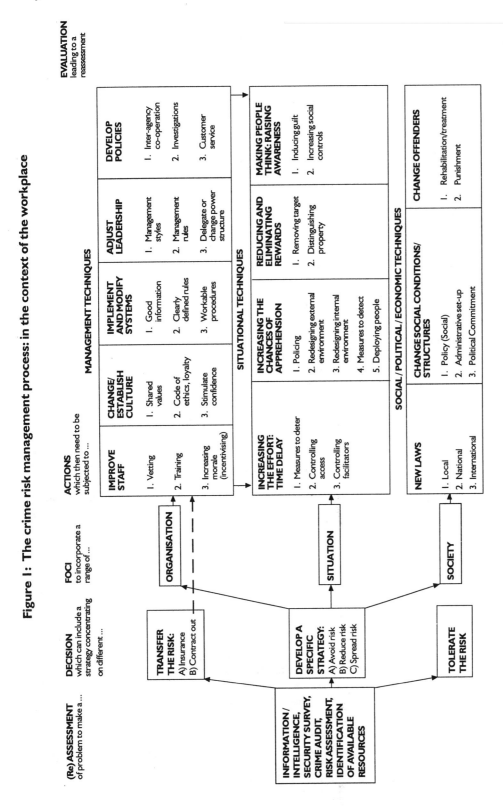

Figure 1: The crime risk management process: in the context of the workplace

Copyright © 1999 Perpetuity Press Ltd, PO Box 376 Leicester, LE2 3ZZ, UK.
Gill, M. (1998) *Crime at Work: Increasing the Risk for Offenders*. Leicester: Perpetuity Press.

Figure 1.1
Gill, M. (1998) CRIME AT WORK: Increasing the Risk for Offenders Leichester: Perpetuity Press P. 15

ENDNOTES

1   Deputy Director, Scarman Center, University of Leicester. The Friars, 154 Upper New Walk, Leicester. LE1 7QA. UK (email: mg26@le.ac.uk).

2   Given that the interest here is in workplaces the use of "business" is contentious. The word "organization" better reflects the fact that workplaces exist in the voluntary and public sectors. It is, however, a less familiar word in this context. In this paper they will both be used to denote workplaces.

3   Thus, in encouraging contributions which are theoretically challenging, the journal will at the same time, encourage "plain English."

4   Rock, P. (1994) The Social Organization of British Criminology, in Maguire, M., Morgan, R. and Reiner, R. (eds) *(The Oxford Handbook of Criminology.)* Oxford: Clarendon Press.

5   See Box, S. (1983) *Power, Crime and Mystification.* London: Tavistock.

6   Speed, M., Burrows, J. and Bamfield, J. (1994) *Retail Crime Costs*, 1993/94 Survey. London: British Retail Consortium.

7   *The Forum of Private Business (1995) Crime and Small Business*. Cheshire: The Forum of Private Business.

8   At the time of writing we are awaiting the publication of the findings from the Home Office Commercial Victimization Survey, although personal communication with a representative has confirmed that (in general terms) they are similar to those found by Speed et al, op cit.

9   Mayhew, P., Elliot, L. and Dowds, L. (1989) *The 1988 British Crime Survey*. Home Office Research Study 111. London: HMSO. Chapter 4.

10   Walker, J. (1995) *Crimes Against Business in Australia. Trends and Issues in Crime and Criminal Justice.* No. 45. Canberra: Australian Institute of Criminology.

11   US Department of Justice (1994) *Violence and Theft in the Workplace.* Crime Brief Data, National Crime Victimization Survey. Washington DC: US Department of Justice, Office of Justice Programs, Bureau of Justice Statistics. July.

12   See Gill. M.L. (1994) *Crime at Work: Studies in Security and Crime Prevention.* Leicester: Perpetuity Press.

13   Speed et al (op cit) concluded that in 1993/4 crime cost the retail industry in the United Kingdom £2.15 billion. Walker (op cit) estimated that in Australia in 1992 the total cost of crime including indirect costs was "somewhere between A\$3.8 billion and A\$4.7 billion." The U.S. Department of Justice study (op cit) which focused on violence and theft at the workplace concluded that an average of 3.5 days per crime were lost by employees and this "resulted in over US \$55 million in lost wages annually, not including days lost by sick and annual leave."

14   Gallagher, D., Lung, K., Mallin, E., Zhou, Y. and Caruso, C. (1989) *Small Businesses, Big Problem: Small Business and Crime in New York City*. New York: Interface.

15   Respondents in this study were asked about incidents that occurred in the previous three years.

16   Clarkson, M. (1994) in *Offenders and Employment in Europe*. The Work of the European Offender Employment Group and Conference Report. July, p 23.

17   See, Tilley, N. (1992) *Safer Cities and Community Safety Strategies*. Police Research Group Crime Prevention Unit Series. Paper 38. London: HMSO.

18   Shapland, J. and Vagg, J. (1988) *Policing by the Public.* London: Routledge, p 178.

19   Wilson, J.Q. and Kelling, G. (1982) *Broken Windows: the Police and Neighborhood Safety*. Atlantic Monthly, March, pp 29–38.

20   Beck, A. and Willis, A. (1995) *Crime and Security: Managing the Risk to Safe Shopping.* Leicester: Perpetuity Press.

21   Speed et al, op cit, p 34.

22   Willis, A. and Beck, A. (1994) *An Analysis of Police Charters with Special Reference to Risk and Security Management.* A Discussion Paper. Prepared for The Risk and Security Management Forum. Center for the Study of Public Order, University of Leicester.

23   Clarkson, C.M.V. (1995) *Corporate Killings.* Inaugural lecture, University of Leicester. 31 October.

24   For a discussion of possible alternatives see Pearce, F. and Toombs, S. (1992) *Realism and Corporate Crime*, in Matthews, R. and Young, J. (eds) *Issues in Realist Criminology*. London: Sage.

25   Hayes, R. (1991) *Retail Security and Loss Prevention.* Stomham: Butterworth-Heinemann.

26   One recent example includes, Bamfield, J. (1994) *Electronic Article Surveillance: Management Learning in Curbing Theft*. In Gill, M.L. (ed) *Crime at Work: Studies in Security and Crime Prevention*. Leicester: Perpetuity Press.

27   Short, E. and Ditton, J. (1995) Does CCTV Affect crime? *CCTV Today*. Vol. 2 No. 2. pp 10–12.

28   See Beck and Willis op cit. Also Hearnden in this issue.

29   There is some overlap between the various decisions shown separately in the diagram. Insurance, a way of transferring the risk may be a method which is used to spread the risk. The main point of the division discussed here is to identify situations where no actions are taken (Accept the risk), actions involving the risk be taken by others (Transfer the risk) or where a policy and response is initiated, which is dependent on specific actions being taken by the company involving the *techniques* shown.

PUBLICATIONS
Perpetuity Press
PO Box 376
Leicester
LE2 3ZZ
UK
tel 44 (0) 116 270 4186
fax 44 (0) 116 270 7742
email: info@perpetuitypress.co.uk

COURSES
Scarman Centre
The Friars
154 Upper New Walk
Leicester
LE1 7QQ
UK
tel: 44 (0) 116 252 3946
fax: 44 (0) 116 252 5766
email: dlsc@le.ac.uk

THE EVOLVING DISCIPLINE OF SECURITY
QUIZ

1.   Businesses/retailers are four times more likely to be burglarized then households.
         ☐ T   ☐ F

2.   The 1988 British Crime survey found that individuals in certain types of jobs are more likely to become victims of crime.
         ☐ T   ☐ F

3.   Crime at the workplace has a direct impact on:
     a)   People
     b)   Increased costs to consumers
     c)   Insurance costs
     d)   Health and safety legislation
     e)   All of the above

4.   _____ is referred to as Security Management.
     a)   Crime control
     b)   Community Safety
     c)   Interpersonal Violence
     d)   Policing

5.   One study found that both the public and management hold very favorable views on security in shopping centers.
         ☐ T   ☐ F

6.   Evaluations of response to crime whether within an organization or in a community setting
        need to take into account:
        a)   Technology factors
        b)   Community standards
        c)   Management factors
        d)   Policing strategies
        e)   A and C
        f)   A and B

7.   Installation of a closed circuit television system can solve all your security problems.
                        □ T   □ F

8.   Rational choice perspective refers to:
        a)   Organizational studies
        b)   How offenders make decisions at the scene
        c)   Disaster management
        d)   Policy choices

9.   The main stages one goes through when planning to tackle crime and other security problems
        are called the:
        a)   Assessment planning techniques
        b)   Specific strategy plan
        c)   Crime risk management process
        d)   Crime issues response

10.   Assessment, decision, foci, actions, evaluations are part of the:
        a)   Learning process
        b)   Security organizational chart
        c)   Crime risk management chart
        d)   Risk minimization strategy

THE FUTURE OF PRIVATE SECURITY
by David L. Ray, B.A., LL.B.

SECURITY INDUSTRY TRENDS

Private security is now the primary protective resource. Studies have shown that security has two and a half times the people in the United States compared with public law enforcement (1.6 million versus 625,000) and private security outspends law enforcement by 73% (64 billion vs. $35 billion). By the year 2000 it is predicted that the national budget for law enforcement will be $44 billion and for private security will be $103 billion. In recent years the security industry has grown at twice the rate of national employment.

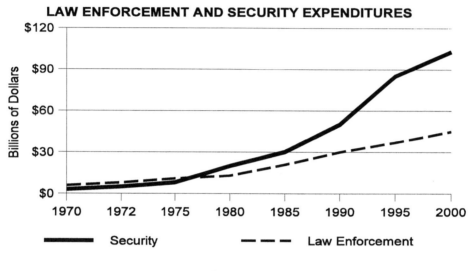

Figure 1.2

REASONS FOR THE TRENDS

The reasons for the trends in growth in private security are complex and varied but some of the major causes are:

Policing

During the late 1970s and early 1980s policing in America grew at a significant rate to keep up with crime trends and with the public's reduced tolerance for crime, especially crimes of violence. Even between 1987 and 1990 expenditures for general purpose law enforcement agencies rose by 19%.[1] With this growth in policing there was a stronger burden on the federal, state and municipal tax base. In the late 1980s and early 1990s with the downturn in the economy the public was no longer willing to accept the tax burden and all government services, including the police, were forced to cut budgets and consequently services.

During the past 25 years there has also been a significant increase in commercial property, especially retail shopping malls and office towers. This increase in retail and commercial space has resulted in a corresponding increase in crime at these sites and a requirement on the part of the property owner to provide security for the tenants, retailers and general public using the facilities. In the same time period there has also been a revolution in the use of computers by business and today enterprises of every size rely on computers for their everyday activity. With this reliance on the use of computers came an increase in computer crime that resulted in significant losses every year.

The end result is that public law enforcement cannot protect against computer crimes, employee theft or fraud or drug trafficking in the workplace. They cannot patrol private facilities such as shopping centers, plants, office buildings and computer centers. Private citizens and enterprise looked to security services to fill the gap left by the police.

The significant tax burden of policing has caused some small municipalities to replace police officers with private security because of the cost savings.[2]

The Justice System and the Courts

The court system has also contributed to the rise in the use of private security. There has been a general reduction in the perception of efficiency in the justice system as a result of lengthy delays in cases going to trial, a view that the courts favor the accused person rather than the victim and the prohibitive cost of civil litigation. This lack of public confidence causes a greater need on the part of the public and private enterprise to ensure that systems are in place to deter crime before it happens rather than force the business to become involved in protracted criminal or civil proceedings.

Crime

The third reason for the rise in demand for private security is the general perception of crime trends especially in the workplace. In the United States it is estimated that business is losing $120 billion annually as a result of crime. Between 1985 and 1991 violent and property crimes increased by 15% on a per capita basis.[3]

Business also suffers where a third party is victimized on company property. Security and crime related lawsuits have risen 17 times faster than the inflation rate and as a result businesses are protecting themselves against legal actions by providing stronger deterrent measures against crime on their businesses.

Cultural Changes

A 1978 University of Minnesota Sociology Department study indicated that there are some significant changes going on in the workplace and with workers. The study reviewed 47 businesses in the cities of Minneapolis-St. Paul, Cleveland and Dallas-Ft. Worth. The businesses under study included 16 retail store organizations, 21 hospitals and 10 electronics firms. They ranged in size from 150–10,000 employees. The purpose was to develop a comprehensive understanding of workplace theft.

Findings

- Workers who stole were preponderantly those who engaged in other counter- or nonproductive behavior on the job.
- The greater the opportunity for theft the greater the likelihood.
- Young employees steal more and do it more frequently.
- Those concerned with advancement and achievement in their careers are apt to steal more than others.
- The employee who is satisfied on and with the job is less likely to steal.
- The greater the fear of detection the less likely the theft.
- Concerted efforts to reduce theft by the employer will reduce loss.
- Almost none of the security programs at the sites surveyed actively strove to reduce employee theft.
- The mere existence of a management policy prohibiting theft was sufficient to reduce incidence.
- About one third of all employees admitted stealing.
- Lack of prosecution and prosecution policies encouraged theft.
- Dismissal from employment is not an effective deterrent, particularly for the young employee.
- Theft on the job does not correlate to external economic conditions including pressure on individual employees.
- Peer attitude towards theft is a major factor in prevalence.
- A combination of peer disapproval and management prohibition is a strong preventative.

Another reason for the increase in the number of work related crimes is that financial crimes pay better than other crimes.

Burglary	**$450 per incident**
Armed Robbery	**$250**
Theft	**$150**
Employee Fraud	**$23,500**
Computer Crime	**$500,000**

A Brigham Young study gives us some insight into the nature of white collar criminals.[4] Compared to bank robbers, fraud perpetrators are/have:
- More likely to be women
- Married
- Less likely to be divorced
- Less likely to have abused alcohol
- Less likely to be tattooed
- More likely to be active church members
- Older, heavier, more children
- Higher education
- First time offenders

Trends in Business

The last reason for the upswing in the use of private security is the general economic conditions over recent years and trends in business. Businesses are seeing reduced profit margins and possibility of financial failure (e.g. one out of three small businesses fail because of employee theft). As a result there is a stronger recognition of the need to protect assets.

The first duty of business is to strive and the guiding principle of business and economics is not the maximization of profit it is the avoidance of loss.

Peter Drucker

Another recent, growing phenomenon is the trend to outsource the non-core area of an enterprise. If a need is established for greater security within an organization there is now a greater likelihood that the organization will approach a security service to provide for its needs rather than hiring internal staff to provide the service.

Economic Conditions

Security management provides some challenges under poor economic conditions. Economic crimes tend to increase because people are strapped for money. Corporations suffer from reduced morale and those intent on theft or fraud find it easier to justify their actions. Insurance costs increase and often companies are forced to take on larger deductibles. Insurers are also not as quick to settle claims and may dispute them.

Litigation increases because companies are seen to have deep pockets and because legal firms are more willing to take clients under a contingency fee arrangement. Environmental legislation also places a strain on budgets. Security departments are generally asked to do more with less and shed all but nonessential services.

The strain on corporate budgets, the changing nature of crime in the workplace and the increased cost of litigation have caused an increased necessity for security to become involved in:
- background checks on new or potential employees;
- training to avoid false arrest, malicious prosecution claims and claims of failure
- to provide security;
- programs to protect employees against workplace violence;

- investigations into compliance with environmental legislation;
- investigations into work place infractions;
- follow up investigations from whistle blowing;
- drug testing; and
- contingency planning.

THE NATURE OF THE SECURITY INDUSTRY

The Hallcrest report identified nine categories of security services.[5]

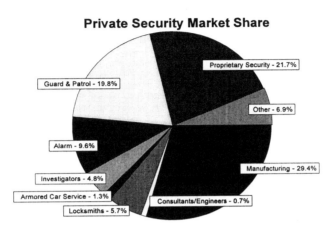

Figure 1.3

"Other" includes:

- guard dog services;
- drug testing/forensic analysis;
- publishing;

- honesty testing;
- uniform rentals and sales.

THE FUTURE

What is the future of security services?

1.   **Outsourcing will continue as a significant initiative**

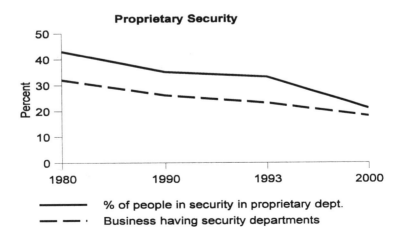

Figure 1.4

Corporations will continue to work hard at reducing overhead and operating costs by hiring contracted services. The Hallcrest study found that between 1990 and 1993 there were 800 fewer in-house security departments in operation in America, and there were layoffs of approximately 22,000 proprietary security personnel.

2.   Private security will continue to provide cost effective protection measures
Availability will be high and competition among security suppliers will continue to provide value. Technology will continue to play an increasing role and technology costs will continue to drop. There will be increased supply of security services to fill an increasing demand.

3.   Security will continue to erode the role of law enforcement
Over time, law enforcement will continue to be under pressure to keep budgets in control. This will cause them to focus on those activities that most require their services and those where there is a high public expectation of response. These will especially include investigations into robberies, sex offences, weapons related offences and other crimes of violence. They will not have the resources to continue with extensive patrols, especially of private property, and they will place a greater expectation on businesses to provide internal investigation on white collar crime.

4.   There will be continued demand placed on inhouse security directors
*   a stronger expectation to justify expenditures
*   more educated
*   broader range of management skills both proprietary and contract
*   integration with other departments such as facilities, HR, risk management or audit departments
*   expectation to do more with less
*   better communicators
*   stronger computer skills
*   flexibility and adaptability

5.   Equipment sales and revenues will continue to be strong
Hallcrest estimated that security equipment sales revenues would increase from $4.6 billion in 1980 to $23.7 billion by the year 2000. Businesses and the community in general are not willing to live with present crime trends and will continue to use private security services to supplement the public police.

The numbers are a reminder that concern about crime has become a major force motivating the corporate world, a weighty business expense, but also for many entrepreneurs a significant new business opportunity.

John Kettle's Future Letter - Sept. 1, 1992

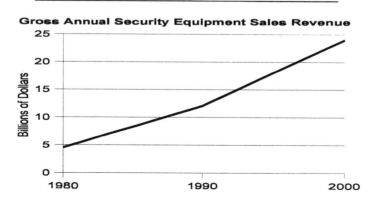

Figure 1.5

BIBLIOGRAPHY

"Theft by Employees in Work Organizations," University of Minnesota, 1985
"Private Security and Police in America," Hallcrest Report I, 1985
"Private Security Trends 1970 - 2000," Hallcrest Report II, 1990

ENDNOTES

1. U.S. Bureau of Justice Statistics, Profile of State and Local Law Enforcement Agencies, 1987 and State and Local Police Departments, 1990, February 1992.
2. Sussex Borough in New Jersey (pop. 2200) approved the replacement of its four officer police department with contract security guards at about half the cost of the former police officers.
3. Based on offences known to the police per 100,000 population. U.S. Federal Bureau of Investigation, *Crime in the United States*, annual.
4. 1982 Brigham Young University Study on White Collar Crime.
5. Hallcrest Report I, Private Security and Police in America, 1985.

THE FUTURE OF PRIVATE SECURITY
QUIZ

1. Private Security will continue to provide _____ _____ protective measures.

2. Security will continue to erode the role of _____ _____.

3. By the year 2000, it is predicted that the national budget for law enforcement will be _____.

4. By the year 2000, it is predicted that the national budget for private security will be _____.

5. In the U.S., it is estimated that business is losing _____ annually as a result of crime.

6. There are two and one half times as many security personnel as police personnel.
    □ T   □ F

7. The University of Minnesota study on theft by employees in work organizations established that theft will take place just as often even if there is a prosecution policy.
    □ T   □ F

8. The average "take" in a computer crime is $500,000.
    □ T   □ F

9. The Brigham Young study on white collar crime established that while collar criminals were more likely to be women.
    □ T   □ F

10. There is more likely to be an expectation that security managers will avoid combining security programs with other departments within an organization.
    □ T   □ F

UNIT TWO
HUMAN RESOURCE MANAGEMENT

Security Personnel Selection
Human Reliability
Personnel: Policies and Procedures
Motivation and Evaluation
Downsizing
Security Officer Scheduling
Discipline

SECURITY PERSONNEL SELECTION
by John T. Brobst, Jr., CPO, CSS

One of the main job responsibilities of the security manager is the hir
This aspect of the profession is often taken for granted by most managers be(
accepted part of managerial duties, and not much thought is given toward th(
the time arrives.

Selecting security personnel is not always an easy task; it takes know(
investigation and instinct to hire personnel who will perform and conform to the high level (
and standards required of today's security officer. Today's standards for hiring should be much more
stringent due to litigation involving negligent hiring and improper training. As well, security officer's
duties are becoming increasingly proactive like those of their public law enforcement counterparts.
You as a security manager must take all of these factors into account when hiring a new officer, and
also keep the hiring procedure streamlined and cost effective. Let us look at the hiring process at each
level from the beginning, addressing various topics, including how to hire and at the same time
avoiding problems such as negligent hiring and discriminatory practices.

SECURITY OFFICER REQUIREMENTS

Before the job is posted or the first advertisement is placed in the media, the applicant
qualifications must be thought of and drawn up if they are not yet decided upon. Some of the more
common requirements are:

1. High school diploma.
2. Minimum of five years of security experience preferred, police, military or other related field considered.
3. Excellent physical condition.
4. Personal skills:
   - Team player
   - Public relations
   - Service attitude
   - Mature personality
   - Decision-making ability
   - Oral and written skills
   - Ability to handle stress
   - No convictions (other than minor traffic violations)

These are not the only requirements and they do not cover the entire scope of responsibility
you may be looking for, however, you should consider them as minimum requirements for your
officers.

By requiring a high school diploma and a certain amount of experience, you can be assured of
a good base of knowledge, both academic and professional. Some managers have raised the question
of hiring people with police experience, stating that police and security job responsibilities are two
different things and that applicants with police experience do not make the transition well. I do not see
any problem with hiring persons with police experience, provided they understand the difference in the
duties (prevention not apprehension) and the security training program in place is sufficient to get the
point across.

If you decide that military experience will be permitted as a requirement, you should look at
what duties the person performed while in the service. An applicant with Military Police experience
would be a qualified candidate, but someone who worked as a cook or a mechanic would not. Any
experience should be related to the security field.

The physical conditioning requirement is a common prerequisite, however, if you get into any
depth with it such as sight, hearing, ability to lift a certain amount of weight, etc., you must be able to
show that it is a duty requirement and not a method to weed out persons with disabilities, which is
illegal. For instance, you should not require an officer to be able to climb ladders if there are no
ladders in his/her patrol area and he/she will never encounter them while on duty.

A security officer's duties place him/her in many situations where interpersonal skills are a
necessity, such as handling complaints and assisting the general public. Security officers must be team
players at all times as their fellow officers depend on them and vice versa. The officer candidate
should have an employment history that shows them having worked as a member of a team. For

---

, a person who was employed as a private investigator usually does not have a demonstrated as a team player since they mainly work alone.

The officer should have good public relation skills. A major part of the security officer's duties involves direct dealings with the various "publics" – employees, visitors and customers. The officer must be courteous and display a service oriented attitude at all times. The manner in which an officer conducts himself in public, in dealing with people and performing his duties, affects the way the "publics" view the individual officer as well as the department as a whole.

A mature personality and decision-making skills work hand-in-hand to help the officer deal with circumstances that arise throughout his/her day to day duties. Oftentimes the officer is called upon to make difficult decisions in which he/she must use good judgement, logic and maturity to make the appropriate call.

Excellent oral and written skills are a very definite requirement for any security officer. On any given day the officer may be required to write clear, concise and accurate reports and also be able to communicate the information verbally to his superiors, the public or other officers.

One aspect of the security officer's job that can be very challenging is the ability to handle stress. A security officer's duties often place him/her in the position of going from routine activity to mind-numbing action within a few seconds, and the ability to handle situations like this with a minimum of stress is of utmost importance.

The personal skills requirements are just as important, if not more important, than education and experience. The security officer's duties place him in the public eye as well as being a representative of the company he is working for. Personal skills are the more difficult requirements to judge through applications and resumes, but if the individual makes it through the initial screening, a more detailed investigation can be made through oral interviews.

None of the applicants should have a criminal record. Except for minor traffic violations, the applicant's record must be clean.

THE JOB DESCRIPTION

The job description is a tool that security managers often overlook. A properly thought out and well-written description will make the hiring process proceed more smoothly. If you already have a job description written for your department's officers, ask yourself when was the last time it was revised. If it has been more than a year, look it over – more than likely something has changed that would require you to make a revision to your description. If you don't have a description of the duties required of your officers, now is the time to make one. Not only will it give you and the new employee a guideline to work from but, in the event of a dispute or a lawsuit, the description could be a financial lifesaver.

The security officer job description should not only contain requirements of the "nuts and bolts" of the duties (patrol, response to incidents, etc.) but also the personal requirements – some of which we touched upon previously. List the minimum entry requirements: education, experience, personal skills, physical skills and any other requirements that are necessary to perform the job in an efficient manner. Go into detail with your requirements – spell out exactly what the minimum requirements are and especially any requirements that are particular to the job in question.

For instance, a hospital security department might include a requirement that an officer must be willing to work with individuals with infectious diseases, or a chemical factory may require that an officer attend training to become a First Responder or EMT.

Make a list of tasks that your officers may perform during their shift, no matter how minor and include them under an "officer responsibility" section of the job description. List what is expected of the officer, including what types of reports they may complete, if they will need to attend court hearings on behalf of the employer, and any special tasks that may arise during their tour of duty. By having this policy in effect and up to date, there should be no questions as to what is expected of the new officer.

ACQUIRING APPLICANTS

Now that your minimum requirements have been set, where do you look for applicants? Some facilities post job openings and allow other employees from the facility with the proper education and training to bid for the position. This type of approach should be avoided, because the quality of the applicant is often questionable due to the fact that they already have made "friends" and "enemies" within the facility, which may have an effect on the officer's job performance. Also, preconceived ideas and knowledge (or lack of it) about the facility, its personnel, and the security department can adversely affect the training process. In other words, if you can start with a "clean slate," do so.

One way to find applicants is through your current employee pool. Your employees may know someone looking for a position and you can generally be assured that the applicant will be of good quality since an employee will usually not recommend a poor candidate because it reflects upon their own judgement. One word of caution – avoid hiring relatives of employees since a person's judgement is often clouded by blood ties.

Call other companies' human resource departments or other security agencies and inquire if they know someone looking for a position. With companies laying off workers and downsizing or closing departments, this can be an ideal method; however, it should be used in conjunction with other types of searches since, depending on the employment situation in your area, you may or may not get a large number of applications.

The use of media to advertise positions is still one of the best methods since it usually gets the most applicants for the time involved. You should place the minimum requirements for the position in the ad; this may cost more in the short term as far as copy costs, however, it will save time and money since you and your staff will not have to search through applications that do not meet your criteria.

THE APPLICATION PROCESS

The application form your company uses should be reviewed and corrected, if needed, since most off-the-shelf application forms contain language that has been made illegal by the ADA or state/local laws in which your company does business. If you are not sure of your application's wording or what constitutes a valid question, consult with an attorney who is well versed in employment law.

No matter what type of application form you use, it should contain an authorization (which the applicant must sign) for a complete background and reference check. It should release the prospective employer as well as others who provide information (former employers, personal references) from any and all liability that may result from the release of the information. This release should also contain language that states that information contained in the application and resume can be provided for the review of the past employers/references if needed. This may assist you in obtaining information from persons hesitant to help you.

Another section of the application should have the prospective employee acknowledge by signature, that any false, misleading or omitted information on the application *will* (not "may") result in either not hiring the individual or, if hired, the termination of the employee regardless of when the discovery is made.

In addition to the application, I recommend requiring a resume, since most applications do not contain enough room for a comprehensive listing of information. You should require specific information on the resume such as listing all past positions held and brief descriptions of job duties. You may add data requirements as you feel necessary but, remember, they must be legal requests and should be directly related to the position in question.

THE RESUME

Have one of your office staff go through the applications and resumes to weed out those that do not meet the minimum job requirements or those that do not meet the informational requirements. Once this is done, you should look through the resumes and applications, deciding on the best candidates to interview.

The resume's format should be organized and information presented in a logical sequence. The way the resume is arranged gives hints as to the person's logic processes and ability to arrange facts and present information.

Is the resume complete? You will want to look for unexplained gaps in the chronological order of the information. This will give you hints as to the unemployment and work history of the individual. If the applicant does not list the periods of employment chronologically, they may be hiding poor performance and/or periods of unemployment. If the applicant uses a different style of writing a resume, checking the chronological order will determine if there may be a problem.

How is the grammar and spelling? Sloppy or misused grammar and incorrect spelling show a lack of attention to details and ability to write required reports with a minimum of problems. This type of difficulty will definitely show up in the future.

Once this initial screening is done, decide on the best candidate to interview, choosing which candidate would be your first choice and so on. Depending on the number of applicants which made it through the two screenings, arrange interviews with the top five or ten prospects.

THE INTERVIEW PROCESS

Preparation

Quite a few managers think of interviews as something that requires a large amount of skill to do, when actually they are something that anyone can do with a minimum of anxiety. The key to the interview game is preparation – applicants have to prepare themselves for an interview and the manager should do the same. A four step approach is basically all you need to conduct great interviews that will make finding your new security officer easy. They are:

1.   Know exactly what type of person you are looking for.
2.   Make a list of questions you will ask each and every applicant to help standardize the interview process.
3.   Keep notes on what the applicant says, your impressions and any other information you feel is important.
4.   Review the information collected and contrast/compare the applicants before you make your decision.

Make out a question sheet in advance; this helps you avoid thinking up questions during the interview and probably missing some important information the applicant has to present. Another reason to write down your questions is that if you don't, you probably aren't asking the same question every time, which makes standardization difficult.

The Interview

The first interview with the applicant is to obtain more data on the person as well as verify information on the application and resume. You want to dig for more information; the more you can get the better – it helps to weed out inaccurate or misleading data.

You should explain to the candidate the requirements and duties that they will be performing as a security officer at your facility, including duties that may be unpleasant or boring. By discussing the duties at this time, it allows the person time to think if they want the job or are capable of handling it.

As each candidate enters the interview area, look at them closely – they should be clean and well dressed and look as if they put some effort into being prepared for the interview. The candidate should have their information available in case you have questions for them; this shows good preparatory skills. Does the person walk confidently or do they seem as if they are uncomfortable or shy? Do they answer questions quickly and decisively? Be aware of behavior and body language during the interview and make notes; you want employees who hold themselves well and act with confidence in stressful situations. By being aware of the applicant's behavior throughout the interview you can often tell what the person is thinking by how they react.

After the first interview with each candidate, choose those applicants you wish to interview again. When you have your list in hand, make some phone calls to verify the information contained in the resumes and applications. You should note who was called, when, what information was called about, who made the call and if the information was correct. Attach the notes to the application or resume; the notes should not contain personal opinions or any information other than what was stated above. If the question of verification comes up, you have written proof that the information was indeed checked.

You should never write on the application or resume unless there is a specific area provided for the interviewer to write in. If there is such an area, only facts should be written, never opinions about the applicant – save personal opinions and other notes for a separate note pad. If the applicant should ever sue claiming discrimination, your notes could be used against you.

After screening the remaining applicants' information, call them back for a second interview. With this interview you are going to look more for the personal skills the applicant has to offer. How much of a team player are they? Ask the applicant to give specific examples of how the duties they perform affect the people they deal with every day, the "publics." Give the person hypothetical situations that may occur on the job (make them realistic) and ask him/her to tell you what they would do; this can give you insight into the person's decision-making capabilities and logic processes. I advise having one or two of your senior officers or other people familiar with the security officer's duties with you in the interview, with all persons asking questions of the applicant.

Give the applicant an opportunity to ask questions of you and your staff and make notes of the types of questions asked. They may give you insight into what expectations they have, as well as their reasoning behind wanting a security position with your company. For instance, if the individual asks what kind of "action" he/she may see, or if they will be carrying "pieces" while on duty, this should raise a red flag in your mind and definitely should be noted. Discuss each candidate with your personnel immediately after each interview and take notes as to what the others have to say.

THE AMERICANS WITH DISABILITIES ACT of 1990 (ADA)

This article is intended for general information only and does not and is not intended to constitute legal advice. The reader should consult with experts/legal counsel in their area to determine how laws or decisions discussed herein apply to their specific circumstances.

The Americans with Disabilities Act (ADA), bans discrimination based on disability. It gives individuals with disabilities civil rights protection like those provided to individuals on the basis of race, sex, nationality and religion. It guarantees equal opportunities for individuals with disabilities in employment, state and government services, public accommodations and transportation.

The ADA defines disability to mean a physical or mental impairment that substantially limits one or more of the major life activities of an individual, having a record of such an impairment, or being regarded as having such an impairment.

How does the ADA affect the security manager? It impacts the types of questions you ask the prospective employee, as well as impacting testing procedures. Some highlights of the law regarding employment are as follows:

1. Employers may not discriminate against an individual with a disability in hiring or promotion if the person is otherwise qualified for the job.
2. Employers may inquire about one's ability to perform a job, but cannot ask if someone has a disability or conduct pre-employment testing that tends to screen out persons with disabilities.
3. Employers will need to provide "reasonable accommodation" to individuals with disabilities if needed. This includes steps such as job restructuring and modification of equipment.
4. Employers do not need to provide accommodations that create an "undue hardship" on business operations.

BACKGROUND CHECK

Background and criminal history checks are one of the most important things that a security manager can do to ensure that the prospective employee is someone who can be trusted to perform the job in question.

In Pennsylvania, it is relatively easy to do a criminal history check through the State Police. All it involves is a little information on a standard form and a ten dollar check. In other areas it may not be as easy. Here are some problems you may face when conducting a background check.

When doing checks through your police or sheriff's department, the data contained in their records may not contain information from local law enforcement or federal agencies. Although this is not often the case, you should keep it in mind when doing any type of criminal history check.

Few employers will release information other than dates of employment and position held, and even fewer will give out information on problems or job performance. This is due in a large part to court cases in which employers are sued because of incorrect information given out about a former employee.

Current right to privacy acts and other legislation can make it difficult for employers to obtain information from law enforcement agencies or other sources such as the Internal Revenue Service or Social Security Office.

Conducting searches of court records is often difficult due to the sheer volume of information involved, as well as the possibility of a person living in a different jurisdiction or having lived out of state.

As you can see, it may not be very easy to do background checks. However, all attempts must be made to verify any and all information. References must be checked and documentation on all checks should be kept in case a lawsuit involving negligent hiring should arise.

TESTING PROGRAMS

In the past, testing programs were often used to keep minorities and other persons deemed "disadvantaged" out of jobs. That changed in 1971 when the United States Supreme Court handed down a decision (*Griggs vs. Duke Power*) barring "discriminatory" job testing. The courts usually agree that any type of test is acceptable if it can be clearly demonstrated that it is needed to protect the business or its customers from damage or theft, or to protect employees from interference or harm.

With reports of security officers committing crimes against the persons they are assigned to protect appearing in the media more frequently, the use of testing as a tool to prevent such situations from occurring is definitely needed.

The ADA and Testing Programs

Under the ADA, an employer may not administer a medical examination (physical and/or psychological testing) before a conditional offer of employment is made. Using the following questions you can determine whether a test might be considered a medical examination under the ADA. A "yes" answer would be an indication of a medical examination.
- Is the test given for the purpose of revealing an impairment or the state of the person's physical or mental health?
- Is the test *designed* to reveal a physical/psychological impairment?
- Does the test measure physiological/psychological responses?
- Is the test administered by a healthcare professional?
- Are the results of the test interpreted by a healthcare professional?
- Is the test invasive? (Blood and urine tests)
- Is the test conducted in a medical setting?
- Is the test conducted with medical equipment/devices?

Physical agility/physical fitness tests that are not medically monitored, psychological tests that measure job related skills, and tests for illegal drugs are not considered medical exams under the ADA. As always, check your state/local laws regarding any type of pre-employment testing to make sure they are legal in your area.

Psychological Testing

A good definition of a psychological test goes like this: it is a written examination used in conjunction with oral interviews and conducted by trained professionals of a person's qualifications, interests and aptitude in order to judge objectively the individual's suitability for a particular job or type of work. This definition addresses the fact that the test must only be used to make sure the applicant has the skills and the interest in the duties to be performed and NOT for discriminatory purposes.

When deciding to use any type of test, investigate all the options and decide which test screens for the information you are seeking. Tests should meet the criteria known as TEST VALIDITY, which is the proven ability to measure what they purport to measure. Talk to other employers (especially those who hire security officers) and find out what has worked for them in the past. Request information from the prospective testing company, and ask them if they meet EEOC and ADA guidelines and what their track record is in legal contests. By using an established testing program, and one that has a reasonably good record, it is much easier to defend the testing program if a lawsuit should arise.

Under the ADA, personality tests are not prohibited provided that they *only* measure a person's honesty, tastes and habits. Any type of psychological test that is designed to, or may reveal a physical/psychological impairment or even sexual preferences is illegal.

Drug Testing

Much has been written on the subject of drug and alcohol testing; some security managers embrace it as a useful tool, while others avoid it at all costs. A well managed program of drug screening, used in conjunction with education after hiring, is one of the best methods of ensuring drug-free employees and reducing liability. If a program of testing is already established at your company, use it by all means. If you are planning to institute a program, you must make sure it encompasses all new employees as well as personnel already employed by your company to avoid accusations of discriminatory practices.

AVOID NEGLIGENT HIRING

We have seen many cases in the past few years where security officers have committed various crimes and even murder against the very people they were hired to protect. When hiring new security officers, the law has placed the burden of making sure that the person is fully qualified on you the security manager. We must make all attempts at verifying the information contained in the application and resume because we can be held liable for any damage or crimes the officer commits while on duty that could have been "foreseeable."

A reasonable attempt should be made to investigate the criminal history of the applicant. Remember, if your employment application asks a candidate if they have ever been convicted of a crime, and you don't check their criminal history, your company can and will be held liable if the employee commits a similar crime. Conduct checks on all the information you are given by the applicant, and document everything you find, as this will show proof that you made a "reasonable effort" to assure that the applicant was telling the truth.

One last thought on avoiding liability: you must exhaust ALL attempts at screening if you will be hiring any candidate who is being considered for "high risk" duties. High risk duties would include, but are not limited to, armored transport, bank security and armed security officers. These candidates should be screened even more carefully as they have more chances to cause damage, theft or injury to the business, its employees or customers. If one of these officers should commit a crime and it is shown that the screening process did not make all attempts at verifying the officer's information, then you can be assured that there is a very good chance your company will be held liable for negligent hiring. The screening process includes your interviews, background checks (criminal and references) and any testing programs your facility utilizes. Finally, be aware of new laws, developments and legislation that arises concerning hiring security personnel in your state as well as other states.

CONCLUSION

As security officer duties have evolved over the years, so has the security manager's responsibilities to hire officers capable of handling them. In today's litigious society, hiring security officers cannot be done haphazardly. It must be done methodically and with a scientific approach, to avoid problems that could arise in the future. Hopefully, by using these guidelines and suggestions, locating and hiring a qualified candidate will not be a task that you dislike, but one that you will look forward to and learn from.

**SECURITY PERSONNEL SELECTION
QUIZ**

1.   By requiring a high school diploma and a certain amount of _____, you can be assured of a good base of knowledge.

2.   A security officer's duties place him/her in many situations where _____ skills are necessary.

3.   One way to find _____ is through your employee pool.

4.   Have one of your office staff go through the applications and _____ to weed out those who do not meet requirements.

5.   The first _____ with the applicant is to obtain more data on the person.

6.   Police officers and people with military experience should never be considered for employment as a security officer.
     ☐ T   ☐ F

7.   The resume's format can give hints as to the applicant's ability to arrange facts, present information and logic processes.
     ☐ T   ☐ F

8.   When explaining the requirements and duties to the candidate, leave out the unpleasant tasks, as it may scare off the applicant.
     ☐ T   ☐ F

9.   The security manager should write all personal opinions on a separate note pad, never on the candidate's resume or applications.
     ☐ T   ☐ F

10.   Posting positions and hiring from the current employee pool is a good way to find your new security officer.
     ☐ T   ☐ F

HUMAN RELIABILITY
by Martin Hershkowitz, M.S.

INTRODUCTION

Violence in the workplace is one of today's greatest management fears. The inability to predict and therefore avoid a violent incident caused by an employee or visitor is a frustration that few managers can successfully cope with since needed protection measures may violate the individual's civil rights. This situation can reach nightmarish proportions when the instrument of protection, the armed security officer, becomes the violent employee. Here is an individual who is trained in the arts and sciences of violence, and carries the weapons of violence with him or her into the workplace.

Fortunately, security management can rely on the principle of "compelling need" to develop protective measures against the likelihood that the security officer becomes the violent employee. When the workplace is a nuclear weapons plant, a nuclear power plant, an explosives production plant or a corrosive chemical plant, the violent act and resulting damage could reach catastrophic proportions and the compelling need for human reliability is quite clear. Under such situations, the compelling need to utilize protective measures that may impact on the individual's civil rights in order to protect the health and welfare of all employees, the employer and the general public becomes the major concern. As the potential for a catastrophic situation decreases, the compelling need decreases more rapidly. Security management, nevertheless, must apply proactive activities that will assure that the security officer displays "good judgement" on the job.

DEFINING GOOD JUDGEMENT

What does the term "good judgement" mean? A simple operational definition is that the employee makes rational decisions in accordance with accepted operational procedures and carries them out in an acceptable manner – regardless of the momentary conditions of the job or the frustrations from personal, family, social and/or financial difficulties. Since some conditions of the job and some personal situations can be overwhelming, the ability to display good judgement becomes an extremely important characteristic.

ASSURING GOOD JUDGEMENT: A HUMAN RELIABILITY PROGRAM

Security management can assure continuing good judgement of its employees through an integrated human reliability program (HRP). A human reliability program is composed of regular medical examinations and evaluations, psychological evaluations, drug-use testing, alcohol-dependency testing, training in peer behavioral observations, national and local criminal records checks, financial stability investigation, and an integrated employee assistance program. Dependent upon the demonstration of compelling need, some of these HRP elements may be considered to be a violation of the individual's civil rights; however, for purposes of this discussion each element will be reviewed herein.

Background Review

The most common way to determine if an individual will display continuing good judgement is to determine if the individual has displayed that good judgement in the past. It follows that a comprehensive pre-employment screening and analysis, including national and local criminal record checks, a credit check, and indicators of spousal or child abuse provides valuable information for determining "human reliability." Prior employment and social contacts should be personally interviewed to determine indicators of judgement that are unacceptable in the workplace. For current employees, the comprehensive screening and analysis should be repeated as a periodic background review, once every year or two.

Although this activity is well defined, it requires professional adjudicators to ensure that the analysis of information leads to a clear determination that the individual has displayed good judgement in the past and will continue to display good judgement in the future. This is true for both pre-employment screening and periodic background review.

Medical Examination and Evaluation

Medical evaluation is a complex undertaking as the individual being examined and evaluated is not the physician's patient as is traditionally the case. The Occupational Medical Physician works for the organization; therefore, the physician is responsible for determining if the individual is both "fit for duty," which traditional medical training equips the physician for, and "displays good judgement," which is not part of the traditional medical training. The former seeks to determine if the individual is physically capable of carrying out the duties of the job. The latter seeks to determine if the individual is mentally and emotionally prepared for the rigors of the job. However, the provisions of the "Americans with Disabilities Act of 1990" may have some legal impact upon this.

The Occupational Medical Program should require both a pre-employment and regular periodic medical examination by a physician trained in occupational medicine who will seek indicators of illegal drug use, prescription drug abuse and/or alcohol dependency; medical limitations on fitness for duty; and the existence of other disqualifying conditions. Finally, the Occupational Medical Director should be able to integrate these results with the findings from other HRP elements and issue a medical statement that there are no existing medical or psychological conditions that could lead to a display of poor judgement in the workplace or that the individual is not or is no longer able to perform in this position.

Drug Testing

Drug testing is not a simple concept. To begin with, drug testing cannot be conducted on a regular, published schedule. In order to be effective, drug testing must be conducted during the pre-employment interview and through 100 percent random sampling of the work force (so that every employee is tested at least once during every testing cycle). To ensure that the results are accurate and that the individual's civil rights are not violated, it is necessary to conduct the drug testing through a three-step process with a rigorous "chain-of-custody" to guarantee evidential purity.

The first step is a screening test to determine if there is an indication of possible drug use. The most commonly accepted screening process is the radio-immune assay using approved thresholds to establish a presumed positive. Each drug has an approved reading threshold, below which the sample is said to be free of the drug. If the sample yields a reading above the threshold, the sample is said to be a presumed positive. Presumed positive should not be mistaken for positive. It is merely an indicator of the need to perform a confirmatory test.

The second step is the confirmatory test to determine if there was in fact a positive finding of drug use. The preferred confirmatory process is the gas chromatography/mass spectrometry (GC/MS) using approved thresholds to establish a confirmed positive. As with the screening process, a reading below the threshold is taken to be a confirmation that there was no drug use; a reading above the threshold is a positive finding of drug use.

In both steps, a rigorous chain-of-custody must be guaranteed or the evidence is tainted and of no value. To repeat the process(es) at this point is of little value as the individual has had sufficient time to cover any drug use through a variety of available techniques.

The third and final step is a review of the drug test results by a Medical Review Officer, a physician who is trained to determine if the positive reading is a result of actual drug use, cross readings from the use of prescribed drugs or the accidental ingestion of material that can result in a false positive. If indicated, the Medical Review Officer may interview the employee to determine the reason for the positive reading.

Psychological Assessment

Psychological assessment results from a two-part process consisting of psychological tests to establish and periodically update a baseline and regular psychological interviews to determine if the individual is beginning to display behavioral problems. This assessment is incorporated into the medical evaluation to provide a complete picture of the individual's ability to display good judgement on the job.

Psychological tests and accompanying interviews are designed to meet a variety of needs. HRP psychological assessments are not designed to determine mental illness as it may or may not be a factor in displaying good judgement; mental illness may be related to "fitness-for-duty," which is a different issue. At the other end of the scale, HRP psychological assessments are not designed to determine fraud or petty theft, which is likewise a different issue. HRP psychological assessments are designed to detect an employee's gradual emotional deterioration due to personal and/or job related stress and an applicant's inability to display good judgement due to psychopathology.

The preferred psychopathologic test is the Minnesota Multiphasic Personality Index II (MMPI-II). Although this test has not been adequately tested in the courts, it is a revision of the original MMPI, which has been tested and found to be legally valid. Another psychopathologic test is the Millon Clinical Multi axial Inventory (MCMI), but this test has not been sufficiently tested in the courts to be used alone. A third test of some interest is the Sixteen Personality Factors (16PF); however, this test is used more to differentiate personalities and is not considered to be a psychopathologic test.

There are many types of psychologists who are proficient in performing a psychological assessment; however, the HRP psychological assessment should require a clinical psychologist. The clinical psychologist is trained to detect psychopathological tendencies and to interpret the ability to display good judgement in the workplace.

Alcohol Dependency

Alcohol abuse takes two forms: acute alcoholism, which is typified by the employee who reports to work drunk; and chronic alcoholism, which describes the individual who is an habitual and excessive user of alcohol. Both forms are a threat in the workplace as they affect both judgement and reaction time. Normally, acute alcoholism in the workplace is taken care of through behavior in the workplace rules; that is, show up drunk and you don't work! In addition to the loss of a day's pay there may be other penalties according to those rules.

Chronic alcoholism affects the thought processes and judgemental reasoning to such an extent that the individual becomes a danger to himself or herself and begins to display very poor judgement in the work place. Due to the nature of this problem, an alcohol dependence testing program must be established for the security officers. Similarly to the drug testing program, alcohol testing should be conducted during the initial interview and through a 100 percent random sampling of the work force (so that every employee is tested at least once during every testing cycle).

The alcohol dependency testing program should contain the following requirements for testing purposes: during the initial interview or pre-screening; during the periodic medical examination; under a random testing procedure; for cause (that is, the employee exhibits signs of being under the influence of alcohol); and after accidents and/or mortal injuries.

The testing program can include one or more of the three common tests for alcohol use; blood test, urine test, or breath analysis. Of the three, breath analysis is the most effective and least invasive, thus more acceptable.

Recognition of Behavioral Change or the Display of Unusual Behavior

Behavioral change or unusual behavior is simply defined to be any change from the way a person usually behaves. Such changes do not have to be permanent to indicate the potential for deteriorating judgement, but they do need to be recognized. In most working relationships a fellow worker or immediate supervisor is in an excellent position to detect such changes. The problem is how to tell when that change is due to some momentary lapse in good judgement and when it is an indicator of a serious deteriorating condition.

All employees and supervisors need to be trained both to recognize behavioral change, including stress, environmental pressures and depression, and to report positive observations to the Occupational Medical Director for further investigation, counseling and treatment. This is not a "snitch" program. Serious behavioral change is a major indicator of a potential deteriorating condition. The employee exhibiting this change in behavior may be about to commit a violent and catastrophic act.

The training program should include the following on-the-job behaviors and work habits that directly impact efficiency, effectiveness and good judgement: change in work quality or quantity, increase in mistakes or bad judgement, decrease in efficiency, difficulty in concentrating, absence from the job, absence "on the job," ignoring company policy, becoming overcautious, becoming overzealous, increase in risk taking, increase in accidents, and change in cooperation with co-workers. In addition, concern over the employee's change in work relationships and social interactions should be part of the training program.

Integrated Evaluation by Management

A simple caution should be observed at this point. All the tests and assessments discussed above are isolated events. A decision made based strictly on one of these data points is likely to be a wrong one. The decision must be based on an integrated review of all results. In particular, the report by the Occupational Medical Director has already integrated many of the tests and assessments and should be considered very carefully; however, the background review is of great importance and should be considered with equal weight. Only the security manager is in a position to integrate all this information and make the vital decision on hiring the applicant or assigning the employee.

Employee Assistance Program

Thus far, the discussion has concentrated on testing the applicant and employee. Unless the organization is prepared to assist the employee to overcome his or her difficulties, all that has been accomplished is that well and expensively trained security officers will be under-used or discharged. This is a poor use of organizational resources. A much better use of those resources is to establish an integrated employee assistance program, where the employee is helped to overcome the medical, health, social and/or financial problem.

It is important that the employee assistance program be sensitive to the security aspects of the employee's duties. A program that ignores this aspect and conceals the employee's problems and deteriorating good judgement is counter-productive to the organization's needs. By integrating this effort into the HRP, security will be retained at a high level of effectiveness.

SECURITY MANAGEMENT RESPONSIBILITIES

There are three levels of security management: the security executive, the security manager, and the security supervisor. In the real world, the responsibilities, functions, and duties of these three levels are not mutually exclusive. There are real and perceived overlaps and occasional gaps; however, for the purpose of this discussion consider that they are mutually exclusive.

The Security Executive

The security executive is primarily concerned with policy, strategic planning, growth, legal issues and profit. With regard to the HRP, the security executive is mostly concerned with establishing, through the corporate counsel, the level of compelling need and with determining, through the comptroller, the number and extent of HRP components to implement in order to get the "most bang for the buck." The security executive is interested in the protection that an HRP can offer to reduce the risk of a catastrophic event occurring due to a security officer displaying bad judgement, but is not interested in paying any more than necessary to achieve that goal.

The Security Manager

The security manager is primarily concerned with operational issues, such as program planning and shift scheduling; identifying, clearing, hiring, and training security officers; identifying and hiring an Occupational Medical Director, Occupational Medical Physician(s) and clinical psychologist(s); contracting with a certified laboratory to conduct screening and confirmatory tests for substance use/abuse (both drugs and alcohol), with the required chain-of-custody control; establishing or contracting for a training unit, to include peer behavioral change observation training; establishing or contracting for an employee assistance program; and establishing an integrated management evaluation team. The security manager has the responsibility for establishing the HRP and making it work properly under the constraints placed on it by the security executive, but only from a programmatic perspective, with an emphasis on operating costs, time management and minimum disruption to shift schedules.

The Security Supervisor

The security supervisor is where "the rubber meets the road." The security supervisor deals with the human being inside the uniform, the individual who might be experiencing deteriorating judgement. The security supervisor has the responsibility for setting the schedules; for ensuring that the security officer attends all training, provides all the necessary samples, and visits the physician and psychologist; for observing any significant changes in behavior that would warrant medical and psychological evaluation; and for ensuring that the security officer anonymously received the full value of an employee assistance program. The single most important principle governing the relationship between the security supervisor and the security officer under the HRP is that "no one gets a free pass"; the security officer cannot know in advance the date of the drug and alcohol tests, cannot miss medical and psychological evaluation appointments, cannot miss important training dates, cannot miss appointments with the employee assistance program.

CONCLUSION

Violence in the workplace is real and increasing rapidly. Although this is not the reason why large, well trained security forces exist, it is clearly a benefit that fellow employees, shoppers, students, hospital patients, and the general public appreciate. However, when a member of the security force, someone who is well trained in the use of violence and who brings those tools of violence into the workplace, begins to display deteriorating judgement, the level of concern becomes intense. It is for this reason that there may be a compelling need to require that security officers submit to tests and procedures that may violate their civil rights.

The collection of tests and procedures are traditionally called a Human Reliability Program (HRP), but has been know by other names as well. The components of the HRP are:
1.   Background Review
2.   Medical Examination and Evaluation
3.   Drug Testing
4.   Psychological Assessment
5.   Alcohol Dependency
6.   Recognition of Behavioral Change or the Display of Unusual Behavior
7.   Integrated Evaluation by Management
8.   Employee Assistance Program

The use of the HRP does not guarantee that the security officer's good judgement will not deteriorate, but it does assure that the early signs of deterioration will be detected and that the security officer who no longer can display good judgement will be removed from the workplace until the problem can be addressed and corrected. In this manner, the on-duty security force is assured to display continuing good judgement.

HUMAN RELIABILITY
QUIZ

1.   Medical _____ is a complex undertaking as the individual being examined and evaluated is not the physician's patient.

2.   Psychological _____ results from a two part process consisting of psychological tests.

3.   Drug testing cannot be conducted on a _____ schedule.

4.   Alcohol abuse takes two forms: _____ alcoholism and chronic alcoholism.

5.   There are three levels of _____ management.

6.   Violence in the workplace is one of today's greatest management fears.
             □ T   □ F

7.   A drug test presumed positive, normally necessitates termination of an employee.
             □ T   □ F

8.   Every Organizational Occupational Medical Program makes it compulsory for a
        pre-employment medical examination.
                        ☐ T   ☐ F

9.   Alcohol abuse takes two forms: Acute alcoholism, which is typified by the employee who
        reports to work drunk, and chronic alcoholism, which describes the individual who is a
        habitual and excessive user of alcohol.
                        ☐ T   ☐ F

10.   The collection of tests and procedures are traditionally called a Human Reliability Program
        (HRP).
                        ☐ T   ☐ F

PERSONNEL: POLICIES AND PROCEDURES
by *Mavis Vet, CPO, CSS*

WHAT IS EXPECTED OF A SUPERVISOR

To properly understand the responsibilities of a supervisor, you have to understand the company structure:

President / Directors
Division Heads
Middle Management
Supervisors
Security Officers

First we will start at the top with the President/Director level. This is where a person or a group of people set the company objective or the "WHY." In the security industry, this objective is to supply security for a client and make a profit.

Next comes the Division Head level. Here is where the policies are set out. You will find these policies in your company manual, a copy of which you received when you were hired. These policies can also be spelled out in a contract if you are unionized. All terms and conditions for employment should be covered along with what the company expects you to do while in their employ.

Our next level is Middle Management. At this stage procedures are set out for the next two levels to follow. In the day-to-day operations, all terms and conditions of employment must be met following governmental guidelines and union-negotiated clauses while remaining in budget. The middle manager is responsible for ensuring supervisors and security officers work effectively and develop their full potential for advancement. The more effectively they do their jobs, the less upper management has to be concerned with the day-to-day dealings.

Now we come to you the supervisor. Supervision means "overseeing." The National Labor Management Relations Act of 1947 (US) was more specific and defined a supervisor as " ... any individual having authority, in the interest of the employer, to hire, transfer, suspend, lay off, recall, promote, discharge, assign, reward, or discipline other employees, or responsibility to direct them, or to adjust their grievances, or effectively recommend such action, if in connection with the foregoing the exercise of such authority is not of a merely routine or clerical nature, but requires the use of independent judgement."

As a supervisor, you have the hardest job of all the above levels. You have to know and understand all the policies and procedures as set out by the company you work for, what each client expects to be done on their site and what each of the security officers working for you expects you to do for them.

First we will take a look at what the company expects of you. In a lot of companies, the supervisor will receive little or no training. When you were promoted, you may have been given a set of instructions that covered an explanation of the company, responsibilities of your job, payroll information, and a breakdown concerning the employees under you with regards to the labor laws.

During your career as a security officer, you displayed potential for promotion, including:
1.   *Job Knowledge* - you set yourself a standard following the company policies and were consistent in your job performance.
2.   *Leadership* - you have a good reputation with your fellow security officers and clients.
3.   *Judgement* - you have demonstrated good judgement in your decisions when dealing with situations as they arise.
4.   *Stability* - you appear to be level-headed and not on a power trip.

Now as a supervisor, your superiors expect you to take these qualities along with their guidelines and apply them to training and directing other security officers.

CHARACTERISTICS OF A GOOD SUPERVISOR

1.   *Knowledge:* know the technical aspect of the job.
2.   *Decisiveness:* gather necessary information, review it, make your decision and put it into effect.
3.   *Communication Skills:* as a supervisor, you must translate company policy into a plan of action, keep employees informed, assess performance, do appraisals, discipline when

necessary and train or take corrective action. What you say, and how, will affect the morale, attitude and performance of the people working for you.

4.   *Establish a Work Ethic:* as a supervisor, you must establish a good work climate. Set performance standards with a no-nonsense atmosphere. Treat each employee equally while following the established rules. Be accessible to the employees so they know they can discuss problems with you.

A sign of a good supervisor is high quality work by employees, a satisfied client and low turnover.

POOR CHARACTERISTICS OF A SUPERVISOR

1.   *Defensiveness*: someone who finds excuses for poor performance and taking all negative comments as attacks on their ability as a supervisor.

2.   *Lack of Emotional Stability:* quick to anger and frustration when events do not go their way. Does nothing to solve problems.

3.   *Poor Delegation:* taking too much on and not being able to finish projects that are started. Not enough time to listen to employee problems. Lacks proper planning to avoid unnecessary problems.

4.   *Inflexibility:* too by-the-book, can cause employees to find ways to circumvent the rules or openly ignore them in times of need.

The overall result of poor supervision is low morale, poor quality of work, high turnover, and a very unhappy client.

Now we will look at what the client expects of a supervisor. As a supervisor you may never even meet the site clients, but you are responsible for what happens on the sites. Leadership defines what they expect of you.

You are to ensure that the security officer working their property has the best guidance to perform the duties according to what the client wants done. It is your responsibility to see that the officers have the proper equipment and the proper training in the equipment's use. If there are any problems concerning this equipment, you should attend to the repair of it.

Sites should be regularly checked to ensure the safety of the officers working them; submit reports to your superiors detailing any problems. All changes should be passed on with the site information being updated to eliminate confusion.

Review the officers regularly to maintain the standards set by the company. Follow up on problems or complaints as soon as possible and submit a full report on how to correct it. Above all, professionalism must be maintained in all your dealings.

Now we get to what the employees expect from you. Everyone likes to hear they are doing a good job. Do not be afraid to tell someone they did good work in dealing with a situation no matter how big or small it was. As a supervisor, you must be aware of what all the employees under you are doing. If an officer needs help, help them. Their problems may seem so small they don't think they should bother getting help, or it may be just a little misunderstanding and easy to correct.

Communication is a very important tool in this industry. Proper information flow can clear up a lot of trouble before it starts. Everyone wants to feel they are involved with the company. Rumors can be very damaging to morale. Successful supervisors keep the lines of communication open by giving the employees the information they need to know and keep them up to date on the major events going on in the company.

Employees look to the supervisor as someone they can go to for help. If an employee is not sure of a legality or the proper procedure to handle a situation, they need someone to talk to, and you are that person. If you are not sure of something, let them know you will find the proper answer for them and get it. Always follow up on what you start.

Another aspect of being a supervisor is loyalty to the people working for you. They need to know that in the time of need, you will "go to bat" for them. With this kind of relationship with their supervisor, employees are encouraged to take on more responsibility and develop in their job; they know that if something goes wrong, the supervisor will be supportive and help them through the situation.

One of the most important things that concerns an employee is tactful discipline. No one likes the embarrassment of being reprimanded in public. Everyone wants guidance and feedback on their performance. If you must be harsh with someone, try and offset it with how well the officer performs in general. Always try to give some good with the bad. Remember, these officers reflect on your ability as a good supervisor.

INFLUENCES AND COMMUNICATION

Understanding how to organize the three influences, you need to develop a game plan for yourself. You have to be able to establish your own checks and balances. Know your limitations and try not to be inflexible. If you are having rouble with areas you do not understand, then seek help from your superior. To be a successful supervisor you need a good relationship with the people above you. Without their support you will not get very far.

All of your three bosses will be communicating problems, praises, changes, and reciprocal information. You will have to make decisions based on what you feel is right for the situation. With boss one, the decision process should be a two-way street; you should feel you can discuss all matters with your manager. Remember, however, they have put you in a position where with your background, you should be able to handle minor problems without bothering them. If you have to go to them, make sure you cannot find a suitable solution without their intervention.

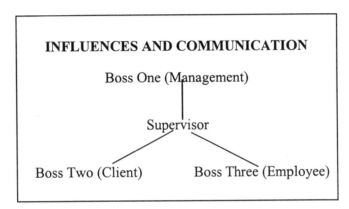

BIBLIOGRAPHY

Canadian Manager The: Cliff G. Bilya, John Wiley and Sons Canada

Effective Manager's Desk Book The: Robert L. Malone, Donald J. Petersen, Parker Publishing Company

Improving Productivity Through Advanced Office Controls: Robert E. Nolan, Richard T. Young, Ben C. DiSylvester, Amacom, A Division of American Management Associations

Management, A Basic Handbook: W.F. Coventry, Irving Burstiner, Prentice-Hall, Inc.

Managerial Mind The: David W. Ewing, A Free Press Paperback, MacMillan Publishing Company Inc.

Managerial Situations and How to Handle Them: William Wachs, Parker Publishing Company Inc.

One Minute Manager The: Kenneth Blanchard, Ph.D., Spencer Johnson, M.D., Berkley Publishing Group

Will To Manage The: Marvin Bower, McGraw-Hill Book Company

PERSONNEL: POLICIES AND PROCEDURES
QUIZ

1. In the day-to-day operation, all _____ and _____ must be met following _____ guidelines and union-negotiated clauses while remaining in budget.

2. You are to ensure that the security officer works _____ the duties according to what the client wants done.

3. As a supervisor, _____ of what all employees under you are doing.

4. Successful supervisors keep the lines of communication open by giving employees _____ _____ and _____ going on in the company.

5. Understanding on how to _____ you need to _____ for yourself.

6. One of the most important characteristics of a supervisor is leadership.
    ☐ T   ☐ F

7. A security officer's performance reflects on the supervisor.
    ☐ T   ☐ F

8. The company clients' ideas are important in how to train a security officer at their site.
    ☐ T   ☐ F

9. During the performance of your duties, flexibility is not a major concern.
    ☐ T   ☐ F

10. As a supervisor, it is important to understand the company structure.

    ☐ T   ☐ F

MOTIVATION AND EVALUATION
by Ronald R. Minion, M.S., CPP, CPO

INTRODUCTION

The line security officer plays a vital role in the success of any security organization. The level of motivation also creates an immediate impression regarding the organization he/she is responsible to protect. First impressions are lasting!

During my 33 years tenure in the contract security business I have worked with high/medium/low performers. A high performer does not necessarily make the best officer. Who gets the job done the best? A long-term solid performer, a protection officer who has been properly screened, trained, uniformed and properly prepared for the job of protecting life and organizational assets

Once the officer is on the job, far too often security managers take the approach; "we're done, out of sight/out of mind." Wrong; this is the time all officers need guidance/support in order to get the job done effectively. Good supervision/coaching leads to positive performance, performance that builds profits (contract or proprietary).

There is no magic to motivating the uniformed security officer. But, for too long, guard force managers have not paid enough attention to the officer's individual professional employment needs. The job can't get done without expending human and financial company resources for officer support/leadership/professional development.

These two resources are indeed precious, hence you must have a program, a plan that will work. Once you commit organizational resources to employee motivation, you had better know what you are doing, how the resources will be managed.

I have owned/operated two successful commercial contract security companies. Both were managed on the premises that the "bottom line" profit resulted directly from the level of motivation of the line security officers. I will discuss what worked for me. You can decide if these methods will work for you!

How company resources are expended to enhance motivation/productivity within the security force is a very important exercise in human resource management! The following step by step program works. But, it likely means a departure from the traditional way protection officers are managed.

OFFICER EVALUATION

Before we discuss rewards/perks/bonuses we must have an accurate record of how well our officers are doing. This can't be a "hit-miss" opinion expressed by a supervisor. We have to score/grade each officer. A report card must be designed/generated. Grade the officers, then grade the site/account. This is the beginning of the "team approach" to guard management.
The following questions must be addressed:
How do we evaluate the officers?
- What are the criteria?
- Who conducts inspections/evaluations?
- How do we verify results?
- How do we link officer performance to team performance?
- How do we "feed-back" results to officer(s)/team(s)?
- What are the rewards for good performers?
- What are the sanctions for bad performers?

Step #1

We must determine what job related officer accomplishments/performance are most important in the evaluation process. The ten most important factors to be assessed are:

Dress/Deportment

How well the officer turns out and conducts him/herself on the job will be a determining factor in the level of performance. How often have you seen a sloppy guard perform well? Have you seen a crisp/sharply turned out officer perform below security management's expectations? The officers must have the tools to work with—a good uniform management program.

Qualifications

There are numerous training/education opportunities available for protection officers. There are official certifications, which accredit the officer's achievements/skills. The most important training programs directly linked to officer performance are; First Aid, CPR, Non-Violent Crisis Intervention, Occupation Health & Safety, Certified Protection Officer (CPO), Protective Security Courses at private/government institutes and professional college security programs leading to an associate or bachelors degree.

Reports/Notes

The officer who is capable of effectively taking notes during his/her tour of duty and able to translate the information to a useful report, is vital to a successful security department. Electronic incident tracking often replaces the manual process, hence, officers must be familiar with how to use computers. Good security depends upon officer contributions to record keeping and statistics.

Site Operating Procedures

All levels of the security unit should participate in the development and maintenance of effective Site Operating Procedures (SOP). Once these indispensable orders are complete, they must be continually updated. Good officers work hard at keeping security procedures current. Officer knowledge and understanding of the application of site/post orders significantly enhances security.

Knowledge of Site

Prior to permanent assignment to any post/site, the officer must be completely familiar with the physical layout of the property/facility to be protected. Site plans, supervised tours, duty checklist, SOP, and a written quiz at the completion of on-the-job orientation are all helpful in gaining a clear understanding of the physical plant.

Attitude

An officer with a positive attitude towards his/her employer, duties, responsibilities and the site, which must be protected, is essential for good security. Bad attitudes equate to bad security. An officer, who has assumed a position in security as a "stop-gap" measure, will seldom possess the right attitude. Good attitudes are developed through joint goal setting. Officers who have a say in how site security is managed generally have the best attitudes.

Public Relations

The protection officer is a public relations envoy for the organization he/she protects. The officer who has paid attention to the need for appropriate dress and deportment, has taken the first step in the creation of a positive first impression with visitors, employees, customers and corporate executives. The officer must understand how to be portrayed as the person in charge. An individual who exhibits a pleasant/upbeat image is vital to a successful protection service program.

Reliability

The ideal officer will come to work early to make sure he/she is fully conversant with the events of the previous shift. Once management recognizes an officer as reliable, he/she will be given more responsibility, advancing a professional career in security. This officer knows his/her work, understands SOP and works harmoniously with other officers on the security team.

Housekeeping

A sloppy guard, a sloppy security office, sloppy records, sloppy notes, sloppy reports, all lead to poor performance and poor security. In the overall pursuit of image enhancement, protection officers must work at looking sharp at all times. They must keep the security area tidy and maintain orderly records and reports. Good housekeeping equates to good security.

Permanency

Turnover is an ugly word in the private security community. New faces create most deficiencies in the life safety/asset protection program. The qualified officer who dresses immaculately, produces quality reports, understands SOP, has the right attitude, exhibits public relations, is reliable and keeps a tidy work station, will stay longer, feel good about the job and will be a credit to his his/her employer and the security profession.

Step #2

Evaluation Format

All professional employees, regardless of their occupation, need feedback. "How am I doing?" "How does my work compare with my coworker's"? "How can I improve?" Protection officers are no exception. If they are left in the dark and can only guess as to how well they are getting their work done, they will soon become demoralized, negatively impacting performance.

The following officer appraisal forms have been developed to accurately assess performance. These reports are based on the 10 most important factors necessary for the attainment of officer success in the security workplace.

Figure 6.1   Illustrates 10 success factors each graded 1 to 10. (1 - unsatisfactory 10 - outstanding)

Inspection Report   **Officer Evaluation Form**

Date: _____ Time: _____ Site: _____
Inspector: _____ Officer: _____

Evaluation Results
Please check mark in applicable box. (See reverse for guidelines.)

	1	2	3	4	5	6	7	8	9	10
Dress / Uniform										
Qualifications										
Quality of Reports / Notes										
Knowledge of Orders										
Knowledge of Site										
Attitude										
Public Relations										
Reliability										
Housekeeping										
Permanency at Site										

Add up all values of the check marks and enter the Total: (Maximum possible = 100 points)   **Total:** _____

Comments: _____

Officer: _____ Date: _____
(Signature)

Figure 6.2   Illustrates grading criteria. What the inspection coordinator looks for to establish scores.

<u>Inspector notes:</u>   Place a check mark in the appropriate value box for each category, e.g. if an officer has four out of five of the requirements for Dress / Uniform place a check mark in the box under 8 against Dress / Uniform. 1 point may be awarded in situations where the officer does not fully meet the required standard, e.g. shirt is clean but not pressed, not fully conversant with content of orders etc.

Dress / Uniform	2 points each for:	Shirt / blouse / jacket clean and pressed Pants / skirt clean and pressed Footwear correct style and clean / polished T-Shirt or tie, clean and of correct form Hair – Men short, clean & clean shaven Hair – Women short, up and off the collar, clean
Qualifications	2 points each for:	First aid/CPR NVCIT OH&S CPO Others
Quality of Reports/Notes	2 points each for:	Notebook – possession Notebook – correctly used Report – neat & tidy Report – properly completed Report – easy to understand
Site Operation Procedures	2 points each for:	Location of orders What is covered in orders Interpretation of orders Application of orders Basic knowledge of orders
Knowledge of Site	2 points each for:	Location of fire suppression equipment Location of exits/entrances incl. fire exits Locations of high security areas Location of alarm panels General layout of building, area and lighting
Attitude	Look for:	Problem solving skills Initiative Personality type Enthusiasm
Public Relations	Look for:	Courtesy, restraint and interest Impartiality Consistency of approach Compliance to procedure
Reliability	Look for:	Punctuality Adherence to work schedule Willingness to work extra shifts Does the officer do the required job?
Housekeeping	Look for:	Accessibility of orders, stationary, forms, etc. Professional appearance of work area, etc.
Permanency at Site	2 points for each month on site, 10 points for 5 months or more	

Rating structure:	2	Unsatisfactory	8	Satisfactory – meets requirements
	4	Requires improvement	10	Outstanding
	6	Satisfactory – room for improvement		

Interpretation:	20 – 40	Officer is unsatisfactory for site	70 – 90	Officer is satisfactory
	40 – 70	Officer requires improvement	90 +	Officer exceeds requirements

Developed by Ron R. Minion CPP, CPO & David P. Williams CPO Copyright 1999

Figure 6.3   ***Results computed to depict officer and team performance ratings.***

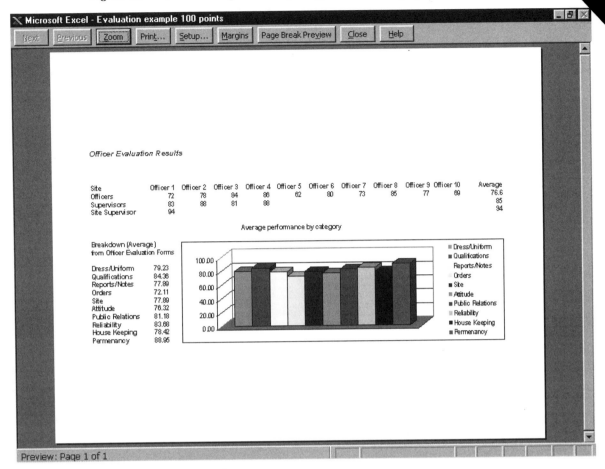

Step #3

Evaluation Process

The completed evaluations are an invaluable document that can be used extensively as a guard force management tool. To effectively evaluate all officers on a particular site, a senior member of the guard force must be appointed to coordinate the project (inspection coordinator).

The inspection coordinator must work closely with the site supervisor, communicating pro-actively. The exercise must not be deemed as a "witch hunt," rather, a positive program designed to recognize good work by all officers.

Once all of the evaluations have been completed, they must remain confidential and be delivered to a senior member of security management.

Step #4

Officer/Team Assessments

Security management is now in possession of very valuable information that can't be left to gather dust. The data must be discussed with the site supervisor, who has also been assessed by the inspection coordinator.

Each officer must be given the opportunity to discuss his/her appraisals. It must be an exercise designed to enhance motivation/performance. It is time to set goals, rather than chastise. Each officer must be told of any shortcomings brought to light in the performance audit. Each officer must be told of the timing of the next evaluation and instructed on how to improve performance as required.

By calculating each officer's rating, it is easy to determine a team score. Simply take the average of

including the supervisor(s). That's the results. Now you have officer/team
you do with this information? The results have been discussed in private with each
:cuss the ratings with the team.

:nt, not only the commercial customer, but corporate management will be
)any security professionals who have worked hard to develop a productive security
taffed with officers whose performance is measured, a process that provides
:o eliminate bad performance among the protection service group.

We now have a level playing field; each officer knows the rules. All team members must be
informed as to when and what to expect from the next scheduled inspection, which should be
conducted within six months.

Step #5

Goal Setting/Motivation

It is time to set realistic goals. If the overall average was 70%, set a new target of 75%. This
gives everyone on the team something positive to strive for. It will be amazing to see how (without
any help from management) the team will establish a norm for good performance. Now, team
members will discreetly sanction poor performers and sometimes not so discreetly. Everyone wants to
play on a winning team.

Ideally, there should be more than one team. If the team consists of a small proprietary
security force, make each shift a separate team. If it is a large in-house group, identify each site as a
team. If it is a contract company, the number of teams are unlimited.

Team standing will become very important to team members, but only with management
impetus. The entire evaluation program has to be managed. Communicating information is vital to the
overall success of the program. By placing a lot of emphasis on the results of the evaluations,
management can significantly improve overall officer performance.

If management, supervisor(s), officers and teams think the results are inaccurate, how can the
rating be validated? If the accuracy of the grades is in doubt, a private security consultant, a member of
the HR or other department within the organization, can be recruited to do spot audits to confirm the
correctness of the data.

How do you sanction poor performers? Certainly a confidential corrective interview is in
order. If the deficiencies are serious, issue a written warning. But most important, allow an
opportunity to improve. Turn a negative to a positive by skillfully communicating with the
low-scoring officer. Individual coaching and encouragement will go a long way to improve future
evaluations.

How do you reward officers? A letter of recognition, a certificate, a plaque, a bonus, gift
certificate, a promotion, a lapel pin, medal of merit, dinner with the boss, a promotion.

How do you reward teams? Publish the standings, tell other departments/divisions in the
organization, a write-up in the company newsletter, monetary reward to be divided by team members,
team jackets, crests, individual/group certificates/plaques, pizza party, drinks on the boss.

The perks/rewards from the initial audit should be minimal. Wait for the results of further
audits. Rewards should only come after a year. For example, an achiever who continually scores more
than 80% ratings may be allowed to use an internal security designation, such as "medal of merit"
(M.M.), after his name. It's prestigious, and officers like recognition.

Most important, however, our goal is to improve performance through heightened motivation
within the security organization. The perks/rewards are secondary to improved on-the-job officer
performance.

How to measure officer performance has always been a puzzle; *you now have the right
yardstick!!*

**MOTIVATION AND EVALUATION
QUIZ**

1.   The _____ security officer plays a vital role in the success of any security
organization.

2.   The job of motivating the officer can't be done without expending _____ and _____ _____ company resources.

3.   Electronic incident _____ often replaces the manual process.

4.   All professional employees, regardless of their occupation, need _____ regarding performance.

5.   Our goal is to improve _____ through heightened motivation.

6.   Security officer motivation has little to do with organization "bottom-line" profit.
        ☐ T   ☐ F

7.   How the officer is turned out for duty has little to do with performance.
        ☐ T   ☐ F

8.   The security officer is responsible for preparing Site Operating Procedures.
        ☐ T   ☐ F

9.   Good housekeeping is a vital part of the overall security operation.
        ☐ T   ☐ F

10.   Perks/rewards as a result of the initial audit should be minimal.
        ☐ T   ☐ F

DOWNSIZING
by David H. Naisby, Jr., CPO

History has often demonstrated that a booming economy is representative of a forthcoming recession. When faced with such a recession, each business entity must conversely react. Each reaction, however, must come in a manner that will result in not only a non-violent manner, but have a positive effect for every entity involved. Therefore, when faced with stagnant or declining revenue, cuts in funding from government and other external sources, and steadily inflating fixed costs, organizations must control or reduce discretionary expenses to keep their budgets in balance. Since staff salaries and fringe benefits are the largest line item in most institutions' budgets, cost containment efforts almost inevitably entail pressure to reduce the staff payroll. The institution is rare that is spared traumatic layoffs, elimination of positions, personnel freezes, and other cost containment measures that threaten staff members' job security. This chapter will examine the importance of a well-planned layoff procedure.

COMMUNICATION

Advance communication with affected employees and other pertinent institutional constituencies is usually desirable if the layoff is to be conducted in the least disruptive way. The rationale for staff layoffs should be developed, justified, and explained honestly and convincingly, and the institution should show that it would emerge from the process stronger and more able to perform its mission.

Layoff decisions often stem from progressive deterioration of the institution's financial position; for example, a shortfall in revenue, unanticipated increase in employee fringe benefit costs, sudden downturn in federal grant and contract support, or surge in utility expense. Months or even years may elapse from the moment of initial revelation to the final decision to implement a layoff plan that covers large units of the institution. The process often begins in the financial vice president's office, proceeds to the president, and quickly widens through concentric circles of the institution's management and constituencies. *The earlier and more coherently the institution can inform its staff of the impending bad news, the better prepared and less bewildered staff members are likely to be.*

As soon as large-scale layoffs are seriously contemplated, a small team of decision-makers should be assembled. The institution's lawyer, risk manager, protection manager, human resource and benefits specialists, and a representative of the financial office should be key members. This small group should develop a coordinated and *consistent* communications strategy. Documents that explain the rationale for layoffs—for example, reports to trustees, minutes of presidential cabinet meetings, charts designed to demonstrate the justification for layoffs, and public statements—should be reviewed carefully before they are finalized and issued. Such documents may play a large part in litigation contesting the layoffs.

Once the official message regarding the layoff has been finalized, it should ordinarily be promptly communicated to the institution's various constituencies. Usually, the message should focus on why layoffs are necessary. Most people react with greater understanding and more sympathetically if they learn of the institution's financial difficulties directly from its spokesperson rather than through the rumor mill.

Briefing sessions should be conducted for trustees and at least in the case of public institutions, key legislators and government officials. "Town meetings" are often a useful setting in which to help explain to employees the financial conditions that have created the need for a layoff. Special communications with employees can take various forms such as an employee newsletter.

Community media merit close attention in the context of large-scale layoffs. In some big cities, even the mass layoff of staff members may not attract the media, but the level of interest is hard to predict. In small towns, where large institutions often have a dominant role in local politics and culture, the layoff of even a few employees can have a community-wide effect that will be front-page news. At the very least, press releases should be prepared and distributed to the local media. In smaller communities, it may be advisable to schedule a press conference to announce the layoffs.

To what extent, if any, should the CEO figure in public communications about a large-scale layoff? This must be determined! Whether the president should be a visible spokesperson may depend on the focus of the layoff. If the layoff is confined to one or a few operating areas, a wise strategy may call for delegation of communications responsibility far down the chain of command. It may be prudent to reserve the president for possible major public controversy. Naturally, the CEO's aptitude for effectively handling such a situation should be taken into account.

Whether the contemplated layoffs involve personnel from many offices and departments or only a few or even one, sensitivity to each affected work unit's culture, specific personnel-management issues, and needs is imperative. Often, the planning of layoffs is necessarily decentralized, with some central administration oversight and, hopefully, prior review. Consultation with the institution's counsel and human resource professionals is no less important where one or a few work units are involved than where institution-wide layoffs are.

IDENTIFYING POSITIONS TO BE ELIMINATED

At many institutions, the personnel policies manual includes a layoff policy. For some organizations, the policy was crafted years before layoffs were imminent. Even at those institutions, however, the policy is often abbreviated and vague, reflecting an era when layoffs were rarely contemplated. An urgent planning group task is to determine, as soon as the possibility of layoffs surfaces, whether the institution's existing policy contains three critical elements:
1. Criteria for determining layoff sequence and selecting individual employees for layoff.
2. Timely opportunity for counsel and other responsible offices, including the risk management, personnel, and affirmative action offices, to review layoff plans before implementation.
3. An equitable but highly efficient process for limited appeal by affected staff members.

If the institution's layoff policy fails to address these elements, the institution is likely to face a choice between, on the one hand, amending the policy shortly before a round of layoffs, thereby increasing breach-of-contract exposure, and, on the other hand, administering an inadequate policy that increases exposure to discrimination and deprivation-of-due-process claims.

In determining the sequence of layoffs, should the policy cite quantitative criteria, such as seniority or years in rank, or qualitative criteria, such as quality of job performance or whether the position is essential to the institution's mission? The question can be difficult. From a legal perspective, use of quantitative criteria such as seniority tends to be safest. Title VII in the Age Discrimination in Employment Act provide that an employer acts legally if it follows a "bona fide seniority system," and the courts have interpreted the law to allow layoffs in reverse order of seniority, provided that seniority is determined fairly.

Most businesses and corporations, however, want to keep their best employees and prefer layoff sequences that are based on supervisors' perceptions of relative performance or job qualifications. While such sequences may be desirable operationally, reliance on qualitative criteria tends to be hazardous legally.

Complicating the legal analysis is the fact that many institutions reduce the size of their work forces not only by laying off employees but also by restructuring and reorganizing operations so that remaining employees perform new jobs. *Layoff decisions based on performance deficiency should be supported by reliable and substantial evidence.*

Experienced human resource professionals familiar with the institution can be valuable guides in the application of layoff criteria and clarification of various related risks. Care should be taken to ensure that, where appropriate confidentiality of communications between such persons and the institution's legal counsel is protected by attorney-client privilege and related legal doctrines.

In tough economic times, many institutions are reacting by reorganizing departments and redeploying personnel. Many, perhaps most, businesses face difficult decisions concerning staffing. This chapter has reviewed the legal risks associated with staff layoffs and methods for managing those risks. The chapter also emphasizes and describes preparation and planning steps designed to minimize legal exposure. It is imperative that the protection officer for any institution be a part of this process.

Staff layoffs usually involve employees entitled to a broad array of substantive and procedural rights. Subsequently, these may be contested in the public eye, and will likely provoke anxiety, anger, and other strong emotions in the workforce. Layoffs can entail such legal risks as claims of breach of contract, discrimination, tortious conduct, violations, collective bargaining agreements, etc. Institutions should manage the risks through intelligent preparation and planning, well-designed procedures, and careful adherence to legally defensible operating standards.

In order to maintain a successful layoff transition, it is recommended that the institution prepares and follows a sequential termination checklist. This not only ensures proper implementation of the plan, but will also assist you when combating unplanned legal ramifications. The following is a suggested pre-termination checklist.

A PRE-TERMINATION CHECKLIST

1.   Develop an overall management plan for the layoffs. The plan should analyze such questions as these:
- Are the layoffs necessary?
- Who are the members of the planning group?
- Who will be the institutional spokesperson?
- Who has been involved in the decision and who has been consulted?
- Have alternatives been considered?
- Is the institution comfortable that its layoff planning and implementation will pass the "front-page test" of media scrutiny?

2.   Plan carefully for identifying persons to be laid-off:
- Does the institution have a workable layoff policy?
- Do managers fully understand the criteria that will be used for identifying positions to be eliminated?
- Are the layoff criteria quantitative or qualitative? If qualitative, how are the criteria to be applied? Is the assessment in each case adequately documented?
- Are the reasons why employees are selected for layoff internally consistent? If work performance is a criterion, does the personnel file of the laid-off employee support the determination that the employee should be laid off while others are not?
- Will there be disproportionate impact on "protected classes" of employees? If so, can there be assurance that the institution can prove that there was no discrimination figured in termination decisions?

3.   Prepare carefully to notify affected employees:
- Tell employees the truth and treat them throughout with dignity and respect.
- Make sure that employees understand the criteria used to determine layoff sequence.
- How much notice will be given?
- Who will be responsible for notifying each individual?
- Insist that managers confer with trained human resource professionals to identify and address questions likely to arise.
- Respect employees' privacy.
- Prepare written materials on severance arrangements, out-placement assistance, re-employment rights, and appeal rights, and have the materials available at individual employee meetings.

4.   Anticipate the reactions and needs of remaining employees:
- Explain any reorganization or job restructuring necessitated by layoffs.
- Use briefing sessions and group counseling to alleviate anxieties.
- Plan an effective means of asset protection.

5.   Debrief afterward:
- Identify a small group of key administrators who will be responsible for monitoring and evaluating the process.
- Consider whether institutional policies and practices should be modified based on the experience during the initial round of layoffs.

Again, an institution that is spared traumatic layoffs, elimination of positions, personnel freezes, and other cost containment measures that threaten staff members' job security is becoming a thing of the past. This chapter examined the importance of a well-planned layoff procedure.

Is the institution comfortable that its layoff planning and implementation will pass the "front-page test" of media scrutiny? Perhaps the largest scrutiny will be that of the media; they will merit close attention in the context of a large-scale layoff. Therefore, covering all the bases prior to the execution of an organizational downsize is imperative. Consultation with the institution's counsel, human resource professionals, and other involved parties is extremely important. This provides safety, security, ease of transition, and legal protection.

Does the institution have a workable layoff policy? At many institutions, the personnel policies manual includes a layoff policy. The criteria for determining layoff sequence and selecting individual employees for layoffs are usually found here. It was designed to be an effective means of control; it should be used.

An organized plan is only as good as those who assist in the execution of such a plan. There should be one person responsible for implementing the plan, not several leaders with their own ideas. However, the "chain of command" is generally the most effective means for executing a plan. In addition, a supervisor should be a good listener, one who is open to suggestions that he or she may have overlooked. However, the manager must remain steadfast in the task at hand. Personal agendas and company politics must be left behind; the security of the organization takes precedence.

This chapter has reviewed the legal risks associated with staff layoffs and the methods for managing those risks. Staff layoffs usually involve employees entitled to a broad array of substantive and procedural rights. Develop an overall management plan for their layoffs.

Prepare for layoffs!

BIBLIOGRAPHY

"Indianapolis' privatizing mayor to share his ideas." As found on the Internet @ www.express-ews.net/auth/pantheon/news-biz/politics/1004bdpa.htm on 15 May 1997.

"Jean therapy." *Business Week.* 17 Nov 1997 n3553 p52(1).

"Preparing financially for hard times." *USA Today.* July 1997, v125 n2626, p8(2).

"Preparing for Layoffs." *The Management Archive.* As found on the Internet @ http://ursus.jun.alaska.edu/archives/odc/msg00482.html on 15 Dec 1997.

"The Axeman Cometh." *Maclean's.* 24 Nov 1997 p105(1).

DOWNSIZING
QUIZ

1. Layoffs are generally the result of three key elements. Which is not one of these?
   a) Elimination of positions
   b) Personnel freezes
   c) Failure to meet job specifications
   d) Cost containment measures

2. At many institutions, the personnel policies manual includes a :
   a) Benefits package
   b) Union guideline memorandum
   c) Layoff policy
   d) Implementation policy

3. What agency will merit close attention in the context of large-scale layoffs?
   a) Community media
   b) Personnel
   c) Bargaining unions
   d) Institutional management

4. To what extent, if any, should the company's president figure in public communications about a large-scale layoff?
   a) A small portion
   b) A great deal
   c) None at all
   d) As little as possible

5.   Staff layoffs usually involve employees entitled to a broad array of substantive and
      a)   Quantitative rights
      b)   Procedural rights
      c)   Qualitative rights
      d)   Reserved rights

6.   When are the layoffs necessary?
      a)   When sales are down
      b)   When government grants warrant cutbacks
      c)   When an institution suspects employee theft
      d)   When an institution deems it necessary on an individual basis

7.   The "front-page test" suggests that:
      a)   The institution is planning a layoff
      b)   The institution is comfortable
      c)   The media has reported the layoff
      d)   The media is exploiting your company

8.   Every institution has a workable layoff policy.
            ☐ T   ☐ F

9.   Should the reasons why employees are selected for layoff be internally consistent?
            ☐ T   ☐ F

10.   Make sure that:
      a)   Employees understand the criteria used to determine layoff sequence
      b)   Your company documents every action
      c)   You explain any reorganization or job restructuring necessitated by layoffs
      d)   All of the above

SECURITY OFFICER SCHEDULING
by Gary Lyons, B.A., CPO, CSS, CPP

PERSONNEL SCHEDULING

For the supervisor or manager who has not dealt with scheduling of personnel—and even for those who have—the correct and efficient use of his or her work force can be extremely challenging. There are an infinite number of ways to construct a working schedule, and wise use of service employees' time has a profound effect on a business' bottom line. Some of the immediate benefits of a good working schedule are increased effectiveness, better relationships, and longer retention of your staff, along with greater client satisfaction. Effective scheduling is often the result of the scheduler's experience and individual creativity. To begin, it is essential to develop a baseline. Remember the old adage: "A failure to plan is a plan to fail."

The following are some fundamental steps for an efficient scheduling process:

1.   *Define what your assignment or mission is.* What is it that you need to accomplish? In most instances, it is simply staffing a post for a defined period of time. In any case, the more specifically the assignment is defined, the better the chances that you'll have a successful final outcome.

2.   *Gather all available information.* This is where the majority of your time should be spent. Be sure to keep all the information you need for future scheduling in an accessible place, such as a notebook or binder. It is very important to keep this information up to date. Sorting through unorganized or unreliable information will only add additional time and frustration to the schedule planning process. There are many sources you can use to gather the needed information. Be proactive. You will find that the search for this information must be initiated by you. Begin by finding out the basic requirements of the post. Note that these are factors that you may have little or no control over. Some of the question you should ask include:
     *   How many hours will this post need to be staffed?
     *   How many personnel will be needed at this post?
     *   Will full or part-time personnel be required?
     *   Is this a mobile post, i.e. foot or vehicle patrol, or is it stationary? This question is necessary in order to figure in the fatigue factor. Staffing a post with a person who is too tired to perform the required basic duties does everyone a disservice. Some positions require frequent breaks to alleviate mental and physical fatigue.

Next, assess factors that you *do* have some, or total, control over:
     *   What is the total number of personnel that you have available? You may need to make adjustments at other posts or inform your human resource department that you need additional hires to carry out your mission.
     *   Do you have full, or part-time personnel?
     *   Do these positions require special training? For example, does the staff need to be armed and, if so, how does this affect your available personnel?

As in any profession, human nature has a great impact on the security field. Most personnel prefer to have a stable and predictable schedule so they can plan their personal lives. *Stability is key to the retention of your staff.* If a post requires multiple time periods, your staff should be informed of the possibility of irregular hours. You should address the impact this may have with each of your workers by noting any concerns in advance. Look for those situations that are a "win-win" for both you and your staff. For example, a college student may prefer the evening and weekend hours that an employee with family responsibilities would find difficult.

Security is very often a 24-hours a day, seven days a week profession. Vacations, holidays, special events, military leave and planned medical leave are all factors that should be addressed in your scheduling plan. Keep a scheduling roster to track these events. This keeps you and your personnel aware of potential scheduling issues in the future and helps you keep a fair and equitable balance of time off, or holidays worked, by employees.

It is important that your company or agency have a clear and precise standard operating procedure for employees to request time off. For example, make it a rule that staff members make requests for time off a minimum of two weeks before the event. This will help control the schedule process and give you time to make the needed adjustments. Of course, emergencies happen. But a standard operating procedure will keep schedule disruption to a minimum.

3.   *Create multiple schedules.* After all pertinent information has been gathered from available sources, it is time to make out the schedule. There is no "set in concrete" way to create a schedule. It is best to do a number of schedules based on the information that you have gathered. Once you have several schedules made, you have the option to implement the schedule that best fits your needs. In addition, you have some back-up schedules to use in case the chosen one did not work as well as you expected. Two schedule templates follow. You will find them an invaluable planning tool. Along with these examples of basic schedules, some common troubleshooting tips have been included.

Schedule I (168 hours total, 24 hours a day, 7 days a week, 3 full time and 3 part-time employees required)

NAME	MON	TUES	WED	THUR	FRI	SAT	SUN
Schedule I							
Officer A.	0800-1600	0800-1600	0800-1600	0800-1600	0800-1600	OFF	OFF
Officer B.	1600-2400	1600-2400	1600-2400	1600-2400	1600-2400	OFF	OFF
Officer C.	0001-0800	0001-0800	0001-0800	0001-0800	0001-0800	OFF	OFF
Officer D.	OFF	OFF	OFF	OFF	OFF	0800-1600	0800-1600
Officer E.	OFF	OFF	OFF	OFF	OFF	1600-2400	1600-2400
Officer F.	OFF	OFF	OFF	OFF	OFF	0001-0800	0001-0800

Schedule II (168 hours total, 24 hours a day, 7 days a week, 4 full time employees required)

NAME	MON	TUES	WED	THUR	FRI	SAT	SUN
Schedule II							
Officer A.	0800-1600	0800-1600	0800-1600	0800-1600	0800-1600	OFF	OFF
Officer B.	1600-2400	1600-2400	1600-2400	1600-2400	OFF	OFF	1600-2400
Officer C.	OFF	0001-0800	0001-0800	OFF	0001-0800	0001-0800	0001-0800
Officer D.	0001-0800	OFF	OFF	0001-0800	1600-2400	0800-1600	0800-1600

Schedule II saves resources in the following areas:

* Workers' Compensation
* Vacation Benefits
* Health Insurance
* Uniforms
* Other "Per Employee" Expenses

The reason for these savings is that two fewer personnel are required for Schedule II. In addition, full-time personnel are not as likely to be a retention issue, which helps create the atmosphere of a long-term career environment. Schedule I would make a good back-up schedule in the event that Schedule II was unable to be implemented.

4.   *Implement the schedule.* The next step would be to implement the best schedule. The chosen schedule should be the best balance of all of the factors in the process including both step one, the mission assignment, and step two, all the factors that are influenced by the client, the security entity itself, and the personnel in the security entity (the human factors).

5.   *Follow up.* One of the most frequently made mistakes is the lack of follow-up by the scheduler. This part of the process is very important. It tells you just how effective your scheduling judgment has been. The best way to follow up is to gather information from the clients you serve, your staff and from personal observation. The schedule should reflect a balance of the gathered information and the mission assignment. Obviously, one needs to cover all the necessary hours. In addition, the schedule should reflect the best needs. After an appropriate period of time, you can make the decision to continue with a chosen schedule, make minor adjustments in the chosen schedule, or implement a new schedule altogether.

Effective scheduling is a continuous improvement process. Employee issues, weather, and clients' needs can change without notice and affect the most solid of schedules. There will be many instances when the planned schedule and the final outcome are inconsistent. Be flexible. Have a planned back-up schedule(s) for each post and a plan for implementing these back-up procedures.

SECURITY OFFICER SCHEDULING
QUIZ

1.   There are in reality only a few ways to create a personnel schedule.
        ☐ T   ☐ F

2.   After you create a personnel schedule you are finished with the process.
        ☐ T   ☐ F

3.   The first schedule you create will always be the best one to use.
        ☐ T   ☐ F

4.   When constructing a schedule you should always consider the "human" factors.
        ☐ T   ☐ F

5.   You should always gather as much information as possible when writing a schedule.
        ☐ T   ☐ F

6.   When scheduling for a foot patrol, physical and mental _____ are factors to consider as far as duration of the shift.

7.   Scheduling stability is a key _____ issue to consider with the working staff.

8.   You should always have a clear and concise _____ to ensure time-off requests are followed properly.

9.   The fundamental planning steps in a schedule are, define your assignment/or mission, _____, create multiple schedules, _____, and follow up.

10.   A schedule should reflect a balance of _____ and _____.

DISCIPLINE
by Michael J. Apgar, CPO and Brion P. Gilbride, CSS, CPO

One of the most unpopular duties of a security manager is to have to discipline a subordinate employee/officer. The reason for its unpopularity rests in the difficulties involved in initiating the disciplinary process, regardless of the organization in which this occurs. Here, we will define *discipline*, explain when it should be used, and most importantly, *how* it should be used.

DEFINING DISCIPLINE

Discipline is, basically, an action taken by a supervisor to correct the behavior(s) of a subordinate employee, generally within that supervisor's department. A good manager "must be prepared to discipline when the need arises."[1] It is helpful to remember that many problems are not deliberate actions on the part of an ungrateful employee, but honest mistakes caused by inexperience, lack of education or improper socialization. An organizations' rules and policies are written to address "routine, day-to-day events."[2] Discipline is generally not looked favorably upon by both supervisors and subordinates, so the least severe action taken to correct a problem will usually be the most effective.[3]

If these two ideas are combined, most disciplinary problems will not result from catastrophe, but from normal operations. For example, Stephen Robbins mentions in his book, *Personnel: The Management of Human Resources,* that "The most serious discipline problems facing managers undoubtedly involve attendance."[4] Next to that are "on the job" behaviors, such as "insubordination, horseplay, fighting, gambling, failure to use safety devices, carelessness and...abuse of alcohol and drugs."[5]

*"Discipline is usually prompted when a mistake is made,
often in the form of a wrong decision."[6]*

THE DISCIPLINARY PROCESS

The whole disciplinary process should contain two steps. The violations must be detected and corrective action must be taken.[7] Managers, when disciplining subordinates, should ask themselves "whether subordinates can learn from their mistakes. If they can, using discipline to teach rather than to punish, is both more humane and better from a business viewpoint."[8] The manager must view the subordinate as an individual, and deal with them on that basis. This will ensure loyalty and support from the subordinate, regardless of the disciplinary actions taken, and will motivate the subordinate to succeed.[9] The entire disciplinary process can be explained with six rules, devised by Charles Sennewald in his book, *Effective Security Management.* They are:

1. *All rules are to be documented. No unwritten rules.*
2. *If you must discipline a subordinate, do it privately.*
3. *Don't get personal / Don't play favorites. Treat employees in a fair and equal manner.*
4. *Don't embarrass them, teach them. Behavioral change, not deliberate humiliation, is the key.*
5. *Keep track of infractions. This provides support for more drastic disciplinary actions if the employee is a chronic offender.*
6. *Be prompt. Don't wait. If there is a violation, correct it immediately or as soon as possible.*[10]

DISCIPLINARY POLICY

If an employer intends to utilize disciplinary procedures, it is a good idea for the management of that company to write a disciplinary policy. This policy can be clearly explained in the company's handbook or employee orientation sessions, posted by the time clock or break room, or other ways. If the employees know the disciplinary policies and procedures, the employees will know what will happen to them if disciplinary action is ever taken, and what is expected of the employee. The following are a few guidelines for what a disciplinary policy should include:

1. *Explanation of Rights* - This is a statement that would inform the employee that the employer has the right to change or modify the policy as they deem necessary, depending on the situation. This statement would not allow the employer to ignore the policy, but it will let the employee know that certain circumstances will be handled differently than others. Circumstances may be based on the number of offenses, frequency, and severity.

2.   *Knowledge of Penalties* - It is important for a supervisor to know what action should be taken to discipline an employee, whether it is docking of pay, suspension, legal action, etc. If an employee is caught stealing a box of pens, the penalty will probably be different than the penalty for stealing a desktop computer. If investigation revealed that the same employee had been stealing a box of pens every Monday for the last 6 months, then the penalty would again change. Although they are still stealing the same item, the dollar amount for the loss to the company would be higher, thus the penalty more severe.

3.   *Standard Operating Procedure* - Most organizations have some sort of SOP (Standard Operating Procedure) manual outlining how the organization is to operate. A section on employee discipline must be included. An organization's SOP should have a code of conduct that employees are required to follow, along with an outline of disciplinary action for various types of infractions. One must accurately plan out a step-by-step procedure that will be the most efficient to utilize, while keeping the disruptions in the organization to a minimum.

4.   *Efficiency* - All disciplinary action should be dealt with in a swift, yet fair manner. The employee must have a chance to defend him- or herself before a decision is made. Therefore, action cannot be delayed. It is important to remember that the violator is still "on the job" while the supervisor decides what, if anything, to do. In some cases, the longer the delay, the greater the difficulties for management when action is finally taken, or if an injured party objects to the delay. Theft cases are fairly straightforward, but a case where sexual harassment is involved becomes much more complicated, especially if the victim seeks legal restitution. This can be harmful both for the employees *and* the public image of the company. If both parties see that the matter is being handled as quickly and quietly as possible, then the need for legal counsel by the outside parties could be avoided.

WHEN TO ENFORCE DISCIPLINARY POLICY

One of the most important things a supervisor must know is *when* disciplinary action is necessary. There are several times that disciplinary action is an appropriate corrective action. Examples of these are:
- Excessive tardiness
- Defective workmanship
- Inadequate work performance
- Poor attitudes that affect morale
- Insubordination [11]

These infractions, except for insubordination, are common, and can be found in virtually every workplace. Insubordination, as defined in *Black's Law Dictionary,* is:

> *State of being insubordinate; disobedience to constituted authority. Refusal to obey some order which a superior officer is entitled to give and have obeyed. Term imports a "wilful" or intentional disregard of the lawful and reasonable instructions of the employer.* [12]

These violations, as compared to criminal law, are *mala in se*. Other violations, or the rules enacted by particular companies for particular reasons, may include break policies, uniform policies, safety regulations, smoking policies, etc. These are the *mala prohibitum* crimes of the workplace.

DETERMINING THE NECESSITY OF DISCIPLINARY ACTION

In order to determine if a violation has occurred, the event/incident must be *investigated*. The investigative process can be broken down into seven items. They are:
1.   What happened? Is there any physical evidence?
2.   Is the infraction serious? Major or Minor? How many people are involved?
3.   Was the violator aware of the rule that was broken? Did the violator have a "reasonable excuse"? Are there any aggravating or mitigating circumstances?
4.   Does the violator have a record of such conduct?
5.   Should the violator receive the same treatment as others for the same offense? Different treatment?
6.   Was the offense documented?
7.   How can the problem be prevented? [13]

A supervisor must also look at the following when investigating an infraction:
1.   *Frequency/Nature of Problem:* Is this a continuing occurrence? Is this rule broken repeatedly by the same individuals?

2.   *Employee's Work History:* How long has the violator been employed? Does the violator perform quality work? A good way to look at work history would be to remember: the longer the tenure, the lesser the discipline.

3.   *Degree of Socialization:* How has management made the employee aware of rules and regulations? Are they written? Informal?

4.   *Organizational Discipline Practices:* How was this infraction dealt with at other times/with other employees? Is management consistent?

5.   *Implications for Co-Workers:* Could disciplinary action against one employee interfere with the morale of the rest?

6.   *Management Backing:* Can the supervisor justify how and why a person was disciplined?[14]

DISCIPLINE METHODS

After a supervisor has investigated an infraction or complaint, and determined it to be true, it is time for that supervisor to take action to *correct* the situation. Notice the emphasis on the word *correct*. Although disciplinary action is a punishment, its goal is to change a behavior, not to merely acknowledge its occurrence.

*"Any punishment connected with discipline should always be a means to an end,
and that end should be organizational, not personal."[15]*

There are six ways to discipline an employee. Five of them are listed here, in order of severity:

1.   *Oral Warning:* The supervisor explains the violation and the seriousness of it to the employee. The supervisor should allow the employee to react to the warning, and then permit the employee to ask questions. The warning must also include the required improvement in behavior, and mention assistance that may be provided by the supervisor or the employer. The penalty, if there is one, should be stated clearly. These warnings should be documented and placed in the employee's personnel file.

2.   *Written Warning:* The procedures are the same for written warnings as for oral ones, but the written warning is used for repeated or more serious infractions, where the oral warning is not. The written warning should be in the form of a letter to the employee, and should be written in a "punitive" tone. A copy of this letter should be kept in the employee's personnel file.

3.   *Suspension:* This action is used only after repeated written warnings or for serious infractions that may not warrant dismissal from employment. Suspensions may also be used if "an unfortunate incident of misconduct on the job requires temporary removal of the employee from the work environment, or where doubt about guilt in some instance necessitates a period of investigation."[16] Like the written warning, a letter should be written to the employee, stating the reason for the suspension and its duration. A copy of this letter should be kept in the employee's personnel file.

4.   *Pay Cut:* This method, though infrequently used, is basically a reduction in an employee's salary or hourly wage, either temporary or permanent. This method is demoralizing to the employee, and defeats the purpose of using discipline as a *corrective* measure. These actions should be documented and placed in the employee's personnel file.

5.   *Demotion:* This method, like the pay cut, is demoralizing to the employee *and* their co-workers. Demotion is used as an "attention getter" by management, and is reserved for tenured employees or those perceived by management as "not easily fired." These actions should be documented and placed in the employee's personnel file.[17]

DISMISSAL: THE "SIXTH" DISCIPLINARY METHOD

This method should be used *only after* all other avenues have been exhausted. The power to dismiss an employee is generally not held by a first or second line supervisor, but by upper management. Some supervisors do have this power, but it is in their best interest to confer with upper management prior to dismissing an employee. A letter should be sent to the employee advising them of the dismissal, and a copy of this letter should be kept in the former employee's personnel file.[18]

Dismissing a subordinate should be the "last resort" of the disciplinary process. It is an important determination that requires accurate information to support the decision. A supervisor/manager must determine what reasons they have for dismissing an employee, and if the employee's record warrants this decision. Documentation of all actions that have been taken in prior instances against the employee, must be kept to protect the employer in case of legal action. Mary A. DeVries, in her book, *The Complete Office Handbook* suggests:

1.   Tell the person why they are being dismissed, and do not make excuses or apologies or appear in any way to be indecisive or unsure of the decision to dismiss.
2.   State the case calmly and unemotionally, using the documentation that has been developed.
3.   Do not engage in a debate or respond to emotional accusations. Simply state the facts and try to focus the discussion on severance conditions.
4.   If you believe the employee will persist in a debate or become hostile, hold the meeting outside the office in a place where there is more than one exit.
5.   Do not attempt to stop or dissuade the person from working out a new professional life elsewhere.
6.   Offer to accept a letter of resignation from the employee and work out an agreeable announcement to co-workers and outsiders.[19]

THE APPEALS PROCESS

If an employee is going to be disciplined, there should exist a way for the employee to appeal the actions taken against them. Although supervisors generally have experience in their field and have demonstrable leadership qualities, they are not perfect. If they were perfect, there would be no employees – just supervisors. Some supervisors do use their disciplinary powers for personal reasons.

Hearings are generally used for more severe actions; a verbal or written warning should not justify an appeal. Suspensions, demotions, and dismissals are arenas in which appeals occur. Appeals should be "heard by a multiple body—often of three persons—which is established by statute or which is appointed ad hoc by the head of the department."[20] The appeal "board" should be as objective and as unbiased as possible. When possible, appeal "boards" should be composed of employees outside the department, and it is better if they are of supervisory rank or higher. If the department is unionized, have a union representative present or even allow one to sit on the appeal "board." This way, there can be no valid accusations that the decisions of the appeal "board" are unfair.

LOW EMPLOYEE MORALE

Sometimes, employees do things that warrant disciplinary action for reasons other than personal gain or poor decision-making skills. "Low employee morale" is the culprit when these types of offenses start occurring, and morale becomes low for a number of reasons. In these cases, sometimes the best way to change an employee's behavior is not to discipline him or her, but to work with them to correct situations that cause low morale. Here are a few examples:

- Poor working conditions
- Poor equipment
- Lack of communication
- Hypocrisy
- Redundancy

When an employee works in a poor environment, their morale is lowered because that employee wishes that conditions were better. Who would want to work in an environment that makes a person feel like there is no way out? This might lead an employee to adopt poor work habits and methods, which may warrant disciplinary action. Supervisors and managers should bear in mind that if *they* would not like working in an environment, other people probably wouldn't either. If the manager's office has carpeting, comfortable chairs, a large finished wooden desk, leather couches, and an advanced phone/computer system, the employees' morale will most likely be lowered if they have old metal chairs and twenty-year-old desks, cold tile floors, inadequate lighting, no couches, rotary phones, and typewriters. An employer should provide a comfortable workplace for employees in order for them to work more efficiently.

Having poor equipment also can have an effect on employee's actions. For example, a security department has a poor two-way radio system. A patrol officer attempts to call their supervisor via radio, but does not get a response. The officer tries again, and again, no response. Then the officer goes to a phone and calls the supervisor, and advises them of the radio difficulties, along with the message that the officer was originally trying to send. That officer may then decide not to patrol as often due to the safety hazard of not having reliable communications with backup officers. If this officer is not patrolling as he/she should be, then that officer is neglecting his or her duties. The supervisor, caring only that patrols are being performed properly, may take disciplinary action against that officer, regardless of the circumstances. To discipline an officer while ignoring circumstances such as these would be unfair to that officer and to the organization. A better alternative would be to discuss the problem with the officer and determine ways to enhance radio performance.

Lack of communication within the organization can also lower morale. The employees might feel like they are "out of the loop," and feel uninformed about certain issues, such as policy changes and other important announcements. A system should be set up to make sure that *all* employees are made aware of new information that affects their job requirements. A chain of command can be used, an email list can be set up, or something as simple as typing or writing a memo can ensure everyone knows what is going on. A sign on the wall or writing information on a bulletin board is not good by itself, because people may not notice it. Employees who are away from work for some reason (whether they are on vacation, taking a personal day, attending job training, etc.), will not be in the area where the information is posted. If everyone knows what is going on, the organization can operate more smoothly.

Hypocrisy in a workplace is another big issue that can commonly be overlooked. If a policy is written, it should be followed by everyone. On the same token, the policy should be enforced by all of the supervisor/managers. If a security supervisor allows one officer to "bend the rules," but another supervisor does not allow this and disciplines that officer, that will also cause problems, particularly within the department. The disciplined employee will point this out to management if he/she appeals the disciplinary action. Management is then faced with deciding *who* needs to be disciplined, as well as why.

Finally, redundancy is probably the most overlooked cause of low worker morale. In other words, a routine is established. If an employee does the same exact thing each day, they tend to lose interest and get bored, leading to the development of poor work habits. Tardiness is one result of redundancy. In most cases, however, this cannot be avoided. A supervisor/manager generally cannot alter the employee's duties so that they are more "exciting." What they can do is add a little something positive to the standard, everyday routine. Buying lunch for the department periodically, holiday parties and an "Employee of the Month" award, are all ways a supervisor/manager can help boost morale. It will give the employees an opportunity to socialize with each other in a more social atmosphere, rather than in a working atmosphere. It can also be viewed by the employees as sort of a "thank you" from upper management, that they are doing a good job, and are appreciated.

BIBLIOGRAPHY

Black, Henry C. *Black's Law Dictionary*. (MN: West Publishing Co., 1990)

Burstein, Harvey. *Security - A Management Perspective*. (Englewood Cliffs, NJ: Prentice Hall, 1986)

Hodgetts, Richard M. *Effective Supervision - A Practical Approach*. (NY: McGraw-Hill, 1987)

Keys, Bernard & Henshall, Joy. *Supervision*. (NY: John Wiley & Sons, 1984)

Robbins, Stephen P. *Personnel - The Management of Human Resources*. (Englewood Cliffs, NJ: Prentice Hall, 1982)

Sennewald, Charles A. *Effective Security Management*. (Boston, MA: Butterworth Publishers, 1985)

Stahl, O. Glenn. *Public Personnel Administration*. (NY: Harper & Row, Publishers, 1971)

Stone, Alfred R. & DeLuca, Stuart M. *Police Administration- An Introduction*. (NY: John Wiley & Sons, 1985)

ENDNOTES

1.   Burstein, Harvey. *Security - A Management Perspective*. (Englewood Cliffs, NJ: Prentice Hall, 1996.) Pg. 72
2.   Stone, Alfred R. & De Luca, *Stuart M. Police Administration*. An Introduction. (NY: John Wiley & Sons, 1985.) Pg. 344
3.   Stahl, Glenn O. *Public Personnel Administration*. (NY: Harper & Row, Publishers, 1971.) Pg. 310
4.   Robbins, Stephen P. *Personnel: The Management of Human Resources*. (Englewood Cliffs, NJ: Prentice Hall, 1982.) pg. 394
5.   Robbins, pg. 393
6.   Burstein, pg. 72
7.   Stone, pg. 350
8.   Burstein, pg. 72
9.   Sennewald, Charles A. *Effective Security Management*. (Boston, MA: Butterworth Publishers, 1985.) pg. 108
10.   Sennewald, pg. 111-112

11.   Hodgetts, Richard M. *Effective Supervision- A Practical Approach.* (NY: McGraw-Hill 1987.) pg. 358
12.   Black, Henry C. *Black's Law Dictionary.* (MN: West Publishing Co., 1990.) pg. 801
13.   Hodgetts, pg. 359
14.   Robbins, pg. 396-397
15.   Sennewald, pg. 107
16.   Stahl, pg. 311
17.   Keys, Bernard & Henshall, Joy. *Supervision.* (NY: John Wiley & Sons, 1984.) pg. 274-275
18.   Keys, Bernard & Henshall, Joy. *Supervision.* (NY: John Wiley & Sons, 1984.) pg. 274-275
19.   DeVries, Mary A. *The Complete Office Handbook.* (Avenal, NJ: Wings books, 1987). p. 32
20.   Stahl, pg. 315

DISCIPLINE
QUIZ

1.   Discipline is basically an action taken by a supervisor to correct the behavior(s) of a subordinate employee, generally within that supervisor's department.
□ T   □ F

2.   Discipline is usually prompted when a mistake is made, often in the form of a _____ ____ _____.

3.   Possible reasons to enforce disciplinary policy may include:
a)   Excessive tardiness
b)   Defective workmanship
c)   Inadequate work performance
d)   All of the above

4.   In order to determine if a violation has occurred, the event/incident must be _____.

5.   Although disciplinary action is a punishment, its goal is to change a behavior, not to merely acknowledge its occurrence.
□ T   □ F

6.   List six ways to discipline an employee:
a)   _____
b)   _____
c)   _____
d)   _____
e)   _____
f)   _____

7.   The power to dismiss an employee is always held by a first line supervisor.
□ T   □ F

8.   _____ in a workplace is another big issue that is commonly overlooked.

9.   If an employer intends to utilize disciplinary procedures, it is a good idea for the management of that company to write a disciplinary policy.
□ T   □ F

10.   The following are a few guidelines for what a disciplinary policy should include: (select best answer).
a)   Explanation of Rights
b)   Knowledge of Penalties
c)   Standard Operating Procedure
d)   Efficiency
e)   All of the above

UNIT THREE
SUPERVISORY PRACTICES

Supervision and Training
Maximizing Personnel Deployment
Dealing with Difficult Employees
Unethical Acts by Security Officers
Appendix A: A Model for Ethical Decision-Making
Multicultural Diversity Training
Interpersonal Communications

SUPERVISION AND TRAINING
by Darren S. Estes, CPO, CSS

CONCEPTS OF SUPERVISION

Supervisors are the link between upper management and line workers. They are responsible for directing the work of others to accomplish company goals and missions. In order to achieve this, a supervisor must possess general knowledge of the company and its mission, technical knowledge of duties performed by subordinates and the human relations skills necessary to gain the cooperation of subordinates in order to manage and direct them.

Supervision is the authority provided to a person by management to direct the work of subordinates. However, merely having the authority to direct employees is not enough to be an efficient supervisor. A supervisor must also be a leader. Leadership is the ability to inspire others to willingly work towards company goals and mission. Management chooses its supervisor; however, a group chooses its leader.

RESPONSIBILITIES TO OTHERS

In order to accomplish company goals and missions, an effective supervisor has a duty to others within the organization. He is responsible for ensuring that subordinates and management can effectively work as a team.

His/Her responsibilities to subordinates include:
   a)   Tailoring jobs to fit the job holder.
   b)   Standing behind them when they act under his orders or with his permission.
   c)   Providing constructive criticism and adequate instruction, training and evaluation.
   d)   Handling their complaints and problems in a fair and just manner.
   e)   Safeguarding their health and welfare while on the job.
   f)   Providing them with a good example.
   g)   Giving them praise for work well done.

His/Her responsibilities to peers include:
   a)   Knowing and understanding each of them as individuals.
   b)   Approaching and cooperating with them as individuals.
   c)   Providing what help is possible to enable them to achieve the measure of satisfaction they desire from their jobs.
   d)   Fostering a spirit of cooperation and teamwork.

His/Her responsibilities to superiors include:
   a)   Transmitting information about problems and recommending solutions.
   b)   Operating within a budget and using company resources effectively.
   c)   Promoting company goals and respecting company policies.
   d)   Striving for efficiency.
   e)   Preparing records and reports on time and in proper form.
   f)   Scheduling work to meet deadlines.
   g)   Showing respect and cooperation.

LEADERSHIP AND HUMAN RELATIONS SKILLS: GETTING OTHERS TO WILLINGLY WORK

Leadership

Leaders command, not demand, respect through their human relations skills and technical knowledge. What a supervisor expects and how he/she treats subordinates dictates performance. Leadership is the ability to cause others to follow willingly in the achievement of goals. Leadership and respect must be earned, not demanded.

Leaders gain the confidence and respect of their personnel by commanding an appreciation of their character and professional knowledge. A supervisor can earn such respect and trust from subordinates by displaying his/her sense of justice, common sense, energy, keenness, forethought, indifference to personal danger, readiness to share hardships, cheerfulness in the face of difficulty, clarity and simplicity in giving orders and firm insistence on their execution and the high value of his/her command.

Leaders are team players. They communicate goals effectively, provide assignments that are meaningful, explain the importance of each assignment, provide growth opportunities for employees, encourage employees to participate in decision-making, encourage suggestions and do not pretend to "know it all." Leaders make it a point to know their people, look out for their welfare and train them to work as a team.

Some common traits of leadership include:

a) *Loyalty.* A supervisor is a symbol of management to his subordinates. Therefore he/she must display loyalty to the company and its goals by not criticizing or slandering the company, its officers, managers or employees, or engaging in dishonest or unlawful activities. If he/she does exhibit such behavior, employees will discredit and distrust the company and fear for their own security within the company.

b) *Positive Thinking.* Effective leaders imagine how things can be accomplished, not why they will fail. In the search for new ideas and alternative plans, they listen carefully to what others have to say, rather than opposing or discrediting that which they hear.

c) *Empathetic and Understanding.* Leaders like and are interested in people. In directing work of another, they try to view things from that person's unique point of view. They may ask themselves, "How would I feel if I was John or Jane? What would help his or her situation?"

d) *Friendly and Approachable.* Leaders make others feel important in their jobs, rather than selfishly displaying their own power and control. They encourage and seek the opinions and advice of their subordinates. They help others attain their goals. They attempt to get to know their workers and take time to meet them for any reason. They admit their mistakes and try to learn from them rather than placing the blame on others. They are conscious of the feelings of others and therefore attempt to increase their employees' sense of self-worth. They understand that people hunger for praise and that sincere praise from a boss is one of the most powerful known stimulants to production.

e) *Initiative.* Leaders continually seek better ways to perform a job. They do not procrastinate; they do not allow a task to wait until tomorrow if it can be done today.

f) *Decisive.* Leaders do not put off, evade or refuse to give a decision. They analyze all the factors, consequences and possible alternatives before issuing a final decision. If a decision is especially difficult, requiring extensive consideration and deliberation, they will ask the person requiring the decision to return at a later time and have the decision when promised.

g) *Tact and Courtesy.* Leaders use tact and courtesy in dealing with others. An efficient supervisor has regard for the feelings of others, based on an understanding of human nature, and provides little considerations to make the job as pleasant and smooth as possible. Leaders treat others with respect and consideration, not merely as tools to be used for their own convenience. Effective leaders do not play favorites or become too friendly with employees because they know that these same employees may require disciplinary actions at some time.

h) *Sincerity and Integrity.* Effective supervisors gain and maintain the respect of others because they always deal squarely and honestly with their personnel. Consistency of thought and action are important if subordinates are to know where they stand. Being strict one day and too lax the next is worse than being consistently strict or consistently lax. Good supervisors strike a happy medium between a firm and relaxed style, then remain consistent.

i) *Humbleness.* Leaders have learned the necessity and importance of being human on the job. Weak supervisors tend to conceal their feelings of inferiority by placing barriers between themselves and their employees, making shows of their authority and assuming false dignity. In contrast, true leaders realize that everyone has something to contribute. They recognize employees who can do things just as well as or better than they. They keep in mind the old proverb, "Every man is in some way superior, and in that I can learn of him." Firmness is essential in handling people; however, it should be tempered with humbleness.

    j)   *Self-Confidence.* Good supervisors have a quiet self-confidence based on thorough knowledge of the job and belief in their own ability. If you have confidence, you inspire confidence in others. Do not ridicule the opinions of others, dominate conversations or be arrogant. People respect and follow the supervisor who has that quiet inner confidence which is expressed through his assured manner, actions and words.

    k)   *Teaching Ability.* A great part of a supervisor's job consists of instructing in one way or another. Giving orders is a form of instruction. A supervisor should train and develop others. Another proverb that is applicable to supervision is, "the man who has a knowledge or skill and who can impart that knowledge or skill to ten others has multiplied his effectiveness ten times."

Although people will produce to the extent that they like and respect their boss, leadership does not equate with friendship. Friendships may develop—they are somewhat inevitable during regular interaction with others; however, an efficient supervisor will avoid developing close, intimate friendships. Close friendships between supervisors and subordinates often create problems in motivation, morale, discipline, work delegation and in many other areas of the employer-employee relationship. For example, employees may feel that the supervisor shows favoritism towards the employee with whom he is a close friend. These employees may then begin to feel envious, even resentful. Soon, their negative feelings will reflect in their attitudes and work performance.

As previously mentioned, supervisors are human and will therefore inevitably make mistakes; however, the following mistakes should be avoided at all costs:

1.   Trying to be liked rather than respected.
2.   Failing to ask subordinates for advice and help, or prohibiting them from being part of the team.
3.   Failing to develop a sense of responsibility in subordinates.
4.   Failing to keep criticism constructive.
5.   Ignoring employees' complaints or suggestions.
6.   Failing to keep persons informed; lack of communication.
7.   Emphasizing rules rather than skills among employees thereby thwarting their personal talents.
8.   Trying to make changes too rapidly.
9.   Dictatorial practices.
10.   Playing favorites.
11.   Failing to delegate work.
12.   Failing to trust subordinates.
13.   Failing to control temper or other inappropriate emotions.
14.   Taking special privileges.
15.   Being too dependant on employees or management.

The "esprit de corps" of the department and the willingness of people to work towards common goals depends to a great extent upon the leadership of the supervisor. A productive unit will be found to be a unit with high morale.

Human Relations

Human relations refers to the study of the problems arising from organizational and interpersonal relations in industry and the actions taken to develop better interpersonal and intergroup adjustments. In other words, human relations is the study and prevention or treatment of problems that occur at work, because of bureaucratic factors (e.g. the company's organizational communications chain, and policies and procedures), and working with other people. A supervisor with good human relations skills:

1.   Understands the principles, standards, rules and regulations necessary for good conduct and practices them.
2.   Relates to his people as individuals and treats them fairly and impartially.
3.   Keeps his employees informed and promptly eliminates rumors – keeps the lines of communication open.
4.   Uses his authority sparingly, avoiding gross displays of power.

5.   Delegates duties properly.
6.   Never makes major issues out of minor infractions or personal issues out of disciplinary matters.
7.   Displays confidence in his subordinates rather than regarding them with suspicion.
8.   Cares for the physical and mental welfare of his subordinates.
9.   Tries to avoid errors but takes responsibility for them when they occur.
10.   Develops loyalty within the group and of the group.

Human relations involves focusing the morale and motivation of all employees in a positive direction. Motivation in the work environment refers to the incentive or drive an individual feels to do the best job they can. Morale refers to the mental and emotional condition (e.g. enthusiasm, confidence or loyalty) of an individual or group, as it relates to the function or tasks at hand, towards the company, its goals and their positions. It refers to an individual's level of psychological well-being based on such factors as a sense of purpose and confidence in the future. In other words, morale is the attitude of each individual in a group towards the group's purposes and goals.

Successful supervision involves power through people instead of power over people. Success and high morale in a department begins with a self-confident supervisor. If a supervisor approaches a task or job with a negative or self-defeating attitude, others will follow the example. This will not only affect the morale and attitudes of other employees, but will also reflect a negative corporate image to those, such as clients, who have contact with the company.

There are as many ways to motivate people as there are people; however, what motivates one person may not motivate another. Motivation usually revolves around the satisfaction of needs. A supervisor must therefore learn to recognize the needs and individuality of all his employees.

Motivation can be looked upon as a three step process. First, there is a need, then a behavior, action or direction to satisfy the need and finally, the accomplishment or satisfaction of the need. A decrease in employee performance suggests a lack of motivation; this can have a drastic effect on other individuals (both inside and outside the company), as well as on the organization.

Factors such as advancement, greater responsibility, promotion, growth, achievement and interesting work are consistently identified as factors that make the work situation enjoyable and motivating. Some surveys have suggested that appreciation for a job well done outranked wages among employees as a motivator. A supervisor should not wait until it is time for formal employee evaluations to give praise. Studies have also shown that morale is higher among employees who have a "listening" supervisor. Listening helps develop an insight into employees' motives and aspirations.

Another strong motivator is employee participation programs. Pride and company teamwork are enhanced through the use of employee advice and suggestion programs. Decision-making procedures which encompass this approach are often more realistic and more tolerable to employees. When employee suggestions are incorporated into decisions, they are strictly followed and appear to last longer because the employees feel that they "own" the decision. Supervisors should therefore seek opinions and be willing to be influenced by the suggestions and criticisms proposed by employees. This, however, does not mean that all decisions should be made by employee participation programs. As in all decision-making, careful analysis of the situation, possible alternatives and good judgement must be employed to reach the best possible solution.

PROCESSES FOR EFFECTIVE LEADERSHIP

Communication

Studies show that most supervisors spend approximately 80% of their time communicating. Communication is the process of transferring and relating information from one or more people to another or others. Real communication flows freely from the sender(s) to the receiver(s) and vice versa. Often, communication is hampered because supervisors devote more attention to informing and commanding than they do to listening, asking and interpreting. When communicating job assignments to employees, it is best to tell them what is to be done, why it is to be done and how it is to be done.

The test of effective communication is comprehension of the message. Communication in its basic form consists of sender, receiver, message and feedback. Communication can be verbal and/or nonverbal. For example, a supervisor who fails to reflect a professional appearance, defames other supervisors or subordinates of the company, or does not comply with company policy is communicating his unprofessionalism and dissatisfaction to every employee and visitor of the company. Other employees may adopt this negative attitude and begin to experience and reflect dissatisfaction and poor performance.

Every supervisor should become a communication expert, one who thinks before he speaks or writes, gets plenty of feedback and is a good listener.

Delegation and Assignment of Duties

The ability to delegate, to assign and entrust another with the responsibility and authority to accomplish a task, is what separates the successful supervisor from the overworked, complaining supervisor. In delegating a task, the supervisor bestows the responsibility and required authority to complete a task upon a specific employee; however, the supervisor still retains overall authority and responsibility, and he/she can revoke all or part of that which is granted to the subordinate. Although the employee is then held accountable to the supervisor for accomplishing the task, the supervisor remains accountable to management. Therefore, he/she must choose the most suitable employee for the job, provide the necessary details for completing the job and evaluate the employee's progress in accomplishing the task.

Prior to assigning a job or task, a supervisor should determine the strengths and weaknesses of each subordinate in order to delegate tasks appropriately. Next, he/she must inform them of why each one was chosen for a specific job and provide them with any necessary training, tools, authority and manpower for successful completion of their tasks. He/she must also communicate the following details of the task:

1. *A clear definition of the job:*
   What is to be done.
   Why it is to be done.
   What results are expected.

2. *Specific goals desired:*
   Specific objectives - what is expected within the department.
   What is expected to have been completed and when.
   Organizational goals - what the company expects from the department.

3. *Imposed limits:*
   The authority and responsibility he is being given.
   Applicable guidelines, policies and procedures.

Once the assigned tasks, organizational goals and specific objectives, responsibilities and guidelines have been communicated to the employees, the supervisor should conduct periodic evaluations on the progress of assignments. The supervisor must maintain open lines of communication. He should check the progress of subordinates as well as evaluate them upon the completion of assignments.

Effective delegation can free a supervisor from time-consuming routine tasks, leaving him/her time for more important and sensitive matters. Some supervisors avoid delegating because they fear that a subordinate may make a costly mistake or perform the task better. Some fear losing control or prestige. However, if employees are adequately trained, given thorough instructions and the supervisor imposes effective controls and makes follow-ups, costly mistakes can be avoided.

Decision-making and Problem Solving

Supervisors must be decisive. When the time for action arrives, the supervisor must take immediate action. Failure to take action may result in confusion, workers' misunderstanding of what needs to be done, and a loss of respect for the supervisor because his failure to make a prompt decision has exhibited a lack of good judgement, knowledge and experience.

Supervisors cannot make all of the decisions that arise each day. Therefore, they should allow subordinates to make some decisions and provide feedback in making other decisions. Some decisions are repetitive and routine. Guidelines can be established to permit subordinates to make these decisions. Decisions that are new or unusual with no pre-established guidelines and procedures, occur less frequently. These decisions are usually more demanding or difficult and should be made by the supervisor. Short-range decisions, involving little risk or uncertainty of the outcome, should be delegated to subordinates. Long-range decisions involving more risk and uncertainty should be made by the supervisor.

There are six steps in successful decision-making:

A	-	Analyze the problem and gather data.
C	-	Consider the alternative solutions.
T	-	Take action - select a solution.
I	-	Implement the solution.
O	-	Ongoing evaluation. Continuously evaluate the solution with feedback from employees.
N	-	Need for change. This is modification of the original solution.

The ability to be decisive as well as to seek advice from others contributes to the decision-making process.

A supervisor must assess the strengths and weaknesses of his/her subordinates as well as himself/herself. A supervisor must acknowledge that reaching goals and objectives requires teamwork from supervisors and employees, not just from employees. When confronted with new tasks, an effective supervisor will therefore ask for and encourage feedback from employees. By using this approach, every member of the staff will feel a sense of belonging and involvement in the setting of solutions and procedures.

Performance Evaluation

Formal evaluations should be conducted at least annually and informal evaluations conducted as often as monthly. There are many reasons for conducting employee performance evaluations. Some of these reasons include:

1. Determining whether each employee is performing his or her job satisfactorily.
2. Determining whether an employee's performance level calls for reward or corrective action.
3. Determining whether an employee has potential for advancement.
4. Determining an employee's attitude to develop a better understanding of his or her needs, wants and expectations.
5. In order to establish a plausible plan of action to remedy any negativity that exists or effect a pleasant working environment for all.

During evaluations, the supervisor should discuss both positive and negative conduct and performance matters. It is just as important to reinforce or reward good performance as it is to curtail or punish poor performance. Praise can be given for positive performance. When discussing poor performance, focus on the process or the reason why the performance is inadequate, not just the negative performance itself. when discussing negative conduct and performance matters, also discuss ways for improvement and the anticipated time-frame for such improvement. Remember an evaluation is a discussion. Both the supervisor and employee discuss the negative performance and ways to improve.

During an evaluation, objectively rate each performance standard. Excellence in one area does not translate into excellence in other areas. Evaluations are also a time to list and clarify your expectations for future performance.

One thing to avoid in evaluations is judging one employee against another. There should be set standards from which you base your evaluation. Do not let your prejudices and biases affect your rating of employees. Do not rate the person, rate the performance.

Discipline

Many supervisors view discipline only as punishment; however, true discipline should be a learning experience. Discipline should be used as a corrective function first and as a last resort for punishment. Using and viewing discipline only as punishment may result in more disciplinary problems. discipline should be fair, firm and consistent to avoid future problems. For example, if a supervisor plays "favorites" in using discipline, resentment will occur. If individuals are permitted to violate rules, morale will decrease along with their respect for the supervisor.

To be effective, discipline should be administered as soon as possible after a violation occurs or a performance problem arises. Whenever possible, disciplinary actions should be conducted in privacy. Discipline should not be used to humiliate the offender, but rather to improve performance, adherence to rules or to remedy a problem. Further, discipline should be commensurate with the infraction.

Prior to disciplining an employee, gather all the facts. Permit the employee to tell his/her side of the story. At this time, if it is apparent that discipline should be administered, inform the employee of the offense, the action you intend to take, the reason for this action, and discuss methods to improve performance. Follow up to ensure adherence to the standards or rules.

Training

Training is used to teach knowledge, skills and attitudes. It is essential in the development of an efficient work force. This is especially true of supplemental or continuing training. Further, training challenges employees and provides an opportunity for growth and a sense of accomplishment. It also makes the employees feel as if the company is interested in them and their careers. Training is an effective motivator. The end result will be a more content, efficient and devoted employee.

Before setting up a training program, it must first be decided what training is needed. To do this, consider the goals and mission of the company and department. Make an inventory of essential skills necessary to perform duties in accordance with the mission and goals. This will provide a list of subjects all employees must learn.

Additional training needs can be determined through performance appraisals, observation of employees (performance not meeting expectations) and employee surveys. Training should also be conducted for new processes or procedures. The greater the knowledge a supervisor has of his/her employees, the easier it is to identify their strengths and weaknesses.

Once training needs are established, instructors must be obtained, lesson plans formulated and instructional aids provided. Training should then be conducted and periodically evaluated through testing or observation of employee performance. Methods and materials for training should suit the course or subject being taught. For example, some subjects may only require classroom instruction, while others may require classroom instruction coupled with hands-on instruction or on-the-job training.

One method of training encompasses identifying the strengths of employees and then allowing them to instruct classes in their area of expertise. This permits employees to learn from one another, have a sense of contribution and feel important.

Active training programs should be established to show employees that they are important and management is interested in increasing the efficiency of operations. An active training program increases employees' willingness to work, improves morale, leads to better communication, improves the company's reputation and fosters public relations through a more efficient and courteous workforce.

Some warning signs that may indicate a need for training are:
        Poor quality or quantity of work
        Failure to meet department obligations
        Low morale or disloyalty
        Excessive turnover
        Confusion
        Poor safety record
        Supervisor is constantly tied up with routine work

Some common training pitfalls to avoid are: teaching too quickly (often leads to a frustrated pupil), trying to teach too much material (a person will only retain so much material in a day), viewing all trainees in the same manner (some people retain material easier than others), not providing adequate time to practice (practice makes perfect), and not providing positive reinforcement (encouragement and praise reinforce the learning process).

Other common mistakes that supervisors make in instructing are:
        Being impatient
        Not judging the learner's interests
        Not adapting the instruction to the individual
        Not keeping the learner interested
        Not finding out the learner's background
        Telling or showing alone
        Not following up on instruction
        Not teaching in logical sequence (simple to complex)
        Lack of preparation for instruction

A.   Training Cycle

1.   *What must be taught.* The instructor must initially decide what general and technical knowledge is required for efficient job performance. He/she should ask himself/herself the following questions:

What steps would I go through to perform this job or task?
What occurs at each step?
What do I have to know about each step?

By asking and answering these questions, he/she should then be able to produce a simple lesson plan. This lesson plan should indicate the name of the course, important steps to complete the task and the key points the learner should know at each step.

2.   *Determine how much to teach.* Once the supervisor has identified the tasks that make up the job, he/she must teach each task in a separate lesson. Each unit or task should be small enough to be covered in a single lesson, complement other lessons, be complete, worthwhile and taught in a logical sequence.

3.   *Conduct the training.* Before beginning instruction, all materials and equipment must be obtained and ready.

4.   *Determine extent of learning.* Oral, written and performance testing of the learners must be conducted periodically to determine whether they are adequately learning the units being taught. If the entire class does poorly on testing, the instructor may need to re-evaluate his teaching methods and adjust them accordingly.

5.   *Maintain records of training.* Maintain documented records of what each person is taught. This information is vital for identifying additional training needs, aiding in litigation avoidance and for decision-making and problem solving situations that may occur.

B.   The Four Step Method of Instruction

Developed by Charles Allen for use in trade instruction, the *Four Step Method of Instruction* has been adopted universally by various governmental and industrial agencies for breaking in new employees and upgrading the knowledge and skills of old employees. The *Four Step Method* is considered simple to learn, easy to apply and economical to use. It consists of a series of steps that are considered equally important, to be adhered to without omissions. It can be applied to any type of instruction, regardless of how simple or complex, and is suitable for both individual and classroom teaching.

1.   *Preparation*—Get the learner's mind ready to receive the instruction—the "warm up."
    a)   Put the learner at ease.
        Project a friendly, helpful attitude.
        Speak slowly.
        Minimize the job—tell the learner that there will be plenty of time to learn.
        Show confidence in the learner's ability.
    b)   Associate present instruction with past knowledge and background of the learner.
        Find out about the background of the learner.
        Show relation of previous jobs or skills to the new one(s).
    c)   Secure attention, arouse interest and create the desire to learn.
        Be enthusiastic.
        State the job to be learned.
        Explain the job's importance and significance.
        Give the overall picture.
        Tell the learner the advantage(s) of learning this job.

2.   *Presentation*—Tell and show.
    a)   Show and explain the job.
    b)   Use the lesson plan (see the previous section, the "Training Cycle").
    c)   Perform the whole job through yourself.
    d)   Repeat the demonstration step-by-step while explaining each step.
    e)   Be sure to define any technical terms and provide related information.
    f)   Position the learner so as to face the same direction as yourself.

g) Emphasize key points and their sequence.
h) Stress any safety points.
i) Go slow—adjust the speed to the learner.
j) Set a good example.
k) Limit details (the average person can only remember about seven points in one lesson.
l) Keep in mind how difficult it was for you to learn the job, what helped and how you learned it step-by-step.

3. *Application*—Check the learner for understanding.
  a) Allow the learner to do the job under supervision.
      Change places with the learner.
      Allow the learner to perform the job while explaining each step prior to their attempt.
      Summarize key points.
  b) Develop confidence.
      Praise.
      Allow the learner to perform the job several times under supervision.
  c) Correct errors.
      Observe carefully and correct errors before they occur.
      Re-instruct when necessary.
      Be patient.
  d) Ensure understanding.
      Ask questions about each step (avoid "yes" or "no" answers by starting questions with "why, how, when, what or where").
  e) Develop good work habits.
      Re-stress key points.
      Emphasize correct practice and allow adequate practice.
      Illustrate "trade tricks" and "shortcuts" to make the work easier without skimping on results.
  f) Re-teach, if necessary.
      Repeat, re-demonstrate.

4. *Follow up*—Final evaluation.
  a) Determine whether the learner can perform the job independently.
      Allow the learner to perform the job alone.
      Inform the learner of where to obtain help.
  b) Display continued interest.
      Check occasionally and give additional information and advice.
      Encourage questions and suggestions.
      Avoid fault-finding.
      Praise.
  c) Determine the extent of learning, areas requiring re-teaching and the efficiency of instruction.
      Conduct performance test.
      Conduct oral test.
      Conduct written test.
      Have discussion.

The following is an example of areas a comprehensive training program for security instruction may cover:

History of Law Enforcement and Security
Field Notes and Report Writing
Observation and Memory
Patrol Techniques
Safety
Traffic Control
Crowd Control
Crime Scene Procedures
Physical Security Systems

Bomb Threats
Alarm Systems
Fire Prevention
Hazardous Materials
Strikes, Lockouts, and Labor Relations
Emergency Planning and Disaster Control
VIP Protection, Hostage Conditions
Human Relations
Interviewing Techniques

Stress Management
Crisis Intervention   Substance Abuse
Security Awareness   Legal Aspects
Security Investigations   Physical Fitness
Managing Employee Honesty   First Aid

The sample program would not only provide knowledge in various essential areas of security, but also would allow for indication of areas of weakness.

In addition to the above sample program, additional training and development of skills such as use of restraints, use of batons and weapons, self-defense, use of fire-fighting apparatus, traffic and crowd control, photography and report writing could be especially useful for security personnel. These can be best developed by allowing personnel to learn and practice these tasks until competency is acquired.

Training is an ongoing function of an effective supervisor. Continuous training not only provides the company with a more efficient workforce, but also a more satisfied one. Training provides advantages for the employee, the supervisor and the company. The advantages for the employee include increased chance for success, improved motivation and morale. The advantages for the supervisor include getting to know the employees better, gaining time by being able to relinquish duties to subordinates as they learn how to perform the duty, furthering his/her career because the supervisor's reputation and leadership abilities reflect positively and subordinates display positive attitudes, and increased work performance and productivity. The advantages to the company are reduced hazards in work performance, more efficient workers, increased productivity, and reduced chance for successful litigation against the company for failure to train, failure to supervise, negligent retention, and for other matters resulting from inadequately trained personnel.

SUPERVISION AND TRAINING
QUIZ

1.   Leadership is the ability to inspire others to willingly work toward company goals and _____ _____.

2.   A supervisor is a symbol of management to his _____.

3.   Human relations is the study and prevention or _____ of problems that occur at work.

4.   Keep the employees informed and promptly eliminate _____.

5.   Studies show that supervisors spend approximately _____ of their time communicating.

6.   Supervision is the ability to inspire others to willingly work toward company goals.
      □ T   □ F

7.   Leadership is the authority given a supervisor by management.
      □ T   □ F

8.   Supervisors have responsibility to subordinates, peers and superiors.
      □ T   □ F

9.   If most employees fail to learn during training, the supervisor should re-examine teaching methods.
      □ T   □ F

10.   Determining the strengths and weaknesses of a subordinate is a step in the delegation process.
      □ T   □ F

MAXIMIZING PERSONNEL DEPLOYMENT
by Alexander M. Hay, CPO, CSS

"Maximizing personnel deployment" means using the officers on your team in the most efficient and cost-effective manner possible to service the range of duties that are within your area of responsibility.

In order to achieve this objective, you will need to have a thorough understanding of the duties for each position together with full knowledge of your officers' skills and abilities. This process will require that you have a basic understanding of the "Canadian Human Rights Act;" some questions, unless directly related to occupational requirements, could be taken as discriminatory, e.g. questions on physical ability, etc. Additionally, you will find that to be successful you will have to utilize a number of the skills dealt with in greater detail in other chapters of this manual, such as interviewing skills including the ability to read body language.

IDENTIFYING POSITION REQUIREMENTS

There are two elements you have to consider:
1.   The position to be filled, and
2.   The person most suited for the position.

These factors need to be studied in detail in order to achieve the closest possible match of any individual officer to a specific position.

In order to develop complete and full knowledge of these two elements, it is necessary to:
1.   Understand the position—examine the position in detail and determine all the elements involved.
2.   Understand your security officers—you have to reach the stage where you have an in-depth understanding of your officers.

Understand the Position

It is necessary to fully comprehend the in-depth requirements of the position to be filled in order to properly understand what will be required by an officer to be assigned to the situation as detailed.

To accomplish this, you will need to establish the following information:
a)   The duties to be performed.
b)   The responsibilities involved.
c)   The qualifications and/or level of training required in order to perform efficiently.

There are basically three ways of gathering this information:
a)   Observation
b)   Interview
c)   Questionnaire

Observation: This is best accomplished by accompanying an officer on the job as it exists. In the case of a new position, you should personally perform the duties listed in order to fully understand exactly what it entails together with the time factor involved. In both cases you will be required to make detailed notes of your observations.

Interview: Hold a discussion session with the incumbent officer to extract the officer's understanding of all the requirements called for. Get as much detail as possible from him/her regarding the duties of the position.

In the case of a newly established position, if you have any questions do not hesitate to discuss all the requirements with your colleagues, and if need be, a superior as to the best way the responsibilities of the position should be performed. You should never be reluctant to seek clarification; remember, the objective is to provide the ultimate possible service.

Questionnaire: Develop a list of questions that includes specifics regarding the duties performed or that will be required in a new position. This list can either be given to an incumbent or provide a basis for use at the interview. In the case of a new position, you yourself will be required to provide, or seek, a complete understanding of all related aspects of the position. Additionally, with respect to an existing position, it can be useful to examine log reports on this specific position for a period of several months to gain additional information.

Regardless of the use made of the question list, some examples of the questions that require answers are:

a)   What specific tasks are to be performed?
b)   What level of knowledge is required to efficiently perform the duties?
c)   What machinery and/or equipment is required to perform the duties?
d)   What are the physical requirements?
e)   Are there special environmental conditions to be taken into account?
f)   What are the stress factors involved?
g)   What, if any, unusual requirements exist?
h)   Are there any hazardous conditions?

Having now gathered all the relevant information, you should undertake a final review of the position by personally performing the duties, and consider all aspects of the job requirements with a critical eye. It is entirely possible that some small but relevant detail may have been overlooked. On completion of this exercise, you should have a complete understanding of all the requirements of the position, including the time required to perform efficiently all phases of the operation, together with the costs involved.

Understanding Your Security Officers

In some respects, gaining information about an officer already on your team is similar to interviewing applicants for a position with your company. However, in a well-organized company, you will have a distinct advantage as information relating to the individual under consideration is available in his/her personnel file. You will also have the advantage of already knowing each individual member of your team.

In achieving understanding of an officer, bear in mind that at this stage you are not trying to match him/her to a specific position; rather, you are interested in his/her ability to undertake progressively increasing responsibilities and authority when the opportunities arise.

When you show that you are interested and care enough to assist an officer to develop the capabilities to advance you can ordinarily be assured that he/she will endeavor to perform to the best of his/her ability at all times.

Review the personnel file carefully and decide what additional information is required in order to allow full and complete understanding of the officer's present and future potential.

You have to be the judge as to the areas wherein you require additional information. The following should provide some guidance to you:

1.   Level of training and understanding of security practices.
2.   Understanding and compliance with the "Protection Officer Code of Ethics."
3.   Awareness of the necessity to handle stressful situations.
4.   Ability to perform in physically demanding situations.
5.   The skill of understanding the importance of not just hearing, but listening and relating to others.
6.   A full and comprehensive understanding of company policies.
7.   The essential and proper interpretation of feedback.

With respect to areas 3, 4 and 5, exercise caution regarding specific questions as you may raise some very sensitive issues. Always ensure that you comply with the standards as set out in the "Canadian Human Rights Act" or, in the United States, "The Equal Employment Opportunity Commission."

1.   Level of Training: It would be advisable to develop some form of security quiz in order to allow proper assessment of the officer's training and understanding of security practices.
2.   Protection Officer Code of Ethics: In lieu of a security industry developed code of ethics, it is recommended that the code of ethics incorporated in the "Certified Protection Officer Training Manual" be adopted. Should the officer concerned be unaware of this program, he/she should be advised of its existence and be provided with a copy of the code. Regardless of the officer's prior knowledge, you must undertake to identify his/her personal ethical standard.

3. Stress Handling Capability: Some assurance regarding this ability can be obtained by observing the officer in the performance of his/her duties and through discussions with the officer. The use and understanding of body language is a very useful skill to apply in this particular instance.

4. Physically Demanding Situations: Most, if not all, security officer positions carry some physical demands, even if it is as simple as performing a foot patrol lasting an hour or more. Other situations could require a considerable amount of stair climbing to high levels.
    As a supervisor you will undoubtedly know the physical demands of positions under your jurisdiction and can therefore assess each officer's ability to perform, not just adequately but effectively.
    In order to achieve this, you have to endeavor to establish if the officer has any physical problems (unable to lift due to back, neck or shoulder problems, fear of heights, etc.). Bear in mind the caution and sensitivity that must be exercised in obtaining this kind of information. Knowledge of this nature can prove to be of value when determining in which position an officer can perform efficiently.

5. Relating to Others: No doubt in your experience you have met the security officer who performs his duties very well, but nevertheless is very abrasive in dealing with people and who listens without hearing. this type of officer does not advance the image of the security industry, and in your capacity as a supervisor you must endeavor to have the officer correct this attitude. This is an important factor to be taken into consideration when trying to achieve your objective of maximizing personnel deployment.

6. Understanding Company Policy: It is very important that the officer has a clear understanding of company policy as it relates to a position. A certain amount of flexibility should be allowed in the performance of the officer's duties, and he/she should be encouraged to discuss the areas wherein he/she considers it more efficient to introduce minor changes in the performance of the specified duties, given that the officer continues to operate within the bounds of company policy.

7. Importance of Feedback: An officer's understanding of feedback is very important. He/she must be made aware that authority, sufficient to permit efficient job performance and to allow him/her to display some initiative, will be delegated to him/her. Consequently, very clear ground rules must be developed with respect to reporting procedures (daily or weekly written reports plus periodic meetings with you to discuss the operation and ensure that actions taken remain within established guidelines). The questionnaire proposed in "Understanding the Position" could prove valuable to you with respect to written reports as it would enable you to assess how he/she expresses himself/herself in writing. Finally, remember that communication is in fact a two-way function. You have to keep him/her current on matters relating to the position and/or changes in policy.

THE FINAL SELECTION

Having completed the foregoing process of establishing the parameters for a specific position, together with your in-depth study of your officers, it now remains to determine the officer most suited to the position in question. It is more than likely that two or more officers prove to be suitable candidates. You, therefore, are faced with having to make the final choice.

In order to resolve this situation you are required to answer the question: "Why should officer A rather than officer B be assigned to this position?"

Unless you are prepared to make an arbitrary choice, the fairest method is to interview each officer for the specific position. The interviews must, for obvious reasons, be conducted with an open mind. Do not make any judgement until all officers have been interviewed.

THE INTERVIEW

Successful interviewing is an extremely useful skill to develop in business. However, it is not the intent to provide in-depth knowledge of interviewing techniques (this is provided elsewhere within this manual), but rather to provide some basic guidelines that you will find beneficial when you conduct interviews.

If, having arranged an interview with an officer, you proceed to ask a series of questions for which you already have the answers, then obviously at the end of the interview you know no more than you did at the beginning. In other words, you were not prepared for the interview and consequently you simply wasted the time of the officer, the company and yourself.

Prior to the interview you must take time to review the relevant position requirements and the officer's history. Then you must assess exactly what further information you require from the officer to enable you to successfully fill the position.

In preparing your list of questions to be asked, remember there are five basic types of questions. These are listed below and followed by a brief explanation of each type:

a)   Closed-ended
b)   Open-ended
c)   Heading
d)   Sensitive
e)   Hypothetical

Closed-ended: These types of questions invariably draw a yes or no answer or a brief factual response. While on the whole they should be avoided, they can be a useful way to obtain specific facts.

Open-ended: This type requires more than a simple yes or no answer; rather it makes the officer give an answer that he/she has had to give some thought. In other words, it allows the officer to respond in his/her own way and at the same time does not make him/her feel defensive. In addition, it causes the officer to carry more of the conversation, making it easier for you to assess his/her thinking and how well she/he communicates.

Heading: Avoid this type as it tends to indicate the answer expected. Examine your questions carefully to be sure that the appropriate answer is not being suggested. After all, you are seeking information, not providing it.

Sensitive: It is unlikely that at this stage you would require to ask any sensitive questions. You have, after all, previously studied his/her personnel file and completed a review of him/her. However, should it prove necessary to include this type of question, it should only be asked once an atmosphere of trust and respect has been established, and it must be handled with considerable tact.

Hypothetical: These types are designed such that by the answer given, you are able to gain insight to the officer's problem-solving and decision-making skills. They do not necessarily require a specific answer; indeed, there could be several acceptable answers. They are the best type of questions to enable you to assess the officer. However, they do require very careful thought to develop.

Having worked your way through all these details you, as a supervisor, are now in the position of having a thorough in-depth understanding of all positions under your control and all the security officers on your team.

However, having expended the energy and time to complete the process it follows that you must remain knowledgeable with respect to both:

a)   The positions, and
b)   Your officers.

The positions: Job positions can and do change. Changes can be major and have an immediate effect, and such corrective action as may be required can be instituted very quickly. Other changes, however, can and often are individually minor, but if a number of changes continue to be made over a period of time they can end up as major changes; this would then require a reassessment of the position.

Major, or an accumulation of minor, changes may very well affect the costs of performing the duties of the modified position. It could reflect increased costs, or the changes could have been introduced in an attempt to reduce operational costs. Either way, this is a factor that you must ensure is reported to your superiors.

If your organization is a public security company serving a number of clients then it may, depending on the extent of the changes that have taken place, be necessary that the contract be renegotiated in order to keep costs in line. On the other hand, if you are part of a company's own security force, the information is still most important as it could materially affect budget considerations.

Your officers: It is equally important that your knowledge of your officers remain current and up to date. This information is vital to you when it comes to the officer's annual review and also in the event that a promotion is being considered. In addition, your officers will be aware of your interest in their development and should respond positively.

SUMMARY

It is essential that in order to achieve the required results, you acquire in-depth knowledge of:
1.   The Positions:
   a)   What are the duties?
   b)   What are the responsibilities?
   c)   What specific qualifications are required?
   This information is obtained by:
   a)   Close observation
   b)   Detailed interview
   c)   Questionnaires related to duties
2.   Your Personnel:
   a)   Their level of training
   b)   Their ethics
   c)   Stress handling
   d)   Physical ability
   e)   Relating to others
   f)   Understanding of company policy
   g)   Reporting procedures
Having obtained as much information as possible, you then are required to match officers to positions. This, as stated, can lead to the necessity of further interviews.

Develop your ability to conduct interviews; this skill will always prove useful to you and could conceivably assist in your future growth within your organization.

Remember that this base of information, regarding both positions and personnel, can be invaluable to you, but only if you are diligent in ensuring that you keep it correct.

MAXIMIZING PERSONNEL DEPLOYMENT
QUIZ

1.   What level of _____ is required to efficiently perform the duties?

2.   Review the personnel _____ carefully and decide what additional information is required.

3.   The Equal Employment _____ Commission.

4.   Regardless of the officer's prior _____, you must undertake to identify his/her personal ethical standard.

5.   Unless you are prepared to make an _____ choice, the fairest method is to interview each officer for a specific position.

6.   It is not important to fully understand the position to be filled.
            ☐ T   ☐ F

7.   Closed-ended questions are useful to obtain in-depth information.
            ☐ T   ☐ F

8.   During an interview you should not ask questions that confirm information you already possess.
            ☐ T   ☐ F

9.   Positions should be filled on a seniority basis.
            ☐ T   ☐ F

10.   Future changes to a position have little or no impact on operating budgets.
            ☐ T   ☐ F

DEALING WITH DIFFICULT EMPLOYEES
by Ivan E. Pollock, CPO, CSS

As a supervisor, you will be dealing with many different people, each one having their own unique personality. Most people, however, fit into a grouping of five different types. It is important that you determine which category applies to each individual employee in order to know the basics of how to deal with that particular person.

DETERMINING PERSONALITY TYPES

1. *Political:* These people are generally more aggressive and demanding; they always look out for themselves and can be very intimidating. To motivate political people, give them some authority and control where possible but make it clear that you are the person in charge. You should be very direct; tell them the end results that are expected and give them a completion date.
2. *Aesthetic:* These people are very creative and this creativity will always show up in some aspect of their work. To motivate these people, give them the freedom to be creative where possible. For set jobs or procedures, explain why specific methods must be used. Tell them what the standard is; then ask them how we can attain it. They will perhaps require time to do this; as the supervisor you will have to determine if the time required is feasible.
3. *Social:* These people interact a lot with others, they are motivated and are generally productive. These people often speak without thinking. To motivate them, set time frames in which to complete tasks. Ensure you praise them for work that is well done. In dealing with these people, it is important to ensure they have enough to do. Lack of sufficient work to fill time will result in this employee disturbing other employees from doing their jobs.
4. *Economic:* These people are analytical by nature. They are very detailed, are good planners and usually do things "by the book." These people are motivated to a great extent by information. Let them know that they are right but at the same time watch that they don't spend too much time doing a simple task. In dealing with these people, you may have to tell why a job is to be done in a specific way.
5. *Theoretical:* These people are highly technically skilled people. They often know more than the supervisor about the job specifics or the mechanics of the job. To motivate these people, communicate deadlines for when a job is to be done. In dealing with these people you could use the word "hypothetically"; they will usually think it out and come back with what you want, but believing it's their idea.

Now that the five personality types have been identified, you would think it would be very easy to put each of your direct reports into one of these categories and use the guidelines I have given for dealing with them. In most cases this will work. In each of these personality types, however, there is the "difficult" employee.

Each of the five personality types can be considered difficult for a unique reason. They can be argumentative, unhappy, angry, talkative or arrogant. Some may be loners or non-talkers while others may complain constantly or be very indecisive.

The following pages identify various traits of employees that make them difficult. These people can cause major problems in your department regardless of the type of business you are involved in. They must be dealt with effectively or morale in the department will most certainly go down.

THE INDECISIVE EMPLOYEE

The indecisive employee is similar to the talkative one and can most certainly take up a lot of your time. These indecisive individuals generally don't trust their own judgement and are often afraid of making the wrong decision.

Some of these approaches should work:

1. Be patient; if you try to rush them, matters will become worse. Suggest that they refer to your company procedures and instruction manual. It is better to point out where to find the answer than to just give it to them. Do, however, follow up to ensure that they found the answer.

2.   Try to create a relaxing environment; if you show understanding and stay calm, you will make them feel more confident and able to make a decision.
3.   Try to set limits; if you can find out ahead of time what they need, you can direct them at that time to research their own answer and therefore make a decision.

THE ANGRY EMPLOYEE

The angry employee delivers this emotion with two basic messages; one is based on fact and the other based on his or her personal feelings. The supervisor must distinguish between the two and get past the feelings to deal with the facts. Avoid saying things like "don't be angry" or "calm down, there is no reason to be upset." Phrases such as these will only make the person angrier.
Try some of these techniques to calm the person:
1.   Keep your own emotions in check and concentrate on the facts being stated and not the words themselves. Try to see past the anger. Very often, the person's anger and frustration have nothing to do with the problem he is having with your company. It may have been brought on by unrelated problems such as an argument with a spouse, or a personal family problem. You can deal with the employee more effectively if you know that there are other contributing factors.
2.   Try not to be defensive or you will feel that the anger is being directed at you. This is rarely the case. Try to be sympathetic even though you may find the person's problem is minor or insignificant. Listen carefully, tell him/her you understand he/she is frustrated and assure him that you will try to help him resolve the problem. Do not, however, agree with criticism of your company. If you agree, you will be telling him/her that he/she is right in being angry, or he/she will lose his respect for you knowing that you, the supervisor, do not support your own company.
3.   Stress what you can do to help resolve the problem, not what you can't do. Negotiate a solution that is acceptable to you and the employee. It is important that you don't promise to do something that you cannot do. It is also important that you do act to bring about the solution to which you agreed.

THE ARGUMENTATIVE EMPLOYEE

The argumentative employee is someone who thrives on arguments. They are always aggressive people who will not agree with anything you say, or at the very least will question what you say. Do not allow yourself to deal with this person on the same level of behavior by disagreeing and arguing back. This is very possibly the only reaction they were trying to get.
Try these approaches:
1.   It is important that you speak softly. Loud speaking will result in a louder response and very quickly result in a shouting match.
2.   Due to their aggressive nature, these employees like to feel that they are in control of the situation. If they feel they are losing that control they will become more argumentative. Try asking that employee for his or her opinion. Often they will have a good idea which they just don't know how to present in any other manner. If there is a positive point that you agree on, be sure to say so.
3.   It is very easy with this type of person to become irritated and angry yourself. If you feel this is happening, ask the person to leave your office and return in five minutes. If the location does not allow for that, excuse yourself from the conversation and take time to regain your composure.

THE NON-TALKER

The non-talker is a particularly difficult employee to deal with because of the fact that he or she is so quiet. He/she may not be sure of himself/herself or may be doing a great job operationally but just has a hard time expressing himself/herself. It is important that this employee first be identified to ensure that he/she does in fact do a good job and to ensure that you don't lose a good employee because he/she feels unnoticed or unimportant.
With the non-talker you must be patient and make him/her feel at ease. Ask questions that require short answers as opposed to long elaborate ones. The employee should feel quite comfortable

with this. Watch for body language transmitted by this employee. He/she may be agreeing verbally with what you are saying, but his/her facial expression is saying something else. Make a point of speaking with this individual at every encounter even if it is simply to say "Good Morning" or "How was your weekend?" These are nonthreatening questions/comments and you should get an open response. It may take time to get this employee to speak freely but do not give up on him or her. They are usually a real asset to your company.

THE HABITUAL COMPLAINER

The habitual complainer doesn't like anybody or anything. This type of person must be considered dangerous to your department as a whole as he/she will bring down morale on his/her shift or team and it can eventually spread through the whole department.
The following techniques may work:
1.   If this habitual complainer speaks to you about a concern, try to be open and let him/her talk. If the complaint is in fact legitimate, take the appropriate action necessary to correct the cause of it.
2.   If you hear of constant complaining in the department, you should speak with the person originating the complaint and make it clear to them that their complaints must be directed to you, the supervisor. At the same time, you should let the employees on the receiving end of the complaints know that they should redirect the complaints and not listen to them.
3.   As a supervisor, it is up to you to distinguish between legitimate and frivolous complaints because it becomes easy to assume, in this employee's case, that none of his/her complaints are legitimate.

CONCLUSION

Dealing with nice employees is easy. Difficult people, on the other hand, can be a challenge. Through proper handling of these challenging people, you will gain loyal employees for your department and therefore your company. You will, at the same time, gain a very rewarding personal satisfaction.
Keep in mind that you will not always be successful in dealing with difficult employees. You may have to ask for the expertise of your personnel department or recommend to the employee that he or she seek the council of the company employee assistance program, if available.
As I have mentioned, each individual personality is unique even though we all fit somewhere in the five personality types. In dealing with all employees, I would put it all into one line by saying: "BE PARTICIPATORY WHEN YOU CAN – BE AUTOCRATIC WHEN YOU HAVE TO BE."
I am sure that you have read many articles dealing with difficult people and the advice given was about the same, just stated in slightly different ways. It is up to you, the supervisor, to use the advice or not. I have personally used it with very successful outcomes and sincerely hope that it will help you.

DEALING WITH DIFFICULT EMPLOYEES
QUIZ

1.   These people are generally more _____ and demanding.

2.   The _____ employee is similar to the talkative one.

3.   The _____ employee is someone who thrives on arguments.

4.   The _____ is a particularly difficult employee to deal with.

5.   Dealing with _____ employees is easy.

6.   Political people are generally aggressive and demanding.
            □ T   □ F

7.   Economic people generally do things their own way.
            ☐ T   ☐ F

8.   Difficult employees can severely alter department morale.
            ☐ T   ☐ F

9.   You should speak loudly and aggressively to an argumentative employee.
            ☐ T   ☐ F

10.   Using the guidelines given, you will always be successful handling difficult employees.
            ☐ T   ☐ F

UNETHICAL ACTS BY SECURITY OFFICERS
by Neal E. Trautman, M.S.

Security administrators must be held accountable for having the courage to "do the right thing" when it comes to instilling integrity and preventing unethical acts by security officers.

The security field is a very demanding profession. While many aspects need improvement, no need is more important than preventing officers from giving in to anger, lust or greed.

THE PROBLEM

Anger, lust and greed devastate good people and destroy great organizations. Many victims suffer; the family or accused officers are humiliated, fellow officers are ridiculed and individuals and companies may be devastated financially.

Some people assert it is unrealistic to believe security officers will abide by high ethical standards while others feel that high ideals and integrity are worthy objectives, yet remain impractical in real life. This is not true.

LEADERSHIP, COURAGE AND PREVENTING CORRUPTION

Most security companies or departments have never provided any form of ethics training. The reason for this is that most administrators must still be educated about the need for this kind of training while others would rather not face the issues of ethics or corruption at all.

Transforming ethics from the backseat to a compelling high priority is difficult. The two essential ingredients required are courage and a better way of ethics training.

Courage usually requires putting your own fears aside to get the job done. As a term, courage is very subjective. Most dictionaries define it with words implying the ability to meet danger or difficulty with unwavering bravery. We are less familiar with another form of courage: the type of courage required for a supervisor or administrator to actively prevent corruption. It is my opinion that chief administrators face more ethical challenges than cops working the street.

Historically, most administrators have failed miserably when it comes to preventing corruption. Few have ever done more than talk about supporting ethics and professionalism. Corrupt security officers are disciplined or fired and administrators seldom do more.

It takes a lot of courage for the person at the top to do the right thing when corruption strikes. Many administrators do little more than what is "politically safe" for themselves, not what is best for their company. The security profession suffers and good security officers gradually experience a loss of self-respect and loyalty.

Leadership is the foundation for preventing unethical acts. Regardless of rank, a leader's actions serve to guide security officers facing ethical dilemmas. Poor supervision generates bad attitudes, and bad attitudes promote unethical acts. Finally, corruption destroys lives.

WHY UNETHICAL ACTS OCCUR IN THE SECURITY PROFESSION

1. The security profession, like most professions, has a history of corruption.
2. Most security officers have never received ethical decision-making training.
3. Some security officers experience temporary selfishness when faced with temptation.
4. Many security officers do not have strong, ethical role models.
5. Many officers are afraid of paying the price for "doing the right thing" as a result of peer pressure.
6. Security companies neglect to provide assistance for stress.
7. The hiring process is inadequate.
8. Internal training is usually inadequate.
9. Very few security companies have a process that prevents unethical acts from occurring.
10. Administrators create a working environment that promotes distrust and resentment instead of loyalty and respect.
11. The security profession has a reactive, not a pre-active view toward unethical acts.
12. The security profession's code of ethics is not meaningful enough.

13.   Security companies lack procedures to identify and deal with officers who exhibit tendencies consistent with unethical behavior.

LEADERSHIP COMMITMENT FOR CHANGE

The first step in preventing corruption is to attain leadership commitment for change. Administrators must show they believe in the pursuit of ethics and the foundation for demonstrating such commitment is a mission statement. Make ethics a vital part of the current mission statement or, if there is no mission statement, write one. Although developing a mission statement is essential, how it's written is just as important. Do not develop it alone; rather, get the entire company involved; ownership will result.

All aspects of the company should be guided by the mission statement which has a clear ethical direction. Goals are then developed to guide all efforts toward achieving the mission, and objectives are written to assist in reaching each goal. Positive leadership will fuel self-esteem and remove obstacles to attaining these goals.

Initial commitment for preventing corruption can be demonstrated by:
- Assisting in the development of the ethical aspects of a mission statement, goals and objectives
- Participating in the organization's first ethics in-service training
- Being an ethical model
- Ensuring all employees are treated with respect and fairness

The path to becoming a truly ethical organization begins with the administration's commitment. Making the commitment may be more difficult than it appears. Most managers and supervisors feel they have already made such a commitment. After all, they are dedicated, sincere and loyal to the highest ideals of the security profession.

It is traditional management that can generate difficulties in carrying out the commitment, where old principles of leadership must often be transformed. Without knowledgeable and respectful supervision, all efforts to prevent corruption will be perceived as meaningless.

TRAINING SECURITY OFFICERS TO MAKE ETHICS RELATED DECISIONS

Under pressure, people react the way they have been trained. Security organizations have never prepared officers to make difficult ethical decisions. They lack the skills and abilities to face ethical dilemmas because no one has provided them.

There are four primary reasons why good security officers do unethical things:
1.   They lie to themselves with excuses
2.   Momentary selfishness
3.   Bad ethics related decision-making
4.   They are afraid of peer pressure reaction for doing the right thing

Ethics decision-making training for officers is not difficult or time-consuming. It can be taught to most officers in 30 minutes. A summary follows.

What "Doing the Right Thing" Requires

It doesn't matter how difficult or stressful the situation, in order for your decision to be right, it must support ethical principles. You do this by:
- First setting aside illegal choices
- Then "doing the right thing"

"Doing the Right Thing" Requires Three Things
- Wanting to be ethical
- Acting on your good intentions
- Being able to think rationally

RATIONAL THINKING FOR ETHICAL DECISIONS

There are four steps to take when thinking about an ethical decision:
- Clearly understand the issues
- Evaluate the facts

- Make the decision
- Follow through

MAKING THE ETHICAL DECISION

When facing an ethical dilemma, run a series of tests through your mind. This will be invaluable in decreasing the emotion and temptation of the moment. Rather, objective, rational thinking will take its place. The tests can be used during a 5-second or 5-week period. Tests for facing ethical dilemmas include:

- How will it make me feel about myself in 20 years?
- What would I decide if I were being videotaped?
- Am I following the golden rule?
- What would I do if my loved ones were standing beside me?
- Is it legal?

ETHICAL TRAINING SCENARIOS

The security profession should do with corruption prevention training what has been done with police firearms training. Realistic, stressful, interactive video training must be developed.

Ethics dilemma scenarios can be developed relatively inexpensively without expensive videotaping. Trainers simply write ethical dilemmas, and officers role play the circumstances which have been presented to them via cassette tape recordings. Realism can be enhanced through sound effects, tape recordings and exercising. Exercising creates many of the physiological reactions an officer experiences during a stressful, ethical crisis.

THE CORRUPTION PREVENTION PROCESS

The security profession has always dealt with corruption by merely investigating charges of misconduct. If warranted, the concerned officer is typically reprimanded, suspended, fired or in extreme cases, arrested.

Developing and carrying out a highly effective and efficient, all-encompassing corruption prevention process is absolutely essential. Failure to have such a process is one of the primary reasons misconduct continues. To be effective the process must govern everything that may influence ethical conduct.

CONCLUSIONS

Ethics is the security profession's greatest training and leadership need. Our need has resulted, for the most part, from the failure of administrators to actively address corruption and ethics training.

Corruption cannot be eliminated. It can, however, be substantially prevented within any security organization. This can be accomplished, in part, by training security officers how to make ethical decisions. Afterwards, realistic dilemma training will allow them to practice making decisions during ethical dilemmas. This will cement the decision-making process into their long-term memory, and they will react the way they have been trained.

Lastly, security companies must stop viewing corruption as something we react to. Instead, it should be considered preventable. Administrators must maintain a process that prevents unethical acts.

UNETHICAL ACTS BY SECURITY OFFICERS
QUIZ

1.   Anger, lust and greed _____ good people.

2.   Historically, most _____ have failed miserably when it comes to preventing corruption.

3.   Security companies lack procedures to identify and deal with officers who exhibit _____ ____ consistent with unethical behavior.

4.   When facing an ethical _____ dilemma run a series of tests through your mind.

5.   The security professional has always dealt with corruption by merely _____ charges of misconduct.

6.   Most security companies or departments have been provided with a form of ethics training.
        ☐ T   ☐ F

7.   The first step in preventing corruption is to attain leadership commitment for change.
        ☐ T   ☐ F

8.   Ethics is the security profession's greatest training and leadership need.
        ☐ T   ☐ F

9.   Under pressure, people do not react the way they have been trained.
        ☐ T   ☐ F

10.   Corruption can be eliminated.
        ☐ T   ☐ F

APPENDIX A: A MODEL FOR ETHICAL DECISION-MAKING
by Christopher A. Hertig, CPP, CPO

Ethics. Ethics is the study of morals within a profession. It is based upon moral theory and applied to situations that present themselves every day. Aside from the theoretical aspects of the study of ethics, ethics is the practice of moral, professional behavior. Applied ethics is what we need to inculcate within the security industry if it is ever to become a true profession. Applied ethics is what security practitioners must master in order to avoid all the problems of making the wrong choices.

Security supervisors need to do all they can to develop ethical behavior among their subordinates. This will require that various, mutually supporting approaches to this be taken. It will mean a "war on several fronts." A few of the approaches that can be taken are:

1. Having a visible code of ethics displayed.
2. Modeling ethical behavior—leading by example.
3. Having officers sign a code of ethics or oath or office when being hired—and at regular (annual) intervals.
4. Maintaining a supervisory relationship where subordinates ask for clarification from supervisors on ethics questions.
5. Proper training in how to perform the job so that the probability of unprofessional behavior being manifested is minimized.
6. Training in ethics that enables officers or investigators to make ethical decisions.

The following acronym—PORT—is an easily employed ethical decision-making model. It provides a framework for how to make an ethical choice. As such it can, and should, be utilized for instructing subordinates in ethical decision-making.

The first component of the acronym is *Problem*. Defining the problem at hand is the first step in solving it. Writing a problem statement is the first step. As ethical dilemmas are conflicts or "hard choices" a problem statement can be composed in a simple manner by stating "There is a conflict between...."

The next step is *Options*. These are courses of action that can be taken by the problem solver. Many instances of poor decision-making occur when all of the available options are not seen by the person "owning" the problem. As with "brainstorming," the trick here is to list all of the imaginable options. Those that are ridiculous should also be listed. By putting all of the conceivable options out for assessment; the chances of picking the best one are improved.

Those options that cannot be seen cannot be employed.

Note that in many cases the best option is a hybrid between several that are listed. Two options are combined into a third option. This is another reason for listing as many courses of action as possible.

In all ethical decisions an option must be chosen and implemented.

The third step is *Responsibilities*. Persons making ethical choices have responsibilities to different entities. A protection officer being asked to ignore and cover up the brutal behavior of a coworker toward a detained person has responsibilities to the following entities:

him/herself	his/her family
the employer	the profession
the client (in some cases)	the public
employees	other officers
the law	local police
the suspect	

The amount of responsibility or obligation owed to each entity can be prioritized. They can be ranked numerically. As part of the decision-making process this should be done.

As with options, as many entities that the officer has responsibility towards should be listed as possible. There will be different entities listed for different situations: victims may be present, contractual relationships may be present, labor unions or media may also be involved. This varies. The important point is to list and prioritize as many entities that are affected by the course of action the officer decides to take as possible.

The final step is _Time_. The test of time. Very simply this is asking oneself about future feelings:

"How will I feel about myself in 20 years?"
"Will I be proud enough of the decision I made to tell my grandchildren about it?"

Instructors can simply present some realistic ethical dilemmas and have those in the class resolve them using the *PORT* acronym. This gives the students/subordinates/learners something useful that can be transferred onto the job.

MULTICULTURAL DIVERSITY
by Timothy D. Michener, M.S., CPP, CSS, CPO

INTRODUCTION

The first time I had heard the phrase "multicultural diversity" was in a training session at a professional seminar. I reluctantly went to the session more out of curiosity than anything else. About halfway through the session I became fascinated with the possibilities and benefits that the topic presented. Within two months of my introduction to multicultural diversity I was training security officers in the subject. I realized, as I hope you will, that multicultural diversity is an important topic for the security professional.

Before you can fully grasp this subject you will need to know some basics: 1) You will need to know that the subject of multicultural diversity is not new;   2) what the term multicultural diversity represents; and   3) why it's important for the security professional to understand it.

This chapter is not intended to change your attitudes toward a particular group of people or their culture; it is only intended to familiarize you with the information and make an effort to learn more about the many different people that you interact with.

ASSIMILATION, CULTURAL PLURALISM, MULTICULTURAL DIVERSITY

Multicultural diversity is a phrase that came into widespread use around 1970. It is sometimes referred to as ethnic diversity. Multicultural diversity is a label that is applied to a viewpoint that maintains that all cultures are important. Accordingly proponents believe, for example, that schools should teach history from the perspective of several different cultures. Before the phrase multicultural diversity, sociologists referred to the general subject area as "cultural pluralism." The theory of cultural pluralism holds that the various minority cultures (ethnic and racial) can retain their own culture while coexisting with the majority culture, thus enjoying equal access to the rewards of society. Of course in reality, the minority culture would not have equal access without having the ability to effect change within the political and economic areas.

Prior to cultural pluralism we referred to this subject area as "assimilation" or "Anglo-conformity." The success or failure of a particular culture in America depended largely upon its ability to be assimilated into the majority culture. Historians refer to Colonial America as a "Melting Pot." U.S. history boasts that persons of all nations were welcome in America. Of course that was not the case. The more similar a culture was to the majority Anglo culture, the easier it was for that culture to assimilate. Blacks, Asians and Native Americans did not fare as well as Germans, Italians or the Irish. From Anglo-conformity to cultural pluralism to multicultural diversity, the descriptive phrases have changed but the concept has been with us for a very long time.

DEFINING MULTICULTURAL DIVERSITY

Before we go any further we need to understand the phrase multicultural diversity. *Funk and Wagnall's Standard Dictionary* International Edition offers the following definitions:
   Multi - much or many
   Culture - The sum total of the attainments and activities of any specific period, race or people including their implements, handicrafts, agriculture, economics, music, art, religious beliefs, traditions, language and story.

Therefore multicultural diversity means the differences between cultures. The areas of diversity that we are concerned with are race, gender, sexual orientation, economic position, religion, and ability.

WHY STUDY MULTICULTURAL DIVERSITY?

There are many important reasons why we as security professionals need to understand diversity issues. Perhaps the most important reason deals with legislation. As security professionals we want to protect the assets of our employers. One way to do so is to eliminate risks of litigation. Many of these risks involve the way in which we deal with employees, co-workers, applicants, customers, guests, and visitors. To eliminate such risks we need to be aware of areas that afford constitutional protections to members of minority groups. We need to be aware of our institution's or company's policy on affirmative action, equal employment, discrimination, sexual harassment and persons with disabilities. Some of the key legislative initiatives in the United States were the Equal Employment Opportunity laws, Affirmative Action laws and the Civil Rights Act of 1964. You should also be aware that there are laws dealing with persons with disabilities, age and immigration.

The Equal Opportunity legislation and policies were designed to protect persons from discrimination based on age, sex, race and national origin. The premise of equal opportunity was that jobs were won by those who were qualified.

Affirmative Action legislation was the perceived cure to correct the racial disparity in certain occupations. Minority groups that were severely under-represented in certain occupations were given preferential treatment with respect to employment.

Title VII of the Civil Rights Act of 1964 prohibits discrimination on the basis of race, color, religion, national origin, and sex.

Secondly, the topic is current. Police officers and security professionals across the continent are being schooled in diversity issues. Take a look at the recent seminar agendas for the national professional security or police associations. Most, if not all, have sessions on multicultural diversity, cultural competence, inter-cultural communication or pluralism.

In 1993 the International Association of Campus Law Enforcement Administrators conducted a general survey of its members. That survey identified the top three issues for campus police and security administrators as: 1) budget/limited resources, 2) cultural diversity, and 3) violence/increased crime on or near campus. One hundred and eighteen out of the 163 respondents stated that their department has offered training on multicultural diversity. It makes sense to learn about the cultures of the people that we deal with. By learning more about them we are able to perform our jobs better.

Thirdly, the United States Department of Labor predicts that by the year 2005, two thirds of the entering work force will consist of minority workers (persons other than white males). As security professionals we need to recognize that the face of America is changing.

WHO WE ARE

Before the arrival of the Europeans in America, the area was inhabited by approximately five million Native Americans who were identified as belonging to about 300 different tribes. Each tribe had its own identity, customs and traditions. By 1890, 75 million people had immigrated to America. By 1890 the American Native population had dropped from nearly five million to less than 250,000. The Native Americans were not assimilated into the European culture. Historians estimate that nearly nine out of ten died as a result of their encounters with the Europeans, mostly as a result of diseases.

The culture in America was that of its European fathers. Initially, there were five main groups in America. The Spanish came to the new world in the early 16th century and settled in the Caribbean, Mexico, Florida and the Western Coast of South America. The French came to the new world in the early to mid 16th century and settled in the area known as the St. Lawrence River Valley. The Dutch and English arrived in the early 17th century and settled in the Mid-Atlantic and Northeastern regions of North America. The fifth group were the Portuguese who settled on the East Coast of South America.

After a number of conflicts North America was divided into the three countries that exist today. U.S. history refers to the United States as a "melting pot," a place that welcomed immigrants from all nations. The diversity of the United States has often been cited as its chief strength. Today the melting pot theory is largely rejected as inaccurate and misleading. The United States was a melting pot for the people who had Anglo features or could "Americanize" their names. It was not a melting pot for people of color.

By examining the United States census statistics you can see the changing face of America over the past four hundred years.

- In 1590, America consisted of approximately 5 million Native Americans.
- In 1690, there were approximately 213,500 people other than Native Americans in the United States.
- In 1790, there were approximately 4 million people other than Native Americans in the United States.
- In 1890, there were approximately 75 million people including 9 million slaves and approximately 250,000 Native Americans.

- In 1990, there were approximately 249 million people in the United States.
  - *White*   *199.6 million*
  - *Black*   *29.9 million*
  - *Hispanic*   *22.3 million*
  - *Asian*   *7.2 million*
  - *Native American*   *1.8 million*
  - *Other*   *9.8 million*

IMPLICATIONS FOR THE FUTURE

The face of America is changing. When Columbus arrived in America (1492), 96% of the population was Indian, the remainder was Pacific Islander. By 1790, 64% was white, 16% was Native American, 11% was black and 4% was Polynesian. By 1990, 74% of the population was white, 10% was black, 8% Hispanic, 3% Asian, 0.7% Native American and 4% other. In the past ten years the Asian population increased by 107%, the Hispanic population increased by 53%, the black population increased by 13% while the white population increased by only 6%. The face of America is changing and what this change means to me is that I need to be able to communicate with a variety of different people under a variety of different circumstances. In short, I need to become culturally competent.

To ensure cultural competence we need to develop a strong foundation. First of all we need to become aware of our own culture in order to learn about different cultures. Secondly, we must learn about the various cultures that we interact with on a daily basis. Finally, we need to understand the dynamics of cultural communication.

UNDERSTANDING OUR OWN CULTURE

How would you describe yourself? What is the color of your skin, your hair, your eyes? What church do you go to? What is your sex? Do you prefer men, women or both as partners? Are you poor, wealthy or middle class?

Our Jewish brothers have established a wonderful cultural training program through the Anti-Defamation League. The program takes the participant through a series of exercises designed to help the participant explore his own culture as well as a different culture via a "New Identify" form.

Use ADL's "New Identity" form to identify the following aspects of someone's culture that is different than your own. (If the person is not American, substitute his national origin/country in place of the word American.)

NEW IDENTITY

My cultural grouping is:
- *African American*
- *Asian American*
- *Caucasian American*
- *Native American*
- *Arab American*
- *Jewish American*
- *Latino American*

My religion is:
- *Catholic*
- *Protestant*
- *Judaism*
- *Moslem*

The economic class of my family is:
- *Poor*
- *Middle Class*
- *Wealthy*

My sexual preference is:
- *Lesbian*
- *Gay*
- *Bisexual*
- *Heterosexual*

My sex is:
- *Male*
- *Female*

My ability is:
- *High Intelligence*
- *Learning Disabled*
- *Blind*
- *Paraplegic*
- *Normal Intelligence*
- *Able Bodied*
- *Deaf*

* Courtesy of the ADL

Now that you have identified the specific aspects of someone else's culture, trade places and record how you feel toward members of your actual cultural group.

DISCOVERING THE CULTURES OF THE PEOPLE AROUND US

As security professionals we should make an effort to understand the cultures of the people that we deal with. One way of accomplishing this is to contact a group and ask them to send a representative to your organization to speak to you about their culture. Most identifiable groups have representatives that would welcome such an opportunity. If you arc unable to identify a representative organization, you may want to ask a member of the group of people that you interact with to address your department. To locate groups that offer educational programs in your area consult the *Encyclopedia of Associations* at your local library. Here are a few examples of representative organizations:

- Gay and Lesbian Alliance Against Defamation, New York, NY (212)807-1700
- National Association for Puerto Rican Civil Rights, New York, NY (212)996-9661
- NAACP Legal and Educational Fund, New York, NY (212)219-1900
- National Alliance Against Racist and Political Repression, New York, NY (212)406-3330

CULTURAL COMMUNICATION SKILLS

It is vital to our success in the security sector to develop communication skills. It is generally accepted that 90% of what we communicate is accomplished through non-verbal means. The problem is that all cultures do not interpret non-verbal language the same way. Our cultures determine how we reason, interpret and think. For example: to an American police officer, a man who gets out of his car when he is pulled over is a threat. A person from Libya not wanting to be rude to the policeman would exit his car and walk back to the policeman's car. The police officer might yell at the man from Libya to get back in his car. The Libyan driver may be very confused by the officer's actions. "Why would the police officer be so angry; didn't I reach him fast enough?"

Here is another example of cultural miscommunication. You are conducting an investigation into a broken window. When you arrive you see seven children playing in the immediate area. You approach the group of children and ask if they know anything about the broken window. An Asian child immediately looks down to the ground. You ask this Asian child directly and he responds but does not look at you when he speaks. Do you have a witness or a suspect? Most Americans would think that the "suspect" is trying to hide something – why else would he hide his eyes. In many Far Eastern cultures children are taught to look down when addressing authority figures. To look at the uniformed officer directly would be a sign of disrespect.

Suppose you are called to take a report of a theft from an office. You notice that the complainant is of Arab descent. Your host offers you a seat next to him. You sit down and cross your legs so that the bottom of your shoe is facing him. Your host appears upset and no longer wants to file a complaint. What went wrong? In the Arab culture it is rude to sit as described above. You have just told your host that you think he is beneath you – why else would you have pointed the bottom of your foot towards him?

The fact is that we do not interpret actions the same way. But how about gestures? Is there any gesture that you can think of that would be translated universally? Most groups that I ask this question to provide the example of an extended middle finger. So we'll examine that gesture. Variations on this gesture can include smacking your forearm while extending a fist. (The fist can be pointed up or down.) You could also convey this same thought by extending your four fingers while curving your thumb towards the palm of your hand. Depending on culture, they all convey the same thought.

For example, imagine that you are driving down the highway and a large sedan (with license plates that identify the occupants as being from the country of Afghanistan) cuts you off. Without hesitation you raise your fist and extend your middle finger. You assume that your fellow motorist understands your "universal" gesture because he responds with a gesture that you interpret as meaning "okay." You now feel you have successfully communicated a thought. The problem is that the Afghanistan national correctly interpreted your gesture and responded with a like gesture. You see, in Afghanistan the hand signal that Americans use for "okay" really means the same as extending your middle finger in America.

The point of this illustration is to demonstrate that different cultures interpret the same gestures differently. We have to recognize that the person we are attempting to communicate with may not understand what we are trying to say.

Dr. Jennifer Lund is a professor at the Georgia State University. In conjunction with the IACLEA she developed a videotape titled "If I Look Confused and Lost, It Is Probably Because I Am." The videotape is about 45 minutes long and is an excellent training tool for instruction in cultural communication. Dr. Lund lists twelve tips for improving communication with foreign students. We can use these twelve tips whenever we deal with people from different cultures.

Dr. Lund's Twelve Communication Tips
1.   *SMILE at me!*
2.   *NAMES are important. Try to pronounce my name. Your efforts will be appreciated.*
3.   *Tell it SIMPLY.*
4.   *WRITE it down for me, STEP BY STEP.*
5.   *If you don't know the answer send me to someone who does.*
6.   *Speak to me. Ask me: "How are you?" Be personal, not mechanical.*
7.   *Listen to my answers. Let me finish my sentence.*
8.   *Talk slower, not louder.*
9.   *Recognize me. I do not know too many people. I need to belong. Be interested. It's okay to ask me about my family and how things are or were done in my country. (Caution: Be sensitive about asking what things were done to or witnessed by students if they are refugees or have political asylum.)*
10. *When I omit something on a form or when I do not do the assigned task, I probably do not know what I am supposed to do. I need help yet I may not know the right question to ask. I may know the question but I may not know how to ask it. Help me by showing me. Your efforts will be appreciated.*
11. *Tell me if it is done differently here.*
12. *If I look lost it is probably because I am. It is your patience and attitude of helpfulness that made it possible for me to approach you, to learn from you.*

Communication is extremely important to the security professional. We need to be aware of what we are saying as well as how we are saying it. By understanding that different cultures may interpret our words or actions in a way other than was intended, we are better prepared to serve our customers.

TRAINING PROGRAMS

The programs listed below are representative of the many fine cultural diversity programs available. If you are interested in getting more information on these programs you should contact the organization directly.
•   Multicultural Competence Training Program of the Jewish Anti-Defamation League. Consult your local telephone book for the nearest organization.
•   Cultural Diversity: A Law Enforcement Perspective Training Program offered by the Michigan State University, School of Criminal Justice (517)355-9648
•   Training is available from your State Human Relations Commission. Consult your local telephone book for the regional address and telephone number.
•   "If I Look Confused and Lost, It Is Probably Because I Am." (Videotape) Excellent training tool for inter-cultural communication. Available from the IACLEA, 638 Prospect Avenue, Hartford, CT 06105-4298 (860)586-7517

SUMMARY

Multicultural diversity means the differences between cultures. The areas of diversity that we are concerned with are race, gender, sexual orientation, economic position, religion and ability.

The subject of multicultural diversity has been with us since the beginnings of civilization. In modern times we have referred to this subject area as assimilation, Anglo-conformity, ethnic diversity, and cultural pluralism.

As security professionals we need to have a general understanding of diversity issues. The following are valid reasons for studying multicultural diversity: 1) Legislative requirements make it necessary to understand diversity issues and how they can impact on the assets of your organization;

2) the topic of diversity is current; and 3) by the year 2005 two thirds of the entering work force will be minority workers – the face of America is changing.

MULTICULTURAL DIVERSITY
QUIZ

1.   It is generally accepted that _____% of what we communicate is accomplished by non-verbal means.

2.   The Civil Rights Act of 1964 prohibits discrimination based on _____, _____ _____, _____, and _____.

3.   As security professionals we need to study diversity issues: the topic is _____. By the year 2005, _____ of the work force will be minority workers; as a means to protect assets we need to be aware of _____ requirements such as equal employment laws.

4.   _____ _____ legislation was the perceived cure to correct the racial disparity in occupations in which minority groups were severely under-represented.

5.   Diversity is not new. In fact diversity has been around since _____.

6.   Today the "melting pot" theory is largely rejected as inaccurate and misleading.
            □ T   □ F

7.   All cultures interpret non-verbal language the same.
            □ T   □ F

8.   Our cultures determine how we reason, interpret and think.
            □ T   □ F

9.   Multicultural diversity in its simplest form means differences between cultures.
            □ T   □ F

10.   Multicultural diversity is a current topic among law enforcement and private security organizations as is evidenced by its inclusion in national association seminars.
            □ T   □ F

INTERPERSONAL COMMUNICATIONS
by *Guy Rossi*

Communication is a fundamental skill for those individuals entrusted to protect people and their property. There is no greater tool in law enforcement than the ability to communicate effectively with others. President Harry S. Truman once said, "We shall never be able to remove suspicion and fear as potential causes of war until communication is permitted to flow, free and open, across international boundaries." Good communication fosters two-way interaction between individuals and groups. Conversely, poor communication only leads to mixed messages, distrust and ultimately conflict. As a law enforcement officer the message delivered may lead to a positive interaction or a negative one. In fact, ineffective communication often is perceived by the listener as officiousness, rudeness and incompetence.

Therefore, interaction between law enforcement personnel and citizens may be categorized into the following basic areas:

1.   Social Dialogue
2.   Information Gathering or Disseminating
3.   Situational Leadership and Supervision
4.   Conflict Management

SOCIAL DIALOGUE: BREAKING THE ICE

I remember as a rookie street cop attending an in-service school on interview and interrogation. The course was presented by two homicide investigators who suggested polishing your social skills, specifically those dealing with initiating a conversation as a tool of a good interviewer. Remember, it is difficult for anyone to share information with another if they feel that they are being ignored or ridiculed. The speaker should avoid an opening line that will illicit a "yes" or "no" answer. When performed correctly the listener's response may be open ended and will likely lead to other avenues of dialogue. For example, asking someone about the weather or how they felt about a recent sports team win would likely result in a one-word response such as "good" or "great." Conversely, asking someone where he or she bought the coat they're wearing or complementing them on a child with them may lead to further explanation, even if it is negative. Once that person is talking to you, you can segue toward that which you wish to solicit. Often, talking to someone about opinion issues will open up pathways to conversation. Here are some examples of icebreakers:

> *"That's a really nice coat you're wearing, do you mind if I ask you where you got it?"*
> *"Do you know how I could get to the admissions office from here?"*
> *"I'm new in town, does it always rain like this?"*
> *"My son used to like to push all the buttons on the elevators too when he was that age."*

Most people like to talk about themselves, their children or their hobbies. Being observant for advertising on T-shirts or items carried by an individual will greatly increase your ability to strike up a conversation. Since body language sometimes speaks louder than words, you must learn to read the cues of self-expression. Approximately seventy percent of what is said is conveyed by body language and voice inflection. Therefore, you should strive to present an open and friendly persona or suffer the loss of the upper hand in "breaking the ice."

INFORMATION GATHERING AND DISSEMINATING

In order to gain the attention of someone to listen, interact or disseminate information you must first persuade them to give you their precious time and attention. In essence, you have thirty seconds or less to turn the listener(s) on or off. The following are suggestions that will assist you in maintaining the attention of the listener or audience:

1.   Sell your position – You must first be willing to share your honest perspective on the situation that is being discussed. A good communicator selects his words and position with forethought. Reacting solely on emotion or the ability to outsmart someone who is a superior arguer than yourself is a sure formula for disaster. Focus on a plan.

2.   Adults are only interested in plans that are "need to know." If the adult learner feels that the speaker is engaging in dialogue that is "nice to know," with little realistic application, they will "turn you off."

3.   Simplify your message – Adults can read through ulterior motives faster than the words can be said. Always directly or indirectly suggest "what's in it for them." Keeping the message simple assures that the listener's perception of what you are saying is the same as yours.

4.   Use terms and quotes that the listener is familiar with. Believing that the listener will be able to decode a term or an analogy that they are not familiar with will become distracting as they attempt to figure it out. In the meantime…they've turned you off!

5.   Use words that are action-oriented, visually stimulating and energized that tend to be remembered long after the interaction occurs.

SITUATIONAL LEADERSHIP AND SUPERVISION

Leadership in a management role is the ability to influence people. Several studies of subordinates regarding their managers and leaders suggested that successful leaders demonstrate the following traits:

- Honesty
- Competency
- Have a Vision
- Are Inspiring
- Are Ultimately Credible

When at their best leaders:

- Challenge the process
- Inspire a shared vision
- Enable others to act
- Model the way
- Encourage the heart – celebrate success and recognize accomplishments!

There are three basic personality traits that a leader may take with his subordinates. These are:

- Autocratic – rules by fear or a compelling pressure to get things done.
- Democratic – flexible, participative, shares responsibility.
- Laissez-faire – a country-club manager, friend to all. Translated from French, meaning, "Let things alone."

Autocratic

There is one significant concept termed "situational leadership." In theory, a supervisor must from time to time be able to demonstrate all of the above leadership styles, depending on the situation that they confront. For example, during a high stress situation supervisors are required to direct priorities. They will likely appear inflexible because of the scenario unfolding before them. This style most parallels military thinking through a chain of command. Although necessary at times, this style is not one that will endear subordinates when used exclusively and the situation no longer dictates a quick decision. Adults will follow this style of leadership when necessary, however they will rebel against it when the situation no longer dictates its use.

The autocratic style may also be used for the subordinate who consistently rebukes the supervisor's authority. A word of caution however, it is critical that a supervisor has the ability to follow up on his commands through discipline, pay or employment. Without authority, the supervisor's command becomes unenforceable.

Democratic

Being flexible as a supervisor and objectively listening to your subordinates is one of the highest forms of respect that may be demonstrated by a supervisor. We have all heard the saying, "There's more than one way to skin a cat." Whenever you have a group of people, "stylistic" differences will surface. The autocrat will never condone "stylistic" differences, because his/her way is the only way! The democratic leader on the other hand looks at the end result. If the task performed differently achieves the same goal without added expense or burden, he/she should condone the procedure as a viable alternative. By objectively considering suggestions the subordinate feels they "buy in to" the organization and that he/she participates in the success or failure of the organization. Take a look at your organization's most respected supervisors and you will conclude that this is a common thread of the successful, respected supervisor.

Laissez-faire

This leadership style works best in one of two situations:
1.   The subordinate is doing an excellent job requiring little supervision. Note: In this scenario the Laissez-faire style reinforces confidence in the subordinate.
2.   The subordinate refuses to follow suggested operating procedures, ignoring a supervisor's warnings.

We have all heard of the saying, "If it's not broke, don't fix it." Laissez-fare leadership is a double-edged sword. Either the supervisor recognizes that the subordinate needs little or no supervision or the subordinate fails to respond to a supervisor's suggestion and has taken his own course of action. The bottom line is that the supervisor may delegate tasks, but he cannot delegate responsibility. The supervisor still has to answer to his superiors. Supervisors usually opt for this style of leadership when an employee has been counseled about deficiencies in the past, and continues to disregard the supervisor's suggestions. This style tends to work when the supervisor has advised the subordinate that if he continues in the same manner that he will face the consequences without his support. When employing this method as a management tool it is important that the supervisor's superiors are made aware of the management style by choice. The latter is significant so that the superiors are aware that the supervisor has intentionally chosen this style rather than by default.

Remember, leadership is not just about leaders, it's about followers as well. It is a reciprocal process, requiring that it occur between people. Lastly, successful leadership depends far more on the follower's perception rather than the leader's abilities. "Perception is reality." If the subordinate perceives that the supervisor is officious, dishonest or incompetent, supervision will be a difficult task.

COUNSELING SUGGESTIONS

It is important that as a supervisor you build and maintain credibility with your subordinates. A good leader asks him/herself first, "What have I done wrong to cause the subordinate's unacceptable behavior?" If the leader can objectively answer this question with, "Nothing," then a counseling session is in order. The following five suggestions may serve to foster a more positive image:
1.   Clarify your values with the subordinates.
2.   Identify what your subordinates want and need.
3.   Build a consensus and work towards the same goal, finding shared values.
4.   Communicate shared values with enthusiasm.
5.   Lead by example.

Basic Ingredients of Effective Counseling
1.   Praise in public, counsel in private.
2.   Be an active listener.
3.   Look at the problem from your subordinate's point of view.
4.   Establish a comfortable relationship/atmosphere during the session.

The Counseling Session
1.   Have a positive feeling about yourself as a supervisor. A positive self-image is crucial for counseling.
2.   Gather all pertinent facts first.
3.   Summarize and review important material.
4.   Stay calm; do not attempt to counsel while emotionally involved in the issue.
5.   Call indirect attention to the subordinate's mistake
6.   Listen with empathy.
7.   Provide feedback.
8.   Invite the subordinate to respond.
9.   Think before you speak.

10.   Restate the problem, using the subordinate's words to ensure clarification.
11.   Identify the policy or proper procedural response for the subordinate.
12.   Set goals and objectives to facilitate remedial training.
13.   Effect completeness.
14.   Celebrate successes.

What You Should Do and Say

1.   Allow the subordinate to determine which of his or her negative behaviors they want to work on first.
2.   Help the subordinate to establish counseling related personal goals.
3.   Help the subordinate to identify logic and/or performance that is self-defeating.
4.   Assist the subordinate to reach self-understanding by examining his or her detrimental behaviors.
5.   Help the subordinate to establish a maintenance system for the concerned behaviors by finding alternatives.

What Not To Do

1.   Warn or threaten.
2.   Order, command or direct.
3.   Moralize or preach.
4.   Lecture or give logical arguments

CONFLICT MANAGEMENT

Often, private and public law enforcement are required to intervene in conflicts that occur within the workplace. Although these skills are very apparent for public law enforcement officers, a new phenomenon has been propelled to the forefront for private law enforcement, i.e. "going postal" (violence in the workplace). Once a police-only trained topic, conflict management may have some real meaning to a private officer in the situation when an employee is being assaulted by a spouse or a recently terminated employee returns to work to seek revenge. Although public officers spend the majority of their police academy time in this area, it would behoove the private officer to have an overview of safety skills required to read a potential conflict and avoid violence which may lead to injury and death.

Response Principals

1.   Never rush into anything without first obtaining information about the type of conflict you are walking into. If need be, attempt to watch the dispute surreptitiously prior to entering the location. Avoid attempting to deal with the situation by yourself without a back-up.
2.   Assess the violence potential. Are you trained in management of aggressive behavior techniques? Do you know how to separate, defuse and mediate? Do you have the authority to arrest individuals and employees by policy or law? Do you know your limitations? Visually frisk the combatants for weapons. Are there potential weapons involved? Are you trained and authorized to deal with weapons? Find out who else is at the location. Speak to everyone present to ensure objectivity as well as to identify other potential assailants. Attempt to keep everyone in sight until public law enforcement arrives.
3.   Stabilize the physical situation in an appropriate manner. Avoid crowding people. Stay away from kitchens, bedrooms and tool shops. Weapons are usually secreted in private areas that are accessible to the combatants. Always attempt to get the parties to interact in a semi-public area such as a conference room, where weapons are less likely to be available. Attempt to get all parties to sit down and to allow one to speak at a time. If the latter is not possible, separate the combatants until they agree they will take turns allowing the other(s) to speak. If you as a peace officer cannot get a word in edgewise, separate the disputants until they agree to interact by taking turns.
4.   Maintain control throughout the situation. Defend yourself at all costs! Unless you have been hired as a bodyguard or police officer you do not get paid to get hurt. Disengage until help arrives. Your lack of training in violent situations relieves you of liability. As long as you follow a policy of notifying the authorities, you have done your job. If you use force and are

not authorized to do so, the company that employs you may claim that there is a "conflict of interest" when a lawsuit is later initiated. When authorization is approved, use "only that force necessary to effect an arrest," or "to protect yourself or another"—no more, no less! Make certain that the incident is documented and that the public law enforcement officers are advised of the tactics that you used to control the individual.

5.   Know your exit! We can learn something from firefighters here; when you walk into any situation, know your way out. Have a plan so that you may disengage quickly if the need arises.

Reading Danger Cues

Body language is defined as unconscious signals sent from the brain that outwardly reflect a person's emotional state. Since words seldom depict the true message hidden behind words, we must learn to rely on the non-verbals as indicators of potential assault. Remember, by law you may protect yourself by meeting force with force in order to disengage for police assistance. Generally, police officers will agree that communication skills, not force, are what commonly defuse conflicts. Therefore, enrolling in a course designed to reduce a subject's anxiety by verbalization should be a priority of public and private law enforcement training. Programs such as REB Security International, "Management of Aggressive Behavior," (M.O.A.B.) identifies common tactics that de-escalate situations with verbal interaction as well as indicators to potential assault. As stated in the M.O.A.B. book by Rolland Ouellette, your verbal communications must be *reasonable*, *enforceable* and *enforced* when necessary, otherwise you will risk loss of credibility and control.

There are many other areas of conflict management training, however they are more directed at psychomotor skills and tactics requiring practice in the presence of a competent instructor. Many police academies and security certification programs now offer certified training in these areas. If you are unable to obtain this information call (716) 266-2459 or e-mail: Rbishop269@aol.com.

For further information on management of force training contact:
REB Security International
P.O. Box 845
Stoddard, NH   03464
(603) 446-9393
NET: www.rebtraining.com

INTERPERSONAL COMMUNICATIONS
QUIZ

1.   Approximately 40% of what is said is conveyed by body expression.
□ T   □ F

2.   How many seconds does one have to turn the listener(s) on or off?
1.   10 Seconds
2.   30 Seconds
3.   15 Seconds
4.   45 Seconds

3.   There are three basic personality traits that a leader may take with his/her subordinates, they are _____, _____ and _____.

4.   Successful leaders demonstrate the following traits:
1.   Honesty
2.   Competency
3.   Have a vision
4.   Are inspiring
5.   All of the above

5.   Democratic personality trait most parallels military thinking through a chain of command.
□ T   □ F

6.   Leadership is not just about the leader, is about _____ as well.

7.   Supervision will be difficult if the subordinate perceives the supervisor is:
      a)   Officious
      b)   Dishonest
      c)   Incompetent
      d)   All of the above

8.   It is against the law to protect yourself by meeting force with force in order to disengage for police assistance.
                        □ T   □ F

9.   Poor communication can lead to:
      a)   Mixed messages
      b)   Distrust
      c)   Conflict
      d)   All of the above

10.   Which personality trait may be used for the subordinate who consistently rebukes the supervisor's authority?
      a)   Democratic
      b)   Autocratic
      c)   Laissez-faire
      d)   None of the above

UNIT FOUR
TRAINING AND PROFESSIONAL DEVELOPMENT

Supervisor's Role in Training
Appendix A: Pitfalls in Training
Orientation for Security Officers
Staff Training and Development
Curriculum Design
Testing for Learning Retention
Professional Certifications

THE SUPERVISOR'S ROLE IN TRAINING
By Christopher A. Hertig, CPP, CPO

DEFINING TRAINING

Training. When we think of training we envision teaching or instruction. We think of lectures, videos, training exercises, "showing a new employee the ropes" and tests. Generally speaking, most of us view training by one of it's aspects or components. *In essence we view training in a very limited manner.* Sometimes we equate it with *classes* held on a particular topic. In still other cases we think of it as learning and practicing a particular skill.

While all of these activities are, indeed, training; they are merely *components* of the *process* of training. They are but pieces of the "training pie." Training can be thought of as an intense learning process where an individual is taught a skill or knowledge that enables him/her to perform a job function. It incorporates various teaching and learning methods. It involves significant amounts of practice. Training is always tested or validated in some manner.

By internalizing the definition above, a supervisor who is charged with some aspect of the training process can better discern the impact of their activities within that process. The common mistake of believing that learning—*a change in behavior or attitude*—has occurred due to a *single learning experience* (a class, meeting, orientation session, etc.) will be avoided. Most people believe that a single well-intentioned learning episode will have a significant impact on job performance because they *want to believe it*. The astute trainer/supervisor/manager knows that job performance improvement requires *significant effort!* The effective supervisor will know how to integrate *training* activities into a comprehensive learning system. By doing this, positive changes in job behavior are far more likely to result.

Supervisors who are charged with training their subordinates must ensure that the training is continuous. The learning must be reinforced through *guided practice* such as periodic in-service instruction, re-certification, drills or scenarios, individual reading or research and attending classes on the topic. *The more separate, yet integrated, learning episodes, the better.*

BENEFITS OF TRAINING

The benefits of training must be examined *prior* to embarking on an expensive, time-consuming training and development process! In order to ensure the greatest return on instructional dollars we must understand both the benefits and the costs. *Some* of the beneficial effects of training are:

- increased job efficiency where specific job tasks are performed better
- better relations between employees and management
- enhanced *professional identity* by protection officers who see positive growth within themselves
- pride and job satisfaction
- increased loyalty to the employer who has shown an interest in the employees by training them
- decreased turnover as there are fewer situations that make the officers feel uncomfortable and incompetent
- fewer mistakes
- decreased accidents
- improved *discretionary* judgement with better decisions being made
- protection from allegations that management is negligent in preparing officers to perform their jobs

DETERMINING TRAINING NEEDS

Determining what areas security personnel need training in is key to successful, cost-effective training. *Training is wasted if it is used to solve problems that are due to inadequate equipment, inadequate resources or inappropriate job design!* Training cannot *by itself* serve to motivate personnel; nor can it solve other problems not related to the development of *knowledge, skills* or *abilities*.

In order to accurately assess training needs, it is first necessary to go through a review of the situation at hand. This will illuminate the problems, causes and possible approaches to addressing them without plunging into an expensive, time-consuming training endeavor.

Some simple questions to ask in this regard are:

1.   *What is the job performance problem?*
2.   *Is the problem a result of inadequate skill or knowledge on the part of security personnel?*
3.   *How can the lack of knowledge or skill deficiency be corrected?*
4.   *Has the knowledge/skill deficiency been corrected?*
5.   *Does the problem still exist?*

Problem: There is a high rate of turnover by contract security personnel at a client's site. Absenteeism is also a problem. Training is minimal as officers are not there long enough to complete anything other than a four (4) hour orientation program. The client is considering changing security service firms.

How should addressing this problem proceed from the standpoint of the supervisor in charge of the account?

TYPES OF TRAINING

Lectures are often used as an instructional technique. They can be effective or ineffective, depending upon the circumstances. Supervisors must always bear in mind that *adults don't like to be lectured*. They must instead be informed and stimulated.

A few things to remember to keep lectures effective are:

1.   Lecture to establish a common base of knowledge *when this base does not exist.*
2.   Use visuals as much as possible as most people are visual learners—video clips are good in this regard.
3.   Use lectures to assess the learners, what they know and how they feel about certain topics.
4.   Keep lectures *short and to the point* as much as possible.
5.   Only use lectures to make two or three points at a time; more information causes overload and learners *BLANK OUT* the learning.
6.   *Reinforce lectures with active learning* such as scenario exercises, discussions, short tests.
7.   Organize the lecture using the same format as a letter: an introduction, main body and closing (which summarizes and reiterates the key points); a simple manner of remembering this is to draw an analogy between other means of communication such as letters and interviews; each of which has three parts:
     *   *An introduction where the topic to be discussed is first mentioned*
     *   *A main body where the topic is discussed in full*
     *   *A closing where there is some degree of summarization or recapping of main points*
     A simple way of remembering this in an instructional setting is:

"Tell 'em what you're gonna tell em.
Tell 'em.
Tell them what you told 'em."

Demonstration is an essential instructional technique for teaching proficiency areas such as equipment use, interviewing, defensive tactics, firefighting, etc. To demonstrate effectively, the following points should be borne in mind:
- explain what you are going to do beforehand
- make sure everyone can see
- make eye contact with everyone during the demonstration
- demonstrate the entire task so that visual learners can grasp what is to be done in a single demonstration
- use video if at all possible to ensure uniformity and documentation of the process to be demonstrated; video also ensures that the whole class can see the procedure being performed
- have the class practice the skill at a slow, easy pace and then refine their proficiency

Coaching or tutoring is also vital for supervisors as *it is the essence of supervision.* Coaching or tutoring can be done in a myriad of situations on the job. A few ideas to be borne in mind include:
- select the appropriate learning method (reading assignments, incident review, computer assisted instruction, research project, etc.) for the learner and what is being taught
- don't be afraid to use *multiple* learning strategies
- *always build on prior learning*
- be patient and don't expect everyone to learn at the same rate
- be flexible and change strategies if the one originally chosen doesn't work
- when editing reports—*a great training opportunity*—make sure to:
  a) *Praise* in some way the work that has been done. Always accentuate the positive in what has been written. Do not trample upon the ego of the writer.
  b) *Question* the writer as to what they are attempting to express.
  c) *Polish* the report with suggestions for improvement.

ROLES OF SUPERVISORS IN TRAINING

Orienting new employees—within the security department or other departments—is a function commonly performed by security supervisors. Orientation is an important juncture in the employment process, combining the selection, training and socialization aspects of the relationship. Supervisors should make the most of it by doing the following:
1. Spread out the learning as much as possible—try and have several sessions/learning episodes.
2. *Instruct in the history and philosophy of the organization. While this is often left out or given minimal treatment, it is essential to develop the ability to make the correct discretionary judgements.* Discretionary judgements are integral to the role of the protection officer. Effective socialization of the employee over the long run is possible, as the officer has the foundation of knowledge to form understanding. An additional added benefit may be that the officer becomes a more effective "sales rep" for their organization: a crucial element for security service firms!
3. Keep the sessions dynamic and ever-changing: use a variety of instructional techniques—mix it up.
4. Make the employee feel a personal bond to people within the organization by introducing him/her to people such as mentors, supervisors and upper level managers. Note: Sometimes inviting upper level managers to meet new employees can elevate the visibility of the Security Department.
5. Prepare the new officer for orientation by informing him/her as to time, place, topics and what to expect in terms of dress, deportment and activities—*reduce the amount of uncomfortable situations the new hire is exposed to at all times.*

In many cases supervisors are called upon to teach in-service classes. These can be *BRUTAL* for both the teacher and the learners! While much of the information concerning overcoming resistance to training is relevant to in-service instruction, the following considerations are essential:

1. Get feedback from the officers as to what *they* want to learn.
2. *Become an expert*—do research and make it interesting by informing them of things they don't already know.
3. Use different instructors—outside experts, personnel from other departments, security officers.
4. *Keep the class moving* with exercises and different activities.

On-the-job training must be provided or overseen by security supervisors! It must be delivered in a professional manner. OJT can be effective if it is structured and formalized. OJT *will* be a waste of time or a euphemism for a lack of a training program without organization and structure.

Perhaps the first important aspect of on-the-job training is *commitment*. OJT must be a priority!

A few tips for delivering on-the-job training are:

1. *Explain and demonstrate each job step.*
2. *Demonstrate each job step while the employee explains the process.*
3. *Have the employee demonstrate and explain each task.*
4. *Stop by later and follow up on the learning.*
5. *Document the training by having a form signed that lists all areas (procedures, equipment and locations) that have been covered.*
6. *Preface the learning by preceding the OJT with a classroom session and/or individual learning experience such as watching a video or reading a manual.*
7. *Follow up the learning by having in-service sessions, drills, etc.*

Job aids can be an effective method of reducing training costs while at the same time increasing job task proficiency. Simply put, *a job aid is an instruction or direction on how to do something*. It can be a sign on a piece of equipment. It may be a procedural manual. It could be a sign or memo that serves as a reminder. The Crisis Prevention Institute sells posters that list steps to be taken for dealing with aggressive persons. Numerous examples of safety posters and posters reminding persons of information security procedures are in workplaces.

Whatever the form a job aid takes, there are several tips to remember about making them effective:

1. *Keep sentences short and to the point.*
2. *List steps to be followed.*
3. *Leave space around each sentence so that it is easy to read.*
4. *Use a plain type style.*
5. *The job aids should be accessible, convenient and user friendly in every respect.*

A mentoring program is where a senior employee guides and assists a new worker on the job. In days gone by this was simply placing a new officer with a more senior one who "showed them the ropes." Such an informal approach enabled the new employee to absorb all the negative traits of the older worker. Mentoring is different because it is more structured. Mentoring may involve a financial incentive to the mentor and should always involve special training and instruction for the mentor.

A few things to bear in mind concerning mentoring programs are:

1. Select a mentor that the new employee should emulate.
2. Provide the mentor with additional, special training and education so that they may act as an effective coach.
3. Introduce the new officer to the mentor at an early stage in the employment relationship such as at orientation.
4. Mentors should be easily approachable by trainees.
5. Mentors must be good teachers who enjoy passing along their knowledge.
6. Mentors should be able to give the neophyte employee *exposure* within the organization.

Evaluating training can be a very complicated matter best left in the hands of specialists who have done graduate work in education or training and development. In most circumstances, this is not within the means of the organization. Some techniques that can be used to assess training are to:

1. Have trainees evaluate the training via a predesigned form or by simply asking them to write an essay on their perceptions regarding the program.
2. Utilize an employee questionnaire before and after training that assesses the perceptions of employees regarding security force professionalism.
3. Analyze incident frequency and severity before and after training to determine if training had a positive effect on how the officers handled incidents.

Another fairly simple method of evaluating training is through the use of supervisory anecdotes. These are simply observations that supervisors make concerning job performance following a training program or session. Anecdotes are simple to use and must be done anyway to evaluate how the new employee is performing on the job.

A few things to bear in mind about supervisory anecdotes are:

1. They must be completely objective and not tarnished by the opinions of other supervisors or preconceived notions of the supervisor making them.
2. Supervisors should have substantial input into training design so that competition, jealousy and general ill-will doesn't develop between trainers—who may not be supervisors—and the supervisors on staff.
3. Use written questionnaires to evaluate so that all observations must be articulated clearly.

PROBLEMS IN TRAINING

Training is often greeted with unbridled enthusiasm. Unfortunately, there are numerous problems involved in the design, development and implementation of training. *If these problems are not addressed, training will not be effective, may serve to demoralize personnel and WILL cause budgetary problems.* Perhaps the worst—and unfortunately a very common—dilemma that can befall training is that training *JUST DOESN'T HAPPEN.* This is both an obvious operational dilemma as well as an ethical lapse on the part of supervisors/managers who have a duty to adequately train their subordinates.

Budget restrictions are perhaps the most common problem in security officer training. Most organizations devote very few resources to training security personnel; some spend nothing at all! There are various approaches to take in addressing this problem:

1. *Hire personnel with as much training as possible.* This in and of itself does not ensure a properly trained protection force—*highly trained persons may not have the exact job skills necessary in a specific application*—but it does address the issue to some degree.

2. *Attempt to have other departments within the parent or client organizations provide instruction.* This can include topics such as customer service, time management, safety, business writing, etc. These topics are certainly of value to security officers and having the officers attend training given by other departments can be a very low-cost option. An additional benefit is the positive exposure of the security department to the rest of the organization. Also, the department gets a good feel for what is happening within the parent or client organization.

3. *Utilize distance education.* Correspondence courses are one approach. Having the security staff complete the *Certified Protection Officer (CPO) Program* is an example. This not only gives the officers a comprehensive exposure to key security topics, but it culminates in a recognized professional credential. While distance education—where the teacher and learner are distant from each other—is not cost-free, it is very inexpensive as it eliminates paying for

overtime so officers can attend classes. It also bypasses the generally insurmountable hurdle of scheduling a class and getting all officers into the class.

Distance education can take a myriad of forms from correspondence study, to Internet courses, to having officers utilize video or audio tapes during quiet times. *Another very simple use of distance education is to have officers read policies and procedures on their own and then answer questions on them.* The questions can be developed by the supervisor in completion, essay or fill-in-the-blank format. Such an approach eliminates costly classroom time spent going over mundane items that the learner has access to on his/her own. It can be incorporated into computerized instructional formats or used in concert with audio or video tapes. Care should be taken to reinforce and clarify the learning with person-to-person instruction (highlighting at training meetings, reviewing with individual officers on post) so as to ensure comprehension. Utilizing distance education in concert with traditional classroom instruction can offer the best of both worlds. Additionally, it can be used before or after a classroom session as a means of *reinforcing* learning. An example would be using the CPO Program chapters on Interviewing or First Aid; the student can read these chapters and answer the questions at the back of them before attending a classroom session on either topic. One cannot effectively teach interviewing or first aid from a book; but one can introduce the topic in this manner. Additionally, one can reinforce and expand upon a classroom learning experience via use of a manual.

4.   *Tuition reimbursement can be used to inspire persons to improve their individual educational/training level.* Many organizations have tuition assistance money earmarked; unfortunately many security departments have not taken advantage of it. While this does not ensure a baseline foundation of knowledge, skill or ability for the entire security force, it *does* help to promote professional development. Professional development always pays for itself in one way or another at some point.

Problem: After suggesting that the security force be enrolled into the Certified Protection Officer program, a supervisor is told by his/her superior that "correspondence study is a bunch of B.S." What arguments could be used to persuade the manager? What facts and scientific research are available to support those arguments?

Scheduling is a serious impediment to traditional training classes for security departments. In order to get everyone in the class, the session must be scheduled *AT LEAST TWICE!* This is to compensate for officers on post, officers out sick, officers on vacation, newly hired officers, etc. *The reality of security training is that unless ALL officers are trained BEFORE being assigned, classroom instruction cannot be used to train everyone.* Unfortunately, few supervisors/managers will fully acknowledge this. The issue is ignored and uniform, comprehensive training does not occur via traditional classroom instruction.

There are a few approaches to overcoming this seemingly insurmountable dilemma:

1.   Distance education that can be achieved at a learner's own pace and own place is key to solving this problem.

2.   Give as much training as possible in the pre-assignment phase of the employment relationship. This eliminates the hassle of attempting to schedule classes later on. It also reduces or eliminates *uncomfortable* situations that new officers are faced with: a key cause of turnover.

3.   Still another approach is to require persons to have certain levels of training prior to being hired or to maintain present levels (first aid, state certifications, weapons certifications). Compensating the officers for doing this is possibly cheaper and less troublesome than attempting to set up "master schedules" for all security force members.

As emphasized earlier, real learning and positive behavioral change does not occur in a single learning episode. People can only learn so much at one time. People only pay attention a fraction of the amount of the time they are in classes. And people must be ready to learn certain things at certain levels of maturity, education, experience, etc. We all learn differently; and we all learn different subjects at different phases of our lives.

Obviously, a comprehensive, continuous learning system is necessary. Reinforcing the learning can be accomplished by:

1.   Periodic in-service instruction such as quarterly qualification with firefighting equipment or weapons.
2.   Drills or scenarios where the *concepts* are applied to actual situations. These can be "table top" exercises, drills affecting only a portion of the facility or protection operation or full blown scenarios involving off-site agencies.
      Problem: Pick a work environment. As a security supervisor within that work environment, what sort of practical scenario exercises could be developed? Making sure that officers are only being tested on what they have previously been taught, what type of exercises could be developed that would not cause operational or safety problems?
3.   *Job aids in the work environment that serve as reminders of how to perform a certain procedure.* These include procedural manuals, signs and sets of instructions on security equipment. Job aids can go a long way in ensuring that performance levels are maintained. They can also reduce costs for instructional sessions. Using job aids effectively can be a very cost-effective training strategy. Performing a study/audit of those in the work environment can be a good first step in employing this strategy.
4.   *Reviewing procedures and post orders with officers at their duty stations.* Spending a few minutes with officers is an essential part of the supervisory process; integrating training into this time is a good way to structure supervisory visits.
5.   *Sending officers to classes on work related topics.* These can be at local community colleges, training academies, professional meetings, etc. Local chapters of professional organizations such as the American Society for Industrial Security can host annual programs for security officers. In some areas groups of security directors at hospitals and colleges are already doing this. *Note: cooperative training sessions, group enrollments into the CPO Program, cooperative purchasing of videos, etc. by security associations may be THE WAY to make training affordable and accessible!*
6.   *Completion of the Safety course offered by the International Association of Healthcare Security & Safety.* This approach is used by many hospital security directors who benefit by developing the safety knowledge of their officers. It is an excellent reinforcement and enhancement of previously learned safety material which serves to expand the capabilities of the protection force. Healthcare protection administrators who have their officers first complete the IAHSS Basic Standard and then the Safety Program during the next year can expect a significant amount of demonstrable, recognized organizational development to occur.
7.   *Completion of distance education programs or professional certifications.* The CPO, CSS and distance education courses offered by various organizations are all examples of progressive learning, growth and development. These can easily be tied in to probationary conditions of employment or horizontal promotion systems.
8.   *Encouraging officers to attain licenses or certifications to use weapons, equipment, administer first aid, lifesaving, Water Safety Instructor, etc.* These activities all help the employee to grow and become more valuable to the organization. They increase the capabilities of the Security Department while at the same time addressing each member's individual learning needs. Note: while not all activities precisely fit the organization's immediate or foreseeable needs, some flexibility is desirable to keep personnel motivated.
9.   *Membership in professional organizations such as IFPO or subscribing to professional publications such as* security *or* police and security news *are other methods of enhancing the*

continuity of learning. An added benefit to this is that protection officers get a *professional identity.* This is no small benefit!

10.   *Incidental learning by making books, magazines, etc. available to officers is another useful technique.* This costs next to nothing, keeps staff abreast of what is going on in the industry and further reinforces the concept of *professional identity.*

     Problem: The general manager of a contract security firm wants to see a new culture of professional growth/identity within the organization. At a branch office employing 1,000 officers which is part of a national firm, how could this strategy be utilized? What specific steps could be taken?

11.   *Overlapping the learning by having class members write descriptions, give class presentations, take notes and conduct interviews throughout the instructional process.* Report writing, for example, cannot be effectively taught in a single session. There must be continuous practice of the writing skills. The same is true of speaking in public (testifying, crowd management, supervision) or interviewing. *By having active participation in problem solving exercises, key skills can be honed and refined.* An example would be having an officer testify in class as to his or her report; the primary purpose is to teach testifying skills, the ancillary objective is to reinforce and refine report writing skills. Another example would be having class members conduct interviews and take notes so interviewing techniques and note-taking methods are taught. Such an exercise could be conducted at some time after a note-taking or interviewing class.

     Bureaucratic training can be a major problem in some environments. This occurs when training is done only to satisfy government requirements. The bureaucrat only trains to minimal legal standards. While legal mandates must be complied with, mere compliance is not enough. Officers quickly see the half-hearted approach to training and are turned off to training! "Going through the motions" is seen as just that. As a result, protection officers are de-motivated to learn and may block out future attempts to enhance their job capabilities.

     Training should serve to create and improve job task performance. Compliance with legal standards—while a necessity—is best thought of as a positive *by-product.* Making compliance the primary goal of training is wasted training! The troops are not impressed. Neither are many government inspectors.

     Problem: A manager whom the supervisor reports to believes that all the training that is necessary is that which is required by the state or province. He/she doesn't want any additional funds spent on training. What arguments could be advanced to persuade this individual that increased training is beneficial?

     Resistance by learners is a significant problem facing those charged with training. In many cases personnel do not want to be in a particular training session or don't want to learn a new procedure. Some methods of dealing with this include:

1.   Take care in scheduling the training so as to interfere with the learner's life/schedule as little as possible.

2.   Recognize the experience, knowledge and *contributions* that each officer can make to the training experience. Adults need to be stroked! A genuine compliment can go a long way towards decreasing resistance to learning.

3.   Ask the trainees what *they want* out of the training. Try to incorporate their needs in the design and implementation of the training as much as possible.

4.   Provide incentives. These can be small or large, depending upon the situation at hand. A list and photograph in the company newspaper is one way to reward those who have completed training. Giving out of certificates and plaques is another. Providing meals and refreshments is also a nice gesture. Letting the class go early is also appreciated by the learners.

5.   Deal positively with trainees who utter questions meant to challenge the instructor or content of the learning. Sometimes these questions can be reflected back with a "How would you handle that?" Asking the class for their input is another strategy. Sometimes telling the

hostile questioner in a classroom setting that the question will be resolved over break—and following through with the promise—is necessary.

"Stuffed Shirts." These are security supervisors who have obtained their positions due to their educational backgrounds. They have a college degree but not enough experience or specific training to be competent. They never went to any type of academy and generally don't understand the realistic applications of firefighting, handcuffing, crowd management, etc. While everyone has weaknesses in their background; it is important to see those weaknesses and work with them in a positive manner. Supervisors are not expected to be experts in everything, but they must be competent at all essential job tasks. They must also be humble and ask for assistance from others. Supervisors shouldn't hesitate to ask one of their subordinates to assist with a training problem. There is no reason why the talents of the security force cannot be harvested! Most security forces are composed of persons with diverse backgrounds (a medic, a firefighter, a soldier, a police officer, a computer person, a safety specialist, etc.). Astute supervisors use their talents.

Training to punish, motivate or gratify management. None of these are **acceptable** reasons to train. All efforts should be made to create a positive, pleasant learning environment. Management must not prescribe "remedial" training unless it can be incorporated into a totally positive learning experience. Training to correct performance deficiencies can leave a bad taste in everyone's mouth. As a result, *ALL LEARNING STOPS.*

Training must be used to improve performance. Period.

Liability for failure to train may be imposed upon supervisors who have training as part of their responsibilities. While most of the court cases in this area deal with public law enforcement personnel; it is illogical to assume that private employers will not be held liable for the torts of their employees and agents. This will become an increasing concern as private security personnel assume more of the roles and functions traditionally performed by public law enforcement agencies. It will grow with the amount of public exposure and responsibility that security forces have.

Obviously, there is liability exposure to organizations and the individual supervisors who work for those organizations where officers are armed. Adequate training, practice and documentation of the training is a necessity in these situations.

Perhaps not so obvious is the potential for liability due to personnel who aren't adequately instructed in how to use emergency equipment or who are expected to provide emergency services. A simple method of uncovering liability exposure in this area is to ask the following questions:

- What are the duties that personnel under my supervision owe to their employer, clients, visitors, etc.?
- What types of emergencies that protection officers must respond to are *reasonably foreseeable?*
- What *specific* functions are they expected to perform during emergencies?
- What types of equipment/weapons can they be expected to use in emergencies?

CONCLUSION

Supervisors play a crucial role in the training process: in the final analysis they are what makes the training process work!

By learning as much as possible about learning theory and instructional techniques, supervisors can significantly enhance their contribution to officer performance. They will also develop their own career aspirations and increase their value to themselves, their families, their employers and the security industry as a whole. They must become *students of training*.

Learning never stops.

BIBLIOGRAPHY

Bunting, Stephen M. "Training Safety: A Supervisory Responsibility" in *Supervisory Survival* by Ed Nowicki (Ed.), 1993, Performance Dimensions Publishing, Powers Lake, WI.

Field, Ginny, "Supervisory Editing" in *Supervisory Survival* by Ed Nowicki (Ed.), 1993, Performance Dimensions Publishing, Powers Lake, WI.

Frantzreb, Richard B., *Training and Development Yearbook* 1990, Prentice-Hall, Inc., Englewood Cliffs, NJ.

Grossi, David M. "The Supervisor's Role in Officer Survival Training," in *Supervisory Survival* by Ed Nowicki (Ed.), 1993, Performance Dimensions Publishing, Powers Lake, WI.

Hertig, Christopher A., *Avoiding Pitfalls in the Training Process*, 1993, International Foundation for Protection Officers, Bellingham, WA.

Minor, Kevin I., Snarr, Richard W. and Wells, James B., "Distance Learning: Examining New Directions and Challenges For Criminal Justice Educations," *ACJS TODAY* January/February, 1998 Vol. 16., No. 4.

Mounts, Harry C.; "Earn Your College Degree At Home," *Police and Security News* January/February 1997, Vol. 13., No. 1.

Nichter, David A., "How MGM Grand Trains Security Officers, Supervisors, Managers," *Hotel/Motel Security and Safety Management* July 1997, Vol. 15., No. 8.

Nilson, Carolyn, *Training Program Workbook* and Kit 1989, Prentice-Hall, Inc., Englewood Cliffs, NJ.

Roberts, Barbara, E., "Supervisory Liability," in *Supervisory Survival* by Ed Nowicki (Ed.), 1993, Performance Dimensions Publishing, Powers Lake, WI.

Wanat, John A., Guy, Edward T. & Merrigan, John J., *Supervisory Techniques for the Security Professional*, 1981, Butterworth-Heinemann, Stoneham, MA.

Zemke, Ron, Standke, Linda & Jones, Philip, *Designing and Delivering Cost-Effective Training—and Measuring the Results*, 1981, Lakewood Publications, Minneapolis, MN.

FOR MORE INFORMATION

American Society of Law Enforcement Trainers, 102 Dock Road, P.O. Box 361, Lewes, DE 19958-0361; (302) 645-4080 Fax (302) 645-4084.

ASLET publishes a journal filled with tips on teaching and where to get information on various topics. The *Law Enforcement Trainer* also has articles on the latest issues and operational concerns of police, security and corrections personnel. The Society also provides members with an extensive amount of discounts on training materials as well as an outstanding annual seminar.

Butterworth–Heinemann, 225 Wildwood Avenue, Woburn, MA 01801; (800) 366-2665 or fax (800) 446-6520.

Butterworth–Heinemann has a large selection of security texts available. Both *The Protection Officer Training Manual* by Ron Minion, CPP, CPO and *The Security Officer's Standard Operating Procedure* by Ed Kehoe, CPP, contain sections that are useful to supervisors charged with training their subordinates.

International Foundation for Protection Officers, #269, 3106 Tamiami Trail, North, Naples, FL 32114; (941) 430-0534 or (941) 430-0533 fax or www.ifpo.com.

The Foundation publishes works such as *Avoiding Pitfalls in the Training Process* which can assist supervisors who must make presentations, design training or educational sessions. IFPO also has Associate Membership which entitles the member to a newsletter, discounts on publications and other Foundation products. Discounts for employers who sponsor their security staffs are also available.

Performance Dimensions Publishing, P.O. Box 502, Powers Lake, WI 53159-0502; (414)279-3850 Fax (414) 279-5758.

Performance Dimensions publishes a variety of texts and videos. The videos are high quality and inexpensive. Texts such as *Supervisory Survival* are excellent references and belong on every supervisor's bookshelf. *Supervisory Survival* has chapters on training safety, supervisory liability, editing reports and various other key topics.

Professional Security Television Network; (800) 942-7786; www.pstn.pwpl.com.

PSTN offers hundreds of videos for the professional development needs of supervisors and officers. There is a monthly subscription service where subscribers receive a new tape each month as well as series of tapes on Casino Security, Healthcare Security, Shopping Center Security, etc. Tapes also come with examinations. The PSTN web site offers a complete catalog as well as a monthly column entitled "A Few Words" which discusses training/education issues.

Professional Training Resources (800) 998-9400 or (802) 447-7832; http://techage.com/ptrbooks

PTR offers hundreds of different book and video titles on a variety of topics for both Security and Law Enforcement personnel. PTR publishes a complimentary newsletter and offers supervisory training services as well.

Special Programs Office, York College of Pennsylvania, York, PA 17405-7199 (717) 815-1451 or 1360 or special-programs@ycp.edu. Fax (717) 849-1607. Web site is www.ycp.edu/.

The Special Programs Office hosts a variety of programs dealing with security-related topics at York as well as offering courses at client locations. Program handout materials are also available for purchase. These consist of detailed outlines, learning exercises and extensive references on where to get additional information on each topic.

SUPERVISOR'S ROLE IN TRAINING
QUIZ

1.   Supervisors who are charged with training their subordinates must ensure that the training is __ _____ .

2.   There are numerous problems in the _____ development and implementation of training.

3.   _____ education, which offers learners the opportunity to work at their own place and their own time, is key.

4.   _____ training occurs when training is done only to satisfy government regulations.

5.   _____ is an essential instructional technique for teaching proficiency in areas such as equipment use.

6.   Job aids serve as reminders as to how to perform a certain task such as operating a piece of equipment.
        □ T   □ F

7.   If one uses distance education to teach policy and procedures, reinforcement in the classroom or via individual meetings is not necessary.
        □ T   □ F

8.   Tuition reimbursement is widely used and fully exploited by most security employers.
        □ T   □ F

9.   When editing a subordinate's work, the supervisor should praise, question and polish.
        □ T   □ F

10.   Supervisors in private security will probably be held liable for the lack of training given their subordinates more often in the future due to the increased responsibilities and public contact on the part of private protection forces.
        □ T   □ F

APPENDIX A
PITFALLS IN TRAINING
by Christopher A. Hertig, CPP, CPO

Training is essential if performance is to be enhanced to any appreciable degree. Unfortunately, the process of training is complex. It is – on it's face – cost prohibitive if not implemented creatively and managed. The following discussion outlines some of the common misperceptions involving the training of protection officers and how these training dilemmas can be avoided or reduced in severity.

THE DEFINITIONAL DILEMMA

"The Definitional Dilemma" begins when managers or trainers don't truly understand what training is. They can't adequately define training and consequently are unable to differentiate training from education or development. Those afflicted with the "Dilemma" throw all three terms around interchangeably, ignorant of the fact that there are distinct differences between them.

To avoid this trap an accurate definition of "training," "education" and "development" is needed. Training is defined by Dr.Leonard Nadler in *Developing Human Resources* (Houston: Gulf, 1970) as:

> *"Those activities which are designed to improve human performance on the job the employee is presently doing or is being hired to do."*

> *"Education" consists of those HRD activities which "are designed to improve the overall competence of the employee in a specified direction and beyond the job now held."*

> *"Development" prepares the employee so that he "can move with the organization as it develops, changes and grows."*

Training prepares the employee through the infusion of knowledge or the acquisition of skills or abilities to perform a specific job. Training focuses on the "how to" do a job task. Training involves practice, repetition and skill development. The training *process* is designed to develop a specific job skill such as driving, using a handgun, patrolling specific points or administering first aid.

Education broadens his/her perspective by increasing the employee's knowledge base. Education focuses on the "why" a job task or duty is being performed. An employee who is educated may not necessarily be able to drive, shoot, patrol or care for casualties; instead he or she will be able to explain the theoretical foundation behind driving. They will understand such things as stopping distance, friction, momentum, etc. They will be better able to make judgements about how to write driving policies and develop safe driving programs.

Development creates growth in the individual and the organization through the combining of training, education and new opportunities. *Experience* acts as a catalyst in the development process, bringing together the knowledge of education and the skill from training to make the employee a better performer. With development, the employee actually evolves into a *different* performer.

Each one has its place within the HRD process and although related to each other, each is a separate, distinct entity. Moreover, each process has differing effects on performance. Training will have a readily identifiable, measurable impact on job performance (provided the training is properly given) whereas education will change attitudes and outlooks. Performance changes may not be as readily discernable with education.

"The Definitional Dilemma" often occurs when managers provide educational opportunities for their subordinates and think that the personnel have been "trained."

Examples include having a guest speaker talk, or sending subordinates to seminars and conferences. These experiences educate but don't train. The "Dilemma" hits when the manager expects the same performance changes with education as with training. The manager is disappointed that extensive performance improvement has not occurred where he sent his officers to a "training session."

In some extreme cases of *"The Definitional Dilemma,"* experience is confused with training. The manager speaks about the training that his personnel have had, when in fact all that they have is experience. Experience is not the best teacher—it is the most expensive teacher; one can learn improper methods through experience and have them reinforced every time the method is used. In other words, "only *perfect* practice makes *perfect* performance."

Training, education, experience and development are all separate entities. A smart manager understands this and uses these professional growth experiences to complement one another.

THE FROG

"The Frog" is a nice fellow who really means to do some wonderful work in the training arena. He wants his officers to be well trained. *"The Frog"* doesn't see the complexities and problems inherent within the training process. He jumps into training without thinking through all of the logistical considerations:
- training needs assessment
- training program development costs
- equipment and materials needed
- scheduling and overtime considerations
- testing and validation methods

"The Frog" enthusiastically jumps into training, then crawls out of it when logistical hurdles appear. The training effort is abandoned for all practical purposes and professional growth is stopped. Often times this occurs when a new manager takes over. In many security organizations this has happened *repeatedly* over the years. The senior security officers have lived through several administrations that were going to have good, strong training programs. In all likelihood, they will out-live the current *"Frog."* Small wonder that the security officers do not take training seriously!

The world was not built on good intentions.

THE PANACEA

Those who subscribe to this theory believe that training can solve any and all personnel performance problems. They fail to recognize that training can only address problems resulting from deficiencies in *skill, knowledge* or *ability.* Unfortunately, job performance inadequacies can also be the result of people not being motivated to perform, being prevented from performing due to some real impediment in the job design, or not knowing how to perform. Training can only solve roughly 20 percent of all performance problems; the remaining 80 percent call for creative, no-nonsense supervision and management.

"The Panacea" is an illogical perspective for trainers or managers to hold. It can be prevented from taking root by a careful analysis of the performance problem in question along with an analysis of the job the problem manifests itself within.

This approach is more likely to identify the problem and consequently solve the problem than rushing headlong into a quick-fix training "solution."

Some steps that can be taken to more accurately diagnose the performance problem include:
- write a problem statement in specific terms
- conduct a job task analysis so that there is a clearer picture of the total job environment
- ask job incumbents what they believe the problem to be
- ask if the problem can be addressed through an increase in knowledge, skill or ability.

BAD MEDICINE

"Bad Medicine" is the prescription of training for problems that training cannot solve. Such a practice may begin by a failure to understand training or the nature of the problem. The person who dispenses *"Bad Medicine"* may be a victim of *"The Definitional Dilemma"* or be suffering from *"The Panacea."* In critical cases both diseases may be present.

"Bad Medicine" hurts the organization by spending money foolishly. It can destroy the image of the training department by utilizing training in cases where discipline would be appropriate. This leaves a bitter aftertaste in the mouths of all involved and is certain to cause employees to view training in a punitive, negative light. Unfortunately, in some organizations labor-management relations have been allowed to degenerate into such a state.

Training and discipline do not mix! Training can, to *some* extent, be a motivator. Motivation can be thought of as the "flip side of discipline"— part of the same "record," but a separate and distinct "song."

Another common manifestation of *"Bad Medicine"* is the prescription of training for correcting personal deficiencies. A trainer named Ed Yager once found a trainee who had taken 30 classes over a period of 10 years and had still not been promoted to supervisor.

Such a practice is common in employment and educational environments. It is a simple, convenient, and highly unethical response to problem employees and students. Managers, trainers, and teachers have a professional responsibility to be honest with their charges and prescribe appropriate treatment. Those who prescribe "snake oil" should not be tolerated.

It should be kept in mind that training should only be prescribed when there is a deficiency in knowledge or skill that is necessary to do the job! It must also be remembered that learning cannot occur in a negative, punitive, stressful, environment.

THE ASSESSMENT ASS

"The Assessment Ass" is not really serious about training. *"The Assessment Ass"* assesses and examines various training strategies, plans and programs. Typically these are complex, sophisticated, trendy ventures. *"The Ass"* is identified by the telltale statement:

"We're assessing ..."

Or words to that effect.

The strategy, plan or program that is being assessed sounds very impressive. In fact, it always *is* very impressive! A manager who would utilize such a strategy, plan, or program would be doing something outstanding, taking training steps that the security industry could emulate. Sending all of the officers to a federal training center sounds great. Having all security personnel given forty (40) hours of classroom instruction is laudable. Using big-name instructors is wonderful. So is entering into a joint training venture with a local community college. Videotaping and critiquing all students on task performance is a marvelous idea.

All of these things sound and are, wonderful. Unfortunately, in the vast majority of cases, none of them will become a reality. There are, after all, roadblocks that must be overcome:
- budgetary limitations
- scheduling shortcomings
- availability of equipment, instructors and facilities

Therein lies the problem with *"The Assessment Ass"*: these brilliant ideas are not likely to happen. And *"The Ass"* knows this. Or at least should know it. *"The Ass"* is either deliberately trying to mislead others or is simply too inept to realize that money doesn't grow on trees.

THE BUDGET BUSTER

This is when a manager has his subordinates attend a training program, generally put on by an outside consultant. In most cases, the outside consultant impresses management greatly. When all the costs of the training are calculated—often *after* the training has occurred—it is found that there is no more money for training left in the current fiscal year. Having the officers undergo the training is not the problem, assessing costs and performance outcomes is. Before embarking on any training initiative, managers must cost out the initiative. This is especially true with "one-time shots." If a program is going to exhaust the budget, it must be worth the price.

Generally speaking, large budgetary allocations should be directed toward programs that are comprehensive and continuous. Sending the staff through the Certified Protection Officer Program or buying a subscription to the Private Security Television Network are examples. Both programs cover numerous subjects, are continuous and provide for testing and evaluation of learning.

Managers must be aware that only so much learning will occur within a given time period. While this varies widely with differences in instructional design and delivery; there is a real limit to what will be learned. One rule of thumb that is good to use is that in a four (4) or eight (8) hour class, a participant will learn three (3) to five (5) things that will be useful on the job.

In cases where expensive, one-shot programs are unavoidable, the learning experience should be made as continuous as possible. Having the class participants read and study the topic before the class is one good strategy. Another is to have them work with the information that has been learned at the end of the class. This can take many forms such as teaching a short class on the topic to others, changing a procedure, or simply personalizing it into their jobs: "What will you change about the way you do your job?"

ROLEAIDS

The *"Roleaids"* manager fails to appreciate the role and function of the contemporary protection officer. While there has not been a great deal of study on this topic, my experience leads me to believe that security officers perform four (4) main functions within an organization:
1.   Intelligence Agent for management via the collection of information that management needs.
2.   Enforcement Agent for management policies.
3.   Management Representative through the enforcement of rules and the providing of information and directions to visitors, employees and customers.
4.   Legal Consultant where the officer has a working knowledge of more areas of the law than any other member of the organization (labor law, administrative regulations such as OSHA, criminal law, civil liability standards).

The *"Roleaids"* manager does not understand this. He thinks of security officers as "guards." As a result he does not develop his subordinate officers. The officers are not socialized as *adjunct members of the management team.* They are not given the human and public relations training necessary to interact with others in a productive manner. Their interpersonal communication skills are not honed so that they can "sell" people on policy adherence. Writing skills are not developed to enable them to record data efficiently.

The solution to *"Roleaids"* is to have the afflicted manager study security officers in some manner. He must become educated about what the officers do. One way of doing this is to conduct a job task analysis. Another is a compensation review by a human resources specialist. Having the manager spend some time with the officers can also be a help. Getting the manager to write a few paragraphs defining "security officers" can be a key to solving this syndrome. Giving the officers a change in job title to more accurately reflect what they do can also help.

TOAD TRAINING

"Toad Training" is a common occurrence in the security industry. It takes place when security officers with limited cognitive ability are hired and trained. Assuming a professional training program is in existence, management will inevitably be disappointed when the new recruits graduate as there will be an abundance of well trained "toads" in the workplace: employees who simply don't have the education, judgement or communication skills necessary to be effective protection officers.

Rather than act as ambassadors for the organization, these employees act as if they were amphibians! There is no excuse for hiring substandard personnel—especially when those employees are representing the organization. Unfortunately, it happens all the time due to a gross and perhaps deliberate misunderstanding of the duties and functions of security personnel (see *"Roleaids"*).

The solution? Research the role of the security officer within the organization. Managers or trainers must perform an in-depth job description based on a scientifically designed job analysis. Trainers must assume the role of consultant rather than hiding within the confines of the classroom. They must become involved in the overall personnel management process including selection, recruitment and evaluation.

Supervisors should beware of getting stuck "holding the bag" when "toad" trainees appear on the job, as graduates of their training program.

MR. UNIQUE

"Mr. Unique" perpetually resists purchasing off-the-shelf training programs because they are generic and not specific enough to his or her work environment. He magnifies the differences instead of linking the similarities between his organization and others. *"Mr. Unique"* thinks that his or her problems are like no other. As no off-the-shelf training program addresses these problems—in his mind—*he does nothing regarding training.*

"Mr. Unique" also does not take advice in solving operational or performance problems from other security managers. He also does not belong to the American Society for Industrial Security (or if he does belong he is not active in attending meetings, seminars, etc.) because his needs are very different than those of other managers.

"Mr. Unique" fails to see that such issues as negative public relations, poor human relations, inadequate reports, sloppy investigations and ineffective enforcement are problems shared by the entire security industry. Rather than learn from other managers, professional organizations, and off-the-shelf training programs, he does nothing. He retreats from addressing the problem under the guise of his situation being unique and therefore, unsolvable.

"Mr. Unique" can be dealt with by assessing the following questions:
1.   What training program is currently in place?
2.   What training program is desirable in the near future?
3.   What would it cost in personnel time and consulting fees to develop a tailor-made training program?
4.   How much budgetary support is currently available?
5.   What will the results of failure to train personnel be in a year from now? Two years from now?

NOTE: *"Mr. Unique"* is very common and often convincing in his arguments.

BIBLIOGRAPHY

Dr. Leonard Nadler as cited in "Why Have A Training And Development Department Anyway" by Dugan Laird which appeared in *Training*, October 1979. Reprinted in *Designing and Delivering Cost-Effective Training and Measuring the Results,* compiled and edited by Ron Zemke, Linda Standke and Phillip Jones; 1981, Minneapolis, MN; Lakewood Publications.

"Front-End Analysis," an interview with Joe Harless which appeared in *Training*, March 1975. Reprinted in *Designing and Delivering Cost-Effective Training and Measuring the Results.*

"Police Performance Problems: Are They Training Or Supervision Issues"; John A. Sample, *The Police Chief,* October 1983, p.58, Volume L, Number 10.

"Caution: Training Is Not A Cure-All"; Ed Yager, which appeared in *Training*, July 1979. Reprinted in *Designing and Delivering Cost-Effective Training and Measuring the Results*

Effective Security Management; Charles A. Sennewald, 1985, Stoneham, MA; Butterworth Publishers, p.97.

"Good In-Service Training: The Chief's Perspective"; International Association of Chiefs of Police Training Evaluation Subcommittee; Larry Brockelsby - Director, *The Police Chief*, November 1986, P.22, Volume LII, Number 11.

ORIENTATION FOR SECURITY OFFICERS
by David H. Naisby, Jr., CPO

First impressions are critical. They establish a foundation for everything that follows. New staff are forming an impression of the supervisor, just as the supervisor is of them. It is suggested that new staff receive a thorough orientation to their new job and the organization for which they will be working. In this way they will get a good impression of the employer, and the supervisor/instructor will provide them with the initial information and tools they need to be successful.

What follows is a list of activities and/or topics that should help new staff become productive colleagues. Each organization should tailor this list to their own unique situation and to the new staff member, and decide who will take responsibility for each item.

Before New Staff Member Arrives

New employee orientation should begin with ease and transition for both the employee and the institution. In order to make that connection, however, it is imperative that all facets of integration are utilized. With respect to the embracing of a new employee, current staff and the prospective newcomer should be aware of their roles as well as those complementary to them.

The new employee should review and become familiar with their job description. This job description should specifically explain how the officers should perform in the organization. It should include control and planning tasks and system-wide obligations. The direct authority for the employees should also be identified to prevent conflicts arising from uncertainty as to who makes the decisions for particular issues. The job description should also reflect the organization's expectations of employees regarding self-management responsibilities and should include temporary job assignments that may happen during employment.

Current staff, on the other hand, should consider the following elements.

1. Distribute an announcement to current staff, including a photograph if possible. Get them to know the new officer.
2. Send the new staff member:
   - A welcome letter
   - A job description
   - Instructions for first day and week
   - When & where to arrive, who to ask for
   - Where to park
   - Suggested attire
   - What to expect for the first few days
   - Orientation to people, job, office, department and organization
   - What to expect regarding meals, breaks and time for personal business
   - Initial work responsibilities
   - Required or recommended reading, such as any publications created by your department
   - Other advance preparation

First Day of Work

At the start of the first day, each new employee shall have a payroll and personnel orientation. The orientation is designed to help new employees better understand personnel policies and procedures. The session should last one hour and will review general payroll and personnel topics such as: meeting the payroll/personnel team, pay rate and schedules, benefits, performance evaluation and standards, holiday schedules, etc.

1.   Meet with supervisor (and others as appropriate) for office orientation, office goals and objectives.
2.   Review primary activities.
3.   Know your relationship to rest of organization, such as :
      •   Service culture
      •   Confidentiality
      •   Ethics
      •   Working with supervisors, colleagues, assistants and/or volunteers
      •   Managing office conflicts
4.   Review and discuss questions about job description and evaluation criteria.
5.   Policies and procedures specific to office, for example:
      •   Working hours
      •   Telephone techniques and etiquette
      •   Correspondence styles
      •   Staff meetings
      •   Budget and accountability
6.   Get assigned work space.
7.   Meet with colleagues and support staff.
8.   Brief overview of their responsibilities and assignments.
9.   Meet with assigned support staff (if appropriate) or "buddy." *
10.   Office organization (files, supplies, etc.).
11.   Handling incoming and outgoing mail.
12.   Office circulation files.
13.   Office resources (directories, dictionaries, style manuals, computer program manuals, staff listing, etc.).
14.   Using the telephone.
15.   Meet assigned "buddy" for orientation to the environment and for informal help.
16.   Office dress code.
17.   Where to put coat and personal belongings.
18.   Restrooms.
19.   Refreshment area, lounges.
20.   Office supplies.
21.   Copy machines.
22.   Review:
      •   Refilling paper supply.
      •   Policies about number of copies and making personal copies.
      •   Fax machines.
      •   Calendars.
      •   Coffee/coffee fund, gift fund.
      •   Where to go for lunch, breaks.
      •   End-of-day routine: lights, telephones, doors, computer, etc.

Within First Week of Arrival

Within the first week of employment, each new employee shall be given a departmental orientation by the immediate supervisor. The orientation will cover the department's *functions*, *organization*, and *goals*. Information given to the employee will also include job responsibilities, annual review, performance evaluation standards and expectations, introduction to department members, tour of department and emergency procedures.

      •   Set up work area.
      •   Start work.

- Supervisor checks in frequently to clarify expectations and answer questions.
- Colleagues check in to answer questions and offer support.
- "Buddy," mentor or field training officer checks in daily to answer questions and offer support.
- Meet with department business manager to cover, as appropriate.
- Time cards.
- Vacation/sick/personal leave policies.
- Keys.
- Access to the office on nights and weekends.
- Telephone: access code, personal calls, paying for personal long-distance calls.
- Stamps, parking permits.
- General review of accounting.
- Listing of account numbers.
- Journal vouchers.
- Travel and reimbursement (especially for business travelers).
- Company credit card.
- Telephone credit card use (saves money over paying the full rate from a hotel room, for instance).
- Paying bills, making deposits, transferring between accounts.
- Meet with company Human Resources Services.
- Complete all necessary paperwork.
- Review company personnel policies and procedures.
- Learn about benefits (health & life insurance, retirement, select benefits, etc.).
- Learn about company orientation.
- Get company ID.
- Get company parking permit (if appropriate).
- Meet with MIS personnel for computer assistance.
- Overview of policies & procedures, including confidentiality and piracy.
- Assessment of knowledge of and comfort with computer hardware and software.
- Hardware: turning on, backing up, printing, shutting down, etc.
- Software: word-processing, data-processing, e-mail, etc. as needed.
- Arrange further training and support as needed.
- Tour the building and immediate area.

Within Six Months of Starting

- Meet key people and offices within the company.
- Meet on a regular basis with supervisor to discuss issues and review job description, expectations and performance.
- "Buddy" checks in on a regular basis to answer questions and offer support.
- Attend company's new staff orientation (provides an overview of company people, departments, policies and procedures, and includes a tour of the company facilities).
- Have 90-day performance dialogue.

    * It would be valuable to assign a "buddy" to a new staff member, preferably a peer from the office area, of whom the new employee can ask any question without fear of reprisals. A colleague who is relatively new to the organization might be the best choice because they have a fresh perspective and they are familiar with questions a new staff member might have. If a buddy is not assigned, someone else should cover these topics.
    Mentoring is a formal process involving mentors who are trained and sometimes compensated for taking someone under their wing. Mentors are generally senior employees who can provide both an example to the new employee and address any concerns that they might have.

Mentors are not supervisors. They perform no evaluative functions. They may represent management insofar as proper codes of conduct and performance are concerned; but they have no authority to discipline.

Mentoring relationships sometimes continue throughout the employment relationship.

Field Training Officers (FTOs) are similar to mentors in that they help to socialize the new hire into the job. FTOs differ from mentors in that they also evaluate the probationary employee. Field Training Officers must be trained in how to teach/train/instruct as well as how to evaluate/supervise.

Because of financial, personal, and legal implications, a lunch companion should not be a formal part of the schedule if lunch is not a reimbursable expense. The new employee should not feel obligated to eat lunch with staff in the event that they feel they cannot afford it, or if they need the time for personal business. A lunch companion may be offered as a courtesy with brown bagging as one option.

Orientation is a critical juncture in socializing the new employee. It "marries" recruitment, training and supervision. Due to the import of first impressions, the reality of security force training today and the critical element of understanding of the organizational culture by protection officers, orientation must be carefully programmed.

BIBLIOGRAPHY

France, Debra R., and Robin L. Jarvis. "Quick starts for new employees." *Training & Development* Oct 1996 v50 n10 p47(4).

Grant, Phillip C. "Job descriptions: what's missing." *Industrial Management*, Nov-Dec 1997 v39 n6 p9(4).

National Orientation Director's Association. As taken from the Internet on 3 July 1998 @ http://www.indiana.edu/~nodal.

Revell, Phil. "First-year shock absorbers." *Times Educational Supplement.* 2 May 1997 n4218 pC4(1).

York County Government Employee Orientation. 1997.

EMPLOYEE ORIENTATION
QUIZ

1.   Orientation of new employees should begin when?
      a)   Once a worker is familiar with his/her position.
      b)   The first day of work.
      c)   At the time of hire.
      d)   When management feels the time is right.

2.   New employees should familiarize themselves with their job description when?
      a)   When a "buddy" is assigned.
      b)   During the hiring interview.
      c)   It should be taught on the job (OJT).
      d)   Before the first day of work.

3.   The "buddy" system is useful because:
        a)   It takes pressure off of the supervisors in the organization.
        b)   One experienced employee can provide useful information without fear of reprisals.
        c)   Employees can become friendly early in one's career.
        d)   Many organizations have employees with nothing else to do anyway.

4.   When should a new employee be introduced to the organization goals, functions and philosophies?
        a)   During the hiring interview.
        b)   Within the first week of arrival.
        c)   Never, it should be something the new employee will inherently pick up.
        d)   The first day on the job.

5.   The first day of work should include:
        a)   Understanding where your work space should be.
        b)   Meeting with colleagues and support staff.
        c)   None of the above.
        d)   All of the above.

6.   When is the "buddy system" necessary?
        a)   Always.
        b)   Until the new hire feels comfortable in his/her position.
        c)   Only in the first week of work.
        d)   During the first month of employment.

7.   Scheduled "Performance Dialogues" are important because:
        a)   The employee will know when he/she is eligible for benefits.
        b)   The institution is obligated to evaluate the employee.
        c)   It is an opportunity for the organization to evaluate and comment on work performance.
        d)   It is an opportunity for the employee to be introduced to new philosophies.

8.   Every institution should have an orientation policy.
                    □ T   □ F

9.   Should the reasons why employees are selected to be a "buddy" be consistent?
                    □ T   □ F

10.   Make sure that:
        a)   New employees understand their new environment.
        b)   The "buddy" documents every action of the new employee.
        c)   You explain any reorganization or job restructuring to the current employees necessitated by a new hire.
        d)   All of the above.

STAFF TRAINING AND DEVELOPMENT
by Charles T. Thibodeau, M.Ed., CPP, CSS

Training is the bedrock of a balanced, stable security force. A well trained security force is more likely to provide required services, in an effective and efficient manner, free of legal liability. The officers operate both as a well orchestrated team and as effective, independent "can do" service personnel. They are usually very visible, approachable and seem always to be in the right place at the right time. They make a positive impression on the people who work at or visit the owner's property.

From a legal perspective, if the company is ever sued by a plaintiff for injuries resulting from a claim of inadequate security, in addition to charges of negligent hiring, negligent supervision, negligent retention, negligent entrustment and negligent assignment, it's likely there will also be a charge of *negligent training*. That is, the plaintiff will charge that either the company failed to provide training, the training that was provided did not meet some standard or the trainer was not qualified due to lack of experience and/or proper credentials.

Some recent settlements related to the negligent training issue include: a $1.25 million award for inadequate training in proper security measures, 32 *ATLA Law Rep.* 366, Oct. 1989; a $100,000 award for negligent training in an assault and battery case, 30 *ATLA Law Rep.*, 272, Aug. 1987; a $12.3 million award for negligent training of employees who improperly used monitoring equipment, 30 *ATLA Law Rep.* 262; a $4.2 million award for failure to teach the use of alarms, and failure to provide a trained and adequate security force, 32 *ATLA Law Rep.* 20, Feb. 1989; and finally a negligent training award of $500,000 for a wrongful death of a shoplifting suspect who was shot by a guard, 29 *ATLA Law Rep.* 39, Feb. 1986.[1]

In order to properly protect a company from legal liability, it is important to ensure that security personnel receive "adequate training" by training the trainer before they are allowed to instruct. One of the greatest mistakes made in the training of security personnel is the use of an untrained instructor. In a lawsuit, one of the first questions that the plaintiff's attorney will ask the trainer is, "please describe all of your education and experience that qualifies you to be a trainer of security personnel" or words to that effect. Unfortunately, in most cases the trainer has no credentials and the plaintiff's case for inadequate training is made. This chapter will provide some direction for putting together an effective training and development program for your security department.

THREE DOMAINS OF TRAINING

First of all it is important to realize that there are three domains of training: *cognitive, psychomotor* and *affective*. A balanced training program will contain all three. The cognitive training domain is most often taught in a classroom and is usually known as pre-assignment training. Cognitive training tackles theory and knowledge and is usually presented using lectures, demonstrations, video presentations, illustrations, readings, tutorial exams and homework.

In many companies the training process is short-circuited at this point by the exclusive use of short videos without an instructor. No one can receive adequate training by merely watching some generic videos about security. It will be extremely difficult for a defense attorney to prove adequate training once the plaintiff's attorney has discovered that all the security officers received by way of cognitive training was six hours of videotapes.

Psychomotor training is the hands-on part of the training process. This is usually taught at the job site and consists of such things as facility orientation, patrol techniques, equipment training, emergency response and department-authorized security procedures. In many companies this is the only training security officers receive. In fact, often the company will send a new recruit out to a facility for fifteen or twenty minutes of training before their first shift. In other words, after fifteen or twenty minutes of training the multimillion dollar building is turned over to the new recruit.

In many cases companies assign new security officers to work with experienced officers for two or three days before they are allowed to take on their own shifts. Three days or more of pre-assignment or on the job training, in conjunction with at least 12 hours of cognitive classroom training will make it much easier for the company's attorney to defend the position that the company provides adequate security officer training.

Affective domain training covers work values and/or professional attitudes. The danger here is that values are automatically and inadvertently being taught by everyone, all the time. The way we dress, our mannerisms, our statements about race, religion, sex – everything we say or do is continually communicated. Our audience, those we communicate with, as well as uninvited listeners, are subjected to our values and attitudes whether we want them to be or not. Our listeners are influenced by our values and attitudes, especially if the listener has great respect for us as teachers, instructors or trainers.

It is important for the trainer to be aware of affective domain training and to include some specific work-related values and attitudes in both the cognitive and psychomotor lesson plans. The way these values and attitudes are delivered is different than the cognitive and psychomotor training. Values and attitudes are not taught as separate subjects, but are linked to the other two types of training. The trainer must be prepared to inject the appropriate value or attitude whenever the opportunity presents itself.

The trainer who comes to work in an unkempt uniform will have a difficult time training others to wear their uniform with pride and to take care with their appearance. The male trainer with long hair and an earring in his ear will have a hard time convincing male students that they must wear their hair short and not wear earrings. If the trainer comes to class late all the time it will be hard for the trainer to criticize tardiness or teach the virtues of being punctual. If the trainer does not follow the sexual harassment, diversity and multiculturalism guidelines of the company, the students will likely have problems in those areas as well. It is not enough to teach in the affective domain; to be believable, the trainer must live this part of the training.

TRAINING PROGRAM DEVELOPMENT

There are four stages of training program development:[2]
1.   Identifying the objectives
2.   Designing programs to meet the objectives
3.   Organizing the programs to meet the objectives
4.   Evaluation of the programs in terms of the objectives

Each stage is separate but related to the other stages. At each step decisions have to be made and problems solved. Throughout the analysis it is important to keep in mind the cost-effectiveness of the training program. In most cases, the determining factor of whether or not you will have a training program is your ability to prove to upper management the cost-effectiveness of your training proposal.

Identify the Objectives of the Program

What are the objectives of the program? Here it is necessary to decide on goals for the training programs which will directly address the real or perceived needs of the company. Review security officer job descriptions and requests for security assistance made by department heads in the company. Review daily activity reports, 911 reports from the public law enforcement and security and safety incident reports to determine threat levels and probability facts. Review the mission statement for the company and department. Prepare objectives to which the upper management, those who have to sign off on the training program, can relate. To do this you may want to survey top management to test their attitude and perceptions of security.

You must be able to clearly define what it is that you want the security officers to be able to do after receiving the training, and to what level you will set your expectations. Consider the following as a general guideline of desired outcomes. The trained security officers should be able to:
1.   Observe, report and take limited action.
2.   Act reasonably.

3.   Perform their duties within the civil law, criminal law, administrative law, company policies and department procedures.
4.   Exhibit high ethical standards.
5.   Be a "can do" company servant.

We commonly find that expectations regarding the performance of security officers include the ability to perform certain skills, to obtain general and specific knowledge of the job and exhibit the proper work values and attitudes.

Design the Program to Meet the Objectives

The program content should include, but not be limited to, the following:

1.   *General:* There will always be a need for cognitive classroom training. This training will carry a standardized curriculum, hopefully containing what every security officer needs to know about security.

2.   *Structured OJT:* At some point the new recruit will need to participate in on-the-job training (OJT). This should normally take place after the classroom training, but it does not have to. As long as the cognitive training is completed within the first 21 days of employment, the OJT can take place first. Since the OJT and cognitive training are fully articulated, each type of training will strengthen and support the other. However, the OJT should be "structured" OJT not just "warm body training."

All security officers should know how to write field notes, how to write a report, how to respond to all emergencies relative to a particular work site, how to do foot patrol as well as vehicle patrol, how to run all of the equipment and systems including alarms, CCTV systems, card access systems, guard tour systems, fire panels. The officer should be highly skilled in human relations, know how to deal with the press, have a professional telephone manner and know how to serve the needs of the people who inhabit the facility to which the officer is assigned.

In some settings the officers must know about the use of force, how to handle a variety of weapons, hand-to-hand combat, handcuffing and the law of arrest. The list of information required goes on and on. It is for the trainer to determine the essentials. At the same time, the trainer must keep in mind cost-effectiveness and the need to satisfy tort law with regard to potential negligent training claims. Be sure that your course content is short enough to be cost-effective but comprehensive enough to defend against charges of negligent training.

What Should Be Included in the Curriculum

Although there are no national standards in private security, by comparing lawsuits over the past ten years, we have attempted to determine what a standard might look like if one did exist. The following are some ideas for your consideration, given that you are about to train an unarmed security contingent:

1.   **BASIC SECURITY OVERVIEW**
      2 HRS.
                  a)   Role of the Security Officer
                  b)   Typical Assignments & "Can Do" Service
                  c)   Facility Orientation
                  d)   Patrol Techniques
                  e)   Access Control
                  f)   Reasonable Observation
                  g)   Reasonable Reporting
                  h)   Limited Actions
                  i)   Pro-active Prevention vs. Reactive Security
                  j)   Liaison with Public Law Enforcement

2.   **LEGAL POWERS AND LIMITATIONS**
      2 HRS.
          a)   Acting under "Color of Law"
          b)   Limited Immunity vs. No Immunity
          c)   Tort Law
                -    Negligence
                -    Intentional Torts
                -    Strict Liability
                -    Contract Law
                -    Imputed Liability
                -    Non-delegable Duties
                -    Selected Case Law
                -    Merchant Privilege Laws
                -    Defenses
                -    The "Reasonable Person Test"
          d)   Criminal Law
                -    Arrest & Detention
                -    Search & Seizure
                -    Burdens of Proof
                -    Probable Cause
                -    Reasonable Suspicion
                -    Defenses
                -    Crime Identification
          e)   Administrative Law
                -    OSHA
                -    ADA
                -    NFPA
                -    EPA-HAZMAT
                -    EEOC & AA
                -    Workers' Comp. Laws
          f)   Constitutional Law
                -    Miranda Warning
                -    Mapp v. Ohio
                -    Burdeau v. McDowell
          g)   Use-of-Force
          h)   Alternatives to the Use of Force
          i)   Defensive Weapons Identification & Use

3.   **EMERGENCY RESPONSE**
      2 HRS.
          a)   Know the Company Policy
          b)   Know & Practice the Department Procedure
          c)   Know How to Identify an Emergency
          d)   Know When to Call 911
          e)   Know How to Respond to Fires
                -    Low Building Fires
                -    High Building Fires
          f)   Know How to Respond to Medical Emergencies
          g)   Know How to Respond to Severe Weather
          h)   Know How to Respond to Criminal Acts
          i)   Know How to Respond to Bomb Threats

j)   Know How to Assist Public Service Personnel

k)   Know How to Deal with Violence in the Workplace

4.   SAFETY & ACCIDENT PREVENTION
2 HRS.

a)   Observing and Reporting Unsafe Conditions

b)   Identify Accident Hazards

c)   Identify Fire Hazards

d)   Identify Hazardous Materials

e)   Know the Safety Rules and Regulations

f)   Know How to Respond to Accident Investigations

g)   Know How to Respond to Report Accidents

h)   Maintain Certifications in First Aid and CPR

5.   REPORT WRITING
2 HRS.

a)   Why Write a Report

b)   The Importance of Note Taking

c)   Elements of a Report

d)   Proper Times, Names and Locations

e)   Giving Physical Descriptions

f)   Facts versus Opinions and Assumptions

g)   The Importance of Good Penmanship

h)   Changes to Reports

i)   Reports as Legal Documents

j)   How to Perform in Court

6.   HUMAN RELATIONS
2 HRS.

a)   General Public Relations Skills

b)   Principles of Good Communications

c)   Proper Telephone Procedure

d)   Listening

e)   Avoiding Confrontation

f)   Dealing with the Media

g)   Dealing with Front Line Rage

h)   Escalation De-escalation Continuum

i)   Escalation Verbal De-escalation Continuum

j)   Break-Aways to Verbal De-escalation

k)   Break-Aways to Escape

The above represents a model curriculum for an unarmed security officer contingent. This is only the author's concept of a model training program. There are many others that are just as good,[3] but this model incorporates all the author has learned from studying the errors of security officers and the lawsuits that have resulted. Armed officers and those who are issued defensive weapons other than firearms, would have to attend the above cognitive pre-assignment training in addition to firearms and defensive weapons training.

Organizing the Program to Meet the Objectives

When considering how to meet the "duty of care" by providing "adequate training" for your security staff, first determine if a contract program is available within your budget constraints. A good place to look for contract services is the local customized training departments of technical colleges and community colleges. This approach has a number of advantages.[4]

Most technical colleges can provide licensed or certified personnel to teach the curriculum; the college can prepare the curriculum, order textbooks or prepare handouts, administer and proctor final exams, keep training records, and, perhaps best of all, mitigate legal problems if your security officers are ever sued; that is, the plaintiff's lawyer may drop the charge of negligent training as soon as the lawyer finds out that training was delivered by outside professionals. In addition, your thoughtful decision to use a well respected educational institution in the community might help to show your company in a favorable light to the jury.

The one negative side of utilizing colleges for training is the cost. Customized training is much more expensive and the cost could easily exceed your training budget. However, it is well worth it to check out the cost of a college program before embarking on the creation of a proprietary training program. The *Job Training Partnership Act* (JTPA), underwrites the most important public programs currently being used to help employers with training activities. The financial aid departments of technical colleges and community colleges will have information regarding this agency. Some programs are controlled by the Private Industry Councils (PICs) and are funded by block grants to the state. If your budget is slim it would be worth it to check into these block grant programs.

Once it has been determined that your company is going to create its own proprietary training program, many logistical matters must be decided upon. These include, but are not limited to, the program's budget constraints, the location and whether the program will be presented on-site or off-site, what materials are needed (such as audio-visual equipment, blackboards, lecterns, etc.), the program schedule, length of the program in hours (in terms of legal liability, what is the standard acceptable number of hours?), are you going to hire a consultant to help prepare the program, where are you going to get trained instructors, who in the department will be designated the official trainer, should you hire a trained and certified person from outside the department to train the officers, what training records you will be required to keep, who will prepare the curriculum (in terms of legal liability), what topics should be included in the training, how can you tie the cognitive domain training to the structured OJT portion of the program, and how will you evaluate the effectiveness of the program?

One of the most important considerations wasn't even touched upon in the above paragraph. The question is, "Is enough money in the budget to pay the security officers to attend the training?" If the company insists on having a proprietary training department, then security officers should be trained off hours and paid for their attendance. When training is mandatory and students are not paid for their attendance, the result will likely be a room full of unmotivated learners – not a great atmosphere for learning. Most likely there will be more sleeping and complaining going on during the sessions than learning.

Scheduling should be done so that the learners are brought in for training after a rest period. That is, don't bring the student into a four hour class after the student has just worked eight hours. Utilize the students' off days or evening hours if they work the day shift. Whatever you do, be sure to remember that in order to learn anything the student must be rested and motivated.

Technical colleges and community colleges can help alleviate scheduling and compensation problems. Your company can make it a policy for security officers to report to the local technical college within a certain time-frame, complete cognitive security officer training and receive a certificate of completion. This would be made a condition of employment. You may even reimburse the officers for their training if they receive a certain grade which you set.

If the colleges only provide a pass/fail grade, then a certificate of successful completion could be used by the security officer to receive reimbursement. Since they must attend the college program on their own time, you can save the cost of paying their wages. There is one company that uses this initial training as a screening device. If you want to have a job you must complete a week or two of training and then compete for the job. Since the people being hired are not employees they receive no pay. After training there is no requirement that the person be hired.

Training The Trainer

Those who are designated trainers, as discussed above, must obtain credentials. The best way to attain teaching credentials is to attend the nearest technical or community college "Train-the-Trainer" course. This course is usually available at most colleges and universities. The fact that the training has nothing to do with security is irrelevant. Learning how to write a lesson plan, how to use different types of teaching methodologies and how to prepare tests are what you need for your credentials. You will add in security topics after receiving the basic training, when applying your knowledge in the classroom.

The trainer should also have some post-secondary or higher level credentials such as holding an AAS or BS degree in Security Management or some other degree in Security Management. Notice that we did not say a degree in Police Science, Criminology or Public Law Enforcement? The reason for this is that there exists a great chasm between public law enforcement and private security. If you have never had a formal education in Private Security, then you may have a terrible time in court trying to prove to a jury that you were qualified to train security officers. Public law enforcement personnel have a very different attitude and perspective than private security practitioners.

In addition, the trainer should have at least five years' experience and a nationally recognized certification such as the Certified Protection Professional Certification (CPP) from the American Society for Industrial Security, a Certified Protection Officer (CPO) or Certified Security Supervisor (CSS) from the International Foundation for Protection Officers, or other such certification.

Imagine a situation where a lawsuit is filed and every one of your officers was trained at the local technical college. The instructor was a professional state licensed instructor who had five years of security management experience prior to becoming an instructor. The instructor had earned the CPP and CSS certifications in addition to his AAS degree in Security Management. Imagine also that each of your security officers has a training file which indicates that they all successfully passed the model curriculum set out above. These facts alone might make a litigious attorney hold off unless the facts of the case were rather lopsided in that lawyer's favor. In any event, negligent training would be very hard to prove.

Imagine the opposite. Let's say that all your security officers receive a few minutes of OJT in the way of training, with an experienced security officer. Compare the difference with the above scenario and determine which situation you would rather be in as a defense lawyer.

Evaluation of the Training Program and the Students

The best evaluation of the program is if it works. Are the security officers performing better? Has their public image and public relations improved? Do the officers seem to take more pride in their work and in themselves than they did before training? Do new recruits seem to reach productive levels faster? Has turnover slowed? Does the program curriculum seem to match the practical application of job tasks? What comments do the officers make about their training experience?

Not only does the program need to be evaluated, but each officer should be evaluated to prove that he/she attained a certain level of knowledge. The training records should be kept in a file separate from personnel files. The cabinet should be of a bar and padlock variety with a secure lock. The files should contain such things as sample tests, student's answer sheets, their grades and any comments made by the instructor. The student grade could be a number, a letter, or a P/F for pass or fail.

A separate file should be kept containing a copy of each revision of the training materials, including dates and times of each revision. A copy of all tests and a copy of the attendance sheet should be kept in this special file.

DEVELOPMENT

Once the security officer is trained and put on the job, the officer should be given a calendar of required CEU credits to be completed and noted by the record-keeper before the end of the first year of employment. Each officer should be in class at least six to twelve hours or more in each 12-month period of employment. This training should not be restricted to cognitive classroom training, but could include hours spent at seminars, specialized OJT for the purpose of cross-training, re-certification in first aid or CPR, self-defense training or college credit courses at a local accredited college.[5]

Nonetheless, the total hours must be calculated and a record kept in each officer's file. Any officer who fails to meet this requirement represents a breach in your legal liability coverage. A supervisor must be assertive in this area and insist on completion of continuous training from your security officer contingent.

Supervisors must also work to encourage the personal growth of their officers and ensure their personnel are satisfied in their current positions. As a supervisor you are charged with the responsibility of evaluating your employees. You should attempt to motivate those under you and provide them with opportunities to achieve goals within the boundaries of your company. Therefore, development is not solely a matter of training, but also entails ensuring that each employee has the chance to move up or even move horizontally within the company. To accomplish this you must:

1.   Analyze job descriptions and identify the skills in which each security officer excels. Find ways to expand the officer's areas of interest within the job description or suggest other similar job descriptions the officer might wish to explore.

2.   Have the officer write down the objectives that he would like to reach and set a time line for their achievement. Discuss strategies on how these goals might be met.

3.   If the security officer requires specialized training to reach the goals, find a way to allow the officer to attend the training.

4.   Monitor and evaluate the officer's progress. If you find the officer backsliding, be quick to confront the officer with the behavior you observed and get the officer back on track.

5.   Most of all, show sincerity and real concern for the future of each security officer. You must be a "can do" supervisor and prove it on a regular basis.

CONCLUSION

Training and development is not only concerned with meeting the needs of the trainee, but meeting the needs of the company as well. In the security industry, whether you operate a contract security business or serve as the proprietary force in a large company, the laws of the state, primarily the civil laws, dictate the training of security officers. Meeting these requirements helps security companies to avoid costly civil litigation. Of course there are other facets of law that must be considered, criminal law and administrative law for example, but most often it is with civil law that security departments become involved. Unfortunately, when a company becomes embroiled in a civil litigation over private security matters, the plaintiff too often wins. It is also true that under the tutored eye of a security expert conducting post-mortems on these losses, most of them can be traced back to inadequate training or no training at all of the security officers.

Therefore, before you put this article down saying "yes, this all sounds nice, but we just can't afford it," read page one, paragraph 3 of this chapter, and ask just one question, "can we afford a $12.3 million dollar loss from a lawsuit right now?" The question is not whether you can afford security training, the question is whether you can afford to go without proper security training.

ENDNOTES

1.   Maxwell, David A., 1993, *Private Security Law*, Butterworth-Heinemann, Boston, 407

2.   Davies, Ivor K., 1981, *Instructional Technique*, McGraw-Hill Inc., New York, pp. 10-11

3.   Gallery, Shari M., 1990, *Security Training Readings From Security Management Magazine*, Butterworths, Boston, MA, pp. 93-113

4.   Mosley, Donald C., et al, 1993, *Supervisor Management, The Art of Empowering & Developing People*, South-Western Publishing Co., Cincinnati, Ohio, p. 354

5.   Hess, Karen M., Wrobleski, Henry M., 1988, *Introduction to Private Security*, 2nd Edition, West Publishing Co., St. Paul, MN, p. 366

STAFF TRAINING AND DEVELOPMENT
QUIZ

1.   In order to properly protect your company from a charge of negligent training, it will be necessary to _____ the _____ before they are allowed to instruct.

2.   There are three training domains. They are _____, _____ and _____ _____.

3.   _____ training consists of theory and knowledge portions of the training.

4.   _____ training consists of the hands-on type of training.

5.   _____ training consists of work values.

6.   Training is a tool that can be used to avoid or mitigate legal problems brought on by the security officers.
        ☐ T   ☐ F

7.   One of the greatest mistakes made in the training of security personnel is failing to train the trainer.
        ☐ T   ☐ F

8.   "Adequate training" as defined by law, consists solely of showing security officers six hours of private security videotapes and having the officers fill out a ten question test after each video.
        ☐ T   ☐ F

9.   Police officers who have never taken private security training and have never worked in private security are good choices to teach private security by virtue of their police training and years of police experience.
        ☐ T   ☐ F

10.   Trained security officers should be able to observe, report and take limited action, in that order.
        ☐ T   ☐ F

CURRICULUM DESIGN
by Daniel R. Baker, Ph.D

INTRODUCTION

Curriculum development and design requires the security training professional to understand, construct, implement and evaluate required training curriculum on a recurring basis. This unit of study provides a starting point for the security professional whose goal is understanding curriculum development and design. To meet that goal there are twelve performance objectives to be mastered.

PERFORMANCE OBJECTIVES

Upon completion of this unit, you as a security supervisor will be able to:
- *Define curriculum*
- *Distinguish between macro and micro curriculum*
- *Select critical elements in the curriculum process*
- *Define competency-based education*
- *Identify the six-step process in determining competency-based outcomes*
- *Identify instructional goals*
- *Conduct instructional analysis*
- *Identify entry-behavior characteristics*
- *Formulate performance objectives*
- *Develop criteria for writing performance-objective test items*
- *Implement an instructional strategy*
- *Select appropriate instructional materials*

Your job as a security training supervisor is to ensure that each individual in your organization develops to the highest degree possible, all the requisite skills to succeed as a professional security officer. When you complete and master this material on curriculum and curriculum design, you should have the skills required to design, construct, implement and evaluate a comprehensive security training program.

Why is it important that you as a supervisor understand and implement a credible security training program? The reduction of liability in security operations is directly related to the level of training provided each officer. To ensure the officer can do and does each task in the appropriate manner as required by policy and procedure is a training function. You are the most important cog in the wheel of security training. The manner in which you do your job developing curriculum that supports organizational requirements can mean life or death to your security practitioners and ultimately to your organization.

This unit of study is broken down into two parts: concepts in curriculum and curriculum design. In Part I, you will develop your skills in articulating and understanding curriculum in general, while in Part II you will master the development and implementation of curriculum in security operations.

PART I: CONCEPTS IN CURRICULUM

Defining Curriculum and Distinguishing Between Macro and Micro Curriculums

Curriculum is normally defined as the sum of the learning activities and experiences that a learner has under the direction of a school or program. It is important to remember that in talking about curriculum you are discussing the sequence, continuity, scope and balance of the materials which will be provided in a classroom or clinical setting. For the professional security curriculum designer *curriculum is best defined as a plan for learning that meets the needs of the organization, the security personnel to be trained, and the public served.*

There are two types of curriculum that can be encountered in security training: micro and macro. *Micro* curriculum is the development of a task training step or unit of training within the confines of a larger course. *Macro* curriculum is the development of a course or complete program of instruction that has multiple units or modules of study. This course is an example of a macro curriculum because it is a complete course of study.

Critical Elements in the Curriculum Process

There are some critical elements that need to be considered when developing a curriculum. Do the training facilities support the desired educational outcome? Do the facilities have the requisite space, accouterments and rest areas necessary to support the students taught? These questions are directly impacted by your philosophy of education. Are you committed to the design and implementation of high-quality curriculum? Do you demonstrate your commitment to excellence in your approach to training policy?

A singularly critical element in the curriculum process, which we will discuss in greater length later, is the selection of students based on fair, consistent, relevant, and measurable standards – the "who is to be taught" issue.

The security curriculum design specialist must understand the importance of instructional media – the materials developed to support the curriculum that has been designed. Finally the security supervisor responsible for the development of curriculum ensures that sound ethical principles, underlying tenets which are incorporated in the education process, are included in designed curriculum.

What then is the most important issue in the curriculum process? The developed curriculum itself – *the plan for learning developed to assist the student in the educational process and those standards employed to ensure excellence.*

Defining Competency-Based Education

Modern security education and training is *competency based.* There are a number of names currently associated with competency-based security training such as:
- Performance-based education or training
- Outcome-based education or training
- Behavior-stated education or training
- Criterion-referenced education and training

For the purpose of this course of study *competency-based education is any educational process that requires the learner to demonstrate a skill, knowledge, or affective behavior based on a task, condition and standard that specifies exact measurable outcomes.* When speaking of performance it becomes what the student can or will be able to do when trained. The behavior exhibited is the level of knowledge demonstrated, or skill displayed. Competency behaviors in curriculum design are broken down into four (4) generalizable categories:
1.   Unskilled - can not do the performance.
2.   Semi-skilled - requires close supervision.
3.   Skilled - can do most parts of the job or task with little supervision.
4.   Mastery skilled - can do all parts of the job or task, requires no supervision, and can teach others how to do the task or job.

Why should all curriculum designed by security professionals be competency based? *The definition of competency-based training answers that question. Competency-based training is the process of setting clearly designed, measurable, observable objectives that the student learner accomplishes to a particular level.* All competency-based training is designed around the development of objectives and the utilization of the developed objectives to measurable performance and/or accomplishment.

A competency is the knowledge, skills and attitudes necessary to do a given task. Competency-based education and training for a security professional is an approach to learning where the student must demonstrate his or her ability to perform at a specific level prior to being certified as a Certified Protection Officer.

Six Steps in Determining Competency-Based Outcomes

What exactly do you need to get started writing competency-based security curriculum? You will need:
- *A job description* for each level of curriculum you intend to write. You use the job description to identify what the entry level, intermediate, or advanced security practitioner needs to know to accomplish the tasks described in the job description.
- *A task analysis* - you use the job description to complete a task analysis. A task analysis is the identification of the steps necessary to accomplish a specific part of the job being taught.
- *A task sequencing* - the analysis of each task from the standpoint of the untrained learner. Simple to complex, known to unknown. The breakdown used by the trainer to identify the training sequence.
- *Performance objectives* for each task. An objective(s) based on task and task sequencing which tells the learner exactly what they must do, know or complete.
- *Measurement standards* for performance that are objective and clearly identified so misunderstanding does not occur.
- *Developed curriculum* that supports the performance objective specified for the competency task the learner is to be trained on. Curriculum that identifies the frequency with which the task will be accomplished or used, the importance of the task to doing the job, and the level of learning difficulty it will take to master the knowledge, skill, ability, or manner of accomplishment.

PART II: CURRICULUM DESIGN

Each of us as security professionals wants to do a good job in training our subordinates. The difficulties faced sometimes seem insurmountable. This unit will give you the tools necessary to increase your ability to incorporate sound systems approaches into your curriculum design. Design, construct, implement and evaluate – those are the catch words of a professional curriculum design specialist. The following materials will familiarize you with the *Systems Approach Model for Designing Curriculum*. It is one of many approaches to curriculum design. For the security supervisor designing curriculum, it is best because of its logical construction and ease of use.

Identify the Instructional Goal

The first step in the systems approach model for designing curriculum requires that you determine exactly what you want the students to be able to accomplish after the training is completed. This design step forces the designer to know exactly what must be taught. It also incorporates all the tasks within a duty to be viewed from the job as a whole. For example the unit of instruction might be; "Provide Entry Control" within a course entitled "Foundations of Security Practices." All of the tasks or units of training for the course come from a comprehensive job description. In developing specific curriculum, the designer utilizes all of the learning domains: the cognitive domain for theory and general knowledge; psycho-motor domain for demonstrated skills requiring use of the hands in performing tasks; and the affective domain for interpersonal, intro-personal or values oriented skills.
The instructional goal may be derived from:
1.   A listing of overall goals of the school, course or unit of study.
2.   A needs assessment—what really needs to be taught.
3.   From practical experience—the common sense approach to curriculum development.

4.   From analyzing how the job is already being accomplished.

Conduct Instructional Analysis

The second step in the systems approach model for designing curriculum is conducting an instructional analysis. This is the process that occurs after you have identified the instructional goal and need to know what type of learning is required on the part of the student. It requires comprehensive analysis on the part of the curriculum designer to:
- Identify subordinate skills that must be learned.
- Determine subordinate procedural steps that must be followed to learn a particular process, skill, ability or performance.
- Create a chart or diagram that depicts required skills and shows relationships among them.

Identify Entry Behavior Characteristics

Step three in the systems approach model for designing curriculum is determining entry behaviors and characteristics that will be required of those participating in the training program. Every course of instruction has a minimum level of competency which must be met. For security, it is normal to require the applicant to be at least eighteen years old, have no history of alcohol or drug abuse and have no felony convictions. These are all entry-level behaviors or characteristics required for employment. But more than these, security applicants should be able to read and write, exercise sound judgement, communicate effectively and demonstrate the ability to control outbursts of temper under stress. These entry-level behaviors and characteristics are normally:
- Required for entrance in the training program.
- Required for successful completion of the training program.
- Required by policy or practice.

Entry behaviors and characteristics are not simply a listing of what the student can do, but specify what is required of the student to participate in the learning process. These required behaviors and characteristics identify any specific characteristic of the learner that may be important to consider in the design of specific curriculum.

Step four in the systems approach model for designing curriculum is writing the performance objectives. Written performance objectives are based on the instructional analysis. They incorporate specific entry behaviors and characteristics and are specific statements of what the learner will be able to do upon completion of the course of study, unit of instruction or task training. All written performance objectives:
- Identify knowledge, abilities, or skills to be learned and the task to be accomplished.
- Identify conditions under which the knowledge, ability or skill must be performed and what will be provided to the student to complete the action required.
- Identify criteria (standards) for successful performance.

One example of a written performance objective would be:

> *"Upon completion of this unit of study each security supervisor participating will (provide pencil, paper and a desk) write one performance objective for a psycho-motor task to the satisfaction of the test examiner."*

The performance objective has a clear statement of the knowledge, ability, or skill that has to be mastered; "write one performance objective." It has two clearly stated conditions: "Upon completion of this course of study" and "provided pencil, paper, and a desk." Finally it has a measurement statement: "to the satisfaction of the test examiner." The standard for successful performance could be without error, to a score of 85%, list six out of ten approaches to curriculum design. It simply must have a statement that the students can utilize to know exactly how they will be evaluated.

Develop Performance Objective Test Criteria

The fifth step in the systems approach model for designing curriculum is the development of the performance-referenced test. The performance-referenced test is based only on the performance objectives specified in the development of curriculum. To that end the performance-referenced test is written before the lesson plans or reference materials to be used in the course of study or training program. It is the formal evaluation instrument that will be used to measure the learners' accomplishment of the specified requirements for successful completion of the competency.

If the performance objective says the learner will write, the performance test question would require writing. Using the performance objective written in step four above, the test question would be a statement: "Write a performance objective for a psycho-motor skill." The directions for the accomplishment of this test item might be: Provided a pencil, paper, a desk, and time to accomplish the task, each student will write a performance objective for a psycho-motor skill to the test examiners' satisfaction.

The test examiner then must be a subject content expert in the construction and evaluation of performance objectives. Why? The measurement standard should be objective and not subjective. Subjective answers are graded only by expert examiners because they require consistency in the standard used to measure accomplishment. In completing the performance objective test task the student would simply have to ensure his or her answer included a:

- statement of the knowledge, abilities or skills to be accomplished.
- condition(s) under which the knowledge, abilities, or skills must be performed and what will be provided to the student to complete the action required.
- measurable standard for identifying successful performance.

Implement an Instructional Strategy

In the sixth step of the systems approach model for designing curriculum, the curriculum developer finally starts to make choices on the instructional style or strategy that will be used to facilitate learning. There are four primary strategies that can be used in curriculum development.

- *Instructor-centered learning.* The instructor provides all the information to the student and evaluates performance. The difficulty of this method is that it is personnel intensive, normally occurs in a lock-step model, every learner learns at the same rate, and does not account for learner differences. The instructor-centered approach is normally lecture oriented.
- *Individual-centered learning.* A plan is developed between the learner and the instructor (supervisor) on what is to be learned, how long the student will take to accomplish the learning, to what level the learning will be measured and how. This method is chosen when the individual is success-oriented, demonstrates a high degree of discipline, and requires low structure in the learning environment. The individual-centered approach works best with individuals studying for advanced outcomes.
- *Interactively centered learning.* A process for developing critical skills. The learner interacts with the environment by verbalizing learning, participating in discussion groups, or demonstrating competencies. This method of curriculum design requires a high degree of motivation on the part of the learner and incorporates case studies, panel discussions, and real time demonstrations in the learning activities. Interactive learning is the hands on approach to skill mastery.
- *Experiential-centered learning.* A process that incorporates cognitive, psycho-motor and affective learning in field or clinical settings. The experiential approach places the student on the job while at the same time requiring ancillary learning by study, drill and practice and evaluation. *Experiential learning is considered the best type of learning because it marries theory with practice.*

In determining the instruction style or strategy to be used in the development of curriculum the security training professional utilizes each previous part of the systems approach model for curriculum design. They also develop a timetable for all pre-instructional activities that must be accomplished. Select the method or methods in which the material to be mastered will be presented. Determine how student feedback will be gathered. Designate the methods to be used in testing and identify testing material needs. They also implement a strategy for follow-through activities to ensure the curriculum is designed, developed, constructed and implemented as planned.

The security training director ensures that all curriculum is based on current research in learning theory, utilizes the best current knowledge available on learning as a process and clearly, concisely, competently, and correctly specifies the content to be taught. The single constraint placed upon the design of the formal curriculum is the mandatory characteristics or behaviors required of the learner to participate in the process.

Select Appropriate Instructional Materials

The final step in the formal construction of security or public safety curriculum is the development and selection of instructional materials. The security training profession provides the learner with a training manual. The manual provides written guidance for successful course completion. It provides the learner with the competency outcomes they will have to master to satisfactorily complete the program of learning and specifies the evaluation process.

Just as the learner is provided a manual, the instructor is also provided with all training materials. The instructor is provided with all the competencies to be taught, lesson plans, student activities sheets, demonstration performance materials, transparency masters, equipment and any other educational materials necessary to conduct the training. Perhaps the most critical teaching tool given to the instructor is the instructor guide. The instructor guide places the unit, course or performance in context with the educational goal. It is the road map used by the instructor to teach the sequenced lessons or facilitate the learners' study.

Testing materials are selected from a created test bank that holds a number of questions written for specific performance objectives. Every performance objective written for the course is tested. If the material does not need testing, a performance objective should not have been written. There are two types of tests. Every unit of instruction should have both of these tests. Validation of learning occurs in the measurement of educational gains between the pre-test, instruction or study and the post-test. If the student demonstrates on the pre-test that they already know the material to a specific standard set in the performance objectives, they should be allowed to move to the next unit without participating in the individual instructional or study unit.

You as the security training supervisor, director or training officer will have to decide if you want to develop new material for your training program. This course and all the work that went into it represents a large investment on the part of the International Foundation for Protection Officers. They made their decision based on a recognition that suitable materials were not available to meet your needs. Remember it is always cheaper to adapt current material than it is to design new curriculum. Another idea is to adopt material that was written for another organization if it is possible and it meets your needs.

In concluding this section on the selection of curriculum remember the four specific questions you should ask:
- What is the cost of designing new materials?
- What materials currently exist that might meet our needs?
- Do the materials that exist support our performance objectives?
- What other organizational criteria need to be considered in the existing material?

CONCLUSION

After you have completed designing your curriculum you aren't through. The final stage in developing curriculum is the evaluation process. Again there are two types of evaluations you should conduct, formative and normative. Formative evaluations are conducted prior to testing the curriculum. The first normative evaluation provides a baseline for further comparisons with follow- up on students or classes. These evaluations are conducted constantly to ensure the curriculum is accomplishing its goal or goals and to keep it current.

Formative evaluation is initiated upon completion of draft instructional materials. It may be accomplished in one of three ways: in one-to-one consultation with another subject content training expert; subjected to evaluation by a small group of training professionals who specialize in the curriculum designed; or in some cases the formative evaluation is conducted in field evaluations if the material is time critical or sensitive. The formative evaluation process may be used for a course, unit of instruction, classroom lecture or demonstration performance.

Normative evaluation is based on some level of acceptable standard. How many days, hours, or questions may be missed and still pass or complete the course? Should the student be able to accomplish the task with no supervision, some supervision or while closely supervised? What are the accepted tolerances? Must the task be accomplished without error, or as indicated, in some other manner?

Normative evaluations should be objective and not subjective. When dealing with theory or cognitive material there should be a written test. The demonstration of a skill requires application in a real work scenario and effective skills are evaluated when the learner models acceptable behaviors.

Both formative and normative evaluation are the first steps in redesigning curriculum in the systems approach for designing curriculum. They identify difficulties experienced by the learner, based on the successful or unsuccessful accomplishment of performance objectives. Formative and normative evaluations identify deficiencies in instruction.

They ultimately attest to the worth of the curriculum design and are used to validate the effect, efficiency and cost effectiveness of the educational process. Formative evaluations are conducted best when someone outside the organization reviews all the material to measure suitability and the accomplishment of stated competency goals. Finally both evaluations are based on quality not quantity.

SUMMARY

The completion of this unit has provided you with the information you will need to: define curriculum, distinguish between micro and macro curriculum, select critical elements in the curriculum process, define competency-based education, identify the six steps to determine competency-based outcomes, identify instructional goals, conduct an instructional analysis, and identify requisite entry-level behaviors and characteristics for entrance into the learning program. You have also learned how to formulate performance objectives, develop the criteria for writing performance objective tests, implement and identify an instructional strategy and select appropriate instructional materials.

With these skills you will be able to construct a comprehensive, performance-oriented training program. The use of the systems approach model for the design curriculum focuses the security training professional on the task at hand: training today's security officers for tomorrow's challenges.

**CURRICULUM DESIGN
QUIZ**

1.   Curriculum development and _____ requires the security training professional to understand, construct, implement and evaluate required training curriculum on a recurring basis.

2.   Modern security education and training is _____ based.

3.   The first step in the systems approach _____ for designing curriculum requires that you determine exactly what you want the students to be able to accomplish after training is completed.

4.   The final step in the formal construction of security or public safety _____ is the development and selection of instructional material.

5.   With these skills you will be able to construct a comprehensive, _____ orientated training program.

6.   Curriculum is best defined as a plan for learning that meets the needs of the organization, the security personnel to be trained, and the public served.
          ☐ T   ☐ F

7.   Micro curriculum is the development of a task training step or unit of training within the confines of a larger course. Macro curriculum is the development of a course or complete program of instruction that has multiple units or modules of study.
          ☐ T   ☐ F

8.   A singularly critical element in the curriculum process is the selection of participating learners based on fair, consistent, relevant, and measurable standards – the "who is to be taught" issue.
          ☐ T   ☐ F

9.   Competency-based training is the process of setting clearly designed, measurable, observable objectives that the student learner accomplishes to a particular known level.
          ☐ T   ☐ F

10.   A job description is not needed when determining competency-based outcomes.
          ☐ T   ☐ F

TESTING FOR LEARNING RETENTION
by Martin Hershkowitz, M.S.

The security supervisor may not be a certified classroom trainer, but he or she is clearly responsible for supervising on-the-job training for security officers under his or her supervision and for selecting formal training courses of value for them. The security supervisor is responsible for ensuring that these security officers attend formal training that is relevant, assures short-term learning from the classroom experience and provides long-term retention of that learning. That is, the training has to pertain to the job; the security officer should have learned something new and be able to display that learning after a suitable period of time.

Once the subject matter of the training has been selected (typically by corporate management or by the corporate training department), the security supervisor is in a position to recommend the local vendor or provider of the training. Since the subject matter has been pre-decided, the supervisor's choices are limited to the way in which the vendor guarantees that learning will take place and how long it will last. This discussion relates to one method for providing that assurance: an in-depth testing program.

In order to demonstrate that short-term learning has taken place, the individual must take a pre-test and post-test on the subject matter and achieve more correct answers on the post-test than on the pre-test. At the conclusion of the training, the security officer should be able to demonstrate sufficient short-term learning to indicate that the learning experience was worthwhile.

In order to demonstrate that long-term retention of the learning has taken place, the individual must take a post-test on the subject matter after a suitable period of time, say six to twelve months. More correct answers must be achieved than on the original pre-test and almost as many correct answers as on the original post-test. The implication being that sufficient learning took place during the training experience to have become internalized and available to be built upon with further training.

The in-depth testing program described above is not typical of most training programs because of the additional cost involved. This does not mean that the testing concept should be abandoned; rather, it means that the security supervisor must demonstrate his or her ingenuity by establishing such a testing program on the job. Actually, this is not too difficult a chore for a good security supervisor who oversees an on-the-job training program.

Remember, the initial pre- and post-test are the same, but given at different times. The second or long-term post-test might be the same as the other two, but at this point the chance that the security officer will become "test-wise" or "test-sensitive" is too great. Rather, the security supervisor should consider an "observational" type of test. That is, the supervisor would have a checklist containing all the activities that the security officer should be performing that directly relate to the training received during the formal training and observe the extent to which those activities are actually being performed.

Consider the following examples:

Example No. 1: The security force is protecting a nuclear power plant and one of the requirements is to search each vehicle entering the plant.
- The new security officers have never conducted a search of a vehicle and have never been instructed on how to conduct one.
- The security officers are given a pre-test, which contains six items on conducting a vehicle search.
- On the average, the security officers guess correctly on only one of the six items.
- The security officers attend formal training, including procedures for searching a vehicle.
- The security officers are given the post-test (the same test as the pre-test), and they average better than five of the six items answered correctly, indicating that short-term learning has taken place for all the security officers.

- Ten months later, the security supervisor has developed a checklist containing 14 specific actions that cover the task of searching a vehicle. As each of the security officers has to search a vehicle as part of their post assignment, the security supervisor covertly grades them on each of the actions on the checklist.
- All but four of the security officers complete 12 of the 14 actions successfully, and the remaining four only complete seven of the 14 successfully, indicating that long-term retention has taken place for most, but not all, of the security officers.
- The security supervisor has determined that the original training was, for the most part, quite successful, and can now plan an on-the-job training effort to correct the deficiencies and reinforce the learning.

Example No. 2: This example is the same as the above except that differences in the testing program results leading to different conclusions.
- The new security officers have never conducted a search of a vehicle and have never been instructed on how to conduct one.
- The security officers are given a pre-test, which contains six items on conducting a vehicle search.
- On the average, the security officers guess correctly on only one of the six items.
- The security officers attend formal training, including procedures for searching a vehicle, given by a contract training organization.
- The security officers are given the post-test (the same test as the pre-test) and they average 11 of the 14 items incorrectly, indicating that short-term learning has not taken place for any of the security officers.
- The security supervisor concludes that the training program is inadequate for the security officers' needs, cancels the training contract and seeks another training contractor.

Example No. 3: This example is the same as the first one except that differences in the testing program results lead to different conclusions.
- The new security officers have never conducted a search of a vehicle and have never been instructed on how to conduct one.
- The security officers are given a pre-test, which contains six items on conducting a vehicle search.
- On the average, the security officers guess correctly on only one of the six items.
- The security officers attend formal training, including procedures for searching a vehicle, given by the security organization's training department.
- The security officers are given the post-test (the same test as the pre-test) and they average 11 of the 14 items incorrectly, indicating that short-term learning has not taken place for any of the security officers.
- The security supervisor concludes that the training program is inadequate for the security officers' needs, informs the training department's curriculum development and instructional staffs about the problems with their course and assists them in correcting the deficiencies.

In summary, the security supervisor plays a very key role in the security officers' learning environment, where he or she determines the adequacy of the training through a suitable testing program and on-the-job observations. If the test items appropriately measure the student's short-term learning and long-term retention, and the results are unsuccessful, then the security supervisor can either seek a better training provider or assist the in-house trainer to improve the training and correct the deficiencies.

TESTING FOR LEARNING RETENTION
QUIZ

1. The security supervisor is responsible for ensuring that security officers attend formal training that is _____.

2. In order to demonstrate that _____ learning has taken place, the individual must take a pre-test and post-test on the subject matter.

3. The security supervisor should have a _____ of all of the activities that the security officer should be performing.

4. The security supervisor plays a key role in the security officer's learning _____.

5. The security supervisor can develop an on-the-job training effort to fill the gaps and _____ the total training experience.

6. The security supervisor has to be less concerned with on-the-job training as opposed to structured classroom instruction.
    ☐ T   ☐ F

7. At the conclusion of the training, the security officers should be able to demonstrate sufficient short-term learning.
    ☐ T   ☐ F

8. In order to demonstrate that long-term retention of the learning has taken place, the individual must take a post-test on the subject matter after a suitable period of time.
    ☐ T   ☐ F

9. To prevent a security officer from becoming "test-wise," the location and length of tests should be altered.
    ☐ T   ☐ F

10. The security officer's learning environment is a critical component to the success of the overall training/learning process.
    ☐ T   ☐ F

PROFESSIONAL CERTIFICATIONS
by Michael A. Hamilton, CSS, CPO, CFSO, BCFE

Today is an exciting time to be working in the security industry. Whether you are working on a guard force, doing investigations, technical surveillance counter measures, forensics or engineering, our industry is experiencing tremendous growth.

With this growth has come increased expectations and demands from the public, private, and government agencies we serve. The days of the "rent-a-cop" are over. Today, anyone working in the security industry is expected to be a professional. To be a professional, one must constantly strive to develop skills and knowledge in order to perform at a maximum level of effectiveness and to experience personal growth.

Professional development is vital for every security professional, but it is absolutely critical for the security professional who is also serving in a supervisory capacity. It is critical because security supervisors provide leadership and a very important part of leadership is professionally developing oneself and those whom you supervise.

There are numerous professional development opportunities available today, many of which lead to certification in a given area of expertise or specialty.

WHY IS CERTIFICATION IMPORTANT?

Certification is important because it provides tangible evidence of skills and knowledge obtained through hard work and study. It also validates one's professional development and conveys a commitment to self-improvement and adherence to increasingly high standards within the security industry. Certification also provides opportunities for personal growth and brings well-deserved recognition from peers and colleagues.

DEVELOPING ONESELF AND OTHERS

Professional development starts with the individual. As security professionals in a supervisory capacity, we have a special responsibility. We must develop ourselves, not only to stay current and advance our careers, but also so we can help to develop those who work for us. This is one of the most important points of leadership. In the U.S. Army, it's called "looking after your troops."

We must be knowledgeable of our own jobs and the jobs of everyone who works for us. The people who work for us will have many questions: "How do we accomplish this?" "Why do we do that?" "Who is responsible in a given situation?" "When can I draw my weapon?" "What is the correct procedure?" "Where is the central alarm station located?" The questions are legion, and you must be prepared to answer all of them.

Looking after those who work for us also means looking after their careers. Provide them with first-class training, give them opportunities for professional development and the chance for greater responsibility.

PROFESSIONAL DEVELOPMENT OPPORTUNITIES

– Talking with colleagues in private or group discussions –
This is a great way to learn. Exchange thoughts and ideas about various topics of concern. Talk about issues important to the security industry and your organization. Play out "what if" scenarios. Playing "what if" provides valuable insights and potential solutions to problems before one has to face them. It prepares us for those moments when immediate action is required and time is at an absolute minimum. Personally, I will never forget when I was in the U.S. Army and attending the Ordnance Officer basic course in 1981. We were having a professional development class and were given the following "what if" scenario:

You are a Captain, commanding a company, engaged in combat and under heavy fire. Suddenly, your first sergeant breaks and runs as fast as he can towards the rear. What do you do? Some in the class said let him run away; most of us, myself included, could not see past regulations. Our answer was "Shoot him for cowardice and desertion under enemy fire." The instructor then gave his solution to the problem. He said to quickly turn to the first sergeant, yell at the top of your lungs, and say "And, first sergeant, don't forget the grenades!" then quickly gather your lieutenants and platoon sergeants and tell them, "I've sent the first sergeant back to get more grenades – we'll hold this position until he returns." Then appoint the senior NCO to be acting first sergeant.

I was stunned when I heard this solution. Prior to hearing it, I was convinced that there were only two possibilities: either shoot him or condone his behavior, neither of which is an acceptable answer. I doubt I will ever be faced with this situation, but if I am, I know exactly what I would do. I would yell at the top of my lungs, "And, first sergeant, don't forget the grenades."

– Join a professional security organization and work towards certification –
Membership in a professional security organization allows us association with like-minded individuals, gives us new insight and fresh perspectives, and keeps us current in our field. In addition, many offer professional certification programs and other training programs that will be of great benefit. The following list outlines some of the membership and certification programs currently available to security professionals.

1.   The International Foundation for Protection Officers (IFPO)

IFPO was established in 1988 for the purpose of facilitating the training and certification needs of protection officers and security supervisors from both the commercial and proprietary sectors. Associate (non-voting) membership is available to any person who is employed in security. Each application for membership must be supported by including, as references, the name and address of two security professionals. Members receive a certificate of membership, identification card, lapel pin, membership directory, *Protection Officer News* (quarterly newsletter) and enjoy a ten percent discount on IFPO sponsored programs. Corporate memberships are also available. A variety of security publications addressing important topics within the security industry can be obtained at a very modest cost. Topics include crime prevention programs, civil liability for security personnel, protection officer survival, special events planning, careers in security and investigation and high-rise building security. IFPO offers two security certification programs: the Certified Protection Officer (CPO) and the Certified Security Supervisor (CSS) programs.

The CPO program is open to all security officers. The program is designed for protection professionals intent on improving their individual security skills and comfortable with a self-paced, home-study style of learning. To earn the CPO designation, candidates must study the "Protection Officer Training Manual" and successfully complete an unsupervised mid-term examination and a proctored final examination. The CPO program covers a variety of important security topics including physical security, investigations, fire prevention, crime scenes, emergency procedures, bomb threats, report writing and crisis intervention. Membership in IFPO is not required for enrollment in the CPO program.

The CSS program consists of a two-part process. First the candidate must enroll in the security supervisor training program. Unique and flexible, this distance learning course of study is designed to meet the needs of the security supervisor or senior protection officer.

Candidates accepted into the program are required to complete an interim and final examination. To earn the program completion certificate, candidates must achieve a score of at least 70 percent on both examinations.

The second step for the candidate who has successfully completed the security supervisor training program is to complete a series of simulated workplace scenarios demanding supervisory action. Candidates must describe the measures they deem appropriate for each scenario and substantiate the recommended actions by using the course text as supportive reference.

Once the candidate has completed the appropriate application and submitted it to the IFPO, the CSS certification committee will review the scenarios and application, along with the candidate's complete file, to determine eligibility for certification.

The CPO and CSS programs both offer excellent training and are an outstanding value, as costs are very reasonable. For information about membership in IFPO, the CPO or the CSS programs, contact:

> Ms. Sandi Davies, Executive Director
> International Foundation for Protection Officers
> #269, 3106 Tamiami Trail, N.
> Naples, FL   34103
> Telephone (941) 430-0534
> Fax: (941) 430-0533
> http://www.ifpo.com
> email: sandi@ifpo.com

2.   The American Society for Industrial Security (ASIS)

ASIS was founded in 1955 and is one of the premier organizations in the security industry. Its purpose is to promote and establish professionalism in the field of security. Membership in ASIS is strictly individual; corporate memberships are not available. New members are required to complete an application, which must be endorsed by a Chapter Officer or Regional Vice President. The prospective member must also be sponsored by an ASIS member in good standing. Membership is open to all security professionals who are currently employed in a position with responsibility for the security function of a business, institution or government agency in a position of responsible charge. The ASIS defines responsible charge to mean "that charge exercised by an individual who makes decisions for the successful completion of objectives without reliance upon directions from a supervisor as to the specific methods or techniques."

Upon membership, you will receive *Security Management*, the official monthly magazine of ASIS. In my opinion, *Security Management* is absolutely the best magazine published by our industry. If you don't become a member of ASIS or you are not eligible to become a member, give them a call and subscribe to *Security Management* magazine. It is well worth the cost. Also included in your membership is the *Security Industry Buyers Guide*. This guide is a very handy resource for locating security services. ASIS also sponsors a wide variety of security training programs and offers the Certified Protection Professional (CPP) program. Membership in ASIS is not required to participate in the CPP program.

To be eligible to sit for the CPP exam, the applicant must meet the following standards:
- Nine years' experience, at least two in a position of responsible charge, or
- An associate degree from a regionally accredited college and seven years of experience, at least two in a position of responsible charge, or
- A bachelors degree from a regionally accredited college and five years' experience, at least two in a position of responsible charge, or
- A masters degree from a regionally accredited college and two years of experience, all in a position of responsible charge.

Each applicant must be endorsed by a CPP in good standing and must affirm adherence to the ASIS code of ethics. The applicant must successfully complete a written exam of 200 questions concerning security knowledge. A second exam of 50 questions concerning legal aspects is also required.

For more information concerning membership in ASIS or about the CPP program, contact:

American Society for Industrial Security
Membership Department, Suite 1200
1625 Prince Street
Alexandria, VA 22314
(703) 519-6200

3.   The American Board of Forensic Examiners (ABFE)

The ABFE was established to advance the profession of forensic examination and consultation by elevating standards through education, basic and advanced training and research. The Board serves as a national center for this purpose and disseminates information and knowledge by lectures, seminars, conferences, workshops and publications. The Board also provides consultation and referral networking to promote new opportunities for its members. In order to qualify as a member, you must be a professional in the field of forensic examination with the government or in private practice, full or part time or in teaching, research or consulting and agree to adhere to the Board's strict Code of Ethical Standards. The ABFE officially recognizes the following forensic fields:

Accident Reconstruction	Interviewing
Accounting	Investigations
Acoustics	Jurisprudence
Anthropology	Linguistics
Arson Investigation	Material Science
Behavioral Profiling	Medicine
Biology	Meteorology
Chemistry	Nursing
Computer Science	Odontology
Criminalistics	Pathology
Crime Scene Analysis	Pharmacology
Criminology	Photography
Engineering	Physics
Eyewitness Identification	Polygraph
Fingerprints	Psychiatry
Financial Crime	Psychology
Firearms	Questioned Documents
Geography	Safety Consultant
Geology	Security and Risk Management
Handwriting Examination	Serology
Hypnosis	Toxicology
Identification	Trace Analysis
Insurance	Voice Identification

The ABFE has numerous training opportunities available in the field of forensic examination. In addition to these training programs, there are three certifications available from the ABFE. They are Board Certified Forensic Examiner (BCFE), Board Certified in Behavioral Profiling (BCBP), and Board Certified in Forensic Documentation Examination (BCFDE).

Only persons who meet the minimum requirement of expertise as defined in the Federal Rules of Evidence, Rule 702.2 and the additional qualifications as established by the ABFE will be considered qualified to receive the designation Board Certified Forensic Examiner. According to the Federal Rules of Evidence, Rule 702.2, an expert must be shown by the party calling him to have scientific, technical or other specialized knowledge. A witness may be qualified as an expert by reason of knowledge, skill, experience, training or education. Under Rule 702.2, a witness may be qualified by any one such factor or upon a combination of any of the five factors. Applicants to be a BDFE must submit written documentation in each of the five prescribed categories: knowledge, skill, experience, training, and education. Candidates must complete the BCFE application form and submit a copy of their resume, have their signature notarized and successfully complete a written ethics exam.

To become Board Certified in Behavioral Profiling (BCBP), the candidate must successfully complete three courses: basic profiling, advanced profiling and forensic profiling. In addition, there is a two year apprenticeship following the completion of the academic courses. The candidate must successfully complete a written ethics exam.

To become a Board Certified Forensic Document Examiner (BCFDE), a candidate must pass the BCFDE standardized test with a score of 75 percent or better. The candidate must also successfully complete a written ethics exam.

For more information concerning membership in ANFE or any of the certification programs, contact:

> Dr. Robert L. O'Block, Executive Director
> American Board of Forensic Examiners
> P.O. Box 4006
> Springfield, Missouri   65808
> Telephone: (417) 881-3818
> Fax: (417) 881-4702

4.   The Business Espionage Controls and Countermeasures Association (BECCA)

BECCA was formed to address the concerns of protecting the proprietary information of the business community. In today's economy, company secrets represent your company's life blood. Protecting your company's secrets is what BECCA is all about. Membership is open to anyone who wants to learn more about this important topic. Membership includes twelve issues of *The Business Espionage Report*, referral service, and a ten percent discount on BECCA training programs. BECCA also offers a professional training program, the Certified Confidentiality Officer (CCO).

The CCO training program consists of five training modules to help you identify and prevent business espionage. Subjects include introduction to business espionage controls and countermeasures, electronic eavesdropping, computers, pretext interviews, and undercover operations. The performance of confidentiality surveys is a core proficiency. BECCA/CCO program participants who successfully complete five surveys may qualify for the Certified Confidentiality Officer designation.

For more information concerning membership in BECCA or the CCO program, contact:

> Dr. Will Johnson, President
> Business Espionage Controls and Countermeasures Association
> Box 260
> Ft. Washington, MD   20749
> (301) 292-6430

5.   The Association of Certified Fraud Examiners (ACFE)

The ACFE was founded as a professional organization for fraud examiners. Its mission is to reduce the incidence of fraud and white-collar crime and to assist the membership in its detection and deterrence. Regular membership is open only to Certified Fraud Examiners. Associate membership is available for individuals who do not qualify as Certified Fraud Examiners but have an interest in matters concerning fraud. Members receive professional publications and periodicals and can benefit from numerous training programs. Persons desiring to become Certified Fraud Examiners (CFE) must study the *Fraud Examiners Manual*, a list of other study references and successfully complete the CFE examination. The exam consists of four parts: financial transactions, investigation, legal elements and criminology. There are 500 true/false and multiple choice practical problem questions.

For more information concerning membership in ACFE, or the CFE program, contact:

The Association of Certified Fraud Examiners
716 West Avenue
Austin, Texas 78701
Telephone: 1-800-245-3321

6.   The Information Systems Security Association

The ISSA was formed in 1982 to address the security concerns of information systems. The primary goal of ISSA is to promote management practices that will ensure availability, integrity, and confidentiality of organizational resources. ISSA offers a variety of opportunities for education in the field of information security. Professional publications include *The Password*, a bi-monthly newsletter, *The ISSA Journal*, and *The ISSA Resource Guide*. Membership is open to professionals who have as their primary responsibility information systems security, educators, students, attorneys, and law enforcement officers having a vested interest in information and data security; or professionals with a primary responsibility for marketing or supplying information security products or services. ISSA also provides a professional certification, Certified Information System Security Professional (CISSP). Requirements for the CISSP designation include experience and/or the successful completion of an examination.

For more information concerning membership in ISSA or the CISSP program, contact:

The Information Systems Security Association
401 North Michigan Avenue
Chicago, Illinois 60611
Telephone: (312) 644-6610

7.   The Academy of Security Educators and Trainers (ASET)

ASET was founded in 1980 and has as its purpose promoting the establishment of security degree programs and training, aiding in curriculum development, serving as a resource for legislative bodies considering regulatory action, sponsoring basic and applied research and facilitating dialogue between teachers, trainers and practitioners. Membership in ASET is open to all persons interested in the improvement of security education and training. ASET offers the professional designation, Certified Security Trainer (CST). To earn the lifetime designation of CST, applicants must proceed through a three-phase process. First, candidates submit a complete resume for credential review and background check and respond in writing to narrative qualifying questions on contemporary security training issues. Second, the candidate must attend the seven-day annual assessment and evaluation program conducted by ASET at the Executive Protection Institute.

Third, the candidate must successfully complete, during the seven-day program, a series of written and oral examinations, personal interviews, training exercises, and three actual presentations for the certification board. Each candidate will also participate in workshops, critique presentations and attend sessions on contemporary issues and problems.

For more information concerning membership in ASET or the CST program, contact:

The Academy of Security Educators and Trainers
Attention: ASET Secretariat
Box 802
Berryville, Virginia 22611
Telephone: (540) 955-1129

8.   **The Operation's Security (OPSEC)
       Professional's Society (OPS)**

OPS was established in 1990 to further the practice of OPSEC as a profession and to foster the highest quality of professionalism and competence among its members. OPSEC is a process used to deny to potential adversaries information about capabilities and/or intentions by identifying, controlling and protecting evidence of the planning and execution of sensitive activities. This process is equally applicable to government, its contractors, and to private enterprise in the protection of their trade secrets and other proprietary information. OPS training sessions and publications emphasize practical and common-sense approaches to solving OPSEC problems. The Society consists of regular, international, corporate, student, honorary and associate members. Regular members must be U.S. citizens who have past or present employment with responsibilities in OPSEC or related fields and have demonstrated ability, opportunity and desire to advance OPSEC and further the aims of the OPSEC Professional Society. OPS established a certification program to identify individuals who meet the highest standards of the OPSEC profession, the OPSEC Certified Professional (OCP). To become an OCP, the candidate must have a given number of years of OPSEC experience and submit papers demonstrating an in-depth understanding of OPSEC.

For more information concerning OPS or the OCP program, contact:

> The Operation's Security Professional's Society
> 120 West Church Street
> Fredrick, Maryland 21701
> Telephone: Mr. Arion "Pat" Pattakos
>   Beta Analytics, Inc.
>   (302) 599-1570

9.   **The International Association for Healthcare Security and Safety (IAHSS)**

IAHSS was founded in 1968 for hospital security and safety administrators. Today IAHSS embraces the entire healthcare industry and has grown to be the largest association of its kind. Membership is open to individuals who are active in the field of hospital/healthcare security and safety. Members receive the *Journal of Healthcare Protection Management*, the *IAHSS Newsletter* and membership directory. IAHSS offers numerous training programs, including the Security Officer Basic Training Certification Standard (40 hours), Supervisory Development Standard (20 hours) and the Safety Training Standard (20 hours). IAHSS also offers the professional designation, Certified Healthcare Protection Administrator (CHPA) to qualified members. Becoming a CHPA is a two-part process.

First, the candidate must be accepted at the nominee level. To achieve nominee status, the applicant must be, or must have been, the security/safety risk management/manager of a healthcare facility. The applicant must submit a completed application clearly documenting the accumulation of ten credits among four categories of education, experience, membership and specialized training. Credits are awarded in each category based on the degree of education, number of years of experience, number of years as a member and the number of specialized training courses completed. Second, the nominee must successfully pass a written examination covering four bodies of knowledge (management, security, safety/life safety and risk management).

For more information concerning membership in IAHSS or the CHPA program, contact:

> The International Association for Healthcare Security and Safety
> P.O. Box 637
> Lombard, Illinois 60148
> Telephone: (630) 953-0990

10.   The Defense Industrial Security Program (DISP)

This program was established by the United States Government to set forth the requirements, policies, and procedures for defense contractors engaged in certain types of government work. Contractors participating in this program are required to appoint a Facility Security Officer (FSO), who is responsible for the contractors' security programs. An FSO must successfully complete four security correspondence courses and attend the Industrial Security Management Course, sponsored by the Department of Defense Security Institute. Once these requirements are met, the FSO can take a proctored exam to obtain certification. Upon successful completion of the exam, the FSO is designated a Certified Facility Security Officer (CFSO). Currently, FSOs do not have to be certified, but the program is currently under review and consideration is being given to making certification mandatory.

If you are working for a contractor involved in this program and have been appointed the FSO, contact the Defense Investigative Service Cognizant Security Officer for information regarding training and certification.

11.   The Executive Protection Institute

The Executive Protection Institute offers training for individuals interested in this exciting career. The training program consists of over 100 hours of instruction, with a minimum of theory and an emphasis upon practical hands-on learning and realistic exercises. Every student will operate a provided motor vehicle, employing defensive and offensive training techniques; design and plan threat assessment models; fire a protective services combat course; become familiar with emergency medical techniques, radio procedures, chemical agents, and ballistics; conduct house and building searches; learn to locate and identify explosive devices; work on advance surveys and escort missions; engage in armed and unarmed defensive tactics; obtain knowledge about dress, protocol, etiquette, and relationships with others; develop countermeasures and operational guidelines, and much, much more. All instructors are acknowledged authorities in the protection field. Upon successful completion of this training, the Executive Protection Institute certifies graduates as Personal Protection Specialists.

For more information concerning this training program and the PPS designation, contact:

> The Executive Protection Institute
> Box 802
> Berryville, Virginia 22611
> Telephone: (540) 955-1128

As you can see, there are many opportunities for security professionals to associate themselves with, many different types of security organizations, and there are many types of security certifications. I am often asked, especially by people who are new to the security field and by personnel managers: "What is the best certification to have?" "Is one higher than the other?" I always give the same answer. It's not a matter of one being better or higher or of more importance than the other. You're comparing apples with oranges. Each of these professional security organizations and each of these certifications was established for a different purpose.

I strongly encourage all security professionals to attempt to earn as many certifications as they can. Start with the ones that concern your specific field (i.e., CST, CFE, PPS, OCP, BCFE, CHPA, etc.) and then move on to the more broad-based ones (i.e., CPO, CPP, CCO, etc.). If your security position is more broad-based, then start with the broad-based certifications and move on to more specific certifications. If you're a security supervisor, it doesn't matter if your mission is of broad or narrow scope: I highly recommend you work toward earning the Certified Security Supervisor (CSS) designation.

– Take advantage of all training opportunities –

Many organizations will have in-house training programs. In-house training allows companies to keep down costs and maximize training time. Most companies, however, are not large enough to provide all the training necessary to accomplish their mission. This is especially true of security training, and the more specialized it is, the more difficult it is to provide in-house. Some thought must be given to external training resources. The organizations mentioned above will be of great benefit in providing information of training opportunities available. There are hundreds of programs available, covering a wide variety of security topics. To mention them all would require a book, but I will mention a few to give you an idea of the broad range of training that is available.

1.   The Institute for Countermeasures Studies (ICMS)

If you are interested in Technical Surveillance Counter Measures (TSCM), this is the place to start. The ICMS offers three different training programs. The Fundamental Countermeasures program is a two-day seminar, designed for the individual who is thinking of becoming a professional "sweeper" or for an organization that is considering whether or not to develop an in-house "sweep" capability.

The Countermeasures Workshops program is three days of intensive study. The workshops deal with electronic eavesdropping and describe the capabilities and vulnerabilities of eavesdropping devices and techniques.

The Management Seminar is a two-day course designed for the security director or supervisor who has the responsibility of establishing and maintaining a defense against electronic eavesdropping.

All of these courses are taught by Mr. Glenn Whidden, who spent 28 years doing TSCM work for the CIA before establishing a private TSCM firm in 1976. He holds five patents for inventions that are currently in use in eavesdropping defense. He is also the author of *The Ear*, a series of publications concerning eavesdropping techniques and their vulnerabilities.

For more information, contact:

The Institute for Countermeasures Studies
Technical Services Agency
10903 Indian Head Highway, Suite 304
Fort Washington, Maryland   20744-4018
Telephone: (301) 292-6430

2.   The Federal Emergency Management Agency's Emergency Management Institute (EMI)

EMI offers several independent study courses with some very nice benefits. First, these courses give you valuable training. Second, if you are an Army, Air Force or Coast Guard reservist, these courses are worth retirement points. Third, most of these courses are worth college credit. Most importantly, these courses are open to anyone who wants to take them and they are free. The courses EMI offers are as follows:

- Emergency Program Manager (IS-1)
- Emergency Preparedness, USA (IS-2)
- Radiological Emergency Management (IS-3)
- Preparedness Planning for a Nuclear Crisis (IS-4) – (NOTE: EMI no longer offers this course but college credit can be obtained for those who previously completed it.)
- Hazardous Materials: A Citizen's Orientation (IS-5)
- Portable Emergency Data System (IS-6)
- A Citizen's Guide to Disaster Assistance (IS-7)

These courses do not have to be completed in any particular order, but you can only enroll in one at a time. Each course has one exam, you must earn a score of 70 percent or better to pass. After you successfully complete each course, you will be issued a certificate of completion. Each course (except IS-6) is worth one semester hour of college credit. What a great way to get a jump on college, for yourself or any member of your family.

Remember, enrollment in these courses is open to everyone and there is no age requirement. For more information on these courses and an enrollment form, contact:

Federal Emergency Management Agency
Emergency Management Institute
Home Study Program
16825 South Seton Avenue
Emmitsburg, Maryland   21727-9986

Once you have completed as many courses as you like, you can obtain college credit. Credit is awarded by Lewis and Clark Community College. The college is fully accredited by the North Central Association of Colleges and Schools. The credit awarded by Lewis and Clark can be transferred to the college of your choice as electives in a program of study leading to an associate or bachelors degree. The tuition charge is a very reasonable $30 per course. For more information concerning college credit for these courses, contact:

Lewis and Clark Community College
5800 Godfrey Road
Godfrey, Illinois   62035

3.   Training for Military Reservists

If you're a member of the U.S. Armed Forces Reserve, see your training NCO right away. (If you're in the Individual Ready Reserve, see the training NCO at the local Armory). The military has hundreds of correspondence courses in security and security related subjects available to reservists. These courses will sharpen your skills and provide you an opportunity to earn retirement points at the same time. The Army Institute for Professional Development (AIPD) has courses available in tort laws; emergency medical care; radiological health; classified document procedures, freedom of information, and privacy acts; safety management; security safeguards, night vision devices, weapons inspections; security operations; radiological safety; fire fighting operations; demolitions; pistols and revolvers; civil disturbances; investigations; interrogation; imagery interpretation; aerial photography; infrared imagery; counterintelligence; explosive ordnance; physical security; traffic control; security management; criminalistics; crypto analysis; radio direction finding; electronic security; and many others.

Another wonderful resource for reservists is the USMC Marine Corps Institute (MCI). MCI was established in 1920 and serves all branches of the U.S. Armed Forces, including the Reserves. See your training NCO. If they aren't familiar with MCI, give them the address below, and they can send for a correspondence course catalog. If you are in the Individual Ready Reserve, you can send for the catalog yourself. The address is:

United States Marine Corps
Marine Corps Institute
Arlington, Virginia   22222-0001

The MCI catalog is well designed and includes information concerning recommended college credit by the American Council on Education (ACE). Many security related courses are available including terrorism counteraction for Marines (1 semester hour (sh) towards a bachelor of arts (BA) ACE); Military functions in civil disturbances (2 sh, BA, ACE); Corrections supervisor (3 sh, BA, ACE). Other courses include communications security, armory procedures, marksmanship and others.

Both the AIPD and MCI operate in a similar fashion. You send for your course materials, complete an exam, and are awarded a certificate of completion. These courses are only available to Active and Reserve Military Personnel. The courses are provided free of charge.

READ AND STUDY

There are thousands of books, documents, and magazine articles covering every conceivable security and security related topic. Take time to read and study. These resources are available from numerous sources including your library, local bookstore and professional security organizations.

Professional development doesn't just happen. You must make it happen. Think about it. A crisis of some kind occurs every day of the year, somewhere in North America. A spy is caught, a robbery prevented, a fire is put out, a life is saved! Most of the time, these positive things happen because someone knew exactly what to do and how to do it. They were professionally developed. Maybe someday, you or someone who works for you will face a crisis. When and if that time comes, will they know what to do? Will you?

A complete list of Academic Security Programs is available through the International Foundation for Protection Officers at www.ifpo.com or by calling (941) 430-0534.

PROFESSIONAL CERTIFICATIONS
QUIZ

1.   Today, everyone working in the security industry is expected to be a _____.

2.   Certification is important because it provides tangible evidence of _____ and knowledge.

3.   Provide them with first-class training, give them opportunity for professional development and the chance for greater _____.

4.   The IFPO was established in 1988 and makes available the _____ and the _____ _____ certifications.

5.   Membership in professional security organizations allow us association with _____ individuals.

6.   There are few opportunities available today for professional development in the security field.
          □ T   □ F

7.   As a security supervisor, you must be knowledgeable of your own job and the job of everyone who works for you.
          □ T   □ F

8.   Playing out "what if" scenarios provides valuable insight and potential solutions to problems before you have to face them.
          □ T   □ F

9.   Membership in a professional security organization helps keep you current in your field.
          □ T   □ F

10.   Each of the security certification programs was established for a different purpose. To compare any of these programs is like comparing apples and oranges.
          □ T   □ F

UNIT FIVE
MANAGEMENT FOUNDATIONS

Evolution of Management
Time and Stress Management
Project Management
Company Policy and Procedures
Total Quality Management

EVOLUTION OF MANAGEMENT
by Christopher L. Vail, M.S.

A person selected for a management position usually brings with them certain attributes – education, job experience, personal contacts or a combination thereof. What they frequently don't have is training or experience as a manager. This chapter is meant to provide the basic concepts and framework for new managers, giving them a brief theoretical overview of management, what the manager's job requires and how to "do it."

Today's practice of management has assimilated many of the theories once prevalent at another time. In other words, the history and evolution of management has given us the framework for what managers do today. Management is nothing new as it has its roots in biblical times. Every organization in the world has used, presently uses and will continue to use, some style of management. In any case, regardless of the style used, management has but one question to address: "what is the best way to accomplish our organization's goals and purposes?"

The first studies of management took the classical approach wherein researchers looked at the bureaucratic structures and formal aspects of the organization. For instance, the study of scientific management tried to find the best method of performing a specific task. Frederick Taylor, the father of scientific management, used time-and-motion studies to support his theory that the manager should do the thinking while the employee did the physical tasks. Max Weber's school of thought introduced the concept of bureaucracy. He proposed rational bureaucratic structures that would include written rules; making jobs routine; division of labor; hierarchy of authority; reliance on technical expertise; and a separation of ownership from administration.

A later school of thought in management studies took the human relations approach that emphasized the informal aspects of the organization. The Hawthorne experiments of the late 1920s and early 1930s theorized that if the physical environment was improved, productivity would increase. While this theory was not supported by the studies, it did open the door for studies into variables other than physical ones such as lighting. This, and subsequent studies, suggested that when management pays attention to the employees, productivity will increase. This school emphasizes communication; shared decision-making; the recognition of strong social norms in the workplace; and leadership.

There have been other approaches to the study of management, such as the behavioral school, the functional, quantitative and others. Modern-day terminology includes TQM, zero-based budgeting, Theory Z and management-by-objectives. Despite the fancy name or label, the purpose of management still remains: "how can we best do the job?" In all likelihood, today's manager will use a little of all the schools of thought. Most workplace situations today are complex and are influenced by more than one factor such as globalization, social relationships, physical surroundings, job specificity or expectations of workers. Therefore, managers should look at the whole picture and match their management approach to the situation. This approach also has a name: situational or contingency management.

DEFINITION OF MANAGEMENT

The dictionary defines management as "the act, manner or practice of managing, supervising or controlling." Inherent in that definition is the implication that management is not a single, identifiable object; nor is it stable. Management is a *process* of directing and controlling people and things so that an organization's objectives can be accomplished. Therefore, today's manager needs to be flexible, yet work within the parameters of established managerial concepts.

THE PROCESS OF MANAGEMENT

The managerial process consists of five functions, each a separate one, but closely tied to the others, that tend to operate in a fairly consistent sequence. In short, these functions are:
1.   *Planning:* setting goals and objectives and developing plans, policies, standard operating procedures, and rules and regulations that will achieve them.
2.   *Organizing:* obtaining, arranging and allocating the right tools, equipment, materials and personnel to get the job done effectively and efficiently.
3.   *Staffing:* recruiting, selecting, hiring, training and developing an adequate number of competent people, then putting them in the right positions in the organization.

4.   *Directing:* activating the employees to achieve organizational goals and objectives through the use of coordination, delegation, motivation, communication and leadership.

5.   *Controlling:* ensuring progress meets organizational goals according to plans by using appropriate reporting systems, performance standards, measuring results, determining and correcting any weaknesses or flaws in the process and taking necessary actions to gain compliance to bring results in line with plans and rewarding people when deserved.

Planning

The first function performed by a manager is planning. This requires forecasting needs and problems and preparing plans to meet them. Good planning provides the framework for the organization by specifying the "who, what, where, when and how" to get the job done. Planning, by it's conceptual nature, consists of setting goals, objectives, plans, policies, procedures, rules and regulations needed to achieve the purpose of the organization. Planning requires a lot of thinking before acting. It also means that contingency plans should be in place in the event of emergencies or crises.

Plans may be administrative, tactical, strategic, fiscal, operational, or procedural. They may be long-term or short-term. Regardless of what the plans pertain to, they will always require detailed thinking and determining what should be done in the future in the organization. One way to assure that all bases have been covered in developing plans is to ask yourself many "what if?" questions throughout the planning stage. Self-imposed questions such as "if we do this, what will happen?" "if they do this, what could happen?" and "if this happens, what should we do?" will suggest an action, or appropriate alternatives, to be taken.

Planning should not be a one-person operation. Using many personnel under his or her command to assist in developing plans has a number of benefits. Involving others in the planning process assures that administrators, supervisors, support, and operational personnel agree on what's to be done. It provides an opportunity to make sure that there are adequate resources available to meet any need. It gives the manager a real insight into what his or her organization can accomplish as a number of different people in the organization will be contributing with ideas, suggestions, and feedback. It's an opportunity for subordinates to become involved in the organization—an action that tends to motivate people. And, it gives subordinates a chance to see how complex their organization really is and how important they are, as individuals, to the organization's success.

Organizing

The second function of a manager, after planning, is organizing. Organizing means acquiring, arranging and distributing work among members of the organization so that the goals of the organization can be accomplished. The basic question addressed in organizing is: "how will the work be divided, who will do it and what do they need to accomplish the work?"

To do this, a chain of command is established that identifies and defines jobs and who will do them. Normally, work teams, units, departments, sections or other entities are created to perform the task(s). The chain of command also defines the appropriate responsibilities and authorities of people. In other words, it assigns accountability throughout the organization. An essential element of the chain of command is the principle that authority is always commensurate with responsibility – they must go hand-in-hand. Clear-cut lines of authority and responsibility will eliminate the problematic "who's in charge?" question. The "golden rule" of management is that no responsibility should be assigned a person unless he has the authority necessary to fulfill it.

The formal chain of command assumes that communications will flow from top to bottom and from the bottom up. Regardless of the formal lines of authority established in a chain of command, most organizations will have an informal one. This is found in the person who just naturally assumes responsibility and exercises authority without anyone spelling them out, such as the file clerk who carries a lot of weight or the mail clerk who knows everyone in the organization. Communications in this informal system may flow in every direction.

A good manager will be aware of and use all communications systems effectively.

The organizing process, particularly when obtaining and assigning manpower and the required materials and supplies, should also consider the two different goals of efficiency and effectiveness.

Efficiency refers to using the least costly and time-consuming efforts to accomplish the organization's goals and purposes. It's a way of getting the best job possible done at the least cost in time, money and manpower. It's "doing things right" while effectiveness is achieving the desired result, or "doing the right things." While the goal of the manager should be to achieve both efficiency and effectiveness, it is not always possible and one or the other may be sacrificed.

Staffing

The third function of management is staffing. Staffing entails recruiting, selecting, and training employees. Sometimes this function is performed by another organization such as a human resources or personnel department rather than the manager's organization. In this case, the manager can have input into job descriptions that will provide a screening process for acceptable job candidates. Otherwise, the manager will be responsible for recruiting the numbers and types of employees needed.

After recruiting the numbers and types of employees necessary to accomplish the job, the right people must be selected. Questions that are unbiased and job-related only should be asked during the job interview to determine if the candidate is qualified to perform the job for which he or she was recruited. Selection of employees should be based upon finding the persons whose qualifications best match the requirements of the job. Resumes should be thoroughly checked. References should be solicited and contacted. Some security positions may require further testing such as polygraph, psychological, performance or other testing methods prior to selection.

The actual hiring may be done by the manager, or again, by the human resources department. At this time, the new employee should clearly understand the job expectations. Company benefits should be explained to the new employee and vacation and sick policies, compensation, insurance and other employee benefits should be understood by the new employee.

Training, although too often overlooked, is vital to the success of any organization. New employees may bring with them some, a little, a lot or no training at all for the job for which they were hired. Management should provide, at the very least, minimum training that will assure that the employee can do the job and do it right. From that point on, it's up to supervisors to make sure that the employee performs adequately. Employee development should consist of an ongoing training program with emphasis on rewarding employees with training, not using training as a "punishment." An important part of the training process should be a new employee orientation program.

One of the goals of staffing should be to assure that the right person is in the right job. After the selection, hiring and training of people, it may be discovered that the employee is not suitable for the job in which he or she is placed. Training may solve the problem, termination may be a viable answer (also a job of the manager), or reassignment to another job may solve the problem.

A performance evaluation system will detect work-related problems through timely appraisals of each employee's performance. A good system will also point out the positive traits of an employee as well as the negative ones. For this reason, performance ratings can be used as a means of selecting people for promotion, reassignment or transfer to a higher position if one is available or becomes available.

Directing

This is perhaps the central core of the manager's role in that it includes coordinating people and things, delegating responsibilities and authorities, motivating others, communicating clearly and concisely and providing strong leadership. Employees look to management for direction; it is in the area of directing that managers "make it or break it." Coordination is merely assuring that the efforts of people and their resources work together to accomplish the goals and objectives of the organization. It is synonymous with directing an orchestra in that one person gets everyone else's cooperation to effectively and efficiently achieve a goal. Coordination is not a "stand-alone" function of management; it is more the result of the manager doing his or her other functions well. It includes aspects of all other managerial functions. During the planning phase, if other people were involved, coordination will occur. In an organization with a well-defined chain of command, everyone knows who they need to work with. With good delegation, coordination is achieved. If the manager selects and places the right people in the right job, coordination will exist. When the manager acts as a leader and motivator, coordination follows.

Delegating authority and responsibility is imperative as a manager. It's far beyond the realm of possibility that one person can perform all the duties and work needed to accomplish an organization's mission. The manager must entrust duties and related authority to subordinates. Lester Bittell and John Newstrom define delegation as "the assignment, or entrustment, to subordinates of organizational responsibilities or obligations along with appropriate organizational authority, power and rights." *(What Every Supervisor Should Know, 6ᵗʰ ed.)*

Not all jobs can be delegated. For instance, the manager may be the only person who has a certain technical, administrative or skill knowledge, in which case he or she should not delegate a job. Anything of a confidential nature should not be delegated. However, the manager who believes that "if you want a job done right, do it yourself" is not trusting subordinates. Proper delegating allows the manager to concentrate on broader issues and activities. It also gives subordinates an opportunity to improve their job skills and knowledge, it develops employees so they can learn to handle more responsibilities and provides motivation as the delegated task(s) shows that the manager has trust and confidence in them. Managers do not relinquish control when delegating; in fact, they are still held accountable and responsible for the completion of the task(s).

Proper delegation requires that the manager tell the employees to whom work is being assigned what they are to do, what you expect from them, how far they can go and how and when you will be checking on them. Communicate your expectations very clearly and then let the employees do the job. Let them do the job their way. They may make mistakes, but proper delegation (as a part of leadership) allows for mistakes. The manager must focus on the end result, not the process. Therefore, a key concept in delegation is *entrusting* others.

Controlling

Often seen in negative, or dictatorial terms, controlling is no more than ensuring that the job is being done according to plans. Controlling is closely tied in with the first function of management – planning. The manager needs to know that the organization's objectives are being met and if not, that appropriate action is taken. The manager must establish acceptable work standards and develop a system of work performance measurements to assure compliance with the organization's plans. When there are deviations, corrective measures should be taken. It is important to have able and capable supervisors to ensure a good control system since they are in more direct contact with the work being performed and the workers performing it.

THE ONE SKILL OF AN EFFECTIVE MANAGER

Any discussion of the skills required of an effective manager would take volumes to write about. There are such words as technically and administratively knowledgeable, experienced, dependable, creative, intelligent and so on. It can also be said that a good manager is tactful, honest, dedicated, has integrity, is fair, understanding, patient, and so forth. Few could argue with any of this. However, one word, perhaps, encapsulates all the skills an effective manager should possess. That one skill is leadership.

Since managers perform five basic functions—planning, organizing, staffing, directing and controlling—it is clear that they require the assistance of other people. In other words, the manager gets others to perform the actual work of the organization and assures that goals and objectives are successfully achieved. Warren Bennis maintains that managers focus on systems, their structure, and processes while leaders focus on people *(On Becoming a Leader, 1989)*.
It is *people* that make systems and processes work, therefore, the manager needs to possess and exhibit leadership aptitude just as much as the supervisor who is "in the trenches."

Management and leadership are not necessarily synonymous. There are managers who cannot lead very well and there are leaders who don't always make good managers. Those who manage without demonstrating leadership skills usually will find a high degree of turmoil, misunderstandings, in-house fighting, sloppy or poor work results and, ultimately, a noticeable loss of productivity and/or profit. Conversely, those who lead find they usually have a smooth-running operation which produces high results.

There are innumerable qualities that leaders should possess and exhibit. Some of those have been listed above. Other desirable qualities an effective manager should have include excellent communications skills, tenacity, dependability, unselfishness, perceptiveness, compassion, intelligence and a positive, winning attitude. Of course, the list could go on and on. Roger Fulton, a noted law enforcement author, suggests the most important quality necessary to be a leader is desire. "The desire to lead the way. The desire to take on difficult problems. The desire to go a step beyond. And, of course, the desire to be a leader of others." *(Common Sense Leadership)*.

One can manage without possessing any of these qualities, but the results will show the lack of leadership in the manager or in management itself. The costs of poor management are high: high personnel turnover, low productivity, low morale, high rates of absenteeism and tardiness, rampant rumor mills and an organizational malaise that refuses to get ahead. On the other hand, when managers are leaders, the opposite holds true.

SUMMARY

As an element of organizational makeup, management, as a function, has been around a long time. Over the years, management has been researched, studied, analyzed and scrutinized. As a result, a number of theoretical models have emerged to describe the types of management found, such as the classical school of management, scientific management, human relations, behavioral, contingency and so on. Regardless of which school of thought one adopts or believes in, the bottom line of management has always been, and is to this day, "what is the most effective and efficient way of accomplishing our organization's stated goals and purposes?" This is the one question management must answer.

Management is defined as "the act, manner, or process of managing, supervising or controlling." In organizational terms, this means that to answer that question, management is responsible for pulling together the people and resources in the organization to achieve its objectives. Management is seen as a process of directing human and material resources, i.e., people and things, so that an organization's purposes can be successfully met.

The process of management consists of five basic functions: planning, organizing, staffing, directing and controlling. Planning is the initial function of management and should not be seen as a unilateral responsibility or duty. Others should be involved in the planning process since there are benefits to be derived both by the organization as well as the people involved.

Planning is looking to the future and developing plans, policies, rules, regulations and procedures to assure that organizational goals and objectives will be attained.

The second major function of a manager is organizing. In order to accomplish the objectives of the organization, work must be arranged and distributed among all the personnel. The manager must ascertain how the work will be divided, who will do it and what they need to accomplish the job. Establishing a chain of command will define appropriate authorities and responsibilities. The chain of command also establishes accountability throughout the organization. A well-defined chain of command not only identifies who does what job and places accountability where it belongs, it also encompasses the "golden rule" of management which is the principle that no responsibility should be assigned to a person unless he has the authority necessary to fulfill it.

Staffing, whether or not it is done by the organization itself or another human resources department, is a management function that entails recruiting, selecting and training employees. During this stage, managers must see that the new employees understand all the company benefits as well as job and management expectations. Training employees, especially new ones, is an important part of management and should include an orientation training program. Making certain that the right person is in the right job is a part of the staffing function. Another important part of this function is that of an effective performance evaluation system. A good system will point out not just negative aspects of an employee, but will indicate the employee's good traits and skills.

The last major function of managers, directing, is the crux of the manager's job. Directing includes coordinating, delegating, motivating, communicating and providing strong leadership. A manager is seen as an orchestra director in that one person coordinates the activities of others by gaining their cooperation to efficiently and effectively achieve a goal. Leadership is the most important skill that an effective manager should possess, for it includes innumerable positive traits and qualities. Management and leadership are not the same for there can be leaders without management skills and managers with no leadership skills. However, efficient and effective managers possess both skills, resulting in higher productivity, high morale, low personnel turnover and fewer personnel problems.

EVOLUTION OF MANAGEMENT
QUIZ

1.   The theory of scientific management tried to find the best method for performing a specific task.
          ☐ T   ☐ F

2.   Management is a process of directing and controlling people and things so that an organization's objectives can be studied.
          ☐ T   ☐ F

3.   Obtaining, arranging and allocating the right tools, equipment, materials and personnel to get the job done effectively and efficiently relates to:
     a)   Staffing
     b)   Organizing
     c)   Controlling
     d)   Planning

4.   The principle that no responsibility should be assigned a person unless he has the authority necessary to fulfill it refers to:
     a)   Organizing
     b)   Leadership
     c)   The "golden rule" of management
     d)   Effectiveness

5.   Considered as probably the central core of the manager's role is:
     a)   Planning
     b)   Supervising
     c)   Directing
     d)   Performance evaluations

6.   _____ authority and responsibility is imperative as a manager.

7.   Often seen in negative, or dictatorial terms, _____ is no more than ensuring that the job is being done according to plans.

8.   The one skill that an effective manager should possess is _____ .

9.   Management and leadership are always synonymous.
          ☐ T   ☐ F

10. If an organization is efficient, it will always be effective.
          ☐ T   ☐ F

TIME AND STRESS MANAGEMENT
by Eric L. Garwood, CPO, CSS

The lack of adequate time management causes stress and can destroy a career. *Stress left unmanaged can cause illness or death.*

"Time management" and "stress" are topics not often associated with one another. However, they are undeniably linked. The lack of time management can create or increase stress. Stress left unchecked will wreak havoc with managing time, and can cause illness or death.

TIME MANAGEMENT

"There aren't enough hours in the day."

The first thing you must accept is that the statement "There aren't enough hours in the day" is true. You cannot do everything in one day, and therefore you must learn to manage your time efficiently.

CONTROL

List the things that affect your time management. Break them into two categories: the things you *CAN* control, and things you *CANNOT* control.

YOU CAN CONTROL	YOU CANNOT CONTROL
Lack of planning	*Emergencies*
Reading junk mail	*Interruptions by superiors*
Procrastination	*Unscheduled events*
Failure to delegate	
Daydreaming	
Phone interruptions	

Review the list of things you can control and then take action accordingly. Lack of planning – you must document and plan tasks and goals. Procrastination – do not put off all tasks you do not like to do or all of your responsibilities will be affected. Phone interruptions – when you sit down to work on a task, let the office staff know that you do not want to be interrupted. Instead, let the secretary or answering machine take incoming calls. Failure to delegate – identify tasks that can or should be completed by co-workers or subordinates and assign them accordingly.

Put simply, take control of the things within your power. Allow flexibility in your planning for the things you cannot control.

PLANNING

The key to time management is planning. Planning tells us where we are and where we are going. By reviewing our plans we can determine if we are on track, or if we need to change course to reach our objectives.

Make a list of your long- and short-range tasks and goals. Assign a number of priority to each (1, 2, 3, etc.). Also assign a deadline for completion of each.

Short Range
Complete theft report 3-30-94 (1)
Meet with work group 4/94 (3)
Give CPR refresher 4-1-94 (2)
Long Range
Introduce new property pass procedure 9/95 (3)
Review visitor pass procedure 5/95 (1)
Institute new training schedule 7/95 (2)

Make several copies of this list and post it in places where you will see it every day, such as your computer terminal and your bathroom mirror. This will be a reminder of the things you need and want to accomplish.

Daily Planning

Now that you have a list of tasks and goals, you can start to plan your day-to-day activities. Each morning set aside 15 minutes to plan your day. Check your list of tasks and goals. List the things that must be done that day. Assign a number of priority to each. Complete the ones with the highest priority first, then go down the list. *JUST DO IT!!*

Monday

> Meet with boss - 4
> Finish manpower survey - 2
> Complete theft report - 1
> Call vendor re: broken camera - 3

As each task is completed, check it off your list. If you do not get to one of the items on your list today, draw an arrow next to it indicating that it will be moved to tomorrow's list. When planning your day remember to allow time for the things you cannot control. Don't schedule meetings back-to-back. Don't list so many tasks that you could not possibly complete them all. *PLAN YOUR WORK —WORK YOUR PLAN.*

STRESS

Effectively managing your time will reduce stress by making it easier to complete tasks. However, it will not do away with stress. Stress is caused by many forms of stimuli. Some of these are:

> *Interpersonal conflict*   *Criticism*
> *Emergencies*   *Poor health*
> *Confrontation*

To deal with stress, we must understand what stress is. The dictionary defines stress as, "To subject to physical or psychological tension." When we are subjected to this tension a natural chemical reaction occurs in the body. This reaction was developed in early man to protect the individual from life-threatening situations and prepares us to "fight or flight." It does this by releasing chemicals such as adrenalin into the body, giving us the energy to physically fight or flight. In today's society we cannot deal with most situations in this manner. Rather, we must cope in an accepted or prescribed manner and in doing so we do not relieve the accumulation of these chemicals. Therefore we must deal with this chemical accumulation in other ways.

The security supervisor is expected to maintain the security of his/her facility and be a public relations officer at the same time. For some people this is very difficult. However, time spent listing and prioritizing these responsibilities allows one to perform both roles with a minimum of stress.

Personal Stress

An essential key to managing stress is identifying the causes of one's personal stress. Make a list of stresses you face, both external and internal. Do this a couple of times a year.

> **External Stress**   **Internal Stress**
> *Physical confrontation*   *Disagreement with superior's decisions*
> *Public speaking*   *Not planning tasks*
> *Criticism*   *Low self esteem*
> *Excessive bills*

Having made a list, go over each item and study them individually. Identify the items you can ignore or let go. Rank the remaining from least to most stressful. Starting with the least stressful items, work out ways to solve the stress. Practice your response to physical situations, discuss your disagreement with superiors and turn criticism into an opportunity to improve yourself.

To survive in this world of ever-growing stress, you must develop coping mechanisms. Start with a healthy lifestyle based on good values and attitudes. My values and attitudes began to develop as a student of martial arts where the head instructor instituted the following "Student Creed," which is reiterated prior to the start of each class.

    1.   I will develop myself in a positive manner and avoid anything that would reduce my mental growth or physical health.

    2.   I will develop self-discipline in order to bring out the best in myself and others.

    3.   I will use what I learn in class constructively and defensively to help myself and my fellow man and never to be abusive or offensive.

These values and attitudes will lead to the appropriate application of time/stress management, exercise, sleep and beneficial family and work relationships.

Another important survival skill is dealing with the body's accumulation of chemicals as discussed in the beginning of this section. If we were walking along the beach looking at the surf and a large wave was headed for us, our bodies would activate the fight or flight mechanism. In order to avoid physical injury, our bodies would trigger us to act immediately. We would run away from the beach, fall to our knees with exhaustion, but feel good that we avoided the danger. This action would return the body's chemicals to their normal levels.

In the field of security we are expected to stand and confront danger. If we see someone committing a crime we are trained not to run but to observe and report what we see. We are trained not to intervene without backup or police assistance. However, our bodies will still activate the fight or flight mechanism. The chemicals will be released and our bodies will energize to deal with the situation. Often, when this type of situation is over, we have not physically exerted ourselves; therefore, the chemicals that have been released have not been burned off. Repeated situations like this without the physical burn-off can result in depression, fatigue and illness.

Since we often cannot physically burn off the chemicals at the time of the incident, we must get regular exercise. Plan regular exercise times into your week—walking, riding a bike, jogging, anything that increases your cardiovascular system and that you enjoy. Exercising three to four times a week for twenty minutes each day will not only reduce stress build-up, but will increase your physical health and well being.

TIME AND STRESS MANAGEMENT
QUIZ

1.   The statement _____ is the first thing you must accept when dealing with time management.

2.   Procrastination is the _____ of time management.

3.   _____ is the key to time management.

4.   When subjected to tension, a natural _____ occurs in the body.

5.   A healthy life style is based on good _____ and _____.

6.   Planning is essential in time management.
        ☐ T   ☐ F

7.   It is appropriate to fight for control of all things in your life.
        ☐ T   ☐ F

8.   You should set deadlines for goals.
        ☐ T   ☐ F

9.   Effectively managing your time will reduce stress.
        ☐ T   ☐ F

10.   Having a good attitude does not reduce stress.
        ☐ T   ☐ F

PROJECT MANAGEMENT
by S. Robert Sherwood, M.S., CPO, CSS

There have been a series of incidents at your bank's ATM sites throughout the city. The customers are demanding better security. As the bank's security manager you have been told to "make it happen."

You are the security director for a large metropolitan hospital. Recently doctors and nurses in the emergency room have been threatened and even attacked by patients and family. You must take action to protect these employees.

As the director of security for a sprawling suburban shopping complex you have noticed the incidence of motor vehicle thefts from the parking lots is on the rise. Retailers are demanding action.

INTRODUCTION

Problem solving is a skill that is required of every person in almost every aspect of life. Seldom does an hour go by without the need to solve some kind of problem. The job of the supervisor is inherently one of problem solving. If there were no problems in organizations, there would be no need for managers. Therefore, it is hard to conceive of an incompetent problem solver succeeding as a supervisor.

Most people, including managers, don't particularly like problems. They're time consuming, they create stress and they never seem to go away. Most people try to get rid of problems as soon as they can. Their natural tendency is to select the first reasonable solution that comes to mind. Unfortunately, the first solution is not often the best one. In normal problem solving, most people implement the marginally acceptable or merely satisfactory solution instead of the optimal or ideal solution. In fact, many observers have attributed the decline in U.S. quality and competitiveness to the abandonment of correct problem solving principles. Short-cuts, they argue, have had a major negative effect on the American economy.

No matter how large the project, how complex the problem, how critical the decision, do not allow yourself to be overwhelmed. The key is to break the problem down into its individual components, prioritize, and solve the series of smaller problems. In the remainder of this chapter you will learn how to do this.

THE BASIC PROCESS

In its simplest terms, problem solving can be broken down into four basic elements. These are:

1. *Describe the problem* – expand your thinking to review the factual symptoms of the problem that you are facing right now. A medical doctor, for example, examines a patient by first looking at the factual events and conditions – the symptoms – which are clues to the underlying problem. In the same way, you begin the problem solving process by noting the most obvious facts – the what, who, where and when of the situation. Then you focus these preliminary observations in a brief description of the problem. This problem description – necessarily incomplete because you're working only with what you know right now – becomes the focal point for a thorough investigation of the problem.

2. *Determine the cause or causes* – open up your thinking by gathering and analyzing information on possible causes of the problem. Seeking out facts and opinions about the causes of a problem will increase your chances of finding a permanent solution. Neglecting this step can prolong the problem solving process and squander precious resources. Begin by listing the possible causes of the symptoms you listed in your description of the problem. Now select two or three probable causes of the problem. If they don't jump out from your list, ask people who are close to the problem which causes they see as most probable. Make a list – facts and figures, background data, people who might have knowledgeable opinions – to focus your efforts in gathering information. The more time you spend gathering information and

walking around the problem, the better your solution is likely to be. Finally, specify the most likely cause or causes of the problem. Any successful remedy must directly address that cause.

3.   *Choose a solution* – expand your thinking once more by generating and evaluating a substantial list of possible solutions. First, identify your goal – the end result you're trying to achieve – and write out a brief goal statement. With the goal in mind, you can now generate a list of solutions that could move you toward that goal. Think of as many solutions as you can – noting each new idea with a brief phrase. Once you have this list, you are ready to decide which solution or combination of solutions is most likely to achieve your goal.

4.   *Plan action steps and follow-up* – consider the various available resources and summarize the details of implementation in a concise action plan. A solution consists of a good idea plus the coordinated efforts of the people who will make that idea a reality. Solving problems, therefore, requires a clear plan with work steps, schedule and follow-up activities. Write up a concise plan specifying action steps, dates, checkpoints and accountability.

DESCRIBING THE PROBLEM

Before effective action can be taken in a complex situation we need to clarify what issues require action. Therefore, an effective approach is to sort out and assess the various parts of the situation. The situation appraisal process is not intended to reach solutions, but to identify the component parts of the situation, break them down into manageable parts, impose order and set priorities so they can be resolved.

Recognizing concerns is a systematic surveying of the work environment for threats and opportunities. The result is a comprehensive list of the areas needing attention. An effective method for recognizing concerns is to list concerns raised in response to this series of questions:

What deviations are occurring?
What decisions need to be made?
What plans should be implemented?
What changes are anticipated?
What opportunities exist?

The purpose of this step is to identify the various concerns or issues that are part of the overall situation.

Once concerns are recognized they should be clarified. Complex concerns should be broken down into sub-concerns and broad or fuzzy concerns should be restated to make them specific statements of fact. By making sure we know precisely what the issue is, or what the elements of a multifaceted concern are, we can avoid wasting time and effort.

After concerns are identified and clarified, priorities can be established. To effectively determine what concerns should be handled first, a priority setting system, based on aspects of the concerns that can be readily determined and compared should be used. There are three areas that consistently appear as highly relevant. These are seriousness, urgency and growth. Questions we should ask are:

What is the impact?
Who is concerned?
What is the deadline for taking action?
When do we start?
What is the future trend?
What will happen if nothing is done?

The answers to these questions provide specific information that can be used to judge the relative priorities of the concerns.

Each concern on the list is assessed first in terms of seriousness. The most serious concern, based on the data, is used as the benchmark for assessing the rest of the list. We can use high, medium and low as indicators of our judgement. Once the assessment for seriousness is complete, we can do the same for the aspects of urgency and growth. Then we can scan the assessments in all three criteria to determine the highest priority concerns.

With priorities in mind, it must then be determined whether we should expand and reorganize our thinking or gather more information. Is more analysis needed? Do we have enough information to make a decision? Involving other people in resolving the concerns and laying out a plan of action should also be considered.

DETERMINING THE CAUSE OR CAUSES

It is important to begin with a clear declaration of the problem before searching for the information necessary to solve it. A problem statement provides a focused starting point for the problem solver. Once the problem is stated clearly, you are in a good position to begin gathering information. Irrelevant information can be readily discarded. It is easy to stay on track once you have a clear statement of the problem at hand. The problem statement should describe, in concise terms, the machine, system, product, person or group having the problem, and what exactly is wrong with it or them. By asking what, where, when and extent questions you can get a clear, complete picture of the problem.

Once you have described the problem completely, you can develop possible causes. Most times, your knowledge, experience and common sense suggest possibilities. You can list the possible causes and begin to evaluate them against the information in the problem description. If these causes fail to explain the deviation or if you have been unable to develop any causes from experience, the following two problem analysis techniques will be helpful.

When you developed the problem statement, you identified not only the "is" but the "is not," with the purpose of establishing clear boundaries around the problem. It is logical to say that whatever caused the problem affected only the "is" side of the analysis since we observe the problem here and not with the "is not." Therefore, the cause of the problem must be acting on something unique about the "is" when compared with the "is not." You should look for the distinctions throughout the entire problem description. Most often, the fruitful sources of distinctions are "is/is not" comparisons that stand out as particularly odd.

Another problem analysis technique is to identify changes. If you have been reaching expectations and then a problem occurs, something must have changed to cause that problem. Find that change and you'll find the cause of your problem. You can expect a vast number of changes to have taken place. Focus in on the changes relevant to the problem and you will be able to determine the cause.

Once you have identified changes that may be relevant to the problem, you can move from gathering facts to making hypotheses. How could each change have caused the problem? We build on past experience, knowledge and common sense to make a specific statement of possible cause. When you have listed several possible causes, the task is to find which cause is the most probable. Examine each possible cause against the facts in the problem description to see if it could explain the deviation being experienced. By testing each possible cause in turn, you can see how well the hypothesis fits the facts by seeing how accurately it explains both the "is" and "is not" facts of our entire problem description.

To this point, the development and testing of causes has been based on available information about the problem, as summarized in the problem specification. The most probable cause, as indicated by your assessment, must now be confirmed as the actual cause of the problem. To do this we must verify any questionable information we have about the cause. The assumptions we noted in the testing step provide a logical starting place. The confirmation process may involve gathering additional facts, observation or conducting tests or experiments. Confirming the true cause may also involve taking action to remove the cause, then tracking the effects to see if the problem indeed goes away.

CHOOSING A SOLUTION

In our personal lives and in the organizations where we work, we are often called upon to choose a course of action or to assess a recommendation presented for our approval. Given the complexity and rate of change of the world today, relying solely on experience and intuition makes little sense. We need a method of decision-making that allows us to efficiently and effectively gather relevant information, reorganize it in a useful way and analyze it rationally and thoroughly.

Once the basic goal of the decision is clearly and specifically identified, objectives are considered and classified. Specific objectives focus on the results to be achieved by the decision and the resources available to achieve those results. The objectives provide the criteria for subsequently evaluating alternative choices and should take into account both short- and long-term effects. Once objectives have been listed we have a clearer statement of the criteria against which to judge the various alternatives. In most decisions, objectives vary in their degree of importance. We need to classify these objectives to reflect their relative influence on the decision.

We divide these objectives into two basic categories. These are "musts" and "wants." Those objectives which are mandatory for the success of the decision are called "musts." Those objectives that, while not essential, are still desirable are called "wants." We now have a clear set of objectives we can use to assess alternatives. It is important that alternatives satisfy the "must" objectives or our decision will not fulfill its purpose.

At this stage we are ready to list the alternatives from which to make our choice. In some decisions the sources for alternatives are clear, while in other situations we must widen the search for alternatives. Generating alternatives is a creative step. We should therefore use any method or technique that releases our creativity.

Once alternatives are listed, we can begin the process of seeing how they perform against the objectives. If our classification of objectives has identified "musts," we can use these to screen out those alternatives that fail to meet our minimum requirements. We can now analyze which of the remaining alternatives best satisfy the "want" objectives.

Considering the risks associated with the remaining alternatives is the third stage of the basic decision-making process: objectives, alternatives, risks. By imaging that the alternative we are considering has been selected, we anticipate what might go wrong during its implementation. Once the risks are noted, we must assess their potential impact on the success of the decision. To fully judge the risk, we must look at two aspects of the threat it poses: the probability that the risk we have identified will occur and the seriousness of the effects should it happen.

The final step in the decision-making process is to commit to the choice by balancing the relative benefits and risks. The judgement and experience we have used in reviewing the information is reflected in our analysis. In making the final choice, we may be prepared to implement an alternative with relatively high risk if the ability of that alternative to satisfy the purpose of the decision is exceptional. Or we may reject the "best" alternative, if the inherent risks are high, in favor of a more conservative choice. Our analysis of the available information, along with an understanding of our personal approach to risk and the posture of our organization, will guide us to the best possible choice.

PLANNING ACTION STEPS AND FOLLOW-UP

Once we make a decision, we sometimes assume that our job is completed. But we must also implement the decision – often in a rapidly changing environment where almost anything can happen. Experience suggests that taking time to analyze and improve our plans before implementing them can help prevent difficulties.

A natural starting point is to identify potential problems, those things that might go wrong and jeopardize the successful implementation of an action or plan, by reviewing the goal or purpose of the action. Now the details of our plan need to be identified by listing the series of actions or activities necessary to reach the goal. The end results of each major step should be identified so that progress can be assessed against specific goals. Responsibility for each step should be assigned and a completion date developed.

With the basic plan in place, we can now step back and look for areas where problems might arise. If we can foresee these potential problems, we can plan actions against them and by doing so improve our plan. Once we focus on the areas most critical to success, we need to identify specifically what might go wrong. The more specifically we can define potential problems, the more likely we will be able to identify effective actions to deal with them.

From this point, our analysis follows the logic of cause and effect. If we can determine what might cause our anticipated problems, we can then plan actions to reduce the probability that the problems will occur. Preventive action serves as a barrier against the cause. Once we have identified preventive actions, they should be included as part of the plan itself. Only then can they actually prevent the problem from arising.

Since it is often impossible to anticipate all the likely causes of a potential problem, the problem may still arise. Contingent action is aimed at minimizing the impact a future problem will have on our plan. To determine the most effective actions to put into place, we must focus on exactly what the effects will be should the problem occur. Reaction plans are then prepared and held ready to be brought into play only if they are needed.

PITFALLS OF PROBLEM SOLVING

There are several common pitfalls that interfere with good decision-making. We have all encountered them at one time or another, if not when making decisions as an individual, then in group decision-making situations. Problem solving is rarely easy. Everyone agrees that when trouble appears, quick, effective action is needed. Unfortunately, several pitfalls in the way people approach problem solving can lead to confusion, wasted efforts and even failure.

When you see no clear pattern emerging from the data, it's easy to get bogged down and forget that analysis alone can't solve a problem. The fact is that sometimes – even after reviewing extensive evidence – you may be unable to identify a clear-cut cause. At that point you may need to talk to someone with a fresh perspective or try out some low risk ideas and see what happens.

Avoid considering possible choices before clarifying what it is you hope to achieve with the decision. Too often, decision-making starts with discussion of the pros and cons of alternatives. Until the objectives of a decision are outlined and agreed upon, discussing the relative merits of possible choices is meaningless.

Sometimes discussion concentrates on the strengths of one alternative and ignores or dismisses other alternatives offhandedly. Such lopsided decision-making interferes with finding the best possible choice. In group decisions, this focus can also lead to frustration and conflict when other alternatives are not explored.

Some people flounder in a mass of information that may or may not be related to the problem. They find it difficult to ferret out the really important facts. Information may be so varied, contradictory and complex that people are not able to clearly focus on exactly what it is they are trying to resolve.

These pitfalls usually arise when one or more of the following conditions exist:

There is pressure to make a decision quickly.

The decision is made by a group of people with widely differing viewpoints.

It is unclear to the people making the decision what information is necessary.

The information is spread out among many people.

To overcome these difficulties, we need a method of decision-making that allows us to efficiently and effectively gather relevant information, organize it in a useful way and analyze it rationally and thoroughly.

CONCLUSION

The word "problem" has taken on a special meaning for each person. It is used indiscriminately to mean a complex situation that requires action, something that has gone wrong (or the cause of what has gone wrong), a difficult choice or even future trouble. These are very different concerns, and each requires a different approach to achieve resolution. Yet elements of all these concerns are intertwined.

Before effective action can be undertaken in a complex situation, we need to clarify exactly what issues require action. Clarification of the situation is achieved through understanding and agreement about the various parts of a major concern. If the word "problem" is defined to mean only those concerns where something has gone wrong, we can readily distinguish between problems, decisions and plans.

PROJECT MANAGEMENT
QUIZ

1.   Problem solving is a _____ that is required of every person in almost every aspect of life.

2.   Seeking out facts and _____ about the cause of a problem will increase your chances of finding a permanent solution.

3.   Before effective _____ can be taken in a complex situation, we need to clarify what issues require action.

4.   It is easy to stay on track once you have a _____ statement of the problem at hand.

5.   The final step in the decision-making process is to commit to the choice by balancing relative _____ and risks.

6.   Identifying the symptoms of a problem will identify the cause.
        ☐ T   ☐ F

7.   The cause of a problem will always be easy to identify.
        ☐ T   ☐ F

8.   Candidate solutions will help clarify the goal.
        ☐ T   ☐ F

9.   The implementation of a solution seldom requires a great deal of effort.
        ☐ T   ☐ F

10.   Gathering, organizing and analyzing information is the key to problem solving.
        ☐ T   ☐ F

COMPANY POLICY AND PROCEDURES
The Security Supervisor's Primer
by John T. Brobst, Jr., CPO, CSS

Policies and procedures—how many times do we hear those words in our day-to-day activities? Someone is quoting them, breaking them or needing a new one for some problem or concern that has arisen.

Unfortunately, many security departments run on an antiquated system of "that's how we've always done it" or "there's a memo here somewhere about that." The front line security officer's duties have grown rapidly in today's society. They are no longer the "guy at the gate"; often times, they are the one responding to crimes in progress, lost children, chemical spills and fires. A company or security department that does not have a written policy and procedure manual is doing itself and the people it protects a great disservice.

As security supervisors, policies become more than something we enforce. They become an added facet of our job; tools we can use to help us, our employees and the security department function more efficiently. The focus of this chapter is to help the security manager understand exactly what policies, procedures and rules are, how they can be written and finally, how they are applied and implemented during everyday activity.

WHAT ARE POLICIES, AND HOW DO PROCEDURES AND RULES INFLUENCE THEM?

Webster's *Dictionary* defines *policy* as "A principle or course of action chosen to guide decision-making."

Policy making for a security department involves a degree of thought and the ability to place those thoughts in a logical and easy to understand document. Policy sets a general outline for a task or idea for a problem or circumstance that an employee will happen upon. For instance, a policy may state; "It is the policy of the Acme Company Security Department to conduct routine patrols of all company grounds and buildings to prevent criminal activity, to locate and report events such as fires, power outages and safety hazards." This statement does not tell the security officer how to patrol, how frequently patrols are to be made, or even to whom to report power outages. It shows that the security department will patrol the area and some reasons why they would patrol. Post orders and procedures take over where a policy stops. The procedure or post orders will tell the officer that patrols are to be made a minimum of three times a shift and to whom to report safety hazards.

Policies can also spell out the stance a company or department takes regarding public and employee issues. For example, a policy may spell out what the minimum requirements are to be employed as a security officer in your facility, or that the company is an Equal Opportunity Employer.

Administrative policies are policies that address a situation that all employees of a facility are to be aware of. For instance, a Smoke Free Workplace policy and an Employee Accident policy are policies that address actions of all company employees. The security supervisor usually does not write Administrative Policies, but may be asked to provide input into their creation.

Departmental policies address situations or procedures that occur or are specific to a certain department. A departmental policy may be a job description, a call-in procedure, or a use of force policy. This type of policy is the one most commonly written by the security manager.

Procedures are often contained in policies and describe the steps taken to produce a desired result. Not all policies require procedures—for instance, a security policy might state that the department is an equal opportunity employer, or list what the chain of command may be. Depending upon what issue the policy is written for, you may have to list a quite lengthy procedure. This is fine if it is thorough and complete. Procedures are more resolute in their function. They are meant to give systematic directions on the actions that are to be performed. The procedure is the most recognizable of all the parts of a policy. In fact, very few policies are written without some form of procedure being contained within it. A procedure often addresses day-to-day activities; for example, signing out a company vehicle, filing incident reports and steps to follow when calling in sick.

Rules serve a function only when they are made about very simple and clear activities. "No smoking in the jet refueling area" is a very clear, understandable and sane rule. "Patrol vehicle will be refueled at the end of the shift" and "all incident reports will be completed before going off duty" are more examples. Rules define exactly what employees are to do—no more, no less.

The use of rules in policies can be a double-edged sword. Use them only when absolutely necessary. Overuse of rules tends to discourage the use of discretion and common sense by the officers and often results in them "only doing what I have to do" to get the job done. Not using rules results in mistakes and mis-communication.

In summary, policies give guidelines and are relatively flexible; procedures spell out steps to take to get to the goal, but are more strict; rules are absolutely clear about what can and cannot be done, and are the most inflexible. Procedures and rules are generally components of policies, however rules should only be used when necessary.

The proper utilization of procedures and rules in policy making provides the manager with an excellent communications tool. Providing employees with current, up-to-date information about what should be done, and how to do it, encourages professionalism and pride in the department and the job function.

Keeping this in mind, let's look at how to begin writing a policy and procedure manual.

PLANNING

Your task as a manager or supervisor is to create policies, procedures and rules to address various subjects and situations that your personnel may encounter while doing their day-to-day activities. In addition, you may need to incorporate administrative policies, security policies and mission statements into your manual. If you have an existing policy manual, review all the policies, taking careful notes about what needs to be changed, deleted or added. Address these changes with your director or administrator for their input.

When preparing to write a new policy, a few things should be addressed. First, is a policy necessary for the task at hand? For example, writing a policy requiring officers to lock the security office door when it is unoccupied is needless since it is an issue that can be addressed by general orientation.

List the goals you want the policy to achieve. A policy cannot be effective if it only reaches half of it's expected purpose. How will your staff follow the policy? Will your policy be an administrative policy affecting the entire facility? An administrative policy regarding package inspections would affect the entire population of your facility. What goals do you expect it to achieve? Theft reduction for fear of being caught would be one goal. Catching thieves in the act could be another. Be realistic and remember that policies are only guidelines to assist your staff in solving problems.

Will the security policy impact other departments directly or indirectly? A policy changing the times an entrance is locked or opened can affect employees and the public. This change could impact deliveries to your entire facility or just one person. Do your homework and speak with the persons affected to gain their input. Involving other staff gives the added benefit that your new policy will be followed since they feel as if they had something to do with its creation.

Creating a new policy manual will require involving administration, supervisory staff from other departments and possibly, your legal counsel. Writing new policies really only involves one extra step—finding out what you're going to be writing about. New security policies should address general security matters as well as site-specific problems. Past events will dictate what your policies and procedures should apply to.

Finding a need for a policy is not difficult; every time a new job function or a new post is added, a policy should be implemented if the activity does not fall under an existing policy. The policy may have a general statement to show the stance the department takes on a particular subject, may list a procedure to follow, or have a rule that *must* be followed to complete the task at hand. Policies should not be created haphazardly and at the pleasure of the manager. Policies need to be applied to situations that are not solved by using common sense or to address specific occurrences at your facility.

WRITING POLICIES

Writing policies and procedures is the easiest part of the entire process. If you have a policy manual in place at your facility, follow the established policy format. Figure 25.1 shows a commonly used policy and procedure format. The heading block shows the name of the company, to what department the policy applies, the subject of the policy addresses, number of the policy, it's effective date, it's revision date and finally the number of pages that should be present. Having the effective and revised dates on the first page will assist the manager when reviewing policies to make sure they are up to date.

The *Policy Statement* is one or two sentences that summarize the goal of the policy. The policy statement should be clear and to the point—any remaining details should be covered by the rest of the policy or a procedure.

The *Purpose* is part of the policy that can be used to further describe the policy statement. In Figure 25.1, the policy statement shows that security will restrict access to company vehicles. The purpose further refines this statement by saying that the reason is to protect the vehicles and to make sure they are used safely.

Not all policies require the purpose statement. The use of a purpose statement is mostly a matter of company or administrative preference. Some policies, as shown in Figure 25.2, do not require a purpose statement because the policy statement makes it clear as to what the goal consists of.

A *Procedure* may or may not be required by your policy. Using procedures may add clarity to some policies, while other times they may complicate it. Make the procedure clear and concise—you do not need to write a blow by blow description of how to do the task. If you feel a procedure will help to clarify the policy, use one. A procedure can be used when a task is out of the ordinary, or something that the officer will encounter infrequently during their tour of duty. For instance, a burglar alarm at a high security building may require a different response than an alarm at another building in the patrol area. The procedure for this example could spell out what should be done, who to call, and how the response itself should be handled. Figure 25.1 shows a procedure for signing out vehicles. It includes rules in its procedure such as where to secure the keys and where to obtain fuel. It addresses various aspects of requisitioning a vehicle, but it does not burden the reader with overly specific or lengthy procedures.

All policies should contain a signature of the person responsible for its origination or directly in charge of the area that the policy addresses. For a security policy, the director or manager would sign; an administrative policy would require the signature of the company president, CEO or vice president.

In today's litigious society, it may be a good idea to include a disclaimer showing that the policy is only a guideline and not in any way an employee contract or guarantee of sorts. Speak with your legal counsel regarding policy disclaimers and if they should be included in your policy manual.

Following the disclaimer, you will find various listings, including but not limited to:

1.   Implementation Date - when the policy came into effect.
2.   Originating Department - who wrote it, or where the policy originated.
3.   Review Date - date policy was last reviewed.
4.   Reviewed - who reviewed the policy on the review date.
5.   Revised - when the policy was last revised.
6.   Cross Reference - any policies or procedures that refer to, or are referred from the policy.

Your facility's policies may include all, some or none of the above listings. The various dates that list when things were done and who did them are tools that the manager can use when reviewing policies for content, applicability and timeliness.

Finally, should there be any new forms or paperwork that need to be filled out in order to comply with the new policy, they should also be included as exhibits with the policy.

The format in which policies are written is not as important as the information they contain. However, a clear and concise style for writing policy is important in that it enables the employee to obtain information in a timely and efficient manner, as well as helping the manager maintain the policy as an effective administrative tool.

IMPLEMENTING POLICIES

Once the initial policy is written, it may need to go through an approval process until the final written form is produced, distributed, and implemented. Some facilities have a policy review board in which all policy and procedure pass through for approval. Others may allow the individual department heads to approve a policy, providing that it affects only that department.

Any time a policy is written or revised, a manager should have his director or administrator review the policy with a critical eye. This will assist in finding any problems or items that should be addressed in the policy. In addition, when the security policy affects another department or the entire facility, administration should be consulted and permitted to review the policy for any issues that may need to be resolved.

The new policy has been written, approved and printed—now it's time to implement it. Making sure that the employees read, understand and know where to find the policy is a concern all managers face when instituting a new policy or procedure. Some suggestions and ideas are included for your review.

Some supervisors post the policy or give a copy to the individual employees and have them sign a sheet (Figure 25.3) stating that they have read and understand the policy. This sheet, once all the officers have signed it, is filed for the future in the event that a problem arises in which an officer states that they never received the policy. You may attach a copy of the policy to ensure that the employees read it. Use daily briefings or staff meetings to tell the officers about the new policy.

You should still have them sign off on a sheet stating that they received and understand the policy.

Making sure that a policy is read company wide is another matter entirely. Issue a memo with the new policy attached to the various department supervisors and have them share the policy with their employees. Although this is not a foolproof method, you will still reach a majority of the employees. Send a general employee memo after the supervisor's memo, telling employees that a new policy was placed into effect and attach a copy of it to the memo.

If the new policy is an administrative or company wide policy, both memos should state where the new policy should be placed and where the employees can find it.

REVIEWING/REVISING POLICIES

Unfortunately, policies and procedures are not eternal; duties are added, changed, and deleted. The security manager is responsible for updating the Security Policy manual to keep it current. Policy manuals should be reviewed and revised a minimum of once per year. This ensures that employees are not getting conflicting information from a new policy when an old one seems to still be in effect.

The easiest way to ensure that the manual is still effective is to update it throughout the year as topics and changes arise. However, it is sometimes difficult to catch every small change as it appears. Read each policy and take notes as to what needs to be changed or removed. Revise the policy and release it just as you did with a new policy. Keep a copy of the original policy as well as each individual revision to it should a question arise in the future about past practice. For example, a lawsuit is brought against the company for an assault on an employee that occurred five years prior. The lawsuit states that security was responsible for being in the parking lots at times when employees are coming into and leaving from work after dark. Current policy states that officers are present at all the parking areas to ensure the safety of employees. However, upon reviewing the policy in effect at the time, it is shown that employees were responsible for calling security when they needed an escort to their cars.

When discontinuing a policy, for example, a monthly lighting survey that security performed, but now maintenance completes, the supervisor needs to inform the officers that the task is not to be performed. A memo will serve the purpose of informing the officers and any other employees that need to be notified. The discontinued policy should be signed and dated as to when the policy was discontinued and filed for future reference.

THE SECURITY POLICY AND PROCEDURE MANUAL

The security policy and procedure manual should be as important to the employee for information as their uniform is for identifying them. The manual should be a place to look for guidance in problem situations and as a tool to help other employees with any security concerns they may have. It is your job as a manager or supervisor to make sure that this information is up to date, complete and available.

As a manager, you should also be making sure that the officers and other employees in your department read and understand the manual. In addition to having the officers initial and date any new policies that come into the department, they should also be required to read the entire policy manual and initial that they have read it and understand it. This can be accomplished simply by having a sheet posted in the front of the manual with each of the officer's names on it. As they read the manual, they initial and date the sheet when completed; this should be done a minimum of once a year. This also should be done for any other policy manuals in your department (administrative, fire and safety, etc.) to ensure that your staff is up to date on the information contained in them.

Finally, review various policies (old and new) with your staff during training sessions, staff meetings or daily briefings. Give a little seminar followed by a quiz. Document any sessions in which you covered policy and who attended them. During employee evaluations include a section on knowledge of policy and procedure. All these ideas are tools the manager can use to make sure that employees are aware of the policy manual and how to use it.

In conclusion, policies and procedures guide us, give us information and are valuable tools that the employee and manager can use to benefit both the department and themselves. Writing policy is not something we look forward to, but it can be one of the simplest tasks to perform. Planning, writing, implementing and revising are steps we take to making that procedure even easier. A well kept, up to date and professional looking security policy manual will benefit more than just the department and its employees. It will benefit the company it protects, as well.

Figure 25.1. Sample Policy with Procedure

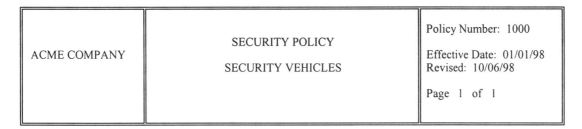

ACME COMPANY	SECURITY POLICY SECURITY VEHICLES	Policy Number: 1000 Effective Date: 01/01/98 Revised: 10/06/98 Page 1 of 1

POLICY STATEMENT

It shall be the policy of the Acme Company's Security Department to restrict the use of the Security Department's vehicles to authorized employees.

PURPOSE

To insure the safe use of company vehicles, the safety of employees and to protect company assets.

PROCEDURE

1. Use of unmarked security vehicles by company employees is permitted, provided:
    a) Vehicle use will be restricted to company employees with a valid driver's license.
    b) Vehicle Requisition must be completed with supervisor's authorization.
    c) Vehicle log in the Security Office will be completed with the destination and the time involved.
    d) Trip Sheet in vehicle will be completed with time out/in and mileage out/in.
2. Marked security vehicles will only be used by company employees if:
    a) An unmarked vehicle is not available or about to become available.
    b) Vehicle is required immediately for an emergency.
    c) Use is cleared by the shift Sergeant.
3. In the event non-security personnel utilize a marked vehicle, the Security Officer on duty will:
    a) Place "OUT OF SERVICE" cover on the roof mounted light bar.
    b) Place magnetic "OUT OF SERVICE" placards over the decals on the door panels.
    c) Remove any security equipment in the vehicle and secure it in the office.
4. All vehicle keys are to be maintained in the security office.
5. Unmarked security vehicles will not be used for personal use without the written authorization of the Company President or the Captain.
6. Marked vehicles shall be used for official security business only.
7. Gasoline will be obtained at the maintenance storage shed.

Captain Joseph Jones Jr.
Acme Company Security Department

NOTE: This policy, as with all policies, is intended as a guideline and is subject to change at the Company's sole and reasonable discretion. Policies are not contracts or employment guarantees for any specific duration.

ORIGINAL IMPLEMENTATION DATE: 01/01/98
ORIGINATING DEPARTMENT: Security
REVIEW DATE: 09/98
REVIEWED: Capt. J. Jones Jr.
REVISED: 10/06/98
CROSS REFERENCE:

Figure 25.2.   Sample Policy: Policy Only

ACME COMPANY	SECURITY POLICY SECURITY ORIENTATION	Policy Number: 2001 Effective Date: 02/01/98 Revised: Page 1 of 1

POLICY STATEMENT

It shall be the policy of the Acme Company Security Department to conduct a security orientation program for new employees. This program is given monthly as part of the general orientation program provided by the Human Resources Department. The following is a list of topics covered in the orientation;

1.   Personal Safety
2.   Security Assistance
3.   Identification Badges
4.   Parking Control
5.   Key Card System

6.   Alarm Systems
7.   Incident Reporting
8.   Package Inspections
9.   Crime Prevention
10. Additional Information as Required

Captain Joseph Jones Jr.
Acme Company Security Department

NOTE: This policy, as with all policies, is intended as a guideline and is subject to change at the Company's sole and reasonable discretion. Policies are not contracts or employment guarantees for any specific duration.

ORIGINAL IMPLEMENTATION DATE: 02/01/98
ORIGINATING DEPARTMENT: Security
REVIEW DATE:
REVIEWED:
REVISED:
CROSS REFERENCE:

Figure 25.3. Employee Information Sheet

TO: Security Officers
FROM: Captain J. Jones Jr.
DATE: 12/20/99
SUBJECT: Security Vehicles Policy Number 1000

Please read the policy, initial and date the form below. If you have any questions, please let me know.
I have read and understand Security Department Policy Number 1000 - SECURITY VEHICLES.

	Initials	Date
1.	*JFB*	*12/21/97*
2.	*SPW*	*12/23/97*
3.	*HBH*	*12/23/97*

COMPANY: POLICY AND PROCEDURES
QUIZ

1. Policy is defined as "a principle or course of action chosen to make rules."
    ☐ T   ☐ F

2. Rules serve a function only when they are made about simple and clear activities.
    ☐ T   ☐ F

3. A procedure:
    a) May or may not be a part of a policy.
    b) Should be clear and concise.
    c) Can be used when a task is out of the ordinary.
    d) All the above.
    e) None of the above.

4. A disclaimer can be used on a policy to help avoid litigation.
    ☐ T   ☐ F

5. Old policies should be shredded when no longer used to avoid confusion.
    ☐ T   ☐ F

6. The manager can review policy with employees:
    a) At the Officer's home.
    b) While on patrol.
    c) At daily briefings.
    d) On lunch break.
    e) None of the above.

7. The security manager commonly writes administrative policy.
    ☐ T   ☐ F

8. Figure 25.1, procedure number 4 is an example of what part of a policy?
    a) A policy
    b) A procedure
    c) A rule
    d) None of the above
    e) All of the above

9. Policy manuals should be reviewed and revised at least once per year.
    ☐ T   ☐ F

10. The purpose can be used to further refine the policy statement.
    ☐ T   ☐ F

TOTAL QUALITY MANAGEMENT
by Tom M. Conley, M.A., B.Sc., B.A., CPP, CFE, CPO

Business is changing rapidly. We are now in a global economy and challenges have never been greater than they are now. Progressive organizations are in the process of transforming from the old way of doing business to the new way of doing business. To be successful now, and in the future, it is essential that security personnel at all levels understand the concepts, benefits and results of Total Quality Management (TQM).

Before we can discuss TQM, we first must attempt to define it. There is no question that TQM is a hot topic in business and academic circles. Business managers are fervently trying to figure out how to do it while academicians are trying to determine what it is. None of them completely agree upon either the definition of TQM or how to put the concept into practice. This disagreement should be expected. First, TQM is ever evolving as new concepts and methods are developed. Second, different organizations are in different stages of transforming to TQM. Third, different organizations may require different forms of TQM to fit their specific needs.

One notable exception to this pervasive disagreement over the concept of TQM is the definition offered by the participants in the Total Quality Forum, a consortium of business and academic leaders who come together annually to study TQM and disseminate their learnings. A study group of the 1992 Total Quality Forum defined Total Quality as:

> *A people-focused management system that aims at a continual*
> *increase in customer satisfaction at continually lower real cost. TQM*
> *is a total system approach (not a separate area or program), and an*
> *integral part of high-level strategy. It works horizontally across*
> *functions and departments, involving all employees, top to bottom, and*
> *extends backwards and forwards to include the supply chain and the*
> *customer chain.*

Not all people will agree with this definition. Some people refuse to acknowledge the existence of TQM, while others are doing all they can to embrace the concepts. Still others are experimenting with TQM and trying to figure out what it means to their business. Whichever position an individual or organization might take, TQM, as a way of doing business in a different way, is here to stay. Our choice is to embrace TQM or be left behind by those who do.

To help us understand where we are now, and where we are going, we need to understand the history of TQM. After World War II, the country of Japan was crippled. Their economy was in ruins and their spirit nearly broken. The United States decided to help them rebuild their economy. A statistician named Dr. W. Edwards Deming, who worked in the U.S. government, was asked to assist on the project of helping Japan. Dr. Deming had previously tried to help companies in the United States, but they turned him away because the U.S. economy was good. There were plenty of workers, and since American companies were leading the world's industrial base, they thought that Dr. Deming had nothing that could help them. So, Dr. Deming went to Japan. When he arrived, the Japanese listened. Dr. Deming taught them the quantitative and qualitative concepts of TQM. They learned ways to do things better and at a lower cost, while still maintaining high quality. The result of the ongoing work with Dr. Deming was remarkable. The Japanese went from having little or no impact in the global economy in the middle to late 1940s to having a significant impact by the 1970s. The major difference was the implementation of TQM.

In the decade of the 1970s, the U.S. economy was not doing very well. Inflation and unemployment hit double digits and American workers continued to want more money and benefits. American companies had lost their competitive edge and were losing in the global economy. By this time, Dr. Deming's work with the Japanese had become widely known and respected by American companies. By the early 1980s, American companies were really hurting. They called on Dr. Deming to help them as he had helped the Japanese. However, unlike the Japanese, most American companies really were not serious about making changes. They wanted a quick-fix to their problems. Dr. Deming was selective in terms of what organizations he would work with. And, he would only deal with the top people in an organization. If those top people were not committed, he was not interested in working with them at all.

Finally, companies like Ford, Chrysler, Westinghouse, Harley-Davidson, and Motorola, as well as a multitude of other organizations, came around and were forced to become committed to TQM for their survival. Dr. Deming helped them. The results of organizations implementing TQM and a new way of doing business were both profound and predictable. The profits of companies increased because the quality of their products increased. By the late 1980s, American automobiles were known for their high quality and were priced competitively. People, once again, were proud to buy American.

In addition to Dr. Deming, there have been a multitude of other people during the last fifty plus years, such as Joseph Juran and Peter Senge, who have worked tirelessly to help organizations become competitive and shift to the new way of doing business.

Dr. Deming used a system known as his "14 points for the transformation of management." He used these as a set of guidelines or operating principles for organizational leaders to focus on the changes they needed to make and to keep the focus on continual improvement. Deming's 14 points for the transformation of management are:

1.   Create constancy of purpose toward improvement of product and service, with the aim to become competitive and to stay in business, and to provide jobs.
2.   Adopt the new philosophy. We are all in a new economic age. Western management must awaken to the challenges, must learn their responsibilities, and take on leadership for change.
3.   Cease dependence on inspection to achieve quality. Eliminate the need for inspection on a mass basis by building quality into the product in the first place.
4.   End the practice of awarding business based on the price tag. Instead, minimize total cost. Move toward a single supplier for any one item, in a long-term relationship of loyalty and trust.
5.   Improve consistently and forever the system of production and service, to improve quality and productivity, and thus constantly decrease cost.
6.   Institute training on the job.
7.   Institute leadership. The aim of supervision should be to help people and machines and gadgets to do a better job. Supervision of management is in need of overhaul, as well as supervision of workers.
8.   Drive out fear, so that everyone may work effectively for the company.
9.   Break down barriers between departments. People in research, design, sales and production must work as a team, to foresee problems of production and in use that may be encountered with the product or service.
10.   Eliminate slogans, exhortations and targets for the workforce asking for zero defects and new levels of productivity. Such exhortations only create adversarial relationships, as the bulk of the causes of low quality and low productivity belong to the system and thus lie beyond the power of the workforce.
11.   Eliminate quotas. Eliminate management by numbers and numerical goals. Substitute leadership.
12.   Remove barriers that rob the hourly worker of his right to pride of workmanship. The responsibility of supervisors must be changed from sheer numbers to quality.
13.   Institute a vigorous program of education and self-improvement.
14.   Put everybody in the company to work to accomplish the transformation. The transformation is everybody's job.

The purpose of Dr. Deming's 14 points are to create a management system that focuses on stopping doing some things and starting doing other things. It is to create an environment or climate in which employees can work with dignity and take pride in their work.

Dr. Deming's 14 points exemplify a profound new way of thinking for the security manager and supervisor. Under the system of TQM, no longer are we there simply to "make certain" that people are doing their job but, rather, the focus is on helping and enabling people do their jobs better through education and support. Ultimately, the objective should be to support the security officer so that officer can support the organization's customer. This applies to proprietary and outsourced security programs.

So what is TQM really and how do we use it? It is imperative that the concept of implementing TQM means a fundamental change in the way an organization does business. TQM *cannot* be implemented simply as a program approach. To be successful and bring the organization and its people profound results, TQM *must* be implemented as a change in the way an organization does business. In a TQM environment, the key stakeholder shifts from the organization's officers and director, to the customer. The organization exists for one primary reason; to service the customer by providing the absolute best quality product or service for the lowest possible cost. The customer must be the primary concern and focus. If an organization takes care of its customers by meeting their needs, there will be ample profits for all people within the organization.

A key factor to implementing TQM in an organization is that top management must be fully committed to the change. This commitment means that leadership must be provided for TQM efforts inside and outside the organization and TQM efforts must be funded. Without the firm, long-term commitment of top management, TQM will not be effective and the needed changes will not occur in an organization. The result will be that the organization will not gain a competitive edge and, over a long term, they may not be competitive whatsoever against other organizations that do implement TQM as a way of doing business.

Organizations must be effective and efficient in everything they do. Effectiveness and efficiency are vital to understand because they lay the foundation for what we do in an organization. Effectiveness is the impact that an organization's product or service has on the market, whereas efficiency relates to the manner in which we employ resources to produce our product or service. The following two examples exemplify how effectiveness and efficiency work together. Take a company that manufactures carburetors for automobiles. They might make the best carburetor for the lowest price, thus they would have high efficiency. But, where is their market? Cars do not use carburetors any longer – they use fuel injection systems. Thus, their effectiveness would be low because there is no longer a market for carburetors. This is an example of *high efficiency*, but *low effectiveness*. Take another company who manufactures fuel injection units for auto makers. They make a great fuel injection unit, but their price is too high, so the auto makers purchase their competitor's fuel injection units because they have the same quality, but are lower cost. This is an example of *high effectiveness*, but *low efficiency*. In order for an organization to compete, their product or service must be highly effective and highly efficient. A combination of both is a competitive advantage and can result in high profits for the organization and the people within an organization. The questions an organization should ask are, "Are we doing the right things?" and "Are we doing things right?" High organizational efficiency and effectiveness is at the core of TQM.

In addition to leadership and a total commitment to organizational change, the concept of TQM involves two disciplines, which are combined and work in conjunction with each other within the concept of TQM. The two disciplines those who work in a TQM environment must understand are qualitative methods and quantitative analysis. Understanding qualitative methods and quantitative analysis is important because everything an organization does involves a process. Some processes are simple, while others can be complicated. Typically, the more complicated the process, the more chance or probability there is for errors and inconsistencies to occur. It is the errors and inconsistencies that cause organizations grief and lost profits. Why? Because errors and other inconsistencies affect the quality of a product or service, which in turn, affects an organization's growth and can affect their very existence.

Imagine for a moment that you are the president of a company that makes hubcaps for automobiles. You sell your hubcaps to auto makers for placement on new cars. It would be important for your hubcaps to be the same size, the same color, and it would be important for you to be able to get the hubcaps to the auto makers, your customers, on time. As long as these criteria were met and your price was competitive, your organization would probably do well. However, let's say that you had a problem with all the hubcaps being the same color, or let's say the size varied from one batch to another. When those hubcaps arrived at your customer's location, some would not fit on the wheel because they would be too large, while others would simply fall off because they would be too small. Are you starting to see how errors and inconsistencies can devastate a business? The key point is that for each process, there is at least one and probably several weak links, or a constraint that limits the overall capacity of the process as a whole. Each process is only as strong as its weakest link. Improvement on any other link does not have nearly the impact on the process as does improving the weakest link. Only identifying and improving the weakest link significantly improves the process, and thus the organization's performance.

Errors and inconsistencies in a process are known as *variance*. The employment of qualitative methods and quantitative analysis are used to control variance and keep the errors and inconsistencies in a process within manageable limits. Qualitative methods are an important part of TQM because they deal with the human skills and conceptual thinking part of TQM. While measurement is important, it is leadership and supporting people that ultimately determines an organization's success or failure. This is especially true in the security profession because security professionals are in the people business. While security officers are required to know how to implement the tools they have to work with (alarms, access control, CCTV, etc.), it is the people skills that make security people valuable to their employers and customers. Qualitative methods help set the structure for organizational processes. Dr. Deming developed a very effective model known as the Plan, Do, Study and Action (PDSA) Cycle. The concept of the PDSA Cycle is to plan the work and process, do the work within the process, study the outputs of the process and then take action upon what needs to be changed or take no action, depending on the results. The PDSA Cycle then repeats with the improvement. This model provides managers and supervisors with a scientific method of learning how to make continuous improvements.

The quantitative analysis tools in TQM involve the actual measurement of outputs and calculate variance. Measuring outputs, calculating and tracking variance and integrating these into a process, is critical to an organization's success in a TQM environment. There is no way to control outputs, only input and processes. In quantitative analysis, variance is tracked and measured in a variety of ways. The idea of tracking and measuring variance is to keep the processes "in control." When a process is in control, it means that the variance in a product or service is within the specifications. When the variance of a product or service is out of control, it means that the process has a problem and the output is no longer within the specifications. Take the hubcap example that I discussed earlier. If the hubcap fits properly on the wheel and it matches the color and strength of the specifications, the production process that made the hubcap was in control. However, if the hubcap has a defect in the coloring or strength, or if it will not fit on the tire because it is too small or too large, then the production process that produced the hubcap was not in control or "out of control." The key to consistent quality is to keep the process of a product or service in control. Ascertaining if a process is in control or out of control is determined by statistical variance. Every process has an upper control limit (UCL) of variance and a lower control limit (LCL) of variance. Back to our hubcap example, if the hubcap is too large, it would be above the UCL. However, if it was too small, it would be below the LCL. In both cases, the hubcap would be out of control. The only way for it to be in control, and not defective, would be for the circumference to measure less than the UCL but more than the LCL.

While determining the UCL and LCL of a process is important, it is important to always be working on ways that will bring the UCL and LCL closer together, thus always be looking for ways to reduce variance even more than it has been reduced in the current process. It is essential that a process be brought in control before attempting to reduce variance within the process. Traditional methods of controlling variance defined an "acceptable" range of variance. Traditional specifications, used in the manufacturing-based approach for quality, define conformity in terms of upper and lower control specification limits. For example, steel rods should meet the engineering specification for length of six inches, plus or minus ten one-hundredths of an inch (6 + or -.10). This approach tends to allow complacency concerning variation within that range. It assumes that a product just barely meeting specifications, just within the limit, is just as "good" as one right in the middle, but one just outside is "bad." Managers, supervisors and line personnel must constantly be looking for ways to improve their systems and reduce variation. In the 1980s, Motorola committed to a campaign called Six Sigma, which is one way of saying that reducing variation so much that the chance of producing a defect is down to 3.4 defects per million, or 99.99966 percent perfect. The difference between the steel rod manufacturer example and Motorola is that the steel rod manufacturer settled for average variation, whereas Motorola reduced their variance until they had an almost perfect process. By keeping the process in control, constant quality is maintained and defects are minimized. This means that production costs are kept to a minimum and customer satisfaction can be kept high. This is a fundamental objective of TQM.

Some of the most common methods and tools used to measure and track processes and variation are Process Control Charts, Histograms, Run Charts, Pareto Charts, Cause and Effect Diagrams, Deployment Charts, Fishbone Diagrams, and Scatter Grams. These tools have their individual purposes and can be used in conjunction with each other. Of course, to be able to employ quantitative analysis tools successfully, the user must have a basic understanding of and competency in general math and basic statistics. An average person normally has the math abilities to add, subtract, multiply and divide. However, it is less common for the average person to have an understanding of statistics. Understanding statistics is fundamental to being able to implement and understand the tools that are used in the TQM environment.

TQM in the security profession is relatively new, but it is coming fast and it's here to stay. Security managers and supervisors who understand TQM and know how to work within the TQM system will be well equipped to help their organizations maximize profits and minimize variance. TQM can be used effectively to help security officers in many ways to do their jobs better and contribute real and measurable value to their customers. Long since past are the days when a security officer can come to work, walk around for the shift, and then go home only to return the following day and do it all over again. The employment of TQM in the workplace is a critical process to results in a security officer being able to contribute maximum value every minute of every shift. As security managers and supervisors, it is essential to provide security personnel with that opportunity.

There are several areas in which security managers and supervisors can contribute to their customers. One major area that security managers and supervisors can contribute to their customers is by formulating a value strategy for their customers. Every quality security department or outsourcing organization must have a value strategy to be successful and maximize the money invested in the security program. The value strategy is a comprehensive and well-defined plan that explains exactly how the security personnel from the security department or outsourcing organization will add value to the customer's organization. If a security department or outsourcing organization cannot explain why they should be there and what value they add to an organization, then they are open to budget cuts and being treated with low levels of corporate esteem. A well-detailed value strategy will prevent any "mutual mystification" about what the mission is of the security personnel and will establish a measurement system to track variance and chart progress. With a clearly defined mission, a process can then be developed that will facilitate the implementation of the mission and identify opportunities for continual improvement through variance reduction. It is essential that the value strategy be communicated to everyone in the organization. This will allow security officers to understand the broader mission of why they are on post and what their job *really* is.

The other major area in which security managers and supervisors can contribute to their customers is to establish and maintain a comprehensive initial and ongoing training program. It is essential that all security personnel, at every level, have adequate security training. Not only does security skills and human relations training provide security personnel with much needed skill sets that enable them to function successfully, it also provides them with a sense of belonging to a team. Training also provides security officers with a belief that the organization truly cares about them as individuals and what happens to them when they are in the field. Of particular value is the effectiveness of training workers with little or no formal education, many of whom may earn low wages. Such employees have much to gain from general workplace and security-specific training because many lack the necessary skills to compete in an increasingly knowledge-dependant economy that is filled with challenges and stress.

So what is TQM? A closing definition of TQM that personnel in security organizations can use effectively is a management system and philosophy that:
1.   Institutes a never-ending process of improvement and innovation.
2.   Is aimed at satisfying and exceeding the customer's needs and expectations.
3.   Reduces costs through the elimination of waste and eliminating bottlenecks in the organization.
4.   Involves all people in the organization.

The focus in all we do needs to be on the customer. The customer needs to be the key stakeholder and understand the value that officers owe, and can add, to their organization for the money they invest in their security program. Anything short of this is unacceptable and will lead to a less than positive outcome. The leadership challenge for today's security supervisor is both daunting and exciting. While the challenges have never been greater than they are now, the opportunity for growth has also never been as good as it is now. The choice of quality is up to each security manager and supervisor. Will you choose quality or mediocrity? One of those two choices will provide the security professional with a satisfying and rewarding career in security that will be a tremendous growth experience, while the other will not. The golden rule is that only the customer is qualified to define quality.

TOTAL QUALITY MANAGEMENT
QUIZ

1.   TQM is an acronym for:
    a)   Total Quality Merit
    b)   Thorough Quantity Management
    c)   Total Quality Management
    d)   Total Quality Maintenance

2. Qualitative methods are the part of TQM that deal with numbers and statistical measurement.
    ☐ T   ☐ F

3. Variation is defined as:
    a)   a defect.
    b)   the point halfway between the upper control limit and the lower control limit.
    c)   an organization's production quotas that are not achieved by the workforce.
    d)   the errors and inconsistencies in a process.

4. The most important aspect of TQM in an organization is:
    a)   organizational leadership and supporting people.
    b)   the measurement of the processes.
    c)   controlling variance.
    d)   ensuring that organization quota are met to keep profits up.

5. Dr. W. Edwards Deming was a _____ by training.
    a)   Math Professor
    b)   History Expert
    c)   Military Officer
    d)   Statistician

6. The Upper Control Limit and Lower Control Limit are essential when determining if a process is, or is not, "in control."
    ☐ T   ☐ F

7. Which of the following is not one of Dr. Deming's 14 points for transformation management?
    a)   Focus on increased quotas and reduced defects.
    b)   Create constancy of purpose toward improvement.
    c)   Drive fear out of the workplace.
    d)   Institute training on the job.

8. It is important for people to understand and be able to perform statistics in a TQM environment because:
    a)   statistics are the key to understanding qualitative methods.
    b)   it is really not important for people to understand and be able to perform statistics in a TQM environment.
    c)   statistical calculations are used to measure and track process variance.
    d)   it is a key part of being able to be promoted in an organization.

9. An organization can be most successful in a TQM environment by measuring and controlling outputs.
    ☐ T   ☐ F

10. The primary reason TQM is effective in the workplace is:
    a)   it increases the organization's profits.
    b)   it reduces operating costs, increases customer satisfaction and increases employee pride.
    c)   it reduces defects and helps control outputs.
    d)   it helps customers receive the products they need when they need them.

UNIT SIX
PROTECTION MANAGEMENT

Risk Management
Safety Attitude Development
Workplace Violence
Crisis Management
Supervising During Emergencies
Supervising During Special Events
Security and Medical Response
Considering Contract Security
Outsourcing in Security

RISK MANAGEMENT
by Johnny May, B.S., M.S., CPP, CPO

Black's Law Dictionary defines risk as "the element of uncertainty in an undertaking; the possibility that actual future returns will deviate from expected returns." We encounter risks in every aspect of our daily lives. When we cross the street, accept a new job or decide what type of automobile we're going to drive, we encounter some degree of risk.

Generally, when one mentions risk management, insurance immediately comes to mind. Risk management is a formal discipline – with its owns jargon closely associated with technical, insurance and legal questions. As such, it has developed a mystique that scares away the uninitiated.

Both loss prevention and risk management originated in the insurance industry. Fire insurance companies, soon after the Civil War, formed the National Board of Fire Underwriters, which was instrumental in reducing loss of property through prevention measures. Today, loss prevention has spread throughout the insurance industry and into the business community. Risk management is also an old practice. The modern history of risk management is said by many insurance experts to have begun in 1931 with the establishment of the insurance section of the American Management Association. The insurance section currently holds conferences and workshops for those employed in the insurance and risk management field.

There are five different types of risk with which organizations consistently have to deal:
1. *Dynamic Risks*: Fluctuate under certain conditions such as weather or location.
2. *Static Risks*: These remain constant, without regard to other factors such as regulations, laws or standards.
3. *Inherent Risks*: These are unavoidable and are associated with a certain product, industry/ business, location and/or procedure.
4. *Speculative Risks*: Occur when an organization initiates any new program, procedure or operation. It also occurs when it enters into any activity, which might subject it to any other risk.
5. *Pure Risks*: Natural disasters or criminal acts that do not fall into any of the above categories.

SOURCE OF RISKS

- *Human Factors*: Probably the greatest single source of risk, including both human error and failure.
- *Mechanical Factors*: Are sources of risk resulting from any reliance on some type of machinery or equipment.
- *Environment, crime risks and civil disorders*.
- *Procedural Factors*: Are those sources of risk caused by the use of certain procedures, routines or operation.

The goal of risk management is to design and implement plans to eliminate loss exposures, wherever possible, and to reduce to a practical minimum, the cost associated with those losses that do occur. This entails using the risk management techniques of loss control and loss financing. The technique of loss control involves reducing the frequency and severity of loss occurrences, while loss financing addresses the minimization of the costs of those losses that do occur.

There are typically four types of losses to which organizations are subject:
1. Property Losses—These types of losses most often come to mind when we think of loss prevention. Property losses involve buildings and their contents (furniture, office equipment, valuables and proprietary information). Protection against property losses involves the reduction of hazards (fire, accidents and crime) that cause loss.
2. Income Losses—Arise when property involving income producing activities such as stores, apartments and other organization owned facilities are subjected to some loss which results in cessation of income produced by such property.
3. Legal Liability Losses—Arise out of duties owed by the organization to members of the society of which the organization is a part. Liability can arise out of statutory law, common law and contract law.
4. Personnel Losses—Result from the loss of services provided by any person in the organization who has a role in that organization's operations. When services

individuals are lost due to illness or accident, the entire organization suffers a loss because these individuals are not available. Often, replacing these services can take place (through use of temporary agencies), but only at some additional expenditure of organizational funds.

✦Another good way to remember how losses occur is through the use of the acronym WAECUP (pronounced wake-up) which stands for Waste, Accident, Error, Crime, Unethical/Unprofessional Practices!

✦Risk management involves the identification and definition of specific problem areas and proper design of measures that will counteract the problem.✦Once a risk is identified, one or more of five specific methods can be selected to reduce exposure. These methods are:

- ➤*Risk avoidance*—Risks can be avoided by taking the threatened object "out of harms way." This approach asks whether or not to avoid the risk.
- ✦*Risk transfer*—The most common method of transferring risk in the business world is insurance. The risk manager works with an insurance company to tailor a coverage program for the risk.
- ➤*Risk abatement*—Risks can be minimized to a level that is compatible with the daily operations of a business. Risks are not eliminated, but the severity of loss is reduced.
- *Spreading the risk among multiple locations reduces risk spreading* – Potential losses.
- ✦*Risk acceptance*—Many business owners do this – they accept (or retain) risk as "part of the cost of doing business" without examining the alternatives available to them. Not every risk can be avoided, transferred, abated or spread, but every effort should be made before a risk is accepted.

What does all of this have to do with security?✦One could say that a marriage of sorts exists between the risk manager and the security manager of a particular organization because of a common goal shared by both – protection of life and property.

The textbook *Suggested Preparation for Careers in Security/Loss Prevention* gives an excellent example (see below).

Suppose the following question was asked of two separate classes. One is a "security management" class and the other is across campus in the college of business and is in "principles of insurance." The question posed to both classes is as follows:

From the following job description you are to identify the person by job title, whose responsibilities within the corporation are as follows. Fill in the blank.

The primary and fundamental objective of the _____ manager is the preservation of assets and earning power from loss or destruction. He or she shall be responsible for identifying all exposures to such loss. The financial risk associated with each exposure to loss must be evaluated as to both its severity and probability of occurrence. An action must then be taken to either eliminate said risks or reduce either the probability of their occurrence or the severity of their consequences. In summation, he/she is charged with preservation of the operating effectiveness of the corporation, by safeguarding both its assets and its potential income.

How do you suppose the two groups answered the question? You can bet the security class thought the job description was right out of their security textbook, and was describing the duties of the security manager. They would have filled in the blank with the word security. The business students, on the other hand, would have recognized that the description of duties fit risk management. Why? Well, one reason is that security is the counterpart of risk. The effective treatment of risks yields security. The two disciplines share some commonalities.

✦Another common interest shared by both risk management and security professionals is disaster planning. Both should focus on taking a proactive approach and formulating plans before tragedies strike. Then when the crisis arises, we need only implement the preconceived plan. An effective disaster plan could substantially reduce the economic impact of a catastrophic event.

Security also plays an important role in the overall risk management process. One of the primary sources of information available to the risk manager is the daily incident report generated by the security department. The reports give a brief description of unusual events that have recently occurred. Security is usually the first responder in the event of an accident, injury or property damage. Incidents such as theft or vandalism are also reported.

The importance of these reports to the risk manager is obvious since they are his or her first indication that loss or potential for loss has occurred. Receipt of these reports enable the risk manager to provide an early response to the incident by putting all necessary legal, loss reporting (for insurance purpose) and loss control activities in motion.

Once a security professional reaches his or her ultimate goal, becoming the director of security, one may ask him/herself now what? Where do I go from here? How about risk management!

As one consultant notes, security people "often consider risk management to require a high level of involvement above and beyond the aspects and intelligence of security." And yet, says another, "a lot of security people don't realize they are already performing the risk management functions."

Assuming the position of risk manager usually means significant increase in responsibility and prestige, but it also means a similar increase in professional headaches as well. Yet, as one risk management consultant contends, "risk management is the natural goal for an aspiring security director... He or she already has the basic abilities of a risk manager. He/she uses the same principles.... {Security} programs revolve around problem identification and problem solving to eliminate hazards. You have to monitor your risk exposures and then try to minimize and reduce them. You do the same thing in risk management."

The risk manager's job varies with the company served. He or she may be responsible for insurance only, or for security, safety and insurance, or for fire protection, safety and insurance. One important consideration in the implementation of a risk management program is that the program must be explained in financial terms to top executives. Is the program cost effective? Financial benefits and financial protection are primary expectations of top executives that the risk manager must consider during decision-making.

Among the many activities of the risk manager are to develop specifications for insurance coverage wanted, meet with insurance company representatives, study various policies, and decide on the most appropriate coverage at the best possible price. Coverage may also be required by law or contract, such as workers' compensation insurance and vehicle liability insurance. Plant equipment should be periodically reappraised in order to maintain adequate insurance coverage. Also, the changing value of buildings and other assets, as well as replacement costs, must be considered in the face of depreciation and inflation.

If one is interested in learning more about risk management, the Insurance Institute of America offers the Associate in Risk Management (ARM) designation. The program is designed for people whose careers include dealing in a cost-effective manner with exposure to accidental losses. Those who would benefit from the ARM program include corporate and governmental risk managers, safety personnel, insurance producers and consultants, security directors and insurance company commercial lines specialists.

The only requirements for earning the ARM designation is successful completion of three national ARM examinations administered by the Insurance Institute of America. The program consists of the following three risk management courses.

ARM 54 – Essentials of Risk Management – Focuses on the first two steps of the risk management decision-making process:
*   identifying and analyzing the loss exposure, and
*   developing alternative techniques for treating each exposure. It also introduces the student to the financial management foundation for the third step – choosing the best risk management alternative, and explores guidelines for selecting the most appropriate technique for handling exposure.

ARM 55 – Essentials of Risk Control – Focuses on the last three steps of the risk management process: selecting appropriate risk control techniques, implementing the chosen techniques, and monitoring the results for effective control and coordination of the organization's total risk management effort. It features further development and application of the guidelines for selecting risk management techniques introduced in ARM 54, especially in relation to the final steps of the risk management process.

ARM 56 – Essentials of Risk Financing – Finishes covering the risk management decision-making process with respect to risk financing techniques. Attention is directed primarily to various form of risk retention and of commercial insurance.

For further information contact: Insurance Institution of America, 720 Providence Road, P.O. Box 3016, Melvern, PA 19355 – 0716

Taking one insurance or risk management course will not suddenly transform a security supervisor into an expert. However, he/she may be surprised to find out that once they become familiar with even a small amount of the vocabulary and methods of the insurance industry, they become much more conversant with the insurance industry and they will become much more conversant with insurance professionals. Just being able to read and understand insurance requirements can make you a better security supervision.

BIBLIOGRAPHY

Chuvala, John, Fischer, Robert J., *Suggested Preparation for Careers in Security / Loss Prevention*, Kendall-Hunt, Dubuque, IA, 1991

Purpura, Philip, *Security and Loss Prevention an Introduction, Second Edition,* Butterworth–Heinemann, Stoneham, MA, 1991

Shaffer, Dale, F., *Public Safety Management Guide, Second Edition*, Public Safety Management, Glenview, IL, 1993

Taitz, Sharyn, *Getting a Job, Getting Ahead, and Staying Ahead in Security Management*, Rusting Publications, Port Washington, NY, 1990

U.S. Small Business Administration, *Small Business Risk Management Guide*, 1994

RESOURCES / PUBLICATION

Risk & Insurance, PO Box 980, Horsham, PA 19044, (2215) 784-0910

Risk Management, 655 3rd Ave, New York, NY 10017, (212) 286-9364

International Journal of Risk, Security, and Crime Prevention, Perpetuity Press, PO Box 376, Leichester, Le2 3zz, United Kingdom, +44 (0) 116 270 4186

APPENDIX A

RISK MANAGEMENT

A.   **KEY TERMS**

Abatement Cost: "The cost of abating a nuisance such as pollution or congestion. In terms of pollution the cost curve will typically slope upwards at an increasing rate as pollution is progressively reduced. This is because it is usually comparatively cheap to 'clean up' some part of a polluted environment, but extremely expensive to remove the last units of pollution. An example would be noise where engines can be muffled, thus, reducing noise by a noticeable amount. Further reductions in noise, might, however, require expensive engine redesign or wholesale changes in road structures, locations, etc." Abatement cost would come from installing keypad locks on doors, which are protecting sensitive equipment. Abatement cost would be the total cost of installation.

Absorption: "1) In accounting, the process of factoring the cost of intermediate products and services into the total cost of the product. Absorption is also known as full costing. 2) In shipping, a gratis service provided by a carrier that is not covered by a published freight tariff or included in freight charges. Premium service includes free wharfage, switching, and so on. Depending on the law jurisdiction in which they are offered, premium services may constitute illegal inducement." Absorption comes when, during planning, a company decides to ignore a particular hazard, for example, a bomb threat. If a bomb is detonated, the company would absorb the costs to repair and replace damage assets.

Asset: Anything of value such as land, buildings, information and image.

Business Continuity Planning: An all encompassing, "umbrella" term covering both disaster recovery planning and business operations following one of a number of disasters that might befall the business systems and resources. In this context, all business resources are considered, and services should not be confirmed.
Example: when your computer system shuts down, what system will you implement so as to continue with daily business, i.e., phone calls, customers and fulfilling orders?

Business Impact Analysis: To build a catalog of threats relating to the continued success of the business and to analyze the associated potential business impacts so as to define priorities for detailed analysis of vulnerabilities and implementation of controls. It is also the process of analyzing all business functions and the effects that a specific disaster may have upon them.
Example: What impact will a fire in a portion of your plant have on your productivity? What additional losses will you incur? Will you be able to function? If so, by what means and for how long?

Contingency Plan: A plan for emergency response, backup operations, and post-disaster recovery that the facility maintains as a part of its security program. A well-designed contingency plan provides many details about each step involved in preparing for, and responding to, an emergency. Although each plan differs in its details, contingency plans contain three major elements:
a)   Background Information
b)   Realistic Scenarios
c)   Response Actions / Countermeasures
        Example: Being able to efficiently evacuate a crowded facility in the case of a bomb threat, fire, or natural disaster.

Countermeasures: Steps taken to combat the loss that has occurred.

Criticality: The impact of a loss as measured in dollars. Replacement costs, temporary replacement, "down time," discounted cash and insurance rate charges are included as well.

Insurance: "Insurance permits individuals to exchange the risk of a large loss for the certainty of a small loss. The losses most commonly insured against are; loss of property, life and income. The purchase of insurance, by payment of an insurance premium, spreads the risk associated with any specified contingency over a large number of individuals. Insurance is said to be 'fair' if the mathematical expectation of gain from purchasing the insurance is zeroed. The existence of administrative costs and any departures from perfect completion in the insurance market tend to make insurance less than fair, although this is frequently balanced by the tax treatment of insurance premia, and in practice insurance may be more than fair, i.e., the mathematical expectation of gain is positive." A company that purchases protection from fire knows that another company will pay for the losses incurred if there is a fire.

Management Generalist: This is a concept where the security manager has expertise in various aspects of management in addition to security. The security manager should attend staff meetings, listen to the problems and concerns of other managers and try to help with his expertise.

Probability: Second step in risk analysis. It is essential to determine the probability of loss. The best way is to make subjective decisions about probability based on location and nature of the business.

Risk Assessment and Analysis: Management decision-making regarding loss-control strategy; implementation of controls; review of the effectiveness of these controls.

Risk Aversion: "The expectation of investors of a higher expected return as compensation for an increase in risk. A risk averter can be a diversifier and spread his portfolio over different assets, or a 'plunger' and invest wholly in bonds or money. A 'risk lover,' however, accepts a higher level of risk for a given expected return. If an individual is 'risk neutral' he would be indifferent between whether or not he accepted 'fair' insurance. Most individuals are generally held to be risk averters."

Risk aversion occurs when a company outsources its security department. If an officer becomes injured due to negligence of those officers, he cannot sue the company, or file workers' compensation claims through the company because he was not hired directly by the company. In this manner, the company is practicing risk aversion.

Risk Management: "Also known as risk minimization, procedures adopted by an organization to reduce its exposure to potential losses. Banks sell commercial risk management services, including credit risk analyses, interest rate and exchange rate hedges, and business loan caps. In international trade transactions, banks and other firms determine country risk, based on evaluations of a specific transaction or the aggregate exposure in a particular country. Among others, risk minimization strategies include purchasing export credit insurance or overseas investment insurance, entering into barter arrangements, and requiring irrevocable letters of credit." Risk management occurs when a company purchases insurance, or hires and places patrol officers at access points, or purchases a CCTV system to observe a sensitive area.

R.O.I.: Return on Investment: This term relates to cost-effectiveness. The business must get back what they put into the business. One formula for calculating R.O.I. is ROI – ALE (old-ALE-(new) – C (cost for protective measure).

Threat: These can be industrial disasters, natural disasters, civil disturbances, crime and other risks.

Threat Assessment: The first step in risk analysis. You must identify the threats and vulnerabilities to the business.

Underwriters: Those who make up the insurance policies based on their experience of events in a certain area, such as fires in certain types of businesses.

Vulnerability: Depends on the security posture, physical location and the attractiveness of the assets to adversaries.
Being susceptible to abuse or misuse, or indiscriminate use; a weakpoint, soft spot or a likelihood for error. In an automated system, situations that can compromise or neutralize a given piece of data or a security measure.
Example: A nation that does not account for, lock down, and guard their national security documents is leaving itself vulnerable to a loss of classified records. This principle is applicable to most every entity and business.

B.   **USES OF RISK MANAGEMENT**

   1.   Risk analysis shows the current security profile of the organization. It is diagnostic, showing management which areas need increased or decreased protection.
   2.   Risk analysis helps to compile facts necessary for the development of cost-effective safeguards through an examination of relevant threats.
   3.   Conducting a risk analysis can increase the security awareness of employees at various levels.
   4.   Can control, compile and audit the cost of loss.
   5.   Can complement insurance protection in regards to lowering insurance premiums.
   6.   Security analysis can dictate procedural design for organization of a security force.
   7.   Through the use of different outside consultants you can gain differing perspectives on loss control within your organization.
   8.   Economic justification of expenditures with the security program.
        a)   increased man hours
        b)   surveillance equipment (CCTV)
   9.   Recognition of vulnerabilities in all aspects of the organization and its security program.
   10.   Access risks and their possible impact on the organization.

C.   **RISK MANAGEMENT PROCESS**

  1.   Identify risk problems via a survey. The first step would be to make up an employee survey. This may not be totally accurate so you might want to study the employees with hidden cameras. By identifying our risks we should target the problems and try to correct or mitigate them. You might want to find the greatest area of weakness and which merchandise has the greatest threat.
  2.   Study the risks uncovered in the survey.
  3.   Collect information on probability, frequency and criticality.
      a)   One way to collect information would be to study past incidences of loss.
      b)   There are many factors you must uncover and study when collecting information. You must find the Annual Loss Expectancy (ALE). To find this you must know the value of the assets in dollar amount (A) and you need to know the probability of how many times a year this might occur (L). You then multiply them together.
      c)   You also want to find Severity (S). There are two levels of this. The two are used to differentiate between a fire that destroys a whole building or a less damaging fire that started in a waste bucket.
      d)   Vulnerability to threat (V) also has two factors ranging from zero to one. It depends upon how secure the asset is, the location and attractiveness of it. When calculating the Annual Loss Expectancy it is now more accurate: $ALE = A \times L \times S \times V$.
      e)   We can also calculate the ALE by multiplying the likelihood by the severity and the vulnerability ratings. This is called the Modified Likelihood: $ML = L \times S \times V$ or $ALE = A \times ML$.
      f)   After devising the new system from this information we have to calculate a modified ALE by multiplying the old ALE by 1 minus the effectiveness of the system: $ALE (New) - ALE (Old) \times (1 - E)$.
      g)   The Annual Cost © must also be found by making it equal to the sum of Depreciation (D) and the annual variable or Operating Cost (OC): $C = D + OC$.
  4.   Analyze various countermeasures
      a)   Determine specific needs, risks and vulnerabilities.
      b)   Choose appropriate countermeasures:
          i)   satisfy needs, risks and vulnerabilities
          ii)   cost effective – 2% of the value of objects you are protecting
          iii)   ones which don't cause problems.
      c)   Have interrelated parts that overlap whenever possible.
      d)   Think in terms of the various responses to risk:
          i)   risk reduction – target hardening.
          ii)   risk avoidance – "If you can't stand the heat, get out of the kitchen."
          iii)   risk transfer – let someone else be financially/legally liable.
          iv)   risk spreading – "don't put all your eggs in one basket."
          v)   risk assumption – it isn't worth worrying about or it can't be avoided.
  5.   Implement countermeasures
      a)   Discreet placement without sacrificing effectiveness
      b)   Appropriate sites for alarms
      c)   Proper installation
  6.   Evaluate countermeasures
      a)   Test for effectiveness – can measures be improved?
      b)   Test under different conditions
          i)   weather – snow, rain, wind
          ii)   daytime and nighttime
          iii)   periods of heavy traffic
      c)   Test for durability

APPENDIX B
Risk Analysis and the Security Survey *by James Broder*
Butterworth–Heinemann 1984

Decision Matrix: A Risk Handling Decision Aid

Frequency of Loss

Severity of Loss	High	Medium	Low
High	Avoidance	Loss prevention and avoidance	Transfer via insurance
Medium	Avoidance and loss prevention	Loss prevention and Transfer via insurance	Assumption and pooling
Low	Loss prevention	Loss prevention and assumption	Assumption

Figure 27.1

APPENDIX C
Introduction to Security 4th Edition *by Gion Green and Robert Fischer*
Butterworth–Heinemann 1987

Probability/Criticality/Vulnerability Matrix

	Probability		Criticality
(1)	Virtually certain	(A)	Fatal
(2)	Highly probable	(B)	Very serious
(3)	Moderately probable	(C)	Moderately serious
(4)	Probable	(D)	Serious
(5)	Improbable	(E)	Relatively unimportant
(6)	Probability unknown	(F)	Criticality unknown

Adapted from: Richard J. Healy and Timothy J. Walsh, *Industrial Security Management* (New York: American Management Association (1971), p.17

Figure 27.2

RISK MANAGEMENT
QUIZ

1.   Generally, when one mentions risk management, _____ immediately comes to mind.

2.   List the five different types of risk with which organizations consistently have to deal:
      a)   _____
      b)   _____
      c)   _____
      d)   _____
      e)   _____

3.   Both loss prevention and risk management originated in the finance business.
                    □ T   □ F

4.   There are several different sources of risk which include: (Select incorrect answer)
      a)   Human Factor
      b)   Mechanical Factor
      c)   Environmental Factor
      d)   Procedural Factor
      e)   Management Factor

5.   The goal of risk management is to design and implement plans to eliminate loss exposures
      wherever possible and to reduce to a practical minimum the costs associated with those losses
      that do occur.
                    □ T   □ F

6.   Define the acronym WAECUP:
      W _____
      A _____
      E _____
      C _____
      U _____
      P _____

7.   Threat assessment is the first step in risk analysis.
                    □ T   □ F

8.   List the four typical losses to which organizations are subject:
      a)   _____
      b)   _____
      c)   _____
      d)   _____

9.   Not all risks can be avoided, transferred, abated or spread, but every effort should be made
      before a risk is accepted.
                    □ T   □ F

10.   R.O.I. is the acronym for:
      a)   Risk Officer Individual
      b)   Return on Investment
      c)   Risk Orientated Individual
      d)   Risk Officer Initiative

SAFETY ATTITUDE DEVELOPMENT
by Randy W. Rowett, CSS, CPO

SUPERVISING CRISIS SITUATIONS

Supervisors know that rarely do people call upon protection staff, or associate with them in most cases, unless in time of need or safety problems. This lack of contact can sometimes produce negative feelings, whereby protection staff feel as if they don't belong. Participation by security staff in local departments or facilities near the work area can assist in building relations and provide protection staff with the opportunity to contribute to the safety of the area or community through positive proactive functions.

Safety planning and the supervisory role is to set forth the correct response in crisis situations and to organize crisis intervention. As well, supervisors must recognize weaknesses and plan accordingly to achieve uniformity in critical areas.

No matter what type of crisis occurs, co-operation between protection staff and the public can be achieved by the following four steps:

a)   Arrange safety meetings between key protection staff and supervisors
b)   Co-ordinate crisis plans through public relations/other departments
c)   Provide leadership and monitor all meetings
d)   Test the results

When the correct formula for training is used, success will be achieved and a safety attitude will prevail.

Protection supervisors are tasked with a variety of functions relating to the safety integration of the public, customers and employees.

Safety in the workplace requires that all personnel be trained in recognizing and rectifying problems before they occur. Examples of safety concerns where the supervisor is involved in training staff are: fire safety, industrial equipment protection and use, unsafe work practices, health related matters (first aid/CPR), sanitation, hazardous materials, employee accidents and reduced injury plans, safety meetings, structural problems (which may cause injury or death), crime prevention and many others.

Attitude plays a key part in safety approach development.

SAFETY COMMITTEE MEETINGS

The safety meeting is more and more becoming a legislated and mandatory function in the workplace. Businesses suffering heavy costs and losses of work-hours due to injuries and illness caused by lack of protective equipment, is another cost factor.

Safety committee meetings should include all sections or departments of a business. Naturally, security officers play a major role in participating in these meetings. Topics covered in these meetings are:

a)   Recent number of accidents per calendar month/year.
b)   Number of employees injured/killed on the job.
c)   Causes of accidents – tripping, falling, improper storage of items, improper safety shoes, malfunctioning safety equipment, structural problems of work areas, slipping on wet floors, insufficient safety training for employees, etc.
d)   Steps to accident correction.
e)   Illnesses caused by accidental or neglected industrial hazards.
f)   Hidden cost of accidents (staff losses, replacements and training of new employees).
g)   Follow-up to results and problems.

As part of the safety approach development process, protection officers should participate in monthly inspections of facilities for accident prevention purposes. Conditions relating to health matters such as unsanitary conditions and fire hazards must also be reported.

SAFETY ATTITUDE DEVELOPMENT

Security supervisors are responsible for the safety education of their officers. Every aspect of safety involves the need for awareness and prevention. The best way to meet that need is to introduce a learning process and safety practices.

There are many ways to start the safety program. For example, when an officer is first hired, incorporate a film on safety into the orientation program. For many years as a security manager, I have instructed new security staff and employees in other departments in the orientation program after hiring. I firmly believe this safety message should be attended by every employee and ideally would be a mandatory program for all new employees.

Methods by which to set up a safety attitude program are numerous and include the following:

a) Films – there are many films on safety and prevention of accidents available from leading safety organizations.

b) Posters – messages such as "Accidents cost jobs and lives" are available from industrial safety companies and safety supply outlets.

c) Safety committee meetings – these will be discussed later.

d) Award programs – award employees who have made a solid contribution to the protection department in the interests of the safety program. Certificates can be created for such a purpose.

e) Guest speakers/seminars by professionals – As a practicing guest speaker for safety/security programs at business colleges, I can attest that students learn from and appreciate these seminars. In the workplace, they enhance learning development and employee morale.

f) For any company or organization that has a newsletter, there should be a security supervisor or director willing to write articles regarding local safety matters. Included in these can be crime prevention notes.

Make a list to find out how many safety methods you can create.

The security supervisor must be familiar with all aspects of protection relating to safety. Part of this responsibility rests with the appropriate understanding, observation and attitude toward existing or potential hazards.

Examples of safety matters are:

a) Fire safety

b) Industrial equipment protection and use

c) Health related safety (including first aid and stocking of materials, etc.)

d) Safe storage of hazardous materials and products

e) Employee accidents and reduced injury plans

f) Electrical hazards

g) Structural problems (which may cause accidents or injury)

h) Fire safety plans/disaster safety plans and many others.

Safety in the workplace or in a facility requires that emergency personnel be trained in the recognition of potential problems before these occur. Prior emergency planning is effective in prevention of accidents. Attitude also plays a key part in safety development. Learn to recognize security hazards and correct them before they cause injuries or even death. Security and protection personnel can assist by watching for hazards such as:

a) Blocked fire exits.

b) Improperly stocked shelves in cupboards or storage facilities.

c) Fire cabinets with improper or missing equipment.

d) Poor lighting in employee traveled areas.

SUPERVISING ACCIDENTS

The protection supervisor is responsible for accurate and concise reporting and initial investigations of the accident scene. Regardless of whether injury has occurred or it was narrowly avoided, the area must be sealed off and an investigation conducted to determine the cause. A review must then be made after the report has been submitted.

Remember the ten steps in supervising the reporting of accidents.

1. Seal off the area and notify emergency personnel (fire, ambulance, police, etc.).

2. Minimize risks to victims or bystanders (electrical wires down, fire, gas leaks) and co-ordinate rescue, etc.

3. Treat victims for injuries (first aid/CPR).

4. Determine cause – i.e. carelessness, vehicle accident, etc.

5. Co-ordinate report – names of victims, addresses, liaison with emergency personnel attending, collect names and badge numbers of workers, etc.

6.   Follow up with results of victim treatment and assign trained safety investigators. (Police investigations will take priority; however, internal investigation can be conducted.)
7.   Interview witnesses to accidents or crimes.
8.   Final examination – determine if the follow up removed existing hazards from scene (to prevent a second incident).
9.   Collect all information for presentation to safety committee and outside agencies.
10.   Review matter with safety committee.

When a person commits him/herself to the task of security, protection or law enforcement work, there is an understanding that we may encounter danger through risks of injury or even death while performing our duties. We also know that, as supervisors, we need to be aware of constant inherent dangers caused by risks such as fire, bombs, threats, domestic family disturbances, etc.

The supervisor who has been on the job for any length of time must be prepared for any eventuality and coordinate training for the protection of his/her staff. These planned training sessions not only involve physical response, but also emotional control and remedial response in an approved professional manner. Safety relates to staff in a variety of work related problems. Some protection staff may be in need of supervisory advice, and supervisors should be familiar with employee assistance programs. Stress related factors can cause carelessness in decision-making; safety approach development should provide for the handling of stress and pressure on the job. The supervisor should be ultimately prepared to intervene if there is a risk of injury to officers or the public due to work/personal problems.

The second rule to safety approach development for the supervisor is, "Be available to address safety concerns." These concerns can be established and created from any person or source.

ENFORCEMENT OF SAFETY REGULATIONS

The security supervisor is part of the management team. It is therefore the supervisor's responsibility to monitor and ensure that all safety regulations are being maintained in compliance with policy.

When violations occur, investigations must be initiated and corrective action taken to correct any fault in the safety protection plan.

Types of safety regulations to enforce include the following:
   a)   Fire safety – trash, papers, non-smoking areas, etc.
   b)   Malfunctioning or missing protective safety equipment – abuse or omitting to wear appropriate devices.
   c)   Workers using unsafe practices – this action can lead to employee injury, injury to bystanders. Another example is staff going into risk areas without proper back-up from officers.
   d)   Non-alert staff – part of the problem may be staff shortages causing fatigue due to extended hours. This is a risk situation. Extra long hours diminish capability and concentration. Proper sleep, diet and lifestyles assist in an alert staff.
   e)   Health/Sanitation – security officers should be instructed to report unhealthy practices relating to risk. An example is unsafe food handling observed.

There are many other areas to be considered. One point of importance is the compliance factor. Security staff must enforce and also comply with existing policies and regulations. Security supervisors have a required duty to assist in monitoring compliance to safety matters. One rule to remember is, "If you enforce the safety rule – don't violate it!"

Types of Conduct/Violations Causing Accidents
   •   Blocked fire exits of insufficient equipment
   •   Electrical problems
   •   Chemical storage (flammable) violations
   •   Improper lighting
   •   Lack of fire equipment
   •   Training insufficiencies – safety policies
   •   Employee carelessness
   •   Insufficient surveillance equipment
   •   Lack of awareness

- Ego errors of employee's judgement

Natural Causes of Accidents
- Aircraft incidents
- Earthquakes
- Floods
- Fires – natural causes – lightning
- Power outages – electrical

Corrective/Proactive Approach
- Frequent inspections – measuring results
- Set up guidelines and policy retraining
- Ensure all equipment (at least minimum acceptable standard) present
- Arrange security/safety awareness program
- Provide first aid, CPR and rescue training
- Coordinate with local authorities
- Ensure all mechanical equipment functions
- Annual retraining, testing with safety programs
- Bring in experts in the field, instructors of safety programs
- Crime prevention activities

FIRE SAFETY SUPERVISORY FUNCTIONS

The following tips are useful for allowing protection supervisors to coordinate, develop and maintain fire safety programs.

- Know types of fire extinguishers to be used. Do not rely on a specific department in a facility to handle situations entirely. Supervisors must train protection officers and facilitate professional liaison with government safety inspectors and law enforcement persons. Therefore a good supervisor will always learn and practice as much about fire safety as is required. Certain fire codes must always be maintained and knowledge of these codes is essential. Check with your local fire department or fire prevention company for courses and information pertaining to codes, prevention and enforcement.
- Coordinate plans for emergency response. Liaise with fire department personnel. Have a meeting with authorities near an airport, sporting facility or major business. Develop evacuation plans and initiate a plan to share shelter and aid with other organizations in the event of an emergency.
- Train security or protection personnel in types of fires, types of extinguishing materials and causes of fires. Develop proposals for fire protection such as cameras, alarms, sensors, smoke detectors. This is useful for both fire safety and regular security duties.
- Introduce and utilize crash carts in every facility. Included should be oxygen, first aid kits, extinguishers, smoke masks, flashlights and any other items required.
- Organize inspections by protection staff on a monthly basis. Any facility or property will benefit from this proactive approach to fire safety.

Protection supervisors have key responsibilities for ensuring the success of safety programs. The following is a list of pertinent duties.

a) Coordination at local command post of accident
b) Policy formulation and awareness programs
c) Reviewing accident statistics and corrective approaches to lower accident numbers
d) Officer safety training and safe response practices
e) Implementing first aid/CPR programs
f) Investigation of actual and observed safety hazards through inspections
g) Liaison with local authorities and businesses.
h) Ensuring all pertinent investigative material is available for local authorities, court or insurance matters. Supervisor must be aware of company or organization regulations pertaining to reporting and command chain of same.

i)   Lists of on-call personnel to dispatch in the event of an emergency. Security staff must have personal phone numbers at the department for call-out purposes.

j)   Arrange awards for outstanding safety contributions

k)   Organize and supervise awareness campaigns such as crime prevention, accident watch, and many others.

SUMMARY

This chapter has been a brief examination of safety. The total emphasis is on observation, prevention, attitude and approach to various problems and procedures. Throughout any organization there are accidents that are tragic in nature. Some are caused by wrongful acts such as crime or negligence. Many more are caused by weaknesses in observation and reporting as well as correction; some accidents still happen due to improper attitude and improper approach to the situation. I would recommend to any supervisor, whether experienced or a career protection officer wishing to advance to a supervisor position, to set up the best protection program possible. Include in this program items related to safety. Integrate safety inspections, crime prevention, equipment usage and protection, committee meetings, employee participation, and safe work practices.

The protection supervisor is tasked with all these duties and more. If you have ever investigated accidents, and knew these were preventable (at less cost to the company, less loss of worker hours due to injury, and terrible records for safety), you as a security supervisor owe it to the department to create a rewarding safety protection plan for the benefit of everyone. The rewards for promoting safety are ongoing. We all chose to work in the protection field. Let's strive to make things as safe as possible.

SAFETY ATTITUDE DEVELOPMENT
QUIZ

1.   When the correct formula for _____ is used, success will be achieved and a safety attitude will prevail.

2.   Every aspect of safety involves the need for _____ and prevention.

3.   Prior emergency _____ is effective in prevention of accidents.

4.   Security staff must _____ and regulations.

5.   Organize and supervise _____ campaigns such as crime prevention and accident watch.

6.   As long as there are some maintenance people on duty in a facility, the supervisor can rely on this experience for full fire protection with minimal involvement in the process.
            □ T   □ F

7.   It is not necessary for security staff to respond to power outage situations.
            □ T   □ F

8.   Supervisors should ensure that only water based types of extinguishers are available for firefighting in work areas.
            □ T   □ F

9.   A crime prevention program focusing on offensive prevention is part of the safety awareness program.
            □ T   □ F

10.   Staffing considerations are of little factor in implementations of safety approach development.
            □ T   □ F

WORKPLACE VIOLENCE
by Stevan P. Layne, CPP

There are a number of contributing causes to incidents of workplace violence. Most involve employees, including those currently employed, former employees, and persons related or involved with employees in either category. The responsibility of the employer, to be monitored, controlled, and enhanced by the security staff, is to provide a safe environment for workers, visitors, and others. This means that the business or institution must be evaluated and prepared in each of the following areas:

1. *Physical Security* - Appropriate barriers, locks, lighting and check points are in place to deny access to unauthorized persons.
2. *Electronic Security* - Intrusion detection, video surveillance systems, panic-duress signals, access controls, and other installed devices are functional, properly serviced and maintained, and properly utilized by staff.
3. *Policies and Procedures* - Appropriate instructions and notifications that give security the legal right to deny access or remove unauthorized persons from company property are in place, properly posted, and available to security management.
4. *Emergency Procedures* - All employees are familiar with and have had a "hands-on" opportunity to practice their assigned roles in emergency evacuation, response or other emergency plans.
5. *Agency Coordination* - Those emergency agencies with designated jurisdiction to respond (police, fire, ambulance, hazardous materials) to incidents, meet with security management and company officials to coordinate response requirements.

Security should assume a leading role in assuring that the above listed elements are present, understood by those employees assigned special responsibilities, and properly documented. Each of these elements is, in itself, a function of violence prevention and must be thoroughly researched, published in a manner so that each employee is aware of and understands their assigned roles, and is prepared to act when called upon. A manual stuffed into a desk drawer does no good when "the flag goes up" and smoke is filling the building.

THREAT MANAGEMENT / CRISIS RESPONSE TEAM

Every organization, regardless of it's size, needs designated individuals to deal with incidents that may lead to violent occurrences. In smaller organizations, one person may assume several roles.

These are the people who, on a daily basis, monitor conditions in the workplace, advise senior management of actual or potential problem areas and provide expertise if an incident should take place. Security plays a vital role in the planning, execution and follow-up of emergency planning.

These positions of responsibility should be designated to accomplish necessary tasks:

Human Resources - conducts pre-employment screening, oversees personnel issues. The human resources staff is responsible for keeping violence-prone employees out of the workforce and for keeping lines of communication open to monitor ongoing problems.

Employee Assistance Program - designated source of help for problems which may include substance abuse, mental instability, personal problems. In many companies, the EAP program is contracted with outside agencies.

Risk Management - encompasses security and safety management, OSHA reporting. Members of this element are responsible for daily management of security and safety related issues, and keeping senior management advised of potentially explosive situations.

Facilities Management - responsible for utilities management, maintenance, other services. In any emergency incident, members of this department are responsible for the shutting down or control of utilities, providing emergency power, establishing communications.

RISK ASSESSMENT

Security provides the technical and professional skills to enable management to make necessary decisions in the purchase and installation of security systems, assignment of staff, and initiation of policies related to the protection of employees. A check list for *most* businesses should include:

> Natural Physical Barriers
> Physical Security Installations
> Access Control Measures
> Personnel Resources
> Policies / Procedures
> Emergency Plans
> Communications Systems
> Evacuation / Safe Shelters
> Response Coordination
> Employee Awareness Training
> Recovery Plans / Procedures

Each of these important elements should be thoroughly evaluated to determine the company's state of readiness to deal with emergency situations. A detailed report of the conditions found should be made available to senior management. Security may choose to conduct this assessment in house, or by contracting with outside agencies who specialize in performing such evaluations. Another alternative is to network with similar businesses, and request an assessment by qualified professionals, in exchange for similar services being performed by the requesting business.

WARNING SIGNS

On a national basis, the percentage of workplace violence incidents involving present employees is highest, followed by past employees, and last but certainly not to be ignored, incidents that began as a domestic dispute and followed one party into the workplace. It would therefore be prudent to observe and report, by any reasonable means, any of the following signs that are apparent in the workforce:

History of Violence - Involvement in previous incidents of domestic violence, verbal abuse, anti-social activities.

Disturbing Behavior - Mood swings, depression, bizarre statements, delusions of persecution.

Romantic Obsession - Beyond sexual attraction. Victim may be unaware of problem.

Chemical Dependence - Alcohol or drug dependence, abuse. Probably the <u>LEADING</u> cause of violent behavior.

Deep Depression - Self-destructive behavior. Withdrawal from social contacts. Unkempt physical appearance. Despair, sluggish decision-making.

Pathological Blamer - Accepts no responsibility for his or her actions. Constantly blames co-workers, the company, government, the system.

Impaired Ability to Function - Poor impulse control. May have been hyperactive as a child, or have brain injuries.

Elevated Frustration with Environment - Disturbance among peers on the job or at home, may trigger violent behavior.

Interest in Weapons - Ownership of guns or gun collection, other offensive weapons. Fascination with shooting skills or weapon-related activity.

Personality Disorders - Anti-social or borderline personality disorders. Anti-social personality is irritable, aggressive, often involved in disputes or fights with others. May steal or destroy property with little remorse. Borderline personality shows moodiness, instability, impulsive action, easily agitated.

Since a large percentage of violent episodes involve present or past employees, it makes good sense to understand the motivating factors behind violent acts. All employees should be aware of the traits, and have the ability to report their observations to a supervisor confidentially.
     * The Warning Sign checklist was developed by S. Anthony Baron, PhD. for his text, *Violence in the Workplace: A Prevention and Management Guide for Businesses*.

COMMUNICATIONS

When workers are disgruntled, involved in criminal acts, involved in substance abuse, or upset about situations outside of the workplace, who do they talk to? The answer is usually fellow workers, often those with similar problems. The company needs to encourage reporting of those situations that warrant intervention, even though they make take place outside of the workplace and not directly affect job performance. It's a thin line between what is appropriate for the employer to be involved in and what is considered protected or private. Your company legal advisor should make the determination.

1.   Encourage direct reporting of any act of violence, threats, use of controlled substances, display of weapons, or presence of unauthorized persons.
2.   *Consider* an anonymous reporting system.
3.   *Act immediately* to interview employees involved, investigate circumstances, and take corrective actions where justified.
4.   *Refer* employees with problems to the appropriate agency or company office.

POLICIES

The company should have in place and security must enforce *and* document, any violations of, or incidents involving these policies:
          Workplace Violence
          Sexual Harassment
          Substance Abuse
          Unauthorized Use of Company Property
          Insubordination
          Unauthorized Access to Restricted Areas

SAMPLE POLICY

It is the policy of this company to maintain a safe workplace, free from any threat of physical violence, emotional abuse or any form or intimidation. Employees, customers, vendors or any visitors to the facility are prohibited from bringing any type of weapon, explosive or destructive material onto company property (except for Company licensed investigators or police officers). Employees will not possess any of the above while engaged in company business. Any acts of vandalism, sabotage or threat of such acts will not be tolerated. Employees are advised to *report any acts*, or threats of acts which are described by this policy, to their immediate supervisor. All complaints, reports or advisements will be thoroughly investigated. *Failure to comply with this policy is a direct violation of foundation rules* and may result in activation of disciplinary procedures up to and including termination of employment. Where criminal violations have occurred, the company will file criminal charges and follow through with prosecution of those involved. This policy is adopted for the mutual protection of all employees and visitors. Employees and others shall not be subjected to nor victimized by threats, intimidation or any form of abuse. All such activities must be reported immediately, by calling the authorities. Callers may remain anonymous if so desired.

     **Management retains the *right to search any lockers, lunch boxes, backpacks, or other containers*, when there is probable cause to believe this policy has been violated. Suspected violators should be present when a search of their property is conducted.

TERMINATION OF EMPLOYMENT

When employees are terminated from further employment because of violations of company policy, criminal acts, or other incidents, security must be a part of the final process. The company policy for ending employment should include an exit interview. While not confrontational, these interviews may escalate to physical violence. Security should be available to respond if needed.

Each employee needs to formally turn in keys, uniforms, and other issued company property. This process must be documented and handled in a professional, non-threatening, non-derogatory manner, so that the departing employee is treated with an element of respect. Security's role is to assist in the turn-in process, and assure that other company property is not removed during the process.

The company may elect to restrict the departing employee from further presence on company property. Security must assure that all officers and entry staff are aware of the restrictions, have a current description of the person(s) involved and understand that police are to be called when such persons return. Note, however, that a copy of the legal notification to the employee, restricting access, must be on file and available to responding officers.

SUMMARY

Workplace violence incidents most often involve employees, but may also be initiated by problems that take place outside of work. Effective communications between employees and a reasonable state of preparedness are necessary to prevent violent acts from taking place.

It is every employee's responsibility to observe and report suspicious circumstances. Security's role is to provide professional and proper assistance, while constantly monitoring the condition of security systems, locks, lighting and other protective measures.

A coordinated effort from police, fire, emergency medical and security agencies is necessary to deal with violent incidents.

BIBLIOGRAPHY

Violence in the Workplace - published by Pathfinder Publishing of California, Ventura, CA 1993

Stay Out of Court - The Manager's Guide to Preventing Lawsuits - Published by Prentice Hall, Englewood Cliffs, NJ 1993

Management of Aggressive Behavior - Published by Performance Dimensions Publishing, Powers Lake, WI 1993

WORKPLACE VIOLENCE
QUIZ

1. _____ are most likely to be involved in incidents of workplace violence.

2. Coordination should be made with police, fire and _____ agencies.

3. A threat management team advises the company about problems which may include: _____ _____.

4. In a termination proceeding, security's role is to _____.

5. Romantic obsession is a trait sometimes present in _____.

6. Fired workers should be taken off the property and advised they may be shot if seen on company property again.
        □ T   □ F

7.   What takes place off of company property is of no concern to the employer.
           □ T   □ F

8.   Employees interested in weapons should be encouraged to form a competitive shooting team to meet after work.
           □ T   □ F

9.   Marital disputes are not considered to be anyone's business but those involved.
           □ T   □ F

10.   When a worker "has had a bad day," leave him alone and the problem will resolve itself.
           □ T   □ F

CRISIS MANAGEMENT:
PLANNING FOR COORDINATED RESPONSES
TO EMERGENCIES AND DISASTERS
by Ernest G. Vendrell, Ph.D.

INTRODUCTION

Most experts today are predicting that corporations, businesses, law enforcement agencies, as well as various other governmental entities in the United States and around the world, will be confronted with critical incidents that are likely to increase in number and level of severity (Sylves and Waugh, 1996; Paschall, 1992; Gigliotti and Jason, 1991). As a result, planning for critical incidents has taken on greater importance as well as a renewed sense of urgency.

Critical incidents are unplanned events such as natural disasters, hazardous materials spills, transportation disasters, workplace violence situations and other similar life threatening events. The extraordinary dimensions of these situations require special organizational skills and abilities on the part of emergency response personnel in order to attain a successful outcome.

Consequently, an emergency response plan that provides the necessary structure for managing critical incidents is of vital importance to any organization. Besides helping to save lives and reduce property loss, a well thought out emergency response plan can serve to lessen an organization's potential liability. Developing a comprehensive emergency response plan is, therefore, one of the most essential functions that a security supervisor or manager can perform.

SCOPE OF THE PROBLEM

Unfortunately, many organizations lack a good emergency response plan. This can ultimately lead to a variety of negative consequences ranging from adverse publicity to significant operating losses as well as loss of life. On the other hand, those organizations that have come to realize that emergency response planning is vital, have created and circulated elaborate policies and procedures designed to deal with a variety of emergency and disaster situations. Moreover, these organizations usually feel confident that they are prepared to deal with any contingency. Their emergency response plans detail specific actions to take in the event of a catastrophic event and outline specific steps that should be employed during the ensuing recovery effort. However, far too often, this is where the planning process ends. Typically, the planning document is filed away and forgotten until a critical incident occurs (Joyce and Hurth, 1997; Reid, 1996).

EMERGENCY PLANNING CONSIDERATIONS

Clearly, no emergency response plan can be applied to every potential crisis situation. However, a comprehensive plan that takes into account potential natural, technological and man-made threats and involves key personnel in the planning process can help an organization to systematically manage emergencies in an effective and efficient manner. Therefore, the planning process is a key element that forces security managers and supervisors to explore viable options that can be employed in the event of a critical incident. For this reason, oftentimes there is considerable discussion regarding which is more important, the plan or the planning process.

The Components of an Effective Emergency Response Plan

Being prepared for critical incidents involves four important components: planning, reviewing, training and testing. These are the cornerstones of any emergency response plan and it should be noted that it is a circular rather than linear process. Perhaps Nudell and Antokol (1988) explain this concept best when they describe the above components, when implemented, as an umbrella of preparation against the thunderstorms of a potential crisis.

According to the American Society for Industrial Security's *Emergency Planning Handbook* (1994, p. 4), effective emergency planning begins with the following:
- Defining an emergency in terms relevant to the organization doing the planning
- Establishing an organization with specific tasks to function immediately before, during and after an emergency

- Establishing a method for utilizing resources and for obtaining additional resources during the emergency
- Providing a recognizable means of moving from normal operations into and out of the emergency mode of operation

Incident Command System

With regard to establishing an organization with specific tasks and a method for utilizing resources, it should be noted that there exists a recognized system with a predetermined chain-of-command as well as a proven structure for an organized response to a critical incident. Referred to as the Incident Command System (ICS), it uses common terminology that is descriptive and decisive, yet not difficult to understand, in order to control personnel, resources and communications at the scene of a critical incident (Woodworth, 1998; Dezelan, 1996).

ICS was developed in the early 1970s after a series of major wildland fires in southern California resulted in a number of recurring problems among emergency responders. Some of these included: nonstandard terminology, nonstandard and nonintegrated communications, unmanageable span of control and lack of the capability to expand and contract as required by the situation.

Although originally a fire service control system, ICS has since been adopted by a wide variety of local, state, and national emergency management and law enforcement organizations due to its many documented successes. Today, it serves as a model all-risk, all-agency emergency management system. ICS principles have been proven over time in government, business and industry. In fact, ICS has been endorsed by the International Association of Chiefs of Police (IACP) and the American Public Works Association (APWA) (FEMA ICS Instructor Guide, 1995).

There is also a legal requirement for using ICS since there are federal laws that mandate its use by individuals responding to hazardous materials incidents. Specifically, OSHA rule 1910.120, which became effective March 6, 1990, requires that all organizations that handle hazardous materials use ICS. Non-OSHA states are also required by the Environmental Protection Agency to use ICS when responding to hazardous materials incidents (FEMA ICS Instructor Guide, 1995).

In essence, ICS is a well organized team approach for managing critical incidents. It uses common terminology, has a modular organization (which means that it can expand/shrink according to the needs of the situation), has a manageable span of control (the number of subordinates one supervisor can manage effectively; usually 3–7, the optimum is 5), and uses clear reporting and documentation procedures. In effect, emergency response personnel can view ICS as an incident management toolbox. Not every tool in the toolbox will be used for every situation, but the tools are available should they become necessary. Additionally, it is important to note that ICS can be used for all types of incidents regardless of size. However, it is essential that all emergency responders understand their specific roles when using ICS (Woodworth, 1998; Arata, Jr., 1995; FEMA ICS Instructor Guide, 1995).

The ICS structure is built around 5 major management activities or functional areas (FEMA ICS Instructor Guide, 1995):

- *COMMAND* - Sets priorities and objectives and is responsible for overall command of the incident.
- *OPERATIONS* - Has responsibility for all tactical operations necessary to carry out the plan.
- *PLANNING* - Responsible for the collection, evaluation and dissemination of information concerning incident development as well as the status of all available resources.
- *LOGISTICS* - Responsible for providing the necessary support (facilities, services and materials) to meet incident needs.
- *FINANCE* - Responsible for monitoring and documenting all costs. Provides the necessary financial support related to the incident.

These five management activities or functional areas form the foundation of the ICS organizational structure. The activities can be managed by one individual in the event of a small incident. Or, a fully staffed ICS structure, addressing all five functional areas, may be needed to manage larger or more complex events. In both cases, it is important to note that the Incident Commander is the individual in charge at the scene of a critical incident until properly relieved. The Incident Commander is also responsible for assigning personnel to the other functional areas (Operations, Planning, Logistics and Finance) as needed.

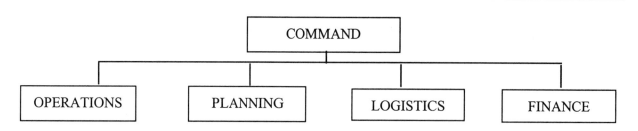

Figure 30.1:   Basic Incident Command System organizational structure.

ICS   organizational structure and procedures enable emergency response personnel to work safely together to take control of a critical incident. It can also assist organizations to effectively and efficiently manage the aftermath of a critical incident.

Common Requirements for Effective Critical Incident Management

Regardless of the type of crisis, Nudell and Antokol (1988, p. 4) point out that there are a series of common requirements that must be taken into account for an organization to be successful when a critical incident occurs. These include:

- Deciding policy
- Assessing threat
- Identifying resources
- Selecting crisis team personnel
- Locating the crisis management center
- Equipping the crisis center
- Training crisis team personnel
- Testing contingency plans and emergency procedures
- Dealing with the media
- Dealing with victims and their families
- Dealing with other affected persons (such as employees)
- Getting the organization's normal work done during the crisis
- Returning to normal after the crisis (both operationally and in human terms)

Vulnerability Analysis

With regard to threat assessment above, many times this procedure can be accomplished by using a simple numerical rating system (scale of 1 to 5 with 1 as the lowest and 5 being highest) to list on a chart potential emergencies (such as fire, flood, terrorist attack, etc.), estimate the probability of each emergency occurring, assess the potential human impact (death and injury), property impact (losses and damages), potential business impact (loss of market share) and finally, the strength of the internal and external resources that may be available (5 being weak resources and 1 indicating strong resources). Next, you would total the score for each emergency, taking into consideration that the lower the score, the better. Although somewhat subjective, the comparisons will be of significant assistance in determining planning priorities. The following example helps to illustrate the process (FEMA Emergency Management Guide for Business & Industry, 1993):

Type of Emergency	Probability +	Human Impact +	Property Impact +	Business Impact +	Internal Resources +	External Resources =	Total
	L 1-5 H	L 1-5 H	L 1-5 H	L 1-5 H	W 5-1 S	W 5-1 S	
Fire	3	5	5	5	2	4	24
Earthquake	2	4	4	4	2	3	19
Hurricane	4	4	4	4	3	4	23

Figure 30.2: Vulnerability Analysis Chart

In the above example, we would be most vulnerable to the fire scenario closely followed by the hurricane threat. We would be less vulnerable to the threat of an earthquake.

The Emergency Operations Center

An Emergency Operations Center (EOC) serves as a centralized area for the management of emergency operations. The EOC is where decisions are made by the emergency management team based on information provided by emergency responders and other personnel (FEMA Emergency Management Guide for Business and Industry, 1993).

The EOC can range from a dedicated, well-equipped center (comprehensive emergency communications capability including radio, telephone, fax, computer and television; self-sustaining power sources; bathroom, eating and sleeping facilities for staff; etc.) to an ad hoc room that is used as circumstances dictate. Of particular importance, is that an organization identify its requirements ahead of time and establish the type of arrangement that best suits its needs (ASIS Emergency Planning Handbook, 1994; Nudell and Antokol, 1988).

Although the EOC should be near senior management, it should not interfere with everyday operations. In addition, an alternate site should always be selected ahead of time. Hawkes and Neal (1998, p. 54) state that "an effective command center ready to respond to any emergency is a critical component of any headquarters security plan." They further contend that "a successful command center is the result of careful planning, clearly defined structure and job descriptions and comprehensive training."

Media Relations

Procedures for dealing with the media is another important area that cannot be overlooked. When a critical incident occurs, the security manager will undoubtedly be pulled in many different directions. Faced with a considerable number of important tasks, the security manager may not view media relations as a primary concern. However, being prepared ahead of time to deal with the media can help an organization to get through the incident without the additional damage that can be caused by misinformation and speculation. In addition, the negative publicity that an organization receives as a result of a critical incident can have far-reaching effects. An organization's image and business can be adversely impacted. Litigation is bound to result as victims, the families of victims, employees, customers and perhaps various interested outside parties, will be seeking to lay blame and recover damages. Attorneys are bound to examine every newspaper account and TV report of the incident. They will, of course, be looking for statements from representatives of the organization for any admissions or confirmation that the organization was in some way negligent (Gardner, 1997).

Nuss (1997, p. 1) defines a crisis as "...an event requiring rapid decisions involving the media, that, if handled incorrectly, could damage the organization's credibility and reputation." He further provides a number of effective crisis communications steps that organizations should consider:
- Have a media plan
- Build a relationship with the media before a crisis strikes
- Train employees in crisis communications
- Maintain a good relationship with the media after [a] crisis

Cooperating with the media provides an organization with a number of important benefits that far outweigh the benefits of denying them access. In particular, it provides the organization with an opportunity to provide its side of the story. This is important since, oftentimes, the spokesman for the organization can make available background information that may provide a different perspective on the situation. Furthermore, working with the media may prevent reporters from seeking out secondary sources that are typically less informed and more likely to misrepresent the organization. Consequently, it is far better to have the organization give an accurate statement of the situation as opposed to leaving it up to the reporter to locate an "informed" source which can lead to speculation and misinformation. Saying nothing also has its own risks. Ignoring bad news will not make the incident go away and usually this tactic raises additional questions (Gardner, 1997).

FEMA (Emergency Management Guide for Business and Industry, 1993, p. 41) provides a number of important considerations for dealing with the media in an emergency:
- Designate a trained spokesperson and an alternate spokesperson
- Set up a media briefing area
- Establish security procedures

- Establish procedures for ensuring that information is complete, accurate and approved for public release
- Determine an appropriate and useful way of communicating technical information
- Prepare background information about the facility

FEMA (Emergency Management Guide for Business and Industry, 1993, p. 41) also provides the following guidelines when providing information to the media during an emergency:

Do's

- Give all media equal access to the information
- When appropriate, conduct press briefings and interviews. Give local and national media equal time
- Try to observe media deadlines
- Escort media representatives to ensure safety
- Keep records of information released
- Provide press releases when possible

Don'ts
- Do not speculate about the incident
- Do not permit unauthorized personnel to release information
- Do not cover up facts or mislead the media
- Do not put blame on the incident

It is quite evident that although safety issues are always a top consideration, a security manager or supervisor cannot overlook the importance of an effective crisis media relations plan. This plan must be implemented quickly during a critical incident in order to provide accurate and timely information while safeguarding the reputation and interests of the organization.

Developing the Emergency Response Plan

Obviously, the development of a comprehensive emergency management plan requires considerable time and effort and sufficient time should be provided for its completion. Representatives from key organizational units must be involved from its inception and upper management support is essential throughout the entire process. Many times this can be readily accomplished by having the chief executive officer or facility manager issue a mission statement that introduces the emergency management plan, its purpose and importance to the organization, and defines the structure and authority of the planning team. Additionally, it is important in the initial planning stages to select an individual within the organization, to assume responsibility for the plan and act as the planning team leader or coordinator.

Ultimately, capabilities and hazards will be analyzed, specific roles and responsibilities will be carefully outlined, and critical company products and services will be identified in order to ensure a coordinated and effective response when a critical incident does occur. This will typically involve meeting with outside groups and establishing mutual aid agreements where appropriate. Gillespie (Drabek & Hoetmer, 1991) emphasizes that mutual aid agreements enhance preparedness and that emergency response is more effective when public and private organizations cooperate.

Some outside groups or agencies could include (FEMA Emergency management Guide for Business and Industry, 1993):
- Local police department
- Local fire department
- Emergency medical services
- City or county office of emergency management
- Local emergency planning committee (LEPC)
- City or county government officials
- Public works department
- Electric utilities
- Telephone companies
- Volunteer agencies such as the American Red Cross, the Salvation Army, etc.

- Essential contractors
- Suppliers of emergency equipment
- Company insurance carriers
- Neighboring businesses
- Trade associations
- National Weather Service

In crisis situations, organizations respond differently based on variations in tasks, level of preparedness, as well as political considerations. Conferring with outside groups or agencies ahead of time will undoubtedly avoid confusion and delays during the response phase of an emergency, improve coordination and communication during the management phase of the incident, and help organizations transition to the recovery phase much faster. However, it is important to note that these agreements should clearly define the type of assistance as well as the procedures for activating the agreement in order to avoid unnecessary conflict.

Reviewing and Integrating the Emergency Response Plan

Once the initial plan is completed, it is essential that its various components be reviewed in-depth by planning team personnel and revised as necessary. The draft plan could then be presented to key management personnel as well as any individuals who may be required to perform or provide support services. Many times, a tabletop exercise provides an excellent opportunity to review potential critical incidents with key personnel since problem areas can be readily identified and discussed. The plan can then be modified accordingly and later presented to the chief executive officer for final approval. Upon approval, the plan can be distributed to all affected personnel who should be required to sign that they have received the document. It is then important that the plan be quickly and clearly communicated to all affected personnel (Gigliotti and Jason, 1991).

It is imperative at this point that the plan be fully integrated into the organization's standard operating procedures (SOPs). According to FEMA (Guide for All-Hazard Emergency Operations Planning, 1996, p. 3-3) "SOPs and checklists provide the detailed instructions that an organization or individual needs to fulfill responsibilities and perform tasks, assigned in the EOP [emergency operations plan]..." Clearly, a comprehensive checklist that includes major planning, implementation, training/testing, response, and recovery components would be an invaluable asset to any organization's emergency response plan.

Training and Testing

After the plan has been finalized, communicated to all affected personnel, and integrated into the organization's standard operating procedures, it must be thoroughly tested. An emergency response plan will not work properly unless realistic training is provided and it is thoroughly tested prior to implementation in an actual emergency. Testing the plan helps to identify problem areas, as well as inherent weaknesses, that must be corrected in order to ensure that the plan will work as designed. Training and testing, thus, serve to identify areas in need of improvement, thereby enhancing coordination and communication among emergency response personnel.

The first step in the training process is to assign a staff member responsibility for developing an overall training plan and the requisite goals and objectives for each component. Additionally, a determination must be made as to the following:

- Who will actually perform the training
- Who will be trained
- What type of training activities will be employed
- What materials and equipment will be needed
- When will the training take place
- Where will the training take place
- How long will the training last
- How will the training be evaluated and by whom
- How will the training activities be documented
- How will special circumstances be handled
- How will training costs and expenses be budgeted

It should be noted that critiques, or evaluations, are an important component of the training process and must be conducted after each training activity. Sufficient time should be allotted for the critique and any resulting recommendations should be forwarded to the emergency planning team for further review and action. Additionally, organizations should consider how to involve outside groups and agencies in the training and evaluation process. As previously mentioned, this could certainly help to avoid conflict and increase coordination and communication when a critical incident does occur. Emergency response training can take a variety of forms. FEMA (Emergency Management Guide for Business and Industry, 1993, p. 22) describes six types of training activities that can be considered:

- *Orientation and Education Sessions* - Sessions designed to provide information, answer questions, and identify needs and concerns.
- *Tabletop Exercise* - This is a cost efficient and effective way to have members of the emergency planning team, as well as key management personnel, meet in a conference room setting to discuss roles and responsibilities and identify areas of concern.
- *Walk-through Drill* - The emergency planning team and response teams actually perform their emergency response functions.
- *Functional Drills* - Designed to test specific functions such as medical response, emergency notifications, and communications procedures, although not necessarily at the same time. The drill is then evaluated by the various participants and problem areas are identified.
- *Evacuation Drill* - Participants walk the evacuation route to a pre-designated area where procedures for accounting for all personnel are tested. Participants are asked to make note of potential hazards along the way and the emergency response plan is modified accordingly.
- *Full-scale Exercise* - An emergency is simulated as close to real as possible. Involves management, emergency response personnel, employees, as well as outside groups and agencies that would also be involved in the response.

Practical "hands-on" training always provides personnel with excellent opportunities to use skills that are taught and to learn new techniques and procedures. For emergency response training, simulations such as tabletop exercises, drills and full-scale exercises, are particularly valuable for practicing decision-making skills, tactical techniques and communications. Moreover, simulations serve to determine deficiencies in planning and procedures that can lead to modifications to the emergency response plan (ASIS Emergency Planning Handbook, 1994; FEMA Emergency Planning Guide for Business and Industry, 1993; Nudell and Antokol, 1988).

"Model City" Simulator

Perhaps one of the most successful and creative ways of teaching critical incident management to emergency response personnel is through the use of a "model city" simulator board. As the name implies, a "model city" simulator represents a small community with a residential area, business district and industrial park. The simulator provides the realistic environment needed to give participants the feeling of actually having managed a critical incident and to immediately see the results of their actions. In essence, students get to practice decision-making skills in a realistic environment where there are no repercussions for making a mistake.

One of the leading companies involved in critical incident management training is BowMac Educational Services, Inc. (BowMac), located in Rochester, New York. This innovative training and development company offers a unique critical incident management training system, which employs a combination of classroom instruction and practical "hands-on" exercises using a transportable "model city" simulator. The goal of this training program is to provide participants with a "game plan" that can make the difference in taking control of an incident or allowing it to mushroom out of control. The primary focus is on training operational personnel to manage the initial thirty minutes of a critical incident by employing a series of critical tasks or decisions. These include:

- *Establish Communications* - Advise dispatch to hold the air and allow only emergency radio traffic or request that a separate frequency be assigned for the incident.
- *Identify the "Hot Zone"* - It is very important to identify the "hot zone" immediately in order to limit additional exposure to danger.
- *Establish an Inner Perimeter* - An inner perimeter should be set up quickly. It is used to control and contain the area and prevent the initial situation from getting worse.
- *Establish an Outer Perimeter* - The outer perimeter is used to control access to the affected area. It is not an offensive position and should be located well outside of the "hot zone."
- *Establish a Command Post* - The command post should be established outside of the "hot zone" between the inner and outer perimeters. It does not need to be located with a view

of the scene. Initially, the command post can be your vehicle or any other suitable temporary location with communications capability.

- *Select a Staging Area* - The staging area should be large enough to accommodate arriving emergency resources for transfer to the scene as needed. It must be located outside of the inner perimeter at a safe and secure location.
- *Identify and Request Additional Resources* - Quickly assess the need for additional resources at the scene and direct resources to the staging area. Examples of additional resources are local police, fire, EMS, HazMat, public works, utility companies, the national guard, federal and state agencies, the American Red Cross, etc.

The advantage of a critical incident management program using a "model city" simulator, such as the system offered by BowMac, is that training shifts from discussing emergency response issues at the "tabletop" level to actually practicing handling an incident in a realistic, simulated environment. Learning to implement a standard set of tasks or procedures under these conditions will undoubtedly assist emergency response personnel to quickly take control and limit the growth of a critical incident, thereby affording a much greater opportunity for bringing the situation to a successful outcome.

Evaluating the Emergency Response Plan

Regardless of the training schedule selected, a formal audit of the entire emergency response plan should be conducted at least once a year. Furthermore, in addition to the yearly audit, the emergency response plan should be evaluated, and modified if necessary, as follows (FEMA Guide for Business and Industry, 1993):
- After each drill or exercise
- After each critical incident
- When there has been a change in personnel or responsibilities
- When the layout or design of a facility changes
- When there is a change in policies or procedures

Of course, any modifications or changes to an emergency response plan should be communicated to affected personnel as soon as possible. Similarly, changes to the planning document should be incorporated and distributed in a timely manner.

PROFESSIONAL DEVELOPMENT

An emergency response plan is a dynamic process that must be kept up to date and consistent with an organization's operations and identified vulnerabilities. Therefore, security managers and supervisors must continually scan their internal and external environments in order to anticipate and plan for problems that could have an adverse impact on their organizations. One way of accomplishing this is for security managers and supervisors to read extensively, become familiar with the numerous emergency/disaster organizations and services available, and maintain an active network with other professionals in their field, as well as in allied disciplines. Two excellent emergency/disaster related resources to consider are the annual *Disaster Resource Guide* as well as the *Emergency Services Sourcebook*. It should also be noted that FEMA, through the Emergency Management Institute (EMI), offers an Independent Study Program consisting of a series of self-paced courses. Each set of course materials includes practice exercises as well as a final exam. The average time of completion is 10–12 hours and individuals who score 75 percent or better are issued a certificate of completion by EMI. There is no charge for enrollment. In addition, for a fee, one semester of college credit may be obtained for each successfully completed course, except one (FEMA Emergency Management Institute, Catalog of Activities, 1997–1998).

SUMMARY

Both public and private sector organizations are becoming increasingly aware of the need to plan for the effective management of critical incidents. Security managers and supervisors are expected not only to prepare well-written plans for these events, but to also have a plan in place that works and is understood by all. This requires that the plan be tested through training thereby ensuring that responding personnel can immediately initiate emergency management operations. Besides helping to define the technical, interpersonal and organizational dynamics of critical incident management, these activities assist emergency responders to become familiar with the roles and responsibilities of all personnel, including outside groups and agencies, at the scene of a critical incident.

BIBLIOGRAPHY

American Society for Industrial Security, Standing Committee on Disaster Management (1994). *Emergency Planning Handbook.* Dubuque, IA: Kendall/Hunt Publishing Company.

Arata, Jr., M. (1995). Finding order amidst the chaos. *Security Management, 39, (9),* 48-53.

BowMac Educational Services, Inc. (1992). *Critical Incident Management Instructor Notebook.* Rochester, NY: Author.

Dezelan, L. (1996). Incident management system. *Law and Order, 44,* (8), Wilmette, IL: Hendon, Inc.

Drabek, T., & Hoetmer, G. (Eds.) (1991). *Emergency Management Principles and Practice for Local Government.* Washington, D.C.: International City Management Association.

Federal Emergency Management Agency (1996). *Emergency Management Guide for Business and Industry.* Washington, D.C.: U.S. Government Printing Office.

Federal Emergency Management Agency (1996). *Guide for All-Hazard Emergency Operations Planning.* Washington, DC: U.S. Government Printing Office.

Federal Emergency Management Agency (1995). *Incident Command System Instructor Guide.* Washington, D.C.: U.S. Government Printing Office.

Gardner, R. (1997). Getting ahead of the headlines. *Security Management, 41,* (7), 115-119.

Gigliotti, R., & Jason, R. (1991). *Emergency Planning for Maximum Protection.* Boston, MA: Butterworth-Heinemann.

Hawkes, K., & Neal, J. (1998). Command performance. *Security Management, 42,* (11), 77-83.

Joyce, E., & Hurth, L. (1997). Booking your next disaster. *Security Management, 41,* (11), 47-50.

Nudell, M., & Antokol, N. (1988). *The Handbook for Effective Emergency Management.* Lexington, MA: Lexington Books.

Nuss, R. (1997). *Effective Media Crisis Communication During a Critical Incident.* Winter Springs, FL: Nuss and Associates, Inc.

Paschall, R. (1992). *Critical Incident Management.* Chicago, IL: The Office of International Criminal Justice.

Rainey, K. (Ed.) (1998). *Disaster Resource Guide.* Santa Ana, CA: Emergency Lifeline Corporation.

Reid, K. (1996). Testing Murphy's law. *Security Management, 40,* (11), 77-78, 80-83.

Smith, D., & Fasano, L. (Eds.) (1993). *Emergency Services Sourcebook, Vols. 1 and 2.* (3rd ed.) New York, NY: Specialized Services, Inc.

Sylves, R., & Waugh, Jr., W. (Eds.) (1996). *Disaster Management in the U.S. and Canada.* Springfield, IL: Charles C. Thomas.

Woodworth, B. (1998). The Incident Command System: A Tool for Business Recovery. *Disaster Resource Guide, 1998 Edition.* Santa Ana, CA: Emergency Lifeline Corporation.

CRISIS MANAGEMENT
QUIZ

1. Preparing for emergencies involves four important considerations: _____, _____ ____, _____ and _____.

2. A particularly important component of the initial planning process is *vulnerability* analysis.

3. _____ are an important component of the training process and must be conducted after each training activity.

4. Emergency response training can take a variety of forms. List three types of training that can be considered: _____, _____ and _____.

5. A formal audit of the emergency response plan should be conducted how often? _____

6. A well thought out emergency response plan can save lives, reduce property loss, and reduce an organization's potential liability.
   □ T   □ F

7. The development of a comprehensive emergency management plan requires considerable time and effort and sufficient time should be provided for its completion. Representatives from key organizational units must be involved and upper management support is essential throughout the entire process.
   □ T   □ F

8. During the planning process, it is not necessary to consider meeting with outside groups and agencies that could be involved in an emergency response.
   □ T   □ F

9. Utilizing the Incident Command System helps to control personnel, resources, and communications at the scene of a critical incident.
   □ T   □ F

10. Cooperating with the media during a critical incident provides an organization with the opportunity to make available background information that may provide a different perspective on the situation.
    □ T   □ F

SUPERVISING DURING EMERGENCIES
by Brion K. O'Dell, CPP, CSS

Supervising a security force can be challenging even during the best of times, but the real test of a supervisor's skill comes when an emergency arises. If not controlled, circumstances can quickly overwhelm both staff and resources with sometimes disastrous results. Depending on the type and severity of the incident, the security supervisor may find it is necessary to cope with the loss of utilities (such as lights and electrical power), property, communications, and transportation. There may also exist the further complication of the medical needs of any victims or the necessity to institute crowd control.

As in other aspects of security, the key to success lies within the supervisor's ability to identify the most probable incidents likely to occur and to formulate adequate response plans to deal with them. These plans must take into account both natural and man-made threats.

PREPARING FOR EMERGENCIES

Developing Emergency Response Plans

When first developing emergency response plans, the wise supervisor will consult with all outside agencies that would be involved during a crisis. These should include local police, fire/rescue department, hospitals as well as utility companies, service vendors or any other organization whose assistance or expertise would be needed during an emergency. Their experience can prove to be a valuable resource in identifying potential threats and formulating suitable responses. Coordinating your response plans with them PRIOR to an emergency will go a long way in avoiding confusion during an actual incident. The supervisor will find that in most instances the heads of these organizations are more than willing to offer their experience and training in assisting with the creation of emergency responses.

During this developmental stage, be certain to include appropriate staff from within your own organization; maintenance, safety, personnel, communications, accounting, management and so on. They will afford additional sources of information needed to formulate an adequate response plan. Adequate emergency equipment (fire extinguishers, first aid kits, two-way radios, flashlights, etc.) must be obtained and kept on hand.

Training/Practice Drills

Once a suitable response plan has been approved it is essential to create a formal training program for all employees to ensure they have a complete understanding of its importance and proper implementation. This training must be comprehensive but also easy to understand. (Bear in mind these plans will be carried out during an emergency ... a time when fear and confusion can cause people to panic.) Whenever possible, your training sessions should include representatives from outside agencies such as the police and fire departments. As previously mentioned, their experience and training can prove to be an invaluable resource to your program. Periodic practice drills that include all employees should be held to help ensure smooth implementation in the event of a real emergency. Oftentimes serious flaws in a response plan can be uncovered and corrected during a practice drill that could otherwise lead to tragedy if left undiscovered.

Copies of the appropriate response plans should be kept accessible to all staff members and posted wherever possible. Evacuation routes must be clearly marked and adequate emergency equipment (such as fire extinguishers and first aid kits) must be readily accessible.

During the Emergency

When an actual emergency arises the security supervisor may be confronted by a myriad of responsibilities and challenges. While it is impossible to list every potential threat, it is possible to identify several areas of response that are common in most situations. It is important to note that the following are NOT listed in order of priority.

Implementation of Response Plans

The security supervisor MUST possess a thorough understanding of:
- The appropriate response plans and the steps that must be taken for their proper implementation.
- What outside agencies to contact in case of fire, medical, or criminal occurrence and what level of action is to be taken pending their arrival. (Note: The level of action taken by security officers will vary according to jurisdiction, state and local law, employer regulations and so on.)
- Which evacuation routes are to be used.
- Which management and/or support personnel within their organization are to be contacted.
- What equipment and/or personnel will be required to contain the incident pending arrival of outside assistance.
- Proper procedures for handling inquiries from the news media, families of victims, employees, etc.

Communication

No matter what the nature of the emergency at hand, the security supervisor MUST be able to maintain reliable communication with the security officers under his/her command and all other outside personnel involved (police, fire, medical, employees, management, etc.). This communication may be electronic, such as two-way radio or telephone or simply verbal. No matter how it is transmitted, information MUST flow between all parties involved. The supervisor must be able to communicate instructions to other officers and receive reports of activities as they occur. Likewise, emergency personnel must be able to provide information/instructions back to the security supervisor. Any major breakdown in the lines of communication could have disastrous consequences.

In today's high-tech world, the most frequently used method of communication is the two-way radio. While it is true that under most conditions radio can be used effectively, there are certain circumstances when their use would be prohibited. One such incident would be the investigation of a bomb threat (the use of a two-way radio could detonate a bomb). Under conditions such as these, alternate means of communication would be required.

The security supervisor must be able to adapt to changing situations and have back-up methods of communication at hand.

Coordination of Activities

During an emergency it is likely that several outside emergency agencies would be involved. This means a large number of personnel may all be working together. In order to prevent confusion (with potentially deadly results) the activities of all involved must be coordinated into an organized effort.

If, for example, the supervisor was confronted with a fire, the activities of the officers under his/her command would need to be directed pending the arrival of the fire department. Once the fire department personnel were at the scene, their command officers would take charge. The security supervisor would need to inform them of the location and nature of the fire, the location and condition of any victims, the actions taken by the security staff and so on. While it is the responsibility of the fire department to contain/control the incident, it is quite possible that the fire department would direct the security staff to assist them in their efforts with such duties as crowd control, aiding victims, locating witnesses and so on. As it is highly unlikely that the security staff would have direct radio contact with the fire department personnel, the job of relaying information and instructions would most probably fall to the security supervisor.

While a fire is only one of the many potential incidents the supervisor may confront, the need for effective coordination of activities holds true in all emergency situations. The security supervisor must be able to cooperate with all other outside emergency personnel and to assist them in successfully bringing the emergency under control.

Protection of Assets

During the height of an emergency, the security supervisor may find the first priority is to assist any victims. While this indeed should be the top priority, the supervisor must not overlook the necessity of protecting the assets of his or her employer. These assets would include all property, equipment, merchandise, vehicles, office supplies and so forth.

The confusion and distractions that can arise as the result of a serious incident can afford others the opportunity to remove or damage property with little or no chance of detection. Additionally, the increase in the number of persons that may be present at the scene of an emergency can cause valuable evidence to be removed or inadvertently destroyed.

The security supervisor must be able to utilize all available officers and resources to contain/preserve the scene while implementing all necessary procedures in order to prevent unauthorized persons from entering the scene regardless of their intentions.

Depending upon the type and severity of the emergency, the supervisor may suddenly be confronted with the loss of resources and equipment that normally are taken for granted. Alarm and intrusion systems may be inoperable. Access controls and barriers such as fences, doors, security screening, etc. may be damaged and no longer able to deter unauthorized entry. Valuable equipment or merchandise may become exposed and vulnerable to attack. It may be necessary to arrange for a temporary increase of security personnel from outside sources or to obtain additional back-up equipment in order to effectively protect the area.

The security supervisor must be able to quickly adapt to changing situations, effectively utilize all available resources and manpower and take whatever actions are necessary to preserve and secure the scene.

CONCLUSION

It is not possible to list all of the possible contingencies the security supervisor may encounter during his or her career. However, it is quite clear that in order to be effective, he or she must be adaptable, able to communicate, possess the ability to remain calm under pressure, be familiar with all applicable procedures and to continually hone his skills through practice and continuing education.

SUPERVISING DURING EMERGENCIES
QUIZ

1. In order to prepare for emergencies the supervisor should identify the most probable _____ _____ likely to occur and formulate adequate response _____ to deal with them.

2. When developing the response plans, the supervisor should consult with all outside _____ _____ and with _____ within their own organization.

3. Once an appropriate response plan has been created, a formal _____ should be held, followed up with routine _____.

4. The supervisor should consult with outside agencies whenever possible because their _____ _____ and _____ can be valuable _____.

5. During certain emergencies, the supervisor may be faced with the loss of _____ that are normally taken for granted.

6. During an emergency, the security staff must handle all situations themselves.
    ☐ T   ☐ F

7. The only form of communication the security supervisor will need during an emergency is two-way radios.
    ☐ T   ☐ F

8.   Once outside emergency personnel have arrived the security supervisor will have no other
        responsibilities or duties.
                          □ T   □ F

9.   During an emergency the security supervisor's top priority is the protection of the employer's
        assets.
                          □ T   □ F

10.   The security supervisor must be able to adapt to changing situations.
                          □ T   □ F

SUPERVISING DURING SPECIAL EVENTS
by Christopher Innace, CPO

The role of a security supervisor is a challenging one, often requiring planning and communicating with various entities. Special events such as rock concerts, athletic events, speeches, autograph sessions, political rallies or stockholder meetings pose a unique set of challenges. There are many potential risks at special events that security supervisors should be aware of, the major one being violent crowds. *This cannot be stressed enough.* Crowds are capable of extensive violence and destruction, oftentimes unleashing their fury in an explosive manner. Effective crowd management is a major step in avoiding a disaster during special events.

Additionally, special events provide an opportunity for image enhancement, both of the protection entity as well as the parent or client organization. In some cases projecting a positive image and relating well to visitors, customers and the public at large is the sole reason for the existence of the parent/client or security organization. Shopping centers, amusement parks and stadiums all exist for the comfort and entertainment of patrons. Supervisory personnel who wish to thrive in their professional careers need to exploit this opportunity to the greatest extent possible!

ASSESS

There are many options to consider when assessing for crowd management. The security supervisor must work with the facility and venue manager to have an effective plan. Together, they should try and ascertain the characteristics of the crowd/audience due at a particular event. Assessing the size and nature of a crowd is important for a security supervisor. The size of a crowd can be determined by ticket sales, counting seats, etc. The nature of the crowd *may* be determined by the event itself. For example, if it is a football game, then crowds tend to be rowdy. One can estimate that alcohol will be a factor in changing some persons' behavior in this type of crowd. If it is a gymnastics crowd, for example, then the crowd tends to be calmer and more relaxed.

There are five different types of crowds that a security supervisor should be aware of:

Acquisitive crowd - is one motivated by the desire to get something. They are concerned with their own interest in buying merchandise, getting an autograph or shaking the hand of a celebrity. As long as their desires are met quickly and efficiently, they are easily managed.

Expressive crowd - usually is when crowd members express their feelings at a protest, demonstration or convention. This type of crowd is usually well-behaved but can easily become hostile if the proper causal factors are present.

Spectator crowd - usually gathers to watch an athletic event or some type of entertainment. A concern here is that emotions can change rapidly; especially during sporting events. Troublemakers must be spotted and dealt with early on and the crowd as a whole continually assessed as to their mood.

Hostile crowd - is motivated by feelings of hate and fear. This type of crowd is ready to fight for what they believe in. This usually occurs at strikes, riots or political demonstrations. Obviously, plans must be made to immediately implement dispersal procedures.

Escape crowd – are crowds that try to flee. This can occur due to an emergency situation such as a fire or other sudden disaster event. Escape crowds can also be created due to mis-management by protection forces. Care must be taken to ensure that crowds do not become too large or confined. There must also be the ability to see and hear by all crowd members, especially those at the extreme front and rear. Quick, efficient, orderly evacuation routes must also be established.

There are five psychological factors of crowd members that a security supervisor should make note of:

Security – Some people possibly will join a crowd because they feel that they will be safe since many others are there as well. For example, this can occur if a gang is threatening citizens and some of the citizens join the gang for security purposes.

Suggestion – By joining a crowd, people accept ideas of the leader and can forget about their own beliefs, values, morals or basic common sense.

Novelty – A person may enter a group to get away from their normal routine or regular duties. They feel like they belong to a new adventure. This is usually due to some influence from the crowd leader.

Loss of Identity – One loses their sense of individuality – and individual accountability – being in a crowd. They believe that they can act with impunity and so will engage in deviant behaviors that they would not normally entertain.

Release of Emotions – In an emotionally charged crowd, one's faults (anger, hostility, etc.) can surface. This gives the crowd member a chance to do things that they normally would not do.

The International Association and Campus Law Enforcement Administrators (IACLEA) offers their members an e-mail service which can be very useful. A security supervisor could gather information via this service from other protection professionals. An example of this is:

```
Date:        Th. 20 Dec. 1998 15:30
From:        "Christopher Innace" <cinnace@ycp.edu>
To:          IACLEA - L@iaclea.org
Subject:          Aerosmith

I am looking for any information on any problem related to the group Aerosmith performing at other
campuses. They will be performing here 2/16/99 and part of their contract is that they will have
security assigned to them on campus.

Thank you.
```

ACCESS CONTROL

Barriers play an important role as to who gets allowed onto the premises. Who gets in and where they can go requires decision-making by the security supervisor and venue management. Criteria for spectators in getting into the facility can be tickets and a guest list. Employees – and in some cases visitors – should have identification cards. These cards should have numbered or colored zones placed on them so the security officer and the employee know where they can and cannot go.

Other decisions depend on if the facility has gates or doors that lock up the outside premises. The security supervisor must decide with facility/venue management when to open and close the facility for employees, performers, athletes, etc. Other barriers that must be checked constantly are entrances and exits. First of all, how many are there and when do they need to be locked or unlocked?

COMMUNICATIONS

Communication is an integral component of preparing for a special event. All communication equipment should be tested prior to the event. The security supervisor should establish a method for security, venue management and law enforcement agencies to be able to contact each other. This can be accomplished via radios equipped with multiple channels. Backup battery packs and spare radios are also essential to the security supervisor. Other communication equipment to be used should include enough telephones, cellular phones, inter-company phones and "bell line" phones to handle the increased traffic required during emergencies. A public address system in the facility can be very useful also as well as portable PA's ('bullhorns') and whistles.

In many facilities large video monitors are placed at strategic locations to provide entertainment, information or emergency instructions to crowd members or employees. These monitors can keep the attention of crowd members focused in a positive manner; especially if there are periods of waiting. Spectators are entertained and not as easily aggravated by having to wait in line. This can easily be tied into the parent or client organizations's marketing effort by providing information on sales, promotions, upcoming events, etc.

Protection officers should have all of their lines of communication checked for both transmission and reception capabilities at the beginning of each shift. There should also be periodic checks to ensure that radio batteries are at proper strength, "dead zones" are avoided, etc. Officers should always think in terms of backup communications in case the primary method of communication is not useable for any reason. This should be stressed and reinforced at every opportunity!

TRAFFIC CONTROL

Traffic control is essential during special events especially when there are emergencies. No emergency plan can succeed without effective traffic control systems in place. It is also important for public relations purposes as it is at this juncture that visitors first come into contact with representatives of the facility – the protection officers directing traffic.

Officers must possess the proper equipment when assigned to traffic control duty. A flashlight, radio and whistle are necessary. Also officers must dress according to the weather so that comfort is assured during long hours. For safety and public recognition purposes, officers should dress so as to be visible. Reflective body vests should be required so that both ease of recognition and officer safety are enhanced.

There should be a separate lane cleared out in case of a fire or other emergency situation. Being able to quickly remove injured persons, evicted individuals, arrestees is important. Being able to bring in fire equipment, vendor supplies or additional personnel efficiently is also key to successful event management. It is also advantageous to be able to do this without crowd members seeing the ambulance, arrestee, additional personnel, etc. arriving or departing. Prudent security supervisors make sure these lanes of approach and exit are kept open!

Training of protection officers in proper traffic control procedures is essential to the security supervisor. Initial and periodic refresher classes must be given to ensure proficiency. Improper procedures, such as incorrect hand signals, could lead to accidents, so training to prevent these behaviors and continuous supervisory assessment on-the-job are essential. Checking the proficiency of officers and the appearance/image of traffic control points is an essential supervisory function. Finding deficiencies and correcting them before they blossom into serious problems is the key.

When officers direct traffic, signals should be simple and distinct. Appropriate sign placement is also essential to both manage traffic and project the proper image. *Supervisors should address the traffic control function from a systems perspective.* Each part of the traffic control system should act in concert with the whole.

EMERGENCY MEDICAL OPERATIONS

The security officer should be trained in first aid. When dealing with a person who is sick or injured, first communicate with the patient if possible. Then the officer should provide basic first aid if necessary. The next step is to call for assistance (911) and to then manage crowds and bystanders. The officer must stay with the patient until medically trained help arrives. Medical personnel (EMTs) to visitors should be a ratio of 1:750. Certified EMTs are essential for the purpose of emergency medical operations.

Provision must also be made for ambulance service. In some facilities, patient transport can be accomplished via golf carts or similar types of patrol vehicles. In-house ambulances may also be used. In all situations external ambulance capabilities must be assessed. Similarly, emergency room capabilities at local hospitals must be factored in, should there be mass casualties.

EVACUATION

In an indoor facility, a six-foot "clear zone" around the inside of the perimeter must be maintained for evacuation purposes. Any equipment must be secure and out of the way in case of a panic situation arising. The security supervisor does not want this to interfere when crowds head towards the exits. For an outside event plans must be made and discussed concerning evacuation routes.

In addition to routes, there must be areas that evacuating crowd members can congregate in. These areas must be large enough to accommodate everyone and provide for the safety of everyone. There should also be consideration given to what crowd members do after evacuating, such as getting in their cars and leaving or assembling and being advised on where to go next.

FIXED POSTS

Fixed posts manned by security personnel are a necessity for any special event. At every fixed post, post orders are a must. Post orders must be clear and understandable so a person unfamiliar with security concepts can comprehend the orders. Every security officer manning the post should know the objective or mission of the post. The location of the post should be included in the post order. Manning orders should also be included to stipulate when the post is operational, as well as what type (unarmed, armed, male, female, etc.) and how many personnel man it.

Any equipment used should be listed and tested regularly. When first manning the post, there should be a sign-in sheet logging the use of any equipment for the security officer to sign. *Some* equipment common to fixed posts are portable radios, flashlights, rain gear, batons, fire extinguishers and CCTV monitors. There are also many other types of possible equipment that may be used, contingent upon the operational and emergency needs of that post. Also, duties must be specified in a post order. This includes area of responsibility and an establishment of a route of retreat, should hostile crowd actions necessitate this.

SAMPLE POST ORDER

Objective: To check and collect tickets.

Location: Aquatic Center - Gate A - Stand right beside turnstile.

Manning: Hours of post are from 1300 - 1600 hours by a single unarmed officer.

Equipment: Sign sheet for portable radios and flashlights. Make sure they both work. Perform a radio check with the command post or CAS every hour.

Duties: Check tickets for date, time and the event to make sure that the tickets are not counterfeit. Rip tickets in half and place one half in the box beside you and return the other half of the ticket to the ticket-holder.

Emergency Route: Exit Gate A and proceed north to parking lot 14. A supervisor will meet you there.

ASSIGNING SECURITY OFFICER'S POSTS

There are a myriad of different assignments at posts. An example of a post order can be checking identifications at an assigned area. Another possible post order can be checking tickets or baggage at the spectator entrance. Another could be observing crowd behavior at a special event, strike or the scene of a recent fire.

Examples of posts for a sporting event include:

Main door	Locker-rooms entrance/exit
Hallways	Spectator entrance/exit
VIP entrance/exit	Seating areas
Media entrance/exit	Parking lots
Athlete entrance/exit	Delivery entrance/exit

PRE-EVENT BRIEFINGS

The security supervisor should have briefings before the security officers go to their posts. These meetings should be brief and explain/remind everyone of what is expected. They should be planned and structured, using a pre-designed outline of what is to be covered. The supervisor should go over different responsibilities, objectives and approaches. They should make sure that everyone has their proper uniforms on and is ready to meet the public! A review and check of equipment should be performed. The supervisor should make sure that officers know how to use everything and that each piece of equipment is functional. This is especially important with weapons and communications equipment.

Most important, ascertain that security officers know exactly what is expected of them! Clearing up any questions they may have is an absolute necessity.

TALKING TO CROWDS

Communicating with crowds properly may prevent problems from occurring. Unfortunately, in many instances proper preparation has not been made to accomplish this. When addressing a crowd there are some steps that a security supervisor—as well as his/her subordinates—should follow:

1. Think before saying something so that the message is *clear* and *concise*.
2. When trying to relay a message, first get the crowd's attention through sound (whistle or clap) or verbal message ("May I have your attention?").
3. Speak slowly and clearly.
4. Project voice to the farthest person but do not try to yell.
5. Use eye contact to express authority. Be somewhat direct with eye contact.
6. Try to make eye contact with every person in the group.
7. Be calm and relaxed.
8. When directing a crowd to move on, do not make exceptions allowing anyone to remain.
9. Be firm. Be assertive.
10. Be polite.

POST-EVENT BRIEFING

Debriefing should *always* take place after the event. Here the security supervisor goes over how everything took place. There should be an overall summary between the security supervisor and venue management. Comments and recommendations should be discussed.

Some tips can include discussions on any possible problems with the security personnel. It also should contain comments on the overall security of the special event. This includes exterior and interior security.

SAMPLE POST-EVENT ASSESSMENT FORM

Event: _____

Date: (From - To) _____

Attendance: _____

# of Supervisors: _____

# of Security: _____

Promoter: _____

# of Accidents/Injuries: _____

# of Incidents: _____

Brief summary of any incidents, accidents or injuries: _____

_____

_____

Comments: _____

_____

_____

Recommendations: _____

_____

_____

The crowd management process can be conceptualized as a system with various components. These components include:
- Selection
- Application/Interviewing
- Testing
- Training

SELECTION

The type of individual hired is a key managerial aspect in any job. It determines the level of performance expected. It is especially important for crowd management. As a security manager, the type of individual hired is one who is smart, calm but decisive, assertive with an ability to communicate precisely and professionally.

Other personal skills should include:
- team player
- service attitude
- mature personality

Many times, security managers hire their personnel en masse for special events without doing any testing or without in-depth interviews. There should be minimum standards established.

SAMPLE SECURITY OFFICER REQUIREMENTS

High School Diploma
Previous training in public relations
State certified security officer license - if applicable
Minimum of 5 years of security experience preferred
Excellent physical condition
Possible college degrees - criminal justice, asset protection, public relations majors
No convictions other than minor traffic violations

RECRUITMENT

Recruitment is essential to acquire efficient security officers. Recruitment establishes the parameters of the selection pool. Recruitment can be accomplished by a variety of approaches. A few that might be applicable to special event staffing are:

Visit different schools:	Recruit students majoring in criminal justice, security programs. Also recruit students with customer service skills and previous security jobs.
Advertising in paper/use of media:	Good method because it will get many applicants but many times it attracts people who want to work a short time before becoming a police officer.
E-mailing:	E-mail security/campus directors at different colleges and universities. This can be an effective way to acquire qualified applicants. This may work well with agencies that only require periodic staffing.

APPLICATIONS/ INTERVIEWING

Applications must be studied carefully, since job seekers tend to exaggerate. Some things to look for during the screening process include:
- Indications of being clearly overqualified
- Unexplained gaps in employment history
- Gaps in residences

- Indications of lack of job stability
- Inadequate references

When interviewing a prospective employee, yes or no questions should not be asked – at least not during the initial phases of the interview. These questions do not require the interviewee to think on the spot and explain themselves clearly and concisely. These latter skills are what is assessed during an interview. They are essential attributes for crowd management personnel to possess. While interviewing, answers to questions should be compared to the application and resume. The job candidate's verbal responses, the resume and the application form should all be audited against each other.

TESTING

After the interview stage, certain specific tests are recommended. These tests may include:

Psychological assessment such as the Minnesota Multi-phasic Personality Inventory (MMPI) – these assessments can reveal habits, fears, sexual attitude and symptoms of mental problems. They may also help to classify a person's personality.

Honesty tests – these help employers screen job candidates because they measure trustworthiness and attitude towards honesty.

Drug tests – can help because employers expect their workers to perform their duties free of intoxicating substances. Also, some security service firms advertise on the basis of their drug screening efforts.

Background investigations should also be required, including a federal background check. An applicant's criminal history is an area of concern to employers especially when an applicant is applying for security employment. Failure to effectively screen personnel who are in positions of trust and who subsequently violate that trust can result in extensive civil litigation.

TRAINING: A SUPERVISOR'S RESPONSIBILITY TO THE EMPLOYEE

When dealing with crowds, it is important that security personnel be trained effectively to handle various situations. There are many approaches that can be taken to training. Essentially what must be done is to ensure that all necessary competency areas are covered thoroughly. A job task analysis should be performed before initiating training to insure that this occurs. Once this is done, a list of topics or competency areas can be constructed.

Sample Training Topics

Crowd control
Report writing
Safety
Patrol techniques
Traffic control
Bomb threats
First aid
Fire prevention/control
Emergency planning
Alarm systems
Hazardous materials
VIP protection
Hostage situations
Public relations

Delivering Instruction:

- Be patient; keep the learner interested; find out learner's background; prepare for instruction.

- Determine what must be taught; decide *how much* to teach.
- Maintain records of training in order to know how much has been taught and which person has been taught what by whom.

Orienting New Officers:

This phase of training tells each new employee what is expected of them and also what the employee expects (feedback). Orientation also provides an overview of job requirements and tasks.

On-The-Job Training Phase:

- Explain and demonstrate each job step.
- Make sure employee comprehends!
- Document training by having forms with all areas that have been covered and taught and have this signed by the employee.

EQUIPMENT

Another integral aspect of a security officer's training is his/her knowledge of equipment. There is a wide variety of equipment that the security officer must be able to handle at any given moment. Magnetometers, hand-held wands, flashlights, radios and first-aid equipment are all indispensable to any security job. Metal detectors can be very important in helping to ensure that weapons do not enter the premises. Specific, documented instruction should be given on each piece of equipment used during both routine and emergency conditions.

CONCLUSION

Preparing for a special event is a considerable undertaking. Persons with supervisory responsibility who are involved in asset protection must approach this task in a serious manner. The supervisor should be detailed, thorough and flexible in his/her approach. Continuous professional growth is strongly recommended. Constant checking of personnel performance is required. Nothing can be left to chance when providing protection at a special event.

BIBLIOGRAPHY

Bishop, P.C. (1998) *Crowd Control Management and Procedures*. In Davies, S.J. & Minion, R.R. (Eds.) *Protection Officer Training Manual*. Boston: Butterworth-Heinemann.

Davies, S.J. & Minion, R.R. (Eds.). (1998). *Protection Officer Training Manual*. Boston: Butterworth-Heinemann.

Estes, D.S. (1995) *Supervision and Training*. In Davies, S.J. & Minion, R.R. (Eds.) *Security Supervisor Training Manual*. Boston: Butterworth-Heinemann.

Hertig, C.A. (1995) *Supervisor's Role In Training*. In Davies, S.J. & Minion, R.R. (Eds.) *Security Supervisor Training Manual*. Boston: Butterworth-Heinemann.

Hertig, C.A. (1985, June). Keep Your Guards Posted. *Security Management, 65-66*.

Holm, A.A. (1998) Traffic Control Procedures. In Davies, S.J. & Minion, R.R. (Eds.) *Protection Officer Training Manual*. Boston: Butterworth-Heinemann.

Millsaps, M.J. (1998, Spring). The F.A.S.T. Approach. *Protection News*.

Poulin, K.C. (1992). *Special Events: Avoiding the Disaster*. Florida: International Foundation for Protection Officers.

Purpura, P. (1991). *Security and Loss Prevention*. Boston: Butterworth-Heinemann.

Tyo K. (1996, Jan-Mar). "Olympic Security: A Crowd Management Interview." Crowd Management, 6-11.

Sherwood, C.W. (1998, August) "Security Management for a Major Event." *Security Management,* 9-16.

Task Force on Crowd Control and Safety, (29 Sept. 1998) *"Crowd Management: Report on the Task Force on Crowd Control and Safety."* http://www.crowdsafe.com.

FOR MORE INFORMATION

Special Events Planning by K.C. Poulin is published by the International Foundation for Protection Officers. Call (941) 430-0534 or visit www.ifpo.com

The Protection Officer Training Manual is the official text for the Certified Protection Officer (CPO) program. The Manual contains chapters on Crowd Management, Public Relations, Emergency Situations, Traffic Control, etc. It is available for purchase from Butterworth-Heinemann. Call (800) 366-2665 or visit www.bh.com.

The Professional Security Television Network has various videos related to Crowd Management, as well as many other titles. Call (800) 942-7786 or visit www.pstn.pwpl.com

York College of Pennsylvania through the Special Programs Office offers seminars in Crowd Management, Public Relations and other related topics. Call (717) 815-1451 or special-programs@ycp.edu or visit www.ycp.edu/.

SUPERVISING DURING SPECIAL EVENTS
QUIZ

1.   In some cases projecting a positive image and relating well to visitors, customers and the public at large is the sole reason for the existence of a security organization.
             ☐ T   ☐ F

2.   List the five different types of crowds:
            a) _____
            b) _____
            c) _____
            d) _____
            e) _____

3.   List the five psychological factors of crowd formation:
            a) _____
            b) _____
            c) _____
            d) _____
            e) _____

4.   In regards to communication at an event the security supervisor should establish a method for _____, _____ and _____ to be able to contact each other.

5.   Protection officers should have all their lines of communications checked for both _____ _____ and _____ capabilities at the beginning of each shift.

6.   What element is most essential during events, especially when there is an emergency?
       a)   Positive image
       b)   Access control
       c)   Traffic control
       d)   Force

7.   Checking the proficiency of officers and the appearance/image of traffic control points is an essential supervisory function.
            □ T   □ F

8.   Medical personnel (EMTs) to visitors should be a ratio of:
       a)   1:500
       b)   1:750
       c)   1:1000
       d)   1:2500
       e)   None of the above

9.   In an indoor facility what is the necessary "Clear Zone" around the perimeter that should be maintained for evacuation purposes?
       a)   Three-foot
       b)   Twenty-foot
       c)   Hundred-foot
       d)   Six-foot

10.   The type of individual hired is a key managerial aspect in a security supervisor's job as it determines the level of performance expected.
            □ T   □ F

SECURITY AND MEDICAL RESPONSE
by David W. Hill, CPO, EMCA

As the subject matter of this chapter is too broad to be taught in depth over the next few pages, this section will demonstrate the relationship between security and emergency response. Rather than providing detailed, "how-to" information, the discussion will focus on the importance of developing a range of skills. It is the responsibility of every security professional to become skilled in security and emergency response through continuing education.

WHAT IS EMERGENCY RESPONSE?

First aid may be defined as the temporary care of the sick or injured. This care extends from the moment you assume responsibility to a time when the patient can be transferred to the care of a medical facility. Temporary care could include the saving of a life and preventing injuries from worsening. The three principles of first aid are:
1. Preserve life
2. Prevent an injury or illness from becoming worse
3. Promote recovery

The growth of emergency medicine as a specialty in the last decade has enhanced the quality of care given to the injured. The competence of all emergency medicine providers has come under close examination.

The Emergency Medical System (E.M.S.) developed and controlled by local provincial and state governments, is the medical system by which patients are transferred to the nearest or required medical assistance. During a basic E.M.S. response the local hospital or ambulance dispatch center receives the emergency call. All pertinent information is quickly recorded through local protocol and an immediate decision is made as to the nature and priority of the call. If an ambulance is required, it is dispatched immediately and the personnel are advised of the situation. The ambulance crew are in constant communication with the dispatch center and relay patient information as they progress through their response. Call information can be relayed from dispatch to the hospital or a radio patch can be initiated enabling the ambulance crew to speak directly to the hospital staff. The patient is then transferred to the hospital which has been notified in advance, as quickly as the nature of the call dictates. Upon arrival at the hospital, the patient's vitals and history are submitted.

ECONOMICS OF SECURITY AND EMERGENCY RESPONSE

Introduction

Over the last ten years we have witnessed an historical revolution in progress. The world population is at an all time high, while unemployment is at an all time low. Famine and crime are rampant and many nations are at war due to intolerance and economic hardship. New diseases such as AIDS are challenging mankind, while forgotten diseases are making a comeback and have arrived in North America. Tuberculosis, to name one, is very contagious and often fatal if left untreated. The security/emergency medical responder would be well advised in today's society to become familiar with all aspects of disease prevention. An ounce of prevention is worth a pound of cure, especially since your life as a medical responder may depend on your knowledge and expertise.

When dealing with patient trauma involving blood, the security officer should wear medical gloves to prevent cross-contamination of diseases such as Hepatitis B, a liver disease. Due in part to such medical considerations, a new breed of security officer, professionals skilled in both security and emergency response, is being created.

Economic Factors

One of the main focuses of corporations today is streamlining the workforce – getting the maximum for the minimum. Effective cost reduction is essential to any corporation wishing to be successful in today's market. Many jobs are being lost due to automation and cutbacks. To ensure your position as a security officer you must seriously consider cross-training.

The old adage of giving someone their money's worth is now becoming a matter of survival in the workplace. An interesting note is that you will often find that many corporations are willing to pay fewer people higher wages in exchange for varied skills.

The various responsibilities of the modern-day security officer are expanding due to cost cutting and the personal safety issue. You must be aware that the workforce of any corporation is a community within itself. Each person has individual life experiences, difficulties and a medical history. As a security officer you may be called upon to respond to a variety of medical emergencies. How well you handle such situations may well be the difference between life or death.

Legal and Medical Obligations

Your responsibilities to your employer and workforce may be legal, medical or both simultaneously. It is important to familiarize yourself with both your legal and medical obligations to ensure you are aware and in control of any given situation.

Consider the following scenario: an employee is observed trying to leave the job while appearing to conceal something. You politely ask the employee what it is and if you may see it. The employee states that he/she is doing nothing wrong and that it really isn't any of your business. You, as a company agent, persist in your questioning and an argument ensues (Note: If this were a store customer you could be getting into legalities with which you should be familiar.). The security officer at this point could be dealing with laws such as assault, unlawful confinement, illegal search and seizure or unlawful arrest if the situation proceeds that far. What if the suspect suddenly keels over clutching their chest? You must be prepared to switch from your role as a security officer to that of an emergency medical responder. The suspect, now referred to as a patient, is still angry at you and refuses your assistance. What would you do and how would you react to this situation? Cross-training could provide you with the appropriate skills to deal with such circumstances.

Everyone Has Rights

If you were to sit down and study the *American Bill of Rights* and the *Canadian Charter of Rights and Freedoms*, you would quickly realize people, including security professionals, have a lot of rights. Through your studies you will become aware of state, provincial and federal laws. Any infringement on a person's rights may lead to losing a case in court and could cause you, your department and your employer great embarrassment. An interesting point is that laws protecting people's rights relating to crime are just as binding when dealing with a medical response. The right of privacy is a basic and fiercely guarded privilege in our society that cannot be violated even for the best of intentions.

We in the security profession are not peace officers, nor do security officers normally have peace officer status. However, the Canadian railway police (security) possess full police powers within a specified distance from railroad property and security officers employed by the Public Service of Canada are designated public officers under the Financial Administration Act. In the United States, some states require that protection officers be "commissioned" or accredited as peace officers by the state. Protection officers in these states are granted full or limited police authority and are also subject to the same legal restrictions placed on this authority by the U.S. Constitution, state statutes and local ordinances.

Even during a medical response, security officers usually have no more powers of arrest than those of an average citizen. While responding to an on-site medical call, you must attain some sort of consent. That is, the person's consent to be touched and aided. The following are guidelines for acquiring consent:
1.   A person may not be coerced into medical treatment if they do not want it.
2.   A person has the supreme legal right to be free from being touched against his/her will.
3.   Treatment given to a person, even if in good faith, and performed with a degree of competence, may still be held to constitute assault unless proper consent has been obtained from the patient.
4.   Consent may be given in writing, given orally or may be inferred by the actions of the patient. Something as simple as a hand being held out for help will suffice.
5.   Consent must be voluntary.
6.   The patient must be mentally and physically able to decide whether or not they want treatment. Watch out for the gray area here. If the patient is deemed incapable of rational decision

regarding their own welfare, quickly contact a doctor and or the police to take the patient into protective custody

7.   If the patient is unconscious, the consent is automatically implied. The law will regard the unconscious patient in immediate need and will assume that the patient would have consented to assistance.

The only occasion where an act can be performed on a patient without his/her consent is an emergency. An emergency allows for the necessary treatment to be undertaken or for the extension of the treatment. Since no consent has been given, the burden of proof rests with the care giver. Thus, the following criteria are necessary and should be well documented to prove that an emergency existed.

1.   A threat to the life or health of the patient must exist.
2.   The threat must be immediate.
3.   It must be impossible to obtain the consent of the patient, either because of physical incapability, such as unconsciousness, or legal incapacity. If the latter is the case, it must also be impossible to obtain the consent of the person legally qualified to consent for the patient.

Good Samaritan Legislation

The Good Samaritan Legislation focuses on the emergency situation that is thrust upon the individual when not at work. Such situations might include the car accident while you are on vacation or the person next to you in a restaurant choking.

In Canada, under Common Law, there is no legal obligation to rescue or assist a person in trouble. The obligation is of a moral or humanitarian one naturally. Good Samaritan Legislation is intended to encourage people to volunteer emergency assistance without fear of liability unless "gross negligence" occurs. Gross negligence could be defined as a standard of care well below the reasonably expected standard due to the circumstances. The law recognizes that a professional who stops to assist at a roadside accident does not usually have their usual "tools" and thus the expected standard of care is modified under the circumstances. Common Law holds the care giver to that standard of care expected of a similar person of similar training and experience in similar circumstances. A good rule of thumb is to only provide first aid measures to the skill level that you are presently certified. Many first aid students have expressed concern over being sued for negligence or a wrongful act during an attempt to save a life. If you follow the above rule of thumb, repercussions will be few and far between. For example, if you were assisting a person who was choking, you would follow your first aid protocols and make your attempt to assist; but you would not take a knife and perform a tracheotomy.

The person providing assistance in an emergency does, however, have an obligation (duty of care) to carry through any assistance initiated. One cannot begin to rescue a victim and then stop.

Roles of Security/Emergency Medical Responder

Corporations today expect and depend on their security staff to be effective during stressful situations. To be an effective officer you must acquire a firm grasp of legalities, roles and responsibilities, and develop the ability to differentiate between legal and medical concerns and act accordingly. Consider the following list of humanitarian duties for the responding officer:

1.   Primary responsibility for the safety of the patient.
2.   The administering of life-saving care and treatment.
3.   Ensure comfort and emotional well-being of the patient.
4.   Maintain respect for the patient's privacy.
5.   Maintain respect for human behavior and religious beliefs.

With regard to different aspects of the role of the security/emergency medical responder, there are other responsibilities which include:

Safety: Ensure the safety at all times of yourself, the patient, public and co-workers in the environment.

Confidentiality: In order to respect the privacy of a patient, all matters must be kept confidential and only pertinent information given to the appropriate authorities. Confidentiality must always be strictly adhered to, both on and off the job.

In the event of an on-site disaster, the responding officer may have to assume two identities. During an emergency medical response, you may also be required to perform a variety of security skills such as traffic control, crowd management, scene and evidence protection, note taking and report writing, human relations, security awareness, considering legal and ethical matters, and keeping management apprized of the situation.

Conduct and Attitude

The manner in which a security/emergency medical responder conducts him/herself and cares for a patient may be as important as the emergency care measures. Try to develop a working rapport with the patient(s), maintain a professional attitude and demonstrate empathy to put the patient at ease. Remember, nothing sounds as good as "you'll be ok" when you are injured or frightened. A simple gesture, such as touching the patient's shoulder when addressing them, will instill trust and enhance responder/patient communication. Apathy, on the other hand, can quickly destroy all patient cooperation, your personal reputation as a care giver and your security department's reputation overall. Emergency medical providers should, therefore, attempt to follow these behavior guidelines:

1.   Always try to maintain control even though the scene around you may be chaotic. A confident and professional manner will be transmitted to the patient and may help to alleviate anxiety and fear.
2.   Conversation should be kept as neutral as possible and should provide constant reassurance to the patient that everything possible is being done for him/her.
3.   Be aware that bystanders and co-workers may also need reassurance during a crisis.

Departmental Training

Unfortunately, there are security/emergency medical professionals who attain their accreditation in their chosen field and then become complacent. Remember that when you achieve your C.P.O. or E.M.S. status, you have just begun your professional training. The three key words are Train! Train! and Retrain!

The sharpest knife will eventually lose it's edge if it is not re-sharpened occasionally. Security departments must continually practice their required skills to maintain an edge. Security and emergency medical response skills must become automatic and second nature if you are to be effective in the field. The time to read the manual is now – not during a crisis situation. There are many varied pieces of rescue equipment involved in security and emergency medical response work. Being familiar with the technology is essential to any successful rescue operation.

One interesting method of maintaining security officers' emergency medical response knowledge is to encourage the officers to volunteer at the local ambulance service. The training they receive will be to local, state or provincial standards and practical experience in emergency medical skills. The benefits received are compounded both for the officer and the security department as a whole. A working relationship between the security department and the local hospital will be firmly established enhancing professional credibility. The hospital will have greater confidence in the corporate security department if the hospital is involved in ongoing emergency medical response officer training. The security officers will seem to be more than just dominant figures at the local "Company." This kind of exposure will definitely strengthen the relationships between the security department and the townsfolk. As the security officer responds to medical emergencies he/she will demonstrate community spirit.

Another way to maintain the skill level of the security department is to have the security officers teach first aid and C.P.R. to the employees. Most corporations today sponsor an ongoing first aid program for employees and sometimes their spouses. This is an excellent opportunity for security and the workforce to meet and develop a mutual understanding and appreciation of their individual roles within the company.

Time should be set aside during staff meetings to discuss security/emergency medical situations that could develop within your organization. This will give each member of the security team a chance to visualize on-site scenarios and related problem solving. Disasters are not predictable, but responses must be. To reiterate, Train, Train and Retrain!!

CONCLUSION

The responsibility to attain professional credibility lies with each security officer. As the responsibilities of security departments increase and security professionals are required to handle situations that were previously dealt with by outside personnel, it becomes most imperative that security officers expand their capabilities. If our profession is to achieve and maintain the standards we are setting for ourselves, we must continually strive to improve our skills and meet corporate expectations through continuing education and training.

Security and emergency response are now considered to be related professions. Can you imagine a more fulfilling and important challenge than being responsible for the life of an injured employee?

SECURITY AND MEDICAL RESPONSE
QUIZ

1. First aid may be defined as the temporary care of the _____ and injured.

2. The competency of all emergency medicine _____ has come under close examination.

3. A person may be _____ into medical treatment if they do not want it.

4. Ensure the safety at all times of _____ the patient, public and co-workers in the environment.

5. Be aware that _____ and co-workers may also need reassurance during a crisis.

6. Cross-contamination of diseases such as AIDS, tuberculosis and Hepatitis B can be prevented by the use of proper safeguarding techniques.
    ☐ T   ☐ F

7. If a workman is injured with a broken arm, he is obligated to let you begin first aid because you are a security/emergency medical responder.
    ☐ T   ☐ F

8. The Good Samaritan Legislation allows a person to take whatever measures necessary in order to save a person's life.
    ☐ T   ☐ F

9. Once you achieve any certification, retraining is not necessary because you will always be competent in your level of skill.
    ☐ T   ☐ F

10. Confidentiality only applies to you while you work.
    ☐ T   ☐ F

CONSIDERING CONTRACT SECURITY
by Christopher A. Hertig, CPP, CPO

Contract security is simply the providing of security services to another entity in exchange for a fee. It generally takes the form of contract guard service where a contract agency supplies a set number of guard man-hours to a client. In most cases a flat fee is charged, although fee structure can be modified if overtime hours are ordered or special services (strike coverage, armed officers, additional supervision, etc.) requested.

Contracting out or outsourcing makes good management sense when one of the following criteria is met:

1. The client cannot perform the service for themselves due to lack of expertise, logistical, cost or legal restrictions.
2. The service is temporary or unusual in nature.
3. Personnel costs (wages, benefits, taxes, etc.) make the service prohibitively expensive for the client organization.

There are many examples of situations where contracting out security service is logical:

1. Nuclear power plants where refueling and repair periods require greater access control, in the form of increased guard posts, due to additional workers onsite with more access points open.
2. Construction projects that require traffic control, fire watch and theft prevention.
3. Stadiums, concerts, colleges or high schools that host public events and need crowd and traffic control.
4. Autograph sessions, auctions, Christmas sales at retail stores, and film debuts that call for increased security and public contact.
5. Strikes, which mandate surveillance, crowd and traffic control.
6. Jewelry stores that need off premises alarm monitoring to meet insurance carrier requirements.
7. Commercial central alarm stations that subcontract alarm response through a local contract security company for their clients.
8. Industrial plants that need supplemental security coverage to cover for in-house guards during vacation.
9. Political figures, business VIPs or entertainment celebrities that require protection from over-zealous spectators; while in transit or after receiving sudden, unexpected threats.
10. Payrolls or bank deposits transported by armored car firms.

The following are generally considered to be advantages to contracting out for security services.

1. Lower cost due to flat billing rate as opposed to incurring wages and attendant labor costs (30% above the wage cost).
2. Administrative streamlining where the client firm only has to pay the bills and make sure they are getting the service they require.
3. Flexibility of manpower if needs change, on a temporary basis.
4. Ease of removing undesirable employees.
5. Elimination/preclusion of guard unions.
6. Ease of rule enforcement due to the outside, independent nature of the security force.
7. Reduction of liability due to independent contractor rule.

Disadvantages of having a contract guard service include.

1. Lower quality of personnel who make inferior wages.
2. Lower loyalty of personnel.
3. Lack of control due to putting in another layer of management via the contract firm. Asset protection is an integral management function that may not be properly outsourced in all circumstances.
4. Poor liaison with law enforcement, which does not want to work with unprofessional personnel.
5. Liability protection is almost always absent due to the client directing and ratifying contractor conduct, strict liability, intentional torts and non-delegable duties. Perhaps more important; having a contractor involved creates an additional target for a plaintiff's lawyers. It makes it easy for them to "divide and conquer" where the contractor and client are fighting each other in court.

Another form of contract security is to hire off-duty police. The advantages to doing this are:
1.   High caliber, professionally screened personnel.
2.   Well trained, experienced officers used to handling a diverse range of situations.
3.   Increased investigative capability due to training, experience and access to official database.
4.   Improved liaison with local law enforcement agencies.
5.   The ability to have armed personnel where legal restrictions may make this capacity unattainable.
6.   Possible utilization of public resources such as vehicles, radios, investigative equipment, etc.
7.   Arrest authority possessed by police can aid in dealing with troublemakers.
8.   Greater deterrent to crime.

Disadvantages to using off-duty police are:
1.   Police react to, rather than prevent problems.
2.   Training/socialization may lead them to be abrasive and /or brutal.
3.   Lack of a customer service ethic or client orientation.
4.   Conflict of interest between public and private role in crime control.
5.   Conflict of interest regarding restricted information.
6.   Police may see their secondary employment as unimportant.
7.   Costs may be high, and there is really no competition.
8.   Legal issues may arise due to the interests that officers were acting to further.
9.   Control over the officers and the ability to terminate the contract is severely limited – clients may fear future reductions in police response time if officers are removed.
10.   There may be illegalities involved due to tax laws, private detective statutes, etc.

Alarm monitoring may also be contracted out. The advantages to doing this are:
1.   Costs, especially start-up expenses, are minimized.
2.   Maintenance and monitoring with all of the associated labor costs/concerns are eliminated.
3.   Insurance company requirements are met and premium reductions obtained.
4.   Off-site storage and management of alarm information.
5.   Administrative streamlining of alarm monitoring and response functions and easier budgeting.

Disadvantages of contract central stations include:
1.   Possible delays in obtaining alarm activity information.
2.   Extra charges for monitoring, response (in some cases) and dedicated lines.
3.   Lack of control over contractor personnel management.

Career success in contract security can be obtained by:
1.   Taking human resources management courses and developing expertise in this area. Most of the daily operational issues in contract security involve recruitment, selection, scheduling and payroll. Competent supervisory and managerial personnel must be knowledgeable of the HR process. They must also master the hiring, training and motivation of personnel in order to provide quick, efficient service on demand.
2.   Studying sales techniques and client relations so that contracts can be obtained – and maintained! While not all service firm providers are sales reps, meeting with current and prospective clients is a key function shared periodically by all management personnel.
3.   Becoming thoroughly conversant with state and local laws that govern contract security services providers. This includes licensing and training requirements. It also encompasses employment laws such as wage and hour laws, civil rights protection acts, etc.
4.   Being knowledgeable about the business that the client firm is in. This enables the contractor to provide higher level of service. Some successful firms specialize in particular market sectors (nuclear, healthcare, shopping center, etc.)
5.   Being able to obtain technical expertise for investigations, security assessments, etc. when needed. Few people in contract security have any real technical expertise; however, the need for this knowledge arises periodically. Smart service providers can deliver it to a client in short order.
6.   Networking in professional organizations, such as the National Burglar and Fire Alarm Association, American Society for Industry trends, as well as to make contact with clients and employers.

7.   Being licensed to carry weapons, conduct investigations or becoming certified as an instructor are also useful in the security service field. The need for armed personnel or investigators may or may not be constant, but sooner or later a potential client will have need of these services. Additionally, being able to instruct in accordance with state or provincial laws or company standards (Crisis Prevention Institute, Pressure Point Control Techniques, Inc., etc.) can give a practitioner added value.

FOR MORE INFORMATION

The Art of Successful Security Management by Dennis Dalton, a noted expert on the successful use of contract security services, discusses management concepts that can be applied to both contract and proprietary settings. Available from Butterworth-Heinemann, 225 Wildwood Avenue, Woburn, MA 01801 (800) 366-2665 or www.bh.com.

Private Security and the Law by Charles Nemeth is an excellent reference book for instructors and graduate students. The book contains chapters on history, regulation and licensing, civil liability, liaison with law enforcement and other legal topics available from Anderson Publishing Co., 2035 Reading Road Cincinnati, OH 45202 (513) 421-4142.

A Primer in Private Security by Mahesh Nalla and Graeme Newman contains much valuable and unique information on the scope of private security, history, legal aspects and how security fits into corporate culture. There are also chapters on Private Security and the Military Model, Security and the Management Model and the Scientific Model: Reducing and Preventing Loss. *A Primer in Private Security* is available from: Harrow and Heston, Publishers, Stuyvesant Plaza, P.O. Box 3934, Albany, NY 12203.

The *National Association of Security and Investigative Regulators,* www.nasir.org., is an organization of those personnel who train, regulate and license investigators and security service firms. Members represent state and provincial regulatory entities throughout the U.S. and Canada. NASIR provides a link between licensees and government regulatory agencies as well as end users of security and investigative services.

The *National Association of Security Companies*, 2670 Union Avenue Extended, Suite 710, Memphis, TN 38112-4416 (901) 323-0173 or (901) 458-0624 fax is a professional organization of contract security firms. NASCO works within the contract security industry through legislative initiatives, information sharing and liaison with other professional organizations.

The *Private Security Services Council* of the American Society for Industrial Security promotes the exchange of information among providers of security equipment and services. The Council can be reached through ASIS headquarters at 1625 Prince Street, Alexandria, VA 22314 (703) 518-1518 or www.asisonline.org.

CONSIDERING CONTRACT SECURITY
QUIZ

1.   Contracting out or outsourcing makes good management sense when one of the following criteria is met: (Select best answer)
   a)   The client cannot perform the service for themselves due to lack of expertise, logistical, cost or legal restrictions.
   b)   The service is temporary or unusual in nature.
   c)   Personnel costs (wages, benefits, taxes, etc.) make the service prohibitively expensive for the client organizations.
   d)   All of the above.

2.	Administrative streamlining, where the client firms only have to pay the bills and make sure they are getting the service they require, is an advantage to contracting out the security services.
	☐ T ☐ F

3.	Another form of contract security is to hire _____ _____.

4.	Police may see their secondary employment as unimportant.
	☐ T ☐ F

5.	Taking _____ _____ _____ courses and developing expertise in this area may add to career success in contract security.

6.	Asset management is an integral management function that may not be properly outsourced in all circumstances.
	☐ T ☐ F

7.	A disadvantage of alarm monitoring contracting is that there may be possible delays in obtaining alarm activity information.
	☐ T ☐ F

8.	Contract security is simply the providing of security services to another entity in exchange for a _____.

9.	It's very difficult to remove undesirable employees in a contract situation.
	☐ T ☐ F

10.	Strikes, which mandate surveillance, crowd and traffic control may be ideal situations to consider contract security.
	☐ T ☐ F

OUTSOURCING IN SECURITY
by Rolland G. Watson, CSS, CPO

Sometime during your career as a security supervisor of a proprietary guard force or protection specialty unit, your corporation will consider outsourcing. Outsourcing is a reduction in personnel caused by a shifting of organizational responsibility to outside agencies. We see this occurring every day in financial institutions and other large organizations. Downsizing or de-cascading reduces cash flow and improves profitability in the short term.

You may be approached by the chief executive officer of your institution and be advised that you must outsource your security service providers. At that moment, you should be able to explain, demonstrate, or provide a cost-benefit analysis either for or against outsourcing. Your officers hope that you, as their representative, can take an approach that can save their jobs.

If you fail to retain your force, your job is going to change; if you retain your force you may have to work more efficiently. No matter what the approach, you will have your job cut out for you. You must be sure that you have all costs, pros and cons, and other specifics for both types of services.

You will become involved in conducting an outsource security survey and the contracting process. These are not to be taken lightly as they will require all your management and human relations skills to ensure your organization has the best security that can be obtained at a price that is affordable to the resource allocators. The selection and contracting process will consume time that would ordinarily be spent in your function as a supervisor – plan on alternatives for completing your day-to-day job.

Even though the corporation has decided to outsource, it doesn't mean they want inferior security services. Every organization wants quality at the most affordable price. Who will be responsible for obtaining and contracting for that quality? You will! The service will be what you make it. With that in mind, let's look at some fundamentals of determining cost.

DETERMINING COST

There are several factors that must be included when costs are determined and each identified factor is as important as the next. You should:

- Conduct a thorough cost-benefit analysis of both your proprietary service and anticipated contract service.
- Identify liability issues and costs. Consult with the supplier of your organization's current liability policy for your proprietary force. Determine:
  - a) What are your present costs?
  - b) What will be saved if you outsource?

In some cases, depending on the type of business, there won't be a savings. Financial institutions, for example, have a blanket liability policy that covers your proprietary force at no additional cost. Determine liability coverage and cost for:
  - a) Armed Proprietary
  - b) Armed Contract
  - c) Unarmed Proprietary
  - d) Unarmed Contract
- Quantify wages and benefits. How do you compensate your proprietary force? What is the cost of your organizational benefit package? Traditionally, a benefit package may be fourteen to forty-one percent in addition to salary. In outsourcing, you should identify:
  - a) Current salary and benefits.
  - b) Locality scales in relationship to benefits and salary.
  - c) Incremental longevity proprietary scales.
  - d) Contract cost per hour versus salary per hour.
  - e) Contract benefits.
  - f) Compare and contrast after analysis retention and turnover rates between proprietary and contract.

It is not unheard of for some contract security forces to experience a turnover rate of over 800% per year. Will a turnover rate of that proportion be tolerated by your directors, suppliers, and customers?

- Provisions—uniforms and equipment. A proprietary force is normally equipped by the organization with uniforms, radios, equipment, office space, phones, etc. When you outsource you need to identify:

  a)   Cost of organization property to be transferred.
  b)   Who will be charged for maintenance or replacement?
  c)   How will telephone bills, lost equipment, breakage, be recovered?
  d)   Key and inventory control processes. Who pays if locks or equipment must be replaced?
  e)   Will the contractor be required to purchase on-hand supplies and materials as a condition of the contract?

These are just a few of the questions that need to be answered when you conduct your cost-benefit analysis in provisions, uniforms and equipment. Other headaches that can occur:

  a)   Who owns the firearms carried by the guards?
  b)   Must the organization maintain an armory?
  c)   What happens to patrol vehicles?
  d)   Who provides weapons and vehicle training?
  e)   How often must officers qualify with firearms and safe driving requirements?

- Training Issues. The number one liability issue in security services is training. More officers, supervisors and corporations are being sued today under the concept of failure to train than ever before in history. When you have a proprietary or contract guard service, the organization, the contract service and all the security supervisors, directors or managers are both corporately and individually liable if they know, allow, or fail to provide training that any reasonable person would conclude was a responsibility of that entity or person.

What types of training will you require to maintain the high image of your corporation? These requirements and costs must be included in the contract as an expense borne by the contractor. This training will need to be documented and proof retained by the contract manager. Training is normally accomplished to some standard set out in the service provider's job description. In security service, some training issues are:

  a)   Use of force.
  b)   Use of deadly force or drawing the handgun.
  c)   Protection of people, organizational assets and the protection officer individually.
  d)   Physical fitness, deportment, conduct.
  e)   Police involvements and conduct prejudicial to organizational standards.

Without a comprehensive list of training requirements, a failure to accomplish a task or duty could have severe liability issues for the organization and contract company. It is your job to identify training needs and to ensure they are specified in the contract, and are conducted and documented.

Other issues that you must consider are:

1.   Identify the strengths and weaknesses of proprietary and contract services.
2.   Create a matrix or checklist that delineates both positive and negative attributes of proprietary and contract security services. Itemize the list to provide a total comparison of both services. Ensure you include:

  - Current costs.
  - Projected costs based on inflation or contractual raises.
  - Training costs.
  - Liability costs.
  - Recruitment, retention, and screening costs.

There are some costs that are intangible but should be entered into the matrix: loyalty, dependability, honesty, integrity and commitment to the organization. These intangibles may cost you more money when outsourced.

SOLICITING THE CONTRACT BID

You should create a specification sheet for the outsourced positions and duties for which you want to contract. Develop a list of current reputable contract services in your area and mail them a solicitation to bid on your contract. Check national publications and state licensing authorities for additional companies to contract. Hold face-to-face interviews, and check with other corporations in your area to see who they use and if they are satisfied. Then check with your local law enforcement agencies to see which companies they have the best rapport with. Go and observe the prospective contractor. Do not use companies that have poorly maintained vehicles and sloppy, overweight guards. Does the prospective contractor reflect your corporate image?

WRITING THE CONTRACT

Your contract must be specific in its requirements – nothing should be left to the imagination or speculation of either party. You need to include such things as initial and ongoing training requirements, who will oversee your contract, hours of coverage, uniforms, equipment and related costs. What will the contract cost be on an hourly basis and what will the guards earn in wages and benefits on an hourly basis? Will the guards receive periodic wage increases, uniform allowances, paid vacation? Who will be responsible for liability costs; make sure that your corporation is covered under the contractor's liability? Include a place for your present proprietary officers to retain their positions with the new contract.

WHAT WILL THE ROLE OF SECURITY BE?

This must be clearly delineated in the contract and must be completely and clearly listed so that there is no doubt what security will do and what is expected of each and every contract guard. The four "C"s of contracting are clear, concise, correct and complete. Make sure you have covered all the bases for your organization or you may be looking for work somewhere else. The role of the security department and its personnel is pivotal in the contracting business.

CONTRACTOR EVALUATION CHECKLIST: SELECTING THE CONTRACTOR

Create a number checklist for each item you want included in the contract and then check each item to ensure compliance. The number or sequencing should be systematic and complete while maintaining an ease of use. Be sure you include all of the items mentioned in this article and any other items important to your organization. Also include such things as branch support, field support and personnel, experience in security (NOT law enforcement), selection, knowledge and professionalism of the contract company representatives. Using this system as a grade, you will be able to determine which contract company matches your requirements.

Finally, it is important that you determine what your role will be in the new or revised security program for your organization. If you are being retained to oversee the contract, then you must obtain additional training. Expand your duties to include life safety, risk management, investigations, and executive protection. If your corporation has decided to outsource your position, then you must make sure you have seen to it that you have included a place with the contractor for yourself. Keep in mind that you are not alone in this. Many other security supervisors have had the same task assigned to them. Besides being able to consult with the other security supervisors in your area, there are many sources available to assist you in this process.

OUTSOURCING IN SECURITY
QUIZ

1. During your career as a security supervisor, your corporation will consider dropping your proprietary staff and outsourcing. Two of the items to consider are _____ and ____ _____.

2. The two major points in putting together a contract staff are the _____ and the ___ _____. Without these you will not be able to run the service properly.

3. Before presenting your recommendations you must complete the _____ and have a thorough knowledge of _____.

4.   In determining the role of your contract force you must determine _____ in the security service _____ to the contract force.

5.   By going to a contract force you do not limit your corporation's _____ or _____ _____ to provide a safe and secure workplace for both customers and employees.

6.   When writing the contract you will not be able to mandate wages and benefits for contract guards.
        ☐ T   ☐ F

7.   In using a contract security company you have no choice in officers.
        ☐ T   ☐ F

8.   The corporation can require their choice of supervisors.
        ☐ T   ☐ F

9.   Your company can specify the equipment to be used by the contractor.
        ☐ T   ☐ F

10.   With contract security you have a risk of using untrained guards.
        ☐ T   ☐ F

UNIT SEVEN
COUNTERMEASURES DESIGN

Security Systems Design and Evaluation
Statistical Analysis
Security Technologies
High-Technology Theft
Designing Operations Centers

SECURITY SYSTEMS DESIGN AND EVALUATION
by Mary Lynn Garcia, M.S., CPP

INTRODUCTION

The design of an effective physical protection system (PPS) requires a methodical approach in which the designer weighs the objectives of the PPS against available resources and then evaluates the proposed design. Without this kind of careful assessment, the PPS might waste valuable resources on unnecessary protection or, worse yet, fail to provide adequate protection at critical points of the facility. For example, it would probably be unwise to protect a facility's employee cafeteria with the same level of protection as the facility's central computing area. Similarly, maximum security at a facility's main entrance would be wasted if entry were also possible through an unguarded cafeteria loading dock. Each facility is unique, even if performing generally the same activities, so this systematic approach allows flexibility in the application of security tools to address local conditions.

The process of designing and analyzing a PPS is described in the remainder of this chapter. The methodology presented here is the same one used by the United States Department of Energy (DOE) when designing physical protection systems for critical nuclear assets.[1] This approach and supporting tools were developed and validated over the past 25 years through DOE funded research and development totaling over $200 million. While other industrial and governmental assets may not require the highest levels of security used at nuclear weapon sites, the approach is the same whether protecting a manufacturing facility, an oil refinery or a retail store. The foundation of this approach is the design of a performance-based system. Performance measures (i.e., validated numeric characteristics) for various system components such as sensors, video or response time, allows the use of models to predict system performance versus the identified threat. This effectiveness measure can then be used to provide the business rationale for investing in the system or upgrade, based on a measurable increase in system performance. A cost-benefit analysis can then be supported by looking at system improvement compared to costs. Before describing this process in more detail, it is necessary to differentiate between *safety* and *security*.

For the purposes of this chapter, safety is meant to represent the operation of systems in abnormal environments, such as flood, fire, earthquake or electrical faults. Security, on the other hand, refers to systems used to prevent or detect an attack by a malevolent human adversary. There are some overlaps between the two, for example, the response to a fire may be the same whether the fire is the result of an electrical short or a terrorist bomb. It is useful, however, to recognize that a fire has no powers of reasoning, while adversaries do. A fire burns as long as there is fuel and oxygen; if these elements are removed, the fire goes out. An attack by a malevolent human adversary, on the other hand, requires that we recognize the capability of the human adversary to adapt and thus eventually defeat the security system.

In the event of a safety critical event, such as a fire, security personnel should have a defined role in assisting, without compromising the security readiness of a facility. In this regard, security personnel should not be overloaded with safety-related tasks, as this may increase exposure of the facility to a security event during an emergency condition, particularly if the adversary creates this event as a diversion or takes advantage of the opportunity. In addition, security personnel may not possess the specific knowledge or training to respond to safety events. For example, in case of a fire, security personnel should not be expected to shutdown power or equipment. This task is better left to those familiar with the operation and shutdown of equipment, power, or production lines. Procedures describing the role of security personnel in these events should be developed, understood, and practiced in order to assure adequate levels of protection and safety.

The design of an effective physical protection system includes the determination of the physical protection system objectives, the initial design or characterization of a physical protection system, the evaluation of the design, and, probably, a redesign or refinement of the system. To develop the objectives, the designer must begin by gathering information about facility operations and conditions, such as a comprehensive description of the facility, operating states, and the physical protection requirements. The designer then needs to define the threat. This involves considering factors about potential adversaries: class of adversary, adversary's capabilities and range of adversary's tactics. Next, the designer should identify targets. Targets may be physical assets, electronic data, people or anything that could impact business operations. The designer now knows the objectives of the physical protection system, that is, "what to protect against whom." The next step is to design the new system or characterize the existing system. If designing a new system, he must determine how best to integrate people, procedures and equipment to meet the objectives of the system. Once a physical protection system is designed or characterized, it must be analyzed and evaluated to ensure it meets the physical protection objectives. Evaluation must allow for features working together to assure protection rather than regarding each feature separately. Due to the complexity of protection systems, an evaluation usually requires modeling techniques. If any vulnerabilities are found, the initial system must be redesigned to correct the vulnerabilities and a reevaluation conducted.

PPS DESIGN AND EVALUATION PROCESS OBJECTIVES

A graphical representation of the PPS methodology is shown in Figure 36.1. As stated previously, the first step in the process is to determine the objectives of the protection system. To formulate these objectives, the designer must (1) characterize (understand) the facility operations and conditions, (2) define the threat, and (3) identify the targets.

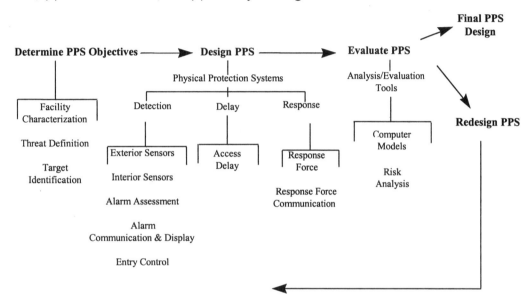

Figure 1 – Design and Evaluation Process for Physical Protection Systems

Figure 36.1

Facility operations and conditions characterization requires developing a thorough description of the facility itself (the location of the site boundary, building location, building interior floor plans, access points). A description of the processes within the facility is also required, as well as identification of any existing physical protection features. This information can be obtained from several sources, including facility design blueprints, process descriptions, safety analysis reports, and environmental impact statements. In addition to acquisition and review of such documentation, a tour of the site under consideration and interviews with facility personnel are necessary. This provides an understanding of the physical protection requirements for the facility as well as an appreciation for the operational and safety constraints that must be considered. Many checklists exist to aid in this process,[2-6] however, since each facility is unique, overreliance on checklists should be avoided. Compromises must usually be made on all sides so that operation can continue in a safe and efficient environment while physical protection is maintained. Additional considerations also include an understanding of liability and any legal or regulatory requirements that must be followed.

Next, a threat definition for the facility must be made. Information must be collected to answer three questions about the adversary:
1.   What class of adversary is to be considered?
2.   What is the range of the adversary's tactics?
3.   What are the adversary's capabilities?

Adversaries can be separated into three classes: outsiders, insiders, and outsiders in collusion with insiders. For each class of adversary, the full range of tactics (deceit, force, stealth or any combination of these) should be considered. Deceit is the attempted defeat of a security system by using false authorization and identification; force is the overt, forcible attempt to overcome a security system and stealth is the attempt to defeat the detection system and enter the facility covertly.

Important capabilities for the adversary include his knowledge of the PPS, his level of motivation, any skills that would be useful in the attack, the speed with which the attack is carried out and his ability to carry tools and weapons. Since it is not generally possible to test and evaluate all possible capabilities of an unknown adversary, the designer and analyst must make assumptions. These assumptions can be based on published information about human performance and the tested vulnerabilities of physical protection elements. Other factors to be considered are the emergency response capabilities and any critical asset tracking and inventory conditions. Consideration of the threat early in the process assures that an appropriate and effective system is designed and implemented. If the primary threat is a vandal, we would not want to implement an expensive PPS that is more suited to a highly trained terrorist. Similarly, if the threat is a motivated criminal, we would implement a system that is capable of detecting and stopping this intruder. For any given facility there may be several threats such as a criminal outsider, a disgruntled employee, competitors or some combination of the above, so the PPS must be designed to protect against all of these threats. This process can be facilitated by choosing the highest credible threat, designing the system to meet this threat and then testing to verify the system performance against the lower threats.

Finally, target identification should be performed for the facility. Targets may include critical assets or information, people, or critical areas and processes. A thorough review of the facility and its assets should be conducted. Such questions as "What asset will cost the most to replace if stolen?" or "What losses will be incurred in the event of sabotage of this equipment?" will help identify the assets or equipment that are most vulnerable or that create an unacceptable consequence.

Given the information obtained through facility characterization, threat definition and target identification, the designer can determine the protection objectives of the PPS. An example of a protection objective might be to "interrupt a criminal adversary with hand tools and a vehicle before he can remove finished CPUs from the shipping dock."

The next step in the process, if designing a new PPS, is to determine how best to combine such elements as fences, barriers, sensors, procedures, communication devices and security personnel into a PPS that can achieve the protection objectives. The resulting PPS design should meet these objectives within the operational, safety, legal and economic constraints of the facility. The primary functions of a PPS are detection of an adversary, delay of that adversary and response by security personnel (guard force).

Certain guidelines should be observed during the PPS design. A PPS system is generally better if detection is as far from the target as possible and delays are near the target. In addition, there is close association between detection (exterior or interior) and assessment. The designer should be aware that detection without assessment is not detection. Another close association is the relationship between response and response force communications. A response force cannot respond unless it receives a communication call for a response. These and many other particular features of PPS components help to ensure that the designer takes advantage of the strengths of each piece of equipment and uses equipment in combinations that complement each other and protect any weaknesses.

Analysis and evaluation of the PPS design begins with a review and thorough understanding of the protection objectives the designed system must meet. This can be done simply by checking for required features of a PPS, such as intrusion detection, entry control, access delay, response communications, and a protective force. However, a PPS design based on required features cannot be expected to lead to a high performance system unless those features, when used together, are sufficient to assure adequate levels of protection. More sophisticated analysis and evaluation techniques can be used to estimate the minimum performance levels achieved by a PPS.

An existing PPS at an operational facility cannot normally be fully tested as a system. This sort of test would be highly disruptive to the operation of the facility and could impact production schedules, as well as security effectiveness (i.e., create a vulnerability). Since direct system tests are not practical, evaluation techniques are based on performance tests of component subsystems. Component performance estimates are combined into system performance estimates by the application of system modeling techniques.

The end result of this phase of the design and analysis process is a system vulnerability assessment. Analysis of the PPS design will either find that the design effectively achieved the protection objectives or it will identify weaknesses. If the protection objectives are achieved, then the design and analysis process is completed. However, the PPS should be analyzed periodically to ensure that the original protection objectives remain valid and that the protection system continues to meet them.

If the PPS is found ineffective, vulnerabilities in the system can be identified. The next step in the design and analysis cycle is to redesign or upgrade the initial protection system design to correct the noted vulnerabilities. It is possible that the PPS objectives also need to be reevaluated. An analysis of the redesigned system is performed. This cycle continues until the results indicate that the PPS meets the protection objectives.

PHYSICAL PROTECTION SYSTEM DESIGN

A system may be defined as a collection of components or elements designed to achieve an objective according to a plan. The designer of any system must have the system's ultimate objective in mind. The ultimate objective of a physical protection system (PPS) is to prevent the accomplishment of unauthorized overt or covert actions. Typical objectives are to prevent sabotage of critical equipment, theft of assets or information from within the facility and protection of people (executive protection or workplace violence). A PPS must accomplish its objectives by either deterrence or a combination of detection, delay, and response. Listed below are the component subsystems that provide the tools to perform these functions.

Detection
> Exterior/Interior Intrusion Sensors
> Alarm Assessment
> Alarm Communication and Display
> Entry Control Systems

Delay
> Access Delay

Response
> Response Force
> Response Force Communications

The system functions of detection and delay can be accomplished by the use of either hardware and/or guards. Response is handled by the guards. There is always a balance between the use of hardware and the use of guards. In different conditions and applications, one is often the preferable choice. The key to a successful system is the integration of people, procedures and equipment into a system that protects the targets from the threats.

Detection, delay, and response are all required functions of an effective physical protection system. These functions must be performed in order and within a length of time that is less than the time required for the adversary to complete his task. A well-designed system provides protection-in-depth, minimizes the consequences of component failures and exhibits balanced protection. In addition, a design process based on performance criteria rather than feature criteria will select elements and procedures according to the contribution they make to overall system performance. Performance criteria are also measurable, so can help in the analysis of the designed system.

PPS FUNCTIONS

Theft and sabotage of the facility may be prevented in two ways: by deterring the adversary or by defeating the adversary. Deterrence occurs by implementing a physical protection system that is seen by potential adversaries as too difficult to defeat; it makes the facility an unattractive target. Examples of deterrents are the presence of security guards in parking lots, adequate lighting at night, posting of signs and the use of barriers, such as bars on windows. The problem with deterrence is that it is impossible to measure. It would be a mistake to assume that because a system has not been challenged by an adversary, the effectiveness of the system has been proven. The deterrence function of a physical protection system is difficult to measure and reliance on successful deterrence can be risky; thus it is considered a secondary function and will not be discussed further in this chapter.

Defeating the adversary refers to the actions taken by the response force to prevent an adversary from accomplishing his goal once he actually begins a malevolent action against a facility. There are several functions that the physical protection system must perform. The primary PPS functions are detection, delay and response. It is essential to consider the system functions in detail, since a thorough understanding of the definitions of these functions and the measure of effectiveness of each is required to evaluate the system. It is important to note that detection must be accomplished for delay to be effective. Recall, the system goal is to protect assets from theft or sabotage by a malevolent adversary. For a system to be effective at this objective, we must start by knowing that we are under attack (detection), then keep the adversary away from the targets (delay), thus allowing the response force time to interrupt or stop the adversary (response).

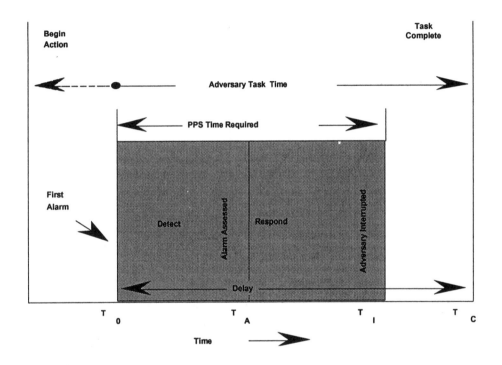

Figure 2 – Adversary Task Time versus PPS Time Requirements

Figure 36.2

The PPS must perform the functions of detection, delay, and response. These functions must be performed in a period of time that is less than the time required for the adversary to complete his tasks. Figure 36.2 shows the relationships between adversary task time and the time required for the physical protection system to do its job. The total time required for the adversary to accomplish his goal has been labeled Adversary Task Time. It is dependent upon the delay provided by the physical protection system. The adversary may begin his task at some time before the first alarm occurs, labeled on the diagram T_0. The adversary task time is shown by a dotted line before this point because delay is not effective before detection. After that alarm, the alarm information must be reported and assessed to determine if the alarm is valid. The time at which the alarm is assessed to be valid is labeled T_A, and at this time the location of the alarm must be communicated to the members of the response force. Further time is then required for the response force to respond in adequate numbers and with adequate equipment to interrupt and neutralize the adversary actions. The time at which the response force interrupts adversary actions is labeled T_I, and adversary task completion time is labeled T_C. Clearly, in order for the physical protection system to accomplish its objective, T_I must occur before T_C. It is equally clear that detection (the first alarm) should occur as early as possible and T_0 (as well as T_A and T_I) should be as far to the left on the time axis as possible.

Detection

Detection is the discovery of an adversary action. It includes sensing of covert or overt actions. In order to discover an adversary action, the following events need to occur:

1. A sensor reacts to an abnormal occurrence and initiates an alarm.
2. The information from the sensor and assessment subsystems is reported and displayed.
3. A person assesses information and judges the alarm to be valid or invalid. If assessed to be a nuisance alarm, a detection has not occurred. Therefore, detection without assessment is not considered detection. Assessment is the process of determining whether the source of the alarm is due to an attack or a nuisance alarm.

Included in the detection function of physical protection is entry control. Entry control means allowing entry to authorized personnel and detecting the attempted entry of unauthorized personnel and material. The measures of effectiveness of entry control are throughput, imposter pass rate and false rejection rate. Throughput is defined as the number of authorized personnel allowed access per unit time, assuming that all personnel who attempt entry are authorized for entrance. Imposter pass rate is the rate at which false identities or credentials are allowed entry.

The measures of effectiveness for the detection function are the probability of sensing adversary action and the time required for reporting and assessing the alarm. A sensor activates at time T_0, then at a later time a person receives information from the sensor and assessment subsystems. If the time delay between when the sensor activates and when the alarm is assessed is short, the probability of detection, P_D, will be close to the probability that the sensor will sense the unauthorized action, P_S. The probability of detection decreases as the time before assessment increases.

Detection can also be accomplished by the protective force or personnel. Guards at fixed posts or on patrol may serve a vital role in sensing an intrusion. An effective assessment system provides two types of information associated with detection: information about whether the alarm is a valid alarm or a nuisance alarm and details about the cause of the alarm—what, who, where, and how many. However, even when assisted by a video assessment system, humans do not make good detectors. Studies have shown that brief instances of movement are missed by 48% of human observers using video monitors.[7]

Delay

Delay is the second function of a PPS. It is the slowing down of adversary progress. Delay can be accomplished by barriers, locks and activated delays. The protective force can be considered elements of delay if they are in fixed and well-protected positions. The measure of delay effectiveness is the time required by the adversary (after detection) to bypass each delay element. Although the adversary may be delayed prior to detection, this delay is of no value to the effectiveness of the physical protection system since it does not provide additional time to respond to the adversary. Delay before detection is primarily a deterrent.

Response

The response function consists of the actions taken by the protective force to prevent adversary success. Response, as it is used here, consists of interruption. Interruption is defined as a sufficient number of response force personnel arriving at the appropriate location to stop the adversary's progress. It includes the communication to the protection force of accurate information about adversary actions and the deployment of the response force. The measure of response effectiveness is the time between receipt of a communication of adversary action and the interruption of the adversary action.

The effectiveness measures for response communication are the probability of accurate communication and the time required to communicate. The time after information is initially transmitted may vary considerably depending on the method of communication. After the initial period, the probability of valid communication begins to increase rapidly. As shown in Figure 36.3, with each repeat, the probability of correct and current data being communicated is increased. There is some delay in establishing accurate communication due to human behavior. On the first attempt to communicate, the operator is alerted that there is a call. Then a request for a second transmission is made, and finally, the operator understands the call and starts to ask for additional details.

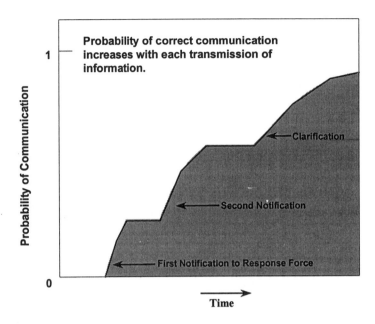

Figure 3 – Variation of Probability of Valid Communication with Time

Figure 36.3

Deployment describes the actions of the protective force from the time communication is received until the force is in position to interrupt the adversary. The effectiveness measure of this function is the probability of deployment to the adversary location and the time required to deploy the response force.

The effectiveness of the PPS functions of detection, delay and response and their relationships have already been discussed. In addition, all of the hardware elements of the system must be installed, maintained and operated properly. The procedures of the physical protection system must be compatible with the facility procedures. Security, safety and operational objectives must be accomplished at all times. A PPS which has been well engineered will include the following characteristics.

- protection-in-depth
- minimum consequence of component failure
- balanced protection

Protection-in-depth means that to accomplish his goal, an adversary should be required to avoid or defeat a number of protective devices in sequence. For example, an adversary might have to defeat one sensor and penetrate two separate barriers before gaining entry to a process control room or a filing cabinet in the project costing area. The actions and times required to penetrate each of these layers may not necessarily be equal, and the effectiveness of each may be quite different, but each will require a separate and distinct act by the adversary as he moves along his path. The effect produced on the adversary by a system that provides protection-in-depth will be:

- to increase uncertainty about the system
- to require more extensive preparations prior to attacking the system
- to create additional steps where the adversary may fail or abort his mission

It is unlikely that a complex system will ever be developed and operated that does not experience some component failure during its lifetime. Causes of component failure in a physical protection system are numerous and can range from environmental factors (which may be expected) to adversary actions beyond the scope of the threat used in the system design. Although it is important to know the cause of component failure to restore the system to normal operation, it is more important that contingency plans are provided so the system can continue to operate. Requiring portions of these contingency plans to be carried out automatically (so that redundant equipment automatically takes over the function of disabled equipment) may be highly desirable in some cases. Some component failures may require aid from sources outside of the facility in order to minimize the impact of the failure. One example of this is the use of local law enforcement to supplement airport security personnel at times of higher alert status.

Balanced protection implies that no matter how an adversary attempts to accomplish his goal, he will encounter effective elements of the physical protection system. Consider, for example, the barrier surface that surrounds a room. This surface may consist of:

- walls, floors and ceilings of several types
- doors of several types; equipment hatches in floors and ceilings
- heating, ventilating and air conditioning openings with various types of grilles

For a completely balanced system, the minimum time to penetrate each of these barriers would be equal, and the minimum probability of detecting penetration of each of these barriers should be equal. However, complete balance is probably not possible or desirable. Certain elements, such as walls, may be extremely resistant to penetration, not because of physical protection requirements, but because of structural or safety requirements. Door, hatch, and grille delays may be considerably less than wall delays and still be adequate. There is no advantage in over-designing by installing a costly door that would take several minutes to penetrate with explosives, if the wall were corrugated asbestos which could be penetrated in a few seconds with hand tools.

Finally, features designed to protect against one form of threat should not be eliminated because they overprotect against another threat. The objective should be to provide adequate protection against all threats on all possible paths and to maintain a balance with other considerations, such as cost, safety, or structural integrity.

DESIGN CRITERIA

Any design process must have criteria against which elements of the design will be measured. A design process based on performance criteria will select elements and procedures according to the contribution they make to overall system performance. The effectiveness measure will be overall system performance.

A feature criteria approach selects elements or procedures to satisfy requirements that certain items be present. The effectiveness measure is the presence of those features. The use of a feature criteria approach in regulations or requirements that apply to physical protection systems should generally be avoided or handled with extreme care. Unless such care is exercised, the feature criteria approach can lead to the use of a "check list" method to determine system adequacy based on the presence or absence of required features. This is clearly not desirable, since overall system performance is of interest, rather than the mere presence or absence of system features or components. For example, a performance criterion for a perimeter detection system would be that the system be able to detect a running intruder using any attack method. A feature criterion for the same detection system might be that the system include two specific sensor types.

The conceptual design techniques presented in this chapter are based on a performance-based approach to meeting the physical protection system objectives. Much of the component technology material will, however, be applicable for either performance criteria or feature criteria design methods.

The performance measures for these functions are:

Detection
    Probability of detection
    Time for communication and assessment
    Frequency of nuisance alarms
Delay
    Time to defeat obstacles
Response
    Probability of accurate communication to response force
    Time to communicate
    Probability of deployment to adversary location
    Time to deploy
    Response force effectiveness

Intrusion Sensors

Intrusion detection is defined as the detection of a person or vehicle attempting to gain unauthorized entry into an area that is being protected. The intrusion detection boundary is ideally a sphere enclosing the item being protected so that all intrusions, whether by surface, air, underwater or underground, are detected. Intrusion detection systems consist of exterior and interior intrusion sensors, video alarm assessment, entry control and alarm communication systems all working together. Exterior sensors are those used in an outdoor environment, and interior sensors are those used inside buildings. The integration of individual sensors into a sensor system must consider specific design goals, the effects of physical and environmental conditions and the interaction of the sensor system with a balanced and integrated physical protection system. Topography, vegetation, wildlife, background noise, climate and weather, and soil conditions and pavement all affect the performance of exterior sensors. Interior sensor application classes include boundary penetration sensors, interior motion sensors and proximity sensors. Various sensor technologies can be applied to achieve protection-in-depth: at the boundary, within the room and at the object to be protected. The designer of a good interior intrusion detection system considers the operational, physical and environmental characteristics of the facility. Also, the designer should be familiar with the sensors that are available, how the sensors interact with the intruder and the environment, and the physical principles of operation for each sensor. Detailed descriptions of various intrusion detection components and technologies have intentionally not been included in this discussion, since it is most important for the security supervisor to understand and apply the process than to be an expert on component hardware. Many technology reviews exist and serve as excellent references for specific sensor types.[8-10]

Intrusion sensor performance is described by three fundamental characteristics:
- probability of detection, P_D
- nuisance alarm rate
- vulnerability to defeat

For the ideal sensor, the P_D of an intrusion sensor is one (1.0). That is, it has a 100% probability of detection. However, no sensor is ideal, and the P_D is always less than 1.0. Even with thousands of tests, the P_D only approaches 1. The probability of detection depends primarily upon:
- threat to be detected
- sensor hardware design
- installation conditions
- sensitivity adjustment
- weather conditions
- condition of the equipment

All of the above conditions can vary and, thus, despite the claims of some sensor manufacturers, a specific P_D cannot be assigned to a piece or set of sensor hardware.

A nuisance alarm is any alarm that is not caused by an intrusion. In an ideal sensor system, the nuisance alarm rate would be zero. However, in the real world all sensors interact with their environment, and they cannot discriminate between intrusions and other events in their detection zone. This is why an alarm assessment system is needed: not all sensor alarms are caused by intrusions.

Usually nuisance alarms are further classified by source. Both natural and industrial environments can cause nuisance alarms. Common sources of natural noise are vegetation (trees and weeds), wildlife (animals and birds), and weather conditions (wind, rain, snow, fog, lightning). Industrial sources of noise include ground vibration, debris moved by wind, and electromagnetic interference. False alarms are those nuisance alarms generated by the equipment itself (whether by poor design, inadequate maintenance, or component failure).

An ideal sensor could not be defeated; however, all existing sensors can be defeated. The objective of the physical protection system designer is to make the system very difficult to defeat. There are two general ways to defeat the system:
- Bypass—Because all intrusion sensors have a finite detection zone, any sensor can be defeated by going around its detection volume.
- Spoof—Spoofing is any technique that allows the target to pass through the sensor's normal detection zone without generating an alarm.

Integration with Assessment System

Many intrusion detection systems use a closed circuit television (CCTV) system to perform alarm assessment. For both the sensor and video systems to perform well, care must be taken to ensure that the designs of the two systems or subsystems are compatible. Assessment may take place via the use of CCTV systems or manually by people. Video assessment automatically tied to sensor activation greatly reduces the amount of time required to determine the alarm source, thereby maximizing the use of any remaining delay and increasing the chance of successful interruption of the adversary. Video assessment also allows remote evaluation of the alarm condition, which eliminates the need to constantly dispatch guards to determine the cause of the alarm, perhaps too late to make an accurate assessment. In addition, as noted previously, people make very poor detectors, so an integrated sensor and video system should only present alarms and associated video to the operator on a single monitor, and not depend on the operator observing multiple monitors or scanning of multiple cameras on one or two monitors to detect suspicious events without the aid of sensors. Studies have shown that use of multiple screens is not as effective as use of one screen and that after one hour of observation, there is significant degradation in the human operator's ability to identify significant events.[11] Presentation of *all* camera formation continuously on several monitors, particularly by scanning, reduces the probability of detection of an event and decreases system performance.

Additional considerations in this area include size of the zone to be assessed and location of the camera. Larger zones require the use of less equipment, while smaller zones can give better resolution. Consideration of the image to be viewed should drive this decision. For example, if it is only important to know that a person has intruded into an area, a wider or longer zone may be used. If, however, specific details of the person are required, shorter zones will be required. For video assessment systems to be effective, the area under surveillance must be adequately lit, to allow a rapid and accurate assessment.

In addition, the camera must be positioned to view the entire area being assessed (i.e., no blind spots). The sensors must be placed so that on an alarm, the camera viewing the zone will have an unobstructed view of the entire zone. To achieve maximum system effectiveness, fixed cameras, aimed at the area of interest, should be used. Use of pan-tilt-zoom (PTZ) cameras should be limited to use for secondary assessment or surveillance only, since it is unlikely that a PTZ camera will be pointing in the appropriate direction on alarm and thus may reduce the chances for an accurate and timely assessment. Technical references on the use and design of CCTV systems and components are readily available.[12,13]

Integration with Barrier Delay System

Balanced integrated physical protection systems usually incorporate some type of barrier or access denial systems to provide delay time for video assessment of the alarm source and for the response force to respond to an intrusion. In many cases this includes some type of barrier installed at the perimeter; however, the barrier should not degrade the performance of the sensors. Perimeter barriers are usually installed on or near the innermost fence so that an intruder cannot tamper with or defeat the barrier without first passing through a detection zone. This placement is important to ensure that the response action is initiated before the delay occurs. Barriers should not distort the sensors' detection volume, cause nuisance alarms, or obscure part of the camera's view.

Response

The meaning of the phrase "response force" varies from facility to facility. A part of or all of the response force may be located on-site or off-site. The response force may include local and state police, and dedicated response teams at the facility. These response forces may be armed or unarmed. In addition, response may be broken into two major categories – immediate on-site response (i.e., timely response) and recovery. Depending on the needs and objectives of a facility, it is prudent to decide in advance which strategy will be used at the site. Different targets may require different strategies. For example, stopping an intruder about to sabotage a critical valve in a refinery may require an immediate on-site response, while recovery may be a better technique for theft of company-owned tools. For a recovery-based response, the use of videotape for after-the-fact review can be very effective and legally acceptable. It should be apparent that timely response will require better detection and delay than a response strategy that focuses on recovery of the asset. The difficulty with recovery as a strategy is that it may not matter if stolen documents or information are recovered, since the adversary may have copied the information. In a like manner, once an incident of workplace violence has occurred, the capture of the perpetrator is commendable, however, there is still the aftermath of the event to consider. This aftermath may include legal action by the victim against the facility, bad publicity for the facility, poor employee morale and regulatory action against the facility.

Due to these variables, it is difficult to generalize about specific procedures or tasks that the response force may be expected to perform. The final result is that the response force must prevent the adversaries from accomplishing their objective. Specific task assignments to accomplish this function will be reflected in variations of qualification standards, training requirements, and performance standards as measured by realistic tests. In this discussion, the physical protection system function of response has been divided into three parts: contingency planning, communication, and interruption.

Contingency planning is an important part of a facility's ability to successfully resolve an incident. Prior planning will help a facility manger identify potential targets, how to respond to different threats, how the facility will interact with outside agencies, as well as what level of force facility personnel will use in various situations. Well-documented procedures should be developed in advance as a major part of contingency planning.

Tactical planning should be part of contingency planning in general. Procedures and plans for guard actions in the event of a true alarm should be well established. The chain of command and the succession of command in case of emergency should be well known. Plans must be made to ensure that members of the response force possess or have rapid access to the proper equipment consistent with the defined threat. Tactical plans must contain specific details for the response force to deploy successfully. Response strategies (contain, deny, assault) must be well planned and practiced.

The role of the response force should also be factored into the facility contingency plan. A response force whose key role is the containment of adversaries until additional help arrives, will deploy differently than a response force capable of recovery operations. It is likely that there will be two sets of guards at a facility – one group checking credentials, patrolling, and serving the deterrence/delay role and another, more highly skilled group with primary responsibility for response.

A critical part of the design and analysis process of a PPS is the identification of potential targets. Supervisors can then evaluate the likely routes an adversary may use to approach the facility boundaries, buildings and rooms, as well as the specific target. This type of information will assist supervisors in developing detailed tactical plans to address various threats to the facility. In addition, it will be useful in determining protective force patrol routes and schedules.

Security supervisors should consider using support from outside (non-facility) agencies as they do their contingency planning. A facility may wish to consider developing support agreements with local or state law enforcement agencies or a Mutual Aid Agreement with other sites. To facilitate this, a written support agreement with outside agencies or sites should be developed. This written agreement should detail the interaction between facility personnel and the neighboring agencies. The agreement should be developed with input from all participants affected by the agreement and approved by each organization. Issues such as the neighboring agency's role in an incident, off-site pursuit by facility response force personnel and communication should be considered. The role of the neighboring agency should be closely examined. Facility security managers may consider use of other agencies for containment and/or recovery support. These decisions will need to be based on the neighboring agency's response time, training, equipment and availability to support the facility. Facility security managers may decide to provide their response force personnel with off-site credentials and authority to facilitate the response force's ability to operate outside of the facility's boundaries. This may be an important consideration during deployment and pursuit.

Communication will be a key factor in the interaction between facility personnel and other agencies. Since different agencies rarely operate on the same radio frequency, supervisors will need to evaluate alternate means of communication. A dedicated land line may be used for initial notification to outside agencies and pre-planned routes and containment positions may help resolve on-scene communications concerns.

A critical factor that will influence the ability for a neighboring agency to successfully support a facility is joint training. Security supervisors should plan and conduct periodic training exercises with outside agencies. The scope of this training will be dictated by the supporting agency's role. If the support agency will act primarily in a containment capacity, then primary containment positions and areas of responsibility should be practiced. However, if the support agency will be conducting recovery operations, more detailed training and facility knowledge will be required.

Different threats will require responding officers to employ a wide variety of force to address any given situation. Response force personnel should have the ability to apply appropriate levels of force to stop an adversary's actions. This will include the guard's presence as a deterrent or delay, the use of intermediate force, and finally the use of deadly force. The facility should have a written policy to provide clear guidelines to the guards in the use of force.

A use of force policy should be based on using the minimum amount of force necessary to stop an adversary's actions. Typically the amount of force used will be dictated by the adversary's actions. For example, an unarmed adversary who is refusing to follow the instructions of a guard but does not present any other threat should be handled with less force than an adversary who is armed and posing a threat to the facility or guards. This type of policy will typically require guards to have the ability to employ intermediate force weapons such as impact (baton) or chemical (mace) weapons.

After developing a use of force policy, supervisors should provide response force personnel with training to ensure all personnel are well versed in the policy and the deployment of their weapons. Managers should consider semi-annual or quarterly training and qualifications to ensure their personnel are capable of successful application of the facility's policy and weapons. Documentation of all training records will be useful in the event of any legal challenges or post-incident reviews.

When designing a training program, it is important to consult the facility security manager and the PPS designer. The facility security manager is most familiar with the functional performance and task requirements of the response force. The facility security manager is also responsible for a separate training agenda that deals with policies, procedures and basic training not specific to system operation (arrest powers, use of force, basic marksmanship, communications).

The physical protection system designer can provide input to the development of training and testing programs. The designer is most familiar with the operations and limitations of the PPS equipment and the other PPS functions (detection, delay). From the designer's point of view, the objectives of the training are to maximize the ability of the response force to use the physical protection system in carrying out its basic mission: protection of the assets of the facility.

In addition to tactical planning and training, it is important for the response force to practice deployment at the specific facility in exercises so they will know what to do in the event of an actual attack. Results of good practice give realistic estimates of response force times. Field exercises should be used to verify that tactical training has resulted in the desired capability and that the overall tactical plan is realistic. In order for the response force to plan and practice, the threat must be quantified either by policy or local assessment. This threat should also address whether the adversary's objective is theft, sabotage, or both.

One test of the response guard's proficiency is to determine if they can arrive in enough time after notification to interrupt the adversary. The responders require skills in addition to speed. Such skills requiring testing include marksmanship, physical fitness, use of force under stress, use of deadly and intermediate force, tactical movement, accurate response communications, target and facility familiarity, and use of physical protection system features to their advantage.

Some of these skills can be evaluated in simulation courses in the classroom. Others, especially the testing of the application of the skills, can only take place in the facility or something quite similar to it. The measure of proficiency being tested under engagement simulation exercises in these circumstances is the response force's ability to stop an attack. The only acceptable level of proficiency in response procedures is the prevention of damage to, or loss of, critical assets.

Communication is a vital part of the response function. The proper performance of all other system functions depends on communication. Information must be transferred through this network with both speed and reliability. Communication to the response force must contain information about adversary actions and instructions for deployment. The effectiveness measures for response communication are the probability of accurate communication and the time required to communicate to the response force. Communication includes voice and other systems that allow members of the protective and response forces to communicate with each other. The successful operation of a physical protection system requires a reliable response force communication network that is resistant to being used to the advantage of knowledgeable and determined adversaries.

ANALYSIS

A PPS is a complex configuration of detection, delay, and response elements. Computerized techniques are available to analyze a physical protection system and evaluate its effectiveness.[14,15] Such techniques identify system deficiencies, evaluate improvements and perform cost versus effectiveness comparisons. These techniques are appropriate for analyzing physical protection systems at individual sites. Also, the techniques can be used for evaluating either an existing protection system or a proposed system design.

An adversary path is an ordered series of actions against a target which, if completed, results in successful theft or sabotage. Protection elements along the path detect and delay the adversary. Detection includes not only sensor activation but also alarm communication and assessment.

At a specific facility, the following factors must be considered:
1.   Specific target(s) must be identified.
2.   Many adversary paths to each target are possible.
3.   The detection, delay and response elements are specific to the protection system.
4.   More than one threat should be considered.

Therefore, the identification and evaluation of adversary paths is usually a complex process.

A team with broad experience is necessary to ensure a complete and accurate assessment of the site is produced. The members of the team should be:
*   Team Leader (Security Supervisor)
*   Security Systems Engineer (Detection and Communications)
*   Locksmith
*   Response Expert
*   Access Delay Expert
*   Modeling Expert
*   Operations Representatives

The team follows the steps of the process described above, including understanding the facility, defining the threat and targets and then designing an appropriate PPS. Once a new PPS or upgrade has been designed, a vulnerability analysis is conducted. It is a systematic way of ensuring the design meets an acceptable level of performance against adversaries identified as the design basis threat. It is important to note that this vulnerability analysis focuses on the performance of the PPS and is not a simple compliance-with-regulations check.

The goal of an adversary is to complete a path with the least likelihood of being stopped by the physical protection system. To achieve this goal, the adversary may attempt to minimize the time required to complete the path. This strategy involves penetrating barriers with little regard to the probability of being detected. If the adversary completes the path before guards can respond, he is successful. Alternatively, the adversary may attempt to minimize detection with little regard to the time required. If the adversary completes the path without being detected, he is successful.

One measure of PPS effectiveness is the comparison of the minimum cumulative time delay along the path compared to the guard response time. An adequate physical protection system provides enough delay for the guards to respond. The disadvantage of this measure of effectiveness is that no consideration of detection is involved. Delay without prior detection is not meaningful since the response force must be alerted in order to respond and interrupt the adversary. Therefore, the minimum time measure alone is not the best measure of system effectiveness.

Another measure of effectiveness is the cumulative probability of detecting the adversary before his mission is completed. An adequate protection system provides high probability of detection. For an effective system, the minimum cumulative detection along the path must be an acceptable value. The disadvantage is that no consideration of delay is involved. Detection without sufficient subsequent delay is not meaningful since the response force may have insufficient time to interrupt the adversary.

Neither delay time nor cumulative probability of detection alone is the best measure of effectiveness. A better measure of effectiveness is "timely detection." Timely detection is the *minimum cumulative probability of detecting the adversary while there is enough time remaining for the response force to interrupt the adversary.* The delay elements along the path determine the point by which the adversary must be detected. That point is where the minimum delay along the remaining portion of the path just exceeds the guard response time. The minimum cumulative probability of interruption (P_I) is the cumulative probability of detection from the start of the path up to the point determined by the time remaining for the guards to respond. This value of P_I serves as a measure of the physical protection system effectiveness. An example of this concept is shown at the end of the chapter.

PHYSICAL PROTECTION SYSTEM DESIGN AND THE RELATIONSHIP TO RISK

The analysis of a physical protection system includes the determination of the physical protection system objectives, characterizing the design of the physical protection system, the evaluation of the design, and possibly, a redesign or refinement of the system. The process must begin by gathering information about the facility, defining the threat and then identifying targets. Determination of whether or not the assets are attractive targets is based mainly on the ease or difficulty of acquisition and desirability of the material. The next step is to characterize the design of the physical protection system by determining the elements of detection, delay, and response. The physical protection system is then analyzed and evaluated to ensure it meets the physical protection objectives. Evaluation must allow for features working together to assure protection rather than regarding each feature separately.

The basic premise of the methodology described in this chapter is that the design and analysis of physical protection must be done from a systems standpoint. In this way, all components of detection, delay and response can be properly weighted according to their contribution to the physical protection system (PPS) as a whole. At a higher level, the facility owner must balance the effectiveness of the PPS against available resources and then evaluate the proposed design. Without a methodical, defined, analytical assessment, the PPS might waste valuable resources on unnecessary protection or, worse yet, fail to provide adequate protection at critical points of the facility. Due to the complexity of protection systems, an evaluation usually requires computer modeling techniques. If any vulnerabilities are found, the initial system must be redesigned to correct the vulnerabilities and a reevaluation conducted. Then the system overall risk should be calculated. This risk is normalized to the consequence severity if the adversary could attain the target. The facility is then able to make a judgement as to the amount of risk that exists and if this is acceptable.

There are some significant considerations of the PPS designer, the facility management and any regulatory authority as they are charged with answering the question "How do we know if the security system is good enough?" In the previous discussion, the concept of probability of interruption of the defined adversary along the most vulnerable path in the facility was developed and identified as the best measure of PPS effectiveness. The next question is, "Given a certain P_I, is that good enough?"

The final question really is "How much risk is the facility willing to accept versus the cost of reducing that risk?" If the facility and regulators understand that there are a limited amount of resources to be applied to physical protection of everything at the facility, then each application of a portion of those resources must be carefully and analytically evaluated to ensure a balanced risk. The remainder of this chapter will briefly explain the method of risk identification and mitigation practiced by Sandia National Laboratories.

The risk equation used is:

$$R = P_A * [1 - (P_I)] * C$$

where the terms are as follows:

R = *Risk to the facility (or stakeholders)* of an adversary gaining access to, or stealing, critical assets. Range is 0 to 1.0, with 0 being no risk and 1.0 being maximum risk.

P_A = *Probability of an adversary attack.* This can be difficult to determine, but generally there are records available to assist in this effort. The value of this probability is from 0 (no chance at all of an attack) to 1.0 (certainty of attack). Usually in the calculation of risk, we assume P_A = 1.0, which means that the risk answer is a "conditional risk." That is, the calculated risk *given* that an attack on a facility will occur.

P_I = *Probability of Interruption.* This is the probability that the defined adversary will be interrupted by the response force in time to stop the adversary from accomplishing their objectives. The principle of timely detection is used in calculating this probability from 0 (the adversary will definitely be successful) to 1.0 (the adversary will definitely be interrupted in their path).

C = *Consequence Value.* This is a value from 0 to 1 that relates the severity of the occurrence of the event. This is the normalizing factor that allows the conditional risk value to be compared to all other risks across the site. A consequence table of all events could be created which would cover the spectrum of loss, from highest to lowest. Therefore, by using this consequence table, the risk can be normalized over all possible events. Then the limited PPS resources can be appropriately allocated to ensure the risk is acceptable across the spectrum.

If we assume that P_A is equal to 1 (there *will* be an attack), this term drops out of the equation. If we then also assume that C is equal to 1, that is, the consequence is the highest we can imagine, this term also drops out. This leaves a conditional risk, R, that is determined solely by the effectiveness of the PPS, which can be useful in establishing the "worst case" risk – i.e., an attack by the most capable adversary on the most valuable target. It is then possible to go back and use different Consequence Values to determine the risk to the enterprise for lower consequence losses. This will allow a prioritization of targets and appropriate protection. Finally, the probability of attack may also be varied, based on available data where possible, and a realistic assessment of risk can be obtained. This three-step process can help in simplifying the complexity of the risk assessment by varying only one term at a time, allowing an appreciation about the influence of each factor on the outcome.

Once the risk value is determined, the security manager can justify the expenditure of funds based on a scientific, measurable and prioritized analysis. This information can be presented to executive management of the corporation or facility to demonstrate how the security risk is being mitigated and how much risk exposure remains. The analysis can then form the basis for a discussion on how much security risk can be tolerated or how much to increase or decrease the budget based on risk. This analysis can also serve to demonstrate to any regulatory agencies that a careful review of the security of the facility has been performed and that reasonable measures are in place to protect people and assets. The analysis will allow the facility to state the assumptions that were made (threat, targets, risk level), show the system design and provide an analysis to show system effectiveness.

This process only describes the evaluated risk of the security system and its effectiveness. It should be noted that there are multiple risk areas for a facility or corporation, of which security is only one part. Other areas of risk that need to be considered within the business enterprise include financial risk management, liability risk financing, property/net income financing, employee benefits, environmental health and safety and property engineering.[16] The facility or corporate Chief Risk Officer must still combine all of the various risks and help the corporation manage total risk. While the security department may be able to aid in mitigation of risk in other areas, the security supervisor is only one of many experts who must be depended on to assure that the corporate enterprise manages and limits their risk exposure. Finally, this approach allows for risk control through two mechanisms. Traditional loss reduction or mitigation, which is the reduction of severity by employing methods to mitigate or minimize the impact of a loss *after* the event occurs (insurance), is very reactive. Another approach is that of loss prevention, which is the reduction of frequency by employing methods to prevent the loss from occurring. This is a more proactive risk control philosophy. Good risk programs should include a combination of risk financing (insurance) and risk control tools to treat the risk.[16]

It should be clear that the security program is one that contributes to the bottom line of the corporation, by protecting assets from malevolent human threats. The security supervisor should be capable of managing available resources to best protect corporate assets and adjusting resources as required in the face of changing threats. This is the role of the security supervisor in the corporate structure.

SUMMARY

This chapter has covered the use of a systematic and measurable approach to the implementation of a physical protection system. The concept of detection, followed by delay and response, was emphasized and a brief description of the relationship of these functions was presented. Specific performance measures of various components of a PPS were described, along with how these measures are combined to support a cost/benefit analysis. The process stresses the use of integrated systems combining people, procedures, and equipment to meet the protection objectives. In support of this concept, the difference between safety and security was described to clarify the contrast between natural disasters and malevolent human attack. The role of training, particularly for the guard force, was also described.

The intent of this chapter is not to create an expert designer, but rather, to instill an appreciation of the relationship between protection objectives and the system that is implemented. This must be accomplished within the constraints of the facility, while at the same time mitigating risk to a known level. The concepts presented here are somewhat unique in the security industry as a whole, but have been demonstrated to be effective in protecting critical nuclear assets for the past 25 years. Although your particular facility may not require the same level of protection, or have the same unacceptably high consequence of loss (the loss of a nuclear weapon or material could result in the death of thousands of people), the process described in these pages can still be applied to protect your targets against the appropriate threats. Ultimately, this leads to an effective system design that can be used to explain why certain security components were used, how they contribute to the system effectiveness, and how this system mitigates total risk to the facility or corporation. This, then, is the goal of the chapter – to allow a security supervisor to discern whether or not an existing or proposed physical protection system has considered all pertinent information and determine if the system is effective at expected levels. Once the supervisor has collected all of this information, supported by application of rigorous criteria and validated analysis, a powerful case can be made to executive management to justify the security department budget and role, and build recognition of the security function as a major part of the corporation's business, not just a non-value-added inconvenience.

Sample Analysis Scenario

Suppose there is a facility with a fence around the boundary, an open space, and then a few buildings with production activities taking place. A single outside criminal, with a hand gun and a cutting torch, decides to break into the facility and steal an asset located in a vault in the building. The perimeter fence has a fence disturbance sensor on the part of the fence that is located at the back edge of the facility. There are two security guards on duty in the lobby of the facility, who monitor multiple pan-tilt-zoom cameras placed on the exterior and interior of the facility though the use of a CCTV system. There are magnetic switch contacts on all doors and Passive Infrared Sensors (PIR) in all rooms and offices in the buildings. The vault has a 4 inch thick steel door and 6 inch thick concrete walls. Inside the vault is a microwave sensor. There are no exterior guard patrols. The response time of the guards at this facility is 4 minutes (240 seconds). Table 1 summarizes the adversary's steps in attacking the facility.

Action	Probability of Detection	Delay Time (seconds)
1. Climb side fence	0.1	5
2. Run to building	0.1	15
3. Open door	0.3	20
4. Move to asset	0.5	30
5. Remove asset	0.4	300
6. Exit building through outer door	0.1	5
7. Cross open area to back fence	0.3	10
8. Leave area by car	0.1	7

Table 1 – Adversary Attack Route, Initial System

The detection values at steps 1 & 2 are assigned by the chance that a guard or employee may spot the attacker climbing the fence or running across the area, with no sensor technology deployed. The delay times reflect the time it takes to climb the fence and run 100 yards to the building. As the attacker enters a side door, the magnetic switch sensor has a P_D of 0.3; the door is locked and it takes 20 seconds to defeat the lock. The attacker then crosses the distance from the door to the office, which has a PIR sensor. The delay time is for the attacker walking across the inner area. Next, the adversary reaches the vault and takes 5 minutes (300 seconds) to defeat the door. The P_D of the interior microwave is 0.4. The adversary then takes the asset and starts his escape by fleeing through the same door he entered, crossing the open area from the side door to the rear of the property and climbing the section of the fence with the sensor, which results in a P_d of 0.3. He then jumps into his car and escapes with the asset. The total adversary task time for this scenario is 392 seconds, or approximately 6.5 minutes.

Computer analysis of this series of events is shown in Table 1. Observe that there is a 67% chance of the adversary being interrupted along this path. This is determined by going back from the target and finding the point where there is more than 240 seconds of delay time left (the amount of time it will take the response force to arrive and interrupt the adversary). This indicates that if the adversary is not detected by the time he reaches the vault door (the first point where over 240 seconds of delay remains), there will not be enough time to stop him. The 0.67 represents the cumulative probability of detecting the adversary by the time he reaches the vault door, which is influenced by the low probability of detection up to the building. Since detection must occur *before* he reaches the vault door for the response force to be successful, the system does not get the benefit of the lengthy delay at the vault door, which favors the adversary. The facility security manager decides that this is not good enough, since loss of this asset would be a high consequence. She decides to add a fence sensor around the remaining three sides of the perimeter to see if this will help. She installs a different kind of fence sensor on the fence and improves the PD to 0.9. The new value is reflected in Table 2.

Action	Probability of Detection	Delay Time (seconds)
1. Climb side fence	0.9	5
2. Run to building	0.1	15
3. Open door	0.3	20
4. Move to asset	0.5	30
5. Remove asset	0.4	300
6. Exit building through outer door	0.1	5
7. Cross open area to back fence	0.3	10
8. Leave area by car	0.1	7

Table 2 – Adversary Attack Route, Upgraded System

Using this new P_D value in the model gives the result shown in Table 2. The probability of interruption has now improved to 93%, due to the addition of improved early detection. Now, the chances of success are much higher, since there is a much higher chance that the intruder will be detected when climbing the fence. Now, *all* of the delay time will be credited since the response force knows they are under attack and has ample time to respond and stop the attack.

This is a simple example, for one path, that shows the usefulness of the systematic approach to security system design and analysis of the system to predict effectiveness.

ENDNOTES

1.   James E. Chapek and Paul Ebel, "Systematic Design of Physical Protection Systems," presented at 12th Annual American Defense Preparedness Association Symposium on Security Technology, June 17-20, 1996, Williamsburg, Va.

2.   Robert L. Barnard, *Intrusion Detection Systems*, Butterworth Publishers, Stoneham, 1988, pp. 7-15.

3.   Howard W. Timm and Kenneth E. Christian, *Introduction to Private Security*, Brooks-Cole Publishing, Pacific Grove, 1991, pp. 124-128.

4.   Harvey Burstein, *Introduction to Security*, Prentice Hall, Englewood Cliffs, 1994, pp. 217-230.

5.   Karen M. Hess and Henry M. Wrobleski, *Introduction to Private Security,* West Publishing, St. Paul, 1996, pp. 723-732.

6.   Lawrence J. Fennelly, *Handbook of Loss Prevention and Crime Prevention*, Butterworth-Heinemann, Newton, 1996, pp. 33-54.

7.   A.H. Tickner, and D.C.V. Simmonds, et al. "Monitoring 16 Television Screens Showing Little Movement," *Ergonomics*, Vol. 15, No. 3, pp. 279-292, 1972.

8.   Neil Cumming, *Security*, Butterworth-Heinemann, Newton, 1992, pp. 79-171.

9.   Lawrence J. Fennelly, *Handbook of Loss Prevention and Crime Prevention*, Butterworth-Heinemann, Newton, 1996, pp. 268-280.

10.   Robert L. Barnard, *Intrusion Detection Systems*, Butterworth Publishers, Stoneham, 1988, pp. 71-217.

11.   A.H. Tickner, and D.C.V. Simmonds, et al. "Monitoring 16 Television Screens Showing a Great Deal of Movement," *Ergonomics,* Vol. 16, No. 4, pp. 381-402, 1972.

12.   Herman Kruegle, *CCTV Surveillance: Video Practices and Technology*, Butterworth-Heinemann, Newton, 1995, pp. 65-126.

13.   Robert L. Barnard, *Intrusion Detection Systems*, Butterworth Publishers, Stoneham, 1988, pp. 221-349.

14.   *Harold A. Bennett, "The "EASI" Approach to Physical Security Evaluation," *SAND Report #760500*, 1977.

15.   *L. D. Chapman and C. P. Harlan, "EASI Estimate of Adversary Sequence Interruption on an IBM PC," *SAND Report #851105,* 1985.

16.   M. Michael Zuckerman, *"Moving Towards a Holistic Approach to Risk Management Education – Teaching Business Security Management, "* presented at 2nd Annual American Society of Industrial Security Education Symposium, August 13-15, 1998, New York, NY.

      * SAND Reports available from:

National Technical Information Service   U.S. Government Printing Office
U.S. Department of Commerce   Superintendent of Documents
5285 Port Royal Road   Federal Depository Libraries Program
Springfield, VA 22161   OR   Washington, D.C. 20402
Phone: 1-800-553-NTIS (6847) or 703-605-6000   Phone: 202-512-1530; 888-293-6498
Fax: 703-321-8547   Fax: 202-512-1262
TDD: 703-487-4639   Email: gpoaccess@gpo.gov
Internet: http://www.ntis.gov/ordering.htm   Internet: http://www.access.gpo.gov

SECURITY SYSTEMS DESIGN AND EVALUATION
QUIZ

1.   Which is NOT an example of a threat tactic?
     a)   Stealth
     b)   Force
     c)   Deceit
     d)   Timely detection

2.   Which of the following would cause a false alarm for an intrusion detection system?
     a)   Rabbit
     b)   Wind
     c)   Blowing trash
     d)   Component failure

3.   Deterrence contributes a measurable amount to an effective physical protection system.
              □ T   □ F

4.   The probability of detection for a sensor depends primarily upon:
     a)   Threat to be detected
     b)   Sensor hardware design
     c)   Installation conditions
     d)   All of the above

5.   In a physical security system, which is NOT a threat scenario?
      a)   Theft
      b)   Sabotage
      c)   Kidnaping
      d)   Earthquake

6.   Which of the following is a performance measure for delay barriers?
      a)   Location of barrier
      b)   Size of barrier
      c)   Time to defeat barrier
      d)   Type of barrier

7.   Which of the following is a performance measure for a sensor?
      a)   Probability of detection
      b)   Placement in the facility
      c)   Technology class
      d)   Detection volume

8.   Detection is not complete until there has been assessment of the alarm.
            □ T   □ F

9.   Which of the following is NOT a performance measure for a sensor?
      a)   Probability of detection
      b)   Sensor application
      c)   Nuisance alarm rate
      d)   Vulnerability to defeat

10.   Which information is NOT required to define a threat?
      a)   Class of adversary—insider, outsiders, outsiders in collusion with insiders
      b)   Adversary tactics—deceit, force, stealth or a combination
      c)   Adversary capabilities—knowledge, motivation, skills, tools, weapons
      d)   Security System—intrusion detection system

STATISTICAL ANALYSIS
by Patricia A. O'Donoghue, CPO, CSS

STATISTICAL ANALYSIS

Statistical analysis ultimately boils down to numerical results: the methods and processes used in obtaining them and the methods and means for estimating their reliability. You do not have to be a mathematical wizard or speak only in theorem(s); even the average person has confidence in a conclusion stated in numerical language and supported by numerical facts and I'm 99.9% sure about the accuracy of that statement.

Simply put, there are three steps involved in the management of a statistical problem that can be summarized as follows:
1.   The collection of data
2.   The organization of data
3.   The analysis of data

In order to grasp the meaning of a vast amount of numerical data, you must reduce its bulk. The process of abstracting the significant facts contained in the data and making clear and concise statements about the derived results constitutes a statistical analysis. Common sense and experience are key elements in the analysis phase of information gathering. It's purpose is to give a summarized and comprehensible numerical description of large amounts of information.

THE COLLECTION OF DATA

Why does a security supervisor need to learn about the collection of data or research methods? The reasons are quite simple: wouldn't it be an asset to any organization if managers could sense, spot and deal with problems before they become serious? Knowing about research and problem solving processes assists managers to identify problems and find out more about the situation.

Staffing Exercise

For example, consider a problem that all managers face at one time or another: the staffing of the work force. As a manager faced with this problem, you will need to collect some data. Here are some things to consider, statistically speaking. First and foremost, what is the total number of individuals that you will need to effectively run your day-to-day operation? Now let's say that seventy percent are considered "old" employees; that is, they have worked in your security department for more than a year. The other thirty percent are "new" employees with the following attrition record:
- Within the first four months of their employment, 50 percent leave.
- Within the second four months, 20 percent leave.
- Within the next four months, 10 percent leave.

Conclusion: only 20 percent make it through the first year: they become "old" employees. Among the old employees, the attrition rate is 30 percent a year (or 10 percent every four months). With these rates in mind, how should you approach the problem of determining a hiring rate that will:
1.   Maintain a stable work force?
2.   Reduce the work force by any given percentage rate annually? or
3.   Increase the work force by any given percentage rate annually?

Once organized and analyzed, this research and data can be a useful decision-making tool rather than a mass of incomprehensible statistical information. In addition, being knowledgeable about research and research methods helps professional managers to (1) identify and solve small problems in the work setting, (2) know how to discriminate good research from bad research, (3) appreciate and constantly remember the multiple influences of factors impinging on a situation, and (4) take calculated risks in decision-making, knowing full well the probabilities attached to the different outcomes.

THE ORGANIZATION OF DATA

When a mass of data has been assembled, it is necessary to classify the material in some compact and orderly form before it can be effectively analyzed. This procedure merely takes the "ungrouped" original information and "groups" or places the information into a specific category to be utilized during periods where the information is tested for accuracy. You want to be able to work easily with the information, and organizing it into categories helps you do that.

Take for example the Affinity Diagram used in many Quality Initiatives;

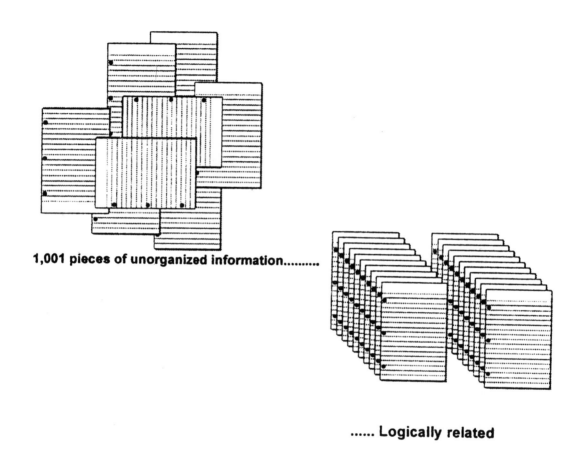

1,001 pieces of unorganized information..........

...... Logically related

Use the affinity diagram when you want to:
1.   quickly organize diverse data and perspectives.
2.   engage everyone in the brainstorming process.
3.   surface different perspectives.
4.   promote a common understanding.

Let's consider a real life example of how to organize data. For the manager of a security force charged with maintaining some type of access control into a facility, the waiting lines and waiting-line behavior of customers is a never ending concern. Waiting in lines (generally referred to as queues), occur when some employee or customer must wait for service and access into a facility. On the average, it is possible to be a member of at least three queues on any given day.

Hurry up and Wait Exercise

From a manager's point of view, here are some of your considerations in trying to solve this problem of the waiting in queue. The manager must try to hit a happy medium where waiting lines are short enough to minimize customer complaints keeping in mind it is clearly not practical to provide such extensive service so that no waiting line or queue can develop. In effect, managers balance the increased cost against the customer complaints (which increases as the average length of the wait increases). Data on time spent waiting in line can be organized and broken down into two categories, (1) the number of arrivals during a certain period of time; and (2) the time lost by personnel waiting for services (see Chart #1). More categories can be constructed to include the sheer numbers of persons waiting in line. This information may be used to determine if another service person should be assigned to the desk during a specific time of day, say between 7:00 and 9:00 o'clock in the morning when the line is the longest.

CHART #1

Period # (Hours)	# of Arrivals	Service Time (Minutes)
1	0	7,7
2	2	
3	0	
4	2	10,10
5	1	5
6	0	
7	4	6,7,9,12
8	7	3,4,6,7,9,10,15
9	5	4,5,5,7,10
10	0	
11	0	
12	2	4,4
13	0	
14	0	
15	0	
16	1	10
17	0	
18	4	5,5,7,10
19	1	8
20	1	10
21	0	

22	0	
23	0	
24	1	10
TOTAL	31	231 Minutes
TIME ANALYSIS: 231 minutes or an average waiting time per arrival of 231/31 = 7.45 minutes.		

As the charts illustrate, it is not only good customer service to provide two access control individuals at the desk but, more importantly, it is cost effective. The Chief Financial Officer (CFO) would love to hear how you saved the company money and utilized your personnel effectively with this one example.

ANALYSIS OF DATA

Since statistics has to do primarily with obscured measurements, which are admittedly approximations, and with processes that are also approximate, it is obvious that any numerical result obtained from them will be an approximation.

Decision-Making

If it were possible to predict the future with complete certainty, the structure of managerial decision would be radically different from what it is. There would be no excess production, no clearance sales, no speculation in the stock market.

As we do not live in a world of complete certainty, we usually try to make decisions by using the probability theory. Usually managers will have some knowledge about the possible outcomes in a decision situation; by collecting and organizing information, as we've spoken about earlier, and considering it systematically, managers often will reach a sounder decision than if they try and guess.

The concept of probability is a part of our everyday lives, both personal and professional. When they predict rain, we change our plans from outdoor activities to indoor ones. Managers who manage inventories go through a series of decision-making situations similar to when we change our original plans of having fun from outside to inside. Both these decision-makers benefit from their own assessment of the chances that certain things will happen.

Probability is the chance that something will happen. In probability theory, an event is one or more of the possible outcomes of doing something. For example, let's examine the classic coin-toss event. We all know if we toss a coin getting a tail would be an event; and getting a head would be another event. This activity of tossing the coin in probability theory is called an experiment.

Most managers, like yourself, are much less excited about coin tossing than they are in the answers to questions like, "Did we order enough blazers?" or "What are the chances that our uniforms will arrive in time for the Annual Meeting?" or "Will the transportation strike affect our shipment of shirts?"

When conducting experiments in probability there are two terms that you should be familiar with: mutually exclusive and collectively exhaustive events.

Events are mutually exclusive if one and only one of them takes place at a time. Consider again the example of the coin toss. We have two possible outcomes, heads or tails. On any single toss, either heads or tails may turn up, but not both. Accordingly, the events heads and tails on a single toss are said to be mutually exclusive. The question you should ask yourself, in determining whether the events are mutually exclusive, is can two or more of these events occur at one time? If the answer is yes, the events are not mutually exclusive.

When you make a list of possible events that can result from an experiment and this list includes every possible outcome, you have a collectively exhaustive list. In the coin toss example, the list "heads and tails" is collectively exhaustive – unless the coin lands on its edge.

In analyzing data and decision-making, most managers should consider and use probabilities. If you do use probabilities, you should be concerned with two situations: (1) the case where one event or the other will occur, and (2) the case where two or more will occur.

Another very important element of analyzing data (in addition to probabilities) is forecasting. Every manager considers some kind of forecast in every decision that he or she makes. Some of these forecasts are quite simple. Take the case of the operations manger who, on Thursday, forecasts the workload she anticipates for Friday in order to give one of her security officers time off. Other forecasts are more complex and usually involve long periods of time, cost and government regulation of some future issue.

No one forecasts with accuracy; nevertheless, decisions must still be made every day and they are made with the best information that is available.

Forecasting Processes

Whether you use one forecasting technique or another, the forecasting process stays pretty much the same.
1.   Determine the objective of the forecast. (What is its use?)
2.   Select the period over which the forecast will be made. (What are your information needs over what time period?)
3.   Select the forecasting approach you will use. (Which forecasting technique is most likely to produce the information you need?)
4.   Gather the information to be used in the forecast.
5.   Make the forecast.

Forecasting Types

There are three basic types of forecasts: judgmental forecasts, extensions of past history, and casual forecasting models.

A.   Judgmental Forecasts

We tend to use these kinds of forecasts when "good" data is not readily available. With a judgmental forecast we are trying to change subjective opinion into a quantitative forecast that we can use. The process brings together, in an organized way, personal judgements about the process being analyzed. Essentially, we are relying primarily on human judgement to interpret past data and make projections about the future.

B.   Extensions of Past History (also called time-series methods)

When we take history as our beginning point for forecasting, it doesn't mean that we think October will be just like August and September; it simply means that over the short run we believe that future patterns tend to be extensions of past ones and that we can make some useful forecasts by studying past behavior.

C.   Casual Forecasting Modes

If considerable historical data are available and if we know the relationship between the variables we want to forecast and other variables we can retrieve, it is possible to construct a casual forecast. This model is an example of forecasts which relate several variables.

Let's take a look at how we might use our decision-making skills and analysis of data in an exercise.

Inventory Exercise

For many security organizations the inventory figure is an extremely large asset. Inventory difficulties can and do contribute to a business' poor image, lack of authority and control and sometimes to the ultimate, failure. In this exercise hopefully you will be able to see that skillful inventory management can make a significant contribution to the security operation.

There are two basic inventory decisions managers must make as they attempt to accomplish the functions of inventory:

1.   How much or rather how many items to order when the inventory of that item is to be replenished.
2.   When to replenish the inventory of that item.

When to order decisions (consider):

a)   *Lead Time*
     If you are calling for home delivery of a pizza and it takes 30 minutes or less for it to arrive, then 30 minutes is the lead time for ordering.

b)   *Lead Time Demand*
     Consider how many pairs of gloves, seasonal items, winter coats or short-sleeve shirts you will need to have in stock, then when stock reaches a certain point, when to order.

c)   *Stockouts*
     Have a contingency plan. Demand of items will continue even in terrible weather (flood, snow, hurricanes), strikes, or even transportation disasters. Consider them all and plan accordingly.

d)   *Safety Stock*
     Hold out some extra items, just in case. The term safety stock refers to extra inventory held as a hedge, or protection, against the possibility of a stockout. It is however, always part of the total inventory.

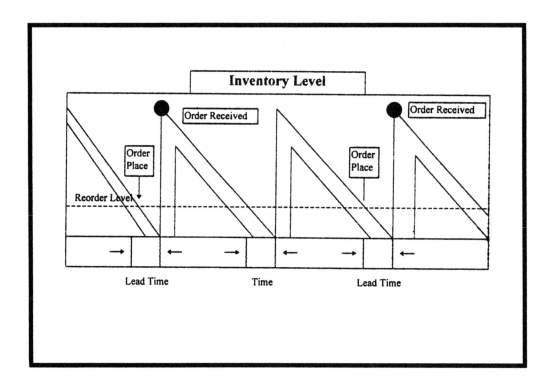

Inventory level with constant demand and lead time.

Graphic Presentations

Columns of numbers have been known to evoke fear, boredom, apathy, and misunderstanding. While some persons seem to "tune out" statistical information presented in tabular form, they may pay close attention to the same data presented in graphic or picture form. As a result you may want to use graphs as opposed to tables.

Here are two very basic examples of how to illustrate your results:

1.   Pie Chart—One of the simplest graphic methods. A circular graph whose pieces add up to 100 percent. Pie charts arc particularly useful for visualizing differences in frequencies among a few normal-level categories.

Pie charts provide a quick and easy illustration of data that can be divided into a few categories.

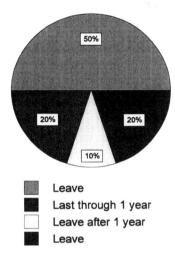

■ Leave
■ Last through 1 year
□ Leave after 1 year
■ Leave

2.   Bar Graphs—The bar graph (or histogram) can accommodate any number of categories at any level of measurement and, therefore, is more widely used.

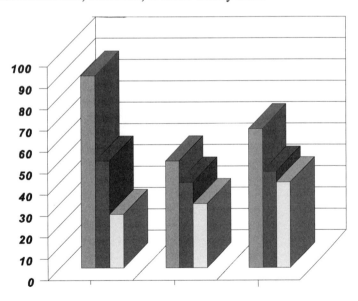

In summary, graphic presentations of data can be used to increase the readability of your findings.

CONCLUSION

Whether trying to influence people or justify your operating budget, look to your everyday experiences as data. Use that information to make predictions about future events and use statistics as an aid in testing your predictions. As with many managerial tasks, there is uncertainty and the use of statistical analysis is no exception; however, utilizing the probability theory and forecasting methods along with simple mathematical formulas and percentages will add authenticity to your decisions and confidence in your conclusions.

STATISTICAL ANALYSIS
QUIZ

1. Statistical analysis is the methods and processes used in obtaining _____ and the methods and means for estimating their reliability.

2. _____ and _____ are the key elements in the analysis phase of information gathering.

3. Events are _____ if one and only one of them takes place at a time.

4. The time-series method of forecasting is also called _____.

5. In _____ forecasting, you are relying primarily on human judgement to interpret past data and make future projections.

6. Even the average person has confidence in a conclusion stated in numerical language and supported by numerical facts.
    ☐ T   ☐ F

7. The waiting lines or queues are a problem for a manager because the manager must balance the increased cost of more help against customer complaints.
    ☐ T   ☐ F

8. Statistics are not approximations.
    ☐ T   ☐ F

9. Probability is the chance that something will happen.
    ☐ T   ☐ F

10. Casual forecasting models have to do with the weather conditions.
    ☐ T   ☐ F

SECURITY TECHNOLOGIES
by Henry C. Ruiz, CPO

INTRODUCTION

As we enter the 21st century, our roles as protection officers are changing at a tremendous rate, particularly where the use of high technology based tools such as computers are involved. To be more effective, protection officers must be well versed in the use of high technology tools.

High technology has influenced our profession and will continue to do so. In our profession high technology is primarily used in electronic access control systems, closed circuit television systems, fire safety/life safety systems, and non-security systems monitored by protection personnel. With the computer as a baseline tool, high technology has changed and enhanced our profession with the concept called Security Systems Integration. Security Systems Integration is a concept that all protection officers must be familiar with.

SECURITY SYSTEMS INTEGRATION

In the past our roles as protection officers primarily concerned the issues of access control and physical security. These roles were limited. As such, we were perceived as unskilled persons whose main functions were to guard gates and shake doors. This changed with advances in technology. Specifically, what affected our profession was the invention of the personal computer. This enabled many security tools to be developed or improved on, such as alarm systems, access control systems and closed circuit television systems.

For many years the security industry was divided into security guard services and alarm services. They were perceived as being separate functions. Today our roles and what we do go far beyond these functions. We provide many services to our customers beyond access control and physical security. We are total protection professionals. With the advances in technology, electronic access control systems, closed circuit television systems, fire safety/life safety systems and related systems, we protection professionals can now meet the needs of our customers more effectively with more tools to work with. This is what is called Security Systems Integration. For the protection officer, the definition of Security Systems Integration is: The unification of computer based security and related systems into one overall system that is controlled by the operator and meeting the needs of any situation.

PERSONAL COMPUTER BASICS

High technology tools affect everything we do. To increase our professional skills, and in fact survive in the 21st century, we must master these tools. The most important tool and the baseline of Security Systems Integration is the personal computer, more commonly called the PC.

Personal Computers in Security Operations

Personal computers have many applications in security operations. As a minimum, they are used to control and monitor electronic access control systems, closed circuit television systems, fire safety/life safety systems and security management systems including patrol tour systems, officer scheduling, parking lot control, key control and incident reporting and investigation management systems. More and more personal computers are becoming major tools in security operations. They are becoming easier to use and make the protection officers more effective in their day to day duties.

What Is a Personal Computer?

A personal computer is an electronic based device or appliance that can perform complex computations, gather data, provide information in data or picture (graphic) form and control various systems including those used in security operations.

In its simplest form a personal computer is similar to other electronic based appliances such as televisions, radios and stereo systems. They are just as simple to understand and operate. A personal computer is composed of what is called hardware and software. PC hardware is usually made up of a console which contains the parts and systems that is the actual computer, a monitor which looks similar to a television, a keyboard similar to that of a typewriter, a printer and other useful devices such as a mouse, which will be described shortly. Software programs are instructions that tell a PC what to do. Software is either stored in the computer in what is called a hard disk drive or in small disks or compact discs that are inserted in the computer when they are used.

Personal Computer Hardware

Console: A PC console is basically a plastic and metal box containing the computer. It can be in the shape of a flat rectangular box called a "desk top" or in a vertical form called a "tower." On the back of the console are connections called "ports" to which are attached the various kinds of hardware including the monitor, keyboard and printer. In the front of the console is the on/off switch or button and status lights that indicate when the computer is on and at least two horizontal slots for software disks or compact discs. Inside the console are the basic components of the computer. The most important components are the microprocessor, random access memory (RAM), hard disk drive, floppy disk drive, CD-ROM disc drive and modem. A brief description of each follows:

Microprocessor: The microprocessor is the most important part of a computer. It is the brains of the computer and controls the flow of information throughout a computer system. Due to the miracles of high technology, the microprocessor is housed in a tiny microchip no larger than a dime. The performance and power of a microchip is based on clock speed which is measured in the electronic measurement of megahertz (MHz) A megahertz is equivalent to one million electrical vibrations per second. The higher the megahertz, the more powerful the microprocessor is. The microprocessor is also called the central process unit or CPU.

Random Access Memory (RAM): RAM is the second most important part of a PC. RAM is where computers temporarily store information while they are in use. RAM is like an electronic work area where you store your work items. RAM is measured in the electronic measurement of megabytes which is over a million bytes or about 500 pages of text. Most PCs need at least 8 megabytes of RAM to function effectively.

Hard Disk Drive: To permanently store software programs and other information, the PC uses magnetic based disks to store information. These disks are stored in devices called drives. The primary kind of disk is called the hard disk drive and is stored in the PC console. A hard disk drive or hard drive contains several disks. These disks rotate very quickly and the information stored on them is read by special heads which can also write data onto these disks. Green or yellow lights on the front of a PC console let you know when the drive is in use. Hard drives store an enormous amount of information from 500 megabytes and up.

Floppy Disk Drive: In every PC there is at least one opening to fit a 3.5 inch sized floppy disk. Floppy disks hold at least 1.44 megabytes of data. Floppy disks are work horses and are used to store information on almost any subject and for almost any application.

CD-ROM Drive: Most PCs have a CD-ROM drive to accommodate compact discs. These discs can hold upwards of 650 megabytes of information and are extremely useful for such applications as animated graphics, sound, and video. These applications are certainly used in security operations. The compact disc is rapidly replacing the floppy disk as the work horse of PC systems.

Modem: Personal computers use telecommunications technology quite extensively, particularly with the use of the Internet. To use telecommunications systems such as telephone and telephone lines, the computer must be able to communicate with these systems. This is accomplished with the use of a device called a modem which converts data and transmits it through telecommunications lines. It is an essential part of personal computers, especially those dealing with security applications.

Other Personal Computer Hardware: As mentioned earlier, other major PC hardware includes the monitor, keyboard, printer and mouse. These and other PC hardware not actually inside the PC console are called peripheral devices. A brief description of each follows:

Monitor: The monitor is very similar to a television set but does more. Monitors have to display a clear and crisp display of text in addition to moving images. Monitors are also configured to produce sound to accommodate what is called "multimedia" applications that enable one to interact with a computer more effectively.

Keyboard: The keyboard is the primary input or entry device for a computer. Similar to a typewriter keyboard, it has many functions. Composed of at least 110 keys, the keyboard controls the functions of a computer including entering/deleting data, calculating, and control functions.

Printer: The printer is the primary output device for a computer. The printer produces output in the form of hard copy paper text, graphs and photographs. Printers come in various shapes and sizes and produce copy of varying degrees of quality.

Mouse: Another major input device is the mouse. A mouse is usually a small control device connected to the computer via a cord. Its shape and cord make it look like a mouse. A mouse performs many functions more effectively and efficiently than a keyboard, particularly control functions. It is a major tool for the computer user.

Peripheral Devices Applicable to Security Operations: Many computer based security application systems have peripheral devices attached to PCs. The most common are badge and identification units used to take photographs and data recorders used in computer based or bar code based patrol tour systems.

Software

When you turn on a computer it will activate most of its components. This process will show up on the monitor as the computer warms up. The system will be ready to use when the computer's "operating system" is activated. The operating system is the software that actually tells the computer what to do. Today the most widely used operating system is Windows. Windows and various versions are very easy to use and very flexible. By itself, Windows offers the user many features including word processing, data management, and system controls. Before Windows the most widely used operating system was disk operating system or DOS. This system is very difficult and time consuming to use.

Although Windows and its various versions offer the user many options and capabilities, a PC will also accommodate other software called "application software." The amount and subject matter of application software is vast. Included are software packages for word processing, database management, spreadsheet analysis, graphics, and control systems. The number and subject matter for security operations used is also extensive and many products are on the market. Many of you work with them. With a PC you can draft incident reports, manage and analyze information, make decisions, and control sophisticated systems including most security and security related systems. In general, a PC enables you to perform your duties more effectively and efficiently.

How Personal Computers Are Used in Security Operations

In security operations computers are commonly used to control and monitor electronic access control systems and other security related systems that are in an integrated environment where all systems work together and communicate with each other. For example, the most widely used security operation controlled and monitored by computers is alarm monitoring of intrusion alarms. A typical system consists of a PC set up described earlier connected to controller systems at alarmed areas or points via telecommunications lines. Alarmed points and areas are programmed and stored in the computer. The alarmed points and areas are displayed on the computer's monitor in graphic form such as maps, diagrams, video, digitized photographs, or alphanumerically. The computer and alarmed points/areas communicate via modems and are continuously monitored by the system controllers. The computer operator has the capability to monitor alarms with various features built in to the alarm monitoring software for the system. When the operator wants to monitor an alarm point or area, the operator enters an instruction into the computer using the keyboard, mouse, or peripheral device unique to the system. This instruction activates the computer's central processing unit (CPU) which reports the alarm status on the monitor, and on hard copy using the printer. When an alarm occurs, it is displayed on the monitor, recorded in memory by the CPU, and printed on hard copy. Most systems also display instructions concerning how to respond to alarms.

How and Where to Learn More about Computers

To become a more effective protection officer, it is to your benefit to learn all you can about personal computer systems. More opportunities will be available to you and you will be more value added to your employer if you are computer literate. Indeed, the trend is toward high technology. There will be fewer opportunities for traditional protection officers as we know it. The protection officer of the future will be a unique professional with a high level skill set and knowledge base including an effective command of computers and related systems.

There are many ways to become more well versed in computer systems. Many courses and training opportunities are available to learn about computers, primarily at the vocational and junior college level. There is a vast amount of literature dealing with computers in libraries and bookstores. You're also encouraged to get your own PC since one of the best ways to learn about computers is to use them.

On the job always seek opportunities to use computers. The best opportunities are in security control operations, security administration, security database management and the maintenance of computer systems and computer based security application systems.

ELECTRONIC ACCESS CONTROL BASICS

Access control is a security method that controls the flow of traffic through the access points and areas of a protected facility. Access control is one of the primary functions of protection officers. The key element of access control is identification. This can be accomplished by having officers posted at access points and areas, using closed circuit television systems and electrical/mechanical controls, or by using computer based electronic access control systems.

What Is Electronic Access Control?

Electronic Access Control (EAC) is a method of access control that uses computer based technology to control and monitor access. Most EAC systems use credit card sized access control cards that are programmed to actuate devices called card readers. These card readers are installed at controlled locations, usually doors. In a typical system, the individual presents his/her card to a card reader at the controlled location. The location could be a door, turnstile, gate or other access point or area. The card reader's sensor extracts information from the card and translates that information into a code number and sends this information to the system's computer. This number is compared with the user's programmed access information and access is either granted or denied. When access is denied, an alarm may be activated, depending on the system. In most cases, there may be a printed record of each access transaction. This provides the system's basic audit trail.

The Basic EAC System

The following describes a basic EAC system:

Access Cards

Proximity Cards
Proximity access cards are the most widely used for EAC systems. They work via the use of passively tuned circuits that have been embedded in a high grade fiberglass epoxy card. To gain access the cardholder holds or presents the card within 2 to 4 inches from a card reader. The reader's sensors detect the pattern of the frequencies programmed in the card. This pattern is then transmitted to the system's computer. If the pattern matches the reader's, the reader unlocks the door and records the transaction. If the pattern doesn't match, no access is granted and this information is recorded and an alarm may activate.

Magnetic Cards

Magnetic cards use various kinds of materials and mediums to magnetically encode digital data onto cards. To gain access, the card user inserts or "swipes" (passes the badges through) the card through a slot in the card reader. As the card is withdrawn from the reader, it moves across a magnetic head, similar to that of the tape recorder head, that reads the data programmed in the card. The information read from the card is sent to the system's computer for verification. If verification is made, the computer sends a signal to the card reader to grant or deny access, and if access is granted, the door is unlocked.

Magnetic cards look like credit cards. The most popular medium for this type of access card is magnetic stripe. With this type of card, a pattern of digital data is encoded on the card's magnetic stripe. This type of card is relatively inexpensive and a large amount of data can be stored on the magnetic stripe that is placed on one side of the card. Magnetic cards tend to chip and break, however, through excessive use. Another type of magnetic card medium uses very small dots of magnetic materials that are laminated between plastic layers of the card. This type of card is cheaper to use than the more widely used magnetic stripe card, but is subject to vandalism and wear and tear.

Weigand Cards

Weigand based access control cards use a coded pattern on magnetized wire that is embedded within the card. When this card is inserted into a reader, the reader's internal sensors are activated by the coded wire. This type of card is moderately priced and will handle a large amount of traffic. It is less vulnerable to vandalism and weather effects than other types of cards. Its main deficiency is that it is subject to wear and tear.

Other Types of Access Cards

Smart cards contain an integrated chip embedded in them. They have coded memories and microprocessors in them, hence, they're like computers. The technology in these cards offers many possibilities, particularly with proximity based access systems.

Optical cards have a pattern of light spots that can be read by a specific light source, usually infrared.

Capacitance cards use coded capacitor sensitive material that is enclosed in the card. A current is induced when the card activates a reader. This current checks the capacitance of the card to determine the proper access code.

Some access devices come in the shape of keys, disks, or other convenient formats that provide users with access tools that look attractive and subdued, but at the same time are functional.

Card Readers

Card readers are devices used for reading access cards. They come in various shapes, sizes, and configurations. The most common reader is the type where the card user inserts the card in a slot or runs or swipes the card through a slot. The other type of reader uses proximity technology where the card user presents or places the card on or near the reader.

Some insertion type card readers use alphanumeric or numeric keypads where after the user inserts the card, the user enters a unique code number on the keypad. This action then grants access.

Biometric Access Control

As we enter the 21st century biometric technology or the use of human biological characteristics for identification and verification is increasingly being used in access control systems. The most popular systems use hand geometry, fingerprints, palm prints, eye retinal patterns, voice prints and signature recognition. When biometric devices are used, they are designed and installed concurrently with card reader systems.

EAC System Applications

An EAC system is ideally used as part of a fully integrated facility management system. In such a system EAC is interfaced and integrated with closed circuit television systems, fire safety/life safety systems, communications systems and non-security systems such as heating, ventilation and air conditioning (HVAC) systems.

In an integrated system EAC systems allow users to be accessed into various areas or limit access. They can track access and provide attendance records. As a safety feature and for emergency response situations, they can determine where persons are located in facilities. In general, EAC systems are flexible and strides in technology are making them even more so.

CLOSED CIRCUIT TELEVISION SYSTEMS BASICS

Closed circuit television (CCTV) systems are among the most effective high technology tools for protection officers. They extend the "eyes" of protection officers and thus enhance the observation and reporting skills of protection officers. CCTV systems range from simple camera and cable systems to sophisticated and complex systems using various technologies and having many applications.

CCTV Equipment and Components

A basic CCTV system consists of a camera, monitor, transmission medium, control equipment, and recording devices. A brief description of each follows:

Camera

The camera used in modern CCTV systems is based on integrated circuit (IC) technology which uses an array of solid state light sensitive elements called pixels arranged on a silicon chip to sense light passed from the scene being televised through the camera's lens. The light passed by the lens falls on the camera's sensors. These sensors release electrons proportional to the intensity of the light striking the pixels. This electron stream is flexible depending on the camera configuration. The most popular type of camera is called a charged coupled device (CCD) camera. This type of camera is extremely powerful and comes in various shapes and sizes depending on its deployment. Cameras will record images in color or black and white depending on the need.

Monitor

The monitor displays the transmitted picture from the camera. The picture quality is similar to very advanced television systems. The picture can be displayed entirely on the monitor screen or via multiple images in a split screen format.

Transmission Medium

The CCTV camera generates a signal to be transmitted as a picture to the monitor by various mediums. The most widely used are coaxial cable, optical fiber, twisted wire pair and microwave.

Control Equipment

Most CCTV systems require control equipment for various purposes. Included are control mechanisms for controlling cameras, transmission mediums, focusing and lighting. Major control equipment for CCTV systems are multiplexors that enable multiple cameras to be used on one single system, signal processors, signal sequencers, video motion detectors, lens controls, switches and pan and tilt devices that control the movement of cameras.

Recording Equipment

Video recorders (VCRs) similar to those used for standard televisions are critical parts of CCTV systems. VCRs for CCTV systems have more advanced features than the typical VCR because of the information they record. VCRs record in real time or time lapse, which is slower than real time, but is more useful for security uses. Most VCRs record the time and date, which is essential for security needs.

CCTV Applications

CCTV applications are only dependent on the needs, creativity, and pocketbook of the end user. Most CCTV systems are used to monitor sensitive areas requiring surveillance. For example, a common application of CCTV is to supplement patrol operations by monitoring perimeter areas that cannot be patrolled continuously.

In an integrated system, CCTV has vast potential and uses. For example, in an access control application, when the access control system registers an alarm, it will signal the CCTV system to pan the area causing an alarm. The system's monitor will then show what is going on in the area, whether it be a tresspassing, burglary or other situation. This information will enable the end user to make the best decisions to deal with the situation. CCTV systems will also assist other components of an integrated system. In a fire safety/life safety situation, the CCTV system could be integrated with certain fire alarm systems and provide an image of an area being affected by fire. This assists first responders in assessing the situation safely without sending the person into harms way.

FIRE SAFETY/LIFE SAFETY AND NON-SECURITY SYSTEMS

Security operations have evolved from basic guard operations concerned only with physical security and the protection of material assets to having responsibility for various areas not traditionally associated with security. As a minimum, this includes fire safety/life safety systems, facility environmental systems and the monitoring of process controls for non-security areas such as manufacturing and laboratories. This concept of having security responsible for monitoring non-security systems is called total facility control (TFC). In TFC various aspects of a facility are connected to security systems via systems integration technology to provide total control over a facility and provide greater safety and comfort for facility occupants and users. Each area of TFC is summarized as follows:

Fire Safety/Life Safety Systems
The major components of fire safety/life safety systems include sprinkler systems, smoke detectors, duct detectors and heat detectors. In an integrated environment these systems are monitored and controlled at a centralized location by security personnel. Monitoring personnel have total control over these systems. They can override or shunt them for various purposes and alarms can be responded to more efficiently and effectively when combined with other systems. For example, a fire in a certain location will set off evacuation alarms, turn on a sprinkler system, lock certain doors to contain a fire and provide the exact location of the fire so it can be responded to by firefighting personnel. With conventional systems most of these functions would be executed separately and not interact with each other in a real time manner. In an integrated environment they would occur simultaneously or in real time.

Environmental Systems
In an integrated environment security personnel monitor and in certain cases respond to problems and situations involving environmental systems. Environmental systems include energy management via heating, ventilation and air conditioning systems (HVAC), lighting, elevator systems control and the control of power systems. These systems ensure that facilities are operating efficiently and providing a safe and comfortable environment for occupants. This applies to both buildings and campus facilities.

In an integrated environment, if a system is malfunctioning an alarm or signal will register on the system control monitored by security personnel. Depending on the type of control system used, the situation can be handled by security or dispatched to the appropriate facility maintenance personnel. For example, a common situation is a power outage or a power surge where the power needs of a facility may be interrupted. In a conventional system the common approach is to inspect every system affected and reset applicable systems. Notification of affected personnel must also be made. This takes time and involves many persons to respond. With an integrated system, systems can be reset from a centralized location (usually the control center) and notification can be made by telecommunications systems connected to the overall system. This saves time and labor costs.

Monitoring Process Controls for Non-Security Areas
The monitoring of process controls involves the profit end of an entity, either concerned with manufacturing/production or research and development. Monitoring process controls includes such systems as freezers, refrigerators, incubators, laboratory systems, water purification systems, and manufacturing and production processes.

In an integrated environment these systems can be connected to security control centers and monitored on specially designed systems. If a process control system alarms, security personnel can assess the situation and notify the proper persons to respond. The monitoring of process controls is value added because security is contributing to the bottom line of profit that these systems are generating.

HOW AND WHERE TO LEARN MORE ABOUT SECURITY SYSTEMS INTEGRATION AND HIGH TECHNOLOGY TOOLS

There are many avenues and opportunities for the protection officer to learn more about security systems integration and high technology tools. The best way to learn about these areas is through hands-on experience, training, and taking advantage of educational opportunities that are available through the following:

- Vocational schools offering courses in computer technology, electronics and related areas.
- Junior colleges offering courses in high technology areas.
- Computer and high technology courses offered by one's employer.
- Job opportunities and assignments involving personal computers, systems integration and high technology tools. Included are Control Room Operator, Security Systems Technician, and Security Specialist positions.

The information base concerning Security Systems Integration and high technology tools is vast, so be prepared for extensive study. The following references will provide you with a start.

BIBLIOGRAPHY

Security, ID Systems and Locks: The Book on Electronic Access Control by Joel Konicek and Karen Little; Butterworth-Heinemann, 1997. This is a very user friendly book about electronic access control.

Total Facility Control by Don T. Cherry; Butterworth, Stoneham, MA, 1986. This book describes in extensive and simplified detail the applications of security systems integration in relation to total facility control.

Access Control and Security Systems Integration. This is an excellent trade magazine and professional journal dealing with high technology security and related systems. It provides the latest information about access control and security systems integration. Address: 6151 Powers Ferry Road NW, Atlanta, Georgia 30339-2941.

More information about the above and other references can be obtained from the International Foundation for Protection Officers.

SECURITY TECHNOLOGIES
QUIZ

1. Security Systems Integration is the_____ of _____ security and related systems into one overall system that is controlled by the operator and meeting the needs of any situation.

2. Protection officers don't need to be concerned about high technology areas such as security systems integration and high technology tools that assist the protection officer.
   □ T   □ F

3. A _____ is a device that can perform complex computations, gather data, provide information in picture form, and control various systems.

4. Personal computers have many applications in security operations.
   □ T   □ F

5. _____ is a _____ method that controls the flow of traffic through the access points and areas of a protected facility.

6. The key element of access control is identification.
   □ T   □ F

7.   A _____ consists of a camera, monitor, transmission medium, control equipment, and
      recording devices.

8.   Proximity based electronic access control systems are inefficient, ineffective and are the least
      used access control system.
            □ T   □ F

9.   The concept of having security responsible for _____ non-security systems is called
      _____.

10.   Closed circuit television systems are among the most effective high technology tools for
      protection officers.
            □ T   □ F

HIGH-TECHNOLOGY THEFT
by Cole Morris, MPA, CSS

Theft in the workplace has been a traditional concern of security practitioners. However, the rapidly evolving technological work environment brings with it new concerns and vulnerabilities. Whether you are charged with the security of a hospital, academic institution, manufacturing plant, library or office complex, the possible theft of high-technology assets is a very real threat.

Much has been written in recent years about "computer security." This highly technical discipline is the realm of specialists concerned with the theft or sabotage of information from computers and networks. The intent of this chapter is not to make you an expert on such complex issues as fire walls and encryption. Instead, this chapter provides awareness and concepts pertinent to the average security supervisor.

The theft of computers and their components is a growing threat. Thieves are increasingly working in elaborate rings of robbers, brokers and fences. Computers vanish from the work site with alarming regularity. The cargo theft of laptop computers—often at gunpoint—is on the rise.

Consider the following news excerpts:

> *"Police recently questioned a man about a string of uptown computer thefts ... They were amazed to find he had keys to a number of office buildings ... More than 25 laptops were stolen from uptown businesses since February ..."*

> *"Two young men have been arrested for selling more than $6 million worth of high-end computer components ..."*

> *"The library's computers were broken into and their memory boards were removed ... The value of the heist is estimated to be over $5,000.00 ..."*

> *"High tech thefts of all types frequently occur with the participation of employees—particularly contract employees ... The American Society of Industrial Security states that more than half of all high-value component thefts are employee related ..."*

> *"The computer was recently purchased by the student counsel ... In addition to the loss of school-related information, the machine will cost $3,600 to replace."*

When even a single laptop or personal computer is stolen from the work site, losses occur in several ways:
1. The company experiences the replacement cost of the computer.
2. The company may experience the cost of lost data that is stored on the computer. This may mean thousands or millions of dollars.
3. The company experiences a loss of productivity while the computer is being replaced.

COMPONENT THEFT

Complete computer systems are not the only assets at risk. Individual computer components also are targeted by thieves. This is a crime that immediately impacts the victimized school, business or library. The usual components stolen are the RAM (random access memory), Pentium chips and sometimes the hard drive. There is a ready market for these types of components.

The losses are staggering. Nationally, this figure approaches $8 billion and is expected to reach $200 billion by the year 2000, according to the American Insurance Service Group.

Chip thefts alone amounted to $40 million in losses in 1993, according to the American Electronics Association. The growing trend of theft is not surprising. After all, computers are everywhere these days. Chips are highly portable. Most are so small they do not have serial numbers. Assets worth thousands of dollars can fit in a shirt pocket. In a manufacturing environment, chips worth $1 million can fit in a gym bag.

The components change hands a dozen or more times in the days after the initial theft. They may even make their way to another country. High-tech theft can take many forms. In addition to armed robbery, there is pilfering of components from within the company or the theft of memory and microprocessor chips from in-use computers or the unauthorized taking of an organization's proprietary data. All of this activity hits the organization hard.

SECURITY SAFEGUARDS

To deter high-tech theft many basic security practices are effective. For example, the security supervisor should examine the perimeter security of the building and make sure it includes appropriate "target hardening" features. Target hardening is the process of setting up a series of physical protection barriers to discourage the thief's success. As in all aspects of physical security, the idea is to have the criminal give up the idea of an attack, give up during the attack, or take enough time for the security force to respond to an attack before it is successful. A building's entrances, exits and utility doors are vulnerable areas that should be the starting point for improved perimeter security.

As a security supervisor you may be expected to make observations and recommendations to either your own management or your client's management. Keep in mind, many business people are focused on their primary profit-making activities. They may consider their site "just" an office building. However, the high-tech equipment found in the average workplace is extremely attractive to outsiders and employees alike. When considering the security posture of the perimeter, ask yourself:

1. Is the building secured at ground level by locked doors, using heavy duty commercial hardware?
2. Are windows at ground level either fixed or locked with heavy duty commercial hardware?
3. Are utility and delivery doors locked or controlled—or are they wide open to strangers?
4. Is there sufficient lighting around the building, including all entrances and the parking?

Some common methods of enhancing perimeter security include:
1. Alarm ground level doors and windows against opening and breakage.
2. Security patrols day and night.
3. Monitor the building perimeter and doors with CCTV.
4. Install security access systems to prevent other tenants in your facility from gaining access to your company's areas.
5. Enhance lighting with tamper-proof lighting fixtures. Position the lighting to prevent deep shadows from the building so intruders can be noticed.

INSIDE THE FACILITY

Once the building perimeter is secured, the security supervisor must then consider how personnel are controlled in the facility. One effective and common method is to have all employees and visitors enter the facility through one entry point, with deliveries arriving at another. Photo ID cards should be worn by employees and all visitors should be logged, issued a visitors' badge, and accompanied by a company escort. Here are a few things to consider for enhanced security inside your facility:

1. Establish reception points with properly trained personnel.
2. Avoid using stairs as a means of entering and exiting the office environment.
3. Establish access controls, either manually, mechanically or electronically.
4. Provide room and building keys only to people who need them.
5. Clearly and permanently mark computer equipment with the company's identification. This will help deter theft and improve the chances of recovery of stolen property.
6. Make police departments and local pawn shops aware of any specific markings on your equipment.
7. Keep portable equipment, such as laptop computers, out of sight in locked desks, automobiles, closets, etc., when not in use.
8. Increase employee awareness of the threat of theft and advise them they need to be alert to the activities of people who do not work in their building or area.

9.   Store recently delivered assets in a secure location until they are set up.
10.   Staff computer labs when in use and lock them at other times.

There are two other procedures that should be considered. With the popularity of laptop computers and similar items, the removal of such company-owned property should be documented with a "property removal pass" signed by an authorized manager. Likewise, in manufacturing environments with large amounts of high-value assets, employees, visitors and their hand-carried items should be "screened" for unauthorized materials upon departure from the facility. Such screening may involve the use of walk-through metal detectors and hand wands. These procedures will provide a deterrent to high-value items simply "walking out the door." Many studies have concluded that employees are the primary cause of high-technology losses in the modern workplace.

When considering screening procedures, the security supervisor should remember thieves at many organizations start out as temporary help, work their way up to positions of authority and may even be issued access cards to get into the building at odd hours. They may even be authorized to sign property removal passes. Putting large numbers of temporary workers close to valuable computer components often leads to high losses. In a warehouse, for example, temporary workers can check out the operation and evaluate your access control procedures. Then they can leave with this information—which is valuable to anyone who wants to steal assets. Individual security officers are often scrutinized to determine who conducts effective departure screenings and who is lax on the job. Therefore, training and sound supervision are imperative to avoid such problems. All screenings must be thorough and consistent. However, they must also be conducted within legal and company guidelines. Internal controls cannot be overstressed.

SPECIALIZED SECURITY DEVICES

There is a huge market for security devices designed to improve the physical security of computers and other high-technology assets. These products provide various means to prevent unauthorized use, intentional damage or destruction, or theft. These include alarms, locks, cabinets, cable kits, lock-down plates and special security screws. The use of security seals, tamper evident labels and ultraviolet detection lamps is also growing. A couple of companies now market theft retrieval software that notifies police of a stolen computer's location.

The effectiveness of such products varies. Some may be useful, but may not be particularly cost-effective. In many cases, it is more cost-effective to protect the work area than it is to tie down or alarm each computer.

It goes without saying that almost all security measures have certain drawbacks. When making recommendations, the security supervisor should understand the drawbacks of various security solutions. For example, labeling, engraving and ultraviolet detection is time-consuming. Likewise, as computers change such efforts are never ending. In fact, some experts believe there is little evidence such methods reduce thefts. Many buyers know an item is stolen but are willing to take the chance of receiving stolen goods because of the low price and the unlikely event of being caught.

Security devices designed to enhance the physical security of computers include cabinets that enclose the entire computer, including the monitor, keyboard, printer and CPU (the Central Processing Unit is the main component of a computer system). They are usually metal or composite materials that are difficult to penetrate. Alarms can be installed either inside or outside the CPU. The alarms do not prevent theft of the computer equipment but they usually act as a deterrent. People working nearby will hear the alarm if the protected asset is tampered with.

Anchoring pads and cables are used to anchor devices to desks and table tops, using high-quality cables or adhesive pads. Once the pad is installed on a desk, it is usually very difficult to remove and often damages the surface of the furniture. Cables are a popular security device. They are relatively inexpensive and feature steel rings through which the cable is passed to attach to the desk. They can prevent people from quickly walking away with an asset, but they can be cut with time. Secure lid locks help prevent intrusion into a computer and thus protect the machine's valuable contents.

Special hardware aside, a record should be kept of all high-tech assets at your facility. For example, in an office environment, serial numbers, part numbers and descriptions should be recorded in the event of theft. This information is crucial if a recovery is made. Quite simply, you must know what is stolen if you have any hope of getting it back.

You may be unfamiliar with computers. The following terms should be understood by any security supervisor tasked with the protection of high-tech assets.

Backup: (Verb) To copy files from a computer hard disk to a floppy disk or tape as a precaution against damage to the hard disk. (Noun) The floppy disk or tape to which the files are backed up.

CD-ROM, Compact Disc, Read-Only Memory: Flat plastic discs similar to music CDs, and capable of storing thousands of pages worth of data. CD-ROM drives can read the information on these discs, but cannot write information to them.

Client-Server Network: A network in which a number of workstations (or "clients") get served with information, programs, and printers from a single, central-server computer. The central server essentially controls and monitors the network system.

Data Recovery: The act of restoring or retrieving information on damaged media, like disks, tapes, hard drives, etc.

E-mail, Electronic Mail: A type of software used to send messages between computers attached to a network.

Ethernet: One of three common standards that govern the design of networks and the way computers share information over a network. The other two common standards are ARCnet and Token Ring.

Expansion Card: A circuit board that fits into a computer and performs a special function such as sending signals to the monitor or allowing sound to be heard on the computer.

Hardware: Any physical device such as a computer, printer, expansion card or microchip used in a computer system.

Interface: (Noun) The commands, menus and on-screen messages that allow the user to control the computer. Software or hardware that enables one type of computer to share information with another type of computer.

Microprocessor: The computer chip that controls the computer, sometimes referred to as the central processing unit or CPU.

Motherboard: The large circuit board containing the computer's essential devices, including the microprocessor, system clock and expansion bus.

License Agreement: A legal contract that allows the use of software under conditions specified by the company that owns the copyright to the software. License agreements usually prohibit the user from sharing or selling copies of the software.

Software: Operating instructions or "programs" that enable the computer hardware to process data, print, communicate or perform other tasks.

Piracy: Illegally copying or using software without paying for it.

Network: A combination of hardware and software that allows computers to share files and send messages to each other.

RAM, Random-Access Memory: The primary memory area of a computer where programs are stored when they are in use so they can be quickly and directly available to the computer's processor.

Pentium: A type of CPU that processes two instructions at a time.

SIMM, Single In-Line Memory Module: A circuit board inside a computer that holds memory chips.

SRAM, Static Random Access Memory: The most expensive type of memory. It works at very high speed and enhances the performance of the computer.

UPS, Uninterruptible Power Supply: A device that protects a computer from damage due to power loss or fluctuations.

Regardless of the type of organization you protect, it will likely have high-tech assets. From warehouses and hospitals to public schools and office buildings, the computer is a fact of life. And the physical security of these important assets will be a growing challenge in the years to come.

HIGH-TECHNOLOGY THEFT
QUIZ

1.   The security of computers and high-technology components is a concern of only those security officers working in high-tech companies.
          □ T   □ F

2.   The theft of a single computer can cost a company millions of dollars.
          □ T   □ F

3.   By the year 2000, high-tech component theft is expected to cost:
     a) $1 million
     b) $15 million
     c) $2 billion
     d) $200 billion

4.   Many basic security practices can be effective in deterring high-tech theft.
          □ T   □ F

5.   Target hardening is:
     a)   the process of setting up a series of physical protection barriers to discourage a thief's success.
     b)   using armed guards and K-9 patrols.
     c)   not required at most facilities.
     d)   inexpensive and easy to accomplish.

6.   Name three types of specialized security devices available to assist in the physical security of computers and other high-tech assets.
     a)   _____
     b)   _____
     c)   _____

7.   Most computers do *not* require a microprocessor.
          □ T   □ F

8.   What is software piracy?
     _____

9.   Components from in-use computers are seldom the target of thieves.
          □ T   □ F

10. According to the American Electronics Association, chip thefts in 1993 amounted to:
     a) $1 billion
     b) $40 million
     c) $2 million
     d)   None of the above.

DESIGNING OPERATIONS CENTERS
by Lowell A. Nelson, B.A., CPP, CPO, CSS

The actual design of an operations center can be as varied as the number of security departments. It would be impossible to create a standard blueprint that one could follow to design a new center. However, there are three general areas that must be considered in the design of all centers: the location and physical construction, equipment contained within and the hiring of personnel. As the supervisor in charge, it will be your decision to determine which factors are the most important considering your monetary restraints. With an eye to the future and one foot firmly planted in the present, you will determine the "look" of your operations center. As it is impossible to describe every component for every imaginable center, the following provides an overview of some of the situations you will encounter.

LOCATION AND PHYSICAL CONSTRUCTION

When choosing a location for your security operations center, your primary consideration should be the basic function the center will fulfill. If the decision was left up to security managers, the location would be easy to determine. The center would be placed in the safest area of the protected premises. It would have 12" thick walls with steel doors and one-way, bullet resistant glass. This, however, is not the norm. Most security departments also perform reception duties. This requires a more open location which can hinder security obligations. With the center more exposed, the visiting public and non-security staff have a clear view of the very area you wish to keep secure. Yet, with careful planning, you should be able to construct an operations center that will satisfy all concerned.

If the operations center will be performing reception duties, the location has to be close to the main entrance of the building. It has to be situated in such a way that pedestrians entering the area are forced to stop at the center before proceeding further. The location should allow the operations officer to safely view people as they approach the immediate area. This can be accomplished by creating barriers through which the public must pass before reaching the center. One way is to use glass doors that enable the officer to view the public, then release an electronic lock to allow them to pass through. This would dissuade people from just showing up unannounced at the command center. The Underwriters Laboratories recommend the following factors be considered when constructing a "central station":

> The central station (operation center) shall have a direct tie-line connection to a police station (this is also known as a "panic button") or to another central station complying with the standard.

> The entrances to the central station shall be kept locked at all times and those requesting admittance shall be positively identified before being allowed to enter.

> The central station should be constructed in such a way that those standing outside of the area can not see the interior. Those windows at grade level shall be either screened or painted. All accessible openings shall be covered with either iron or steel bars or a wire-mesh or at least No. 16 MSG expanded sheet steel or No. 10 AWG steel wire with openings not greater than two inches.

As stated before, it is impossible to list and explain all the things involved in planning the location and construction of the operation center. The above information forms only a small part of the things you need to consider when designing the command center. It is recommended that all available sources be utilized. This includes, but is not limited to, consultants trained in this area, publications printed by Underwriters Laboratories and fellow security managers.

EQUIPMENT CONTAINED WITHIN THE OPERATIONS CENTER

The modern operations center consists of many components, including video monitoring switching and recording equipment, card access control and/or alarm monitoring equipment, fire annunciation equipment, intercoms, radio and telephone communication equipment and consoles. We will take a closer look at two of these components: video monitoring and card access and alarm monitoring.

Closed Circuit Television (CCTV)

If the modern radio communication system is the "ears" of the security department, then the CCTV system is the "eyes" of the operation. It is difficult to imagine a command center without a bank of monitors showing, in real time, what is happening in the protected areas. However, there are some considerations that should be addressed before the purchase and installation of video equipment.

Will the monitoring equipment be in color or black and white?

It is a fact that color equipment is more expensive but there are times when the color image is a factor in the safety/security of the department or it is vital for identification. Also, a color image is easier on the eyes over an extended period of time. On the other hand, a black and white image generally has better resolution than color, giving it an advantage in low light situations.

How many cameras will be needed?

A rule of thumb is that a camera should be placed wherever you need twenty-four hour coverage. This can mean at entrances and exits, potential areas of danger (money storage areas) or areas in which constant visual image input is desired. Most systems will grow over time, so it is important that your switcher/controller choices are either modular in concept or expandable.

Will your system be monitored at all times?

If your system is not to be monitored at all times, then it is important that you have accurate recording for archival retrieval. Sometimes, during extremely busy periods or if careful study is required to understand the importance of an event, real time monitoring is not beneficial. By recording all that the system monitors, personnel can review the tapes to gather information or even detect crimes that ordinarily would have been missed. Another method is to have the recording system respond to alarms. This allows the recorders to remain dormant until signaled to "lite up." Instead of watching hours of non-activity, you now have a record of alarm activity.

What type of transmission medium will be used?

The standard means of transmitting video imagery is through the use of RG-59u coaxial cable. If you intend to use fiber optics cable, then you will need to make provisions in your console design that will enable you to accommodate the fiber optic receivers.

One of the more recent developments in CCTV is the advent of the "multiplexor." A multiplexor allows the viewing and recording of up to 16 images on one monitor and one recorder in nearly real time.

Card Access Control—Alarm Monitoring

This system is the heart of the operations center. Without it, you would have to station an officer at every entry and exit of the building. You would also need twenty-four hour coverage in all areas to ensure a degree of security and/or safety. Once the system is installed, you can:

Control the times that doors are locked or unlocked. This allows you to control the entry and exit of those who are permitted in that area. You will be able to enable and disable alarms to allow traffic in the area during working hours and then "alarm" the area automatically when everyone should be clear.

The system can be used as a "log book" showing what has transpired during a time period. By examining the printout, you can determine who entered an area, what time the area was entered, and what time the person left. By using the message area, your operations officer can enter information relative to the alarm that will explain what has transpired.

STAFFING THE OPERATIONS CENTER

One of the more critical decisions to be made concerning the operations center is the selection of officers that will be responsible for its activity. The officers working the operations center must:

- Be able to handle various emergencies that arise during the shift, including security functions, fire alarms and medical responses.
- Understand how to use the computers (entering and retrieving information).
- Have a high degree of communication skills. This would include report writing, radio communication and telephone requests.

The Underwriters Laboratories states that the central station "shall have a minimum of one operator and one runner or serviceman trained and equipped in the performance of their duties, constantly on duty to immediate attention to all signals received and prompted service to the protected area." It goes on to state, "the operator shall be on duty to receive and act on signals from the protected premise," and the runner "shall be on duty at all times at one station or in a vehicle in constant radio contact with the central station." Furthermore, all circuits from the central station shall be manually tested in intervals not exceeding 12 hours.

As you can see, it is impossible to design a generic operations center suitable to all security departments. However, with a knowledge of the basic requirements and an understanding of what is required from the operations center, you will be able to tailor the center to your needs.

DESIGNING OPERATIONS CENTERS
QUIZ

1.   The most important consideration in designing an operations center is _____.

2.   The Underwriters Laboratories recommends that _____ officer(s) be stationed in the operations center.

3.   A multiplex allows _____.

4.   Why is it important that the operations center be a secured area? _____
        _____.

5.   If the windows to the operations center are on grade level, the Underwriters Laboratories recommends that you _____ and _____.

6.   The decision of where to locate the operations center and determining the function it is to perform usually just involves the security manager.
             ☐ T   ☐ F

7.   Standardization of an operations center is critical to the overall protection process.
             ☐ T   ☐ F

8.   Sometimes security considerations are sacrificed to accommodate an easy access environment.
             ☐ T   ☐ F

9.   Security centers should be constructed in such a way that those outside of the area cannot see the interior.
             ☐ T   ☐ F

10.   The standard means of transmitting video imagery from the security center to the monitor is through the use of low level light transmitting technology.
             ☐ T   ☐ F

UNIT EIGHT
INVESTIGATIONS

Investigations
Developing Report Writing Ability in Subordinates
Testifying in Court

INVESTIGATIONS
by Robert Metscher, B.S., CSS, CPO, PPS

INTRODUCTION

Security supervisors throughout the security industry are responsible for managing investigations. Whether they include interviewing unwanted visitors or taking a report for a customer accident they are still investigations that need to be monitored to ensure completeness. After all, a poorly completed accident report could cost a company a significant amount, should it lead to litigation. It is because of this often concealed responsibility that security supervisors should be able to adequately manage investigations.

KEY MANAGEMENT SKILLS

Communication

The skill of communication is somewhat vague, particularly in the context of being a manager or supervisor. Security departments essentially have several different customers including the organizational management, employees, vendors, customers and any member of the public that may have a legitimate reason to be on the premises. Concise communication is necessary in three separate contexts to lay the foundation for successful information transfer within an organization. Communication with the security staff cannot be underrated, as it is these individuals that you must count on to accomplish the mission you are supervising. Communication with organizational management can be a tricky endeavor often because security must report to more than one department. Thirdly, communication with organization members, and in this case through committees or when responding to a complaint, can make or break the overall security program. A quick look at these aspects may provide insight as to how they are approached and handled in respect to investigations. Whenever disseminating information to persons or groups outside of the security department it can be useful to utilize an information dissemination checklist (see end of chapter) to aid in organizing data, clarifying issues involved and preventing the release of information or sources that could hinder future security operations.

Departmental: Within the security department information should be shared fairly readily. Even so, there is a certain level of formality that must be maintained. Where that level exists is truly a departmental or organizational matter. Moving information from one shift to another can become a monumental task which can be overcome with a pass-on book or a simple desk log (see conclusion of chapter). Oncoming members can verify that a note has been read by initialing the information. Simple desk logs can be useful in reviewing activity levels and officers can also use this as a reference. Memoranda should be reserved for formal communication pertaining mainly to personnel action issues and office policies, while incident information should be contained in departmental report format. Open communications within the department is a key factor in bringing all available investigative resources into use but security professionals must respect the need to compartmentalize some information.

Organizational Management: With respect to investigations in general and internal investigations specifically, this can be extremely sensitive, as managers often want to know "everything." If no policy exists then the security supervisor must come to an agreement with those to whom he or she reports. It is not always prudent to share all current information considering that, should a leak develop within management then a relationship of continuous conflict will evolve. In addition it is important to act impartial to management decisions based upon investigations. Investigators seek answers and explanations not convictions or terminations. If an opinion or suggestion is solicited then be forthright and logical, but in any other case your impartiality should be from a professional standpoint.

Organizational Staff: If there are no current employee committees on security topics then it may be worthwhile to organize one. It is through this type of involvement and communication with line employees that you as supervisor can get a feel for how security services are *perceived* by one of your customers. Acting on information gained in such meetings will greatly increase the security department's credibility. For it is your department's credibility in providing quality service that will ultimately dictate the level of involvement in security matters by line employees. Put the minutes from these meetings in a monthly bulletin to further increase communication. If you the supervisor lack the time or informational content for a purely security bulletin then consider sharing with a related department such as Safety or Human Resources. The more line employees that mention the security department's capabilities or consider it a resource, the more likely management will take notice and provide more resources.

Filing Systems

The finest investigation in the world is all for naught if the information is not stored in an easily retrievable and logical manner. Consequently, it is the responsibility of the supervisor to maintain or develop a strong filing system. Such a system must make accommodations for documents dealing with a wide variety of subject matter as well as various access levels. Contained below are some important issues in forming a worthwhile and flexible filing systems.

Incident/Activity Numbering Practices: Numbering systems associated with cases, incidents or activity reports can be a deciding factor in the quality of a filing system. Creativity is the key that allows a numbering system to provide quick reference information while remaining uncomplicated. While the most simplistic system would be to just number incidents from 1 – 9999, little information about the activity involved can be ascertained without physically searching the file. On the other hand, by using just the names of those involved as a means for sorting can raise issues of privacy and may cause complications for multiple incidents or similar names. A numbering system that contains some portion of the activities' date, location, type of incident/investigation and a counting sequence can provide easy reference. With the increase in the use of computer reporting and storage systems, such numbers can allow for the sorting of databases to measure the levels of various types of occurrences.

98-0102-4-2-123

The above style of number could represent an event occurring on January 2, 1998 (98-0102) at a specific location or zone (4), and was a customer accident (2) which by a simple count was the 123 event that year. Such numbering systems provide a great deal of flexibility that can be directly translated into a tracking tool for both activity monitoring, focusing audit efforts and lead development within investigations. Moreover, for larger case files it is perfectly feasible to have a Master Incident number such as the one above and further assign an additional dash number (-1, -2, etc.) for each document within the case or file. This extra effort can be of great use should any information within the case file need to be specifically referenced in a later report.

Card Support Filing Systems: With just a little extra effort, index cards can become a most valued tool in furthering investigations or just saving time while compiling information. For organizations not fortunate enough to have a computer reporting database or one not configured to sort necessary information, card filing systems can take the place of the machine without too much effort. The card filing system can be as complicated as is necessary, allowing key pieces of information from different activities to be sorted in an easily retrievable fashion. Some specific types of cards and their uses are (see also conclusion of chapter):

1. Reference Card: This card will often contain general information about the activity that created the case file. Included on this card is a reference number, which could be the master incident number or a separately generated sequence, and lists the documents that are associated with the case file as well as any other types of cards that have been filed. The reference card is sorted by reference number and acts as the base for the card file structure.
2. Information Card: An information card is a miniature incident report with key information about the individual involved, located at specific points on the card. By placing information at convenient points on the card, it becomes possible to "flip-through" a stack of cards to locate a specific characteristic such as height, sex, aliases or associates. This can be of value during future investigations. Sort these cards by the last name of the individual described on the card.
3. Identification Card: These cards contain key information taken from the identification presented by an individual detained, arrested or interviewed successfully. Placing information in specific locations on the card makes "flip-through" review possible for such facts as the state of presented identification or the type of identification presented. This allows for quick

cross-referencing to determine any other incidents in which the individual may have also been involved.

4. License Tag Card: In a retail environment this can be extremely useful in tracking professional shoplifters and smash-and-grab operators. In a general office setting this can be incorporated into a parking identification system providing for quick notification of employees whose vehicles need some type of attention (headlights, accidents, vandalism). License cards should be sorted by tag number but can also be sorted by the color of the tag itself (first noticed in most situations).

5. Purge Date Card: This card is of great importance in maintaining a useful card reference system, otherwise the sheer volume of cards will make all but the most meager searches impractical. Keep in mind that the purpose of the card system is to allow for quick cross-referencing of incident information to identify trends, problem persons or areas. As a result, most cards can be purged within a year of creation, however, extending this can easily be done on a case by case basis. If your facility has a very low volume of activity it may be possible to maintain several years of cards with little trouble. Whenever cards are purged (and destroyed) this should be noted on the purge card or a document destruction log to include the date, specific documents and the agent/officer actually destroying the information.

Location of Files

Files should be carefully separated as much as space will allow. This aids in preventing information being accidentally "shared" or shared unnecessarily. Divisions of files can be based on the type of investigation involved, with internal investigations being of the most sensitive and important to protect from unnecessary perusal. Realistically, members of the security staff not directly involved with the investigation do not need full access to internal files. They do however need to know the type of activity the individual was conducting if they are to prevent it in the future. Security managers and supervisors should also carefully restrict access to internal training or personnel files maintained within the department. These are in essence partial mirrors of documents maintained in the Human Resource Department and should be provided the same level of confidentiality.

Some specific types of files that should be separated as much as possible are:
>   Internal training files
>   Security department activity tracking forms
>   Customer accident reports
>   Employee accident reports
>   Internal investigation files
>   External investigation files
>   Equipment maintenance records
>   Exception reports – new and old

Keep in mind that as a manager you are responsible for tracking people, their activity and activity within the organization in general. It is important to share all the appropriate information with your staff, but to provide the same level of individual privacy as does a human resource department in dealing with security staff personnel records. It can be hard to keep some files locked away from your staff and it can cause some questions to be raised about trust, but these can be addressed from a standpoint of the nature of the information and an employee's expectation of privacy. Remember that your employee's curiosity is an important ingredient in preventing or investigating activities, but as their supervisor you must keep this in check in regards to personnel information.

PERSONNEL CONCERNS

Assigning Investigators

Often, investigators are assigned to investigations merely by being the first to answer the phone or arrive at a scene. Needless to say this is certainly not the optimal method for matching skills to problems, but it may be the most reasonable under the circumstances. Ideally in an environment with limited manpower, investigators should be equally capable to handle any investigation. This may very well be the case but keep in mind that there can be factors within an investigation that warrant the attention of a person with a specific interest. When an individual is an investigator or dons the investigation "cap," it is their imagination, creativity and most of all their curiosity that ensures a successful outcome. Consequently, officers that are only concerned with the "what" and not the "why" may not be strong investigators and should be encouraged to be more inquisitive.

In a perfect world a supervisor would have all the resources and a specialized investigator for any situation, but as a general rule this is not the case. Supervisors must be able to remove or add investigators to an investigation without overlooking the impact on those individuals involved. To avoid conflicts resulting from reassigning investigators supervisors should consider possibilities such as using partnering or specializing/centralizing some activities.

It may be very difficult to maintain partner teams in an environment with normally limited resources, but it is possible for a supervisor to assign a secondary or investigative partner on a case-by-case basis. This allows the flexibility to place skills where they are best suited while avoiding problems caused by removing individuals from an investigation. This can also create an even distribution of extra work should an investigator leave the organization. With a fixed partner team the termination of one partner leaves that individual's entire caseload on the partner, which could become quite burdensome if these should require court appearances or liaison with outside organizations. By having investigators maintain an individual case log, it becomes rather easy to redistribute a departing investigators cases. Case logs should be designed to reflect the aspect of investigations that are choke points within your investigative process.

Another option available to supervisors is the designation of longer-term activities to one individual. For instance if your organization has a problem with vandalism or more specifically "tagging," it may be more efficient to assign one officer to handle all these investigations. This does not mean that other officers cannot conduct the initial inquiry and photograph the evidence but it does imply that the designated individual should track this activity and conduct liaison with the appropriate outside agencies. This is a useful method for lateral promotions that give senior officers more responsibility and experience. This also assists in developing a complete and standardized reporting system for a particular type of activity.

Motivating / Tracking / Evaluating Investigators

The backbone of a good investigation is not generally exciting high-profile work but rather laborious surveillance and endless document review. This can cause an investigator to cut corners or to become more cursory in their work. An ironhanded supervisor can impede investigations by stifling the necessary initiative within investigators, yet a passive supervisor would indirectly cause investigations to falter or become weaker. Motivational methods can be directly tied to supervisory tracking and evaluation efforts of investigators, however the supervisor must know each member of their team and what motivates them as individuals. Efforts to motivate the individual separate from the team must be made as is necessary and to strengthen the investigator's tie to the team. Here are some useful tools to encourage, track and evaluate an investigative team. There are, however, a limitless number of ways to motivate and a supervisor must use some creativity and sound judgement when developing these efforts.
1.   Develop a monthly review/counseling program. These need not be long counseling sessions but merely a 15–20 minute session for each agent at the beginning or end of each month. The supervisor can write a few objectives and points of improvement for the investigator to reach within the month and identify topics that the agent will receive training on in that month. The agent in turn can write concerns or suggestions about the points listed and any comments about the department's operations. This not only provides useful documentation to support an annual review, but also gives the individual a feel for their overall performance. For the supervisor this can offer valuable insight into the attitudes of the department and likely avenues for future motivation and improvement. It should also be noted that supervisors must be prepared to receive some fairly harsh criticism from their staff and that such criticism must be acted upon but not retaliated against. If the staff is willing to write their criticism then they are concerned about their workplace and are not simply "punching the clock." This is positive and can be harnessed.
2.   Hold well defined meetings regularly. Keep these as short as possible by using a standard naming system that helps to identify the purpose. Names such as solution meetings, planning meetings and organizational affairs meetings can create the right mindset prior to attendance. Limit the agenda to one or two topics in a meeting and strive to keep these under 30 minutes in length. Never forget that meetings should ultimately increase productivity and not become a

barrier. If necessary, designate an individual to act as a facilitator to prevent the meeting from being sidetracked.

3.   Allow the staff some say in general operations. Foster an open environment that encourages suggestions that can streamline operations. Don't be afraid of using some of these ideas! By incorporating everyone's ideas the staff gains a feeling of ownership of the department and consequently their interest and concern will increase further.

4.   Develop a lessons learned journal. This can consist of a list of all cases with short entries describing the circumstances. Also included are actions that should not be repeated (hence lessons learned) as well as compliments for activities that were handled exceptionally and that agent's name. This provides a lasting acknowledgment of an investigator's achievements.

5.   Various charts can be used to show progress and organize activity. Flowcharts (see conclusion of chapter) can be used to graphically guide investigations and as a reminder as to who is responsible for finding different information. Load charts (see conclusion of chapter) can be a quick reference to show the number and length of investigations for which each officer is responsible. The example makes it plain that Smith is dealing with far fewer investigations than his peers are and this can be a tool in motivating Smith. Smith may not realize how much less he is doing and such a graphic representation is undeniable.

To help level the work load and to ensure that mundane tasks are not too mundane, internal audit activities can be developed by a supervisor. These audits can be a natural extension of patrol or other activity that aids in enforcing or monitoring protection standards—perhaps monitoring the use of safety equipment by line employees or searching back areas for concealed merchandise.

INVESTIGATION ISSUES

Initiating and Prioritizing Investigations

Investigations are initiated for many reasons and in diverse circumstances; however, the security supervisor is often directly responsible for those generated by exception reports, audits, or unique incidents. These investigations must be prioritized and worked into the department schedule. The security supervisor should seek to have a staff investigator handle much of the so-called "legwork" so as not to cause a slighting of supervisory duties. This in no way implies that the supervisor can simply pass off the work he or she just does not feel like doing, but instead offers training and experience opportunities for other investigators. Supervisors can use all investigations in which they are directly involved as an opportunity to mentor another experienced investigator.

Once an investigation has been initiated, lead sheets, which for practical purposes can be index cards, should be created for each lead that is discovered. These can then be systematically researched or divided up among agents for follow-up. These lead sheets should contain basic information about the investigation (incident number, type of incident, date, etc.) as well as the lead itself. Similar leads can be grouped onto the same sheet, as they will most likely be researched at the same time. Any information that is discovered from the lead should be briefly noted on the lead sheet since any evidence (receipts, photographs, vouchers, etc) would most likely be kept separate from the lead sheet itself. Completely researched leads that provide no further leads can then be returned to the primary investigator or the case file, while any further leads can be noted on the original sheet before a new sheet is created and researched. Lead sheets are of unquestionable value when an investigation is paused or stopped, especially if the primary investigator leaves the organization during this time. In addition, this type of documentation allows the supervisor to quickly review investigations to determine the level of effort and effectiveness of an investigator.

Prioritizing investigations should not occupy more than a few minutes of a supervisor's time, but these decisions can have a great effect on the security department, the parent organization and the public's opinion of the organization. Careful consideration must be given to high-profile incidents or when senior executives are implicated in wrongdoing. Failing to properly judge the amount of emotion behind an investigation or the opinions of organizational staff, management and the public could cause serious embarrassment to the parent organization. Factors for prioritizing investigations include but are not limited too:

Emotionally charged issues (i.e. workplace violence, hate crimes, stalking)
High-profile incidents (media or prominent figure involved)
Organizational management interest
Total investigative resources available

Total protection obligations
Likeliness that activity investigated will cease quickly
Number and quality of leads
Solvability factors considered and reviewed:
       Was there a witness?
       Can the suspect be: Named
                               Located
                               Described
                               Otherwise identified
Can a suspect vehicle be identified?
Is stolen property traceable?
Is a clear suspect MO present?
Is there significant physical evidence present?
Is there a positive report concerning physical evidence by a trained technician?
Is it reasonable to conclude that the case may be solved by normal effort?
Was there clear limited opportunity for anyone but the suspect to have committed the crime?

Investigative priority is a frequently changing situation with investigations being set aside for periods of time when necessary. A word of caution goes with this and that is to avoid unnecessary shuffling of investigations. If an investigation is nearly complete there is little reason to drop it simply because of an artificial priority system.

Investigative Follow-Up

The security supervisor is directly responsible for ensuring the completeness of case files and all documentation included within, and therefore must take several actions during and after an investigation. The supervisor must monitor progress, coach investigators and be prepared to summarize the investigation to management upon its completion. This is a tall order but is essential to building departmental credibility with organizational management and outside agencies.

As discussed previously, progress reporting can occur in several different ways as well as being an inherent part of the coaching process. It is important to identify an investigator's improper actions as quickly as possible to prevent them from occurring again and to recognize proper actions in an equally timely fashion. One coaching method includes three steps upon identifying the incorrect action. First a positive activity is recognized and encouraged, followed by the incorrect actions being verbalized to the individual and the correct way explained or demonstrated. The positive reinforcement can be placed at the end but it illustrates one way to correct behavior while avoiding an unconcerned presentation of the supervisor's interest. As the investigator is coached through the investigation the progress can be easily monitored. It is with more experienced investigators who may not seek assistance often that progress must be monitored through other techniques.

Another extremely important tool for coaching investigators is to play "devil's advocate." So long as the investigators know you are not attacking them personally or questioning their character in a real sense this can be very useful and often quite fun. Simply question all aspects of the investigator's report and try to put yourself in the shoes of a defense attorney. By attempting to find holes in the report or case and picking at them it becomes possible to search for other information and aid the investigator in remembering the important aspects of the investigation. At the right time this can be very enjoyable for all involved and is also useful in offering newer investigators a feel for questions they may be confronted with in the future. The operating terms here are informal and impersonal. In all ways prevent the investigators from feeling that their peers are personally attacking them.

In addition to ensuring that parts of a case file are complete, take the time to make sure the case file contains all the appropriate parts. Develop checklists that aid in keeping files complete from start to finish. Checklists should seek to eliminate relevant problems through prevention rather than merely identifying the existence of a problem after the fact. For example, begin with the completeness of the prepared case file to ensure all necessary forms are present at the start, which also serves as a reminder of the requirements of the various parts of the case file. Again, try to keep paperwork to a minimum, as it should contribute to the overall productivity rather than creating extraneous work.

Once the investigator has completed the case file the supervisor can write a summary of the case in the lessons learned journal. Later, this can be used as an executive summary in memos forwarded to organizational management. The summary should be extremely brief, identifying unique aspects of the case as well as actions taken and the current disposition. Below is an example of such a summary:

> *Review of alarm access reports identified access activity at the*
> *satellite location outside of normal business hours. Subsequent*
> *surveillance and investigation identified a total of approximately*
> *$5,000 in potential loss through property theft, and identified newly*
> *hired manager John Smith's code as the one used for access. During*
> *the interview, Smith admitted to the theft of property totaling $5,000*
> *from the satellite location as well as $2,300 in fraudulent invoices for*
> *undelivered services. Subject agreed to pay restitution in full and*
> *criminal charges have been filed. Total loss in this case is*
> *approximately $7,300 and a new exception report has been developed*
> *to aid in a more timely identification of similar loss opportunities.*

After the case file is completed the supervisor must review further aspects of the case such as evidence preservation and conduct one last review of all the paperwork. Proper preservation of evidence can prevent uncomfortable courtroom situations. The local prosecutor's office should be contacted and preservation practices reviewed. Any time evidence may be maintained outside of a police evidence operation it is likely that some questions will be raised about chain of custody and access. A little extra time spent on this matter may lend considerable credibility to one's department in the future. Moreover, it is important for the supervisor to review all cases with investigators prior to their court appearances. The investigators should do the same for the supervisor on the days of his or her appearances. The fact that court appearances can occur months or even years after an investigation is completed makes this review and drilling of great importance. This is just another application of the old adage, "...a gallon of sweat in training is better than a pint of blood in battle." Keep this in mind when an investigator grumbles about the extra effort.

Information / Intelligence

Investigative supervisors are expected to have volumes of current information literally at their fingertips at any given time. They need to have a firm understanding of local and regional trends that could affect their organization. Collecting and maintaining information can be a very useful tool with little extra effort in the long run. Using a card filing system like the one mentioned earlier, it is possible to track activity in the vicinity of the organization, which quite possibly becomes the source of a lead in a later incident.

Information can be located from a variety of open sources such as newspapers, phone books, criss-cross directories and the World Wide Web. Newspapers often have a section on police reported incidents in the area. This can be of tremendous value in recognizing activity trends in the immediate area. When one is at a court appearance, it only makes sense to listen to the other cases being heard and if any are for activities related to your organization then make note of this. It is possible that a robbery could occur in a mall parking lot while the tenant stores remained unaware of this activity. If your organization were located in or around the area this information might be useful in determining staffing needs and informing employees. As with any information collection and storage function, it is important to regularly purge the records to maintain just those that will be useful.

Any information provided by an individual, whether solicited or not, must be carefully reviewed to determine credibility. The following questions represent the minimum scrutiny such provided information should receive.

Why did this event happen?
    At this particular time?
    At this location?
Why is this information being provided to us?
Presented in this fashion with this slant?
Why does or doesn't this information stand up when compared to all other information available?
Why or how will someone or some group benefit by others believing this information?

Always keep in mind that information that is received or developed may be false or incorrectly organized. This may be intentional or not, however, the result is the same. Investigators must seek to corroborate any information to ensure its accuracy.

CONCLUSION

Nearly all security supervisors are responsible for managing investigations of one type or another. An accident investigation in one organization may be as important as a theft investigation is to another organization. It is the supervisor's responsibility to ensure that investigations are complete, accurate, timely and meet the needs of the organization. Minutes spent preparing can save hours in unnecessary effort. Supervisors need to create strong investigation support measures such as filing, mentoring and information storage to provide the greatest long-term value from the investigative process.

INFORMATION DISSEMINATION CHECKLIST

Check Existing Notes
Update Facts and Data
> Identify information that, if leaked, would be detrimental to the intended security department activity and remove mention of as much as possible.

Consult with Other staff (Other departments as appropriate)
Identify Target Audience
> Primary – *i.e. Vice-President of Operations*
> Secondary – *i.e. CEO or President and all other Vice-Presidents*

Prepare Key Messages (*i.e.*)
1. *This activity directly affects operational efficiency*
2. *This activity impacts on profitability*
3. *This activity impacts on morale*
4. *This activity can be largely prevented*
5. *Our suggestions are necessary to effectively prevent negative impacts of this activity*

Develop Positioning Statement
Develop Theme
List Example or Analogy
Provide Quotes
> Sound or Video Bites
> Excerpts from reports and written statements

Role Play Potential Questions & Answers

DAILY ACTIVITIES LOG

DATE _____
DAY _____

OPENING	CLOSING
____ FITTING ROOMS	____ FILE AUDITS
____ MAIL	____ CLEAN OFFICE
____ CLEAN INTERVIEW ROOM	____ CHECK DOORS

DAILY AUDIT EXCEPTIONS:

____ REGISTER AUDIT: REG # ____   RESULT _____
                                     SEARCH _____

____ REGISTER AUDIT: REG # ____   RESULT _____
                                     SEARCH _____

____ REGISTER AUDIT: REG # ____   RESULT _____
                                     SEARCH _____

____ INKTAG COMPLIANCE: SECTION _____   # UNTAGGED ____
                          RESULT _____

____ HOLDS COMPLIANCE: RESULTS _____

LP SCHEDULE
NAME   HOURS

EXECUTIVES
NAME   HOURS

TIME	INCIDENT/ CASE NUMBER	DESCRIPTION/ CASE NAME	ACTION TAKEN/ RESULTS	BY WHOM

REFERENCE CARD

Ref #   Type
Last Name   First Name MI
Aliases:
DL#   State
TAG #   Color Make Model
Documents: ____
1
2
3   AGENT

PURGE DATE CARD

Ref#   open MM/YY
MM/YY of Scheduled Purge
Note extensions

Total Documents: #Purged:
Purging Agent:
Witness
Witness
Doc#   AGENT

INFORMATION CARD

Last Name   Ref #   Type
First Name   Middle   Sex   Race
Address: Ht   Wt
City   ST   Zip DOB/Age
Phone #
Aliases: Associates:

Doc #   *details on back*   AGENT

LICENSE TAG CARD

TAG#   State   REF#   Type

Color Make Model   Year

ID'ing information

Details of information

Doc#   AGENT

IDENTIFICATION CARD

ID#   State   REF #   Type
EXP
Last Name   First Name   MI
Address
City   ST   Zip
Phone

Doc #   AGENT

ACTIVITY FLOWCHART

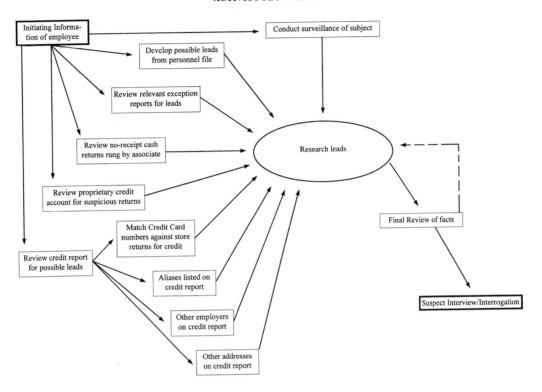

LOAD CHART

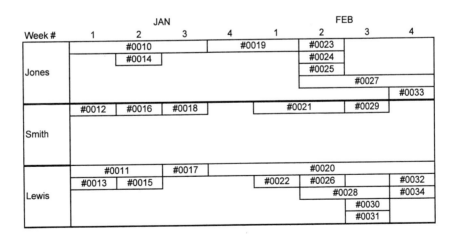

INVESTIGATIONS
QUIZ

1. It is important to act impartial to management decisions based upon investigations.
   □ T   □ F

2. An extremely important tool for coaching investigators is to play _____.

3. Managing investigations is the responsibility of the:
   a)   Security Director
   b)   Team Leader
   c)   Human Resource Department
   d)   Security Supervisor

4. Three examples of information cards are _____, _____ and _____.

5. Factors for prioritizing investigations include but are not limited to:
   a)   Organizational management interest
   b)   Total protection obligations
   c)   Number and quality of leads
   d)   All of the above

6. Gathering information is the primary role of the investigator. It is not necessary that the investigator seek to corroborate any information to ensure its accuracy.
   □ T   □ F

7. One of the most valued tools in furthering investigations is:
   a)   Binoculars
   b)   Tape recorder
   c)   Index card filing system
   d)   None of the above

8. To avoid conflicts resulting from re-assigning investigators, supervisors should consider possibilities such as using partnering or specializing or centralizing some activities.
   □ T   □ F

9. _____ _____ are expected to have volumes of current information literally at their fingertips at any given time.

10. Failing to properly judge the amount of emotion behind an investigation or the opinions of organizational staff, management and the public could cause serious embarrassment to the parent organization.
    □ T   □ F

DEVELOPING REPORT WRITING ABILITY IN SUBORDINATES
by Christopher A. Hertig, CPP, CPO

If one were to query most security supervisors about the most pressing problems they have with their subordinates, there is an excellent chance that the reply would be:

"Poorly written reports."

Report writing is a *process*. It consists of obtaining information—usually through interviewing —making notes on it and organizing it into a readable, useful format. Whichever format is used, the essential elements are the same. Unfortunately, professional report writing is difficult. Many people have never been taught how to do it; some lack the literacy skills necessary and others simply don't want to do it. All of these obstruct the process and create problems for supervisors.

In assessing report writing competency, the supervisor should be on the lookout for these problem behaviors:

- *Avoiding writing the reports.* This can take the form of delaying and procrastinating as much as possible the writing of the report. It can also manifest itself in avoidance of incidents that would give rise to having to write a report. Some of these officers become "World Class Avoiders" and seemingly never have incidents or conditions of concern on their shifts. Others invariably arrive late at the scene of incidents.
- *Failing to log or note all pertinent conditions.* This may be simple laziness or the emulation of an inappropriate role model. It may also stem from the officer not realizing the importance of complete documentation. A few questions to ask in regards to diagnosing this problem are:
  1. Who reads the reports?
  2. How is feedback on reports given to the officers?
  3. Are officers educated—not merely told—of how the reports will be used by insurance carriers, accreditation agencies or courts?
- *Failing to proofread the report.* This is probably the most common mistake for we are all our own worst editors. Few of us can adequately critique our writing effectively. Some methods of overcoming this are:
  1. Have a fellow protection officer review the report.
  2. Provide immediate and constant supervisory review so that every report gets scrutinized—pounce on the reports!
  3. Have officers sign the reports so that they feel a sense of formality, of commitment to their work product
- *Inadequate detail/descriptions.* Have them make rough sketches. Also consider making or using existing codes for areas of the facility and proximity to subjects (#2 Position, etc.)
- *Inadequate command of the English language.* Educational levels must be increased! The role of the protection officer must be fully understood and appreciated in terms of the communications aspects of the position. Job descriptions must make mention of this and hiring practices must reflect it.
- *The demeaning of officers who write well by other officers.* This does not occur in all workplaces, but it can easily take root if supervisors don't manage the employee socialization process effectively. When one hears comments such as: *"OK, here we go again 'Dark and Stormy Night' is gonna write another report"*; the obvious inference is that negative, counterproductive forces are at play. This cannot be tolerated. Supervisors must take every opportunity to advance and advocate for higher education, increased training and greater professionalism within the protection organization.
- *Lecturing or complaining by supervisors about inadequate reports when practice sessions in report writing have not been given!* This is a problem *owned and controlled* by the supervisor. He or she must give practice in writing in order for the skill to develop. Along with this practice—usually preceding it—is the presentation of a model behavior. Show "The Troops" a well-written report.

"WRITING ACROSS THE CURRICULUM"

Colleges have taken the position that students do not learn to write in English composition courses; rather they learn to write by applying the basics of writing learned in English composition in other courses. They write in various writing intensive courses.

Note taking—notes are the foundation of the report. A simple way of remembering this is the equation:

$$NO\ NOTES = NO\ REPORT$$

Note taking can be and should be taught throughout any instructional process. The most casual review of class participants will usually reveal those with college and those without as the college educated take notes. They have learned not to trust their memories. More importantly, they have learned to take notes on information in an organized, retrievable manner.

One technique for teaching writing is to have class members read each other's notes. In this way they can share perspectives, are on notice that they must be active participants and get practice in this crucial skill. Having them take notes in "bullet" format with some space between each line is a good practice. This leads in to writing reports—and memos—in a "bullet" format. This format is accepted in business circles and easier on both the writer and reader.

Perhaps most important in having class members read each other's notes is that it moves them towards that most difficult of roles: editor!

Interviewing—without conducting an effective interview, there will be no useful information to make notes on. As most information comes from people, interviewing is a critical investigative skill.

Violence Management—the documentation phase of the violent event. Obviously any use of force must be documented completely. Note that encounters don't have to be physically violent in order to require thorough and complete documentation; simply enforcing a rule, evicting someone from the property or taking away a privilege all call for complete documentation. All are situations where the officer's actions and judgement will be called into question.

Crime/Incident Scenes—similar to violence management, the protection officer's observations and actions need to be documented at the scene of all crimes and incidents. Short note taking and report writing practice sessions can be meshed in with instructional sessions on crime/incident scene management. In instances where doing an actual writing practice is not practical, it is good practice to review verbally the items that must be noted. In this way, students can develop "an eye for documentation."

Testifying—testifying in legal (criminal or civil court) or quasi-legal (disciplinary hearings, administrative agency hearings, labor arbitration hearings) proceedings is the final product, the epitome of an investigation. There are some who believe that testimony starts with the taking of notes. One could probably argue that it starts earlier, with the interview or initial approach to the incident under review.

Whichever is the case, testimony is the presentation of an investigation. It is where the officer shows his or her work on the case. It is also, like report writing, an exercise in communication.

When teaching testifying, it is relatively easy to tie in report writing; one need only to challenge or attack the report that was written by a student. Challenges to the descriptions of persons and objects drive home the import of attention to detail. Questions about the officer's sources of information illustrate the criticality of attributing everything learned to its proper source. Queries regarding the definitions of words in the report emphasize the need to use simple terms, avoiding technical jargon or "legalese."

Note that there are other benefits to emphasizing testifying, such as improved presentation skills for conducting meetings, enhanced public speaking ability for dealing with crowds and a better understanding of the legal/quasi-legal environment. An astute instructor could use testifying to develop public speaking skills that are normally avoided by adults.

Supervisors must ensure that quality reports are written by *all* protection officers. The supervisor must be a role model *and* a coach in the report writing process.

DEVELOPING REPORT WRITING ABILITY IN SUBORDINATES
QUIZ

1. If one were to query most security supervisors about the most pressing problems they have with their subordinates, there is an excellent chance that the reply would be poorly written reports.
    ☐ T   ☐ F

2. Report writing is a process that includes: (Select best answer)
    a)   interviewing
    b)   making notes
    c)   organizing it into a readable, useful format
    d)   all of the above

3. Avoiding writing the reports in a timely fashion has no bearing on the overall process.
    ☐ T   ☐ F

4. Proofreading of the report should be left solely to the supervisor on duty.
    ☐ T   ☐ F

5. Note taking is the foundation of the _____.

6. An effective technique in note taking is: (Select best answer).
    a)   always utilize capitals
    b)   utilize a shorthand method
    c)   utilize bullets
    d)   none of the above

7. Without conducting an effective _____ there will be no useful information to make notes on.

8. Non-physical violent events need not be reported on.
    ☐ T   ☐ F

9. Testimony is the presentation of a _____.

10. The supervisor must be a _____ _____ and a coach in the report writing process.

TESTIFYING IN COURT
by Christopher L. Vail, M.S.

Testifying in court is like firing your weapon in the line of duty – it's unlikely you'll ever have to do it, but if you do, you'd better be accurate! There is always the possibility that you, as a security officer, will have to testify in a court of law. Court appearances can be intimidating and frightening to those who have little or no experience in testifying. This chapter will do more than just alleviate fear of testifying. It will prepare the security officer to present his or her testimony in a confident and professional manner.

GRAND JURY VS TRIAL JURY

The grand jury, the initial step in the trial process, decides whether or not to prosecute based on the strength of the evidence offered by the prosecutor. This evidence may include oral testimony of a security officer. The grand jury environment is ordinarily a relaxed and informal setting in which the prosecutor presents the case to a jury, usually consisting of between 6 to 24 jurors. Grand jury proceedings are conducted in secret and are closed to the defense counsel, press and the public. Nevertheless, the grand jurors get an immediate impression of the professional training, skills and abilities of the testifying officer and his or her agency.

Since testimony presented in front of trial (petit) juries is done in open forum, the press and public can closely scrutinize a testifying officer's professional conduct. Testimony should be presented in a confident and professional manner. Trial juries consist of 6 or 12 jurors who consider your testimony, the oral testimony of other witnesses and physical evidence to decide on the guilt or innocence of the accused.

EXPERT VS REGULAR WITNESS

An expert witness is considered to be one who is qualified to speak with authority by reason of his or her special or unique training, skills or familiarity with a particular subject. An expert witness is allowed to render opinions and draw conclusions (in contrast, witnesses not qualified as experts are generally not allowed such latitude). A person becomes qualified as an expert witness by demonstrating to the judge, or sometimes the jury, that he or she has the required education, knowledge, training and/or experience to qualify as an expert in the subject matter under consideration.

Most police and security officers do not qualify as expert witnesses as their duties are usually more general in nature. In most cases, an investigating security officer can testify only to that information of which he or she has personal knowledge. For example, while the case may have involved questioned documents, the officer can only testify as to what he or she knows about the documents and cannot testify as to the authenticity of the documents themselves. The document examiner in the case would be the expert witness.

PREPARATION FOR COURT

Probably the most important part of being a successful and confident witness in court is your preparation before testifying. The first step in this preparation is to realize that you may be called upon to testify on any official act you perform in your job as a security officer. Preparation actually begins at the scene of a crime or when conducting the initial investigation. Officers should consider every call, complaint and investigation as possible material for a future court case. In every case and in every investigation, think ahead about the possibility of having to testify to all your actions in that particular case. The easiest way to do this is to picture the judge, jury and/or defense counsel looking over your shoulder as you perform your duties and ask yourself such questions as "How will I explain this on the stand?", "What if they ask me about this?" and "Can I explain this action in court?"

Review your case in detail before going to trial. You may have forgotten just enough to present some inaccurate information and put reasonable doubt in the mind of the jury. If you are going to testify concerning a situation that happened months or even years earlier, you will have to refresh your memory. Refer to the notes you took at the scene of the incident. Review any reports you wrote regarding the incident. Talking with co-workers who may have knowledge of the situation may help you to recall forgotten details. But, do not try to develop a common story. Remember your testimony must state what you recall, not what somebody else told you.

Let's take a quick look at notes as they may be of assistance to you in court. Officers who perform their job professionally are well aware of the necessity to take good field notes, maintain good field notebooks and prepare well written and accurate reports in all cases. Field notes and the notebooks in which they are kept, represent the basic source of information drawn upon when writing the incident, offensive or investigative report. They are very valuable and of great assistance when the officer testifies in court.

Field notes should begin with the officer's assignment to a case and continue until the case is closed. The time and place to get factual data and information is at the scene during the initial investigation. Anything omitted or overlooked is either lost or must be ascertained later. That is usually a difficult, time-consuming task which often leaves out important facts that may be crucial testimony or evidence in court.

If you pictured the judge, jury and/or defense counsel watching over your shoulder during the investigation and listening to your interviews, you will find that your notes, which may be introduced as evidence in a trial, and your reports (written from your notes), will be more complete, thorough and accurate. Your self-confidence will be evident to the judge and jury, and you will actually feel better.

If documents, photographs, records, etc. are going to be introduced into evidence in your case, gain some familiarity with them. You don't need to be an expert, but you should become generally familiar with their use, purpose and how they are used in the normal course of business.

SPEAKING AND ACTING WITH CONFIDENCE IN COURT

It is said that an audience remembers 7% of what you say, 38% of how you sound and 55% of how you look. A jury, like any other audience, is made up of real people. It can and will have feelings about you as a person, not only as a witness. They may like or dislike you, respect and admire you or look at you as an incompetent idiot. Juries, like other audiences, are not easily deceived. If what the jurors see and hear is believable, they will believe it. You can win their trust, respect and admiration by appearing confident, self-assured and by telling the truth. Even before getting into court, there are some things you should do which will assist you in presenting a winning case. Following these guidelines will help you to develop that feeling of self-confidence that can help your case.

1.   Know which courtroom you'll be testifying in. If you are unfamiliar with the particular courthouse or courtroom, check it out before the trial so you will appear to know your way around.
2.   Know who the major players are: the prosecutor, defense counsel and judge. Learn something about them if possible; the more you know about them, the more comfortable and confident you'll be.
3.   Do not discuss anything about the case in public or where your conversation may be overheard. You just don't know who could be a juror or defense witness!
4.   Treat people as if they are the judge, defense counsel, defense witness or juror in your case going to trial. Your professionalism, politeness and courtesy will be noted and remembered – especially by those who do see you in court as a witness.
5.   Do not discuss your personal life, official business, biases, prejudices, likes and dislikes or controversial subjects in public for the same reasons above. You might create a poor impression on a judge, juror, defense counsel or witness.
6.   Always be on time for your case. Know what time you will be expected to be called.
7.   Dress appropriately at all times. Look businesslike and official. If in uniform, it should be clean, neat and complete. (If you don't know, check in advance if you need to leave your weapon off.) If not in uniform, a neat and clean sport coat and slacks is as appropriate as a business suit (male and female officers alike).
8.   Try to avoid the defense counsel and any defense witnesses before the trial. You should assume that they will try to take advantage of you and get you to say something about the case. If you do say something, look for it to appear later, in a way to discredit you and your testimony.

Now that you have started to develop your self-confidence and are beginning to realize that you can handle testifying, let's discuss how to be even better prepared.

The famous Dale Carnegie way of building self-confidence works extremely well to prepare yourself for doing something that most people fear the most – speaking in public. In the 1977 best seller, *The Book of Lists*, speaking before a group was the number one fear listed in a category called "the fourteen worst human fears" (the fear of death was listed sixth). Fear is the strongest enemy of good communications. It is shown by nervousness, tension and self-consciousness. After starting his course, Dale Carnegie said: " ... little did I realize that this training would prove to be one of the best methods ever yet devised to help people eliminate their fears and feelings of inferiority. I found that learning to speak in public is nature's own method of overcoming self-consciousness and building up courage and self-confidence."

The Carnegie approach to self-confidence is potent medicine for those who, like the 85% of the public (security officers included), dislike or absolutely fear speaking in public. After all, testifying in court is public speaking, isn't it? Even in closed grand jury proceedings, you are speaking before others. The "stomach butterflies" which grow into flailing monsters in many people don't know the difference between courtroom testifying, grand jury proceedings or speaking to an audience of hundreds.

A very brief summary of Carnegie's self-confidence development course (see *The Quick and Easy Way to Effective Speaking*, Dale Carnegie, Dale Carnegie & Associates, Inc., (1962) will help you to be a self-confident witness. The basic tenets of this excellent program are:
1.   Realize that you are not alone in being afraid to speak in public.
2.   A certain amount of stage fright is useful. It is nature's way of preparing us to meet unusual challenges in our environment. Be aware of this and keep those psychological preparations (pulse beating faster, respiration speeding up) within limits. Doing so will make you capable of thinking faster, talking more fluently and generally speaking with greater intensity than under normal circumstances.
3.   Most professional speakers never completely lose all stage fright.
4.   The chief cause of your fear is simply that you are unaccustomed to speaking in public. For most people, public speaking is an unfamiliar experience, and therefore, it brings out many anxiety and fear factors. The way to beat this is to practice as much as possible.
5.   Be prepared: "Only the prepared speaker deserves to be confident."
6.   Preparation does not include memorizing.
7.   Predetermine your mind to success; lose yourself in your subject. In law enforcement terms, this means "know your case well." Keep your mind off the negative stimuli that may upset you and it is especially important to keep your attention off yourself. Give yourself a "pep talk"; "psych" yourself up.
8.   Act confident. Take a deep breath; sit or stand up straight; look your audience straight in the eyes and talk as confidently as if every one of them owed you money.
9.   If you have prepared yourself all along, you will be more confident.

If you follow and practice the Carnegie method for developing self-confidence, you will be more confident about your testimony in court. You will be able to explain not only what you did (or didn't do) but why you did (or didn't) do it. Many of your answers will have already been prepared at the scene or during the investigation. These principles are tried and true. Go back and read them again, learn them – they do work.

Knowing and practicing effective techniques of public speaking is synonymous with winning; you feel positive, confident and self-assured. You reflect the presence that says you are strong, determined, persuasive and in control. The jury will listen to you, you will gain and hold the attention of the jury and you will effectively sell your case and yourself to the jury.

The first step in effective public speaking is to be comfortable. You must appear to be both comfortable and in control. Use erect posture as this suggests authority. If you are standing, your feet should be about shoulder width apart, suggesting solidity and confidence. Your hands should rest comfortably at your side, showing you to be a natural and comfortable person. If you're sitting, lean slightly forward, but do not slump in the chair. Have your hands in a comfortable position and do not play with rings, pencils, your notes, etc.

Overcome your fear of speaking in front of a group by learning how to breathe properly. Proper breathing requires taking deep breaths, but not allowing your shoulders to heave so you look stiff, scared or intimidated. Deep breaths shouldn't be seen above the rib cage; your lungs need to expand outward, not upward.

Relax by first tightening your muscles, then relaxing them. An easy way to do this is to get out of public view. Do this at home or in a private location before going into court. Take a few deep breaths to clear the air in your lungs, then tighten and relax the muscles in your body a few times. Be careful you don't get a cramp, though.

When testifying, what the jury sees is sometimes more important than what they hear. Your appearance should be neat, clean and you should show confidence, not cockiness. Your tone, eyes, face and appearance all send signals; they have the power to make a strong impression that can contribute to whether or not you win your case.

Be careful when using gestures. Do not cross your arms over your chest. Do not raise your fists or pound the air as if you are making a dictatorial presentation. Use no pointing gestures towards the jury or defense counsel. While you may wipe the sweat off your brow occasionally, do not let it indicate nervousness. Don't show signs of nervousness, such as playing with rings on your fingers, pencils, notebooks and frequent crossing and uncrossing of your legs.

Use your voice to your advantage. The presentation should be loud enough to be heard by the juror furthest from you. But use a natural voice, only speaking with the volume needed to be heard clearly. Don't use a monotonous pitch when talking. Raise or lower the pitch to make certain points in your testimony. Control the rate of speech; be deliberate, but not tiresome. Try to balance volume, pitch and rate. Listen to yourself speaking and practice when alone – you will only help yourself when it's your time to testify.

Eye contact is very important. Make the jury, prosecutor or defense counsel feel that you are talking directly to them and not into thin air. Don't start, just find a comfortable place on their face (or above their heads) and keep your eyes there. Don't let your eyes wander as this can make you look dishonest or untrustworthy.

The most important element of speaking is your face. How many times have you thought to yourself, "I don't like his looks" or "He looks sneaky to me"? A jury also forms similar opinions when seeing a witness for the first time. Frowning indicates you are either unsure of yourself (no self-confidence) or you are unfamiliar with what is going on (loss of control). A "blank" face is one on which nothing but the mouth moves. Wear the same face you use everyday – be natural. By elevating your eyebrows and letting horizontal lines appear in your brow, you are indicating an interest in what is going on. It also shows self-confidence on your part. When you feel comfortable and wear a natural expression in front of a jury, you'll be trusted, more convincing, and more likely to be believed. You'll appear to be self-confident and in control of yourself and the situation.

GIVING YOUR TESTIMONY

Hopefully, you have prepared yourself mentally, emotionally and physically for testifying by now. You've got the butterflies under control, you know your case (without memorizing it) and you feel confident. So let's go to court and see how to give your testimony in a winning way.

1.   First, in your mind, review and practice everything we've discussed so far.
2.   Avoid undignified behavior such as loud laughter, telling jokes, etc. from the moment you enter the courthouse or courtroom. Normally, smoking and chewing gum are permitted in the hallways of courthouses, but not in courtrooms.
3.   Stand upright and erect when taking the oath – it shows confidence in yourself and in your knowledge of the case in which you'll be testifying.
4.   Control signs of nervousness. There is no reason to be scared or nervous if you've done your homework by reviewing the case carefully and preparing yourself.
5.   When you take the oath, you swear that you will tell the truth. DO IT!
6.   Speak directly to the members of the jury if it is a jury trial, otherwise, speak directly to the judge. Speak loudly enough so the juror furthest from you can hear you without difficulty.
7.   Speak in your own words and do not use slang or police type jargon.
8.   Listen carefully to each question and make sure you understand it before you start to answer. Have the question repeated if necessary.
9.   Be alert for any question that will lead you to make conclusions (remember, only expert witnesses can give opinions and draw conclusions).
10. Try to answer with a simple "yes" or "no" if possible. Avoid saying "I think," "I believe," "to the best of my recollection" types of answers. You should be testifying only to the facts as you know them.
11. Answer only the question asked, then stop. Do not volunteer any information as your answer may become legally objectionable under the technical rules of evidence. Do not exaggerate anything.
12. Sometimes, you just have to answer "I don't know." There's nothing wrong with this; just minimize doing it.
13. If you find that you gave a wrong or unclear answer to a question, correct it immediately yourself by asking the judge if you can do so.

14.   Refrain from showing or indicating emotions such as happiness, joy, disgust or disappointment about anything that occurs in the courtroom or during the trial.
15.   Always be polite and maintain your composure. Do not be argumentative or sarcastic or get involved in verbal fisticuffs with counsel.
16.   Finally, the officer who presents honest testimony and maintains a professional bearing during testimony has nothing to fear during cross examination.

CONCLUSION

While testifying in court may be intimidating and cause swarms of butterflies to appear in the stomach, learning and practicing a few things will help officers gain self-confidence and present winning testimony in court. Preparation is the key to successful testifying; prepare your case and prepare yourself.

Always review your case before going to court. Know where the courthouse and courtroom where you'll be testifying are located. Go over the facts in your case but don't memorize the case. You will be testifying to facts, no opinions or beliefs. Know the facts as they happened by reviewing your field notes, notebooks and relevant reports.

Prepare yourself by practicing the proven Dale Carnegie principles of self-development. Practice techniques of public speaking so you'll be comfortable and confident when testifying. When in court, carry yourself with an air of authority, confidence and self-assurance, but do not look cocky or smug. Stand or sit upright, speak clearly, look directly at the jury, judge or counsel, and by all means, tell nothing but the truth. If you've done your homework and prepared yourself to testify, you will be an outstanding and credible witness.

TESTIFYING IN COURT
QUIZ

1.   The _____ jury is the initial step in the trial process.

2.   Most security and police officers do not qualify as _____ witnesses.

3.   Know who the major players are: the prosecutor, defense counsel and _____.

4.   The famous _____ way of building self-confidence works extremely well.

5.   When _____, what the jury sees is sometimes more important than what they hear.

6.   An expert witness is allowed to render opinions and draw conclusions in court.
            ☐ T   ☐ F

7.   Probably the most important part of being a successful and confident witness in court is the preparation for testifying.
            ☐ T   ☐ F

8.   The petit jury is the initial step at which time the decision to prosecute or not is made based on the strength of the evidence offered by the prosecutor.
            ☐ T   ☐ F

9.   When in court as a witness, a security officer should always wear his or her uniform or a business suit.
            ☐ T   ☐ F

10.   Officers may not refer to their field notes or notebooks when testifying in court.
            ☐ T   ☐ F

UNIT NINE
PUBLIC RELATIONS

Customer Service and the Protection Officer
The Supervisor's Role in Customer Service
Uniforms and Image Enhancement
Marketing the Security Function
Appendix A: Ten Commandments of Marketing
Crime Prevention / Community Relations

CUSTOMER SERVICE AND THE PROTECTION OFFICER: GUIDELINES TO ACHIEVING EXCELLENCE
by Randy J. Rice, CSS, CPO

There have been many challenges through the years in the security profession. One of these challenges is customer service and it's this challenge that many companies are starting to look at very closely. Customer service and the protection officer work hand in hand with each other. Most protection officers have a very difficult time with customer service due to the notion *"How can the protection officer provide customer service when they are dealing with a large portion of incidents where customers are doing something wrong?"* The protection officer can use customer service techniques in everything they do and still have poor customer relations. This chapter will discuss customer service ideas from the beginning and throughout the protection officer's career.

SELECTION

We must first begin with the hiring procedures of the protection officer. When an applicant is being interviewed for a position as a protection officer, the employer should prepare a series of questions to ask the applicant during the oral interview. Some of the questions that should be asked are scenarios of different types of incidents with people that are most common to the place of business. An example of this would be, "How would a protection officer handle a patron of a mall that was smoking in a non-smoking mall?" Have the applicant explain in their words how they would resolve the problem using customer service skills. Another example would be to inform the driver of an illegally parked vehicle to move their car. Once the oral interview is conducted, proceed with a detailed background check. Check the past employment history and find out how they have dealt with others they've worked with in the past. Did they have any type of behavior problems while employed with that company? Once a complete and detailed background has been performed and you decide to hire the applicant, customer service training has begun.

IMAGE ENHANCEMENT

The next step begins with the image of the company and the protection officer. The new protection officer should be provided with basic information on the job and what's expected. During this stage the protection officer should be informed what their role is and how they are involved in the customer service aspect of the company. After providing a detailed explanation of customer service do's and don'ts, the protection officer is ready to move to the next step: the appearance of the protection officer. Appearance is approximately 55% of the message the protection officer sends out to a person. A protection officer should never underestimate the powers of their appearance. As the saying goes *"you never get a second chance to make a first impression."* A professional image speaks well of the employer and the protection officer. Following a few simple guidelines can assist the protection officer in getting it right the first time. These simple guidelines are:

Neat: Shirt tucked in, shirt is neat and pressed, gig line straight, shoes tied and polished, hair well kept and groomed, clean shaven, duty belt kept in order, all insignias shined and clean, equipment working and worn uniformly.

Clean: Clothing is cleaned and pressed, hands washed, fingernails cleaned.

Jewelry: Simple and not excessive, makeup is light, not too much cologne or perfume.

A person will always respond more positively to someone who appears neat and has a professional manner.

TRAINING AND BEHAVIOR

The next step is training and training is what "makes or breaks" the protection officer and their employer in the area of customer service. Let's start off with some basic examples of how a protection officer can have poor customer service techniques.

- Bad Attitude
- Incompetence
- Rumor Spreading
- Irresponsibility
- Impoliteness
- Abusive Authority

- Crude Speech
- Griping
- Disinterest
- Irresponsibility
- Exploiting People
- Failure to Communicate

The protection officer wants to avoid these at any cost. It's the role of the supervisor and training officers to instruct the protection officer on the proper personality traits so they understand how their personality traits and working relations affect themselves and others around them.

Following these six basic steps will assist the protection officer in maintaining a high regard for customer service:

1. *Taking the Initiative* – Exceptional customer service begins simply by getting involved with something. Make an opening move to show the person care and concern. Keep this in mind whenever dealing with a person; you decide whether you want to act or react. It's your choice and you have to determine which one will best promote customer service. Most places with poor customer service are just *reacting* to a customer, always reacting.

    The protection officer must keep in mind that reacting is tiring, self-defeating and is usually too late. By acting and taking the initiative protection officers are able to gain the proverbial upper hand and take the early advantage. People expect others to react and when the protection officer acts first they are surprised and impressed. An example of taking the initiative would be, you're a protection officer at a mall and observe a young mother attempting to exit the mall and having a hard time opening the doors. Taking the initiative and opening the door before being asked provides a high level of customer service. In this simple act the protection officer has influenced the person's behavior.

2. *Be Positive* – Another choice, once the protection officer has decided to act, is one of these three:

    - Be positive – upbeat, affirming, personable, interested, respectful and considerate
    - Be Neutral – indifferent, bland, flat, matter of fact or distant
    - Negative – unpleasant, mean, angry, rude, defensive or uncooperative

    Being *positive* is where customer service begins to pay off. This gets the relationship started in the right direction. When the protection officer acts, they challenge the customer to react in a positive way. The protection officer must keep in mind that under normal situations the person will respond in a similar behavior. Keep in mind this may not always be true. The protection office must remember that when a customer is rude, negative and generally difficult, the odds are that the protection officer is not the target, just in *range*. If the protection officer comes under attack, don't take it personally. No matter how unpleasant a customer can be, remain positive. Here are some tips to stay positive:

    - Body Language
      a) Keep direct eye contact
      b) Use open body language (no folded arms, hands, legs crossed, hands in pockets)
      c) Smile, Smile, Smile
    - Voice
      a) Calm
      b) Even tones (not shaky, cracky or tentative)
      c) Even volume (not too hard, not too soft, just right)
    - Wording
      a) Don't use negative words like "no," "I can't" or "but"
    - Self-confidence – Most Important
      a) Positive attitude

Post-Encounter Critique: *After dealing with a customer think of ten things that were done well and write them down.*

3.   *Make the Customer Feel Special* – Just keep this in mind; "The customer you make feel special will become a special customer." *There was never a customer that liked being treated like a number.* The protection officer might deal with the same or similar situations ten times a day, but each encounter remains a special and personal matter to each new customer the protection officer deals with. The idea is simple. Just provide such remarkable service that you surprise the customer and people around them. Make the customer feel honored by going above and beyond the call of duty. If the officer approaches each and every customer *like they're your only customer*, they will stay satisfied and happy. Make the customer feel important and don't over deliver in the way or manner you help them. The protection officer must remember that they may not be able to fully help the customer or give the customer what they ask for, but you can make them feel special. When the protection officer does this, it makes the customer more tolerant and they become more openminded, forgiving and kinder towards you. *The protection officer must remember, the easier the customer is to work with, the easier the job will be for them.*

4.   *Listen and Understand* – The first thing the protection officer must do is to identify the problem and focus on the customer. Give the customer 100% attention. The protection officer must concentrate on getting "in tune" with the customer, finding that same wavelength. Make that person's point of view their own at that point. The protection officer must demonstrate their interest in understanding the situation. They must also establish a common ground by looking at things from the customers perspective.

If you were that person what would you want?

Think Like a Customer!

The protection officer should sniff out the other person's concerns, wants and needs. Ask questions in order to obtain facts and listen carefully. Try to read between the lines, because the customer may be confused or lack necessary facts or simply can't explain things well. Pitfalls the protection officer needs to avoid are:
*   jumping to conclusions
*   prejudging
*   placing blame
*   arguing
*   becoming defensive
*   starting to solve the problem before analyzing it

The protection officer should welcome bad news with open arms. Problems give the protection officer a chance to leave a mark on the mind of a customer. They can turn them into real opportunities. It's an opening for the protection officer to do something special.

Listening, however, is always the hardest and most important part of this step. Here are a few tips to assist the protection officer with developing good effective listening skills:

DON'TS
*   Interrupt the customer.
*   Look away from customer.
*   Doodle, pace, frown or make strange facial expressions.
*   Put words in the customer's mouth or attempt to finish their statement.
*   Answer questions with a question.

DO'S
*   Hear the customer out, concentrate on what is being said.
*   Maintain direct eye contact.

- Let the customer know you're paying attention.
- Paraphrase to clarify.

Of all the don'ts and do's listed above, the most important "do" is paraphrasing what the customer has informed the officer on. Simply restate what the customer has said in your own words. Paraphrasing is important as it demonstrates to the customer that the protection officer was paying attention and understands what they have told the officer. It provides the customer and the officer with the opportunity to clear up any misunderstandings or gaps in the communications process.

Please note that paraphrasing is only to ensure and demonstrate understanding, not to state a position or try to solve the problem.

5. *Be Helpful*—Once the protection officer has truly listened and through paraphrasing has a good handle on the situation, the protection officer now knows what the customer's expectations are, their wants and needs, or concerns. Now the officer can address the top priorities. The protection officer should take personal responsibility for satisfying the customer. They should consider themselves an agent of the customer. For a brief moment, be on the customer's side and put both heads together and create options. Search for alternatives to the customer's problems. Do some joint problem solving, keeping in mind the resources that can be brought to bear on the situation, because the officer has a better idea of what is available to work with than the customer does.

    The idea of this step is simply to help, or in the case of a problem or complaint, to fix things. Whatever the need, take care of it following the company's policy and procedures. Provide help even if it's the customer's fault and avoid pointing the finger and run-arounds. Just put forth the effort that clearly says, "*The buck stops here.*"

    The protection officer will always be able to help the customer in some way.

    Sometimes the protection officer can't give the customer everything they want, but every time the officer can give something the customer wants, they walk away pleased and feeling good. Never dodge problems. Don't think of them as an aggravation, but as a valuable opportunity. This is one of the important "moments of truth" in customer service. Customers who have had their problems and complaints handled effectively will become the company's most loyal customer and probably the most pleasant ones. They will trust and believe in the officer as well as his/her employer.

6. *Follow-up*—This is the part where the officer takes the personal responsibility for the customer and makes sure that the plans the officer has made and the actions that the officer took made a difference. If the protection officer is simply answering questions, it can be made simple by asking if there was anything else you could do for them? Provide the officer's name and tell the customer that if they need anything in the future to please contact him/her. If the customer has a problem or a more complicated request, it could involve offering to follow-up with a phone call or asking a supervisor if they remembered to take care of the things on their end.

    There are many different approaches that the protection officer can use to seize the initiative, be positive and make the customer feel special. Likewise, various alternatives can work as the officer tries to understand, offer help and follow-up. Think about what works for the officer, what more or less comes naturally, what the officer can do well. Don't try to be someone else. Customer service, as the protection officer provides it, will reflect on the officer's individual style—one's very own magic touch.

    Finally, when dealing with angry customers remember the following tips:
    - Let them vent.
    - Don't get emotionally involved.
    - Don't rationalize or justify.

- Give empathy.
- When all else fails:
  a)   Make them aware of their behavior.
  b)   Say, " I'd like to help and I will when you can calm down."
- When the officer has stuck to the basics, draw that line and call the supervisor.

TELEPHONE PERSONALITY

No matter what position a person holds in a company, they have to spend time on the phone. This is one of the most powerful tools at one's disposal. When making or receiving phone calls, the officer is representing the entire organization. To a caller, the officer is representing the whole company. When a caller finds a competent, courteous, and efficient person on the other line, they are likely to form a positive and lasting impression of the organization. When people can't see the officer, on as on the telephone, the customer only has a voice to deal with and make them feel comfortable. Tips to improve the officer's phone personality include:

- Provide full attention to the caller.
- Use enthusiasm as a tactical advantage.
- Deal with the customer like they are right in front the officer.
- Use simple straightforward language – no slang or technical terms.
- Talk directly into the mouth piece.
- Use the caller's name; if unsure ask for it.
- Always thank the caller at the end of the conversation.

When using the phone sit up straight, keep the head held high and smile while speaking.

Using the few tips above will provide the officer with confidence and heighten the customer's confidence in the officer.

TELEPHONE STANDARDS

It is essential that the protective service organization establishes a set of telephone standards the officer can use:

Answering the phone

- Answer the phone by the third ring – be timely and alert.
- Use a friendly greeting:

  " Thank you for calling _____. This is Officer _____ speaking. How may I help you?"

- Always get the customer's name.
- Talk slowly and distinctly.
- *Be helpful.*

Putting a caller on hold

- Usually there are three reasons to put a caller on hold:
  a)   Already on the phone with another person.
  b)   If the caller would like to speak with someone else.
  c)   Obtaining information for the caller that is not readily available.
- In any case the officer must always ask the caller if they would mind being put on hold.
- If the caller elects to be placed on hold, thank them.
- If they are going to be on hold for a long period, pick up and let them know they haven't been forgotten.

Ending a Call

- Always end the call with a positive statement:

" Thank you for calling. If I may be of further assistance please let me know."

In conclusion, this chapter has touched the surface of customer service and the protection officer. It discussed the beginning stage of customer service from the hiring process to training of the protection officer. There are a lot more types of training classes a protection officer should go through, but following the guidelines set forth in this chapter will greatly assist them in achieving the goal of excellent customer service. Customer service will always continue to be a challenge for the protection officer, now and in the future.

Customer Service Checklist for Protection Officers

Yes   No

Did I have a professional image?
Did I avoid poor communications traits?
Did I listen clearly?
Did I paraphrase properly?
Did I take initiative?
Was I positive?
Did I use correct body language?
Did I keep good eye contact?
Did I make the customer feel special?
Did I understand the message?
Was I helpful?
Did I follow-up after the situation?
Did I use good telephone techniques?

BIBLIOGRAPHY

Crown America Corp, (1997) *Customer Service Excellence Training Material*

Satterfield, P.,   (1989) *The Security Officer's Performance Manual*, Cypress, CA

Salter D., (1998) Interview – *Public Relations and Security*

Thibodeau, C., Hertig, C. & Barnett, G., (1998) "Public Relations" in *Protection Officer Training Manual* (International Foundation for Protection Officers), Butterworth-Heinemann, Woburn, MA

Wanat, J., (1981) *Supervisory Techniques For The Security Professional*, Butterworth-Heinemann, Boston, MA

CUSTOMER SERVICE
QUIZ

1. The protection officer can use customer service techniques in everything they do and still have poor customer relations.

    ☐ T   ☐ F

2.   It's a good idea during the hiring/interview process to prepare a series of scenarios in which customer service skills must be applied and addressed to determine the level of ability of the potential employee.
        ☐ T   ☐ F

3.   Appearance represents what percentage of the message the protection officer sends out to a person?
        a)   5%
        b)   75%
        c)   55%
        d)   90%

4.   You never get a second chance to make a first _____.

5.   Poor customer service techniques might include the following. (Select the best answer)
        a)   Impoliteness
        b)   Irresponsibility
        c)   Bad attitude
        d)   All of the above

6.   Paraphrasing is important as it demonstrates to the customer that the protection officer was paying attention and understanding what they have told the officer and it provides the customer and the officer with the opportunity to clear up any misunderstanding or gaps in the communication process.
        ☐ T   ☐ F

7.   It is not essential that the protective service organization establish a set of telephone standards that the officers use.
        ☐ T   ☐ F

8.   Taking the _____ and opening the door before being asked provides a high level of customer service.

9.   Give the customer what percentage of attention?
        a)   25%
        b)   50%
        c)   100%
        d)   95%

10.   It is the role of the _____ and _____ _____ to instruct the protection officer on the proper personality traits so they understand how their personality traits and working relations affect themselves and others around them.

THE SUPERVISOR'S ROLE IN IMPROVING CUSTOMER SERVICE
by Christopher A. Hertig, CPP,CPO

The asset protection/security supervisor is a key player in both establishing and maintaining an appropriate customer service orientation within the protection force. To better understand how the supervisor functions, we must first examine the role of the supervisor; then assess the development of an organizational philosophy.

ROLE OF SUPERVISORS

• The person who represents higher authority—the *core philosophy* of the organization—to subordinates.
• The person who must ensure compliance with policies and procedures and quality performance in the customer service area.
• The individual who is the first responder to any and all situations—as such a supervisor must be a model diplomat. He or she must model diplomacy in trying circumstances (accidents, investigations, personnel issues) when there are competing interests (subordinates, other departmental supervisors, higher management, customers, law enforcement agencies, etc.) involved.
• A master of communications, especially interdepartmental and interagency communications. Again, other departments (human resources, physical plant, etc.) and external organizations such as local police, vendors, clients and regulatory agencies must be dealt with.

CORE PHILOSOPHY OF PARENT OR CLIENT ORGANIZATION

In order to gain a firm foothold in public or customer relations, one must first understand what the philosophical foundations are within the parent or client organization. Each organization is different; they do not simply all want "to make money" as the uninformed may believe. Each organization may indeed want to make money, but in their own manner. Each takes a different path. Some rely on innovations in technology. Some work on customer loyalty. Others focus on cost containment. Still others place great emphasis on close ties to the community.

Whichever guiding beliefs lie at the center of the organization, these must be firmly understood by those who wish to effectively represent that organization to customers. A key question to be addressed is:

*What makes my employer and/or client unique
from other entities in the same field of endeavor?*

Organizational philosophy is founded in the history of the concern. Each organization is established at some point and evolves over time. The original beliefs may be modified somewhat, or they may remain unchanged and be further cemented into the organizational culture. Whatever the case may be, an important question to be asked when studying an organizations's culture is:

What is the history of my employer?

This is especially important for security service firms such as Pinkerton and Burns International which have an illustrious history. The founders of both firms were highly successful entrepreneurs. They both were prominent citizens who played key roles in the history of the United States and the development of investigative practice. Smaller, newer firms may also have founders and principals who were industry pioneers. Each organization has a unique history which can illustrate important lessons. *Knowing this history helps to make each officer a more effective company representative.* Unfortunately, this may not be capitalized upon as effectively as it should be.

Organizational philosophy is framed in the policies of the organization. Reading and understanding these policies is essential to comprehending the philosophy of the organization—as well as knowing what the rules are to be enforced. A question to be mulled over is:

What do the policies of my employer state?

Organizational philosophy is more precisely articulated in the procedures of the concern. These specify the "what" and "how" of the policies. They state how the policy—philosophy—is executed. When reading procedures, some introspection can be given to the following inquiry:

What do the procedures explain?

Once policies and procedures are fully comprehended, it becomes necessary to examine the role of the security department in advancing the organizational philosophy. Upper management has delegated certain functions to the security department. Efficient use of resources and organizational survival mandate that the following question be addressed:

*What is the role of the asset protection/security department
in advancing that philosophy?*

ENSURING OPTIMAL PERFORMANCE AND ADHERENCE TO "BEST PRACTICES"

Supervisors must ensure that their charges perform to the best of their ability. They must also work to achieve quality through adherence to recognized standards of performance or "best practices." There are several steps to take toward this end. The first step is to conduct a job task analysis to determine roles and functions of officers. Once this is done, a clear picture emerges as to what officers do, what their key competencies are. From there, recruitment, selection, training and the remainder of the human resource management process can occur.

*What is the customer service role of a protection officer
in our organization?*

Protection officers are often highly involved in public relations/customer service. At a seminar given some years ago by this writer, an officer stated that "public relations is 90% of this job." It was interesting to note, as the class was at a manufacturing facility where public/customer contact is not as great as it would be in a shopping center, college campus, park or office building.

Some organizations such as shopping centers, hotels and amusement parks utilize security personnel as customer service agents to a large extent. Sam's Clubs "greeters" serve to welcome a customer into the store while at the same time ensuring that they are members. In many hotels a similar function is performed by protection officers in the hotel lobby. Lounges employ "Lounge Hosts" to welcome customers and keep out troublemakers. The sample job description given below for "HAPPY TIME RESORTS" provides ample evidence of the customer service role for security personnel:

> *Job Title*: Lounge Host
> *Organizational Unit*: Asset Protection
> *Accountability*: Security Shift Supervisor
> *Job Summary*: to provide for a safe, enjoyable atmosphere for our guests.
> *Duties and Responsibilities*:
> > Greeting customers in the Lounge.
> > Controlling access to Lounge.
> > Maintaining an accurate customer count.
> > Ensure the safety of the Lounge and the surrounding area.
> > Maintain order in the Lounge.
> > Ensure compliance with Alcoholic Beverage Commission regulations.
> > Customer assistance as appropriate.
> *Interaction*: Lounge manager, Bartender
> *Prepared By*: Director of Asset Protection
> *Approved By*: Vice-President, Human Relations

Training and certification of protection officers. Specific, *recognized* and *documented* training of protection staff is essential to projecting a positive image. It is also integral to making officers competent to provide a meaningful level of service.

State and provincial licensing or certification. This is essential where required by law. It also helps to give the protection force recognition. While there are serious deficiencies in state training and licensing requirements (the failure of most governmental entities to regulate proprietary forces, as an example), there is likely to be more regulation in the future (licensing is attractive as it provides a revenue stream to the state, county or city). Astute managers should see the direction that legislation is taking and be both proactive and supportive. State mandated standards are generally minimal in regards to training and screening. Professional managers ensure that their organizations go beyond the minimal and embrace "best practices."

Company certification. These credentials are given by private companies, generally in the use of equipment or techniques. Some examples of company certification programs common within the protective services arena are the Crisis Prevention Institute, REB Training International, PPCT Management Systems, and Powerphone, Inc. Each company establishes it's own criteria for certification and sells its services to customers. These certifications may be important as they are "best practices"; only those organizations interested in being on the leading edge of professionalism embrace these programs.

Of note is the use of instructor certification programs. CPI, REB and PPCT all have instructor certification processes where an individual becomes certified to teach. Having one or more individuals certified as instructors who teach non-security staff, is a valuable customer service within an organization.

Professional certification programs such as the Certified Protection Officer (CPO) and Certified Fraud Examiner (CFE). Similar to company certifications, attaining these credentials affords one industry recognition. Security staffs who are professionally certified are at a higher level of professional development. As such, they are providing more service to their customers. Professional certifications make one stand out; they enable the organization who has certified employees to demonstrate a superior level of professional development. This is markedly different than simply claiming professional status without proffering any evidence. Having professionally certified staff members is a very powerful marketing tool as Pinkerton's and others have discovered.

Industry certification. This includes such things as the International Association of Health Care Security and Safety's Basic Standard. This is a definite standard within healthcare protection that should be obtained by security forces. As specialized, vertical market sectors of security grow and develop, more of these types of programs may appear. The International Association of Campus Law Enforcement Administrators has established a Campus Protection Officer program. As the needs of campus asset protection are unique and relatively few schools have police academy trained staffs, this program will probably become heavily utilized.

Systematic, automatic professional development is necessary! For employees to function at optimal levels, they must be constantly learning. There are several programs that aid protection supervisors and managers in this regard:

- The *Safety Standard of the IAHSS* which is a logical means of organizational development for healthcare protection organizations. The Safety Standard helps to enhance the safety orientation of protection officers so that they can provide additional services. This not only expands the services of the protection organization, but presents them in a more positive manner. No longer is security seen as a paramilitary, law enforcement type organization. Instead they are viewed more as helpers. And "helpers" who assist the parent/client firms in complying with OSHA regulations are a valuable asset.
- The *Professional Security Television Network (PSTN)* offers subscribers monthly training tapes. Each month a different topic is covered so that a subscriber firm can enjoy continuous professional development for its staff. Tests are also included with each month's tapes so that learning is measured and employees are not simply "watching tapes."
- Periodic guest speakers from police departments, local colleges and civic organizations (Red Cross, Chamber of Commerce, volunteer fire department, etc.) can also aid in continuous professional development. Having representatives of these organizations speak to protection forces also raises the level of visibility of the security department.

FEEDBACK LOOP: AUDITS, CUSTOMER COMPLAINTS

The quality assurance aspect of the supervisory process can be accomplished via two different evaluative techniques: audits of individual officers and an analysis of customer complaints. Audits can take the form of "shopping" an organization by having someone unknown to the protection officer ask for directions or assistance. Phone inquiries can also be made and the results of each contact documented. Investigators can use pre-designed forms to rate pleasantness, appearance, knowledge, responsiveness or any other criteria deemed appropriate.

While a formal assessment performed by an independent entity may be preferable—and indeed quite appropriate—to large protection force operations, informal audits can also be used. The latter are much more common and easy to implement. Care must be taken, however, not to use slipshod methods when evaluating or disciplining an officer.

Customer complaints are another source of valuable intelligence. Inappropriate customer service practices, such as surly officers, can be detected through customer complaints. More importantly, systemic deficiencies such as inadequate staffing levels, substandard procedures, shoddy maintenance or poor personnel traffic flow patterns can be spotlighted. A series of complaints focused on a particular area gives managers a clear signal that something is amiss. The challenge is to design a system where the information (complaints) can be easily retrieved, analyzed and acted upon. Interdepartmental relations may be key here as personnel in other aspects of the organization may be aware of the problem areas. Meeting with them and having open lines of communication can keep the security department apprised.

FOR MORE INFORMATION

Layne Consultants International offers a seminar on Customer Service:
Layne Consultants International
(970) 468-5522
(970) 468-7832 fax
globalriskconsultants@compuserve.com

The Professional Security Television Network has numerous video programs on Public Relations, Customer Complaints, etc.

Professional Security Television Network
(800) 942-7786
www.pstn.pwpl.com

The *Special Programs Office* at York College of Pennsylvania offers a seminar on Public Relations.

Special Programs Office - York College of Pennsylvania
(717) 815-1451 or 1360
(717) 849-1607
special-programs@ycp.edu
www.ycp.edu/

THE SUPERVISOR'S ROLE IN IMPROVING CUSTOMER SERVICE
QUIZ

1. The asset protection/security supervisor is a key player in both establishing and maintaining an appropriate customer service orientation within the protection force.
   ☐ T   ☐ F

2. Knowing the organization's _____ helps to make each officer a more effective company representative.

3. Supervisors must ensure that their charges perform to the best of their ability. They must also work to achieve quality through adherence to recognized standards of performance or "_____ _____ _____."

4.   What percentage of an officer's job is related to public relations?
       a)   10%
       b)   50%
       c)   30%
       d)   90%

5.   Specific, recognized and documented training of the security department personnel is essential
       to projecting a positive image.
                    □ T   □ F

6.   For employees to function at optimal levels, they must be constantly _____.

7.   Having guest speakers from police departments, representative from local colleges and civic
       organizations (Red Cross, Chamber of Commerce, Volunteer Fire Department, etc.) can aid in
       continuous professional development.
                    □ T   □ F

8.   Astute managers should see the direction that legislation is taking and be both _____
       and _____.

9.   Understanding the organizational philosophy is only important to the management team.
                    □ T   □ F

10.   Some examples of organizations that may utilize security personnel as customer service
       agents to a large extend may include: (Select best answer)
       a)   Shopping centers
       b)   Hotels
       c)   Amusement parks
       d)   All of the above

UNIFORMS AND IMAGE ENHANCEMENT
by Daniel J. Benny, M.A., CPP, CPO, CSS

UNIFORMS

The determination on whether or not security officers will wear uniforms, and if so the type to be worn, needs to be based on the environment and location to which the officers will be assigned. Their specific mission and assignments must also be considered.

In most situations the professional security officer will wear a uniform. This allows the officer to be easily recognized, which serves both as a deterrent to criminal activity and as a means to be easily identified should their assistance be required. Uniforms also provide the officers with the symbol of authority when enforcing company regulation and, where applicable, local and state laws. The uniformed security officer is an asset to the overall loss prevention program.

The type of uniform selected will depend on the environment, work location and duties assigned. Most uniformed security officers wear a police or military type of uniform. It is important to ensure that the uniforms and badges, patches and other identifying symbols worn on them do not violate any local or state laws. This type of uniform is generally utilized by contract security officers and proprietary security officers working in industrial, governmental, transportation, parking, education, resort, and retail mall locations where a high profile is desirable.

In some work locations, such as museums, hospitals, and sports arenas, security officers wear a blazer or a business suit type of uniform along with a badge, patch or identifying name tag on the pocket. This presents a softer, less authoritative image while still allowing the security officer to be identifiable. At many work locations, there is a blend of both of these uniforms based on specific duties. An example would be to have security officers working in the parking area of a museum wear the police or military type uniform and those working in the galleries inside the museum to wear blazers.

Other specialized uniforms may also be considered based on the uniqueness of a specific assignment. Officers assigned to special duties such as bike or motorcycle patrol, beach patrol, equestrian patrol, water craft or aviation patrol and patrol in cold environments will require uniforms that are adapted to those specific environments and work situations. These may include golf shirts and shorts for bicycle and beach patrol, riding breeches and boots for mounted patrol, or full coverage jump suits for officers assigned to long-term traffic control in cold conditions. Each situation must be evaluated to determine what is the best type of uniform for a particular site.

After a type of uniform has been selected, it is important to examine the type of material from which the uniform is constructed. Basic considerations include looking for a uniform that is durable, easy to care for, comfortable for the officer, and professional looking.

Based on the mission of the officers, it may be the decision that no officers or only a percentage of them will wear uniforms. Situations such as this may include the area of retail security where officers dress as customers in order to detect and apprehend shoplifters. Non-uniformed security officers may be used for stealth or undercover security coverage during protective service details, crowd control, or counter terrorism assignments.

IDENTIFICATION

Regardless of whether the security officer is in uniform or plain clothes, photo identification cards should be issued and carried by the officer at all times when on duty. The only exception to this would be in cases where the officer is working in a true undercover assignment and the discovery of their identity and position as a security officer could result in a dangerous situation.

The purpose of identification is to provide the officers with an authentic means of identifying themselves as an agent of the organization for which they work. This is especially important for non-uniformed officers, as it is the only means they have of identifying themselves should this be necessary.

EQUIPMENT

Equipment issued to or utilized by officers can be divided into several categories including routine operational equipment, protective equipment, communications equipment and weapons.

Routine operational equipment includes items such as leather gear, flashlights, traffic control aids such as whistles and notepads. Regardless of the type of operational equipment issued, it is important that it be of good quality and maintained by the officers.

The protective equipment issued to an officer may vary based on his or her assignment and the potential threat level. This equipment should include rubber gloves and face shields for protection from blood or body fluids. Safety shoes, hats and eyeglasses should be issued to officers working in an industrial or construction area. Officers assigned to bicycle, motorcycle or mounted patrol will require special helmets and other protective clothing. Should an officer be assigned to water craft patrol, they will require a personal flotation device (PFD) or life jacket. To provide the officer with personal protection from assault, equipment such as protective vests and handcuffs should be considered based on the threat assessment.

The communications equipment issued to officers is vital to their safety and the effective performance of their duties. It is one of the security officer's roles to report information in a timely manner. The best means to facilitate this is through the use of a two-way radio. The radios selected should be licensed in accordance with federal regulations and meet the requirements for distance at the site where they will be used. Radios should be as compact as possible and be equipped with a lapel speaker mike for the officers' convenience.

As a back-up to the two-way radio systems, many security officers are also equipped with cellular telephones. This is especially important in contacting emergency services such as police, fire or medical personnel through telephone lines.

Whether or not weapons or protective equipment will be issued depends upon local and state laws, the threat to the security officer at the particular site, and management's decision on what the role of the security officer will be. Weapons and protective equipment commonly issued includes handcuffs, oleo capsicum spray and batons such as the PR-24 or ASP. Based on the threat to the security officer, management must decide whether any of these types of weapons are to be issued. Officers working alone in isolated areas, providing money escorts, or working in known high-threat environments are often issued the oleo capsicum spray, batons, and even handguns.

Handguns, in most cases, are not utilized by security officers; if they are, certain issues must be considered. State and local licensing and training requirements must be adhered to. Officers should also be required to attend an annual weapons training program. This should include a review of weapons safety, proficient use of and qualifying with their weapon, and a review of relevant laws and policies related to use of force.

If the decision is made that the officer will carry a handgun, as part of the force continuum, other non-lethal force options must be provided to the officer by allowing them to carry the PR-24 or ASP baton, OC spray and handcuffs. Security officers should never be placed in a situation in which their only option beyond the verbal command level of the force continuum is the use of deadly force with a handgun. The officer must be provided with the proper protective equipment so that they can respond at any level of the force continuum.

Officers who are issued protective equipment other than firearms, such as the PR-24 or ASP baton, OC spray, and handcuffs, should also receive annual proficiency training in the use of these protective devices, as well as a review of use of force laws and procedures related to this equipment.

CONCLUSION

The decision to provide uniforms and the type to be used, as well as the equipment to be utilized by the security officer, is a management decision. The decision must take into account the safety and comfort of the officers, their role and mission, the work location, and the impact on other employees, patrons, or visitors to the location. The uniforms and equipment selected should be functional, durable, and professional in appearance.

The uniformed security officer often provides the first impression that a patron or visitor to an establishment will have of that organization. A professionally uniformed and equipped security officer will be a credit to the security department, the organization, and the security profession as a whole.

UNIFORMS AND IMAGE ENHANCEMENT
QUIZ

1.   Uniforms also provide officers with a _____ of authority.

2.   Based on the _____ of the officers, it may be the decision that no officers or only a percentage of them will wear uniforms.

3.   Equipment issued to or _____ by officers can be divided into several categories.

4.   _____ in most cases, are not utilized by security officers.

5.   The uniformed security officer often provides the first impression that _____ or visitors to an establishment will have of that organization.

6.   Security officers are usually required to wear uniforms so that they can be easily recognized.
            ☐ T   ☐ F

7.   The type of uniform selected depends on what the individual officer prefers to wear.
            ☐ T   ☐ F

8.   All security officers should be issued a photo ID.
            ☐ T   ☐ F

9.   Most security officers carry firearms.
            ☐ T   ☐ F

10.   A use-of-force policy is not needed if security officers do not carry firearms.
            ☐ T   ☐ F

MARKETING THE SECURITY FUNCTION
by Benn H. Ramnarine, M.A., CSS, CPO
Ramdayal K. Ramdeen, CSS, CPO

INTRODUCTION

The increasingly competitive security service markets of today are leading to a change in attitude towards marketing concepts in the security industry. More and more security organizations are taking marketing seriously and are seeking to attain a professional stand in their marketing drive.

SECURITY MARKET NEEDS

As security markets grow and services become diverse, the competitiveness of the industry will force organizations to conduct assessments of themselves and consider the following:
a)   Their understanding of their client/customer needs
b)   Client/customer attitudes
c)   Client/customer buying power and behavior
The security organization will need to package their services and gear the corporate image to become competitively attractive.

THE CONCEPT OF SERVICES MARKETING

Services marketing has increased in importance over the last decade with the resultant increase in competition. The question of what constitutes a service has to be explored with a view to providing the precise service:

"A Service is an activity which has some element of intangibility associated with it, which involves some interaction with customers or with property in their possession and does not result in a transfer of ownership. A change in condition may occur and production of the service may or may not be closely associated with a physical product." (Adrian Payne, *The Essence of Services Marketing,* Prentice Hall International (U.K.) Ltd. 1993)

The question of what constitutes a "product" in the security service is quite vague. Terms such as "product," "service" or "product service" may be used quite loosely to indicate the same service.

In an effort to market the security product, one should not be too concerned with a definition per se but rather with the "requirements" of the client and what the security organization "offers" to it's customers.

SECURITY SERVICES MARKETING

When involved in security services marketing you are dealing basically with an intangible product, as versus security equipment and supplies which tend to have tangible characteristics. Security services cannot be produced before they are required and stored to meet a demand (for example, a bottle of detergent). The service is therefore most likely "used up" whilst it is being performed and invariably the consumer of the service is actually involved in its consumption.

The main difference between goods and services in the industry is that the services offered by the security service are "performed" whereas the foods are "produced." The service, therefore, is physically intangible and cannot be seen, heard, smelled, tasted or touched.

Security services marketing therefore has a variety of unique challenges for security administration or the company:
1.   How can security achieve a unique corporate image?
2.   How to offer a service differentiation.
3.   How to achieve a distinctive reputation in the market place.
In a competitive market, your security marketing skills must be precise and clear in order to satisfactorily market services and liaise with the client.

SELLING THE SECURITY SERVICE

"Selling is the art of developing relationships." For the security practitioner, this includes practicing qualities consistent for selling the services, which includes:

1. Acting with Integrity
2. Honesty
3. Professionalism
4. Commitment
5. Customer Relations
6. Trustworthiness
7. Market Oriented

All these qualities are translated into consultive behaviors. The security supervisor should:

1. Learn about consultive behavior
2. Become knowledgeable about the customer's business
3. Become excellent listeners
4. Become excellent communicators
5. Understand the customer's customer

Having achieved this, the security supervisor then becomes a clearing house of information leading from the customer's organization back to the security company. The security company will then be in a position to deal with these definite possibilities:

1. Recognize new opportunities within the customer's identified needs.
2. Handle potential and/or problems early.
3. Become highly effective in preparing and delivering services to the customer. Contingency planning is very important here.

The security supervisor who operates as an effective consulting/marketing person obtains substantially more information quickly and currently. Information of this caliber serves the security company in a variety of ways:

1. It allows the organization to assess its quality and strength
2. It allows for measured performance
3. It allows for improved strategic planning
4. It allows for faster effective decisions
5. It determines where to target for measured efforts
6. It allows the company to hold and maintain that competitive edge

Each security supervisor involved in the selling of services, skills and behaviors should use their knowledge of the customer's business to identify their business problems, potential problems and solutions for increased business and security effectiveness.

ORGANIZATIONAL STRATEGIES (FUNCTIONAL)

The security company's strategic plans need to establish what kind of business the company will become engaged in and the specific objectives for each. A more comprehensive planning mechanism then needs to be developed in conjunction with the security department, illustrating its role in the strategic planning process.

The security department should provide information for management to prepare a detailed organizational plan, which will show how the security department will integrate itself overall and outline the functional areas to accomplish its objectives.

The "strategic plan" defines the company's overall mission and objectives. The alert security administrator/company will rely on marketing as one of the major systems for monitoring and integrating the changes in the market place.

Marketing the security service is not just selling or advertising but rather a detailed process which compares and contrasts the organizational plan to the marketing opportunities available. This marketing management function can best be achieved by:

1. Analysis and Planning – examining the company's market environment to identify opportunities. To also decide on a marketing strategy that is co-related with the security company's strategic objective.

2. Implementation – all departments of the company must blend their resources together in a comprehensive, cohesive working unit (finance, purchasing, services/manufacturing).

3.   Control – mechanisms to ensure objectives are met.
                        - measure performance levels
                        - identify the causes and flaws in the performance levels of officer/staff
                        - determine corrective/remedial measures

The security company should, however, take time out to review its overall performance and approach to the market place. The basic objective is to verify that the company's mission, objectives, policies, strategies and programs are current and feasible within the changing environment.

MISSION STATEMENT

The development of a mission statement is most important in services marketing given the intangibility of the security service. Companies/organizations need to develop a clear "mission," a statement of performance to ensure that adequate planning and supervision is directed towards achieving those critical elements of the strategic plan.

While organizations prepare mission statements for a variety of reasons, they should reflect elements of the strategies of the organization and focus on the organization's business activities. Specifically, it should outline a long-term plan of the company indicating what it wants to be and the direction it plans to take. The mission statement is an absolute mechanism for developing and reviewing the strategic market and service options of the security department.

Communicating the Mission Statement

After a mission statement has been developed it should be communicated to persons both internally and externally. This can be done in a variety of ways:
1.   Posters
2.   Plastic cards for distribution to staff
3.   Company newsletter
4.   Desk plaques
5.   Personal memo pads/organizers
6.   Training programs/workshops
7.   On memos

Service Oriented Mission Statement

It is particularly important in the security industry to avoid a mission statement that reflects "product" rather than "service." The mission should be defined in a way to reflect customer needs rather than product features. "Service needs" should be of major concern for the security director when making a decision about the nature of what services they will offer. Such a statement should contain some of the following components:
a)   Who are my customers?
b)   Range and type of services – the diversity of services offered
c)   Market – where does the security service compete?
d)   Long- and short-term objectives – immediate action plan, long-term action plan
e)   The organization as a good corporate citizen – concern for the security service public image
f)   Employee satisfaction – the company's attitude towards the security officer and client
g)   Marketing strategies – value, plans and projections to capture market segment
h)   Total Quality Service

THE CUSTOMER - SECURITY SERVICE INTERFACE

The security supervisor has a responsibility to sell services personally. In doing so he has to consider:
1.   Personal contact and relationship between the security department and the customer
2.   Development and training in marketing and total quality service
3.   Service is the product and it must be quality oriented

The relationship between the customer and the security supervisor must be an ongoing relationship. He/she can sell the services through:

1.   Good communication skills
2.   Sales planning
3.   Handling conflict/negative input
4.   Analysis of target market
5.   Good negotiation of agreement(s)

The Security Interface Must Include

1.   Personal contact – Client/customer should be managed through personal contact
2.   Customer/security satisfaction – intimate and professional contact provides the basics for the relationship between customer and security
3.   The security supervisor is the first line marketing officer. He/she acts as the first line sales person because of positioning to communicate details of services to:
      a)   Clients
      b)   Customers
      c)   Potential customers
      d)   Advertising agencies
      e)   Security publications

THE SECURITY SURVEY

The security supervisor's interface will also come into play in conducting security surveys. This enables the supervisor to ascertain the security status and identification of deficiencies or other vulnerabilities of a potential client. The survey is important as it gives the supervisor his "mechanism" to determine clients' needs. While the survey serves to provide an objective insight into the security needs of a customer, it can also be used to market security services to current customers and future potential ones.

The Responsibilities of the Supervisor in Conducting Surveys

The supervisor should conduct the survey as part of his/her initial marketing plan. Here are some suggested guidelines:
1.   Goals and objectives should be clear
2.   Identify the time, support and availability of other resources that can assist you
3.   Conduct research on the history and background of the location or facility, include geographical location
4.   Check the interactions the location or facility has with the community and clients
5.   Check the crime situation in the area
6.   Review policies, rules, regulations and standard operating procedure
7.   Check plans, other architectural drawings and previous surveys
8.   Compile a list of services you can sell the client in order of priority, this excludes the original requirements identified by the client
9.   Compile your survey report – exclude your list of potential services
10.   Your list of services to the client should reflect a cost effective approach or even package deals

There is no set method for marketing your identified services; however, the supervisor must be aware of costs and what the competition is like. The final presentation to the client should be:
1.   Clear
2.   Well prepared
3.   Customer oriented
4.   Confident in approach and presentation
5.   Organized with total quality service in mind and nothing should be left to chance

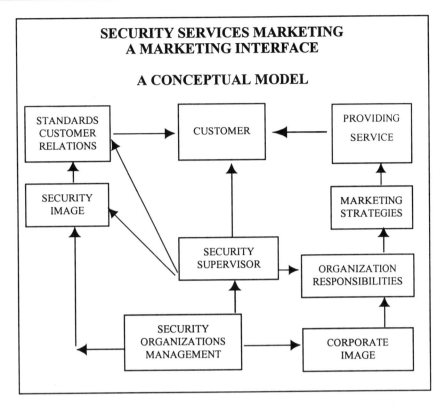

Figure 47.1

SUMMARY

Services marketing provides that competitive edge for many a company. The effectiveness of it is dependent on companies recognizing the differences between the marketing activity and the process to achieve it. The security supervisor's continuous contact with the customer and reaction to research, planning, selling, advertising and interfacing with the entire security organization, regarding customer needs and requests, will cause a cross-fertilization of activities to emerge. This will further serve to enhance a total quality service package depending on whether the security company has a total quality management system.

The supervisor must also be aware that in striving to market his security services, the training and development of staff is essential. It must not be thought that higher quality means higher cost, for it is more of building quality into services, preventing failures from occurring and eliminating financial waste. Personnel is the key to your quality service becoming a success.

Services will emerge through the provision of quality service. In striving to provide a "top notch" service to client/customer, communicate as you never have before, involve management in leading roles, measure for success, train like crazy and give recognition where it is deserved.

Services will emerge through the provision of quality service and reliability. The entire company has to become involved in providing that "top notch" security service.

BIBLIOGRAPHY

J. Bateson, *Managing Services Marketing*, Text and Readings, Dryden, Chicago, 1984

D. Cowell, *The Marketing of Services*, Heinemann, London, 1984

Paul Connolly, Ph.D., Clark Wilson, Ph.D., *The Survey of Quality Values in Practice*, Clark Wilson Publishing Company, 1992

J. M. Rathmell, *Marketing in the Service Sector*, Winthrop Publishing, Cambridge, Mass., 1974

D. L. Riddle, *Service-Led Growth*, Pradger, New York, 1986

Mike Robson, *Quality Circles-A Practical Guide*, Gower Publishing Company Ltd., Aldershot, Hants, England, 1984

P.L. Towsend, *Commit to Quality*, Wiley, Chichester, 1986

A. Wilson, *Practice Development for Professional Firms*, McGraw Hill, London, 1984

PERIODICALS

Supervisor Management, Publisher: American Management Association, P.O. Box 58155, Boulder, CO. 8033-8155, U.S.A.

Management Review, Publisher: American Management Association AMA Publications, Box 408, Saranac Lake, NY 12983-0408, U.S.A.

International Management, Publisher: Reed Business Publishing, Quadrant House, The Quadrant, Sutton, Surrey, SMZ 5AS, U.K.

International Journal of Strategic Management, Publisher: Pargamon Press Inc., 660 White Plains Road, Tarrydown, NY 10591-5153, U.S.A.

International Business Week, Publisher: McGraw Hill Inc., 1221 Avenue of the Americas, New York, NY 10020, U.S.A.

International Security Review, Publisher: FMJ International Publishers Ltd., Queensway House, 2 Queensway, Redhill, Surrey RH2 1QS, U.K.

Public Relations Quarterly, Publisher: Public Relations Quarterly, 44 West Market St., Rhineback, NY 12572, 914-876-2081, U.S.A.

Security, Publisher: Cahners Publishing Company, Div. of Reed Publishing Company U.S.A., 275 Washington St., Newton, MA 2158-1630, U.S.A.

MARKETING THE SECURITY FUNCTION
QUIZ

1.   Services marketing has increased in importance over the last decade with resultant increase in _____.

2.   The main difference between goods and services in the industry is that the services offered by security service is _____, whereas the goods are _____.

3.   Become knowledgeable about the customer's _____.

4.   The security company should take "_____" to review its overall performance and approach to the market place.

5.   It is particularly important in the security industry to avoid a mission statement that reflects "product" rather than "_____."

6.   Marketing is a critical function of the security organization.
             ☐ T   ☐ F

7.   Selling is the art of developing relationships.
                    □ T   □ F

8.   An understanding of the customer's business is not important for the security supervisor in
        marketing security services.
                    □ T   □ F

9.   The strategic plan defines the company's overall image.
                    □ T   □ F

10.   The security supervisor has a responsibility to sell services personally.
                    □ T   □ F

APPENDIX A:
THE TEN COMMANDMENTS OF MARKETING
by Christopher A. Hertig, CPP, CPO

I.   A positive image is always reflected in the bottom line.

II.   Target markets must be identified in terms of customer profiles (demographics, buying motives, buying patterns).

III.   Quality is defined by the customer, *not* by the producer.

IV.   Pricing must be determined in terms of costs and market conditions in order to be attractive to the customer.

V.   "People only buy something after they hear about it 3 times."

VI.   Negative customer service is the most powerful advertising tool.

VII.   Visualization of the product or service via charts, graphs, etc. is important to influencing buying decisions as is documentation where facts and figures are offered as evidence of product/service worthiness.

VIII.   Association of the product or service with something noteworthy or appealing to the target market helps to sell it.

IX.   Physical representation via logo or trademark helps establish a product/service identity.

X.   Market development—the exploration of new markets—should occur in order to keep the product/service in demand.

CRIME PREVENTION / COMMUNITY RELATIONS
by Mark Gleckman, M.S., CPO

The National Crime Prevention Institute defines crime prevention as the anticipation, recognition and appraisal of a crime risk and the initiation of action to remove or reduce it.

Crime prevention generally focuses on the reduction of criminal opportunity rather than working to inhibit the desire or the skill to commit the crime. Potential victims can reduce criminal opportunity by understanding criminal attack methods and taking precautions against them. Convincing community members to take basic precautions is the main task of crime prevention.

Crime prevention practitioners work to inform the community that criminal opportunity arises out of carelessness. Inadequate locking devices or poorly secured doors are all the criminal needs.

Crime prevention practitioners want the community to be aware that criminal opportunity arises because of carelessness, inadequate or lack of elementary locking devices and doors that any novice could get through.

The crime prevention specialist must possess a wide variety of general knowledge in crime prevention theory and practice. They must be adept at public speaking and promote good community-police relations at all times. Further, they must have a thorough knowledge of the area, the people in it, their needs and projects and programs that will aid the community in developing a comprehensive crime prevention program.

COMMUNITY WATCH

Whether called community watch, citizen alert, business watch, neighborhood watch or block watch, the idea is the same – neighbors watching out for each other. The concept involves developing a crime prevention program in which citizens work with each other and with local law enforcement agencies to reduce crime and vandalism in their community.

Everyone must adopt the attitude that they may be the next victim of a crime and take preventative measures. Crime plays no favorites.

Criminals gravitate to places where they feel safe and secure. They stay out of neighborhoods where they are likely to get caught. The goal of community watch programs is to make criminals aware that their activities are being watched and will be reported to the police. In neighborhoods where people watch after each other, burglary rates are lower.

Participation in a community watch program does not require a great deal of time. However, it does require you to become slightly more observant in your daily routine and maintain open lines of communication with your neighbors and with local law enforcement. If everyone participates, a community watch can work to reduce crime and make your neighborhood a safer place to live.

THE SECURITY SURVEY

A security survey is an on-site physical examination of a home or business, its surroundings and its environment. The security survey will evaluate the security of the property, identify any deficiencies or security risks, make recommendations to reduce or eliminate any threats and/or vulnerabilities and determine the degree of protection needed.

A qualified crime prevention specialist should be used to conduct the survey. The specialist should review any information that may be available from previous studies and recommendations. A checklist should be created and used to facilitate the gathering of pertinent information. The checklist is considered to be the backbone of the survey and will serve to systematically guide the specialist through the areas that must be examined.

Checklists can be presented in many forms. They can be a simple list of questions requiring only a yes or no response or they may ask open-ended questions that will require a more in-depth narrative response. It doesn't matter how it is designed as long as it provides a logical way to record information and assures that no important questions go unasked.

At the conclusion of the survey the specialist should prepare a complete professional report. The specialist should then discuss the results with the client and explain the recommendations.

HOME SECURITY

According to the U.S. Department of Justice, 42 percent of all household burglaries occur without forced entry by opportunists who happen to spot an open window or door, an unlocked gate, an open garage, or a house that looks like the occupants have not been around for a while.

The following security tips offer some common sense measures that will help in developing a home crime prevention plan.

*   Lock your doors and windows whenever you leave your house.
*   Never hide a key outside. Burglars know all your hiding places.
*   Never leave a note stating that you have left and will return at a certain time.
*   Use UL rated automatic timers to turn on and off your lights, radio and television. Set the radio or television to a talk show or news station.
*   Engrave your valuables with your driver's license number.
*   Photograph items that cannot be engraved.
*   Keep an inventory list of your valuables, with serial numbers.
*   Make two copies of all computer disks. Keep one off premises.
*   Keep your gates and garage door locked.
*   Trim your hedges below window sills. Prune tree branches six feet up and away from your home.
*   Don't let newspapers or mail accumulate. Keep your lawn and shrubs cut.
*   Light up all exterior doorways and shadowed areas. Use motion detectors or photoelectric sensors.
*   Install an alarm system.
*   Get a dog. Even a small dog may discourage a burglar.
*   Secure doggie doors when you are not at home.
*   Make sure that all exterior doors are solid core and that all exposed hinges are pinned or spot welded.
*   Use deadbolt locks with a one in long throw on exterior doors.
*   Use auxiliary locks on all windows and sliding glass doors.
*   To ensure windows cannot be lifted out of their tract, install sheet metal screws into the upper tract.
*   House numbers should be at least four inches high, illuminated and mounted on a contrasting background.
*   Participate in a neighborhood watch program.
*   If you come home and find signs of forced entry, don't go in. Go to the nearest phone and call the police.

Home security does not have to cost a lot of money. It just takes a little extra time and some common sense. Eliminate the opportunity and you may prevent yourself from becoming the next victim of a residential crime.

ROBBERY PREVENTION

Violent crimes, such as robbery, can cost the business owner not only a financial loss but a loss of life or serious injury. Isolated stores like convenience stores and small mini-marts at gas stations are especially vulnerable to robbery. Retail robbery targets include cash registers, cash rooms and cash deposit runs.

A typical robber is male, between 20 and 29 years old, and armed with a handgun. He is likely to be nervous and may become violent if surprised by a sudden motion, an audio alarm or the arrival of police. The average robbery takes about 90 seconds, with one robbery occurring in the United States every minute.

The most effective robbery deterrents are to decrease the amount of cash on hand and increase the visibility of clerk areas. Security hardware such as cash storage devices, metal detectors or CCTV has proven to be effective in reducing robberies. The following are some suggested robbery prevention methods:

*   Train employees in robbery reaction procedures.
*   Keep safes and money boxes locked when not in use.
*   Keep the amount of cash in the register to a minimum – under $75 is recommended.

- Use a time delay cash drop safe.
- Never display cash in public view.
- Post signs stating that employees cannot unlock the safe.
- Reposition window signs or displays that may be blocking the view of the register area.
- All entrances should be kept well lit.
- Any entrance door not being used should remain locked.
- Use "bait" money (numbered bills) to assist in the apprehension of a robber.
- When taking a cash deposit to the bank, be totally unpredictable. Constantly change routes, times, methods of cash concealment and deposit personnel.
- Advise employees not to wear expensive jewelry to work.
- Check security equipment daily and fix anything that is not working.
- After closing, never re-open for anyone.

Robbery prevention will involve a combination of training and security hardware. An effective robbery prevention plan can be designed and implemented by determining local trends and the store's high-risk areas.

INTERNAL THEFT

Internal crime costs American business 40 million dollars a year. One insurance company estimates that 30 percent of all business failures are the direct result of employee theft. The National Association of Convenience Stores estimates 50 to 70 percent of an organization's losses are directly related to internal theft.

The most common form of employee theft is the removal of merchandise or company property. Articles are removed by carrying or wearing them out of the building. Employees will also steal cash directly from cash registers by manipulating their cash sales. This usually involves the under-ringing of the sales amount. Employees also steal money by inappropriately using discounts, ringing sales up as a "void" or "no sale," or through fraudulent CODs. This list of techniques used by the dishonest employee is endless.

Employee theft is a crime of opportunity. Systems should be instituted that will reduce the opportunities and increase the risk of getting caught. The best security measures are simply good management practices. For example:

- Check applicant references before hiring.
- Rotate employees in high-risk areas.
- Clean up piles of trash. Stolen goods can be hidden in the pile and retrieved at a later time.
- Take physical inventories on a regular basis.
- Spot check all operations on an irregular and unannounced basis.
- Issue package passes for items being carried off the premises.
- Control cash.
- Restrict employees from parking near the building.
- Effectively use CCTV and electronic article surveillance systems.

Company policies and rules regarding theft should be posted in convenient locations. Employees need to be educated to understand that security is part of their job description.

SHOPLIFTING

Shoplifters come in all sizes, ages and sexes. They come from varying ethnic, educational and economic backgrounds. According to a survey conducted by Commercial Services Systems Inc., 55% of the people caught shoplifting are adults, 63% of whom are under 30 years of age. Females dominate the overall statistics, while males account for the majority of juvenile shoplifters.

Shoplifters fall into two categories, the amateur and the professional. Generally, the amateur shoplifter steals on impulse without any type of preconceived plan. The loss resulting from each amateur shoplifting incident is relatively small compared to the loss from each professional theft. Professional shoplifters account for a greater financial loss per shoplifting incident because professional shoplifters steal strictly for profit.

The retailer's best defense against shoplifters consists of:
- Train employees in the methods of shoplifting.

- Offer employees a reward for deterring shoplifting.
- All customers should be greeted immediately upon entering the store.
- Maximize visibility by raising the cash register area, use convex mirrors, one-way mirrors and closed circuit television cameras.
- Use an electronic article surveillance system (EAS).
- Post signs in plain view stating that all shoplifters will be prosecuted.
- Keep cash registers locked and monitored at all times.
- Use cable tie-downs
- Watch for price switching.
- Monitor all delivery men.
- Cashiers should check every item sold that might hide other merchandise.
- Have the cashier staple the customer's bag closed with the sales receipt attached.
  The best shoplifting prevention programs are those that are basic and uncomplicated.

CONCLUSION

An effective crime prevention/community watch program is so extensive that it will demand a concerted and coordinated community effort. Citizens must be educated to recognize certain conditions and situations that contribute to crime and must be motivated to report and eliminate them. Individuals must come to realize the need to protect themselves against crime and to safeguard their neighborhoods. Practical and effective crime prevention programs should lead to increasing proportions of failed attempts compared to the total number of crimes being committed.

CRIME PREVENTION / COMMUNITY RELATIONS
QUIZ

1. The National Crime Prevention Institute defines crime prevention as the anticipation, _____ _____ and appraisal of crime risk.

2. Whether called community watch, citizen alert, _____ watch, neighborhood watch or block watch, the idea is the same.

3. A qualified crime _____ specialist should be used to conduct a security survey.

4. Never leave a _____ saying you will return at a certain time.

5. Violent crimes, such as robbery, can cost the business owners not only a financial loss but a loss of life or _____ injury.

6. The crime prevention specialist should limit their knowledge only to preventive measures.
    ☐ T   ☐ F

7. A security survey is an on-site physical examination of the property.
    ☐ T   ☐ F

8. One of the most effective robbery deterrents is to increase the visibility of clerk areas.
    ☐ T   ☐ F

9. Robbery prevention involves a combination of security hardware and employee training.
    ☐ T   ☐ F

10. Bank deposits should be done at the same time every day.
    ☐ T   ☐ F

UNIT TEN
LEGAL ISSUES

Legal Aspects of Security
Managing / Supervising to Reduce Liability
Sexual Harassment
Contracts in Asset Protection

LEGAL ASPECTS OF SECURITY
by Christopher A. Hertig, CPP, CPO

INTRODUCTION

Protection professionals work within a complex array of legal standards. Their daily functioning requires them to be knowledgeable of laws governing the employment relationships present in the workplace, civil and criminal law, standards of practice, as well as a myriad of government regulations. Added to this mixture is the burgeoning repertoire of professional standards enacted by such entities as the Joint Commission on the Accreditation of Healthcare Organizations, the International Association of Campus Law Enforcement Administrators and others.

Unfortunately, traditional texts on legal aspects have focused too narrowly on criminal law and civil liability. Scant coverage of administrative or regulatory law has been given. Almost no attention has been paid to the vast and complex spectrum of employment law. This chapter will provide a brief introduction of the various legal aspects of which protection supervisors must be knowledgeable. It is an introduction from which the reader is encouraged to expand. It is for educational purposes and is not to take the place of competent legal counsel.

KEY TERMS AND CONCEPTS

Action - a formal legal proceeding by one party against another. *Cause of action* is the right that one party has to institute a legal proceeding. *Actionable* means furnishing legal grounds for an action.

Agent - an individual authorized to act for or in place of another (principal) who represents that person.

Americans With Disabilities Act (ADA) - a law signed by George Bush on July 6,1990, that is designed to ensure equal opportunities to employment based on merit.

Title I covers employers of 15 or more employees, state and local governments, employment agencies and labor unions and is under the jurisdiction of the Equal Employment Opportunity Commission.

Title II provides for nondiscrimination on the basis of disability in state and local governments. Title II covers public entities such as state and local governments and public transportation. It is enforced by the Department of Justice.

Title III provides for nondiscrimination on the basis of disability in public accommodations and commercial facilities, such as hotels, office buildings, retail stores, etc. Places of worship and private clubs are not covered by Title III. Title III is under the jurisdiction of the Department of Justice.

Arbitrary and Capricious - willful and unreasonable action taken without regards to the facts or the law. Arbitrary and capricious is the standard by which courts will overturn the rulings made by an administrative agency such as the Occupational Safety & Health Administration or Federal Communications Commission.

Bloodborne Pathogens Act - OSHA's Occupational Exposure to Bloodborne Pathogens; Final Rule, Standard 29CFR, part 1910.1030 became effective on March 6,1992. Known as the "Bloodborne Pathogens Act," this standard requires employers having one or more employees with occupational exposure to bloodborne pathogens to have an exposure control plan, adopt universal precautions to prevent the spread of bloodborne pathogens such as AIDS and hepatitis B, educational training programs and medical record keeping.

Burden of Proof - the obligation of establishing a requisite degree of belief in the trier of fact in a legal proceeding. The degree of proof necessary to prevail. The burden of proof varies between different legal processes.

Reasonable Suspicion - the degree of facts and circumstances necessary to make a prudent and cautious person believe that criminal activity is afoot. Reasonable suspicion is more than mere suspicion for it must be based on articulable facts and circumstances. Police officers in the United States may conduct a search for weapons of the outer clothing (pat down) of persons whom they have a reasonable suspicion of committing, having committed or be about to commit a criminal offense. Similarly, school officials under *New Jersey v. TLO* can search students for contraband if they have reasonable suspicion.

Probable Cause - also known as "reasonable cause"; enough evidence for a belief in the alleged facts. An apparent state of facts found after a reasonable inquiry. Circumstances sufficient in themselves to warrant a reasonable man believing the accused to be guilty. The necessary evidence used for arrest, search or the issuance of an arrest or search warrant. Probable cause is also necessary to defend against suits for false arrest.

Prima Facia - at first sight; evidence sufficient on its face to establish proof. The amount of evidence necessary to support a fact at issue without rebuttal by the opposing party. Prima facie is used at preliminary hearings to bind a case over to trial in criminal cases. It is enough to send a case to trial but not enough to convict.

Preponderance of Evidence - the majority or greater weight of the evidence. More probable than not. Preponderance of the evidence is the standard used in civil cases.

Clear and Convincing Proof - the amount of proof that results in reasonable certainty of the fact at issue. More than a preponderance of evidence but less than beyond a reasonable doubt. Often used in labor arbitrations.

Beyond a Reasonable Doubt - fully satisfied; entirely convinced to a moral certainty. Reasonable doubt is the degree of doubt that would cause a prudent person to hesitate in acting on matters of great import to them. This is the standard of proof necessary in criminal cases.

Certiori - a writ issued by a superior court (appellate court, Supreme Court) to an inferior court (court of first instance, lower court, trial court) requiring that the inferior court produce records of a particular case. Certiori is used to inspect the lower court's actions in order to uncover irregularities.

"Color of Law" - the misuse of lawful authority by a government agent. The power vested in the official is exercised unlawfully and is only done so due to the appearance of lawful authority. Actions taken under pretense of law and clothed in state authority that violate the rights of citizens. Unlawful acts done by an official must be done while that person is exercising lawful authority; the acts could not have occurred, but for the authority that the official possessed. Under 42 U.S.C.A., Section 1983, private persons can be found to be acting "under color of law" when there is significant state involvement in the activity. Such persons can be found civilly liable—as well as criminally liable—under federal law for civil rights violations.

Contract - an agreement containing a promise or set of promises the breach of which is actionable. Contracts can be either express (manifested in written or spoken words) or implied (shown by actions rather than words). Contracts consist of several key parts:

1. An agreement to do or not do a certain thing.
2. Between legally competent parties (consulting adults).
3. Based on genuine consent of the parties.
4. Supported by consideration (profit or benefit accruing to each party).
5. Made for a lawful objective; not in violation of public policy.
6. In the form required by law.

Equal Employment Opportunity Commission - an administrative agency created by Title VII of the Civil Rights Act of 1964. The Commission works to end discrimination based on race, color, religion, sex, age or national origin in employment. The EEOC promotes voluntary programs of equal opportunity and also seeks to resolve disputes. The Commission may also assist in bringing actions based on a violation of Title VII on behalf of the aggrieved parties in the federal courts. The EEOC also enforces the Age Discrimination in Employment Act of 1967, Equal Pay Act of 1963 and those sections of the Americans with Disabilities Act that deal with employment.

Evidence - Proof of a fact at issue. Any testimony, writings, exhibits, physical objects, etc. that may help prove the existence or nonexistence of a fact.

Negligence:

Simple negligence is failing to exercise the degree of care that would be exercised by ordinarily prudent persons.

Gross negligence is the intentional failure to perform a duty in reckless disregard of the consequences of nonperformance. Gross negligence is a conscious and voluntary act or omission likely to cause serious injury to another and of which the "tortfeasor" is aware. Gross negligence usually bars limitations of liability in contracts. Such contracts may include exculpatory clauses which bar suit in cases of simple negligence. These are generally held to be valid, but instances of gross negligence are found to be in violation of public policy and are, therefore, not enforceable.

Public Policy - public conscience and morals that are applied throughout the community. Supported by public opinion, public policy relates to those matters that promote the general health, welfare and safety of all persons. Public policy consists of those tangible, noticeable duties that each man must extend to his fellowmen. The *public policy doctrine* affords courts the right to refuse to enforce contracts that violate the law or public policy.

Qualified Immunity - an affirmative defense to civil prosecution held by public officials. Qualified immunity is extended to governmental agents so that they may exercise discretionary authority. They are immune to prosecution if their actions did not violate statutory laws or constitutional safeguards. Government officials acting with probable cause cannot be held civilly liable.

Reasonable and Due Care - that degree of care that a reasonably prudent person would exhibit in similar circumstances. The degree of care necessary to prevent an action of negligence.

Reasonable Belief - facts sufficient to cause a reasonable and cautious man to believe that a certain set of circumstances is true, such as, that a person committed a felony.

Recovery - the amount of damages awarded to the plaintiff. The restoration of a right to an aggrieved party by a judgement of a court (damages, injunctive relief).

Statute of Limitations - In Pennsylvania the limits vary between torts; actions must be filed within one year for libel, slander or invasion of privacy. The limit extends to two years for assault, battery, false imprisonment, false arrest, malicious prosecution, wrongful death or claims for forfeiture.

Substantial Evidence Rule - substantial evidence that a fact is true is sufficient to let stand an administrative agency ruling by a court reviewing that ruling. Under the rule, all evidence is competent and may be considered, regardless of its source, if it is reasonable to support a conclusion. Substantial evidence is more than a mere scintilla, but less than a preponderance.

Summary Judgement - A decision rendered by a court when there is no dispute as to the facts of a case and there is only a question of law to be addressed. Summary judgements allow the expeditious handling of civil complaints whereby one party believes he will prevail as a matter of law. This party makes a motion for summary judgement.

ARREST AND DETENTION

Arrest - Depriving a person of liberty by legal authority in order that he may answer to a criminal charge. Generally citizen's arrest can be performed for the following reasons—*which vary considerably from state to state:*

1. Commission of a felony
2. Felony committed in arrestor's presence
3. Felony witnessed by arrestor
4. Breach of the peace resulting from a felony or misdemeanor being committed

Most jurisdictions require that a felony has been committed in fact, that the person making the citizen's arrrest has reasonable grounds to believe the person being arrested has committed the felony and that the felony was committed in the arrestor's presence.

There are also specific circumstances under which certain persons may make arrests in various states; in Pennsylvania, a train car conductor may make an arrest of a person carrying a bomb on a train.

Citizen's arrest is not looked upon favorably by employers or the courts as there is often no privilege or *qualified immunity* from civil prosecution for private persons. While police officers who have *probable cause* are immune from civil actions due to false arrest, private persons are not. Additionally, if the arrest is invalid, the police are not obligated to take the arrestee into custody. This makes for a very troublesome situation.

Arrest Procedures

- Notify the arrestee of the purpose of the arrest.
- Be certain to use only reasonable or necessary force.
- Restrict searches of arrestees to cursory crushing of the outer clothing for weapons.
- Do not keep the person in custody any longer than is necessary.
- The police should be notified as soon after the arrest as possible and the arrestee delivered to the police without delay.

Juveniles

Juveniles being arrested or detained give rise to special problems. Many states have complicated and changing rules concerning juveniles. In general, the protection officer should bear in mind the following when taking a juvenile into custody:

Consider legal relationship to juvenile—in loco parentis ("in place of the parent") exists when a person assumes temporary supervision of a child in the absence of a parent such as teachers at schools.

1. Know and follow all state laws—these vary *considerably*.
2. Notify appropriate authorities—police, juvenile probation, truant officers.
3. Notify parents or guardians.
4. Release to parents (summary offense or civil recovery), police or juvenile authorities at earliest opportunity.
5. Children under 7 years of age cannot be taken into custody for a crime.

DETENTION

Detention is the act of temporarily stopping someone's freedom of movement. This may be done to protect oneself or another whom the officer has a *duty* to protect against an assault, to stop a trespasser, to conduct an entry or exit search or to recover merchandise. Detention could result in arrest, but in the overwhelming majority of cases it is not performed with the intent of bringing someone before a court. Generally, detention does not involve the use of force and should not involve the use of force if at all possible. Detention authority is specified in state statutes regarding shoplifting and library theft, but most states—*and legal texts*—are mute on the subject when applied to the more common performance of detention at entry points, in schools, in high security facilities, etc.

Merchant's privilege statutes vary considerably between the states. *Generally* they extend qualified immunity which allows merchants, their employees or agents to take persons into custody with *reasonable* or *probable cause* that the person has committed a retail theft for the following purposes:

- To request and verify information.
- To ascertain if the person has un-purchased merchandise in his or her possession.
- To inform a peace or police officer of the detention and surrender that person to the officer.

The following points serve as evaluative tools by which protection professionals can assess detention practices:

1. Know and articulate specific purpose of detention—self-defense, recovery of merchandise, protection of others, prevention of trespass, etc. Officers must be able to demonstrate clearly why they are restricting someone's freedom.
2. Have a written policy on detention which is implemented via specific procedures, post orders, etc.
3. Develop policy after assessing state statutes, regulatory requirements, case law and local law enforcement agency procedures.
4. Know the policy and operating procedures of responding law enforcement agencies.
5. Call police as soon as possible in those cases requiring their assistance—where persons are violent and/or where criminal charges will be brought against someone.
6. Record the times of calls to the police, the results of such calls, and the arrival times, numbers and names of responding police officers.
7. Use effective and legally correct (truthful, accurate) verbalization when detaining.
8. Tell the detainee what is transpiring, but no more than is necessary. Provide a basic explanation, but do not engage in protracted dialogue about the reason, the officer's authority, etc. Lengthy discussions create room for argument!
9. Be as polite and considerate as possible to the detainee. Scrupulously avoid referring to them in demeaning terms.
10. Assess the detainee and environment for safety—avoid areas with a lot of glass, easy access to weapons, hazardous materials or the inability to secure the room from associates of the detainee—before initiating the contact.
11. Avoid physical contact and document in detail *any and all* physical contact that occurs.

12.   Understand the relationship of the detainee to your employer as much as possible. An employee can be spoken to longer in the eyes of the courts as they are being compensated for their time via an established business relationship.

13.   Detain in a safe, secure area under your control. Control is the issue. Whose "turf" the detention occurs on will play a large role in determining which area to use.

14.   Detain in a private place. A quiet, somewhat secluded, comfortable office environment is best to minimize interpersonal tensions between the officer and detainee. A private setting also helps to preclude any embarrassment the detainee may feel.

15.   Have witnesses to the detention the same sex as the detainee.

16.   Search the detainee in an appropriate manner: visual scan, cursory search for weapons, consent search of purse, etc. Employer policies will dictate the type and nature of the search. Officers should always have some reasonable degree of assurance that the detainee is not armed.

17.   Restrain the detainee in an appropriate manner; have them sit with hands in view, handcuff, four-position restraints, etc.

18.   Separate detainees from each other.

19.   Question detainees for basic information and record their statements.

20.   Debrief the detainee as appropriate by complimenting them, explaining the impropriety to them, getting their acknowledgment of their inappropriate actions, etc.

21.   Document the detention completely, being sure to include all statements, admissions, threats, etc.

CONSIDERATIONS REGARDING THE USE OF FORCE

The lawful—and *safe*—use of force by private security personnel is a growing concern. Private security personnel are apt to encounter aggressive and potentially violent individuals in shopping centers, theaters, restaurants, amusement parks, "gated communities" and other places. In such environments, security personnel are largely taking the role of the old time cop on the beat in a downtown urban environment. As there is more privatization of protective services in courthouses, municipal buildings, public parks, municipal garages and housing projects, so too the potential for use of force encounters.

Use of Force Continuum

Developed by Dr. Kevin Parsons, the Use of Force Continuum is a guide to using only that degree of force necessary to effect the immediate purpose for its employment. Other continuums have been developed by PPCT Management Systems, Larry Smith Enterprises, etc. All of them consist of a series of logical steps toward escalating the level of force used against an assailant. Officer presence would be followed by verbal controls, which would be followed by soft empty hand control. After this would be striking with the hands, impact weapons and, finally, deadly force. Note that there are differences of opinion among the experts regarding these continuums. Also note that the particular circumstances involving the use of force vary from situation to situation. An untrained officer using a lateral vascular neck restraint is a far cry from a trained and proficient individual employing the same technique. Similarly, the modification of any weapons used will change their place on the continuum. Adding CS or CN agent to oleoresin capsicum ("pepper spray") will change the content and effect of the aerosol.

Deadly Force

That force which is readily capable of causing death or *serious bodily injury*.

Serious Bodily Injury

Bodily injury which creates a substantial risk of death or results in permanent disfigurement, or the protracted loss of use of any bodily member or organ.

Evaluating the Use of Force

The following are some basic standards that courts use to evaluate the use of force by police and security personnel:

Ability - does the person the officer is using force against have the ability to cause bodily harm to the officer or someone he/she has a duty to protect?

Opportunity - does the assailant have the opportunity to assault at the instant of the use of force by the officer?

Jeopardy - is the assailant placing the officer or others whom the officer has a duty to protect in imminent physical jeopardy?

Preclusion - is the officer precluded from using force by taking some *alternative* action such as verbal persuasion, hard verbal commands, retreating, or the use of a lesser degree of force? As almost all encounters with persons do not call for the use of force, some attention to supportive communications is in order:

    a)   Honor subject's personal space.
    b)   Introduce yourself.
    c)   Employ *active listening* techniques.
    d)   Use "we" rather than "you," which tends to be accusatory and inflammatory.
    e)   Have subject sit down.
    f)   Offer subject something to drink—other than hot coffee or alcoholic beverages!
    g)   Ask open ended questions which require some explanation by the subject.
    h)   Use *paraphrasing* and *reflection* to clarify what the subject says.
    i)   Beware of your fears and prejudices!

Some questions the officer can use to determine what, if any, force to employ in a given situation are:

- Am I in *imminent physical jeopardy?*
- Is someone whom I have a *duty* to protect in *imminent physical jeopardy?*
- Is my *mission* in jeopardy—preventing trespass, protecting assets from destruction, preventing theft, maintaining order, preventing escape ?
- Do I have another *alternative*—persuasion, "hard" verbal techniques such as screaming, retreat, subsequent criminal or civil redress—to using force?
- How will my actions be viewed by others—supervisors, police, courts, the public/community—who may evaluate them?

Specific Circumstances

There are certain state statutes that enable private persons to use force in specific situations such as mental health commitments, in schools, where required by law to maintain order, where persons are assembled, etc. These statutes create both a legal justification for the use of force and a professional obligation. The obligation is not to be taken lightly! Officers should become familiar with local laws regarding this.

Juveniles

Also, there are varied standards for using force when juveniles are involved. In many cases these statutes relate to the arrest of juveniles. State statutes on juveniles should be read and studied by those in the business of protection or teaching protection officers!

Post-Event Actions

Much of the legal and public/community relations difficulty associated with the employment of force occurs after the incident. Unprofessional behavior after an encounter with an aggressor can sway the verdict in both the legal system and the "court of public opinion" against the officer involved. This may be true even if the use of force was appropriate. For this reason, extreme care must be taken following a use of force encounter. Complete documentation of the incident and control of statements and media coverage is crucial! At a minimum, the following should be recorded in use of force situations:

- Complete, *professional* description of subject's aggressive behavior. This includes verbal *and* non-verbal behavior. It must include all behavior that lead to the employment of force against the subject.
- Complete, *professional* description of officers' actions to control subject.
- All witnesses and *points of contact* such as home and work phone numbers, email, addresses, etc.
- Listing of *all* persons who assisted and responded to the incident. Often witnesses recall seeing a large number of security and/or police officers at the scene of a fight. The perception is that a large number of officers were using force against the subject. In fact, most of the "uniforms" present have arrived after the incident is over. Unfortunately, witnesses—and cameras—see a lone subject being overwhelmed by "an army" of officers. Care should be taken to specify the arrival time of each officer.
- Description of medical care given—note that officer has a *duty* to provide medical care to an assailant. Information on ambulance response time, hospital care and any and all medical care given should be noted. If medical care is offered and refused, this should also be noted.
- Chronological detailing of facts, leading up to the most aggressive actions by the subject. This will "walk the reader" through the scenario so that he/she can completely understand it. Note that a good report is one that enables the reader to feel almost as if they were at the scene of the incident.
- Factual agreement between all accounts!

Media and public statements should be minimized. Statements to the media should only be given by a designated media representative. Statements by the officer should not be given to *anyone* except his or her supervisor and/or attorney. These persons should be briefed as soon as practicable. *THE MORE THE OFFICER CAN BE KEPT AWAY FROM THE PUBLIC AND THE LESS HE OR SHE SAYS, THE BETTER.*

CIVIL LIABILITY

Civil law impacts upon the actions *and* inactions of protective forces each and every day. The potential liability of being sued—having to pay attorneys and spend an extensive amount of man-hours on the case—mandates that circumstances that could create lawsuits should be discovered and avoided! Should a suit make it to court (out-of-court settlements are given by the defendant in 90% of the cases) and the plaintiff prevail, the potential of having to pay plaintiff's legal fees, compensatory damages and possible punitive damages raises the stakes even further.

INTENTIONAL TORTS

Assault
- An intentional act causing an apprehension of imminent physical contact.
- No contact must be made.

Battery
- Unconsented, unlawful touching.
- No apprehension of touching necessary.
- Any degree of physical contact can be battery.
- May also include causing contact with the person by his or her clothing such as knocking off someone's hat.

False Arrest
- Unlawful restraint of another.

False Imprisonment
- An act that completely confines a plaintiff within fixed boundaries.
- An intent to confine.
- Defendant is responsible for or causes the confinement.
- Plaintiff was aware and knowledgeable of the confinement or was harmed by it.

Defamation
- False accusations.
- Injury to another's reputation.
- Can be written (libel) or spoken (slander).
- Accusation of commission of a crime is defamation per se.

Invasion of Privacy
- Unlawful, unreasonable intrusion upon another's privacy.
- Can be physical or mental privacy.
- Can include unconsented publication of a private fact to a third person.

Malicious Prosecution
- Bringing groundless criminal charges against another.
- Lack of probable cause is key.
- Criminal proceeding terminates in favor of the defendant.

Negligent Infliction of Emotional Distress
- An act that is deemed extreme or outrageous.
- The intent to cause another severe emotional distress.
- Actual suffering of severe emotional distress.
- Causation—defendant is the actual cause of the emotional distress.
- May need to be caused by physical contact—this is now a minority view with the contiguous test.
- Can be limited as a *parasitic* action in that it must follow another tort action such as assault, defamation, etc. Whether or not this is true in a particular state, infliction of emotional distress does give the plaintiff another avenue of recovery.

Conversion
Wrongful appropriation of the property of another. Depriving the owner of the property for an indefinite time. Altering something or exercising control over something so that the owner's rights are excluded. Conversion is the civil aspect of theft.

Wrongful Discharge or Termination
An action by an at-will employee alleging that the employer discharged the employee in violation of a law or a contractual agreement. This tort is growing and the at-will doctrine will probably be a thing of the past in a few years. Employment at-will is modified by the following factors:
- contractual relationships which have been established—any violation of the terms of the agreement by the employer would enable the employee to bring an action for wrongful termination
- public policy (a state or federal statute) such as the Americans With Disabilities Act (ADA) or various whistleblower statutes which have been enacted by both the federal government and many states. An example of this would be an employee in an OSHA regulated workplace lodging a complaint with the Administration concerning a safety violation.
- an implied employment contract where promises were made to the employee ("You'll always have a job here as long as you want one").
- an implied covenant of good faith where the employer must behave honestly and conscientiously. If trickery, deceit or duress are applied to the employee, there may be grounds for a wrongful termination action.

In some cases parasitic actions for emotional stress are filed due to the loss of the job, status and income. Depending upon the jurisdiction, these charges can add substantially to the amount recovered by the plaintiff.

Negligence
Negligence actions can easily be lodged against an organization. In some cases, managers can be held *personally liable* for their negligence. Negligence is failing to prevent loss/harm/injury when there was a duty owed to the plaintiff and *reasonable and due care* would have prevented the injury from occurring. In essence, negligence consists of five elements:

1.   The existence of a duty as established via law or contract.
2.   A failure to perform that duty.
3.   Harm or injury to a party to whom the duty was owed.
4.   The harm was reasonably foreseeable.
5.   The harm was caused by the failure to perform the duty.

One aspect of liability is suits based on the principle of respondeat superior ("let the master answer"). This means that employers can be held liable for the actions of their employees that are committed within the scope of employment. Scope of employment is generally defined by:

1.   Time - was the employee on-duty when the action occurred?
2.   Place - was the employee on employer's property at time of offense?
3.   Purpose - was the act committed in furtherance of the employer's interests?

Other sources of liability can accrue if the employer was negligent—*failing to take reasonable and due care to prevent a foreseeable injury that he had a duty to prevent*—in any of the following areas:

1.   *Selection* - hiring someone without properly screening them and placing them in a position of trust (accountant) or where they have access to keys (maintenance personnel in apartment complexes or schools) or where others may be exposed to dangerous propensities that they may have (convicted pedophiles in day care centers or convicted rapists in colleges).
2.   *Retention* - continuing the employment of someone with whom the defendant knows or *should have known* has dangerous proclivities.
3.   *Entrustment* - entrusting a dangerous item to another whom the provider knew, or should have known, is likely to use such item in a reckless manner likely to cause harm to others. This could be a driver of a vehicle or the arming of a protection officer who has been known to be untrustworthy of handling a weapon. Obviously state licenses and certifications in the use and carrying of weapons are important to acquire *and* maintain.
4.   *Supervision* - not properly supervising personnel in situations where someone suffers injury due to the failure. This could include having an inadequate span of control or an absence of supervisory checks.
5.   *Instruction* - failing to properly direct a subordinate so that a third party—or the subordinate—suffers harm.
6.   *Training* - failing to properly train someone to perform job duties with the result that an injury is caused.

Some basic questions that should be addressed in suits regarding training liability are:

1.   Was the employee given instruction in the area at issue?
2.   What type of instruction was given—video, manual review, lecture, etc?
3.   What type and how much practice was the employee given to ensure task proficiency?
4.   For emergency skills, what type and frequency of refresher training was given?
5.   How was the learning tested or evaluated?
6.   What were the qualifications of those giving the instruction?
7.   Are there recognized instructional standards for the area of instruction, such as certifications?
8.   Are there statutory (state or federal laws) or administrative/regulatory standards (OSHA, Department of Energy, etc.) regarding the area of training?

Independent Contractors

These are individuals or firms who/that perform work for the principal (client) but the principal does not have control over them. The principal is not vicariously liable for the acts of an independent contractor except in the following circumstances:

1.   The activity being carried out is inherently dangerous.
2.   The activity is personal in nature and thus non-delegable; safety and security functions are often found by courts to be non-delegable.
3.   Ratification of the act by the principal occurs.

Section 1983 and 1985 Actions

The Ku Klux Klan Act of 1871 was enacted to ensure the 4th Amendment rights of recently freed slaves. A provision in the Act, Title 42, Section 1983, provides for civil redress in federal courts for those person whose 4th Amendment rights are infringed upon by those acting *under color of law.* Section 1983 provides an *additional remedy* for tortious conduct within the federal court system.

> *Every person who, under color of any statute, ordinance, regulation, custom, or usage, of any State or Territory, subjects, or causes to be subjected, any citizen of the United States or other persons within the jurisdiction thereof to the deprivation of any rights, privileges, or immunities secured by the Constitution and laws, shall be liable to the party injured in an action at law, suit in equity, or other proceeding for redress.*

A few key points concerning Section 1983 actions are:
- the defendant must be acting under color of law
- private corporations can not be held *vicariously liable* for the actions of employees
- private party defendants cannot assert *qualified immunity* defenses to suits as can publicly employed police officers
- private corporations can be held liable for attorneys' fees in 1983 suits if they employ a public (off-duty) officer

Section 1983 actions will probably escalate with increasing privatization and closer relations between police and security organizations

Additionally, *criminal penalties* may be imposed in certain circumstances for civil rights violations. Title 18, United States Code, Section 242, provides for criminal prosecution for anyone who, under color of law, statute, ordinance, regulation or custom, willfully subjects an inhabitant of any State, Territory or the District of Columbia to the deprivation of any rights, privileges, or immunities secured or protected by the Constitution of the United States, or to different punishments, pains, or penalties, on account of such an inhabitant being an alien, or by reason of his color or race, than are prescribed for the punishment of citizens, shall be fined not more than $1,000 or imprisoned not more than one year, or both. If bodily injury results, they may be subject to ten years imprisonment. If death occurs they may be subject to any term of years or for life.

Section 1985 of 42 U.S.C. provides for recovery by plaintiffs where a *conspiracy* exists to deprive someone of their rights, privileges and immunities secured by the Constitution and laws of the United States.

Strict Liability

Strict liability is applied in cases where there is no intent to cause harm or injury; the act itself is ultra-hazardous. It is dangerous enough to cause unconditional or *absolute* liability. Activities that qualify for strict liability include:
- keeping wild animals
- using explosives
- underwater gear
- firearms in some cases
- "Certificates of Authority" issued by government agencies to private entities may also create absolute liability

CRIMINAL LAW AND CRIMINAL LIABILITY

Criminal law is of obvious import to protection professionals who generally deal with a limited set of behaviors (crimes) within their respective work environs. Security personnel must be knowledgeable of these offenses. They must know the elements of each and be skilled at prosecuting each. Note: aside from the obvious benefit this knowledge has in terms of job proficiency, it is also essential for avoiding liability and preserving good relations with law enforcement and local district attorneys. Police should be called to make valid, "solid" arrests. The officer calling should know the elements of the offense in question to make the police officers' job easier.

Another issue is with new or unique offenses. Sometimes new laws are written and police are uncomfortable enforcing them. Protection professionals should attempt to learn as much as possible about the new laws. They may have to seek legal counsel or meet with prosecuting attorneys to understand the nuances behind the new legislation. They should also be knowledgeable of other offenses that the defendant may be charged with during the same course of conduct. Examples of these would be indecent or sexual assault in cases of rape; receiving stolen property in cases of robbery or burglary (the perpetrator had stolen property on his or her person); conspiracy in cases regarding controlled substances.

TRESPASSING
Model Penal Code, Section 221.2
1.   Buildings and occupied structures: A person, knowing that he/she is not licensed or privileged to do so, enters or surreptitiously remains in any building or occupied structure, or separately secured or occupied portion thereof.
2.   Defiant Trespassers: A person, knowing that he/she is not licensed or privileged to do so, remains in any place in which notice against trespass is given by:
   •   Actual communication to the person
   •   Posting in a manner prescribed by law
   •   Fencing or enclosure manifestly designed to exclude intruders
3.   Defenses: Affirmative defenses for charges under this section are as follows:
   •   The building or occupied structure involved with a trespassing offense is *abandoned*.
   •   The premises, at the time, were open to members of the public, provided that all lawful conditions pertaining to access have been complied with.
   •   The trespasser believes that the owner would have authorized his/her presence there.

Dealing with Trespassers

        Protection officers are often called upon to evict persons from the property they are hired to protect. Performing this function can involve a host of difficulties that are generally not foreseen by property managers. Property/facility managers simply desire a certain "culture" or ambience within the boundaries of the facility or property. They leave the details to the protection officers as to how to be the "preservers of the corporate culture." Such a role is complex and challenging. How effectively the protection officer can secure the property he/she is employed to protect will determine the degree of legal, operational and safety problems that are confronted. For these reasons, evicting trespassers should be done *professionally*. Below is a list of recommended practices for controlling trespass to property.
1.   A polite request to leave should be employed. This can be prefaced with an interview as to what the person is doing so as to better assess the situation. Persons will not have to be evicted in every case; some will simply comply with the protection officer's request.
2.   Conduct the process in private as much as possible to preclude acting-out behavior in front of an audience as well as to avoid exposure to defamation/invasion of privacy actions.
3.   Avoid invading the personal space of the evictee! A respectable distance—at least a leg length —must be maintained *at all times*. When there are indications that the person is violent, this distance should be increased to at least 10 feet. Care should be taken so as not to corner the person when first approaching them or going through a doorway. The latter scenario is a common cause of aggressive behavior when evicting someone from a room. For information on this see Roland Ouellette's book and video *Management of Aggressive Behavior*, available from Performance Dimensions Publishing (800/877-7453).
4.   Accompany the evictee all the way off the property so as to monitor and influence their behavior. Being too far from the evictee can make them feel unsupervised and rebellious. Acting-out behavior such as shouting, cursing and threatening is likely to escalate. Aside from being detrimental to the decorum, this behavior can incite problems from nearby crowds of people.
5.   Document the action in a daily log, etc. This lists the basic information regarding a routine eviction. Should there be a substantial problem or the person being evicted has been a problem in the past, a complete incident report should be prepared. Also consider video, still shots and audio documentation.
6.   Evict with a partner/witness. Security officers can use the "Contact/Cover" concept where one officer communicates with the subject and the other oversees from an appropriate distance/location for safety purposes. See *Total Survival* by Ed Nowicki from Performance Dimensions Publishing (414)279-3850 for a more detailed description of this concept.

7.   Obtain police assistance if force must be used. Advise police of the problem when calling them. If the person has been violent, threatening or has caused prior disturbances, the police should know this.

8.   Advise the resistant person of the legal consequences of his/her actions—a trespassing charge as well as any other appropriate charges. Knowledge of the law serves to establish the officer's professionalism and authority; few persons will argue if the officer knows what he/she is doing. Legal knowledge also helps to maintain a positive relationship with local police!

9.   Use the phrases "private property" or "_____ (company, college, hospital, etc.) property." Most people have a degree of respect for private property, realize they are on someone else's "turf" and comply with reasonable directions. Even chronic troublemakers are thrown off guard by the phrase "private property."

10.   Give persons being evicted very specific parameters as far as time limits, routes to take, etc. Be fair and firm with this. Document it.

11.   Enforce only lawful and *reasonable* rules. If the rules are not clear and concise, do not attempt to enforce them! Ambiguous, unenforceable rules will lead to trouble with police after they are summoned to arrest a trespasser and do not feel obligated to do so. Such encounters destroy the credibility of security, management and the police.

12.   Consider utilizing prepared notices on company letterhead to mail as certified or registered letters. Such trespass letters should specify the unauthorized activity and dates of occurrence. In public places such as shopping centers, there should be several instances of arrests and evictions indicated as the person is being banned from a whole host of retail establishments. Prepared in a slightly different format, these can also be handed to trespassers. *The Retailer's Guide to Loss Prevention and Security* by Donald Horan from CRC Press (800/272-7737) provides an excellent discussion of both trespass procedures that can be applied to a retail environment as well as some outstanding tips on establishing relationships with law enforcement agencies.

13.   Provide the trespasser with the option of behaving or leaving and document that this was done. The trespasser made the decision to remain on the property.

14.   Discuss with police and other parties such as managers after they have evicted or arrested persons how to improve upon the process. Make sure everyone can share perspectives on the process!

Eviction of trespassers is a challenging undertaking which must be professionally handled in order to ensure that civil rights, property rights and the appropriate rules/culture/decorum are preserved. *Management representatives*—protection officers—who serve as *the ambassadors of the organization* can do no less.

LABOR LAW, DISCIPLINE AND DISMISSAL

As security personnel are the representatives of their employers, they serve as liaison between employees and management. Whether these employees are line or managerial level personnel, there are certain legal and ethical standards governing the employee/employer relationship. Labor law encompasses statutory law (legislation), administrative or regulatory law, contract law, civil law, court decisions and a smattering of criminal law. Unfortunately, labor law has traditionally been overlooked in texts and courses for protection officers.

Employment-at-Will

Absent an express agreement to the contrary, either party may terminate the employment relationship. No cause must be shown. The employment-at-will doctrine is largely eroded. One problem is the myriad of state and federal employment laws; while an employer may believe that he can terminate an employee-at-will, there may be in existence—unbeknownst to him—a state or federal statute that prohibits such action. Aside from these specific exceptions, there are some general exceptions to the employment-at-will doctrine. Some of the more notable general exceptions are:

1.   *Public policy* - not hiring or firing someone because they are on jury duty, in the reserves, etc. Another example would be not hiring someone or firing someone who has lodged a complaint

with a state or federal agency against an employer. In this latter example, "whistleblower" statutes *specifically* forbid discriminatory treatment of employees who file complaints.
2.   *Good faith* - employers must treat employees in a fair, honest manner.
3.   *Implied contracts* - promises made by employers must be adhered to. Promises can be made in job interviews, in employee handbooks, memos, etc. A systematic review of employee handbooks and other orientation materials should always be conducted!

Wagner Act of 1935 (National Labor Relations Act)
•   Created the National Labor Relations Board.
•   Employers cannot interfere with efforts of employees to form, join or assist labor organizations, or to engage in concerted activities for mutual aid or protection.
•   Domination of a labor organization or contribution of financial or other support to it.
•   Discrimination in hire or tenure of employees for reason of union affiliation.
•   Discrimination against employees for filing charges or giving testimony under the Act.

Court Injunctions

Injunctive relief can be obtained from the courts in labor disputes provided that the petitioner has complied with all lawful obligations and has taken reasonable steps to resolve the conflict through negotiation. In general, courts will issue restraining orders when they find that:
1.   Unlawful acts have been either threatened or committed and will continue to be committed unless they are restrained by the court.
2.   Damage of a substantial, irreparable nature will be done to the complainant's property.
3.   The complainant will suffer greater injury by not having the order than the defendants will suffer by having it.
4.   The complainant does not have an adequate remedy at law (civil or criminal).
5.   Public authorities are unable or unwilling to protect the complainant's property

Fair Labor Standards Act of 1938

Passed in 1938 to help pull the country out of the Great Depression by making employers hire more workers due to the overtime provision. It also helped to raise people's standards of living by requiring that minimum wages be paid. The Fair Labor Standards Act established the following:
1.   Minimum wages must be paid to workers
2.   Wage and Hour Division of the Department of Labor
3.   Overtime pay at time and a half of the regular rate of pay—not discretionary pay such as merit pay, bonuses, etc.—must be paid for hours worked over 40 within one week's time.
4.   Children under 14 cannot be employed save for children employed by parents, in agriculture after school, as child actors or newspaper deliverers. Children under 18 are not authorized to work in hazardous occupations, as determined by the Secretary of Labor. Children over 16 may be employed in non-hazardous work; 16 is the basic age at which children may work.
5.   Retention of payroll, employment contracts and collective bargaining agreements for three years. Time cards, earning records, overtime records, work schedules, etc. must be kept for two years.
"Hours worked" is any activity participated in which is job-related and which benefits the employer that the employer *doesn't prohibit*. The employer must control the work; they must know how much off-duty work is being performed; if the work is not stopped by the employer, the employer must pay for it. Employees have no obligation to stop or control the work being performed.

Overtime exemptions under the Act:
1.   The burden of proof for exemptions rests with management.
2.   "High level management" personnel are exempt from overtime pay. Job descriptions—*not mere titles*—that delineate the work being performed as managerial in nature are required.
3.   Management personnel must be paid on a salary basis in pre-determined amounts each pay period. Pay is unrelated to hours worked.

4.   Compensatory time can be paid to employees with the following stipulations:
   - There must be an agreement with the union.
   - Compensatory time is an "alternative currency" for wages and as such is equal to wages.
   - Comp time cannot be controlled or restricted by management unless it is a serious business interruption.
   - There can be no "use it or lose it" stipulation.
   - Upon termination of employment, all comp time is cashed out at today's rate.
   - Enforcement of the Act via the Department of Labor or civil suit involving:
   - Time and a half back pay for all hours worked.
   - Interest—liquidated damages—at double the principal.
   - Two year statute of limitations is in effect.
   - Reasonable attorneys' fees.
   - Punitive damages if the employer discriminates against the employee for lodging a complaint

Taft-Hartley Act of 1947

Taft-Hartley shifted the balance of power back toward management. It established a series of management rights and provisions for governmental control of unions. Note that unions reached their zenith during 1946–47. The Act provided that:
   - Unions could be found to engage in unfair labor practices such as requiring excessive union fees, forcing an employer to bargain with an uncertified union and forcing an employer to pay for services not rendered.
   - Provided for back pay awards for employees who have been reinstated in cases of unfair labor practices.
   - Removed supervisors from protection as employees.
   - Removed closed shop agreements which required an employee to join a union *prior* to being hired. Note: some employers—particularly small ones in construction and the maritime industries—draft agreements with unions that require the employer to *offer* the union an opportunity to fill vacant work assignments.
   - Provided for emergency intervention by the President in the case of strikes that threaten national security.
   - Prohibited guards from belonging to the same unions as other employees.
   - Established the Federal Mediation and Conciliation Service to help in the settlement of unresolved disputes.
   - Permitted suits by and against labor organizations for violating labor contracts.
   - Prohibited union officials from accepting money from supervisors.
   - Extended coverage of the Act to employees of private nonprofit hospitals in 1974.

Landrum-Griffin Act of 1959

Continuing the trend set by Taft-Hartley, this Act established more controls over union activities including:
   - Provided freedom of speech, equal voting rights, control of dues, increases, retention of the right to sue and rights to copies of labor agreements under which they worked.
   - Required financial disclosure by unions and reports by employees of financial transactions with unions.
   - Required bonding of union officers and prohibited recently convicted felons from holding office.
   - Made illegal "hot cargo" agreements wherein employees agree not to use nonunion goods.

Strike Surveillance

Section 158 (a) (1) of the National Labor Relations Act prohibits an employer from any activity that would interfere with, restrain or coerce employees who are exercising their lawful rights of collective bargaining. Activities such as picketing, union meetings, or accepting handbills from union organizers are protected. As photographing and conducting surveillance of people has an inherently intimidating effect, the National Labor Relations Board has ruled that surveillance of persons engaged in collective bargaining activity constitutes an unfair labor practice. Exceptions to this are when the activity being documented is unlawful or when the information being collected is to be used in a petition for an injunction.

- Firms should seek advice from legal counsel about conducting surveillance to be used at an injunction hearing. Such evidence should actually be used at the hearing.
- Surveillance should not be undertaken prior to thorough documentation of the activities of strikers.

Polygraph Protection Act of 1988

Due to increasing concern by liberal members of Congress—such as Ted Kennedy—that employers were encroaching upon the rights of workers, Congress passed the Polygraph Protection Act of 1988. This debate had been going on for a period of years in Congress. While the various states had laws restricting the use of polygraph testing (e.g., in Pennsylvania an employer cannot require a prospective applicant to take a polygraph exam), until 1988 the federal government had no laws regarding the use of polygraphs in employment. The Polygraph Protection Act impacts upon commercial businesses—government agencies, school systems and correctional institutions are not affected. There are also exemptions for businesses under contract with the federal government, businesses in counterintelligence, armored car companies, security alarm or service firms or those firms that manufacture, distribute or dispense controlled substances. The basic provisions of the Act are:

- Employers cannot suggest or require an applicant for employment to take a polygraph test.
- Employers can suggest—*but not require*—current employees to take polygraph tests.
- Employers can suggest employees take polygraph examinations when the following conditions have been met:
  a) The request must be related to a specific, ongoing investigation.
  b) The employee must have access to the property, money or area under investigation.
  c) The employer must have reasonable suspicion that the employee was involved in the incident under investigation.
  d) At least forty-eight (48) hours written notice be given prior to the examination.
  e) The examination must follow certain procedures such as lasting at least ninety (90) minutes.
  f) A statement must be read to the examinee, that includes his or her rights under the Act.

Discipline
- Keep employee handbook current!
- Document all transgressions and advise employees of this.

Dismissal
- Ensure that there are clear policies regarding terminable offenses.
- Avoid telling employees that they will never be fired without just cause, as this can create an implied employment contract.
- Ascertain that all employer policies have been followed leading up to the termination.
- Select a neutral location.
- Have a witness who does not talk, only listens.
- Have a written termination notice that specifies all previous disciplinary problems the employer has encountered with the employee.
- Be objective and a good listener; do not argue! Minimize attempts at reasoning with the to-be-terminated employee who is probably too emotional to be rational.
- Provide the employee with a written notice of the termination.
- Avoid using ambiguous terms such as "layoff."
- Avoid giving notice at the end of a work day, prior to a holiday or when the employee has just returned from vacation.

Federal False Claims Act of 1863

This law was enacted to protect the Union Army from unscrupulous contractors who were defrauding the government. The Act provides for civil penalties of $5,000 and $10,000 for each false payment demand, bill, etc. In addition the defendant is liable for up to three times the amount of damages the government suffers due to the fraud. Other provisions entitle "whistle-blowers" to receive between 15 and 30% of the amount that the government recovers.

LEGAL STANDARDS REGARDING PRIVACY

Privacy Act

Enacted in 1974, the Privacy Act requires federal agencies to collect and maintain only necessary information about citizens. It specifies:
- citizens can see, copy and correct files kept on them
- while there is no response time mandated by the Act, a reply in 10 days is customary in many agencies
- intelligence and law enforcement agencies can exclude entire systems of records from disclosure

Freedom of Information Act

Passed to improve citizens' access to records kept by the executive branch of government. Records will be disclosed unless they fall into one of the following categories:
- information on litigation
- internal agency memos
- trade secrets
- law enforcement activities
- CIA activities
- classified documents
- personnel, medical or other files that are matters of personal privacy
- confidential government sources

All 50 states have set up their own version of open-records laws.

Fair Credit Reporting Act of 1970

The purpose of this act was to regulate the collection and dissemination of consumer credit information. Consumer credit information can be personal credit histories; the language of the 1997 amendment suggests that it also affects criminal backgrounds, motor vehicle checks, and other types of public records checks normally performed during pre-employment screening of job applicants. Investigative reports such as reference checks with employers, neighbors, friends and associates are also considered consumer reports if they are obtained from an organization in business to provide such information. It regulates businesses that assemble reports for other businesses, such as:
- credit bureaus
- investigative reporting companies
- detective and collection agencies
- lender's exchanges
- information reporting companies

The Fair Credit Reporting Act basically establishes the following rights of consumers:
- Right to notice that the information is being reported
- Right of access to the information contained in consumer credit reports
- Right to correct any erroneous information in consumer credit reports

Note: There are also state acts that regulate the collection and reporting of consumer credit information. These are generally more restrictive than the federal law.

Trade Secrets

Trade secrets are formulas, patterns, processes, devices or compilations of information that are used in one's business to gain an advantage over competitors who do not have the information. A trade secret has continuous use in the operation of the business. Some examples of trade secrets are:
- processes used in manufacturing
- patterns for a machine
- lists of customers
- codes for determining discounts or rebates
- methods of bookkeeping

The basic elements of a trade secret are:
- It must be secret, not known to others.
- It must be used in the business of the owner of the secret in order to obtain an advantage.
- There must be continuous or consistent business application of the secret.

Not all information used in business is a trade secret. Some factors used in determining whether information constitutes a trade secret are :
- To what extent is data known to the outside world?
- To what extent is data known by the holder's employees?
- What type of protective measures has the holder taken to safeguard secrecy of the data?
- What is the value of the information to the business and the competition?
- How much effort and money was spent in developing the data?
- How easily could this data be acquired legitimately by competitors?

ADMINISTRATIVE LAW

Administrative agencies have been created to regulate both business and government so that rapidly changing technology can be effectively controlled. Administrative agencies have a tremendous impact on the day-to-day operations of a business—one that is substantially greater than that of the courts or legislatures. Agencies differ in their jurisdiction and authority. While most have some form of judicial review, some do not. Some agencies, such as the Nuclear Regulatory Commission, enforce their rules through an internal appellate process prior to external judicial review; others such as the National Labor Relations Board must have the courts enforce their orders. In general, administrative agencies have the following types of authority:

1. *Rule-making or quasi-legislative power* as enumerated in the enabling statute that created the agency.
2. *Quasi-judicial.* Agencies hold hearings that are not limited by the formal rules of evidence or procedure used in court. The hearings must follow due process, the agency's own rules and regulations, provisions of the Administrative Procedures Act and the Fifth Amendment protection against self-incrimination.

Judicial review of an agency decision can occur. With some agencies this is more common than with others; largely this is determined by the agencies, enabling statute which specifies the amount of authority that it has. Other factors include the impact of its rulings; those with minimal impact are unlikely to be appealed to a court while those creating major financial burdens will be.
    Some factors that a court will examine on review are :
- Whether the agency was empowered to act as it did.
- Whether the agency followed statutory procedures or its own published procedures.
- Whether the agency acted in an arbitrary and capricious manner.
- Whether the record shows at least some facts on which the decision could rest. *Substantial evidence* that a reasonable mind would accept to support a conclusion; somewhat less than would be required for a preponderance of evidence.

Judicial review of agencies is limited. Courts are reluctant to overturn agency rulings as the "doctrine of administrative expertise" decrees that the legislative body that created the agency

determined that agency's expertise. Therefore, the agency should rule on matters it has expertise in rather than the courts:
- When the Administrative Procedures Act or the agency's enabling statute prohibit review.
- When administrative remedies have not been exhausted.
- When the party requesting the review has no standing.
- When the government is not subject to suit.
- When the agency has statutory discretion to act or not to act and has not acted.

Investigative: where the agency can investigate and issue subpoenas for persons to testify at hearings and to produce documents. Subpoenas are enforced by the appropriate court via contempt citations, fines, imprisonment.

Federal Agencies
- OSHA
- EEOC
- NRC
- EPA
- NLRB
- FCC
- FAA

State Agencies
- OSHA
- Human Relations Commission
- Department of Environmental Resources

Municipal Agencies
- Zoning Commission
- Board of Health

Because administrative agencies can fine, suspend, or revoke licenses to operate as well as sue, management is very concerned about compliance. Surviving an audit by a government inspector is important; learning an agency's rules, and the interpretation of them, is crucial to success for security managers. Federal agencies publish their rules in *The Federal Register* as well as via press releases.

Administrative Language

Administrative language is important for security managers to understand. When reading regulations the meanings of the following key words must be kept in mind:

"Shall" - this means "must." There is a requirement to do a certain thing. Managers must ascertain that every "shall" is complied with!

"Should" - this means recommended. While not specifically required, today's "shoulds" can become tomorrow's "shalls." Additionally, auditors look more favorably upon businesses that take the "high road" rather than those who merely do enough to get by.

"May" - this means that the activity discussed is optional. It is completely at the discretion of the business, neither required nor recommended.

AUDITS

Being audited is a fact of life for most businesses. While the points listed below relate to audits conducted by regulatory agencies, the same principles apply when being audited by an insurance carrier or professional accreditation body (CALEA, JCAHO, etc.)

The Ten Commandments of Winning Audits

1. *Have up-to-date documentation of the standards being audited against.*
2. *Understand the formal authority of the auditing organization.*
3. *Know the history of the auditing organization.*
4. *Know and appreciate the philosophy of the auditing organization.*
5. *Assess the background and perspectives of the individual auditor.*
6. *Assess probable areas of specific inquiry and develop retrievability of data to match the inquiries.*

7.   *Neatness/image is everything!*
8.   *Use the language of the auditing entity.*
9.   *Educate all personnel in the organization about the audit process.*
10.   *Internalize the audit process—seek out suggestions from the auditing organization and develop internal audits.*

INTERROGATION

*Interrogation—focused interviewing—*is often performed by protection professionals. Sometimes this is done as part of an investigation and is a planned activity; sometimes it is rather spontaneous, such as, when catching someone in the act of commission. Whatever the case, interviews must be held that are free from duress and coercion of the subject. The resulting admissions, statements or confessions must be valid!

The following cases address interrogation by private security personnel:

Miranda v. Arizona (1966) required that before police interrogate a person they have taken into *custody* or deprived of his freedom in any significant way, they must provide the following warnings:
1.   You have the right to remain silent
2.   Whatever you say may be used against you
3.   You have the right to a lawyer
4.   If you cannot afford a lawyer, one will be provided to you
Interrogation under Miranda may only proceed after the suspect makes a "knowing and intelligent waiver" of his rights. This should be in writing!
Security personnel, operating as security personnel, free and clear of government direction or control, are not obligated to give Miranda warnings in most states (California and Montana being exceptions). Security personnel acting in furtherance of a government interest would be subject to Miranda as well as all other constitutional protections.

Garrity v. New Jersey (1967) - employers cannot require employees to give statements regarding disciplinary matters and then use them in criminal prosecution. Employees giving statements that might incriminate them should note that the statement is being given pursuant to an employer's directive and cannot be used in a criminal action.

Weingarten v. National Labor Relations Board (1975) - employers who have entered into collective bargaining agreements with employees and are interviewing employees in a situation where the employee *reasonably believes* disciplinary action could result must:
•   inform the employee of the time, place and nature of the interview
•   allow the employee representation by a union steward or interested co-worker—*not an attorney*—at the meeting *if it is requested*

Employers are *not* required to:
•   advise employees of their right to representation
•   bargain with the representative
•   suspend the interview if the representative is not readily available

Key Points on Interrogation
•   Review case thoroughly—know as much as possible about both the event(s) and subject.
•   Keep the interrogation in a private setting. This precludes publication of private information such as accusations. There may be another investigator, supervisor, union representative or same-sex witness present, but privacy is the key element. Each person in the room should have a legitimate interest in the case. They must be there for a reason!
•   Try to be as non-accusatory as possible.
•   Make no promises that can't be kept, such as promising not to prosecute criminally if restitution is made.

- Keep statement preambles short—a few words to the effect that the statement is "free and voluntary" is sufficient. Avoid "policespeak" jargon which is complicated and, in almost all cases, convoluted and confusing to the reader.
- With procedural violation statements, be sure to include sufficient biographical and work history data to indicate the employee's level of training and experience so that they are accurately depicted as untrained (didn't know any better) or were trained (knew better) and are subject to disciplinary procedures.
- Make sure that the statement is given free of duress and is in the subject's own words.
- It may be advisable for the investigator to write the statement with the subject; in this way words and phrases that establish the key elements of culpability can be put into the statement.
- Be aware of—and scrupulously follow—any state laws regarding juveniles. Generally this means having the parents or guardians involved. Giving the parents/guardians time alone with the juvenile and then starting the interview may be the appropriate course of action.

SEARCH AND SEIZURE

Search and seizure by private persons is not normally controlled by the Constitution. Exceptions would be where a governmental interest or instigation were present. The following cases illustrate court decisions on searches by private parties.

Burdeau v McDowell (1921): the U.S. Supreme Court found that evidence turned over to a government official by a private person could be used in prosecuting that person even though it was not seized within the confines of the Fourth Amendment. It also cannot be obtained by instigation of the government; the search must be performed for a private interest.

People v. Santiago (1967): a security officer arrested Santiago for shoplifting and subsequently searched Santiago's coat and found a loaded weapon. The search was contested on the grounds that the security officer didn't have the authority to search a person incidental to an arrest. The court found that the search was valid, as arrests made by citizens justify searches just as do those by government agents.

Many authors believe that a cursory search of a suspect for weapons (frisk, pat down) can be performed by security personnel just as it can by police who have reasonable suspicion to believe that criminal activity is afoot and that their *personal safety* is at stake. The justification of having no reasonable alternative to searching, so that personal safety—and the safety of others nearby—is preserved, should be present.

NJ v. TLO: - school officials and protection officers assigned to school environments may conduct searches of students if they have reasonable suspicion that the student is violating an administrative regulation of the school. Criminal behavior—in the above named case the possession of marijuana—can be prosecuted if discovered subsequent to an administrative search.

Simpson v. Commonwealth of Pennsylvania Unemployment Compensation Review Board: stipulated that an employer can suspend an employee for insubordination for refusing to submit to a search where the search was a recognized, posted procedure. The employee was not entitled to unemployment compensation during the period of his suspension.

Searches by private entities are often governed by collective bargaining agreements.

Employers should have a clause in their union contract that stipulates management's rights to search and investigate. Additionally, there should be published/posted notices of management's rights to search. *Maintaining* the right to search should be accomplished by conducting searches periodically, so as to keep the policy active.

Similarly, property owners can perform searches of persons entering or remaining on their property. These searches should be for specific, lawful purposes (combatting the introduction of weapons or explosives or the theft of materials or equipment). They should be written into policy and specific procedures developed for their implementation. There should be notices posted regarding the search requirement. The example below might be appropriate for a museum or similar type of facility.

NOTICE: All bags must be checked. Receipts will be issued. Purses, briefcases and other similar items are subject to search.

Additionally, the use of consent forms is suggested. If people are going to be given a hands-on search for weapons, they should sign a form giving their consent. Consent forms can be signed at the point of entry. Such forms can also include an acknowledgement of the rules for entering and remaining on the property. At a nuclear facility or R & D center, escort procedures would apply. Public events where people come into contact with VIPs and celebrities would also use consent forms containing an outline of entry rules.

Searches by private protection officers also are faced with the spectre of civil liability. Obviously tort actions for invasion of privacy, assault, battery, false arrest/false imprisonment or negligent infliction of emotional distress can result in improper searches.

Evaluating Searches

1. What is the objective of the search—what is being looked for?
2. In whose interest is the search being conducted?
3. What is the searchee's reasonable expectation of privacy?
4. What is the written policy on searches?
5. What policy is being carried out in actual practice?
6. What has past practice been in similar search situations?
7. How has consent been given? Is there actual consent or implied consent as a condition of employment or as part of a collective bargaining agreement?
8. Does the person giving consent have the authority to do so?
9. Is there an alternative to searching?
10. Should the search be performed by another entity?
11. Who is witnessing the search?
12. How is the search documented?
13. Will others who may see the search view it as reasonable?

REGULATIONS GOVERNING THE SECURITY INDUSTRY

There are various regulations that affect the security industry; most of these are at the state level, some are at the federal level. In general, states tend to regulate the following classes of personnel:
1. Armed security officers
2. Contract security service firms
3. Private investigators
4. Alarm dealers and installers

In some cases polygraph operators and others are regulated by individual states. A continuous problem is that the state regulation is generally minimal at best. Another concern is that state regulatory bodies are usually made up of personnel from the law enforcement community who are not really security professionals and who often grant licenses to those who are in their network but make unreasonable demands on those who are not!

States such as New York and Florida have extensive regulation of training for security personnel. These laws require 16 hours of pre-assignment training and an additional 4 hours of annual in-service training for unarmed officers. Armed personnel must also complete additional training. In Virginia, Personal Protection Specialists (PPS) are required to complete a state recognized training program.

The federal government appears likely to enter into this in the near future. Currently federal regulation is confined to:

1. Bank Protection Act of 1968, as amended in 1991
2. FAA and NTSB security regulations
3. Nuclear Regulatory Commission (NRC) regulations
4. Department of Defense (DOD) security regulations for DOD contractors
5. Department of Energy regulations

With expanding privatization, federal regulations concerning security are likely to grow. There is also a movement to support crime control measures that are financed by private industry.

STANDARDS

Standards are of extreme import in the arena of protective services. Standards are created by the surrounding community, the security industry itself, insurance organizations such as Underwriter's Laboratories or Factory Mutual, or professional organizations. Standards are important because they:

1. Provide a recognized level of excellence
2. Create a possible marketing opportunity for service providers
3. Establish what constitutes "reasonable and due care" in negligence cases
4. Mandate what measures must be taken per insurance policies

Standards are important to individual protective services careers, as compliance with standards is very important in certain industries. Healthcare facilities that don't comply with Joint Commission on the Accreditation of Healthcare Organizations security standards may lose JCAHO accreditation. This could mean the loss of federal grant monies.

Types of Standards

There are various types and sources for the promulgation of standards within the security industry. These can be broken down into the following categories:

Government mandated standards that are set by legislation—the Bank Protection Act, licensing laws for private investigators, local ordinances on false alarms or the securing of parking lots. There are also those set by administrative agencies of the government—licensing *requirements* for security service firms, Physical Security Plan and Contingency Plan mandates for U.S. Nuclear Regulatory Commission licensed power plants. Government standards can also be set by non-administrative agencies, such as the Department of Defense mandates that DOD contractors must follow for the protection of classified information. In some cases government agencies specify requirements that security service firms must comply with. They may require certain screening and training procedures in Requests For Proposals dealing with providing security to city, county, state or federal property. Note that municipal standards such as robbery prevention measures in convenience stores or security practices at parking garages are being adopted throughout the country.

Industry standards are generally accepted practices within an industry. These can be formally established through professional organizations such as the National Burglar and Fire Alarm Association or the American Society for Industrial Security or can simply be those practices commonly followed within the hotel, shopping center or telecommunications industry. ISO 9000 standards can be thought of as industry standards regulating those businesses conducting foreign commerce.

Community standards are those practices generally accepted within a geographical area. Examples would be the use of armed guards in shopping centers or CCTV in the lobbies of hotels or doormen in office buildings. Some cities see this as being common; others do not.

Some of the standard setting organizations in the security industry are:
- *National Fire Protection Administration* which has established a committee charged with establishing premises security standards as has the American Society for Testing and Materials. Both efforts have been thwarted by the American Hotel and Motel Association and the International Council of Shopping Centers.
- *AAA* which sets standards for physical security of hotels and motels.
- *Building Owners and Managers Association* which mandates construction specifications such as having handrails at a height of 34".
- *International Association of Campus Law Enforcement Administrators* who accredit campus police departments by adopting several of the standards set by the

Commission on the Accreditation of Law Enforcement Agencies. IACLEA has also established a 40 hour *Campus Protection Officer* training program.
- *International Association of Healthcare Safety & Security* which has training standards for security officers and supervisors as well as specifications for healthcare security. There is also a safety training certification program for protection officers in the healthcare industry.

GIVING DEPOSITIONS AND TESTIFYING IN LEGAL AND QUASI-LEGAL PROCEEDINGS

Security personnel are often required to testify in disciplinary hearings for their employers, preliminary or probable cause criminal hearings, criminal trials, civil trials, hearings conducted by administrative agencies (unemployment, workers' compensation, OSHA) and labor arbitration. They are also often asked to give depositions in civil cases. Testimony is important for the following reasons:
1. It can mean the difference between successful completion of an investigation or failure.
2. It is stressful to the officer and so must be mastered before it masters the officer's health and well-being.
3. Testimony in one proceeding can be used in another proceeding! Single incidents often are heard in a variety of hearings. A criminal trial's testimony could be used later in a civil proceeding, often to the detriment of the officer.
4. Effective testimony establishes professionalism, while ineffective testimony destroys credibility.
5. The proficiency of testimony can be the determining factor in relationships with local police, clients, etc.

Whatever the setting, the following points are key to being successful:
- Prepare by having all notes and evidence in good order.
- Have proof of corporate existence via a certified copy of the articles of incorporation.
- Be able to establish value of merchandise or extent of damage through a professional assessment. A store buyer, contractor's estimate, etc. should be brought to court.
- Meet with counsel.
- Keep answers short.
- Make eye contact with the trier of fact.
- Be polite, addressing everyone by "sir," "ma'am" or their proper title.
- Avoid absolutes such as "always" and "never."
- Do not guess, speculate or answer hypothetical questions.
- If unsure about a question, wait for an objection and a ruling on it.

Depositions

Depositions are often engaged in by security personnel in civil proceedings as part of the discovery process. They are usually given at an attorney's office after notices to appear have been sent out to the persons being deposed (deponent). Depositions are formal legal proceedings with court reporters and legal counsel present. Lists of questions are prepared in advance by attorneys and paralegals. Litigation assistants also take notes at the deposition.

While the formal, legal reasons for conducting depositions are to obtain testimony out of court where having such testimony in court is impractical, there are several tactical reasons for depositions:
- Observe and assess the witness.
- Assess the recollection of the opposing witness when they are confronted with unexpected questions.
- Gauge the testimony of the witness and predict what it will be in a subsequent court appearance.
- Obtain testimony in writing for possible impeachment later.
- Identify witnesses known to the witness.
- Require that documents be produced via a Request for Production.

Being Deposed
•   Take the proceeding seriously. Don't be sarcastic or cocky; be very careful that a
deposition is taken seriously—even if the setting is relaxed and informal.

Interrogatories
Interrogatories are sets of written questions submitted by one party in a case to the other as part of the discovery process. Interrogatories are usually given under oath, with the person answering them signing a sworn statement that they are true. Interrogatories are submitted to a jury.

BIBLIOGRAPHY

Anderson, R.A, Fox, I. & Twomey, D.P. *Business Law,* 1984, South-Western Publishing Company; Cincinnati, OH

Apo, A.M. "Is it Time for Premises Security Standards?", *Security Management*, April 1996

Bequai, A. *Every Manager's Legal Guide to Hiring*, 1990, Dow-Jones-Irwin; Homewood, IL

Black, H.C. *Black's Law Dictionary*, 1990, West Publishing; St. Paul, MN

Cohen, D. "Giving Notification Where It's Due," *Security Management*, March 1998

Corley, R.N. and Black, R. L. *The Legal Environment of Business,* 1973, McGraw-Hill, New York, NY

Givens, B. *The Privacy Rights Handbook: How to take Control of Your Personal Information*, 1997, Avon Books, New York, NY

Hartman, J.D. *Legal Guidelines for Covert Surveillance Operations in the Private Sector*, 1993, Butterworth-Heinemann, Stoneham, MA

Hertig, C.A. *Civil Liability for Security Personnel*, 1992, International Foundation for Protection Officers, Bellingham, WA

Horan, D.J. *The Retailer's Guide to Loss Prevention and Security*, 1996, CRC Press, Boca Raton, FL

Inbau, F. E., Farber, B.J. & Arnold, D. W. *Protective Security Law,* 1996, Butterworth-Heinemann, Newton, MA

Klotter, John C. *Criminal Law*, 1990, Anderson, Cincinnati, OH

Nadell, B.J. "Timeliness of Records Now Critical," *Security Management*, March 1998.

Nemeth, C.P. *Protective Security and the Law*, 1995, Anderson, Cincinnati, OH

Schiff, T.K. "Demystifying Worker's Comp Calculations," *Security Management*, March 1998

Thibodeau, C.T. "Use of Force, Alternatives to the Use of Force, Legal Aspects of the Use of Force," August 1995, A seminar by Q/A Systems & Consultants, Minneapolis, MN

LEGAL ASPECTS OF SECURITY
QUIZ

1.   Reasonable suspicion is more than mere suspicion for it must be based on
_____, _____ and _____.

2. Simple negligence is the intentional failure to perform a duty in reckless disregard of the consequences of non-performance.
    ☐ T   ☐ F

3. Arrest procedures include: (Select incorrect answer).
    a)   Notify the arrestee of the purpose of the arrest.
    b)   Be certain to use only reasonable or necessary force.
    c)   Restrict searches of arrestees to cursor crushing of the outer clothing for weapons.
    d)   Detain arrestee for as long as possible.

4. Children regardless of age can be taken into custody.
    ☐ T   ☐ F

5. Detention may occur for the following reasons: (Select best answer).
    a)   Protect against assault
    b)   Stop a trespasser
    c)   Conduct an entry or exit search
    d)   Recover merchandise
    e)   All of the above

6. Should a suit make it to court, what percentage of out of court settlements are given by the defendant?
    a)   10%
    b)   60%
    c)   90%
    d)   30%

7. Interrogation under Miranda may only proceed after the suspect makes a "knowing and intelligent waiver" of their rights.
    ☐ T   ☐ F

8. There are various regulations that affect the security industry; most of these at the _____ ____ _____, and some are at the _____ _____.

9. Employers can require employees to give statements regarding disciplinary matters and then use them in criminal prosecution.
    ☐ T   ☐ F

10. Search and seizure by private persons is not normally controlled by the _____.

MANAGING / SUPERVISING TO REDUCE LIABILITY
by Steven R. Ruley, CPP, CFE, CPO

Managing and supervising in the security field is a dynamic and exiting task which provides the opportunity to make a real difference in the safety and security of others. It is also a difficult and demanding job which requires considerable insight and skills to help your employees become effective and productive security officers.

Perhaps the most wide-reaching facet of managing and supervising security personnel, and the issue that can cause the most grief, is that of legal liability; it not only affects relationships with our customers, but it also directly affects relationships with our own employees and with the organization for which we all work.

As a manager and/or supervisor you are in a unique position due to your responsibilities to help your organization meet its goals and objectives. Your task of managing and supervising is special, and your work is different from that of other employees because of the following five principles:

1.   Supervising and managing are different from other types of general work.
2.   Supervisors and managers are generally responsible for planning, organizing, directing, staffing and controlling the work of others.
3.   You play a key role in applying skills to meet the needs of your organization.
4.   Your performance will be judged, in part, by the results you are able to obtain with the resources you are given.
5.   Your actions will be guided by the dynamics of each situation, and your ability to interpret and apply rules and regulations.

You will have three basic roles as a security supervisor or manager. Each of the following roles is critical to your ability to reduce liability:

Interpersonal Role - This is where your ability to inspire and lead other people comes to the forefront. As a supervisor you will be working directly with employees. It is in this role that you have a tremendous opportunity to project honesty, integrity and the type of attitude that is critical to the overall success of a security organization. This is also where you will be dealing with employees on an individual basis, and where you must ensure that your employees are treated in accordance with the laws that are designed to guarantee fairness and safety in the working environment. This role will also expose you to the intricacies of selecting and hiring security employees. This is another area of potential liability where you can play a key role in managing risk.

Informational Role - In this role you are expected to be a fountain of legally correct information and to disseminate that information to each of your employees so that they clearly understand their jobs, what is expected of them and what they legally can and cannot do in the context of their employment. In your informational role you are responsible for TRAINING. Most employees actually WANT to do an outstanding job, and are eager to learn. Your role is to provide them with the best information to help them perform their duties in an efficient and legal manner.

Decisional Role - This final role is what people often think about when considering the responsibilities of supervisors and managers. Your decisional role is a form of crisis handling; you will be the leader who must decide how best to handle unusual situations. This role will place you in the position of making decisions that will directly affect your customers, the public and often your own employees. These decisions may range from who is working on what shift to how many people will be assigned to work a particular event or detail. Each of these decisions creates a potential exposure to liability.

Each of the three basic roles in which you will serve as a supervisor presents various problems. You will need three types of SKILLS to successfully handle these roles and reduce the unnecessary exposure of liability of your employees, your customers and yourself:

Conceptual Skills - These are basic managerial skills that give you the ability to analyze situations, interpret laws, rules and regulations, and to solve problems in a reasonable manner. If you have poor conceptual skills you will be inclined to misinterpret situations and to apply incorrect or improper methods of handling problems. This can lead to an unnecessary liability exposure.

Conversely, good conceptual skills will enable you to quickly recognize and avoid problem areas and to provide sound decisions that reflect good risk management.

Human Relations Skills - These are perhaps the most important of the skills you need to manage and supervise. They are important because they enable you to interact with the public and your employees in a way that is effective and efficient. Good human relations skills are displayed in your ability to be pleasant with people whenever possible, to be firm when necessary, and to be fair at all times. Managers and supervisors with good human relations skills have employees and customers who genuinely respect them and communicate with them freely. Communication is another key element in avoiding liability situations. Human relations skills are extremely important because they enable you to avoid problems in the first place and to diffuse and negotiate through problems which are sometimes unavoidable. For this reason alone good human relations skills are often able to make up for minor deficits in the other skill areas.

Technical Skills - These skills are the basic skills you possess that allow you to operate in the security environment. They include your basic training and management training and relate directly to the technical aspects of your job and the jobs of each of your employees.

LIABILITY: WHAT IS IT???

Black's Law Dictionary defines liability as a "broad legal term which has been referred to as of ' the most comprehensive significance, including almost every character of hazard or responsibility, absolute, contingent or likely." In simpler terms, liability is a legal concept under which a person (you) may be held responsible by another person and required to make good on any loss or damages you may have caused. It is a simple concept which has become extremely complex due to a large body of conflicting legal decisions.

Liability is a RISK just like all of the other risks which we face every day. But because it is a RISK, it can be MANAGED by the application of RISK MANAGEMENT TECHNIQUES.

These techniques include the following:
1.   *Recognition* - It is important to recognize the various types of liability exposure.
2.   *Education* - Liability can be reduced and minimized if both management and employees are thoroughly trained in the aspects of their jobs, and in liability avoidance techniques.
3.   *Supervision* - The best educational programs will not be effective in reducing liability if they are not accompanied by effective supervision.
4.   *Documentation* - Report writing and documenting facts are a basic part of security work. Yet, when it comes to incidents where we are exposed to liability, there is often an amazing lack of documentation. We must document ALL of our activities in order to reduce our liability exposure. This includes security incidents, the training and counseling we provide, complaints we receive and evaluations we make about our employees. Each of these records must thoroughly and honestly document the facts because someday they may be important in the defense of a liability case.

Liability exists in two basic forms:
1.   *Civil Liability* - in which you may be subjected to a lawsuit for your actions, and
2.   *Criminal Liability* - in which you may be subjected to potential criminal charges for acts performed.

It is also possible to face BOTH CIVIL and CRIMINAL liability.

CIVIL LIABILITY

Civil liability is presented when an act, known as a TORT, is committed against another. In the security field, we are concerned with the following torts:

1.   *Intentional Torts* - these are torts in which an act occurs and you COULD HAVE or SHOULD HAVE known that it would be likely to cause damages. To prove an intentional tort, you must have the following:
     a)   The Act
     b)   Intention of Consequences

c)   Causation (what you did caused the result)
d)   Damages

Intentional torts can be committed against PERSONS. Examples of torts against persons would include:

a)   *Battery* - harmful or offensive contact judged by a "reasonable person" standard. No action damages are required.
b)   *Assault* - Reasonable fear of immediate battery. (The apparent ability to cause harm is insufficient). An overt act IS required. (Words coupled with conduct). No proof of actual harm is required.
c)   *False Imprisonment* - Act or omission of confinement to a bounded area. Awareness of the confinement. The length of time is immaterial.
d)   *Intentional Infliction of Emotional Distress* - This is a frequent tort seen in the security field. This tort requires an act of *EXTREME* and *OUTRAGEOUS* conduct towards someone of known sensitivity (children, pregnant women, sick people, elderly, sensitive adults, etc.). Actual damages are required and would include evidence of physical harm of extreme outrage.

Intentional torts can be committed to PROPERTY:

a)   *Trespass to Land* - This requires a physical invasion of the land. Under common law (traditional case law) no proof of actual damages is required. The person committing the tort is liable for all consequences.
b)   *Trespass to Chattel* - An act that interferes with a person's right of possession of property. This is a tort occasionally seen in security work when a person is wrongfully restricted from entering or using his property.

There are several defenses that may be used to defend against intentional torts. These include the following:

a)   *Consent* - Consent may be given voluntarily. A person giving consent must be capable of giving it, i.e., the person cannot be incompetent, intoxicated, a young child, etc. Consent must not be induced by fraud.
b)   *Self-Defense* - You must have a reasonable belief as to the necessity of the act. You must show any force used was proportional to the apparent harm.
c)   *Defense of Others* - You may argue that you acted to defend another person.
d)   *Defense of Property* - This is limited to the preventing of the commission of a tort, except in cases of "hot pursuit." The use of DEADLY FORCE IS NOT ALLOWED in the defense of property.
e)   *Necessity* - You may defend an intentional tort if the threatened injury is SUBSTANTIALLY MORE SERIOUS than invasion.

The other area of concern in civil liability to the security supervisor or manager is that of NEGLIGENCE. A significant portion of liability exposure to you, your company and your employees will come in this area of law.

In order to prove a case of NEGLIGENCE, four elements must be present:

1.   *Duty* - (usually a duty to protect against unreasonable risk of injury). This duty is normally that of a reasonable, ordinary and prudent person. However, professionals have a HIGHER DEGREE OF DUTY and must act to the level of skill, knowledge and care of a practitioner in a similar community. This simply means that security personnel are expected to act with the same degree of skill as is generally accepted in the profession.
2.   *Breach of Duty* - To prove breach of duty you must show the facts of an occurrence AND show that the action taken was unreasonable under the applicable standard of care. Along with this, proof needs to be shown that the injury would not have happened without negligence and that what caused the injury was in the exclusive control of the defendant.
3.   *Causation* - This means that the act was either the cause in fact OR the proximate cause of the injury.
4.   *Damages* - This is the actual injury or loss that happened because of the negligence. Injured parties have a duty to mitigate or minimize their injuries. If negligence results in personal injury, the victim is entitled to compensation for all damages. If negligence results in property

loss or damage, the victim is entitled to REASONABLE cost of repair OR the FAIR MARKET VALUE. In some cases, PUNITIVE DAMAGES may be available. Factors considered in assessing punitive damages include the defendant's level of culpable fault, economic gain and financial wealth, and the victim's compensatory damages.

There are also several defenses to the tort of negligence. These include:
1. *Contributory Negligence* - This means that the victim was also negligent and because of that, "contributed" to the cause of the damages.
2. *Comparative Negligence* - This defense assigns various percentages of negligence to each party and allows recovery in a ratio to fault.
3. *Assumption of Risks* - This theory states that the victim either expressed or implied voluntary assumption of the known risk.

As you can see, there are many instances in security work where negligence can be claimed. This can include negligent hiring of personnel, negligent retention of unsuitable employees who should have been terminated, negligent training and negligent supervision. All of these areas of negligence directly impact on YOU, the supervisor.

OTHER GENERAL AREAS OF LIABILITY

Now that you have been briefly introduced to the intentional torts and to negligence, you should also be aware of a few more areas in which the security industry is particularly vulnerable to liability. These areas include the following:
1. *Nuisance* - Which is defined as being either PRIVATE or PUBLIC.
A Private Nuisance is the substantial, unreasonable interference with another person's use or enjoyment of property.
A Public Nuisance is the unreasonable interference with health, safety or property rights of the community.
Legal remedies for nuisance can involve payment of money damages to the victim(s) and/or *Injunctive Relief* in which the court issues an order to stop doing whatever it is you were doing that was a nuisance.
2. *Defamation* - This is a very sensitive area for liability in the security industry. It is most often seen when an improper arrest has been made and the victim has lost status as a result of the improper arrest. It is occasionally seen in investigative cases in which information is improperly disseminated and the victim loses status or reputation or is otherwise damaged by leaked information that should have remained confidential.

Defamation is subdivided into two general categories:
Libel, which requires the publication of permanent recording of defamatory information, i.e., it is put into writing and disseminated to others, and;
Slander, which is the spoken word including defamatory information about the victim.
There are different standards of proof required to prove defamation between a "public figure" and a private citizen.

Defenses to charges of defamation include: *Consent* (the victim consented to your actions), *Truth of Statement* (if you are telling the truth, you cannot be defaming the person), *Absolute Privilege* (which occurs in judicial, legislative and executive proceedings), if you are *forced* into your actions against your will, communications between *spouses*, and *qualified privilege* (such as public reporting or the special interest of the recipient, such as your client).

Another area of tort liability of special interest to the security field is that of *invasion of privacy*. There are several actions that would constitute this tort, but, from a security standpoint, it is most often an act of prying or intruding into another person's private affairs that would be objectionable to a reasonable person. Also, publication of facts which portray the victim in a "false light" and the public disclosure of private facts that a reasonable person with ordinary sensibilities would find objectionable, could also constitute this tort. If you do any of these things and actually cause damages (emotional distress is sufficient) you are liable for this action.

As with the tort of Defamation, this tort can be defended if you had *consent* to perform your actions by the victim or if you had a *privilege* to perform your actions.

It is important for you to recognize that all of these civil liabilities will affect not only your employees, but also may very well affect you and your organization. Because of a legal doctrine known as *vicarious liability*, you and your company may be held liable for the actions of your employees. This is defined even further under the *Doctrine of Respondent Superior*, which clearly makes employers liable for torts committed by their employees *if the employee was acting within the scope of his or her employment.*

This Doctrine of Respondent Superior is the legal theory under which employers may be held liable for intentional acts of their employees and is where you can be held liable for such things as negligent hiring, negligent supervision, negligent entrustment, negligent retention of the employee or negligent selection of the employee.

EMPLOYMENT LIABILITY

In addition to the general areas of civil liability that can involve you and those you supervise, you are also personally exposed to liability in your actions as a manager and supervisor.

For the past several years, employment laws have been changing in order to guarantee certain rights and privileges to employees. As a manager and supervisor, your employees are your most valuable asset and it is beneficial to have these protective laws in place. However, you must also recognize that each of these laws, rules and regulations will restrict you in the manner in which you staff and supervise your operation.

The laws governing employees may be categorized into three general areas:

1. **Assurance of Equal Employment Opportunities**
    These laws guarantee the right to be employed and to advance in employment based on merit, ability and potential without discrimination because of race, color, religion, sex, age or national origin. These laws are enforced by the Equal Employment Opportunity Commission (EEOC).
2. **Assurance of Safe and Healthful Working Conditions**
    These laws guarantee employees' safety on the job by requiring provision of safety equipment where needed, by requiring training on safety matters, and by requiring that employees be made aware of hazards in the workplace and how they are to be handled. Most of these laws were implemented under the Occupational Safety & Health Act of 1970 (OSHA) and are enforced by either federal or state occupational safety agencies.
3. **Assurance of Fair Compensation and Collective Bargaining**
    These laws concern minimum wages and working conditions, and also cover general labor relationships between workers and management. The National Labor Relations Board (NLRB) enforces collective bargaining issues.

Each state has its own set of labor and employment laws, and you should make every effort to be at least familiar with them and their provisions.

You should also be acquainted with the major federal laws concerning Equal Employment. These include:
1. *Equal Pay Act of 1963.* Provides for equal pay for equal work between men and women.
2. *Title VII of the Civil Rights Act.* Prohibits discrimination.
3. *Age Discrimination in Employment Act.* This was amended in 1978 to protect workers between the ages of 40 and 70 from being forced into retirement or other positions.
4. *Pregnancy Discrimination Act of 1978.* Protects pregnant women from job discrimination.
5. *Americans with Disabilities Act of 1991.* Prohibits discrimination based on disabilities.

All of these laws are voluminous and beyond the scope of this chapter. However, each of them is important and can result in liability to you or your organization if they are not properly observed and enforced. Time spent learning about the laws under which you must work is time well invested and will be very helpful to you in reducing your exposure to liability.

One final area of employment law that is receiving a great deal of attention in both the courts and the media is that of SEXUAL HARASSMENT. This is a form of gender discrimination that violates Title VII of the 1964 Civil Rights Act and also violates the discrimination laws of most states.

In the employment setting, there are two types of sexual harassment:
1.   *Quid Pro Quo* - where employment decisions (hiring, firing, promotions, assignments, etc.) are based on an employee's willingness to grant or deny sexual favors.
2.   *Hostile Environment* - where verbal and/or non-verbal behavior on the job is sexual or gender based in nature, is unwanted or unwelcome and is severe or pervasive enough to affect the victim's work environment.

Suffice it to say that the cost of defending on the these lawsuits is tremendous, not to mention the costs in terms of public relations and employee morale. With proper training, good attitudes and prevention, these lawsuits may be avoided entirely.

Prevention of sexual harassment charges requires you or your organization, to prepare and distribute a clear and concise policy prohibiting gender harassment. As a supervisor you need to make certain this policy is well publicized and discussed among your employees. You should provide in-house training and awareness seminars and you should develop a complaint procedure.

If you are unfortunate enough to have one of these complaints presented to you, the complaint should be evaluated and investigated without undue delay. The investigation should be documented. If the complaint is valid, appropriate corrective action should be taken immediately.

This is a very sensitive issue that requires all of your abilities as a supervisor to reassure the complainant, investigate fairly and impartially and to communicate to all involved parties what is being done.

CRIMINAL LIABILITY

Besides the civil liabilities we have already discussed, security personnel are also subject to criminal liability, just like any other citizen, if they violate the law.

The criminal areas most often affecting security employees include the following:

> *trespass*
> *harassment*
> *entrapment*
> *conspiracy*
> *impersonating*
> *reckless endangerment*
> *obstructing public rights of way*

There are as many potential criminal liabilities as there are criminal laws. You can avoid unnecessary criminal liability for your organization by proper screening of personnel, by conducting regular training of your personnel, and by doing your job in providing adequate supervision to prevent and correct problems while they are still minor.

WHAT DOES IT ALL MEAN???

Now that you have had a brief introduction to some of the things that can go wrong and result in legal liability, you may be asking yourself if it would be safer to just quit your job, lock yourself up in a dark room and wait quietly until your time on this planet is over! With all the problems out there, is it really worth it?? OF COURSE IT IS!!

The security profession is a critically important part of our society. We protect and serve people, just as doctors, paramedics, lawyers, police officers and firefighters do.

All of this liability business sounds serious, and it should. It is serious. But by reading this introduction you have taken the first step to reduce your risks.

If you prepare yourself as a supervisor and as a manager, and do your job as it should be done, you have already won more than half the battle. As a supervisor you have both a personal and professional interest in selecting the best people to work in our industry, training these people as often and as well as you can, promoting their development as security officers and providing strong and effective supervision.

YOU ARE THE KEY TO REDUCING LIABILITY IN OUR PROFESSION.

BIBLIOGRAPHY FOR FURTHER READING

1.   BINTLIFF, Russell L., *The Complete Manual of Corporate and Industrial Security.* Prentice-Hall, 1992

2.   BITTEL, Lester R., *The McGraw Hill 36 Hour Management Course.* McGraw-Hill Publishing Co, 1989

3.   BLANCHARD, Roderick D., *Litigation and Trial Practice for the Legal Professional.* West Publishing Company

4.   FENNELLY, Lawrence J., *Handbook of Loss Prevention and Crime Prevention.* Butterworth-Heinemann, 1989

5.   HARTMAN, John Dale, *Legal Guidelines for Covert Surveillance in the Private Sector.* Butterworth-Heinemann, 1993

6.   INBAU, Fred & ASPEN, Marvin E. & SPIOTO, James E., *Protective Security Law.* Butterworth-Heinemann, 1993

7.   STATSKY, William P., *Torts: Personal Injury Litigation.*   West Publishing Company, 1982

MANAGING / SUPERVISING TO REDUCE LIABILITY
QUIZ

1.   Supervisors and managers are generally responsible for planning, _____ and directing.

2.   In order to provide a case of _____, four elements must be present.

3.   Slander is the spoken word including _____ ınformation about the victim.

4.   Assurance of _____ and healthful working conditions.

5.   Besides the _____ liability, security personnel are also subject to criminal liability.

6.   The two basic forms of liability are Civil Liability and Criminal Liability.
                    ☐ T   ☐ F

7.   Assumption of risk is one defense to the Tort of Negligence.
                    ☐ T   ☐ F

8.   The substantial, unreasonable interference with another person's use or enjoyment of property is a PUBLIC NUISANCE.
                    ☐ T   ☐ F

9.   Libel is the spoken word, including defamatory information about the victim.
                    ☐ T   ☐ F

10.   As a supervisor/manager in the security field, your employer accepts all responsibility, so you need not worry about personal liability.
                    ☐ T   ☐ F

SEXUAL HARASSMENT
by Brion P. Gilbride, CSS, CPO

In recent years, sexual harassment in the workplace has become more and more evident, just as more focused efforts have been made to prevent it. As a security manager, one might be called upon to deal with this type of behavior, especially in larger companies where many employees are female. In order to cope with sexual harassment, the security manager must be aware of what it is and what remedies may be used to correct it.

Most people are aware of what sexual harassment is now that recent case law has brought the issue into public discourse. Statistics as of 1997 indicate that the increased awareness of sexual harassment is changing things. Some of these changes are beneficial, and some are not. Anita Hill, in an editorial in the *New York Times*, stated that "Last year, more than 17,000 sexual harassment claims were filed with the EEOC."[1] An article on insurance for sexual harassment indicated another statistic. "Federal reports of sexual harassment have more than doubled, from 6.883 in 1991 to 15,889 in 1997."[2] The judgments in these cases that are decided in favor of the victim are also interesting. "A jury awarded $80.7 million to a former UPS employee for accusing a co-worker of poking her in the breast," and from 1991 to 1997 "monetary awards in federal sexual harassment suits rose from $7.1 million to $49.4 million."[3] In a court case decided in February 1998, "Astra USA, Inc., a pharmaceutical company in Westboro, MA, agreed to pay $9.85 million in a sexual harassment settlement."[4]

DEFINITIONS

The first thing that should be done when examining *sexual harassment* is to define it. The first place to look would be federal statutory law. In 1964, Congress passed the Civil Rights Act. Within that act, specifically in Title VII (46 USC § 2000e-2), it states that it is an "unlawful employment practice" to *fail or refuse to hire or to discharge any individual, or otherwise to discriminate against any individual with respect to his compensation, terms, conditions, or privileges of employment, because of...sex.*[5]

This law (46 USC § 2000e-2) applies to most businesses and employers, "*if they employ fifteen or more employees.*"[6] The Act also provides for five kinds of relief:
1.   reinstatement/promotion
2.   back pay/benefits
3.   monetary damages
4.   injunctive relief
5.   attorney's fees.[7]

Any of these would be damaging to an employer; not just financially but from a public relations standpoint as well.

Another source for the definition of *sexual harassment* would be the guidelines for the Equal Employment Opportunity Commission (EEOC). This definition can be found in Code of Federal Regulations in 29 CFR 1604.11(a). It reads:

> *Harassment on the basis of sex is a violation of [the law]. Unwelcome sexual advances, requests for sexual favors and other verbal or physical conduct of a sexual nature constitute sexual harassment when:*
> * *Submission to such conduct is made either explicitly or implicitly a term or condition of an individual's employment*
> * *Submission to or rejection of such conduct by an individual is used as the basis for employment decisions affecting such individual, or*
> * *Such conduct has the purpose or effect of unreasonably interfering with an individual's work performance or creating an intimidating, hostile or offensive working environment.*[8]

The actual behaviors that are listed by the EEOC to constitute harassment include, but are not limited to:

1.   sexual advances, propositions or attempts to obtain sexual favors from an employee;
2.   hostility toward women employees, all or a particular one;
3.   sexual/pornographic pictures, jokes or language that permeates the workplace.[9]

In the final part of setting down a definition of *sexual harassment*, the two types of harassment that exist today must be included. The first, called *quid pro quo* harassment, is the easiest to understand, and the most obvious. Quid pro quo harassment occurs when "an employee is confronted with sexual demands to keep her job or obtain a promotion." The second type of harassment, which is somewhat more vague, is *hostile environment* harassment. This type of harassment is not actually defined, but rather "is used to describe other types of cases in which the threat is not direct."[10]

LIABILITY

Having defined *sexual harassment*, the next thing that must be defined is *liability* as it relates to this issue. Both of these definitions are based on statutory and case law at the time of this writing. The state and local laws regarding *sexual harassment* and *liability* may vary from place to place. In *Forbidden Grounds*, a book by Richard Epstein, he states

> *"In a quid pro quo case, the corporate defendant is strictly liable for
> the supervisor's harassment ... when a supervisor requires sexual
> favors as quid pro quo for job benefits, the supervisor, by definition,
> acts as the company."*

Epstein notes that this liability standard is for quid pro quo harassment only. What this means to the security manager is that the employer could be successfully sued even if the employer, other than the instigating supervisor, had no knowledge that the harassment occurred. This is because the supervisor is considered to be acting within the scope of his or her duties. Regarding hostile environment harassment, Epstein writes

> *"In a hostile environment case, no quid pro quo exists. The
> supervisor does not act as the company; the supervisor acts outside
> 'the scope of actual or apparent authority to hire, fire, discipline, or
> promote' ... "*

What this means to the manager is that a suit against the employer for sexual harassment may not be successful because the supervisor is acting outside his or her duties. In summation, Epstein states

> *"corporate liability, therefore, exists only through respondent
> superior; liability exists where the corporate defendant knew or
> should have known of the harassment and failed to take prompt
> remedial action against the supervisor."* [11]

In simpler terms, where the supervisor is directly involved in the harassment, both the supervisor and the company are liable. In cases where the supervisor is not directly involved in the harassment, but ignores it or fails to stop it, the supervisor is liable but the company is not, unless the company also was aware of the harassment.

Most of the applicable case law on the subject of *sexual harassment* and *liability* comes from a landmark Supreme Court decision from 1986; the case of *Meritor Savings Bank v. Vinson* (477 U.S. 57). In *Meritor*, the Court made several decisions that have established precedent in sexual harassment cases. In the decision, it was stated that

> *In that case, the EEOC believes, agency principles lead to:
> a rule that asks whether a victim of sexual harassment had reasonably
> an avenue of complaint regarding such harassment, and, if available
> and utilized, whether that procedure was reasonably responsive to the
> employee's complaint. If the employer has an expressed policy
> against sexual harassment and has implemented a procedure
> specifically designed to resolve sexual harassment claims, and if the*

victim does not take advantage of that procedure, the employer should
be shielded from liability absent actual knowledge of the sexually
hostile environment (obtained, e.g., by the filing of a charge with the
EEOC or a comparable state agency).[12]

More recent cases on the subject touch upon the idea that a company *can* defend itself against a sexual harassment suit. In a recently decided Supreme Court case, *Faragher v. City of Boca Raton* (000 U.S. 97-282), the Supreme Court clarified the subject of vicarious liability regarding harassment cases. The Court held that although the employer is vicariously liable, the employer may successfully defend itself based on "the reasonableness of the employer's conduct as well as that of the plaintiff and victim." Essentially, this means that if the employer took appropriate action against the harasser, or the harassment was not properly reported through that employer's procedures, that the employer's liability may be significantly reduced.[13]

Another case that deals with the liability issue is *Burlington Industries, Inc. v. Ellerth*. In this case, unlike *Faragher*, the Supreme Court held that

under Title VII, an employee who refuses the unwelcome and
threatening sexual advances of a supervisor, yet suffers no adverse,
tangible job consequences, may recover against the employer without
showing the employer is negligent or otherwise at fault for the
supervisor's actions, but the employer may interpose an affirmative
defense.[14]

What this means, basically, is that the burden of proof in these cases is shifted largely to the employer. Although the opinion states that an affirmative defense is possible, it is much easier for the victim to claim harassment and win and much more difficult for the employer to defend itself successfully. The affirmative defense becomes possible when a satisfactory grievance procedure is in place *and* all interviews, complaints, reports, etc. are documented and available if and when the case goes to trial. The victim must also have failed to reasonably utilize the policy for preventing / controlling sexual harassment.

PREVENTION AND RISK REDUCTION

Many companies already have policies regarding sexual harassment complaints, since "major employers are deemed desirable targets for lawsuits." Spartan Oil Company, which is based in Dover, New Jersey, has a very effective policy on sexual harassment. In 1991, when Spartan Oil had approximately 125 employees, thirty percent of whom were female, management decided to write a sexual harassment policy with the assistance of their corporate counsel. In the opening of the policy, it defines the types of harassment, and it then states that "Spartan Oil Company will not tolerate any such types of sexual harassment of an employee by one or more other employees." The policy then defines sexual harassment, which it lists "in general, it is any conduct that is sexually offensive, intimidating, or hostile or interferes with an individual's work performance where the conduct is either verbal or physical in nature and is of a sexual nature."[15] The policy lists guidelines of what is considered sexual harassment. These guidelines include eleven types of behavior. The policy then states that two individuals "have been designated as representatives of Management to whom any employee can in complete confidence discuss any problem or any potential problems which they believe exists with respect of the possibility of sexual harassment in their employment with Spartan Oil Company."[16] The two individuals that Spartan Oil designated include a *male* and a *female*. Since October 29, 1991, when the policy was put into effect, Spartan Oil Company has not been involved in sexual harassment litigation, and the policy has remained unchanged as of the time of this writing.

The reaction of companies to sexual harassment has varied, especially within the last year. Companies have also taken unusual steps to avoid sexual harassment. Some companies "discouraged associates of the opposite sex from dining together or traveling together on business."[17] One company even went so far as to state that "male supervisors were not allowed to give performance reviews to female subordinates unless a lawyer was present."[18] Whatever the case, a policy, at least, would be helpful to any employer in reducing liability.

Another remedy that was pioneered in 1988 by the E. I. DuPont de Nemours and Company (DuPont), based in Wilmington, Delaware, is to have a program that addresses and explains sexual harassment. DuPont's program is called "A Matter Of Respect." This is a class, typically four hours long, which is offered frequently and usually involves twenty to twenty-five employees, plus two facilitators. During the class, the employees watch videotapes of situations, and they are then called upon to determine if each situation would be considered harassment. They discuss the issue amongst themselves until they come up with an answer. The facilitator asks the employees some questions and makes some statements to assist them in their analysis.[19] Currently, sixty-five percent of DuPont's employees have participated in the program.

The program goes far beyond the class that is offered. The facilitators offer a list of their names, phone numbers, and a list of other internal contact people, should an employee wish to discuss "any of the issues or problems they're having in more detail."[20] The facilitators of the program receive five to thirty days of training, which allows them to counsel other employees and to be involved in the initial investigation of any complaints. They learn to talk to worried employees, as well as listen to them.[21]

TRANSFER/INSURANCE

One of the remedies that has arisen since the early 1990s is what is referred to as *employment practices liability coverage*, or EPL. Basically, it is insurance against lawsuits charging unlawful employment practices, such as sexual harassment. "Five years ago, premiums for companies with fewer than 100 employees were in the $50,000 to $100,000 range. Today, premiums on the same policy might run an employer $5,000." Originally, few insurers would allow coverage against these suits. Now, however, large companies such as "Chubb, Lloyds of London, and Reliance, offer EPL." This has caused the cost of EPL to "plummet."[22]

INVESTIGATION

Investigation is the key to determining if there is a valid complaint, determining what actions need to be taken against a harasser, and preventing litigation. The most important thing about investigating a sexual harassment complaint is to do it immediately. "A prompt and objective investigation should be the standard response to any complaint of sexual harassment"[23] in order to decrease liability.

"Investigating all possible instances of harassment, regardless of how they come to the employer's attention, reduces the potential for liability."[24]

Provided the employer already has a policy against sexual harassment, the employer must then designate a person or persons that can hear sexual harassment complaints and act on them without bias; preferably someone in a different chain of command than the complainant. The security manager can be that person, however, the security manager should have alternate people to perform investigative duties in the event that there is a conflict. Conflicts would include personality conflicts with the complainant or the alleged harasser. It may even become necessary to hire an independent investigator.[25]

From there the investigation should begin. The investigator should attempt to get whatever information possible from the complainant, the alleged harasser and witnesses. The information should include:
1. The identity of the person(s) accused of the offensive action and any witnesses to the alleged harassment;
2. What specific conduct is objectionable;
3. How many times and over what period of time the conduct has occurred;
4. Whether any other employees have experienced this type of offensive conduct;
5. Whether there have been any previous complaints to fellow employees, the harasser or others about the offensive conduct; and
6. Whether there is any pattern to the offensive conduct.[26]

The objectives for the investigation should also be clear. Know *why* an investigation is being initiated and *what* is intended to come because of it. The manager, by initiating an investigation should:
1. Determine whether a basis of fact exists to formally accuse the employee;
2. Serve, if an accusation has already been made, as the basis of fact for determining if the accusation was warranted, and if warranted, as the basis for initiating some type of

discipline;

3. Serve, if some type of disciplinary action has been effected, such as a suspension from duties pending the outcome of an investigation, as the basis for either sustaining or rescinding the action;

4. Determine if a basis of fact exists for imposing discipline over and above what already may have been given relative to the misconduct investigated.[27]

There are even recommended guidelines for interviewing individuals who have relevant knowledge to the complaint being investigated. They are:

1. Disclose information only on a need-to-know basis.

2. Ask broad and open-ended questions that are not limited to the specific facts of the complaint. Let the alleged victim know that the employer takes the matter seriously and will promptly investigate it.

3. Take notes and follow up on any leads that the questioning reveals, even if they are not directly or specifically related to this complaint.

4. Conduct the interview in a non-threatening environment, in a manner that encourages the interviewee to be forthcoming. If the interviewee feels uncomfortable, probe gently or return to the question or subject later in the interview.

5. Remind interviewees that there will be no retaliation for participating in this interview.[28]

Occasionally, there are witnesses to the harassment. This is especially so if the case regards a hostile environment. If a complaint is being investigated, there will probably be witnesses involved. When a security manager decides to include witnesses in his or her inquiry, that manager should consider the following:

1. If the allegations are such that the accused will likely admit to them, you may want to postpone your witness interviews. Then, if all material allegations are admitted, your employer may not see a need to involve potential witnesses.

2. If the material allegations are denied, then you have an unresolved factual dispute, and witness interviews are needed to attempt to resolve the dispute.[29]

In cases where the accused does not admit to the allegations, but instead denies them, it is entirely possible that the accused is not telling the truth. If the security manager suspects that the accused is lying, that manger may wish to consider these options:

1. Cease interviewing and proceed directly into an interrogation. Conduct this in accordance with acceptable interrogative techniques you would use in any other type of investigation.

2. Commit the accused to a false exculpatory statement. The value of such a statement is that it is documentary proof of deception. Such a statement is based on the accused denying facts that can be proven true.

3. Carry out both of the above suggestions; if the interrogation fails to produce a confession, a false exculpatory statement can then be obtained.[30]

Sometimes, the investigation does not clearly state if the alleged harasser did commit the action for which he or she has been accused. This is not uncommon. If this is the case, inform the harasser that if the additional evidence surfaces at a later time, the investigation will be re-opened and appropriate action will be taken.[31]

DISCIPLINE

If the employer has determined that sexual harassment did take place, then disciplinary action must occur. Otherwise, the investigation and the efforts of various people will have been wasted.

One of the most important things to remember about disciplining people is to be "objective and consistent."[32] For discipline to be effective, it must correct the act, not belittle the person. The discipline that is given should depend upon the offender's previous behavior. Keeping a file on employee infractions, that is, to document each violation and keep that information sorted by employee/offender, allows the record to be easily accessed to determine if the offender is a repeat offender or if he or she has committed other violations.[33] If action is to be taken, in order to be effective it must be taken promptly. If there is a tremendous time lapse between the offense and the disciplining, then the offender may not recall why he or she is being disciplined. That practice would cause low employee morale. Also, when disciplining, the manager should remember that "the discipline should fit the severity of the conduct and be calculated to immediately put a stop to the offensive conduct."[34]

One option that may be used to discipline an employee is termination from employment. If the employee is found to have committed sexual harassment after an investigation, the safest course of action would be to fire that person. This is not always practical, however. If alternative forms of discipline are to be utilized instead, certain things should be considered:

1. Determine the presence and degree of guilt prior to disciplining.
2. Because of intense emotions surrounding a sexual harassment accusation, be careful to separate fact from fiction as emotion will distort an employee's claims.
3. Sexual harassment *could* be symptomatic of an emotional illness; medical treatment could be considered for use as constructive discipline.
4. There must be a well-communicated sexual harassment policy in existence prior to the accusation.
5. Understand that things said in jest may not be similarly interpreted. In determining the degree of guilt, motive is as important as what was actually said or done.[35]

CONCLUSION

Even though much relevant information on sexual harassment has been stated here, laws and court decisions continually change the way that the issue is viewed. The best way to ensure that sexual harassment is avoided is to have a clear and concise policy on the subject, and to be sure that the policy is updated periodically to include any changes made by the courts or by federal, state, and local legislative actions. Once policy has been established, adhere always to the procedures that have been outlined. Where possible, attempt to eliminate the problem, not the employee. Finally, remember *confidentiality* above all things. Sexual harassment accusations, be they true or not, are extremely damaging to all concerned.

BIBLIOGRAPHY

Ahmad, Shaheena. (1998, March 2). Get Your Sex Insurance Now. *U.S. News & World Report.* Pg. 61

Associated Press. (1998, March 23). Insurers Issuing More Policies to Help Handle Harassment. *York Daily Record.* Pg. 3a

Bryant, Adam. (1998, February 16). Companies Watch Scandals For Clues To Own Policies. *New York Times.* Pg. A11

Burlington Industries, Inc. v. Ellerth., 000 U.S. 97-569 (1998).

Chapman, Bryan A. *Information is Power.* Available: http://www/baclaw/#promptly and objectively.

Eisaguirre, Lynne. (1993). *Sexual Harassment—A Reference Handbook.* Santa Barbara, CA: ABC-CLIO.

Epstein, Richard A. (1992). *Forbidden Grounds.* London, England: Harvard University Press.

Faragher v. City of Boca Raton., 000 U.S. 97-282 (1998).

Flynn, Gillian. (1997, October). A Pioneer Program Nurtures A Harassment Free Workplace. *Workforce.* Pg. 38-43

Hill, Anita. (1998, March 19). A Matter of Definition. *New York Times.* Pg. A25.

Meritor Savings Bank v. Vinson., 477 U.S. 57 (1986).

Sennewald, Charles A. (1985). *Effective Security Management.* Boston, MA: Butterworth Publishers.

Spartan Oil Company. (1991, October 29). *Company Policy of Spartan Oil Company Regarding Sexual Harassment.*

Sutherland, Karen. (1997). *Investigating Sexual Harassment Claims-What's A Business Owner To Do?* Available: http://www.omwlaw.com/pubs/sutherland/00014.html

ENDNOTES

1.   Hill, Anita. (1998, March 19). A Matter of Definition. *New York Times.* Pg. A25.
2.   (1998, March 23). Insurers Issuing More Policies to Help Handle Harassment. *The York Daily Record.* Pg. 3A.
3.   Ahman, Shaheena. (1998, March 2). Get Your Sex Insurance Now. *US News and World Report.* Pg. 61.
4.   *Insurers Issuing More Policies to Help Handle Harassment.* Pg. 3A
5.   Civil Rights Act of 1964, 42 USC § 2000e-2 *et seq.* (Internet Law Library, 1-21-96) Available: http://law2.house.gov/uscode-cgi.
6.   Eisaguirre, Lynne. Pg. 56.
7.   Eisaguirre, Lynne. Pg. 56.
8.   Eisaguirre, Lynne. (1993). *Sexual Harassment - A Reference handbook.* Santa Barbara, CA: ABC-CLIO. Pg. 57.
9.   Eisaguirre, Lynne. Pg. 58.
10. Eisaguirre, Lynne. Pg. 57
11. Epstein, Richard A. (1992). *Forbidden Grounds.* London, England: Harvard University Press. Pg. 363.
12. Meritor Savings Bank v. Vinson, 477 U.S. 57 (1986).
13. Faragher v. City of Boca Raton, 000 U.S. 97-282 (1998).
14. Burlington Industries, Inc. v. Ellerth, 000 U.S. 97-569 (1998).
15. Spartan Oil Company. (1991, October 29). Company Policy of Spartan Oil Company Regarding Sexual harassment. Pg. 1.
16. Spartan Oil Company. Pg. 1.
17. Bryant, Adam. (1998, February 16). Companies Watch Scandals for Clues to Own Policies. *New York Times.* Pg. A11.
18. Bryant, Adam. Pg. A11
19. Flynn, Gillian. (1997, October). A Pioneer Program Nurtures A Harassment Free Workplace. *Workforce.* Pg. 38-40.
20. Flynn, Gillian. Pg. 40.
21. Flynn, Gillian. Pg. 41.
22. Ahmad, Shaheena. Pg. 61.
23. Chapman, Bryan A. Recommended Guidelines for the Employer. Available: http://www.baclaw.com/#promptly and objectively. Pg. 6.
24. Sutherland, Karen. (1997). Investigating Sexual Harassment Claims - What's a Business Owner To Do? Available: http://www.omwlaw.com/pubs/sutherland/00014.html. Pg. 1.
25. Sutherland, Karen. Pg. 2
26. Sutherland, Karen. Pg. 2.
27. Imundo, Louis V. (1985). *Employee Discipline: How To Do It Right.* Belmont, CA: Wadsworth Publishing Company. Pg. 76.
28. Sutherland, Karen. Pg. 2.
29. Connell, Michael E. (1987, December). How To Investigate Sexual Harassment. *Security Management.* Pg. 35.
30. Connell, Michael E. Pg. 35.
31. Sutherland, Karen. Pg. 2.
32. Sennewald, Charles A. (1985). *Effective Security Management.* Boston, MA: Butterworth Publishers. Pg. 111.

33.   Sennewald, Charles A. Pg. 112.
34.   Sutherland, Karen. Pg. 2.
35.   Immundo, Louis V. Pg. 242.

SEXUAL HARASSMENT
QUIZ

1.   Sexual harassment includes:
      a)   a male employee propositions a female employee for a sexual favor
      b)   a female employee makes derogatory statements about a male employee's genitalia
      c)   a and b

2.   The supervisor is liable for sexual harassment if:
      a)   the supervisor has no knowledge of the harassment
      b)   the supervisor issues a warning to a harasser and there are no further incidents
      c)   the supervisor is aware of the harassment but takes no action to correct the situation

3.   The sexual harassment victim's case would be strengthened by:
      a)   lack of a corporate policy prohibiting sexual harassment
      b)   the usage, at least once, of an established grievance procedure
      c)   having no evidence to substantiate the claim of harassment
      d)   a and b

4.   Policies written to address sexual harassment should *not* include:
      a)   definition and explanation of types of sexual harassment
      b)   names and numbers of persons to contact to discuss or file a complaint
      c)   information about searches and seizures

5.   Employment Practice Liability Insurance offers:
      a)   financial protection against losses in sexual harassment cases
      b)   a complete shield against all liability in sexual harassment claims
      c)   the right of an employer to permit sexual harassment in the workplace

6.   DuPont's sexual harassment program and Spartan Oil Company's sexual harassment policy *both* included:
      a)   the viewing of taped scenarios
      b)   a system that designated people for victims to contact if they wished to discuss/report sexual harassment
      c)   an explanation of Employment Practices Liability insurance

7.   The investigation should try to determine:
      a)   who performed the harassment
      b)   the approximate age of the victim
      c)   what was said/done by the harasser
      d)   a and c

8.   Questioning of the victim, the accused and the witnesses should be conducted:
      a)   at any convenient time
      b)   as soon after the initial complaint as possible
      c)   never, they will provide all necessary and pertinent information
      d)   within one week of receiving the complaint

9.   Disciplinary action should be taken with *what* in mind?
      a)   punishment only
      b)   correction of the harassment
      c)   insurance that the harassment will not be repeated
      d)   b and c

370 - Sexual Harassment

10. Disciplinary action, when taken, should consider which of the following:
  a) The harasser's personal preference for discipline;
  b) The discipline requested by the victim;
  c) The nature of the actions taken by the harasser; whether they were performed in jest or with malicious intent;
  d) The work performance record and general credibility of the victim.

CONTRACTS IN ASSET PROTECTION
by Christopher A. Hertig, CPP, CPO and Sidney S. Sappington, M.B.A., J.D.

As any asset protection professional can attest, contracts are an extensive part of protective services. While their import is expanding with privatization and outsourcing for security services, legal texts and even articles in professional periodicals give scant treatment of them. Some common examples of contracts within the security profession are:

- contract security services
- alarm installation, monitoring and response agreements
- investigative services
- consulting services
- training services
- security equipment installation and maintenance
- employment contracts for individuals
- collective bargaining agreements
- releases from liability

As the services provided by contract firms continue to diversify into such areas as risk assessment, time and attendance, scheduling and training, so too will the use of contracts to regulate the provision of these services. *There will be more contractual relationships entered into, mandating a sound understanding of what contracts are all about for those involved in asset protection.*

Contracts are essentially *agreements between two or more parties to perform an act or to not perform a particular act*. Contracts are legally enforceable agreements. They are *binding*. They consist of several key elements:

1. *An agreement* that is not a *mere offer* or an *invitation* to negotiate. There must be acceptance of the offer. Agreements can be either *express*—declarations of the intention of the parties and the terms of the transaction—or *implied*—where the contract is demonstrated by the acts and conduct of the parties. Examples in employment contracts could include promises made by supervisory personnel during employment interviews ("You've got a job as long as you want one") or passages from employee handbooks (a mention of an annual salary can be construed as a promise of a full year's employment). Similar implied agreements can be interpreted in service contracts through advertising, promises by sales representatives, etc.

   Agreements are reached after negotiation. This process can consist of *distributive* (competitive) *bargaining, integrative* (collaborative) *bargaining* or *contingency* (variation) *bargaining*. Negotiation proceeds from a "time and event" perspective, beginning with the *preparation of planning*, which consists of research, information gathering, communications factors, etc. It then enters the *preliminary stage* which sets the parameters and scope of the negotiation. The actual negotiation takes place covering the substance of the contract. This is followed by the *conclusion* where the parties have agreed to the terms and conditions in principle with minor provisions to be carried out as performance takes place. Finally, there is *follow-up* where contingencies or new conditions come into play.

2. *Between competent parties* who have the capacity to understand that a contract is being made and to comprehend its general nature. Minors, intoxicated persons or mental incompetents cannot make contracts. Agreements cannot be made when one party is under duress. Agreements not to sue, being signed by detainees, are generally not enforceable for this reason.

3. *Consideration* means that the promise or performance of the parties be *legally sufficient* and the promise must be of *value* in the eyes of the law. There must be to the parties either a detriment, the giving of something of legal value or a benefit, the receiving of legal value. It must be bargained for and given in exchange for the promise made. Releases from liability signed by persons who have been detained must have some consideration in the form of money or goods. This should be of some substance rather than a nominal amount. Additionally these agreements should always be witnessed. Obviously persons falsely arrested can still bring a suit for same, as the contract is not legally binding. It is, in effect, an agreement to do something illegal.

4. *Mutuality of agreement* where both parties must genuinely agree.

5.   *Mutuality of obligation.* Both parties are bound or neither is bound.

6.   *Made for a lawful objective.* Not in violation of law or public policy.

7.   *In the form required by law.* In some cases there are statutory requirements as to how a contract must be designed.

For contracts to be used effectively, the following points should be borne in mind:

*   *Contract language should be specific.* There should be no ambiguity in contract language. If such ambiguity exists, the intention of the parties can be taken from the "four corners" rule—the instrument as a whole. Intention may also be taken from the circumstances surrounding the execution of the contract. Terms such as "security" should be specified so that their meaning is clearly understood. The contract should spell out what particular asset protection services are meant by "security." In this way implied duties to provide protection are not created.

*   *Third parties—such as patrons at a shopping center—can be beneficiaries of a contract and can bring an action for breach of contract if the contract was made out for their benefit.* Examples would be patrons at a shopping mall, theme park or office building. While such persons had no *privity*—they were not parties to the signing of a contract to provide security patrol services—they were the intended beneficiaries. As such they may be able to bring suit for breach of contract if the property was not patrolled.

*   *Contracts must be in writing!* An old law school saying goes: *"An oral contract is not worth the paper it's written on."* They must also be written in accordance with prevailing legal standards. In the state of New York, the Secretary of State requires licensed security agencies to have written contracts. There are, however, circumstances where courts will find that a contract existed even though there was no specific contract form written. In these cases the courts will look at other documents from which an agreement can be implied. They will also consider oral agreements and customary practices to make this determination. Employment promises where the employee has been promised a job, relocated, taken the offer of employment and then been laid off in a short time ("turfed") is a fairly common example of an implied contract.

        In the enforcement of a contract the *Parol Evidence Rule* applies. According to Section 213 of the *Restatement of the Law of Contracts (Second Edition): "Oral testimony will not be permitted to alter or vary the terms of a written completed contract."* (Courts commonly state that such prior statements and negotiations are merged into the final written agreement. The Parol Evidence Rule may not apply in cases of fraud, ambiguity or gross errors.

*   *Enforcement of contracts will not occur where there is a lack of voluntary assent in such cases as undue influence,* or if there has been fraud, duress, mutual mistake, impossibility or unconscionability (obviously unfair).

*   *Limitations of liability* appear in many alarm and security service contracts. These clauses impose a cap on the amount of liability that the contractor will assume. Courts generally validate these clauses as they recognize that alarm companies are not insurance companies. Where such agreements are valid and enforceable, they may expose the client firm to extensive liability. In some cases, the limitations on liability are struck down as being against public policy, unconscionable or unclear. Findings of gross negligence on the part of the contractor, or conduct showing willful and wanton misconduct, are usually not enforceable. Actions in these cases can be brought for breach of contract as well as for negligence. *Exculpatory clauses* must also not grow out of unequal bargaining power (residential apartment leases where the lessee is at a

distinct disadvantage), or attempt to remove from the vendor a public duty to perform (public utility company). *Clauses cannot be hidden or obscured within the contract.*

- *Releases from liability* are of great psychological value, as are waivers. They may not have much legal weight as they are not supported by consideration. Liability releases *should be supported by consideration, such as a cash payment.* Releases from liability should be obtained from persons who are under Accelerated Rehabilitation Disposition (ARD) or Adjourned in Contemplation of Dismissal (ACD) dispositions from courts. These agreements allow first offenders to have a clean record after a specified period of time if there are not future arrests or convictions for other crimes. The existence of these agreements should also be noted in the court record.

- *Service agreements* are another cause of concern in contracts where equipment maintenance and repair are covered.

AGENCY

The concept that one party may act on behalf of the other. The contractor (agent) acts on behalf of the client (principal) and is under the *control* of the principal. *The actions of the agent bind the principal.*

INDEPENDENT CONTRACTOR

One who contracts with a principal or client and is free to perform the work according to his own methods. Independent contractors perform work for a client, but choose their own methods for doing so. They are not controlled by the principal, save for the final work or product. Independent contractors may or may not be agents of the principal. Clients may escape civil liability for the actions of an independent contractor. *The test is which party was in control when the tortious or negligent actions occurred.* Control is determined by:
1.   Who has control according to the contract.
2.   Who has control in actual practice. This is determined by such facts as:
- Who provides uniforms and equipment?
- Who hires and fires?
- Who gives daily duties or assignments?
- Who supervises?
- Who evaluates?
- Who pays the employee?

Obviously, client organizations who utilize a hybrid protection force consisting of contract agency employees supervised by a proprietary staff, would most probably be in control. Also in control would be those organizations having long-standing contracts with a particular service firm or who have a very close working relationship with the site supervisor for the contract agency.
Principals are not vicariously liable for the tortious acts of independent contractors unless:
1.   The activity is inherently dangerous. Armed guards may be considered so.
2.   The activity is personal in nature and thus non-delegable—safety and security functions usually are.
3.   The principal ratifies the act of the contractor. Ratification can occur by affirming a tortious act or failing to correct tortious behavior by a subcontractor with the knowledge that such an act occurred.

The use of *subcontractors* is another factor that tends to complicate the contractual relationship in both the legal *and* ethical arenas. *Ethics* and *professionalism* are the keys to success for service providers. The desire to enter into a *mutually beneficial partnership*—which is legally binding —is essential to successful outsourcing by client firms.

CHECKLIST FOR SERVICE CONTRACTS

1. *Is the contract lawful, meeting the requirements of local, state and federal law?*
2. *Is the contract enforceable, containing the essential elements of a contract (mutual agreement, supported by consideration, made between competent parties, genuine assent of the parties) and is it in the form required by law?*

    Are conditions in the contract spelled out in sufficient detail? These can include *conditions precedent*—those that must be fulfilled before a party's performance can be required, such as a contractor providing proof of licensing or insurance; *conditions concurrent*—those that must be fulfilled simultaneously by each party, such as payment for services; or *conditions subsequent*—when a condition operated to terminate a party's absolute promise to perform, such as failure to provide service.
3. *What is the time of performance?* If time is of the essence it must be stated in the contract.
4. *Are standards of performance in place that require the parties to perform to a measurable standard and to develop controls to monitor such standards?*
5. *Are rates for service, method of payment and credit terms specified?*
6. *Are performance and behavioral liabilities of the parties specified?* These include financial responsibilities, proof of insurance and limitations of liability.
7. *Is a mechanism for resolving disputes identified?* This could be in-house, via third party negotiation or arbitration such as that provided by members of the American Arbitration Association.
8. *Are there provisions for contract modification, extension or cancellation?* There should be some flexibility written in to account for legal changes, such as wage rate increases, etc.
9. *Is there a contract forum selection clause designating the forum in which disputes will be litigated?* This relates to legal jurisdiction and is very important when business is conducted between entities operating in multiple states or countries.

The foregoing is a fundamental discussion of contracts as they relate to asset protection. It is offered as a beginning point in the continued exploration of the issues they raise. It is not intended as a substitute for legal advice. Obviously, such factors as individual state laws, consumer protection acts, etc. impact the specific legal ramifications of any contract.

BIBLIOGRAPHY

Anderson, Ronald A., Fox, Ivan and Twomey, David P. (1984). *Business Law.* South-Western, Cincinnati, OH.

Bequai, August. (1990). *Every Manager's Guide to Hiring.* Dow Jones-Irwin, Homewood, IL.

Black, Henry C. (1990). *Black's Law Dictionary.* West Publishing, St. Paul, MN.

DeCenzo, David A. and Robbins, Stephen P. (1996). *Human Resource Management.* John Wiley & Sons, New York, NY.

Horan, Donald J. (1997). *The Retailer's Guide to Loss Prevention and Security.* CRC Press, Boca Raton, FL.

Inbau, Fred E., Farber, Bernard J. And Arnold, David W. (1996). *Protective Security Law.* Butterworth-Heinemann, Newton, MA.

Maxwell, David, A. (1993). *Private Security Law: Case Studies.* Butterworth-Heinemann, Newton, MA.

American Law Institute (1981). *Restatement of Contracts (Second Edition),* West, St. Paul, MN.

Tryon, David C. (1998). "Guarding Against Legal Problems," *Security Management,* August, Vol. 42., No. 8.

CONTRACTS IN ASSET PROTECTION
QUIZ

1. Contracts are essentially agreements between two or more parties to perform an act or to not perform a particular act.
   □ T   □ F

2. An _____ is not worth the paper it's written on.

3. Enforcement of contracts will not occur where there is lack of voluntary assent in such cases as undue influence. What factors may contribute to this?
   a) fraud
   b) duress
   c) mutual mistake
   d) impossibility or unconscionability
   e) all of the above

4. Releases from liability are of no psychological value, as are waivers.
   □ T   □ F

5. The use of _____ is another factor that tends to complicate the contractual relationship in both the legal and ethical arenas.

6. Independent contractors may or may not be agents of the principal.
   □ T   □ F

7. Principals are not vicariously liable for the tortious acts of independent contractors unless:
   a) the activity is inherently dangerous
   b) the activity is personal in nature and thus non-delegable
   c) the principal ratifies the act of the contractor
   d) all of the above

8. Clauses cannot be hidden or obscured within the contract.
   □ T   □ F

9. _____ __ _____ appear in many alarm and security service contracts.

10. As the services provided by contract firms continue to diversify into such areas as risk assessment, time and attendance, scheduling and training, so too will the use of contracts to regulate the provision of these services.
    □ T   □ F